Coins of Northern Europe & Russia

Edited By George S. Cuhaj & Thomas Michael

Published by

krause publications

An Imprint of F+W Publications

700 East State Street • Iola, WI 54990-0001
715-445-2214 • 888-457-2873

Our toll-free number to place an order or obtain
a free catalog is (800) 258-0929.

Library of Congress Catalog Number: 2006930833
ISBN 13-digit: 978-0-89689-428-0
ISBN 10-digit: 0-89689-428-2

Designed by: Sandra L. Morrison
Edited by: George Cuhaj and Tom Michael

Printed in the United States of America

Table of Contents

Introduction

Welcome to this first edition of the *KP Official Guide to Coins of Northern Europe & Russia.*

Condensed in this volume you will find the same great coin information that collectors, dealers and the casual reader have come to expect from the Krause Publications *Standard Catalog of World Coins* series. This unique volume, the first of four, provides a streamlined version of the data, while encompassing a broader historical timeframe than the current century-specific books, and covering a popular geographic region for collectors.

Countries covered in this volume include: Belarus, Belgium, Czech Republic, Czechoslovakia, Danzig, Denmark, Estonia, Faeroe Islands, Finland, German States, Germany (Empire), Weimar Republic, Germany during the Third Reich, the German Federal Republic; the German Democratic Republic; Great Britain, Greenland, Guernsey, Iceland, Ireland, Irish Republic, Isle of Man, Jersey, Latvia, Lithuania, Luxembourg, Netherlands, Norway, Poland, Russia, Slovakia, Spitzbergen and Sweden.

The starting and ending dates of the presentations are different for each of the countries contained within. For those countries which existed in the 19th century, a natural break in coinage types, either due to a new ruler or that of a major coinage change has been selected. For countries formed after World War I, this natural starting point has been maintained. Finally, for countries that resumed coinage after the breakup of the U.S.S.R. those issues are included.

The ending dates of the countries presented generally come up to the present. In a very few cases, particularly Guernsey, Isle of Man and Jersey, listings terminate in 1971 due to the large number of non-circulating legal tender issues produced by those countries after that date. These issues can be found in the *Standard Catalog of World Coins – 1901-2000, and 2001-present.*

This book has been compiled in a streamlined form for ease of identification and providing a handy, portable guide for the dealer, collector, and buyer on the go. A photograph, denomination and medal are presented along with the type description, and the full date and mintmark listing has been truncated to a date range format that includes base line pricing for the type.

We hope that users of this book will enjoy this simplified format for portability and convenience. For additional information on the coins presented in this book, please consult our regular *Standard Catalog of World Coins* series, or visit us on the web at www.numismaster.com.

The editors,
Iola, Wisconsin, October 2006.

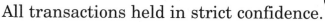

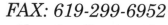

Acknowledgements

Jan Olav Aamlid
David Addey
Esko Ahlroth
Joel Anderson
Yuri Barshay
Alex Basok
Mitchell Battino
Anton Belcev
Al Boulanger
Christopher Budesa
Doru Calin
Ivo Cerny
Jerry Crain
Eric Dawson
Jean-Paul Divo
Stephen Eccles
Wilhelm Eglseer
Esko Ekman
Kent Froseth
Tom Galway
Dennis Gill
Mark Goldberg
Dieter Gorny
Ron Guth
Flemming Lyngbeck Hansen
Martin Rodney Hayter
James Higby
Anton Holt
Serge Huard
Martin Jacobowitz
Robert Johnston
Robert Julian
Børge R. Juul
Alex Kaglyan
Dmitry Korzhkov
Peter Krix
Matti Kuronen
Joseph Lang
Thomas Lautz
Claire Lobel
Richard Lobel
Harrington Manville
Jeff Means
Franck Medina
Juozas Minikevicius
Dr. Richard Montrey

Paul Montz
Horst-Dieter Müller
Arkady Nakhimovsky
Michael Nielsen
Frank Passic
Jens Pilegaard
Romain Probst
Gerhard Schön
Michael Sedgwick
Alexander Shapiro
Evzen Sknouril
Vladimir Suchy
Benjamin Swagerty
Mehmet Tolga Tanner
M. Louis Teller
Gunnar Thesen
Anthony Tumonis
Robert Van Bebber
J. Van der Schueren
Erik Van Loon
R Walter
Stewart Westdal

Auction Houses

Dix-Noonan-Webb
Heritage World Coin Auctions
Thomas Høiland Montauktion
Hess-Divo Ltd.
Münzenhandlung Harald Möller, GmbH
Ponterio & Associates
Laurens Schulman BV
Stack's
UBS, AG
World Wide Coins of California

Societies

American Numismatic Association
American Numismatic Society
British Museum
British Royal Mint
Central Bank of Russian Federation
Mint of Finland
Numismatics International
Royal Dutch Mint
Smithsonian Institution

Whatever your specialty, Heritage has coins – and information – for you!

Over the last several years, Heritage has auctioned more than $25 million in ancient and world coins – including many individual rarities and entire collections from Russia and Northern Europe. The information on every lot – descriptions, prices realized, and full-color, enlargeable images – is available in our Permanent Auction Archives, exclusively at HA.com. This incredible resource is fully searchable, so whether your focus is on Borodino or Gustaf IV, you can easily find the information you need. All this is included with your free membership – sign up now from the homepage at HA.com.

Whatever your collecting specialty, Heritage wants to be your #1 choice when buying or selling. We invite you to contact us at 800-872-6467
Warren Tucker, World Coin Director, Ext. 287,
or e-mail WTucker@HA.com

> **HA.com/Join** *(free and quick). Enter reference #5348 for bonus auction catalog or book of your choice.*

Foreign Exchange Table

The latest foreign exchange fixed rates below apply to trade with banks in the country of origin. The left column shows the number of units per U.S. dollar at the official rate. The right column shows the number of units per dollar at the free market rate.

Country	Official	Free
Afghanistan (New Afghani)	49.6	–
Albania (Lek)	102	–
Algeria (Dinar)	70.8	–
Andorra uses Euro	.83	–
Angola (Readjust Kwanza)	80	–
Anguilla uses E.C.Dollar	2.70	–
Antigua uses E.C.Dollar	2.70	–
Argentina (Peso)	3.08	–
Armenia (Dram)	450	–
Aruba (Florin)	1.79	–
Australia (Dollar)	1.35	–
Austria (Euro)	.83	–
Azerbaijan (Manat)	4,600	–
Bahamas (Dollar)	1.00	–
Bahrain Is.(Dinar)	.377	–
Bangladesh (Taka)	68	–
Barbados (Dollar)	2.00	–
Belarus (Ruble)	2,150	–
Belgium (Euro)	.83	–
Belize (Dollar)	1.98	–
Benin uses CFA Franc West	545	–
Bermuda (Dollar)	1.00	–
Bhutan (Ngultrum)	44.3	–
Bolivia (Boliviano)	8.00	–
Bosnia-Herzegovina (Deutschmark)	1.63	–
Botswana (Pula)	5.50	–
British Virgin Islands uses U.S.Dollar	1.00	–
Brazil (Real)	2.15	–
Brunei (Dollar)	1.63	–
Bulgaria (Lev)	1.63	–
Burkina Faso uses CFA Fr.West	545	–
Burma (Kyat)	6.42	1,250
Burundi (Franc)	975	–
Cambodia (Riel)	4,100	–
Cameroon uses CFA Franc Central	545	–
Canada (Dollar)	1.14	–
Cape Verde (Escudo)	91.8	–
Cayman Is.(Dollar)	0.82	–
Central African Rep.	545	–
CFA Franc Central	545	–
CFA Franc West	545	–
CFP Franc	99.3	–
Chad uses CFA Franc Central	545	–
Chile (Peso)	525	–
China, P.R. (Renminbi Yuan)	8.037	–
Colombia (Peso)	2,255	–
Comoros (Franc)	410	–
Congo uses CFA Franc Central	545	–
Congo-Dem.Rep. (Congolese Franc)	430	–
Cook Islands (Dollar)	1.73	–
Costa Rica (Colon)	503	–
Croatia (Kuna)	6.09	–
Cuba (Peso)	1.00	27
Cyprus (Pound)	.48	–
Czech Republic (Koruna)	23.8	–
Denmark (Danish Krone)	6.21	–
Djibouti (Franc)	175	–
Dominica uses E.C.Dollar	2.70	–
Dominican Republic (Peso)	32.5	–
East Caribbean (Dollar)	2.70	–
Ecuador uses U.S. Dollar	1.00	–
Egypt (Pound)	5.74	–
El Salvador uses U.S. Dollar	1.00	–
England	.57	–
Equatorial Guinea uses CFA Franc Central	545	–
Eritrea (Nafka)	15	–
Estonia (Kroon)	13.02	–
Ethiopia (Birr)	8.73	–
Euro	.83	–
Falkland Is. (Pound)	.57	–
Faroe Islands (Krona)	6.21	–
Fiji Islands (Dollar)	1.75	–
Finland (Euro)	.83	–
France (Euro)	.83	–
French Polynesia uses CFP Franc	99.3	–
Gabon (CFA Franc)	545	–
Gambia (Dalasi)	28.3	–
Georgia (Lari)	1.83	–
Germany (Euro)	.83	–
Ghana (Cedi)	9,160	–
Gibraltar (Pound)	.57	–
Great Britain	.57	–
Greece (Euro)	.83	–
Greenland uses Danish Krone	6.21	–
Grenada uses E.C.Dollar	2.70	–
Guatemala (Quetzal)	7.63	–
Guernsey (Pound Sterling)	.57	–
Guinea Bissau (CFA Franc)	545	–
Guinea Conakry (Franc)	4475	–
Guyana (Dollar)	200	–
Haiti (Gourde)	41.9	–
Honduras (Lempira)	18.9	–
Hong Kong (Dollar)	7.76	–
Hungary (Forint)	210	–
Iceland (Krona)	66.2	–
India (Rupee)	44.3	–
Indonesia (Rupiah)	9,200	–
Iran (Rial)	9.130	–
Iraq (Dinar)	1,523	1,930
Ireland (Euro)	.83	–
Isle of Man (Pound Sterling)	.57	–
Israel (New Sheqalim)	4.71	–
Italy (Euro)	.83	–
Ivory Coast uses CFA Franc West	545	–
Jamaica (Dollar)	63	–

Country (Currency)			Country (Currency)		
Japan (Yen)	117.6	–	Portugal (Euro)	.83	–
Jersey (Pound Sterling)	.57	–	Qatar (Riyal)	3.64	–
Jordan (Dinar)	.71	–	Romania (New Leu)	2.89	–
Kazakhstan (Tenge)	130	–	Russia (New Ruble)	27.93	–
Kenya (Shilling)	72	–	Rwanda (Franc)	545	–
Kiribati uses Australian Dollar	1.35	–	St.Helena (Pound)	.57	–
Korea-PDR (Won)	2.2	500	St.Kitts uses E.C.Dollar	2.70	–
Korea-Rep. (Won)	975	–	St.Lucia uses E.C.Dollar	2.70	–
Kuwait (Dinar)	.292	–	St.Vincent uses E.C.Dollar	2.70	–
Kyrgyzstan (Som)	417	–	San Marino uses Euro	.83	–
Laos (Kip)	10,400	–	Sao Tome e Principe (Dobra)	7100	–
Latvia (Lat)	.58	–	Saudi Arabia (Riyal)	3.751	–
Lebanon (Pound)	1,500	–	Scotland (Pound Sterling)	.57	–
Lesotho (Maloti)	6.24	–	Senegal uses CFA Franc West	545	–
Liberia (Dollar) "JJ"	57	-	Serbia (Dinar)	72.8	–
Libya (Dinar)	1.34	–	Seychelles (Rupee)	5.52	6.40
Liechtenstein uses Swiss Franc	1.297	–	Sierra Leone (Leone)	2,950	–
Lithuania (Litas)	2.88	–	Singapore (Dollar)	1.63	–
Luxembourg (Euro)	.83	–	Slovakia (Sk. Koruna)	31	–
Macao (Pataca)	7.99	–	Slovenia (Tolar)	200	–
Macedonia (New Denar)	51	–	Solomon Is.(Dollar)	7.59	–
Madagascar (Franc)	2,220	–	Somalia (Shilling)	1600	–
Malawi (Kwacha)	135	–	Somaliland (Somali Shilling)	1,800	4,000
Malaysia (Ringgit)	3.71	–	South Africa (Rand)	6.24	–
Maldives (Rufiya)	12.8	–	Spain (Euro)	.83	–
Mali uses CFA Franc West	545	–	Sri Lanka (Rupee)	102	–
Malta (Lira)	.36	–	Sudan (Dinar)	230	300
Marshall Islands uses U.S.Dollar	1.00	–	Surinam (Dollar)	2.74	–
Mauritania (Ouguiya)	270	–	Swaziland (Lilangeni)	6.24	–
Mauritius (Rupee)	30.7	–	Sweden (Krona)	7.86	–
Mexico (Peso)	10.69	–	Switzerland (Franc)	1.29	–
Moldova (Leu)	13	–	Syria (Pound)	52.2	–
Monaco uses Euro	.83	–	Taiwan (NT Dollar)	32.5	–
Mongolia (Tugrik)	1,200	–	Tajikistan (Somoni)	3.21	–
Montenegro uses Euro	.83	–	Tanzania (Shilling)	1,200	–
Montserrat uses E.C.Dollar	2.70	–	Thailand (Baht)	38.8	–
Morocco (Dirham)	9.73	–	Togo uses CFAFranc West	545	–
Mozambique (Metical)	26,850	–	Tonga (Paíanga)	2.05	–
Myanmar (Burma) (Kyat)	6.42	1,250	Transdniestra (Ruble)	6.51	–
Namibia (Rand)	6.24	–	Trinidad & Tobago (Dollar)	6.29	–
Nauru uses Australian Dollar	1.35	–	Tunisia (Dinar)	1.35	–
Nepal (Rupee)	70.9	–	Turkey (New Lira)	1.31	–
Netherlands (Euro)	.83	–	Turkmenistan (Manat)	5,200	–
Netherlands Antilles (Gulden)	1.79	–	Turks & Caicos uses U.S.Dollar	1.00	–
New Caledonia uses CFP Franc	99.3	–	Tuvalu uses Australian Dollar	1.35	–
New Zealand (Dollar)	1.52	–	Uganda (Shilling)	1,825	–
Nicaragua (Cordoba Oro)	17.15	–	Ukraine (Hryvnia)	5.06	–
Niger uses CFA Franc West	545	–	United Arab Emirates (Dirham)	3.67	–
Nigeria (Naira)	130	–	United Kingdom (Pound Sterling)	.57	–
Northern Ireland (Pound Sterling)	.57	–	Uruguay (Peso Uruguayo)	24.3	–
Norway (Krone)	6.64	–	Uzbekistan (Som)	1,200	–
Oman (Rial)	.385	–	Vanuatu (Vatu)	113	–
Pakistan (Rupee)	59.9	–	Vatican City uses Euro	.83	–
Palau uses U.S.Dollar	1.00	–	Venezuela (Bolivar)	2,150	2,000
Panama (Balboa) uses U.S.Dollar	1.00	–	Vietnam (Dong)	15,915	–
Papua New Guinea (Kina)	3.10	–	Western Samoa (Tala)	2.74	–
Paraguay (Guarani)	5,970	–	Yemen (Rial)	195	–
Peru (Nuevo Sol)	3.33	–	Zambia (Kwacha)	3,300	–
Philippines (Peso)	51	–	Zimbabwe (Dollar)	100,000	–
Poland (Zloty)	3.19	–			

How To Use This Catalog

This catalog series is designed to serve the needs of both the novice and advanced collectors. It provides a comprehensive guide to well over 100 years of world coinage. It is generally arranged so that persons with no more than a basic knowledge of world history and a casual acquaintance with coin collecting can consult it with confidence and ease. The following explanations summarize the general practices used in preparing this catalog's listings. However, because of specialized requirements, which may vary by country and era, these must not be considered ironclad. Where these standards have been set aside, appropriate notations of the variations are incorporated in that particular listing.

Arrangement

Countries are arranged alphabetically. Political changes within a country are arranged chronologically. In countries where Rulers are the single most significant political entity, a chronological arrangement by Ruler has been employed. Distinctive sub-geographic regions are listed alphabetically following the country's main listings. A few exceptions to these rules may exist. Refer to the Country Index.

Diverse coinage types relating to fabrication methods, revaluations, denomination systems, non-circulating categories and such have been identified, separated and arranged in logical fashion. Chronological arrangement is employed for most circulating coinage, i.e., Hammered coinage will normally precede Milled coinage, monetary reforms will flow in order of their institution.

Within a coinage type coins will be listed by denomination, from smallest to largest. Numbered types within a denomination will be ordered by their first date of issue.

Identification

The most important step in the identification of a coin is the determination of the nation of origin. This is generally easily accomplished where English-speaking lands are concerned, however, use of the country index is sometimes required. The coins of Great Britain provide an interesting challenge. For hundreds of years the only indication of the country of origin was in the abbreviated Latin legends. In recent times there have been occasions when there has been no indication of origin. Only through the familiarity of the monarchical portraits, symbols and legends or indication of currency system are they identifiable.

The coins of many countries beyond the English-language realm, such as those of French, Italian or Spanish heritage, are also quite easy to identify through reference to their legends, which appear in the national languages based on Western alphabets. In many instances the name is spelled exactly the same in English as in the national language, such as France; while in other cases it varies only slightly, like Italia for Italy, Belgique or Belgie for Belgium, Brasil for Brazil and Danmark for Denmark.

This is not always the case, however, as in Norge for Norway, Espana for Spain, Sverige for Sweden and Helvetia for Switzerland.

Some other examples include:
DEUTSCHES REICH - Germany 1873-1945
BUNDESREPUBLIC DEUTSCHLAND - Federal Republic of Germany.
DEUTSCHE DEMOKRATISCHE REPUBLIK -
German Democratic Republic.
EMPIRE CHERIFIEN MAROC - Morocco.
ESTADOS UNIDOS MEXICANOS - United Mexican States (Mexico).
ETAT DU GRAND LIBAN - State of Great Lebanon (Lebanon).

Thus it can be seen there are instances in which a little schooling in the rudiments of foreign languages can be most helpful. In general, colonial possessions of countries using the Western alphabet are similarly identifiable as they often carry portraits of their current rulers, the familiar lettering, sometimes in combination with a companion designation in the local language.

Collectors have the greatest difficulty with coins that do not bear legends or dates in the Western systems. These include coins bearing Cyrillic lettering attributable to Bulgaria, Russia, the Slavic states and Mongolia; the Greek script peculiar to Greece, Crete and the Ionian Islands; the Amharic characters of Ethiopia; or Hebrew in the case of Israel. Dragons and sunbursts along with the distinctive word characters attribute a coin to the Oriental countries of China, Japan, Korea, Tibet, Viet Nam and their component parts.

The most difficult coins to identify are those bearing only Persian or Arabic script and its derivatives, found on the issues of nations stretching in a wide swath across North Africa and East Asia, from Morocco to Indonesia, and the Indian subcontinent coinages which surely are more confusing in their vast array of Nagari, Sanskrit, Ahom, Assamese and other local dialects found on the local issues of the Indian Princely States. Although the task of identification on the more modern issues of these lands is often eased by the added presence of Western alphabet legends, a feature sometimes adopted as early as the late 19th Century, for the earlier pieces it is often necessary for the uninitiated to laboriously seek and find.

Except for the cruder issues, however, it will be found that certain characteristics and symbols featured in addition to the predominant legends are typical on coins from a given country or group of countries. The toughra monogram, for instance, occurs on some of the coins of Afghanistan, Egypt, the Sudan, Pakistan, Turkey and other areas of the late Ottoman Empire. A predominant design feature on the coins of Nepal is the trident; while neighboring Tibet features a lotus blossom or lion on many of their issues.

To assist in identification of the more difficult coins, we have assembled the Instant Identifier and Monogram sections presented on the following pages.

They are designed to provide a point of beginning for collectors by allowing them to compare unidentified coins with photographic details from typical issues.

We also suggest reference to the Index of Coin Denominations presented here and also the comprehensive Country Index, where the inscription will be found listed just as it appears on the coin for nations using the Western alphabet.

Dating

Coin dating is the final basic attribution consideration. Here, the problem can be more difficult because the reading of a coin date is subject not only to the vagaries of numeric styling, but to calendar variations caused by the observance of various religious eras or regal periods from country to country, or even within a country. Here again, with the exception of the sphere from North Africa through the Orient, it will be found that most countries rely on Western date numerals and Christian (AD) era reckoning, although in a few instances, coin dating has been tied to the year of a reign or government. The Vatican, for example dates its coinage according to the year of reign of the current pope, in addition to the Christian-era date.

Countries in the Arabic sphere generally date their coins to the Muslim era (AH), which commenced on July 16, 622 AD (Julian calendar), when the prophet Mohammed fled from Mecca to Medina. As their calendar is reckoned by the lunar year of 354 days, which is about three percent (precisely 2.98%) shorter than the Christian year, a formula is required to convert AH dating to its Western equivalent. To convert an AH date to the approximate AD date, subtract three percent of the AH date (round to the closest whole number) from the AH date and add 622. A chart converting all AH years from 1010 (July 2, 1601) to 1450 (May 25, 2028) may be found elsewhere in the catalog under the name Hejira Date Chart.

The Muslim calendar is not always based on the lunar year (AH), however, causing some confusion, particularly in Afghanistan and Iran, where a calendar based on the solar year (SH) was introduced around 1920. These dates can be converted to AD by simply adding 621. In 1976 the government of Iran implemented a new solar calendar based on the foundation of the Iranian monarchy in 559 BC. The first year observed on the new calendar was 2535 (MS), which commenced March 20, 1976. A reversion to the traditional SH dating standard occurred a few years later.

Several different eras of reckoning, including Christian and Muslim (AH), have been used to date coins of the Indian subcontinent. The two basic systems are the Vikrama Samvat (VS), which dates from Oct. 18, 58 BC, and the Saka era, the origin of which is reckoned from March 3, 78 AD. Dating according to both eras appears on various coins of the area.

Coins of Thailand (Siam) are found dated by three different eras. The most predominant is the Buddhist era (BE), which originated in 543 BC. Next is the Bangkok or Ratanakosindsok (RS) era, dating from 1781 AD; followed by the Chula-Sakarat (CS) era, dating from 638 AD. The latter era originated in Burma and is used on that country's coins.

Other calendars include that of the Ethiopian era (EE), which commenced seven years, eight months after AD dating; and that of the Jewish people, which commenced on Oct. 7, 3761 BC. Korea claims a legendary dating from 2333 BC, which is acknowledged in some of its coin dating. Some coin issues of the Indonesian area carry dates determined by the Javanese Aji Saka era (AS), a calendar of 354 days (100 Javanese years equal 97 Christian or Gregorian calendar years), which can be matched to AD dating by comparing it to AH dating.

The following table indicates the year dating for the various eras, which correspond to 2006 in Christian calendar reckoning, but it must be remembered that there are overlaps between the eras in some instances.

Christian era (AD)	-2006
Muslim era (AH)	-AH1427
Solar year (SH)	-SH1384
Monarchic Solar era (MS)	-MS2565
Vikrama Samvat (VS)	-VS2063
Saka era (SE)	-SE1928
Buddhist era (BE)	-BE2549
Bangkok era (RS)	-RS225
Chula-Sakarat era (CS)	-CS1368
Ethiopian era (EE)	-EE2000
Korean era	-4339
Javanese Aji Saka era (AS)	-AS1939
Fasli era (FE)	-FE1416
Jewish era (JE)	-JE5766

Coins of Asian origin - principally Japan, Korea, China, Turkestan and Tibet and some modern gold issues of Turkey - are generally dated to the year of the government, dynasty, reign or cyclic eras, with the dates indicated in Asian characters which usually read from right to left. In recent years, however, some dating has been according to the Christian calendar and in Western numerals. In Japan, Asian character dating was reversed to read from left to right in Showa year 23 (1948 AD).

More detailed guides to less prevalent coin dating systems, which are strictly local in nature, are presented with the appropriate listings.

Some coins carry dates according to both locally observed and Christian eras. This is particularly true in the Arabic world, where the Hejira date may be indicated in Arabic numerals and the Christian date in Western numerals, or both dates in either form.

The date actually carried on a given coin is generally cataloged here in the first column (Date) to the right of the catalog number. If this date is by a non-Christian dating system, such as 'AH' (Muslim), the Christian equivalent date will appear in parentheses(), for example AH1336(1917). Dates listed alone in the date column which do not actually appear on a given coin, or dates which are known, but do not appear on the coin, are generally enclosed by parentheses with 'ND' at the left, for example ND(1926).

Timing differentials between some era of reckoning, particularly the 354-day Mohammedan and 365-day Christian years, cause situations whereby coins which carry dates for both eras exist bearing two year dates from one calendar combined with a single date from another.

Countermarked Coinage is presented with both 'Countermark Date' and 'Host Coin' date for each type. Actual date representation follows the rules outlined above.

Numbering System

Some catalog numbers assigned in this volume are based on established references. This practice has been observed for two reasons: First, when world coins are listed chronologically they are basically self-cataloging; second, there was no need to confuse collectors with totally new numeric designations where appropriate systems already existed. As time progressed we found many of these established systems incomplete and inadequate and have now replaced many with new KM numbers. When numbers change appropriate cross-referencing has been provided.

Some of the coins listed in this catalog are identified or cross-referenced by numbers assigned by R.S. Yeoman (Y#), or slight adaptations thereof, in his Modern World Coins, and Current Coins of the World. For the pre-Yeoman dated issues, the numbers assigned by William D. Craig (C#) in his Coins of the World (1750-1850 period), 3rd edition, have generally been applied.

In some countries, listings are cross-referenced to Robert Friedberg's (FR#) Gold Coins of the World or Coins of the British World. Major Fred Pridmore's (P#) studies of British colonial coinage are also referenced, as are W.H. Valentine's (V#) references on the Modern Copper Coins of the Mohammedan States. Coins issued under the Chinese sphere of influence are assigned numbers from E. Kann's (K#) Illustrated Catalog of Chinese Coins and T.K. Hsu's (Su) work of similar title. In most cases, these cross-reference numbers are presented in the descriptive text for each type.

Denominations

The second basic consideration to be met in the attribution of a coin is the determination of denomination. Since denominations are usually expressed in numeric rather than word form on a coin, this is usually quite easily accomplished on coins from nations which use Western numerals, except in those instances where issues are devoid of any mention of face value, and denomination must be attributed by size, metallic composition or weight. Coins listed in this volume are generally illustrated in actual size. Where size is critical to proper attribution, the coin's millimeter size is indicated.

The sphere of countries stretching from North Africa through the Orient, on which numeric symbols generally unfamiliar to Westerners are employed, often provide the collector with a much greater challenge. This is particularly true on nearly all pre-20th Century issues. On some of the more modern issues and increasingly so as the years progress, Western-style numerals usually presented in combination with the local numeric system are becoming more commonplace on these coins.

Determination of a coin's currency system can also be valuable in attributing the issue to its country of origin. A comprehensive alphabetical index of currency names, applicable to the countries as cataloged in this volume, with all individual nations of use for each, is presented in this section.

The included table of Standard International Numeral Systems presents charts of the basic numeric designations found on coins of non-Western origin. Although denomination numerals are generally prominently displayed on coins, it must be remembered that these are general representations of characters, which individual coin engravers may have rendered in widely varying styles. Where numeric or script denominations designation forms peculiar to a given coin or country apply, such as the script used on some Persian (Iranian) issues. They are so indicated or illustrated in conjunction with the appropriate listings.

Mint and Privy Marks

The presence of distinctive, but frequently inconspicuously placed, mintmarks indicates the mint of issue for many of the coins listed in this catalog. An appropriate designation in the date listings notes the presence, if any, of a mint mark on a particular coin type by incorporating the letter or letters of the mint mark adjoining the date, i.e., 1950D or 1927R.

Coin Alignment   Medal Alignment

Coin vs Medal Alignment

Some coins are struck with obverse and reverse aligned at a rotation of 180 degrees from each other. When a coin is held for vertical viewing with the obverse design aligned upright and the index finger and thumb at the top and bottom, upon rotation from left to right for viewing the reverse, the latter will be upside down. Such alignment is called "coin rotation." Other coins are struck with the obverse and reverse designs mated on an alignment of zero or 360 degrees. If such an example is held and rotated as described, the reverse will appear upright. This is the alignment, which is generally observed in the striking of medals, and for that reason coins produced in this manner are considered struck in "medal rotation". In some instances, often through error, certain coin issues have been struck to both alignment standards, creating interesting collectible varieties, which will be found noted in some listings. In addition, some countries are now producing coins with other designated obverse to reverse alignments which are considered standard for this type.

The presence of mint and/or mintmaster's privy marks on a coin in non-letter form is indicated by incorporating the mint letter in lower case within parentheses adjoining the date; i.e. 1927(a). The corresponding mark is illustrated or identified in the introduction of the country.

In countries such as France and Mexico, where many mints may be producing like coinage in the same denomination during the same time period, divisions by mint have been employed. In these cases the mint mark may appear next to the individual date listings and/or the mint name or mint mark may be listed in the Note field of the type description.

Where listings incorporate mintmaster initials, they are always presented in capital letters separated from the date by one character space; i.e., 1850 MF. The different mintmark and mintmaster letters found on the coins of any country, state or city of issue are always shown at the beginning of listings.

Metals

Each numbered type listing will contain a description of the coins metallic content. The traditional coinage metals and their symbolic chemical abbreviations sometimes used in this catalog are:

Platinum - (PT)	Copper - (Cu)
Gold - (Au)	Brass -
Silver - (Ag)	Copper-nickel- (CN)
Billion -	Lead - (Pb)
Nickel - (Ni)	Steel -
Zinc - (Zn)	Tin - (Sn)
Bronze - (Ae)	Aluminum - (Al)

During the 18th and 19th centuries, most of the world's coins were struck of copper or bronze, silver and gold. Commencing in the early years of the 20th century, however, numerous new coinage metals, primarily non-precious metal alloys, were introduced. Gold has not been widely used for circulation coinages since World War I, although silver remained a popular coinage metal in most parts of the world until after World War II. With the disappearance of silver for circulation coinage, numerous additional compositions were introduced to coinage applications.

Most recent is the development of clad or plated planchets in order to maintain circulation life and extend the life of a set of production dies as used in the production of the copper-nickel clad copper 50 centesimos of Panama or in the latter case to reduce production costs of the planchets and yet provide a coin quite similar in appearance to its predecessor as in the case of the copper plated zinc core United States 1983 cent.

Modern commemorative coins have employed still more unusual methods such as bimetallic coins, color applications and precious metal or gem inlays.

Precious Metal Weights

Listings of weight, fineness and actual silver (ASW), gold (AGW), platinum or palladium (APW) content of most machine-struck silver, gold, platinum and palladium coins are provided in this edition. This information will be found incorporated in each separate type listing, along with other data related to the coin.

The ASW, AGW and APW figures were determined by multiplying the gross weight of a given coin by its known or tested fineness and converting the resulting gram or grain weight to troy ounces, rounded to the nearest ten-thousandth of an ounce. A silver coin with a 24.25-gram weight and .875 fineness for example, would have a fine weight of approximately 21.2188 grams, or a .6822 ASW, a factor that can be used to accurately determine the intrinsic value for multiple examples.

The ASW, AGW or APW figure can be multiplied by the spot price of each precious metal to determine the current intrinsic value of any coin accompanied by these designations.

Coin weights are indicated in grams (abbreviated "g") along with fineness where the information is of value in differentiating between types. These weights are based on 31.103 grams per troy (scientific) ounce, as opposed to the avoirdupois (commercial) standard of 28.35 grams. Actual coin weights are generally shown in hundredths or thousands of a gram; i.e., 0.500 SILVER 2.9200g.WEIGHTS AND FINENESSES

As the silver and gold bullion markets have advanced and declined sharply over the years, the fineness and total precious metal content of coins has become especially significant where bullion coins - issues which trade on the basis of their intrinsic metallic content rather than numismatic value - are concerned. In many instances, such issues have become worth more in bullion form than their nominal collector values or denominations indicate.

Establishing the weight of a coin can also be valuable for determining its denomination. Actual weight is also necessary to ascertain the specific gravity of the coin's metallic content, an important factor in determining authenticity.

Troy Weight Standards
24 Grains = 1 Pennyweight
480 Grains = 1 Ounce
31.103 Grams = 1 Ounce

Uniform Weights
15.432 Grains = 1 Gram
0.0648 Gram = 1 Grain

Avoirdupois Standards
27-11/32 Grains = 11 Dram
437-1/2 Grains = 1 Ounce
28.350 Grams = 1 Ounce

Bullion Value

The simplest method for determining the bullion value of a precious metal coin is to multiply the actual precious metal weight by the current spot price for that metal. Using the example above, a silver coin with a .6822 actual silver weight (ASW) would have an intrinsic value of $6.65 when the spot price of silver is $9.75. If the spot price of silver rose to $11.00 that same coins intrinsic value would rise to $7.50.

Valuations for most of the silver, gold, platinum and palladium coins listed in this edition are based on assumed market values of **$11.50** per troy ounce for silver, **$625** for gold, **$1200** for platinum, and **$300** for palladium. To arrive at accurate current market indications for these issues, increase or decrease the valuations appropriately based on any variations in these indicated levels.

Homeland Types

Homeland types are coins which colonial powers used in a colony, but do not bear that location's name. In some cases they were legal tender in the homeland, in others not. They are listed under the homeland and cross-referenced at the colony listing.

Countermarks\Counterstamps

There is some confusion among collectors over the terms "countermark" and "counterstamp" when applied to a coin bearing an additional mark or change of design and/or denomination.

To clarify, a countermark might be considered similar to the "hall mark" applied to a piece of silverware, by which a silversmith assured the quality of the piece. In the same way, a countermark assures the quality of the coin on which it is placed, as, for example, when the royal crown of England was countermarked (punched into) on segmented Spanish reales, allowing them to circulate in commerce in the British West Indies. An additional countermark indicating the new denomination may also be encountered on these coins.

Countermarks are generally applied singularly and in most cases indiscriminately on either side of the "host" coin.

Counterstamped coins are more extensively altered. The counterstamping is done with a set of dies, rather than a hand punch. The coin being counterstamped is placed between the new dies and struck as if it were a blank planchet as found with the Manila 8 reales issue of the Philippines. A more unusual application where the counterstamp dies were smaller than the host coin in the revalidated 50 centimos and 1 colon of Costa Rica issued in 1923.

Photographs

To assist the reader in coin identification, every effort has been made to present actual size photographs of every coinage type listed. Obverse and reverse are illustrated, except when a change in design is restricted to one side, and the coin has a diameter of 39mm or larger, in which case only the side required for identification of the type is generally illustrated. All coins up to 60mm are illustrated actual size, to the nearest 1/2mm up to 25mm, and to the nearest 1mm thereafter. Coins larger than 60mm diameter are illustrated in reduced size, with the actual size noted in the descriptive text block. Where slight change in size is important to coin type identification, actual millimeter measurements are stated.

Valuations

Values quoted in this catalog represent the current market and are compiled from recommendations provided and verified through various source documents and specialized consultants. It should be stressed, however, that this book is intended to serve only as an aid for evaluating coins, actual market conditions are constantly changing and additional influences, such as particularly strong local demand for certain coin series, fluctuation of international exchange rates, changes in spot price of precious metals and worldwide collection patterns must also be considered. Publication of this catalog is not intended as a solicitation by the publisher, editors or contributors to buy or sell the coins listed at the prices indicated.

All valuations are stated in U.S. dollars, based on careful assessment of the varied international collector market. Valuations for coins priced below $100.00 are generally stated in full amounts - i.e. 37.50 or 95.00 - while valuations at or above that figure are rounded off in even dollars - i.e. $125.00 is expressed 125. A comma is added to indicate thousands of dollars in value.

For the convenience of overseas collectors and for U.S. collectors doing business with overseas dealers, the base exchange rate for the national currencies of approximately 180 countries are presented in the Foreign Exchange Table.

It should be noted that when particularly select uncirculated or proof-like examples of uncirculated coins become available they can be expected to command proportionately high premiums. Such examples in reference to choice Germanic Thalers are referred to as "erst schlage" or first strikes.

Restrikes/Counterfeits

Deceptive restrike and counterfeit (both contemporary and modern) examples exist of some coin issues. Where possible, the existence of restrikes is noted. Warnings are also incorporated in instances where particularly deceptive counterfeits are known to exist. Collectors who are uncertain about the authenticity of a coin held in their collection, or being offered for sale, should take the precaution of having it authenticated by the American Numismatic Association Authentication Bureau, 818 N. Cascade, Colorado Springs, CO 80903. Their reasonably priced certification tests are widely accepted by collectors and dealers alike.

Non-Circulating Legal Tender Coins

Coins of non-circulating legal tender (NCLT) origin are individually listed and integrated by denomination into the regular listings for each country. These coins fall outside the customary definitions of coin-of-the-realm issues, but where created and sold by, or under authorization of, agencies of sovereign governments expressly for collectors. These are primarily individual coins and sets of a commemorative nature, marketed at prices substantially in excess of face value, and usually do not have counterparts released for circulation.

Edge Varieties

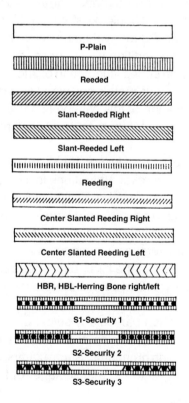

P-Plain

Reeded

Slant-Reeded Right

Slant-Reeded Left

Reeding

Center Slanted Reeding Right

Center Slanted Reeding Left

HBR, HBL-Herring Bone right/left

S1-Security 1

S2-Security 2

S3-Security 3

New Issues

All newly released coins dated up to the year 2006 that have been physically observed by our staff or identified by reliable sources and have been confirmed by press time have been incorporated in this edition. Exceptions exist in some countries where current date coin production lags far behind or information on current issues is less accessible.

Conditions/Grading

Wherever possible, coin valuations are given in four or five grades of preservation. For modern commemoratives, which do not circulate, only uncirculated values are usually sufficient. Proof issues are indicated by the word "Proof" next to the date, with valuation proceeded by the word "value" following the mintage. For very recent circulating coins and coins of limited value, one, two or three grade values are presented.

There are almost no grading guides for world coins. What follows is an attempt to help bridge that gap until a detailed, illustrated guide becomes available.

In grading world coins, there are two elements to look for: 1) Overall wear, and 2) loss of design details, such as strands of hair, feathers on eagles, designs on coats of arms, etc.

The age, rarity or type of a coin should not be a consideration in grading.

Grade each coin by the weaker of the two sides. This method appears to give results most nearly consistent with conservative American Numismatic Association standards for U.S. coins. Split grades, i.e., F/VF for obverse and reverse, respectively, are normally no more than one grade apart. If the two sides are more than one grade apart, the series of coins probably wears differently on each side and should then be graded by the weaker side alone.

Grade by the amount of overall wear and loss of design detail evident on each side of the coin. On coins with a moderately small design element, which is prone to early wear, grade by that design alone. For example, the 5-ore (KM#554) of Sweden has a crown above the monogram on which the beads on the arches show wear most clearly. So, grade by the crown alone.

For **Brilliant Uncirculated** (BU) grades there will be no visible signs of wear or handling, even under a 30-power microscope. Full mint luster will be present. Ideally no bags marks will be evident.

For **Uncirculated** (Unc.) grades there will be no visible signs of wear or handling, even under a 30-power microscope. Bag marks may be present.

For **Almost Uncirculated** (AU), all detail will be visible. There will be wear only on the highest point of the coin. There will often be half or more of the original mint luster present.

On the **Extremely Fine** (XF or EF) coin, there will be about 95% of the original detail visible. Or, on a coin with a design with no inner detail to wear down, there will be a light wear over nearly all the coin. If a small design is used as the grading area, about 90% of the original detail will be visible. This latter rule stems from the logic that a smaller amount of detail needs to be present because a small area is being used to grade the whole coin.

The **Very Fine** (VF) coin will have about 75% of the original detail visible. Or, on a coin with no inner detail, there will be moderate wear over the entire coin. Corners of letters and numbers may be weak. A small grading area will have about 66% of the original detail.

For **Fine** (F), there will be about 50% of the original detail visible. Or, on a coin with no inner detail, there will be fairly heavy wear over all of the coin. Sides of letters will be weak. A typically uncleaned coin will often appear as dirty or dull. A small grading area will have just under 50% of the original detail.

On the **Very Good** (VG) coin, there will be about 25% of the original detail visible. There will be heavy wear on all of the coin.

The **Good** (G) coin's design will be clearly outlined but with substantial wear. Some of the larger detail may be visible. The rim may have a few weak spots of wear.

On the **About Good** (AG) coin, there will typically be only a silhouette of a large design. The rim will be worn down into the letters if any.

Strong or weak strikes, partially weak strikes, damage, corrosion, attractive or unattractive toning, dipping or cleaning should be described along with the above grades. These factors affect the quality of the coin just as do wear and loss of detail, but are easier to describe.

In the case of countermarked/counterstamped coins, the condition of the host coin will have a bearing on the end valuation. The important factor in determining the grade is the condition, clarity and completeness of the countermark itself. This is in reference to countermarks/counterstamps having raised design while being struck in a depression.

Incuse countermarks cannot be graded for wear. They are graded by the clarity and completeness including the condition of the host coin which will also have more bearing on the final grade/valuation determined.

	PROOF	UNCIRCULATED	EXTREMELY FINE	VERY FINE	FINE	VERY GOOD	GOOD	POOR
U.S. and ENGLISH SPEAKING LANDS	PRF	UNC	EF or XF	VF	F	VG	G	PR
BRAZIL	—	(1)FDC or FC	(3) S	(5) MBC	(7) BC	(8) BC/R	(9) R	UT GeG
DENMARK	M	0	01	1 +	1	1 ÷	2	3
FINLAND	00	0	01	1 +	1	1?	2	3
FRANCE	FB Flan Bruni	FDC Fleur de Coin	SUP Superbe	TTB Très très beau	TB Très beau	B Beau	TBC Très Bien Conservée	BC Bien Conservée
GERMANY	PP Polierte Platte	STG Stempelglanz	VZ Vorzüglich	SS Sehr schön	S Schön	S.G.E. Sehr gut erhalten	G.E. Gut erhalten	Gering erhalten
ITALY	FS Fondo Specchio	FDC Fior di Conio	SPL Splendido	BB Bellissimo	MB Molto Bello	B Bello	M	—
JAPAN	—	未 使 用	極 美 品	美 品	並 品	—	—	—
NETHERLANDS	— Proef	FDC Fleur de Coin	Pr. Prachtig	Z.f. Zeer fraai	Fr. Fraai	Z.g. Zeer goed	G	—
NORWAY	M	0	01	1 +	1	1 ÷	2	3
PORTUGAL	—	Soberba	Bela	MBC	BC	MREG	REG	MC
SPAIN	Prueba	SC	EBC	MBC	BC +	BC	RC	MC
SWEDEN	Polerad	0	01	1 +	1	1?	2	—

Sending Scanned Images by Email

Over the past several years, we have been receiving an ever-increasing flow of scanned images from sources worldwide. Unfortunately, many of these scans could not be used due to the type of scan, or simple incompatability with our systems. We appreciate the effort it takes to produce these images and accuracy they add to the catalog listings.

Here are a few simple instructions to follow when producing these scans. We encourage you to continue sending new images or upgrades to those currently illustrated and please do not hesitate to ask questions about this process.

- Scan all images at 300 dpi
- Size setting should be at 100%
- Scan in true 4-color
- Save images as 'jpeg' or 'tiff' and name in such a way, which clearly identifies the country of origin
- Please email with a request to confirm receipt of the attachment
- Please send images to Randy.Thern@fwpubs.com

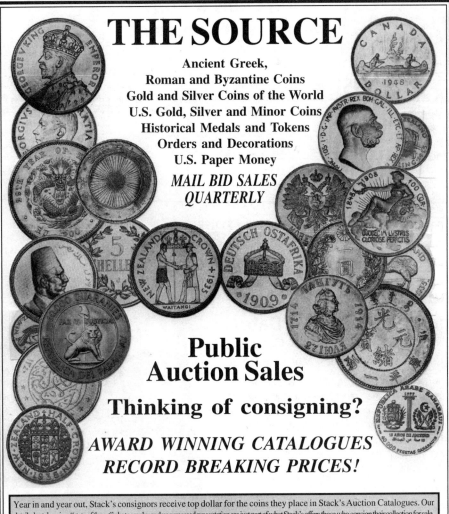

Expand Your Coin Collecting Library!

World Coins & Currency
Warman's® Companion
by Allen G. Berman

Make smart on-the-spot decisions at shows, coin shops, or during online auctions by turning to this handy coin and currency companion. Availability of world coins and paper money is at an all time high, and now is the time to take advantage of opportunities to expand your collection.

Inside this new guide, you'll discover:

- 700+ detailed color photos for quickly and confidently identifying currency
- Tips for spotting counterfeit pieces, and saving you from making costly investment errors

Softcover • 5 x 8 • 304 pages • 700+ color photos

Item# Z0303 • $17.99

Standard Catalog of®
World Coins, 2001 to Date
by Colin R. Bruce, II Senior Editor, George Cuhaj, Editor, and Thomas Michael, Market Analyst

This book may be half the size of the mammoth coin guides that make up the Standard Catalog of® World Coins series, but its just as detail heavy and price precise as the rest of the "family." This guide takes you on a thorough review of modern coins, minted since 2001, and covers many of the details you need to accurately and easily identify and price your collection.

Inside you'll find:

- 5,000 large-format images of all world coins minted since 2001
- Covers hundreds of new issues, sets, European listings, bi-metallic and tri-metallic coins

Softcover • 8-1/2 x 11 • 336 pages
5,000 b&w photos

Item# Z0360 • $30.00

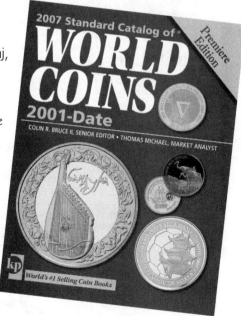

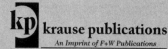

Discover Essential Details About Your Coins

Coins & Currency of the Middle East
A Descriptive Guide to Pocket Collectibles
Edited by Tom Michael & George S. Cuhaj

This one-of-a-kind guide helps you explore the coins, currency, and variety of military-related collectibles to come out of the Middle East in the last 25 years. Packed with more than 400 full-color, many featuring the people, culture and soldiers within the Middle East, this guide is truly unique in its coverage of this newly developing collecting arena. From coins and paper money to POGs and propaganda materials, the details of this diverse collecting arena are covered in this thorough new guide.

Softcover • 6 x 9 • 272 pages • 400+ color photos, illus.
Item# MDET • $17.99

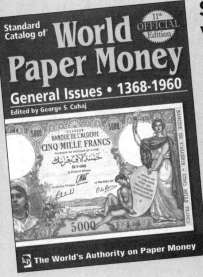

Standard Catalog of® World Paper Money, General Issues
11th Edition
Edited by George S. Cuhaj

Whether you're a general paper money enthusiast, expert world note collector, or dealer, there's no better choice for world paper money details than the Standard Catalog series. This book is the leading internationally distributed world-paper money reference, and the guide both general collectors and dealers turn to.

Inside this new edition of the ultimate guide to general issues you'll find:

- 5,800 detailed photos and illustrations for quick identification
- Nearly 45,000 expertly analyzed and updated prices for all circulating world paper money from 1368-1960

Reap the rewards of today's ultra active world paper money market by accurately determining the worth of your collection.

Softcover • 8-1/4 x 10-7/8 • 1,248 pages • 5,800 b&w photos
Item# PM11 • $70.00

krause publications
An Imprint of F+W Publications

700 East State Street • Iola, WI 54990-0001

To order call 800-258-0929 Offer NUB6
OR
Visit booksellers nationwide and your favorite coin shops for these and other expert guides from Krause Publications.

Belarus

Belarus (Byelorussia, Belorussia, or White Russia- formerly the Belorussian S.S.R.) is situated along the western Dvina and Dnieper Rivers, bounded in the west by Poland, to the north by Latvia and Lithuania, to the east by Russia and the south by the Ukraine. It has an area of 80,154 sq. mi. (207,600 sq. km.) and a population of 4.8 million. Capital: Minsk. Chief products: peat, salt, and agricultural products including flax, fodder and grasses for cattle breeding and dairy products.

MONETARY SYSTEM
100 Kapeek = 1 Rouble

REPUBLIC

STANDARD COINAGE

KM# 31   ROUBLE
7.9800 g., 0.9167 Gold .2532 oz. AGW **Subject:** United Nations 50th Anniversary **Obv:** National arms **Rev:** Crane flying over map and U.N. logo

Date	F	VF	XF	Unc	BU
1996 Proof	Value: 185				

KM# 6   ROUBLE
Copper-Nickel **Subject:** 50th Anniversary - United Nations **Obv:** National emblem **Rev:** Crane flying over map and UN logo

Date	F	VF	XF	Unc	BU
1996	—	—	—	12.50	—

KM# 6a   ROUBLE
28.5100 g., 0.9250 Silver .8479 oz. ASW

Date	F	VF	XF	Unc	BU
1996 Proof	Value: 35.00				

KM# 7   ROUBLE
Copper-Nickel **Subject:** Olympics **Obv:** National arms **Rev:** Gymnast on the rings

Date	F	VF	XF	Unc	BU
1996	—	—	—	12.50	—

KM# 8   ROUBLE
Copper-Nickel **Subject:** Olympics **Obv:** National arms **Rev:** Ribbon dancer

Date	F	VF	XF	Unc	BU
1996	—	—	—	12.50	—

KM# 34   ROUBLE
Copper-Nickel **Subject:** Olympics **Obv:** National arms **Rev:** Biathalon skier with rifle

Date	F	VF	XF	Unc	BU
1997	—	—	—	12.50	—

KM# 36 ROUBLE
Copper-Nickel **Subject:** Olympics **Rev:** Two hockey players

Date	F	VF	XF	Unc	BU
1997	—	—	—	12.50	—

KM# 20 ROUBLE
Copper-Nickel **Subject:** 200th Anniversary - Birth of A. Mitskevich - Poet **Obv:** National arms **Rev:** Mitskevich portrait, dates

Date	F	VF	XF	Unc	BU
1998 Proof		Value: 11.50			

KM# 9 ROUBLE
Copper-Nickel **Subject:** Third Anniversary of Independence **Obv:** National arms **Rev:** Monument

Date	F	VF	XF	Unc	BU
1997	—	—	—	12.50	—

KM# 21 ROUBLE
Copper-Nickel **Subject:** Olympics **Obv:** National arms and denomination **Rev:** Hurdlers, Olympic crest

Date	F	VF	XF	Unc	BU
1998 Proof		Value: 11.50			

KM# 18 ROUBLE
Copper-Nickel **Subject:** Architecture of Belarus **Obv:** National arms **Rev:** Castle at Mir

Date	F	VF	XF	Unc	BU
1998 Proof		Value: 11.50			

KM# 22 ROUBLE
Copper-Nickel **Subject:** Cities of Belarus **Obv:** National arms **Rev:** Minsk view with city arms

Date	F	VF	XF	Unc	BU
1999 Proof		Value: 11.50			

KM# 19 ROUBLE
Copper-Nickel **Subject:** Cities of Belarus **Obv:** National arms **Rev:** Walled City of Polatsk with city arms

Date	F	VF	XF	Unc	BU
1998 Proof		Value: 11.50			

KM# 23 ROUBLE
Copper-Nickel **Subject:** 100th Anniversary - Birth of Mikhas Lynkou **Obv:** National arms **Rev:** Head of Lynkou facing right

Date	F	VF	XF	Unc	BU
1999 Proof		Value: 11.50			

KM# 40 ROUBLE
14.5000 g., Copper-Nickel **Subject:** G.N. Glebats **Obv:** National arms **Rev:** Glebats portrait with two smaller portraits, dates **Edge:** Reeded

Date	F	VF	XF	Unc	BU
1999 Proof		Value: 11.50			

KM# 41 ROUBLE
Copper-Nickel **Subject:** 2000 Years **Obv:** National arms **Rev:** Bethlehem view

Date	F	VF	XF	Unc	BU
1999 Proof		Value: 11.50			

KM# 63 ROUBLE
14.3600 g., Copper-Nickel, 32.8 mm. **Subject:** Jubilee 2000 **Obv:** National arms **Rev:** Logo and three churches **Edge:** Reeded

Date	F	VF	XF	Unc	BU
1999 Proof		Value: 12.00			

KM# 48 ROUBLE
13.2000 g., Copper-Nickel, 31.9 mm. **Subject:** Architecture **Obv:** National arms **Rev:** Church **Edge:** Reeded

Date	F	VF	XF	Unc	BU
2000 Proof		Value: 12.50			

KM# 47 ROUBLE
13.1400 g., Copper-Nickel, 31.9 mm. **Obv:** National arms **Rev:** Bison **Edge:** Reeded

Date	F	VF	XF	Unc	BU
2001 Proof		Value: 15.00			

KM# 50 ROUBLE
12.8000 g., Copper-Nickel, 28.6 mm. **Subject:** 2002 Winter Olympics **Obv:** National arms **Rev:** Two freestyle skiers **Edge:** Reeded

Date	F	VF	XF	Unc	BU
2001 Proof		Value: 10.00			

KM# 44 ROUBLE
13.1400 g., Copper-Nickel, 31.9 mm. **Obv:** National arms **Rev:** Beaver and young **Edge:** Reeded

Date	F	VF	XF	Unc	BU
2002 Proof		Value: 15.00			

KM# 54 ROUBLE
13.1200 g., Copper-Nickel, 31.9 mm. **Obv:** National arms **Rev:** Mute swans **Edge:** Reeded

Date	F	VF	XF	Unc	BU
2003 Proof		Value: 15.00			

KM# 55 ROUBLE
13.1000 g., Copper-Nickel, 31.9 mm. **Obv:** State arms **Rev:** Herring Gull in flight **Edge:** Reeded

Date	F	VF	XF	Unc	BU
2003 Proof		Value: 15.00			

KM# 56 ROUBLE
13.1000 g., Copper-Nickel, 32 mm. **Obv:** National arms **Rev:** Church of the Savior and Transfiguration **Edge:** Reeded

Date	F	VF	XF	Unc	BU
2003	—	—	—	12.00	—

KM# 61 ROUBLE
12.5000 g., Copper-Nickel, 32 mm. **Obv:** National arms **Rev:** Wrestlers **Edge:** Reeded

Date	F	VF	XF	Unc	BU
2003 Proof			Value: 10.00		

KM# 60 ROUBLE
13.1000 g., Copper-Nickel, 31.9 mm. **Obv:** National arms **Rev:** Two Common Cranes **Edge:** Reeded

Date	F	VF	XF	Unc	BU
2004 Proof			Value: 15.00		

KM# 75 ROUBLE
15.9200 g., Copper-Nickel Antiqued Finish, 33 mm. **Subject:** "Kupalle" **Obv:** Folk art quilt design **Rev:** Flower above ferns **Edge:** Reeded

Date	F	VF	XF	Unc	BU
2004	—	—	—	10.00	—

KM# 76 ROUBLE
15.9200 g., Copper-Nickel, 33 mm. **Subject:** "Kalyady" **Obv:** Folk art cross design **Rev:** Stylized sun flower **Edge:** Reeded

Date	F	VF	XF	Unc	BU
2004	—	—	—	10.00	—

KM# 78 ROUBLE
15.9000 g., Copper-Nickel, 33 mm. **Obv:** National arms **Rev:** Radziwill's Castle in Neswizh **Edge:** Reeded

Date	F	VF	XF	Unc	BU
2004	—	—	—	—	12.50

KM# 80 ROUBLE
15.9000 g., Copper-Nickel, 33 mm. **Subject:** Defenders of Brest **Obv:** Soviet Patriotic War Order **Rev:** "Courage" monument **Edge:** Reeded

Date	F	VF	XF	Unc	BU
2004	—	—	—	12.50	—

KM# 97 ROUBLE
14.5000 g., Copper-Nickel, 33 mm. **Subject:** Almany Bogs **Obv:** Blooming plant on frosted design **Rev:** Great Grey Owl **Edge:** Lettered

Date	F	VF	XF	Unc	BU
2005 Proof			Value: 15.00		

KM# 24 10 ROUBLES
16.9600 g., 0.9250 Silver .5044 oz. ASW **Subject:** 200th Anniversary - Birth of A. Mitskevich **Obv:** National arms **Rev:** Portrait Mitskevich facing left, dates

Date	F	VF	XF	Unc	BU
1998 Proof			Value: 28.50		

KM# 25 10 ROUBLES
16.9600 g., 0.9250 Silver .5044 oz. ASW **Subject:** G.N. Glebats - Theatre Artist **Obv:** National arms **Rev:** Glebats portrait with two smaller portraits, dates

Date	F	VF	XF	Unc	BU
1999 Proof			Value: 27.50		

KM# 26 10 ROUBLES
16.9600 g., 0.9250 Silver .5044 oz. ASW **Subject:** 100th Anniversary - Birth of Mikhas Lynkou **Obv:** National arms **Rev:** Head of Lynkou facing right, dates

Date	F	VF	XF	Unc	BU
1999 Proof			Value: 27.50		

KM# 64 10 ROUBLES
16.8200 g., 0.9250 Silver 0.5002 oz. ASW, 32.9 mm. **Obv:** National arms **Rev:** Jakub Kolas (1882-1956) **Edge:** Reeded

Date	F	VF	XF	Unc	BU
2002 Proof			Value: 27.50		

KM# 13   20 ROUBLES

33.8400 g., 0.9250 Silver 1.0064 oz. ASW   **Subject:** Olympics **Obv:** National arms and denomination **Rev:** Olympic crest, gymnast on rings

Date	F	VF	XF	Unc	BU
1996 Proof		Value: 50.00			

KM# 11   20 ROUBLES

34.7400 g., 0.9000 Silver 1.0052 oz. ASW   **Subject:** Russia-Belarus State Treaty **Obv:** National emblem **Rev:** 2 city views with respective national emblems

Date	F	VF	XF	Unc	BU
1997 Proof		Value: 45.00			

KM# 14   20 ROUBLES

33.8400 g., 0.9250 Silver 1.0064 oz. ASW   **Subject:** Olympics **Obv:** National arms **Rev:** Ribbon dancer

Date	F	VF	XF	Unc	BU
1996 Proof		Value: 50.00			

KM# 12   20 ROUBLES

31.4800 g., 0.9990 Silver 1.0110 oz. ASW   **Subject:** 75th Anniversary - Banking System **Obv:** National emblem **Rev:** Bank building

Date	F	VF	XF	Unc	BU
1997 Proof		Value: 50.00			

KM# 10   20 ROUBLES

34.7400 g., 0.9000 Silver 1.0052 oz. ASW   **Subject:** Monument of Independence **Obv:** National emblem

Date	F	VF	XF	Unc	BU
1997 Proof		Value: 45.00			

KM# 15   20 ROUBLES

31.0300 g., 0.9250 Silver .9228 oz. ASW   **Subject:** Olympics **Obv:** National arms **Rev:** Biathlon skier

Date	F	VF	XF	Unc	BU
1997 Proof		Value: 35.00			

KM# 16 20 ROUBLES

31.1500 g., 0.9250 Silver .9264 oz. ASW **Subject:** Olympics
Obv: National arms **Rev:** Two hockey players

Date	F	VF	XF	Unc	BU
1997 Proof		Value: 35.00			

KM# 29 20 ROUBLES

33.5200 g., 0.9250 Silver .9969 oz. ASW **Subject:** Olympics **Obv:**
National arms and denomination **Rev:** Hurdlers, Olympic crest

Date	F	VF	XF	Unc	BU
1998 Proof		Value: 32.50			

KM# 27 20 ROUBLES

33.5200 g., 0.9250 Silver .9969 oz. ASW **Subject:** Architecture
of Belarus **Obv:** National arms **Rev:** Castle and Mir and seal

Date	F	VF	XF	Unc	BU
1998 Proof		Value: 35.00			

KM# 17 20 ROUBLES

33.9000 g., 0.9250 Silver 1.0082 oz. ASW **Subject:** 80th
Anniversary - Financial System **Obv:** National arms **Rev:**
Anniversary logo

Date	F	VF	XF	Unc	BU
1999 Proof		Value: 30.00			

KM# 28 20 ROUBLES

33.5200 g., 0.9250 Silver .9969 oz. ASW **Subject:** Cities of
Belarus **Obv:** National arms **Rev:** Polatsk with city arms above

Date	F	VF	XF	Unc	BU
1998 Proof		Value: 35.00			

KM# 30 20 ROUBLES

33.5200 g., 0.9250 Silver .9969 oz. ASW **Subject:** Cities of
Belarus **Obv:** National arms **Rev:** Minsk view with city arms

Date	F	VF	XF	Unc	BU
1999 Proof		Value: 35.00			

KM# 42   20 ROUBLES

33.8600 g., 0.9250 Silver 1.0070 oz. ASW **Subject:** 2000 Years of Christianity **Obv:** National arms **Rev:** Bethlehem view **Edge:** Reeded

Date	F	VF	XF	Unc	BU
1999 Proof		Value: 35.00			

KM# 43   20 ROUBLES

33.8600 g., 0.9250 Silver 1.0070 oz. ASW **Subject:** Jubilee 2000 **Obv:** National arms **Rev:** Three churches

Date	F	VF	XF	Unc	BU
1999 Proof		Value: 35.00			

KM# 66   20 ROUBLES

33.8500 g., 0.9250 Silver 1.0067 oz. ASW, 38.5 mm. **Obv:** National arms **Rev:** Borisoglebsk church in Grodno **Edge:** Reeded

Date	F	VF	XF	Unc	BU
1999 Proof		Value: 40.00			

KM# 52   20 ROUBLES

31.4500 g., 0.9250 Silver 0.9353 oz. ASW, 38.6 mm. **Subject:** 2002 Winter Olympics **Obv:** National arms **Rev:** Discus thrower **Edge:** Reeded

Date	F	VF	XF	Unc	BU
2000 Proof		Value: 37.50			

KM# 68   20 ROUBLES

33.8500 g., 0.9250 Silver 1.0067 oz. ASW, 38.5 mm. **Obv:** National arms **Rev:** Synkovichi church **Edge:** Reeded

Date	F	VF	XF	Unc	BU
2000 Proof		Value: 40.00			

KM# 46   20 ROUBLES

33.7300 g., 0.9250 Silver 1.0031 oz. ASW, 38.6 mm. **Subject:** Wildlife **Obv:** National arms **Rev:** Bison **Edge:** Reeded

Date	F	VF	XF	Unc	BU
2001 Proof		Value: 45.00			

KM# 49   20 ROUBLES

28.3200 g., 0.9250 Silver 0.8422 oz. ASW, 38.6 mm. **Subject:** 2002 Winter Olympics **Obv:** National arms **Rev:** Marksman **Edge:** Reeded

Date	F	VF	XF	Unc	BU
2001 Proof		Value: 42.50			

KM# 51   20 ROUBLES

33.6500 g., 0.9250 Silver 1.0007 oz. ASW, 38.6 mm. **Subject:** 2002 Winter Olympics **Obv:** National arms **Rev:** Two freestyle skiers **Edge:** Reeded

Date	F	VF	XF	Unc	BU
2001 Proof		Value: 47.50			

Belarus

KM# 45 20 ROUBLES
33.7300 g., 0.9250 Silver 1.0031 oz. ASW, 38.8 mm. **Obv:** National arms **Rev:** Beaver and young **Edge:** Reeded

Date	F	VF	XF	Unc	BU
2002 Proof			Value: 45.00		

KM# 57 20 ROUBLES
31.1000 g., 0.9250 Silver 0.9249 oz. ASW, 38.6 mm. **Obv:** National arms **Rev:** Church of the Savior and Transfiguration **Edge:** Reeded

Date	F	VF	XF	Unc	BU
2003 Proof			Value: 50.00		

KM# 59 20 ROUBLES
28.6300 g., 0.9250 Silver 0.8514 oz. ASW, 38.6 mm. **Obv:** National arms **Rev:** Arctic bear with two cubs **Edge:** Reeded

Date	F	VF	XF	Unc	BU
2002 Proof			Value: 45.00		

KM# 70 20 ROUBLES
33.8500 g., 0.9250 Silver 1.0067 oz. ASW, 33.43 mm. **Obv:** National arms **Rev:** 80th Anniversary - National Savings Bank **Edge:** Reeded

Date	F	VF	XF	Unc	BU
2002 Proof			Value: 40.00		

KM# 71 20 ROUBLES
31.1000 g., 0.9250 Silver 0.9249 oz. ASW, 38.6 mm. **Subject:** "Kupalle" **Obv:** Folk art quilt design **Rev:** Fern flower with inset red synthetic crystal **Edge:** Reeded

Date	F	VF	XF	Unc	BU
2004	—	—	—	45.00	—

KM# 53 20 ROUBLES
33.8400 g., 0.9250 Silver 1.0064 oz. ASW, 38.5 mm. **Obv:** State arms **Rev:** Two Mute swans in pond **Edge:** Reeded

Date	F	VF	XF	Unc	BU
2003 Proof			Value: 45.00		

KM# 72 20 ROUBLES
31.1000 g., 0.9250 Silver 0.9249 oz. ASW, 38.6 mm. **Subject:** Defense of Brest **Obv:** Multicolor Soviet Order of the Patriotic War **Rev:** "Courage" monument **Edge:** Reeded

Date	F	VF	XF	Unc	BU
2004 Proof			Value: 50.00		

KM# 73   20 ROUBLES
31.1000 g., 0.9250 Silver 0.9249 oz. ASW, 38.6 mm.   **Obv:**
National arms **Rev:** 2 common cranes **Edge:** Reeded

Date	F	VF	XF	Unc	BU
2004 Proof		Value: 40.00			

KM# 77   20 ROUBLES
31.1000 g., 0.9250 Silver 0.9249 oz. ASW, 38.6 mm.   **Subject:**
"Kalyady" **Obv:** Folk art quilt design **Rev:** Stylized sunflower with
inset blue synthetic crystal **Edge:** Reeded

Date	F	VF	XF	Unc	BU
2004	—	—	—	45.00	—

KM# 79   20 ROUBLES
31.1000 g., 0.9250 Silver 0.9249 oz. ASW, 38.6 mm.   **Obv:**
National arms **Rev:** Radziwill's Castle in Neswizh **Edge:** Reeded

Date	F	VF	XF	Unc	BU
2004 Proof		Value: 50.00			

KM# 82   20 ROUBLES
28.7200 g., 0.9250 Silver 0.8541 oz. ASW, 38.6 mm.   **Subject:**
WW II Victory **Obv:** Multicolor Soviet Order of Victory **Rev:** Soviet
soldiers raising their flag in the Reichstag in Berlin **Edge:** Reeded

Date	F	VF	XF	Unc	BU
2005 Proof		Value: 50.00			

KM# 92   20 ROUBLES
28.6300 g., 0.9250 Silver 0.8514 oz. ASW, 38.6 mm.   **Obv:** Two
children sitting on crescent moon **Rev:** Violinist and inset orange
color glass crystal **Edge:** Plain

Date	F	VF	XF	Unc	BU
2005	—	—	—	50.00	—

KM# 93   20 ROUBLES
28.6300 g., 0.9250 Silver 0.8514 oz. ASW, 38.6 mm.   **Subject:**
Kalyady's star **Obv:** Two children sitting on a crescent moon **Rev:**
Blue glass crystal inset on forehead, flower **Edge:** Plain

Date	F	VF	XF	Unc	BU
2005	—	—	—	50.00	—

KM# 94 20 ROUBLES

28.6300 g., 0.9250 Silver 0.8514 oz. ASW, 38.6 mm. **Obv:** Two children sitting on a crescent moon **Rev:** White glass crystal inset above landscape with fox **Edge:** Plain

Date	F	VF	XF	Unc	BU
2005	—	—	—	50.00	—

KM# 95 20 ROUBLES

28.6300 g., 0.9250 Silver 0.8514 oz. ASW **Obv:** Two children sitting on a crescent moon **Rev:** Yellow glass crystal inset in flower design **Edge:** Plain

Date	F	VF	XF	Unc	BU
2005	—	—	—	50.00	—

KM# 96 20 ROUBLES

33.6600 g., 0.9250 Silver 1.001 oz. ASW, 38.6 mm. **Obv:** Quilted star design **Rev:** Yellow glass crystal inset in candle flame above basket **Edge:** Reeded

Date	F	VF	XF	Unc	BU
2005	—	—	—	50.00	—

KM# 98 20 ROUBLES

33.6300 g., 0.9250 Silver 1.0001 oz. ASW, 38.6 mm. **Subject:** Almany Bogs **Obv:** Blooming plant on frosted design **Rev:** Great Grey Owl **Edge:** Reeded

Date	F	VF	XF	Unc	BU
2005 Proof			Value: 40.00		

KM# 32 50 ROUBLES

7.7800 g., 0.9990 Gold .2499 oz. AGW **Subject:** Olympics **Obv:** National arms **Rev:** Ribbon dancer

Date	F	VF	XF	Unc	BU
1996 Proof			Value: 220		

KM# 33 50 ROUBLES

7.7800 g., 0.9990 Gold .2499 oz. AGW **Rev:** Gymnast on rings

Date	F	VF	XF	Unc	BU
1996 Proof			Value: 220		

KM# 35 50 ROUBLES

7.7800 g., 0.9990 Gold .2499 oz. AGW **Rev:** Skier with rifle

Date	F	VF	XF	Unc	BU
1997 Proof			Value: 220		

KM# 37 50 ROUBLES

7.7800 g., 0.9990 Gold .2499 oz. AGW **Rev:** Two hockey players

Date	F	VF	XF	Unc	BU
1997 Proof			Value: 220		

KM# 38 50 ROUBLES

7.7800 g., 0.9990 Gold .2499 oz. AGW **Rev:** Two hurdlers

Date	F	VF	XF	Unc	BU
1997 Proof			Value: 220		

KM# 58 100 ROUBLES
155.5000 g., 0.9250 Silver 4.6245 oz. ASW, 64 mm. **Obv:**
Theater building **Rev:** Two ballet dancers **Edge:** Reeded **Note:**
Illustration reduced.

Date	F	VF	XF	Unc	BU
2003 Proof	Value: 150				

KM# 74 1000 ROUBLES
1000.0000 g., 0.9990 Silver 32.1186 oz. ASW, 100 mm. **Subject:**
2004 Olympics **Obv:** National arms **Rev:** Ancient charioteer **Note:**
Illustration reduced.

Date	F	VF	XF	Unc	BU
2004 Proof	Value: 500				

Belgium

The Kingdom of Belgium, a constitutional monarchy in northwest
Europe, has an area of 11,780 sq. mi. (30,519 sq. km.) and a population
of 10.1 million, chiefly Dutch-speaking Flemish and French-speaking
Walloons. Capital: Brussels. Agriculture, dairy farming, and the processing of raw materials for re-export are the principal industries. Beurs
voor Diamant in Antwerp is the world's largest diamond trading center.
Iron and steel, machinery motor vehicles, chemicals, textile yarns and
fabrics comprise the principal exports.

MONETARY SYSTEM
100 Centimes = 1 Franc
1 Euro = 100 Cents

LEGENDS
Belgian coins are usually inscribed either in Dutch, French or
both. However some modern coins are being inscribed in Latin or
German. The language used is best told by noting the spelling of
the name of the country.
(Fr) French: BELGIQUE or BELGES
(Du) Dutch: BELGIE or BELGEN
(La) Latin: BELGICA
(Ge) German: BELGIEN
Many Belgian coins are collected by what is known as Position
A and Position B edges. Some dates command a premium depend-
ing on the position which are as follows:
Position A: Coins with portrait side down having upright edge
lettering.
Position B: Coins with portrait side up having upright edge let-
tering.

KINGDOM
DECIMAL COINAGE

KM# 1.1 CENTIME
Copper **Note:** Wide rims. Some were overstruck on Netherlands
1 Cent, KM#47.

Date	VG	F	VF	XF	Unc
1832-1835/2	2.00	10.00	70.00	150	300

KM# 1.2 CENTIME
Copper **Note:** Narrow rims.

Date	VG	F	VF	XF	Unc
1835-1863	0.50	1.50	10.00	30.00	50.00

KM# 1.3 CENTIME
Copper **Rev:** Without dash below CENT.

Date	VG	F	VF	XF	Unc
1857-1860	3.00	6.00	40.00	90.00	135

KM# 1.4 CENTIME
Copper **Rev:** Without stop in signature

Date	VG	F	VF	XF	Unc
1862	2.00	4.00	10.00	30.00	50.00

KM# 33.1 CENTIME
Copper, 18 mm. **Obv:** Legend in French

Date	F	VF	XF	Unc	BU
1869-1907	0.20	0.50	1.50	4.00	—

KM# 33.2 CENTIME
Copper **Note:** Thin flan.

Date	F	VF	XF	Unc	BU
1882-1902	0.50	1.50	4.00	12.50	—

KM# 34.1 CENTIME
Copper **Obv:** Legend in Dutch

Date	F	VF	XF	Unc	BU
1882-1907	0.25	0.50	1.50	4.00	—

KM# 34.2 CENTIME
Copper **Note:** Thin flan.

Date	F	VF	XF	Unc	BU
1887-1902	1.00	1.50	8.00	25.00	—

KM# 33.3 CENTIME
Copper **Rev:** Additional stop in signature... BRAEMT.F.

Date	F	VF	XF	Unc	BU
1902	1.00	2.00	10.00	30.00	—

KM# 76 CENTIME
Copper **Obv:** Legend in French **Edge:** Reeded

Date	F	VF	XF	Unc	BU
1912-1914	0.20	0.50	2.50	7.00	—

KM# 77 CENTIME
Copper **Obv:** Legend in Dutch **Edge:** Reeded

Date	F	VF	XF	Unc	BU
1912	0.20	0.50	1.50	4.00	—

KM# 4.1 2 CENTIMES
Copper **Note:** Wide rims. Some were overstruck on Netherlands 1/2 Cent, KM#51.

Date	VG	F	VF	XF	Unc
1833-1835	2.50	8.00	60.00	150	285

KM# 4.3 2 CENTIMES
Copper **Note:** Medal alignment.

Date	VG	F	VF	XF	Unc
1833-1834	10.00	20.00	110	300	—

KM# 4.2 2 CENTIMES
Copper **Note:** Narrow rims.

Date	VG	F	VF	XF	Unc
.1835.-1865	0.50	1.00	6.00	20.00	40.00

KM# 4.4 2 CENTIMES
Copper **Rev:** Without stop in signature

Date	VG	F	VF	XF	Unc
1844-1861	0.75	2.50	10.00	30.00	55.00

KM# 4.2a 2 CENTIMES
Bronze

Date	VG	F	VF	XF	Unc
1845-1859	30.00	40.00	200	400	—

KM# 84 2 CENTIMES
Copper **Counterstamp:** Script LII **Note:** Counterstamp in monogram on Netherlands 1 Cent, KM#47.

Date	VG	F	VF	XF	Unc
ND	120	450	900	1,400	—

KM# 35.1 2 CENTIMES
Copper **Obv:** Legend in French

Date	F	VF	XF	Unc	BU
1869-1909/5	0.15	0.50	3.00	10.00	—

KM# 35.2 2 CENTIMES
Copper **Note:** Thin flan.

Date	F	VF	XF	Unc	BU
1902	3.00	5.00	35.00	75.00	125

KM# 36 2 CENTIMES
Copper **Obv:** Legend in Dutch

Date	F	VF	XF	Unc	BU
1902-1909	0.15	1.00	4.00	12.00	—

KM# 65 2 CENTIMES
Copper **Obv:** Legend in Dutch

Date	F	VF	XF	Unc	BU
1910-1919	0.15	0.35	0.75	3.00	—

KM# 64 2 CENTIMES
Copper **Obv:** Legend in French

Date	F	VF	XF	Unc	BU
1911-1919/4	0.15	0.25	1.00	3.00	—

KM# 5.1 5 CENTIMES
Copper

Date	VG	F	VF	XF	Unc
1811-1861	1.00	2.00	10.00	30.00	65.00

KM# 5.1a 5 CENTIMES
Bronze

Date	VG	F	VF	XF	Unc
1833-1859	35.00	75.00	500	1,200	—

KM# 5.2 5 CENTIMES
Copper **Rev:** Without stop in signature

Date	VG	F	VF	XF	Unc
1833-1852	1.00	2.00	10.00	30.00	65.00

KM# 5.3 5 CENTIMES
Copper **Rev:** Large S in CENTS

Date	VG	F	VF	XF	Unc
1858-1859	2.00	3.00	40.00	120	175

KM# 21 5 CENTIMES
Copper-Nickel **Note:** Varieties exist.

Date	VG	F	VF	XF	Unc
1861-1864	0.15	0.50	3.00	7.00	15.00

KM# 40   5 CENTIMES
Copper-Nickel   **Obv:** Legend in French

Date	F	VF	XF	Unc	BU
1894-1901	1.00	4.00	9.00	20.00	—

KM# 41   5 CENTIMES
Copper-Nickel   **Obv:** Legend in Dutch

Date	F	VF	XF	Unc	BU
1894-1900	1.00	4.00	9.00	20.00	—

KM# 44   5 CENTIMES
Copper-Nickel   **Rev:** Lion of different design

Date	F	VF	XF	Unc	BU
1901	3.00	8.00	35.00	70.00	—

KM# 45   5 CENTIMES
Copper-Nickel   **Obv:** Legend in Dutch **Rev:** Lion of different lower design

Date	F	VF	XF	Unc	BU
1901	3.00	8.00	35.00	70.00	—

KM# 46   5 CENTIMES
Copper-Nickel   **Obv:** Legend in French, small date

Date	F	VF	XF	Unc	BU
1901-1903	0.25	1.50	7.00	22.00	—

KM# 47   5 CENTIMES
Copper-Nickel   **Obv:** Legend in Dutch, small date

Date	F	VF	XF	Unc	BU
1902-1903	0.15	1.50	7.00	22.00	—

KM# 54   5 CENTIMES
Copper-Nickel   **Obv:** Legend in French, large date

Date	F	VF	XF	Unc	BU
1904-1907	0.15	0.35	2.00	6.00	—

KM# 55   5 CENTIMES
Copper-Nickel   **Obv:** Legend in Dutch, large date

Date	F	VF	XF	Unc	BU
1904-1907	0.15	0.35	2.00	7.00	—

KM# 66   5 CENTIMES
Copper-Nickel   **Obv:** Legend in French **Rev:** Plain field above 5

Date	F	VF	XF	Unc	BU
1910-1928	0.10	0.35	1.25	4.00	—

KM# 67   5 CENTIMES
Copper-Nickel   **Obv:** Legend in Dutch **Rev:** Plain field above 5

Date	F	VF	XF	Unc	BU
1910-1928/3	0.10	0.35	1.25	4.00	—

KM# 80   5 CENTIMES
Zinc   **Obv:** Legend in French **Note:** German Occupation WW I

Date	F	VF	XF	Unc	BU
1915-1916	0.10	0.60	2.00	7.00	10.00

KM# 94   5 CENTIMES
Nickel-Brass   **Obv:** Legend in Dutch **Rev:** Star added above 5

Date	F	VF	XF	Unc	BU
1930-1931	0.10	0.20	0.35	3.00	—

KM# 93   5 CENTIMES
Nickel-Brass   **Obv:** Legend in French **Rev:** Star added above 5

Date	F	VF	XF	Unc	BU
1932	0.10	0.20	0.35	3.00	—

KM# 110.1   5 CENTIMES
Nickel-Brass   **Obv:** Legend in French

Date	F	VF	XF	Unc	BU
1938	0.10	0.20	0.75	2.00	—

KM# 110.2   5 CENTIMES
Nickel-Brass **Note:** Medal alignment.

Date	F	VF	XF	Unc	BU
1938	1.25	3.00	8.00	30.00	—

KM# 111   5 CENTIMES
Nickel-Brass **Obv:** Legend in Dutch

Date	F	VF	XF	Unc	BU
1939-1940	0.10	0.20	0.75	3.00	—

KM# 123   5 CENTIMES
Zinc **Obv:** Legend in French **Note:** German Occupation WW II

Date	F	VF	XF	Unc	BU
1941-1943	0.10	0.20	1.00	4.00	—

KM# 124   5 CENTIMES
Zinc **Obv:** Legend in Dutch

Date	F	VF	XF	Unc	BU
1941-1942	0.10	0.20	1.00	4.00	—

KM# 2.1   10 CENTIMES
Copper

Date	VG	F	VF	XF	Unc
1832-1856	9.00	25.00	130	400	550

KM# 2.2   10 CENTIMES
Copper **Note:** Medal alignment.

Date	VG	F	VF	XF	Unc
1832	75.00	140	600	1,400	—

KM# 22   10 CENTIMES
Copper-Nickel

Date	VG	F	VF	XF	Unc
1861-1864	0.10	0.50	3.00	6.00	20.00

KM# 42   10 CENTIMES
Copper-Nickel **Obv:** Legend in French

Date	F	VF	XF	Unc	BU
1894-1901	0.75	3.00	7.00	15.00	—

KM# 43   10 CENTIMES
Copper-Nickel **Obv:** Legend in Dutch

Date	F	VF	XF	Unc	BU
1894-1901	0.75	3.00	9.00	20.00	—

KM# 48   10 CENTIMES
Copper-Nickel **Obv:** Legend in French, small date

Date	F	VF	XF	Unc	BU
1901-1903	0.15	1.00	3.00	7.00	—

KM# 49   10 CENTIMES
Copper-Nickel **Obv:** Legend in Dutch, small date

Date	F	VF	XF	Unc	BU
1902-1903/2	0.20	1.00	2.50	7.00	—

KM# 52   10 CENTIMES
Copper-Nickel **Obv:** Legend in French, large date

Date	F	VF	XF	Unc	BU
1903-1906/5	0.15	0.60	2.00	7.00	—

KM# 53   10 CENTIMES
Copper-Nickel **Obv:** Legend in Dutch, large date

Date	F	VF	XF	Unc	BU
1903-1906/5	0.10	0.50	2.00	7.00	—

KM# 81   10 CENTIMES
Zinc **Obv:** Legend in French **Note:** German Occupation. All of KM#81 have dots after the date. The 1916 is distinguished by a period after the date.

Date	F	VF	XF	Unc	BU
.1916-1917	0.15	0.75	3.00	10.00	—

KM# 85.1 10 CENTIMES
Copper-Nickel **Obv:** Legend in French

Date	F	VF	XF	Unc	BU
1920-1929	0.10	0.20	1.00	4.00	—

KM# 85.2 10 CENTIMES
Copper-Nickel **Rev:** Single line below ES of CES

Date	F	VF	XF	Unc	BU
1920-1921	0.50	1.00	5.00	15.00	—

KM# 86 10 CENTIMES
Copper-Nickel **Obv:** Legend in Dutch **Rev:** Plain field above 10
Edge: Plain

Date	F	VF	XF	Unc	BU
1920-1930	0.10	0.20	1.00	4.00	—

KM# 95.1 10 CENTIMES
Nickel-Brass **Obv:** Legend in French **Rev:** Star added above 10

Date	F	VF	XF	Unc	BU
1930-1932	5.00	10.00	20.00	50.00	—

KM# 95.2 10 CENTIMES
Nickel-Brass **Rev:** Single line below ES of CES

Date	F	VF	XF	Unc	BU
1931-1932	2.00	8.00	20.00	50.00	—

KM# 96 10 CENTIMES
Nickel-Brass **Obv:** Legend in Dutch **Rev:** Star added above 10

Date	F	VF	XF	Unc	BU
1930-1931	0.30	0.75	3.00	10.00	—

KM# 112 10 CENTIMES
Nickel-Brass **Obv:** Legend in French

Date	F	VF	XF	Unc	BU
1938-1939	0.10	0.25	0.50	1.50	—

KM# 113.1 10 CENTIMES
Nickel-Brass **Obv:** Legend in Dutch

Date	F	VF	XF	Unc	BU
1939	0.10	0.25	0.50	1.50	—

KM# 113.2 10 CENTIMES
Nickel-Brass **Note:** Thin flan.

Date	F	VF	XF	Unc	BU
1939	1.25	3.00	10.00	35.00	—

KM# 125 10 CENTIMES
Zinc **Obv:** Legend in French **Edge:** Plain **Note:** German Occupation WW II.

Date	F	VF	XF	Unc	BU
1941-1943	0.15	0.25	1.50	4.00	—

KM# 126 10 CENTIMES
Zinc **Obv:** Legend in Dutch **Edge:** Plain

Date	F	VF	XF	Unc	BU
1941-1946	0.15	0.25	1.50	4.00	—

KM# 19 20 CENTIMES
1.0000 g., 0.9000 Silver .0289 oz. ASW

Date	VG	F	VF	XF	Unc
1852-1858	3.00	12.00	45.00	80.00	135

KM# 20 20 CENTIMES
Copper-Nickel

Date	VG	F	VF	XF	Unc
1860-1861	1.00	3.00	10.00	32.00	100

KM# 146 20 CENTIMES
Bronze **Obv:** Legend in French **Edge:** Plain

Date	F	VF	XF	Unc	BU
1953-1963	0.10	0.10	0.10	0.50	—

KM# 147.1 20 CENTIMES
Bronze **Obv:** Legend in Dutch **Edge:** Plain

Date	F	VF	XF	Unc	BU
1954-1960	—	—	0.10	0.50	—

KM# 147.2 20 CENTIMES
Bronze **Obv:** CENTIMES touching rim **Edge:** Plain

Date	F	VF	XF	Unc	BU
1954-1960	—	0.15	0.75	2.50	—

KM# 62　25 CENTIMES
Copper-Nickel　**Obv:** Legend in French

Date	F	VF	XF	Unc	BU
1908-1909/8	0.50	4.00	20.00	50.00	—

KM# 63　25 CENTIMES
Copper-Nickel　**Obv:** Legend in Dutch

Date	F	VF	XF	Unc	BU
1908	0.50	4.00	20.00	50.00	—

KM# 69　25 CENTIMES
Copper-Nickel　**Obv:** Legend in Dutch

Date	F	VF	XF	Unc	BU
1910-1929	0.10	0.25	2.00	6.00	—

KM# 68.1　25 CENTIMES
Copper-Nickel　**Obv:** Legend in French

Date	F	VF	XF	Unc	BU
1913-1929	0.10	0.25	2.00	6.00	—

KM# 68.2　25 CENTIMES
Copper-Nickel　**Rev:** Single line below ES of CES

Date	F	VF	XF	Unc	BU
1920-1921	0.35	0.75	5.00	15.00	—

KM# 82　25 CENTIMES
Zinc　**Obv:** Legend in French **Note:** German Occupation WW I

Date	F	VF	XF	Unc	BU
1915-1918	0.50	2.00	7.00	15.00	—

KM# 114.1　25 CENTIMES
Nickel-Brass　**Obv:** Legend in French

Date	F	VF	XF	Unc	BU
1938-1939	—	0.25	1.00	4.00	—

KM# 114.2　25 CENTIMES
Nickel-Brass　**Note:** Medal alignment.

Date	F	VF	XF	Unc	BU
1939	1.75	3.00	10.00	30.00	—

KM# 115.1　25 CENTIMES
Nickel-Brass　**Obv:** Legend in Dutch

Date	F	VF	XF	Unc	BU
1938	—	0.25	1.00	3.00	—

KM# 115.2　25 CENTIMES
Nickel-Brass　**Note:** Medal alignment.

Date	F	VF	XF	Unc	BU
1938	5.00	10.00	20.00	30.00	—

KM# 131　25 CENTIMES
Zinc　**Obv:** Legend in French **Note:** German Occupation WW II.

Date	F	VF	XF	Unc	BU
1942-1946	—	0.20	0.75	3.00	10.00

KM# 132　25 CENTIMES
Zinc　**Obv:** Legend in Dutch

Date	F	VF	XF	Unc	BU
1942-1946	—	0.20	0.75	3.00	10.00

KM# 153.1　25 CENTIMES
Copper-Nickel　**Obv:** Legend in French **Note:** Struck at Brussels
Mint. Mint mark - Angel Head. Mintmaster Vogeleer's privy mark - Bird.

Date	F	VF	XF	Unc	BU
1964-1975	—	—	—	0.10	0.15

Belgium

KM# 153.2 25 CENTIMES
Copper-Nickel **Note:** Medal alignment. Struck at the Brussels Mint. Mint mark - Angel Head. Mintmaster Vogeleer's privy mark - Bird.

Date	F	VF	XF	Unc	BU
1964-1974	—	—	5.00	12.00	—

KM# 154.1 25 CENTIMES
Copper-Nickel **Obv:** Legend in Dutch **Edge:** Plain **Note:** Struck at Brussels Mint. Mint mark - Angel Head. Mintmaster Vogeleer's privy mark - Bird.

Date	F	VF	XF	Unc	BU
1964-1975	—	—	0.10	0.15	—

KM# 154.2 25 CENTIMES
Copper-Nickel **Edge:** Plain **Note:** Medal alignment. Struck at Brussels Mint. Mint mark - Angel Head. Mintmaster Vogeleer's privy mark - Bird.

Date	F	VF	XF	Unc	BU
1964-1972	—	—	5.00	12.00	—

KM# 26 50 CENTIMES
2.5000 g., 0.8350 Silver .0671 oz. ASW **Obv:** Legend in French

Date	F	VF	XF	Unc	BU
1866-1899	1.00	25.00	100	175	—

KM# 27 50 CENTIMES
2.5000 g., 0.8350 Silver .0671 oz. ASW **Obv:** Legend in Dutch

Date	F	VF	XF	Unc	BU
1886-1899	2.00	20.00	65.00	125	—

KM# 50 50 CENTIMES
2.5000 g., 0.8350 Silver .0671 oz. ASW **Obv:** Legend in French

Date	F	VF	XF	Unc	BU
1901	2.00	5.00	30.00	75.00	—

KM# 51 50 CENTIMES
2.5000 g., 0.8350 Silver .0671 oz. ASW **Obv:** Legend in Dutch

Date	F	VF	XF	Unc	BU
1901	2.00	5.00	30.00	75.00	—

KM# 60.1 50 CENTIMES
2.5000 g., 0.8350 Silver .0671 oz. ASW **Obv:** Legend in French

Date	F	VF	XF	Unc	BU
1907-1909	1.00	2.50	10.00	30.00	—

KM# 60.2 50 CENTIMES
2.5000 g., 0.8350 Silver .0671 oz. ASW **Obv:** Without period in signature

Date	F	VF	XF	Unc	BU
1907-1909	2.00	5.00	12.00	35.00	—

KM# 61.1 50 CENTIMES
2.5000 g., 0.8350 Silver .0671 oz. ASW **Obv:** Legend in Dutch

Date	F	VF	XF	Unc	BU
1907-1909	1.00	2.50	9.00	30.00	—

KM# 61.2 50 CENTIMES
2.5000 g., 0.8350 Silver .0671 oz. ASW **Note:** Medal alignment

Date	F	VF	XF	Unc	BU
1909	12.50	15.00	45.00	135	—

KM# 61.3 50 CENTIMES
2.5000 g., 0.8350 Silver .0671 oz. ASW **Obv:** Without periods in signature

Date	F	VF	XF	Unc	BU
1909	2.00	6.00	17.50	50.00	—

KM# 70 50 CENTIMES
2.5000 g., 0.8350 Silver .0671 oz. ASW **Obv:** Legend in French

Date	F	VF	XF	Unc	BU
1910-1914	0.85	1.25	2.00	6.00	—

KM# 71 50 CENTIMES
2.5000 g., 0.8350 Silver .0671 oz. ASW **Obv:** Legend in Dutch

Date	F	VF	XF	Unc	BU
1910-1914	0.85	1.25	2.00	6.00	—

KM# 83 50 CENTIMES
Zinc **Obv:** Legend in Dutch **Note:** German Occupation WW I

Date	F	VF	XF	Unc	BU
1918	0.50	3.00	10.00	25.00	50.00

KM# 87 50 CENTIMES
Nickel **Obv:** Legend in French

Date	F	VF	XF	Unc	BU
1922-1933	0.15	0.25	0.50	3.00	—

KM# 88   50 CENTIMES
Nickel   **Obv:** Legend in Dutch

Date	F	VF	XF	Unc	BU
1923-1934	0.20	0.25	0.50	3.00	—

KM# 118   50 CENTIMES
Nickel   **Obv:** Legend in French **Note:** Striking interrupted by the war. Very few coins have been officially released into circulation.

Date	F	VF	XF	Unc	BU
1939	200	400	800	1,300	—

KM# 144   50 CENTIMES
Bronze **Obv:** Legend in French **Rev:** Helmeted mine worker, miner's lamp at r. Large head, tip of neck 1/2 mm from rim **Edge:** Plain

Date	F	VF	XF	Unc	BU
1952-1955	—	0.10	0.10	0.35	—

KM# 145   50 CENTIMES
Bronze **Obv:** Legend in Dutch **Rev:** Helmeted mine worker, miner's lamp at right, large head **Edge:** Plain

Date	F	VF	XF	Unc	BU
1952-1954	—	0.10	0.10	0.35	—

KM# 148.2   50 CENTIMES
Bronze **Edge:** Plain **Note:** Medal alignment.

Date	F	VF	XF	Unc	BU
1953-1980	—	—	15.00	30.00	—

KM# 149.1   50 CENTIMES
Bronze **Rev:** Helmeted mint worker, miner's lamp at r. Smaller head, legend in Dutch **Edge:** Plain

Date	F	VF	XF	Unc	BU
1956-2001	—	—	0.10	0.10	—

KM# 149.2   50 CENTIMES
Bronze **Edge:** Plain **Note:** Medal alignment.

Date	F	VF	XF	Unc	BU
1953-1981	—	—	15.00	30.00	—

KM# 148.1   50 CENTIMES
Bronze **Obv:** Legend in French **Rev:** Helmeted mine worker, miner's lamp at right, smaller head, tip of neck 1mm from rim **Edge:** Plain

Date	F	VF	XF	Unc	BU
1958-2001	—	—	0.10	0.10	—

KM# 8   1/4 FRANC
1.2500 g., 0.9000 Silver .0362 oz. ASW **Note:** Varieties exist with and without periods in signature.

Date	VG	F	VF	XF	Unc
1834-1844	8.00	20.00	120	200	300

KM# 14   1/4 FRANC
1.2500 g., 0.9000 Silver .0362 oz. ASW

Date	VG	F	VF	XF	Unc
1849-1850	85.00	175	1,000	2,000	3,000

KM# 6   1/2 FRANC
2.5000 g., 0.9000 Silver .0723 oz. ASW **Note:** Varieties exist.

Date	VG	F	VF	XF	Unc
1833-1844	15.00	30.00	175	300	600

KM# 15   1/2 FRANC
2.5000 g., 0.9000 Silver .0723 oz. ASW

Date	VG	F	VF	XF	Unc
1849-1850	125	275	1,300	2,500	4,000

KM# 7.1   FRANC
5.0000 g., 0.9000 Silver .1447 oz. ASW **Note:** Coin alignment.

Date	VG	F	VF	XF	Unc
1833-1844	20.00	40.00	250	400	700

KM# 7.2   FRANC
5.0000 g., 0.9000 Silver .1447 oz. ASW **Note:** Medal alignment.

Date	VG	F	VF	XF	Unc
1833	100	300	1,000	2,000	—

KM# 16.1   FRANC
5.0000 g., 0.9000 Silver .1447 oz. ASW **Note:** Edge varieties exist.

Date	VG	F	VF	XF	Unc
1849-1850	125	250	1,200	2,100	3,500

KM# 16.2 FRANC
5.0000 g., 0.9000 Silver .1447 oz. ASW **Obv:** Without period in signature

Date	VG	F	VF	XF	Unc
1850	150	300	1,400	2,500	4,000

KM# 28.1 FRANC
5.0000 g., 0.8350 Silver .1342 oz. ASW **Obv:** Legend in French

Date	F	VF	XF	Unc	BU
1866-1886/66	1.50	20.00	100	170	—

KM# 38 FRANC
5.0000 g., 0.8350 Silver .1342 oz. ASW **Subject:** 50th Anniversary of Independence

Date	F	VF	XF	Unc	BU
1880	4.00	35.00	100	140	—

KM# 28.2 FRANC
5.0000 g., 0.8350 Silver .1342 oz. ASW **Obv:** Without period in signature

Date	F	VF	XF	Unc	BU
1886	2.00	30.00	75.00	150	—

KM# 29.1 FRANC
5.0000 g., 0.8350 Silver .1342 oz. ASW **Obv:** Legend in Dutch

Date	F	VF	XF	Unc	BU
1886-1887	3.00	25.00	100	150	—

KM# 29.2 FRANC
5.0000 g., 0.8350 Silver .1342 oz. ASW **Obv:** Without period in signature

Date	F	VF	XF	Unc	BU
1886-1887	2.50	25.00	100	150	—

KM# 56.1 FRANC
5.0000 g., 0.8350 Silver .1342 oz. ASW **Obv:** Legend in French

Date	F	VF	XF	Unc	BU
1904-1909	2.50	10.00	30.00	45.00	—

KM# 56.2 FRANC
5.0000 g., 0.8350 Silver .1342 oz. ASW **Obv:** Without period in signature

Date	F	VF	XF	Unc	BU
1904-1909	2.50	10.00	30.00	45.00	—

KM# 57.1 FRANC
5.0000 g., 0.8350 Silver .1342 oz. ASW **Obv:** Legend in Dutch

Date	F	VF	XF	Unc	BU
1904-1909	2.50	10.00	30.00	50.00	—

KM# 57.2 FRANC
5.0000 g., 0.8350 Silver .1342 oz. ASW **Obv:** Without period in signature

Date	F	VF	XF	Unc	BU
1904-1909	3.00	10.00	30.00	45.00	—

KM# 72.1 FRANC
5.0000 g., 0.8350 Silver .1342 oz. ASW **Obv:** Legend in French

Date	F	VF	XF	Unc	BU
1910-1918	BV	2.00	3.50	7.00	—

KM# 72.2 FRANC
5.0000 g., 0.8350 Silver .1342 oz. ASW **Note:** Medal alignment.

Date	F	VF	XF	Unc	BU
1914	4.50	12.50	50.00	125	275

KM# 73.1 FRANC
5.0000 g., 0.8350 Silver .1342 oz. ASW **Obv:** Legend in Dutch

Date	F	VF	XF	Unc	BU
1910-1918	BV	2.00	3.50	7.00	—

KM# 73.2 FRANC
5.0000 g., 0.8350 Silver .1342 oz. ASW **Note:** Medal alignment.

Date	F	VF	XF	Unc	BU
1914	4.50	12.50	50.00	125	275

KM# 89 FRANC
Nickel **Obv:** Legend in French **Edge:** Reeded

Date	F	VF	XF	Unc	BU
1922-1934/24	0.15	0.25	1.00	3.00	—

KM# 90 FRANC
Nickel **Obv:** Legend in Dutch **Edge:** Reeded

Date	F	VF	XF	Unc	BU
1922-1935/23	0.15	0.25	1.00	3.00	—

KM# 119 FRANC
Nickel **Obv:** Legend in French

Date	F	VF	XF	Unc	BU
1939	0.15	0.25	0.50	1.50	—

KM# 120 FRANC
Nickel **Obv:** Legend in Dutch

Date	F	VF	XF	Unc	BU
1939-1940	0.15	0.25	0.50	1.50	—

KM# 127 FRANC
Zinc **Obv:** Legend in French **Note:** German Occupation WW II.

Date	F	VF	XF	Unc	BU
1941-1947	0.20	0.75	1.50	5.00	10.00

KM# 128 FRANC
Zinc **Obv:** Legend in Dutch

Date	F	VF	XF	Unc	BU
1942-1947	0.20	0.75	1.50	5.00	10.00

KM# 142.1 FRANC
Copper-Nickel **Obv:** Legend in French **Edge:** Reeded

Date	F	VF	XF	Unc	BU
1950-1988	0.10	0.10	0.10	0.30	—

KM# 142.2 FRANC
Copper-Nickel **Edge:** Reeded **Note:** Medal alignment.

Date	F	VF	XF	Unc	BU
1952-1988	—	10.00	30.00	60.00	—

KM# 143.1 FRANC
Copper-Nickel **Rev:** Legend in Dutch **Edge:** Reeded

Date	F	VF	XF	Unc	BU
1950-1988	—	0.10	0.10	0.30	—

KM# 143.2 FRANC
Copper-Nickel **Edge:** Reeded **Note:** Medal alignment.

Date	F	VF	XF	Unc	BU
1951-1981	—	10.00	30.00	60.00	—

KM# 170 FRANC
Nickel Plated Iron **Obv:** French legend **Rev:** Legend in French

Date	F	VF	XF	Unc	BU
1989-1993	—	10.00	30.00	0.35	—

KM# 171 FRANC
Nickel Plated Iron **Obv:** Dutch legend **Rev:** Legend in Dutch

Date	F	VF	XF	Unc	BU
1989-1993	—	10.00	30.00	0.35	—

KM# 187 FRANC
Nickel Plated Iron **Obv:** Albert II **Rev:** Legend in French **Note:**
Struck at Brussels Mint. Mint mark - Angel Head. Unknown
mintmaster's privy mark - scales.

Date	F	VF	XF	Unc	BU
1994-2001	—	—	—	0.30	—

KM# 188 FRANC
Nickel Plated Iron **Rev:** Legend in Dutch

Date	F	VF	XF	Unc	BU
1994-2001	—	—	—	0.30	—

KM# 9.1 2 FRANCS (2 Frank)
10.0000 g., 0.9000 Silver .2894 oz. ASW **Note:** Edge inscription
inclined to left.

Date	VG	F	VF	XF	Unc
1834-1844	100	175	1,000	2,000	—

KM# 9.2 2 FRANCS (2 Frank)
10.0000 g., 0.9000 Silver .2894 oz. ASW **Note:** Edge inscription inclined to right.

Date	VG	F	VF	XF	Unc
1834-1844	75.00	150	750	1,600	2,500

KM# 10 2 FRANCS (2 Frank)
10.0000 g., 0.9000 Silver .2894 oz. ASW **Note:** This coin was not officially released into circulation.

Date	VG	F	VF	XF	Unc
1849-1865	400	900	4,500	8,000	—

KM# 30.1 2 FRANCS (2 Frank)
10.0000 g., 0.8350 Silver .2685 oz. ASW **Obv:** Legend in French **Note:** Edge varieties exist.

Date	F	VF	XF	Unc	BU
1866-1868	5.00	80.00	325	500	—

KM# 30.2 2 FRANCS (2 Frank)
10.0000 g., 0.8350 Silver .2685 oz. ASW **Rev:** Without cross on crown

Date	VG	F	VF	XF	Unc
1866-1868	6.00	20.00	125	450	700

KM# 39 2 FRANCS (2 Frank)
10.0000 g., 0.8350 Silver .2685 oz. ASW **Subject:** 50th Anniversary of Independence **Rev:** Legend in French

Date	F	VF	XF	Unc	BU
1880	15.00	150	300	600	—

KM# 31 2 FRANCS (2 Frank)
10.0000 g., 0.8350 Silver .2685 oz. ASW **Obv:** Legned in Dutch **Rev:** Cross on crown **Note:** Edge varieties exist.

Date	F	VF	XF	Unc	BU
1887	35.00	300	1,300	2,200	—

KM# 58.1 2 FRANCS (2 Frank)
10.0000 g., 0.8350 Silver .2685 oz. ASW **Obv:** Legend in French

Date	F	VF	XF	Unc	BU
1904-1909	.3.50	6.00	25.00	50.00	—

KM# 58.2 2 FRANCS (2 Frank)
10.0000 g., 0.8350 Silver .2685 oz. ASW **Obv:** Without period in signature

Date	F	VF	XF	Unc	BU
1904-1909	9.00	15.00	60.00	200	—

KM# 59.1 2 FRANCS (2 Frank)
10.0000 g., 0.8350 Silver .2685 oz. ASW **Obv:** Legend in Dutch

Date	F	VF	XF	Unc	BU
1904-1909	3.50	6.00	25.00	50.00	—

KM# 59.2 2 FRANCS (2 Frank)
10.0000 g., 0.8350 Silver .2685 oz. ASW **Obv:** Without period in signature

Date	F	VF	XF	Unc	BU
1904-1909	7.00	15.00	45.00	90.00	—

KM# 74 2 FRANCS (2 Frank)
10.0000 g., 0.8350 Silver .2685 oz. ASW **Obv:** Legend in French

Date	F	VF	XF	Unc	BU
1910-1912	BV	4.00	10.00	30.00	—

KM# 75 2 FRANCS (2 Frank)
10.0000 g., 0.8350 Silver .2685 oz. ASW **Obv:** Legend in Dutch

Date	F	VF	XF	Unc	BU
1911-1912	BV	4.00	10.00	25.00	—

KM# 91.1 2 FRANCS (2 Frank)
Nickel **Obv:** Legend in French

Date	F	VF	XF	Unc	BU
1923-1930/20	0.50	1.50	8.00	20.00	—

KM# 91.2 2 FRANCS (2 Frank)
Nickel **Note:** Medal alignment

Date	F	VF	XF	Unc	BU
1923	5.00	8.00	45.00	110	—

KM# 92   2 FRANCS (2 Frank)
Nickel **Obv:** Legend in Dutch

Date	F	VF	XF	Unc	BU
1923-1930/20	0.25	1.50	10.00	25.00	—

KM# 133   2 FRANCS (2 Frank)
Zinc Coated Steel **Obv:** Legend in French **Edge:** Plain **Note:**
Allied Occupation issue. Made in U.S.A. on blanks for 1943 cents.

Date	F	VF	XF	Unc	BU
1944	0.25	0.50	1.50	5.00	10.00

KM# 133a   2 FRANCS (2 Frank)
Silver **Note:** Made in error in U.S.A. on blanks for Netherlands
25 cents.

Date	F	VF	XF	Unc	BU
1944	100	200	300	400	—

KM# 11   2-1/2 FRANCS
12.5000 g., 0.9000 Silver .3617 oz. ASW **Obv:** Legend in French

Date	VG	F	VF	XF	Unc
1848-1849	20.00	50.00	300	500	700

KM# 12   2-1/2 FRANCS
12.5000 g., 0.9000 Silver .3617 oz. ASW **Note:** Larger head.

Date	VG	F	VF	XF	Unc
1848-1865	30.00	100	450	700	1,200

KM# 3.1   5 FRANCS (5 Frank)
25.0000 g., 0.9000 Silver .7234 oz. ASW **Note:** Incuse lettered edge.

Date	VG	F	VF	XF	Unc
1832-1844	16.00	30.00	250	550	800

KM# 3.2   5 FRANCS (5 Frank)
25.0000 g., 0.9000 Silver .7234 oz. ASW **Note:** Raised lettered edge

Date	VG	F	VF	XF	Unc
1847-1849	9.00	12.00	80.00	200	400

KM# 17   5 FRANCS (5 Frank)
25.0000 g., 0.9000 Silver .7234 oz. ASW

Date	VG	F	VF	XF	Unc
1849-1865/55	7.00	10.00	35.00	100	—

KM# 24   5 FRANCS (5 Frank)
25.0000 g., 0.9000 Silver .7234 oz. ASW **Obv:** Smaller head,
engraver's name near rim, below truncation

Date	F	VF	XF	Unc	BU
1865-1876	6.50	6.00	20.00	60.00	—

KM# 25   5 FRANCS (5 Frank)
25.0000 g., 0.9000 Silver .7234 oz. ASW **Obv:** Larger head, engraver's name below truncation

Date	F	VF	XF	Unc	BU
1865-1868	275	1,700	2,500	4,000	—

KM# 97.1   5 FRANCS - 5 FRANK (Un / Een Belga)
Nickel **Obv:** Legend in French **Rev:** Value: UN BELGA **Note:** All dates exist in position A and B, values are the same.

Date	F	VF	XF	Unc	BU
1930-1934	1.00	4.00	10.00	20.00	—

KM# 97.2   5 FRANCS - 5 FRANK (Un / Een Belga)
Nickel **Note:** Medal alignment. Edge varieties exist.

Date	F	VF	XF	Unc	BU
1930	17.50	50.00	150	350	—

KM# 98   5 FRANCS - 5 FRANK (Un / Een Belga)
Nickel **Obv:** Legend in Dutch **Rev:** Value: EEN BELGA **Note:** All dates exist in position A and B, values are the same.

Date	F	VF	XF	Unc	BU
1930-1933	1.50	6.00	12.00	25.00	—

KM# 108.1   5 FRANCS - 5 FRANK (Un / Een Belga)
Nickel **Rev:** Legend in French **Note:** Both dates exist in position A and B, values are the same.

Date	F	VF	XF	Unc	BU
1936-1937	6.00	10.00	30.00	70.00	—

KM# 108.2   5 FRANCS - 5 FRANK (Un / Een Belga)
Nickel **Note:** Medal alignment.

Date	F	VF	XF	Unc	BU
1936	17.50	55.00	150	350	—

KM# 109.1   5 FRANCS - 5 FRANK (Un / Een Belga)
Nickel **Rev:** Legend in Dutch **Note:** Both dates exist in position A and B, values are the same.

Date	F	VF	XF	Unc	BU
1936	4.00	15.00	35.00	50.00	—

KM# 109.2   5 FRANCS - 5 FRANK (Un / Een Belga)
Nickel **Note:** Medal alignment. Edge varieties exist.

Date	F	VF	XF	Unc	BU
1936	15.00	50.00	150	325	—

KM# 116.1   5 FRANCS - 5 FRANK (Un / Een Belga)
Nickel **Obv:** Legend in French **Note:** Milled edge, lettering with crown.

Date	F	VF	XF	Unc	BU
1938	0.20	0.75	4.00	10.00	—

KM# 116.2   5 FRANCS - 5 FRANK (Un / Een Belga)
Nickel **Note:** Milled edge, lettering with star.

Date	F	VF	XF	Unc	BU
1939	350	700	1,500	3,000	—

KM# 116.3   5 FRANCS - 5 FRANK (Un / Een Belga)
Nickel **Note:** Milled edge, without lettering (error).

Date	F	VF	XF	Unc	BU
1938	40.00	70.00	135	300	—

KM# 117.1   5 FRANCS - 5 FRANK (Un / Een Belga)
Nickel **Obv:** Legend in Dutch **Note:** Milled edge, lettering with crown.

Date	F	VF	XF	Unc	BU
1938-1939	7.00	15.00	50.00	125	—

KM# 117.2   5 FRANCS - 5 FRANK (Un / Een Belga)
Nickel **Note:** Milled edge, lettering with star.

Date	F	VF	XF	Unc	BU
1938-1939	0.15	0.50	2.00	5.00	—

KM# 117.3   5 FRANCS - 5 FRANK (Un / Een Belga)
Nickel **Note:** Milled edge, without lettering (error).

Date	F	VF	XF	Unc	BU
1939	30.00	60.00	175	350	—

KM# 129.1 5 FRANCS - 5 FRANK (Un / Een Belga)
Zinc **Obv:** Legend in French **Edge:** Reeded **Note:** German Occupation WW II.

Date	F	VF	XF	Unc	BU
1941-1947	0.35	0.75	2.00	12.00	—

KM# 129.2 5 FRANCS - 5 FRANK (Un / Een Belga)
Zinc **Note:** Medal alignment.

Date	F	VF	XF	Unc	BU
1943	5.00	15.00	50.00	130	—

KM# 130 5 FRANCS - 5 FRANK (Un / Een Belga)
Zinc **Obv:** Legend in Dutch

Date	F	VF	XF	Unc	BU
1941-1947	0.30	0.50	2.50	10.00	—

KM# 134.1 5 FRANCS - 5 FRANK (Un / Een Belga)
Copper-Nickel **Obv:** Legend in French **Edge:** Reeded

Date	F	VF	XF	Unc	BU
1948-1981	1.00	1.00	0.20	0.35	—

KM# 135.1 5 FRANCS - 5 FRANK (Un / Een Belga)
Copper-Nickel **Obv:** Legend in Dutch **Edge:** Reeded

Date	F	VF	XF	Unc	BU
1948-1981	1.00	1.00	0.20	0.50	—

KM# 134.2 5 FRANCS - 5 FRANK (Un / Een Belga)
Copper-Nickel **Note:** Medal alignment.

Date	F	VF	XF	Unc	BU
1949-1977	—	4.00	10.00	30.00	—

KM# 135.2 5 FRANCS - 5 FRANK (Un / Een Belga)
Copper-Nickel **Note:** Medal alignment.

Date	F	VF	XF	Unc	BU
1950-1974	—	4.00	10.00	30.00	—

KM# 163 5 FRANCS - 5 FRANK (Un / Een Belga)
Brass Or Aluminum-Bronze **Rev:** Legend in French

Date	F	VF	XF	Unc	BU
1986-1993	—	—	0.35	0.65	—

KM# 164 5 FRANCS - 5 FRANK (Un / Een Belga)
Brass Or Aluminum-Bronze **Rev:** Legend in Dutch

Date	F	VF	XF	Unc	BU
1986-1993	—	—	0.35	0.65	—

KM# 189 5 FRANCS - 5 FRANK (Un / Een Belga)
Aluminum-Bronze **Obv:** Albert II **Rev:** Legend in French **Note:** Struck at Brussels Mint. Mint mark - Angel head. Mintmaster R. Coenen's privy mark - Scale.

Date	F	VF	XF	Unc	BU
1994-2001	—	—	—	0.50	—

KM# 190 5 FRANCS - 5 FRANK (Un / Een Belga)
Aluminum-Bronze **Rev:** Legend in Dutch **Note:** Struck at Brussels Mint. Mint mark - Angel head. Mintmaster R. Coenen's privy mark - Scale.

Date	F	VF	XF	Unc	BU
1994-2001	—	—	—	0.50	—

KM# 18 10 FRANCS (10 Frank)
3.1662 g., 0.9000 Gold .0916 oz. AGW **Note:** 54,890 pieces dated 1849 and 1850 were withdrawn from circulation.

Date	VG	F	VF	XF	Unc
1849-1850	9,876	500	1,200	2,000	3,000

Belgium

KM# 18   10 FRANCS (10 Frank)
3.1662 g., 0.9000 Gold .0916 oz. AGW   **Note:** 54,890 pieces dated 1849 and 1850 were withdrawn from circulation.

Date	F	VF	XF	Unc	BU
1849-1850	9,876	500	1,200	2,000	3,000

KM# A33   10 FRANCS (10 Frank)
3.1662 g., 0.9000 Gold .0916 oz. AGW

Date	VG	F	VF	XF	Unc
1867	9,876	1,800	3,200	6,500	—

KM# A33   10 FRANCS (10 Frank)
3.1662 g., 0.9000 Gold .0916 oz. AGW

Date	F	VF	XF	Unc	BU
1867	9,876	1,800	3,200	6,500	—

KM# 100   10 FRANCS - 10 FRANK (Deux / Twee Belgas)
Nickel   **Obv:** Conjoined heads of Leopold I, Leopold II and Albert I left **Rev:** Legend in Dutch **Note:** Exists in position A or B, values are the same.

Date	F	VF	XF	Unc	BU
1930	30.00	75.00	140	250	—

KM# 99   10 FRANCS - 10 FRANK (Deux / Twee Belgas)
Nickel   **Subject:** Independence Centennial **Rev:** Legend in French **Note:** Exists in position A or B, values are the same.

Date	F	VF	XF	Unc	BU
1930	25.00	70.00	130	200	—

KM# 155.1   10 FRANCS - 10 FRANK (Deux / Twee Belgas)
Nickel   **Rev:** Legend in French **Edge:** Plain **Note:** Struck at Brussels Mint. Mint mark - Angel head. Mintmaster Vogeleer's privy mark - Bird.

Date	F	VF	XF	Unc	BU
1969-1979	—	—	0.40	0.70	—

KM# 155.2   10 FRANCS - 10 FRANK (Deux / Twee Belgas)
Nickel   **Note:** Medal alignment. Struck at Brussels Mint. Mint mark - Angel head. Mintmaster Vogeleer's privy mark - Bird.

Date	F	VF	XF	Unc	BU
1969-1978	—	6.00	12.00	30.00	—

KM# 156.1   10 FRANCS - 10 FRANK (Deux / Twee Belgas)
Nickel   **Rev:** Legend in Dutch **Edge:** Plain **Note:** Struck at Brussels Mint. Mint mark - Angel head. Mintmaster Vogeleer's privy mark - Bird.

Date	F	VF	XF	Unc	BU
1969-1979	—	—	0.40	0.70	—

KM# 156.2   10 FRANCS - 10 FRANK (Deux / Twee Belgas)
Nickel   **Note:** Medal alignment. Struck at Brussels Mint. Mint mark - Angel head. Mintmaster Vogeleer's privy mark - Bird.

Date	F	VF	XF	Unc	BU
1971-1976	—	6.00	12.00	35.00	—

KM# A23.1   20 FRANCS (20 Frank)
6.4516 g., 0.9000 Gold .1867 oz. AGW   **Edge:** Lettered

Date	F	VF	XF	Unc	BU
1834-1841	950	4,800	8,000	—	—

KM# 23   20 FRANCS (20 Frank)
6.4516 g., 0.9000 Gold .1867 oz. AGW   **Note:** Approximately 1/3 of the 1865 mintage was struck in 1866. Each variety of name below the bust exists both in positon A and position B, with values being the same.

Date	F	VF	XF	Unc	BU
1865	—	BV	125	150	250

KM# 32   20 FRANCS (20 Frank)
6.4516 g., 0.9000 Gold .1867 oz. AGW   **Obv:** Heavy coarser beard

Date	F	VF	XF	Unc	BU
1867-1870	—	—	BV	125	130

KM# 37   20 FRANCS (20 Frank)
6.4516 g., 0.9000 Gold .1867 oz. AGW   **Obv:** Finer beard

Date	F	VF	XF	Unc	BU
1870-1882	—	—	BV	125	—

KM# 78   20 FRANCS (20 Frank)
6.4516 g., 0.9000 Gold .1867 oz. AGW   **Obv:** Legend in French

Date	F	VF	XF	Unc	BU
1914	—	—	BV	125	—

KM# 79   20 FRANCS (20 Frank)
6.4516 g., 0.9000 Gold .1867 oz. AGW   **Obv:** Legend in Dutch

Date	F	VF	XF	Unc	BU
1914	—	—	BV	125	150

KM# 101.1   20 FRANCS - 20 FRANK (Vier / Quatre Belgas)
Nickel **Obv:** Legend in French **Note:** All dates exist in position A and B, values are the same.

Date	F	VF	XF	Unc	BU
1931-1932	15.00	45.00	95.00	140	175

KM# 101.2   20 FRANCS - 20 FRANK (Vier / Quatre Belgas)
Nickel **Note:** Medal alignment. Edge varieties exist.

Date	F	VF	XF	Unc	BU
1932	65.00	175	400	600	—

KM# 102   20 FRANCS - 20 FRANK (Vier / Quatre Belgas)
Nickel **Obv:** Legend in Dutch **Note:** All dates exist in position A and B, values are the same.

Date	F	VF	XF	Unc	BU
1931-1932	15.00	40.00	90.00	130	175

KM# 103.1   20 FRANCS - 20 FRANK (Vier / Quatre Belgas)
11.0000 Silver .6800 Silver .2405 oz. ASW   **Obv:** Legend in French

Date	F	VF	XF	Unc	BU
1933-1934	—	BV	4.00	10.00	—

KM# 103.2   20 FRANCS - 20 FRANK (Vier / Quatre Belgas)
11.0000 g., 0.6800 Silver .2405 oz. ASW   **Note:** Medal alignment.

Date	F	VF	XF	Unc	BU
1934	35.00	80.00	190	400	—

KM# 104.1   20 FRANCS - 20 FRANK (Vier / Quatre Belgas)
11.0000 g., 0.6800 Silver .2405 oz. ASW   **Obv:** Legend in Dutch

Date	F	VF	XF	Unc	BU
1933-1934	—	BV	4.00	6.00	—

KM# 104.2   20 FRANCS - 20 FRANK (Vier / Quatre Belgas)
11.0000 g., 0.6800 Silver .2405 oz. ASW   **Note:** Medal alignment.

Date	F	VF	XF	Unc	BU
1934	30.00	70.00	170	350	—

KM# 105   20 FRANCS - 20 FRANK (Vier / Quatre Belgas)
11.0000 g., 0.6800 Silver .2405 oz. ASW   **Note:** Both dates exist in position A and B, values are the same. Coins dated 1934 exist with and without umlauts above E in BELGIE.

Date	F	VF	XF	Unc	BU
1934-1935	BV	3.50	5.50	8.00	—

KM# 140.1   20 FRANCS - 20 FRANK (Vier / Quatre Belgas)
8.0000 g., 0.8350 Silver .2148 oz. ASW   **Obv:** Legend in French **Edge:** Reeded

Date	F	VF	XF	Unc	BU
1949-1955	—	BV	3.50	7.00	—

KM# 140.2   20 FRANCS - 20 FRANK (Vier / Quatre Belgas)
8.0000 g., 0.8350 Silver .2148 oz. ASW   **Edge:** Plain **Note:** Medal alignment.

Date	F	VF	XF	Unc	BU
1949-1950	15.00	35.00	75.00	125	—

KM# 141.1   20 FRANCS - 20 FRANK (Vier / Quatre Belgas)
8.0000 g., 0.8350 Silver .2148 oz. ASW   **Obv:** Legend in Dutch **Edge:** Reeded

Date	F	VF	XF	Unc	BU
1949-1955	—	BV	3.00	7.00	—

KM# 141.2   20 FRANCS - 20 FRANK (Vier / Quatre Belgas)
8.0000 g., 0.8350 Silver .2148 oz. ASW   **Edge:** Reeded **Note:** Medal alignment.

Date	F	VF	XF	Unc	BU
1949-1951	15.00	35.00	85.00	135	—

KM# 159   20 FRANCS - 20 FRANK (Vier / Quatre Belgas)
Nickel-Bronze   **Rev:** Legend in French

Date	F	VF	XF	Unc	BU
1980-1993	—	—	0.70	2.00	—

KM# 160   20 FRANCS - 20 FRANK (Vier / Quatre Belgas)
Nickel-Bronze   **Rev:** Legend in Dutch

Date	F	VF	XF	Unc	BU
1980-1993	—	—	0.70	2.00	—

KM# 191   20 FRANCS - 20 FRANK (Vier / Quatre Belgas)
Nickel-Bronze   **Obv:** Albert II **Rev:** Legend in French **Note:** Struck at Brussels Mint. Mint mark - Angel head. Mintmaster R. Coenen's privy mark - Scale.

Date	F	VF	XF	Unc	BU
1994-2001	—	—	0.70	1.00	—

KM# 192   20 FRANCS - 20 FRANK (Vier / Quatre Belgas)
Nickel-Bronze   **Rev:** Legend in Dutch **Note:** Struck at Brussels Mint. Mint mark - Angel head. Mintmaster R. Coenen's privy mark - Scale.

Date	F	VF	XF	Unc	BU
1994-2001	—	—	0.70	1.00	—

KM# 13.1   25 FRANCS
7.9155 g., 0.9000 Gold .2291 oz. AGW   **Ruler:** Leopold I **Note:** 16.5% of the total mintage of KM#13.1 and 13.2 was melted. Actual number melted per date is unavailable.

Date	F	VF	XF	Unc	BU
1848-1849	600	1,400	2,000	3,400	—

KM# 13.2   25 FRANCS
7.9155 g., 0.9000 Gold .2291 oz. AGW   **Ruler:** Leopold I **Obv:** Larger head **Rev:** 900/M

Date	F	VF	XF	Unc	BU
1850	800	1,800	3,000	4,500	—

KM# 13.3   25 FRANCS
7.9155 g., 0.9000 Gold 0.2291 oz. AGW   **Ruler:** Leopold I **Obv:** Larger head **Rev:** 900 M

Date	F	VF	XF	Unc	BU
1850	900	2,000	3,300	5,000	—

KM# B23.1   40 FRANCS (40 Frank)
12.9032 g., 0.9000 Gold .3734 oz. AGW   **Edge:** Lettered

Date	F	VF	XF	Unc	BU
1834-1841	2,500	8,000	—	—	—

KM# B23.2   40 FRANCS (40 Frank)
12.9032 g., 0.9000 Gold .3734 oz. AGW   **Note:** Medal alignment.

Date	F	VF	XF	Unc	BU
1834	1,500	8,000	—	—	—

KM# 106.1   50 FRANCS (50 Frank)
22.0000 g., 0.6800 Silver .4810 oz. ASW   **Subject:** Brussels Exposition and Railway Centennial **Obv:** St. Michael slaying

dragon (Brussels' patron saint) **Rev:** Brussels train station, legend in French **Note:** Exists in positions A and B, values are the same.

Date	F	VF	XF	Unc	BU
1935	40.00	70.00	110	180	350

KM# 106.2 50 FRANCS (50 Frank)
22.0000 g., 0.6800 Silver .4810 oz. ASW **Note:** Medal alignment. Exists in positions A and B, values are the same.

Date	F	VF	XF	Unc	BU
1935	200	300	500	825	—

KM# 107.1 50 FRANCS (50 Frank)
22.0000 g., 0.6800 Silver .4810 oz. ASW **Obv:** St. Michael slaying dragon (Brussels' patron saint) **Rev:** Brussels railway station, legend in Dutch **Note:** Exists in positions A and B, values are the same.

Date	F	VF	XF	Unc	BU
1935	50.00	100	150	225	—

KM# 107.2 50 FRANCS (50 Frank)
22.0000 g., 0.6800 Silver .4810 oz. ASW **Note:** Medal alignment. Exists in positions A and B, values are the same.

Date	F	VF	XF	Unc	BU
1935	300	600	900	1,500	—

KM# 121.1 50 FRANCS (50 Frank)
20.0000 g., 0.8350 Silver .5369 oz. ASW **Rev:** Legend in French **Note:** Both dates exist in positions A and B, values are the same.

Date	F	VF	XF	Unc	BU
1939-1940	BV	8.00	12.00	18.00	—

KM# 121.2 50 FRANCS (50 Frank)
20.0000 g., 0.8350 Silver .5369 oz. ASW **Rev:** Without cross on crown **Note:** Both dates exist in positions A and B, values are the same.

Date	F	VF	XF	Unc	BU
1939-1940	BV	8.00	12.00	18.00	—

KM# 122.1 50 FRANCS (50 Frank)
20.0000 g., 0.8350 Silver .5369 oz. ASW **Rev:** Legend in Dutch **Note:** Both dates exist in positions A and B, values are the same.

Date	F	VF	XF	Unc	BU
1939-1940	BV	8.00	12.00	18.00	—

KM# 122.2 50 FRANCS (50 Frank)
20.0000 g., 0.8350 Silver .5369 oz. ASW **Rev:** Without cross on crown **Note:** Both dates exist in positions A and B, values are the same.

Date	F	VF	XF	Unc	BU
1939-1940	8.00	15.00	35.00	55.00	—

KM# 122.3 50 FRANCS (50 Frank)
20.0000 g., 0.8350 Silver .5369 oz. ASW **Rev:** Triangle in third arms from left, cross on crown **Note:** Both dates exist in positions A and B, values are the same.

Date	F	VF	XF	Unc	BU
1940	15.00	25.00	40.00	85.00	—

KM# 122.4 50 FRANCS (50 Frank)
20.0000 g., 0.8350 Silver .5369 oz. ASW **Rev:** Without cross on crown **Note:** Both dates exist in positions A and B, values are the same.

Date	F	VF	XF	Unc	BU
1940	30.00	60.00	100	200	—

KM# 136.1 50 FRANCS (50 Frank)
12.5000 g., 0.8350 Silver .3356 oz. ASW **Obv:** Legend in French

Date	F	VF	XF	Unc	BU
1948-1954	—	BV	4.50	6.00	—

KM# 136.2 50 FRANCS (50 Frank)
12.5000 g., 0.8350 Silver .3356 oz. ASW **Note:** Medal alignment.

Date	F	VF	XF	Unc	BU
1949	10.00	30.00	90.00	175	—

KM# 137 50 FRANCS (50 Frank)
12.5000 g., 0.8350 Silver .3356 oz. ASW **Obv:** Legend in Dutch

Date	F	VF	XF	Unc	BU
1948-1954	—	BV	4.50	6.00	—

KM# 150.1 50 FRANCS (50 Frank)
12.5000 g., 0.8350 Silver .3356 oz. ASW **Subject:** Brussels World Fair **Obv:** Legend in French

Date	F	VF	XF	Unc	BU
1958	—	BV	6.50	10.00	—

KM# 150.2 50 FRANCS (50 Frank)
12.5000 g., 0.8350 Silver .3356 oz. ASW **Note:** Medal alignment.

Date	F	VF	XF	Unc	BU
1958	18.00	45.00	100	180	—

Belgium

KM# 151.1   50 FRANCS (50 Frank)
12.5000 g., 0.8350 Silver .3356 oz. ASW   **Obv:** Legend in Dutch
Edge: Reeded

Date	F	VF	XF	Unc	BU
1958	BV	5.00	7.50	10.00	—

KM# 151.2   50 FRANCS (50 Frank)
12.5000 g., 0.8350 Silver .3356 oz. ASW   **Note:** Medal alignment.

Date	F	VF	XF	Unc	BU
1958		15.00	35.00	75.00	125	—

KM# 152.1   50 FRANCS (50 Frank)
12.5000 g., 0.8350 Silver .3356 oz. ASW   **Subject:** King
Baudouin's marriage to Doña Fabiola de Mora y Aragon

Date	F	VF	XF	Unc	BU
1960	BV	4.50	6.00	9.00	15.00

KM# 152.2   50 FRANCS (50 Frank)
12.5000 g., 0.8350 Silver .3356 oz. ASW   **Note:** Medal alignment.

Date	F	VF	XF	Unc	BU
1960	12.50	30.00	60.00	120	—

KM# 168   50 FRANCS (50 Frank)
Nickel   **Rev:** Legend in French

Date	F	VF	XF	Unc	BU
1987-1993	—	—	2.00	4.00	—

KM# 169   50 FRANCS (50 Frank)
Nickel   **Rev:** Legend in Dutch

Date	F	VF	XF	Unc	BU
1987-1993	—	—	2.00	4.00	—

KM# 193   50 FRANCS (50 Frank)
Nickel   **Obv:** Albert II **Rev:** Legend in French **Note:** Struck at

Brussels Mint. Mint mark - Angel head. Mintmaster R. Coenen's
privy mark - Scale.

Date	F	VF	XF	Unc	BU
1994-2001	—	—	—	3.00	—

KM# 194   50 FRANCS (50 Frank)
Nickel   **Obv:** Albert II **Rev:** Legend in Dutch **Note:** Struck at
Brussels Mint. Mint mark - Angel head. Mintmaster R. Coenen's
privy mark - Scale

Date	F	VF	XF	Unc	BU
1994-2001	—	—	—	3.00	—

KM# 213.1   50 FRANCS (50 Frank)
Nickel   **Subject:** European Soccer Championship **Obv:** Head of
Albert II left **Rev:** Soccer ball, legend in French **Edge:** Reeded

Date	F	VF	XF	Unc	BU
2000	—	—	—	6.00	—

KM# 213.2   50 FRANCS (50 Frank)
Nickel   **Note:** Medal alignment.

Date	F	VF	XF	Unc	BU
2000 Proof		Value: 22.00			

KM# 214.1   50 FRANCS (50 Frank)
Nickel   **Subject:** European Soccer Championship **Obv:** Head of
Albert II left **Rev:** Soccer ball, legend in Dutch **Edge:** Reeded

Date	F	VF	XF	Unc	BU
2000	—	—	—	6.00	—

KM# 214.2   50 FRANCS (50 Frank)
Nickel   **Note:** Medal alignment.

Date	F	VF	XF	Unc	BU
2000 Proof		Value: 22.00			

KM# 138.1   100 FRANCS (100 Frank)
18.0000 g., 0.8350 Silver .4832 oz. ASW   **Obv:** Legend in French
Rev: Conjoined heads left of Leopold I, Leopold II, Albert I and
Leopold III.

Date	F	VF	XF	Unc	BU
1948-1954	—	BV	6.50	9.00	—

KM# 138.2   100 FRANCS (100 Frank)
18.0000 g., 0.8350 Silver .4832 oz. ASW   **Note:** Medal alignment.

Date	F	VF	XF	Unc	BU
1948-1950	10.00	40.00	90.00	200	—

KM# 139.1   100 FRANCS (100 Frank)
18.0000 g., 0.8350 Silver .4832 oz. ASW **Obv:** Legend in Dutch **Rev:** Conjoined heads left of Leopold I, Leopold II, Albert I and Leopold III

Date	F	VF	XF	Unc	BU
1948-1951	—	BV	6.50	9.00	—

KM# 139.2   100 FRANCS (100 Frank)
18.0000 g., 0.8350 Silver .4832 oz. ASW **Note:** Medal alignment.

Date	F	VF	XF	Unc	BU
1948-1951	7.50	30.00	75.00	160	—

KM# 215   200 FRANCS (200 Frank)
Silver **Subject:** The Universe **Obv:** Legend in French

Date	F	VF	XF	Unc	BU
2000	—	—	—	15.00	—

KM# 216   200 FRANCS (200 Frank)
Silver **Subject:** Nature **Obv:** Legend in Dutch

Date	F	VF	XF	Unc	BU
2000	—	—	—	15.00	—

KM# 217   200 FRANCS (200 Frank)
Silver **Subject:** The City **Obv:** Legend in German

Date	F	VF	XF	Unc	BU
2000	—	—	—	15.00	—

KM# 157.1   250 FRANCS (250 Frank)
25.0000 g., 0.8350 Silver .6711 oz. ASW **Subject:** Silver Jubilee of King Baudouin **Obv:** Legend in French **Edge:** Reeded **Note:** Struck at Brussels Mint. Mint mark - Angel head. Mintmaster Vogeleer's privy mark - Bird.

Date	F	VF	XF	Unc	BU
ND(1976)	—	—	BV	9.50	—

KM# 157.2   250 FRANCS (250 Frank)
25.0000 g., 0.8350 Silver .6711 oz. ASW **Edge:** Stars **Note:** Struck at Brussels Mint. Mint mark - Angel head. Mintmaster Vogeleer's privy mark - Bird.

Date	F	VF	XF	Unc	BU
ND(1976)	—	—	—	15.00	—

KM# 158.1   250 FRANCS (250 Frank)
25.0000 g., 0.8350 Silver .6711 oz. ASW **Obv:** Legend in Dutch

Edge: Reeded **Note:** Struck at Brussels Mint. Mint mark - Angel head. Mintmaster Vogeleer's privy mark - Bird.

Date	F	VF	XF	Unc	BU
ND(1976)	—	—	BV	9.50	—

KM# 158.2   250 FRANCS (250 Frank)
25.0000 g., 0.8350 Silver .6711 oz. ASW **Edge:** Stars **Note:** Struck at Brussels Mint. Mint mark - Angel head. Mintmaster Vogeleer's privy mark - Bird.

Date	F	VF	XF	Unc	BU
ND(1976)	—	—	—	15.00	—

KM# 195   250 FRANCS (250 Frank)
18.7500 g., 0.9250 Silver .5571 oz. ASW **Subject:** BE-NE-LUX Treaty **Note:** Struck at Brussels Mint. Mint mark - Angel head. Mintmaster R. Coenen's privy mark - Scale.

Date	F	VF	XF	Unc	BU
ND(1994)	—	—	—	15.00	—

KM# 199   250 FRANCS (250 Frank)
18.7500 g., 0.9250 Silver .5571 oz. ASW **Subject:** 60th Anniversary - Death of Queen Astrid (car death) **Rev:** Bust of crowned Queen Astrid 1/4 facing right **Note:** Struck at Brussels Mint. Mint mark - Angel head. Mintmaster R. Coenen's privy mark - Scale.

Date	F	VF	XF	Unc	BU
ND(1995)	—	—	—	10.00	—

KM# 202   250 FRANCS (250 Frank)
18.7500 g., 0.9250 Silver .5571 oz. ASW **Subject:** 20th Anniversary - King Baudouin Foundation **Obv:** Royal couple and monogram **Rev:** Denomination, stylized design and royal monogram

Date	F	VF	XF	Unc	BU
ND(1996)	—	—	—	15.00	—

KM# 207   250 FRANCS (250 Frank)
18.7500 g., 0.9250 Silver .5571 oz. ASW **Subject:** 60th Birthday
- Queen Paola **Obv:** Denomination **Rev:** Portrait **Note:** Struck at
Brussels Mint. Mint mark - Angel head. Mintmaster R. Coenen's
privy mark - Scale.

Date	F	VF	XF	Unc	BU
1997	—	—	—	15.00	—

KM# 208   250 FRANCS (250 Frank)
18.7500 g., 0.9250 Silver .5571 oz. ASW **Subject:** King
Boudewijn - Queen Fabiola **Obv:** Heads of King and Queen, queen
in profile facing left, king 1/4 facing left **Rev:** Pelican with nestlings

Date	F	VF	XF	Unc	BU
ND(1998)	—	—	—	15.00	—

KM# 209   250 FRANCS (250 Frank)
18.7500 g., 0.9250 Silver .5571 oz. ASW **Subject:** 40th Wedding
Anniversary - King Albert and Queen Paola **Obv:** King and Queen's
conjoining busts left **Rev:** St. Gudule Cathedral and city hall **Edge:**
Reeded

Date	F	VF	XF	Unc	BU
ND(1999)	—	—	—	15.00	—

KM# 218   250 FRANCS (250 Frank)
18.7500 g., 0.9250 Silver .5571 oz. ASW **Subject:** Marriage of
Prince Philip and Princess Mathilde **Rev:** Two hands joined on a rose

Date	F	VF	XF	Unc	BU
1999	—	—	—	15.00	—

KM# 161   500 FRANCS (500 Frank)
Silver Clad Copper-Nickel **Subject:** 150th Anniversary of
Independence **Obv:** French legend **Rev:** French legend **Note:**
Struck at Brussels Mint. Mint mark - Angel head. Mintmaster
Vogeleer's privy mark - Bird.

Date	F	VF	XF	Unc	BU
ND(1980)	—	—	—	9.00	—

KM# 161a   500 FRANCS (500 Frank)
25.0000 g., 0.5100 Silver .4099 oz. ASW **Obv:** French legend
Rev: French legend **Note:** Struck at Brussels Mint. Mint mark -
Angel head. Mintmaster Vogeleer's privy mark - Bird.

Date	F	VF	XF	Unc	BU
ND(1980) Proof	Value: 20.00				

KM# 162   500 FRANCS (500 Frank)
Silver Clad Copper-Nickel **Obv:** Dutch legend **Rev:** Dutch legend
Note: Struck at Brussels Mint. Mint mark - Angel head. Mintmaster
Vogeleer's privy mark - Bird.

Date	F	VF	XF	Unc	BU
ND(1980)	—	—	—	9.00	—

KM# 162a   500 FRANCS (500 Frank)
25.0000 g., 0.5100 Silver .4099 oz. ASW **Rev:** Dutch legend
Note: Struck at Brussels Mint. Mint mark - Angel Head. Mintmaster
Vogeleer's privy mark - Bird.

Date	F	VF	XF	Unc	BU
ND(1980) Proof	Value: 20.00				

KM# 165   500 FRANCS (500 Frank)
25.0000 g., 0.5100 Silver .4099 oz. ASW **Obv:** KM#161 **Rev:**
KM#162 **Note:** Mule. Struck at Brussels Mint. Mint mark - Angel
head. Mintmaster Vogeleer's privy mark - Bird.

Date	F	VF	XF	Unc	BU
1980	—	—	—	1,000	—

KM# 178   500 FRANCS (500 Frank)
22.8500 g., 0.8330 Silver .6120 oz. ASW **Subject:** 60th Birthday
of King Baudouin **Rev:** Dutch legends

Date	F	VF	XF	Unc	BU
1990	—	—	—	20.00	—

KM# 179   500 FRANCS (500 Frank)
22.8500 g., 0.8330 Silver .6120 oz. ASW **Subject:** 60th Birthday of King Baudouin **Rev:** French legends

Date	F	VF	XF	Unc	BU
1990	—	—	—	20.00	—

KM# 180   500 FRANCS (500 Frank)
22.8500 g., 0.8330 Silver .6120 oz. ASW **Subject:** 60th Birthday of King Baudouin **Rev:** German legends

Date	F	VF	XF	Unc	BU
1990	—	—	—	20.00	—

KM# 196   500 FRANCS (500 Frank)
22.8500 g., 0.8330 Silver .6120 oz. ASW **Subject:** 40th Year of Reign **Obv:** Stylized design around **Rev:** Crown above, denomination, year below, Dutch legend

Date	F	VF	XF	Unc	BU
1991	—	—	—	12.00	—

KM# 197   500 FRANCS (500 Frank)
22.8500 g., 0.8330 Silver .6120 oz. ASW **Subject:** 40th Year of Reign **Obv:** Stylized design around **Rev:** Crown above, denomination, year below, French legend

Date	F	VF	XF	Unc	BU
1991	—	—	—	12.00	—

KM# 198   500 FRANCS (500 Frank)
22.8500 g., 0.8330 Silver .6120 oz. ASW **Subject:** 40th Year of Reign **Obv:** Stylized design around **Rev:** Crown above, denomination, year below, German legend

Date	F	VF	XF	Unc	BU
1991	—	—	—	15.00	—

KM# 186   500 FRANCS (500 Frank)
22.8500 g., 0.8330 Silver .6120 oz. ASW **Subject:** Europalaia - Mexico Exposition **Note:** Struck at Brussels Mint. Mint mark - Angel head. Mintmaster R. Coenen's privy mark - Scale.

Date	F	VF	XF	Unc	BU
ND(1993)	—	—	—	25.00	—

KM# 212   500 FRANCS (500 Frank)
22.8500 g., 0.9250 Silver .6975 oz. ASW **Subject:** Brussels - European Culture Capital **Obv:** Denomination and European map **Rev:** Portraits of Albert and Elizabeth in ruffled collars **Edge:** Plain

Date	F	VF	XF	Unc	BU
ND(1999)	—	—	—	30.00	—

KM# 219   500 FRANCS (500 Frank)
22.8500 g., 0.9250 Silver .6975 oz. ASW, 37 mm. **Subject:** Europe: Charles V **Obv:** Map and denomination **Rev:** Charles V of Spain and building **Edge:** Plain

Date	F	VF	XF	Unc	BU
ND(2000)	—	—	—	30.00	—

KM# 222   500 FRANCS (500 Frank)
22.8500 g., 0.9250 Silver .6795 oz. ASW, 37 mm. **Subject:** Europe: Europa and the Bull **Obv:** Map and denomination **Rev:** Europa sitting on a bull **Edge:** Plain

Date	F	VF	XF	Unc	BU
2001 Proof			Value: 50.00		

KM# 210   5000 FRANCS
15.5500 g., 0.9990 Gold .4994 oz. AGW **Subject:** Brussels - European Culture Capital **Obv:** Denomination and European map **Rev:** Portraits of Albert and Elizabeth in ruffled collars **Edge:** Plain

Date	F	VF	XF	Unc	BU
ND(1999) Proof			Value: 500		

KM# 220   5000 FRANCS
15.5500 g., 0.9990 Gold .4994 oz. AGW, 29 mm. **Subject:** Europe: Charles V **Obv:** Map and denomination **Rev:** Charles V of Spain with building **Edge:** Plain

Date	F	VF	XF	Unc	BU
ND(2000) Proof			Value: 500		

KM# 223   5000 FRANCS
15.5500 g., 0.9990 Gold .4994 oz. AGW, 29 mm. **Subject:** Europe: Europa and the Bull **Obv:** Map and denomination **Rev:** Europa sitting on a bull **Edge:** Plain

Date	F	VF	XF	Unc	BU
2001 Proof			Value: 500		

TRADE COINAGE
European Currency Units

KM# 166   5 ECU
22.8500 g., 0.8330 Silver .6120 oz. ASW   **Subject:** 30th
Anniversary - Treaties of Rome **Rev:** Bust of Charles V right

Date	F	VF	XF	Unc	BU
1987-1988	—	—	—	12.00	—

KM# 183   5 ECU
22.8500 g., 0.8330 Silver .6120 oz. ASW   **Rev:** Charlemagne

Date	F	VF	XF	Unc	BU
1991 Proof	Value: 55.00				

KM# 185   5 ECU
22.8500 g., 0.9250 Silver .6796 oz. ASW   **Subject:** Belgian
Presidency of the E.C. **Obv:** King Baudouin

Date	F	VF	XF	Unc	BU
1993 Proof	Value: 45.00				

KM# 200   5 ECU
22.8500 g., 0.9250 Silver .6796 oz. ASW   **Subject:** 50th
Anniversary - United Nations

Date	F	VF	XF	Unc	BU
1995 Proof	Value: 35.00				

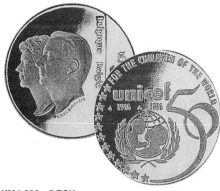

KM# 203   5 ECU
22.8500 g., 0.9250 Silver .6796 oz. ASW   **Subject:** 50th
Anniversary - UNICEF **Obv:** Royal couple **Rev:** UNICEF logo

Date	F	VF	XF	Unc	BU
1996 Proof	Value: 45.00				

KM# 205   5 ECU
22.8500 g., 0.9250 Silver .6796 oz. ASW   **Subject:** 40th
Anniversary - Treaty of Rome **Obv:** Portraits of Albert II and
Baudouin **Rev:** European Union map

Date	F	VF	XF	Unc	BU
1997 Proof	Value: 45.00				

KM# 221   5 ECU
22.8500 g., 0.9250 Silver .6796 oz. ASW   **Subject:** 50th
Anniversary - Human Rights Declaration

Date	F	VF	XF	Unc	BU
1998 Proof	Value: 45.00				

KM# 172   10 ECU
3.1100 g., 0.9990 Gold .1000 oz. AGW   **Rev:** Charles V bust right

Date	F	VF	XF	Unc	BU
1989-1990 Proof	Value: 140				

KM# 176   10 ECU
Bi-Metallic Gold center in Silver ring   **Subject:** 60th Birthday of
King Baudouin

Date	F	VF	XF	Unc	BU
1990 Proof	Value: 75.00				

Belgium

KM# 181   10 ECU
Bi-Metallic Gold center in Silver ring **Subject:** 40th Year of Reign of King Baudouin

Date	F	VF	XF	Unc	BU
1991 Proof			Value: 90.00		

KM# 177   20 ECU
Bi-Metallic Gold center in Silver ring **Subject:** 60th Birthday of King Baudouin

Date	F	VF	XF	Unc	BU
1990 Proof			Value: 160		

KM# 182   20 ECU
Bi-Metallic Gold center in Silver ring **Subject:** 40th Year of Reign of King Baudouin

Date	F	VF	XF	Unc	BU
1991 Proof			Value: 185		

KM# 173   25 ECU
7.7750 g., 0.9990 Gold .2500 oz. AGW **Rev:** Diocletian bust right

Date	F	VF	XF	Unc	BU
1989-1990	—	—	BV	170	—

KM# 167   50 ECU
17.2800 g., 0.9000 Gold .5000 oz. AGW **Subject:** 30th Anniversary - Treaties of Rome **Obv:** Charles V bust right

Date	F	VF	XF	Unc	BU
1987-1988	—	—	BV	340	—

KM# 174   50 ECU
15.5550 g., 0.9990 Gold .5000 oz. AGW **Rev:** Charlemagne seated on dais

Date	F	VF	XF	Unc	BU
1989-1990	—	—	BV	340	—

KM# 184   50 ECU
15.5550 g., 0.9990 Gold .5000 oz. AGW **Rev:** Charlemagne bust right

Date	F	VF	XF	Unc	BU
1991 Proof			Value: 450		

KM# 213   50 ECU
15.5550 g., 0.9990 Gold .5000 oz. AGW **Subject:** Belgian Presidency of the E.C.

Date	F	VF	XF	Unc	BU
1993 Proof			Value: 375		

KM# 201   50 ECU
15.5550 g., 0.9990 Gold .5000 oz. AGW **Subject:** 50th Anniversary - United Nations

Date	F	VF	XF	Unc	BU
1995 Proof			Value: 400		

KM# 204   50 ECU
15.5550 g., 0.9990 Gold .5000 oz. AGW **Subject:** 50th Anniversary - UNICEF **Obv:** Conjoined busts of Royal couple left **Rev:** UNICEF logo

Date	F	VF	XF	Unc	BU
1996 Proof			Value: 450		

KM# 206   50 ECU
15.5550 g., 0.9990 Gold .5000 oz. AGW **Subject:** 40th Anniversary - Treaty of Rome **Obv:** Conjoined heads of Albert II and Baudouin **Rev:** European Union map

Date	F	VF	XF	Unc	BU
1997 Proof			Value: 500		

KM# 211   50 ECU
15.5550 g., 0.9990 Gold .5000 oz. AGW **Subject:** 50th Anniversary - Human Rights Declaration

Date	F	VF	XF	Unc	BU
1998 Proof			Value: 500		

KM# 175   100 ECU
31.1030 g., 0.9990 Gold 1.0000 oz. AGW **Rev:** Bust of Maria Theresa, stateswoman, right

Date	F	VF	XF	Unc	BU
1989-1990	—	—	BV	675	—

EURO COINAGE
European Economic Community Issues

KM# 224   EURO CENT
2.2700 g., Copper Plated Steel, 16.2 mm. **Ruler:** Albert II **Obv:** King's portrait **Rev:** Denomination and globe **Edge:** Plain

Date	F	VF	XF	Unc	BU
1999-2005	—	—	—	0.35	0.75

KM# 225   2 EURO CENTS
3.0300 g., Copper Plated Steel, 18.7 mm. **Ruler:** Albert II **Obv:** King's portrait **Rev:** Denomination and globe **Edge:** Grooved

Date	F	VF	XF	Unc	BU
1999-2004	—	—	—	0.50	1.00

KM# 226   5 EURO CENTS
3.8600 g., Copper Plated Steel, 21.2 mm. **Ruler:** Albert II **Obv:** King's portrait **Rev:** Denomination and globe **Edge:** Plain

Date	F	VF	XF	Unc	BU
1999-2005	—	—	—	0.75	1.25

KM# 227   10 EURO CENTS
4.0700 g., Brass, 19.7 mm. **Ruler:** Albert II **Obv:** King's portrait **Rev:** Denomination and map **Edge:** Reeded

Date	F	VF	XF	Unc	BU
1999-2005	—	—	—	0.75	1.25

KM# 228   20 EURO CENTS
5.7300 g., Brass, 22.1 mm. **Ruler:** Albert II **Obv:** King's portrait **Rev:** Denomination and map **Edge:** Notched

Date	F	VF	XF	Unc	BU
1999-2005	—	—	—	0.75	1.25

KM# 229   50 EURO CENTS
7.8100 g., Brass, 24.2 mm. **Ruler:** Albert II **Obv:** King's portrait **Rev:** Denomination and map **Edge:** Reeded

Date	F	VF	XF	Unc	BU
1999-2005	—	—	—	0.75	1.25

KM# 230   EURO
7.5000 g., Bi-Metallic   Copper-Nickel center in Brass ring, 23.2 mm. **Ruler:** Albert II **Obv:** King's portrait **Rev:** Denomination and map **Edge:** Reeded and plain sections

Date	F	VF	XF	Unc	BU
1999-2005	—	—	—	2.50	4.50

KM# 231   2 EURO
8.5200 g., Bi-Metallic Brass center in Copper-Nickel ring, 25.7 mm. **Obv:** King's portrait **Rev:** Denomination and map **Edge:** Reeded with 2's and stars

Date	F	VF	XF	Unc	BU
1999-2005	—	—	—	3.50	5.50

KM# 240   2 EURO
8.5200 g., Bi-Metallic Brass center in Copper-Nickel ring, 25.7 mm. **Ruler:** Albert II **Subject:** Schengen Agreement **Obv:** Albert II of Belgium and Henri of Luxembourg **Rev:** Value and map **Edge:** Reeding over stars

Date	F	VF	XF	Unc	BU
2005	—	—	—	5.00	7.50

KM# 241   2 EURO
8.5200 g., Bi-Metallic Brass center in Copper-Nickel ring, 25.7 mm. **Ruler:** Albert II **Obv:** Atomic model **Rev:** Value and map **Edge:** Reeding over stars and 2's

Date	F	VF	XF	Unc	BU
2006	—	—	—	—	3.50

KM# 233   10 EURO
18.9300 g., 0.9250 Silver 0.563 oz. ASW, 32.9 mm. **Subject:**
Belgian Railway System **Obv:** Value, head at right transposed on
map **Rev:** Train exiting tunnel **Edge:** Reeded

Date	F	VF	XF	Unc	BU
ND (2002) Proof	Value: 40.00				

KM# 235   10 EURO
18.9300 g., 0.9250 Silver 0.563 oz. ASW, 32.9 mm. **Subject:**
"Simenon" **Edge:** Reeded

Date	F	VF	XF	Unc	BU
2003 Proof	Value: 40.00				

KM# 234   10 EURO
18.7500 g., 0.9250 Silver 0.5576 oz. ASW, 33 mm. **Ruler:**
Albert II **Obv:** Value **Rev:** Western Europe map and Goddess
Europa riding a bull **Edge:** Reeded

Date	F	VF	XF	Unc	BU
2004 Proof	Value: 40.00				

KM# 236   10 EURO
18.9300 g., 0.9250 Silver 0.563 oz. ASW, 32.9 mm. **Ruler:**
Albert II **Subject:** "Tintin" **Edge:** Reeded

Date	F	VF	XF	Unc	BU
2004 Proof	Value: 75.00				

KM# 237   100 EURO
15.5500 g., 0.9990 Gold 0.4994 oz. AGW, 29 mm. **Subject:**
Founding Fathers

Date	F	VF	XF	Unc	BU
2002 Proof	Value: 550				

KM# 238   100 EURO
15.5500 g., 0.9990 Gold 0.4994 oz. AGW, 29 mm. **Subject:** 10th
Anniversary of Reign

Date	F	VF	XF	Unc	BU
2003 Proof	Value: 475				

KM# 239   100 EURO
15.5500 g., 0.9990 Gold 0.4994 oz. AGW, 29 mm. **Subject:**
Franc Germinal

Date	F	VF	XF	Unc	BU
2004 Proof	Value: 475				

GHENT
GERMAN OCCUPATION WWI
TOKEN COINAGE

KM# Tn1   50 CENTIMES
Brass-Plated Iron   **Note:** Similar to KM#Tn1a, thin "50".

Date	F	VF	XF	Unc	BU
1915	7.00	15.00	25.00	40.00	100

KM# Tn1a   50 CENTIMES
Brass-Plated Iron   **Rev:** Thick "50"

Date	F	VF	XF	Unc	BU
1915	7.00	15.00	25.00	40.00	100

KM# Tn2   FRANKEN
Brass-Plated Iron

Date	F	VF	XF	Unc	BU
1915	7.00	15.00	25.00	40.00	100

KM# Tn2a   FRANKEN
Brass-Plated Iron   **Rev:** 11. 1919 instead of 1.1. 1919

Date	F	VF	XF	Unc	BU
1915	8.00	17.00	26.00	45.00	120

KM# Tn3   FRANKEN
Gilt Copper **Obv:** Lion in circle, STAD GENT VILLE DE GAND around
Rev: 1915 1 FR in circle, UIT BETAALBAAR 1 JANUARI 1918
REMBOURSABLE 1 JANVIER 1920 along sides of square **Shape:**
Square **Note:** This token was struck in 1920 for the benefit of charity.

Date	F	VF	XF	Unc	BU
1915	50.00	200	350	600	—

KM# Tn4   2 FRANKEN
Brass-Plated Iron

Date	F	VF	XF	Unc	BU
1915	10.00	25.00	40.00	60.00	150

KM# Tn5   2 FRANKEN
Gilt Copper **Obv:** Arms in circle, STAD GENT FIDES ET AMOR
around **Rev:** 1928 2 FRANK in circle, UIT BETAAL BAAR
JANUARI 1922 PAX ET LABOR around **Note:** This token was
struck in 1920 for the benefit of charity.

Date	F	VF	XF	Unc	BU
1918	45.00	175	300	550	900

KM# Tn6 5 FRANKEN
Brass-Plated Iron

Date	F	VF	XF	Unc	BU
1917	17.50	30.00	45.00	100	175

KM# Tn7 5 FRANKEN
Brass-Plated Iron

Date	F	VF	XF	Unc	BU
1918	15.00	27.00	40.00	90.00	160

Czech Republic

The Czech Republic was formerly united with Slovakia as Czechoslovakia. It is bordered in the west by Germany, to the north by Poland, to the east by Slovakia and to the south by Austria. It consists of 3 major regions: Bohemia, Moravia and Silesia and has an area of 30,450 sq. mi. (78,864 sq. km.) and a population of 10.4 million. Capital: Prague (Praha). Agriculture and livestock are chief occupations while coal deposits are the main mineral resources.

MONETARY SYSTEM
1 Czechoslovak Koruna (Kcs) = 1 Czech
  Koruna (Kc)
1 Koruna = 100 Haleru

REPUBLIC
STANDARD COINAGE

KM# 6 10 HALERU
0.9900 Aluminum 0.6 oz., 15.5 mm. **Obv:** Crowned Czech lion **Rev:** Value and stylized river **Edge:** Plain **Note:** Two varieties of mint marks exist for 1994.

Date	F	VF	XF	Unc	BU
1993-2004	—	—	—	0.20	—

KM# 2.1 20 HALERU
0.7400 g., Aluminum, 17 mm. **Obv:** Crowned Czech lion **Rev:** Linden leaf within value; Closed 2, "h" above flat line **Edge:** Milled **Note:** Medallic coin alignment.

Date	F	VF	XF	Unc	BU
1993-1997	—	—	—	0.30	—

KM# 2.2 20 HALERU
Aluminum, 17 mm. **Obv:** Crowned Czech lion **Rev:** Linden leaf and value, "h" above flat line, closed 2 in denomination **Note:** Coin alignment.

Date	F	VF	XF	Unc	BU
1993	—	—	—	4.00	—

KM# 2.3 20 HALERU
Aluminum **Rev:** Open 2 in denomination, "h" above angle line **Note:** Medallic coin alignment.

Date	F	VF	XF	Unc	BU
1998-2004	—	—	—	0.30	—

KM# 3.1 50 HALERU
Aluminum 0.9 oz., 19 mm. **Obv:** Crowned Czech lion **Rev:** Large value **Edge:** Part plain, part milled repeated **Note:** Two styles of "9" exist for 1994; prev. KM#3.

Date	F	VF	XF	Unc	BU
1993-2001	—	—	—	0.50	—

KM# 3.2 50 HALERU
0.9000 g., Aluminum, 19 mm. **Subject:** Outlined lettering and larger mint mark

Date	F	VF	XF	Unc	BU
2001-2005	—	—	—	0.50	—

KM# 7 KORUNA
Nickel Clad Steel, 20 mm. **Obv:** Crowned Czech lion **Rev:** Value above crown **Edge:** Milled **Note:** Two varieties of mint marks exist for 1996. 2000-03 have two varieties in the artisit monogram.

Date	F	VF	XF	Unc	BU
1993-2005	—	—	—	0.60	—

KM# 9 2 KORUN
3.7000 g., Nickel Clad Steel, 21.5 mm. **Obv:** Crowned Czech lion **Edge:** Plain **Shape:** 11-sided **Note:** Two varieties of designer monograms exist for 2001-04.

Date	F	VF	XF	Unc	BU
1993-2005	—	—	—	0.65	—

KM# 8 5 KORUN
4.8000 g., Nickel Plated Steel, 23 mm. **Obv:** Crowned Czech lion **Rev:** Large value, Charles bridge and linden leaf **Edge:** Plain

Date	F	VF	XF	Unc	BU
1993-2005	—	—	—	1.00	—

KM# 4 10 KORUN
7.6200 g., Copper Plated Steel, 24.5 mm. **Obv:** Crowned Czech lion **Rev:** Brno Cathedral **Edge:** Milled **Note:** Position of designer's initials on reverse change during the 1995 strike.

Date	F	VF	XF	Unc	BU
1993-2005	25.00	75.00	150	1.50	—

KM# 42 10 KORUN
7.5200 g., Copper Plated Steel, 24.5 mm. **Subject:** Year 2000 **Obv:** Crowned Czech lion **Rev:** Clock works above denomination **Edge:** Reeded

Date	F	VF	XF	Unc	BU
2000	—	—	—	1.50	—

KM# 5 20 KORUN
8.4300 g., Brass Plated Steel, 26 mm. **Obv:** Crowned Czech lion **Rev:** St. Wenceslas (Duke Vaclav) on horse **Edge:** Plain **Shape:** 13-sided **Note:** Two varieties of mint marks and style of 9's exist for 1997.

Date	F	VF	XF	Unc	BU
1993-2004	—	—	1.00	2.50	—

KM# 43 20 KORUN
8.6000 g., Brass Plated Steel, 26 mm. **Subject:** Year 2000 **Obv:** Crowned Czech lion **Rev:** Astrolab and denomination **Edge:** Plain **Shape:** 13-sided

Date	F	VF	XF	Unc	BU
2000	—	—	—	2.50	—

KM# 1 50 KORUN
9.7000 g., Bi-Metallic Brass plated Steel center in Copper plated Steel ring, 27.5 mm. **Obv:** Crowned Czech lion **Rev:** Prague city view **Edge:** Plain

Date	F	VF	XF	Unc	BU
1993-2005	—	—	2.50	7.50	—

KM# 10 200 KORUN
13.0000 g., 0.9000 Silver .3440 oz. ASW, 31 mm. **Subject:** 1st Anniversary of Constitution **Note:** 22 pieces, Unc and Proof, were melted by the Czech National Bank in 1997.

Date	F	VF	XF	Unc	BU
1993	—	—	—	12.50	14.50

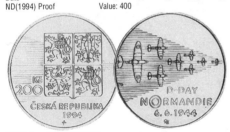

KM# 11.1 200 KORUN
13.0000 g., 0.9000 Silver .3440 oz. ASW, 31 mm. **Subject:** 650th Anniversary **Rev:** St. Vitus Cathedral and Archbishop's arms **Edge:** Reeded **Note:** See note with KM#11.2.

Date	F	VF	XF	Unc	BU
ND(1994)	—	—	—	12.50	14.50

KM# 11.2 200 KORUN
13.0000 g., 0.9000 Silver .3440 oz. ASW, 31 mm. **Subject:** 650th Anniversary **Rev:** St. Vitus Cathedral and Prague Archbishop's Arms **Edge:** Plain **Note:** 22 pieces, Unc and Proof of KM#11.1 and 11.2, were melted by the Czech National Bank in 1997.

Date	F	VF	XF	Unc	BU
ND(1994) Proof	Value: 400				

KM# 12 200 KORUN
13.0000 g., 0.9000 Silver .3440 oz. ASW, 31 mm. **Subject:** 50th Anniversary - Normandy Invasion **Rev:** Spitfires in formation **Note:** 6,445 pieces, Unc and Proof, were melted by the Czech National Bank in 1997.

Date	F	VF	XF	Unc	BU
1994	—	—	—	16.50	18.50

KM# 13.1 200 KORUN
13.0000 g., 0.9000 Silver .3440 oz. ASW, 31 mm. **Subject:** 125th Anniversary of Brno Tramway **Edge:** Reeded **Note:** See note with KM#13.2.

Date	F	VF	XF	Unc	BU
1994	—	—	—	14.00	16.00

KM# 13.2 200 KORUN
13.0000 g., 0.9000 Silver .3440 oz. ASW, 31 mm. **Subject:** 125th Anniversary Brno Tramway **Edge:** Plain **Note:** 22 pieces, Unc and Proof, were melted by the Czech National Bank in 1997. Beginning with KM#14, all 200 Korun strikes come either reeded, or plain edges with the inscription, "CESKA NARODNI BANKA".

Date	F	VF	XF	Unc	BU
1994 Proof	Value: 50.00				

KM# 14 200 KORUN
13.0000 g., 0.9000 Silver .3440 oz. ASW, 31 mm. **Subject:** Environmental Protection **Note:** 22 pieces, Unc and Proof, were melted by the Czech National Bank in 1997.

Date	F	VF	XF	Unc	BU
1994	—	—	—	14.00	16.00

KM# 15 200 KORUN
13.0000 g., 0.9000 Silver .3440 oz. ASW, 31 mm. **Subject:** 50th Anniversary - Victory Over Fascism **Note:** 22 pieces, Unc and Proof, were melted by the Czech National Bank in 1997.

Date	F	VF	XF	Unc	BU
ND(1995)	—	—	—	14.00	16.00

KM# 16 200 KORUN
13.0000 g., 0.9000 Silver .3440 oz. ASW, 31 mm. **Subject:** 200th Anniversary - Birth of Pavel Josef Safarik **Note:** 22 pieces, Unc and Proof, were melted by the Czech National Bank in 1997.

Date	F	VF	XF	Unc	BU
1995	—	—	—	14.00	16.00

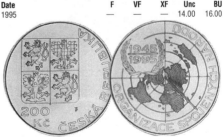

KM# 17 200 KORUN
13.0000 g., 0.9000 Silver .3440 oz. ASW, 31 mm. **Subject:** 50th Anniversary - United Nations **Note:** 25 pieces, Unc and Proof, were melted by the Czech National Bank in 1997.

Date	F	VF	XF	Unc	BU
ND(1995)	—	—	—	14.00	16.00

KM# 22   200 KORUN
13.0000 g., 0.9000 Silver .3440 oz. ASW, 31 mm. **Subject:** Czech Philharmonic **Rev:** Building and musical instruments **Note:** Three varieties in the artisit's monogram exist. 25 pieces, Unc and Proof, were melted by the Czech National Bank in 1997.

Date	F	VF	XF	Unc	BU
1996	—	—	—	14.00	16.00

KM# 23   200 KORUN
13.0000 g., 0.9000 Silver .3440 oz. ASW, 31 mm. **Subject:** Karel Svolinsky **Note:** 25 pieces, Unc and Proof, were melted by the Czech National Bank in 1997.

Date	F	VF	XF	Unc	BU
ND(1996)	—	—	—	14.00	16.00

KM# 24   200 KORUN
13.0000 g., 0.9000 Silver .3440 oz. ASW, 31 mm. **Subject:** Jean-Baptiste Gaspard Deburau

Date	F	VF	XF	Unc	BU
1996	—	—	—	14.00	16.00

KM# 25   200 KORUN
13.0000 g., 0.9000 Silver .3761 oz. ASW, 31 mm. **Subject:** 200th Anniversary - Czech Christmas Mass by Jakub J. Ryba

Date	F	VF	XF	Unc	BU
ND(1996)	—	—	—	14.00	16.00

KM# 26   200 KORUN
13.0000 g., 0.9000 Silver .3761 oz. ASW, 31 mm. **Subject:** Centennial - First Automobile in Bohemia **Obv:** National arms **Rev:** Side view of antique automobile - Prasident

Date	F	VF	XF	Unc	BU
ND(1997)	—	—	—	14.00	16.00

KM# 27   200 KORUN
13.0000 g., 0.9000 Silver .3761 oz. ASW, 31 mm. **Subject:** Millennium - St. Adalbert's Death **Obv:** Unbordered arms **Rev:** Bishop's portrait

Date	F	VF	XF	Unc	BU
ND(1997)	—	—	—	14.00	16.00

KM# 28   200 KORUN
13.0000 g., 0.9000 Silver .3761 oz. ASW, 31 mm. **Subject:** Czech Amateur Athletic Union **Obv:** Unbordered arms **Rev:** Runners

Date	F	VF	XF	Unc	BU
ND(1997)	—	—	—	14.00	16.00

KM# 29   200 KORUN
13.0000 g., 0.9000 Silver .3761 oz. ASW, 31 mm. **Subject:** 650th Anniversary - Na Slovanech-Emauzy Monastery **Obv:** National arms **Rev:** Seated saintly figure

Date	F	VF	XF	Unc	BU
ND(1997)	—	—	—	14.00	16.00

KM# 30   200 KORUN
13.0000 g., 0.9000 Silver .3761 oz. ASW, 31 mm. **Subject:** 650th Anniversary - Charles University in Prague **Obv:** National arms **Rev:** Charles IV portrait and document seal

Date	F	VF	XF	Unc	BU
ND(1998)	—	—	—	14.00	16.00

KM# 31 200 KORUN
13.0000 g., 0.9000 Silver .3761 oz. ASW, 31 mm. **Subject:** 200th Aniversary - Birth of Frantisek Palacky **Obv:** National arms **Rev:** Head of Palacky loft

Date	F	VF	XF	Unc	BU
ND(1998)	—	—	—	14.00	16.00

KM# 32 200 KORUN
13.0000 g., 0.9000 Silver .3761 oz. ASW, 31 mm. **Subject:** 800th Anniversary - Coronation of King Premysl I. Otakar **Obv:** National arms **Rev:** Half facing head of the king at right, coin design at left

Date	F	VF	XF	Unc	BU
ND(1998)	—	—	—	14.00	16.00

KM# 33 200 KORUN
13.0000 g., 0.9000 Silver .3761 oz. ASW, 31 mm. **Subject:** 150th Anniversary - Birth of Frantisek Kmoch **Obv:** National arms **Rev:** Head of Kmoch facing left, dates

Date	F	VF	XF	Unc	BU
ND(1998)	—	—	—	11.50	13.50

KM# 34 200 KORUN
13.0000 g., 0.9000 Silver .3761 oz. ASW, 31 mm. **Subject:** 50th Anniversary - NATO **Obv:** Undivided national arms **Rev:** NATO style cross **Edge Lettering:** CESKA REPUBLIKA CLENSKA ZEME NATO 1996

Date	F	VF	XF	Unc	BU
ND(1999)	—	—	—	14.00	16.00

KM# 35 200 KORUN
13.0000 g., 0.9000 Silver .3761 oz. ASW, 31 mm. **Subject:** 200 Years - Prague Fine Arts Academy **Obv:** Stylized national arms **Rev:** Stylized design **Edge:** Reeded

Date	F	VF	XF	Unc	BU
ND(1999)	—	—	—	14.00	16.00

KM# 36 200 KORUN
13.0000 g., 0.9000 Silver .3761 oz. ASW, 31 mm. **Subject:** 100 Years - Brno University of Technology **Obv:** Undivided national arms **Rev:** Stylized design

Date	F	VF	XF	Unc	BU
ND(1999)	—	—	—	14.00	16.00

KM# 37 200 KORUN
13.0000 g., 0.9000 Silver .3761 oz. ASW, 31 mm. **Subject:** 100th Birthday - Ondrej Sekora **Obv:** National arms **Rev:** Ant holding flowers

Date	F	VF	XF	Unc	BU
ND(1999)	—	—	—	14.00	16.00

KM# 46 200 KORUN
13.0000 g., 0.9000 Silver .3761 oz. ASW **Subject:** 700th Anniversary - Currency Reform

Date	F	VF	XF	Unc	BU
2000	—	—	—	15.00	—

KM# 47   200 KORUN
13.0000 g., 0.9000 Silver .3761 oz. ASW   **Subject:** 100th Anniversary - Birth of Poet Vitezslav Nezval

Date	F	VF	XF	Unc	BU
2000	—	—	—	15.00	—

KM# 51   200 KORUN
13.0000 g., 0.9000 Silver 0.3762 oz. ASW, 31 mm.   **Subject:** Jaroslav Seifert **Obv:** National arms **Rev:** Head of Jaroslav Seifert right

Date	F	VF	XF	Unc	BU
ND(2001)	—	—	—	15.00	17.00

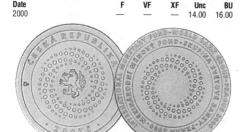

KM# 48   200 KORUN
13.0000 g., 0.9000 Silver .3762 oz. ASW, 31 mm.   **Subject:** 150th Anniversary - Birth of Zdenek Fibich, Musical Composer **Obv:** National arms **Rev:** Portrait

Date	F	VF	XF	Unc	BU
2000	—	—	—	14.00	16.00

KM# 52   200 KORUN
13.0000 g., 0.9000 Silver 0.3762 oz. ASW, 31 mm.   **Subject:** Soccer **Obv:** National arms **Rev:** Rampant lion on soccer ball

Date	F	VF	XF	Unc	BU
ND(2001)	—	—	—	15.00	17.00

KM# 49   200 KORUN
13.0000 g., 0.9000 Silver .3762 oz. ASW, 31 mm.   **Subject:** International Monetary Fund and Prague World Bank Group **Obv:** Crowned lion in swirling dots **Rev:** Circle of swirling dots

Date	F	VF	XF	Unc	BU
2000	—	—	—	14.00	16.00

KM# 53   200 KORUN
13.0000 g., 0.9000 Silver 0.3762 oz. ASW, 31 mm.   **Subject:** 250th Anniversary - Death of Kilian Ignac Dientzenhofer **Obv:** National arms, denomination **Rev:** Doorway and caliper

Date	F	VF	XF	Unc	BU
ND(2001)	—	—	—	15.00	17.00

KM# 50   200 KORUN
13.0000 g., 0.9000 Silver .3762 oz. ASW, 31 mm.   **Subject:** New Millennium **Obv:** National arms **Rev:** Stylized phoenix design

Date	F	VF	XF	Unc	BU
2000	—	—	—	14.00	16.00

KM# 54   200 KORUN
13.0000 g., 0.9000 Silver 0.3762 oz. ASW, 31 mm.   **Subject:** Euro Currency System **Obv:** National arms **Rev:** Prague gros coin design

Date	F	VF	XF	Unc	BU
ND(2001)	—	—	—	15.00	17.00

Czech Republic

KM# 58 200 KORUN
13.0000 g., 0.9000 Silver 0.3762 oz. ASW, 31 mm. **Subject:**
Frantisek Skroup **Obv:** National arms **Rev:** Portrait and name

Date	F	VF	XF	Unc	BU
ND(2001)	—	—	—	15.00	17.00

KM# 55 200 KORUN
13.0000 g., 0.9000 Silver 0.3762 oz. ASW, 31 mm. **Subject:** St.
Zdislava **Obv:** National arms **Rev:** Saint feeding sick person

Date	F	VF	XF	Unc	BU
ND(2002)	—	—	—	15.00	17.00

KM# 56 200 KORUN
13.0000 g., 0.9000 Silver 0.3762 oz. ASW, 30.9 mm. **Subject:**
Emil Holub **Obv:** National arms **Rev:** Traveller and African dancers

Date	F	VF	XF	Unc	BU
ND(2002)	—	—	—	15.00	17.00

KM# 57 200 KORUN
13.0000 g., 0.9000 Silver 0.3762 oz. ASW, 30.9 mm. **Subject:**
Jiri of Podebrady **Obv:** Overlapped arms **Rev:** Head of Podebrady

Date	F	VF	XF	Unc	BU
ND(2002)	—	—	—	15.00	17.00

KM# 59 200 KORUN
13.0000 g., 0.9000 Silver 0.3762 oz. ASW, 31 mm. **Subject:**
Mikolas Ales **Obv:** Four coats of arms above denomination **Rev:**
Horse and rider **Edge:** Reeded

Date	F	VF	XF	Unc	BU
ND(2002)	—	—	—	15.00	17.00

KM# 60 200 KORUN
13.1400 g., 0.9000 Silver 0.3802 oz. ASW, 31 mm. **Subject:**
Jaroslav Vrchlicky **Obv:** Denomination and quill **Rev:** Portrait with hat

Date	F	VF	XF	Unc	BU
ND(2003)	—	—	—	15.00	17.00

KM# 62 200 KORUN
13.0000 g., 0.9000 Silver 0.3762 oz. ASW, 30.9 mm. **Subject:**
Josef Thomayer **Obv:** National arms **Rev:** Portrait **Edge:** Reeded

Date	F	VF	XF	Unc	BU
ND(2003)	—	—	—	15.00	17.00

KM# 63 200 KORUN
13.0000 g., 0.9000 Silver 0.3762 oz. ASW, 31 mm. **Subject:**
Tabor-Bechyne Electric Railway **Obv:** Portrait **Rev:** Railroad
station scene

Date	F	VF	XF	Unc	BU
ND(2003)	—	—	—	16.00	18.00

KM# 64 200 KORUN
13.0000 g., 0.9000 Silver 0.3762 oz. ASW, 31 mm. **Subject:**
Bohemian Skiers' Union **Obv:** Portrait **Rev:** Skier **Edge:** Reeded

Date	F	VF	XF	Unc	BU
ND(2003)	—	—	—	16.00	18.00

KM# 70 200 KORUN
13.1000 g., 0.9000 Silver 0.3791 oz. ASW, 30.8 mm. **Subject:**
300th Anniversary - Death of Pond builder Jakub Krcin **Obv:** Coat
of arms above value with reflected design below **Rev:** Two
fishermen in boat with reflection on water below

Date	F	VF	XF	Unc	BU
ND(2004)	—	—	—	16.00	18.00

KM# 71 200 KORUN
13.1000 g., 0.9000 Silver 0.3791 oz. ASW **Subject:** Entry into the European Union

Date	F	VF	XF	Unc	BU
2004	—	—	—	16.00	18.00

KM# 72 200 KORUN
13.1000 g., 0.9000 Silver 0.3791 oz. ASW **Subject:** Prokop Divis

Date	F	VF	XF	Unc	BU
2004	—	—	—	16.00	18.00

KM# 73 200 KORUN
13.1000 g., 0.9000 Silver 0.3791 oz. ASW **Subject:** Leos Janacek

Date	F	VF	XF	Unc	BU
2004	—	—	—	16.00	18.00

KM# 74 200 KORUN
13.1000 g., 0.9000 Silver 0.3791 oz. ASW **Subject:** Kralice Bible

Date	F	VF	XF	Unc	BU
2004	—	—	—	16.00	18.00

KM# 44 2000 KORUN
34.2140 g., 0.9990 Bi-Metallic Gold And Silver .9990 oz., 40 mm. **Subject:** Millennium **Obv:** National arms hologram on gold inlay **Rev:** Stylized 2000 **Edge Lettering:** *CNB* Ag 0.999* 31.103 g *CNB* AU 999.9 *3. 111 g* **Note:** With a 3.1110 gram, .999 gold, .0999 ounce actual gold weight inlay.

Date	F	VF	XF	Unc	BU
ND(1999)	—	—	—	85.00	100

KM# 75.1 2000 KORUN
6.2200 g., 0.9999 Gold 0.2 oz. AGW, 20 mm. **Obv:** Ornamental porch below three heraldic animals **Rev:** Hluboka Castle with coat of arms in foreground **Edge:** Reeded

Date	F	VF	XF	Unc	BU
2004	—	—	—	—	145

KM# 75.2 2000 KORUN
6.2200 g., 0.9999 Gold 0.2 oz. AGW, 20 mm. **Edge:** Plain

Date	F	VF	XF	Unc	BU
2004 Proof		Value: 165			

KM# 76 2500 KORUN
31.1040 g., 0.9990 Bi-Metallic Gold And Silver .9999 Gold 7.776g center in .999 Silver 23.328g ring 0.999 oz., 40 mm. **Subject:** Czech entry into the European Union **Obv:** Value within circle of shields **Rev:** "1.5.2004" within circle of dates and text **Edge:** Lettered **Edge Lettering:** " CNB * Ag 0.999 * 23,328 g * Au 999.9 * 7,776g * "

Date	F	VF	XF	Unc	BU
ND (2004) Proof		Value: 265			

GOLD BULLION COINAGE

KM# 18 1000 KORUN
3.1103 g., 0.9999 Gold .1000 oz. AGW, 16 mm. **Subject:** Historic Coins - Tolar of Silesian Estates 12-1/2 tolar 1620.

Date	F	VF	XF	Unc	BU
1995-1997	—	—	—	—	100

KM# 38 1000 KORUN
3.1103 g., 0.9999 Gold .1000 oz. AGW, 16 mm. **Note:** Karlstejn Castle.

Date	F	VF	XF	Unc	BU
1998-1999	—	—	—	—	85.00

KM# 65 2000 KORUN
6.2200 g., 0.9999 Gold 0.2 oz. AGW, 20 mm. **Subject:** Znojmo Rotunda **Obv:** Three heraldic animals **Rev:** Farmer and round building

Date	F	VF	XF	Unc	BU
ND(2001)	—	—	—	—	145

KM# 66   2000 KORUN
6.2200 g., 0.9999 Gold 0.2 oz. AGW, 20 mm. **Subject:** Vyssi
Brod Monastery **Obv:** Three heraldic animals above Gothic design
Rev: Man holding church building model

Date	F	VF	XF	Unc	BU
2001	—	—	—	—	145

KM# 61   2000 KORUN
6.2200 g., 0.9999 Gold 0.2 oz. AGW, 20 mm. **Subject:** Litomysl
Castle **Obv:** Three heraldic animals above mermaid **Rev:** Aerial
castle view and mythical creature

Date	F	VF	XF	Unc	BU
2002	—	—	—	—	150

KM# 67   2000 KORUN
6.2200 g., 0.9999 Gold 0.2 oz. AGW, 20 mm. **Subject:** Kutna Hora
Fountain **Obv:** Three heraldic animals **Rev:** Fountain enclosure

Date	F	VF	XF	Unc	BU
2002	—	—	—	—	145

KM# 68   2000 KORUN
6.2200 g., 0.9999 Gold 0.2 oz. AGW, 20 mm. **Subject:** Slavonice
House Gables **Obv:** Three heraldic animals above city view **Rev:**
City arms

Date	F	VF	XF	Unc	BU
2003	—	—	—	—	145

KM# 69   2000 KORUN
6.2200 g., 0.9999 Gold 0.2 oz. AGW, 20 mm. **Subject:**
Buchlovice Palace **Obv:** Three heraldic animals above palace
Rev: Palace view

Date	F	VF	XF	Unc	BU
2003	—	—	—	—	145

KM# 19   2500 KORUN
7.7759 g., 0.9999 Gold .2500 oz. AGW, 22 mm. **Subject:** Historic
Coins - 1620 Tolar of Moravian Estates

Date	F	VF	XF	Unc	BU
1995-1997	—	—	—	—	250

KM# 39   2500 KORUN
7.7759 g., 0.9999 Gold .2500 oz. AGW, 22 mm. **Rev:** Seal of
Karel IV with legal document

Date	F	VF	XF	Unc	BU
1998-1999	—	—	—	—	175

KM# 20   5000 KORUN
15.5517 g., 0.9999 Gold .5000 oz. AGW, 28 mm. **Subject:**
Historic Coins **Rev:** Bohemian Maley Gros of 1587

Date	F	VF	XF	Unc	BU
1995-1997	—	—	—	—	560

KM# 40   5000 KORUN
15.5530 g., 0.9999 Gold .5000 oz. AGW, 28 mm. **Rev:** Karel IV,
Charles University founder

Date	F	VF	XF	Unc	BU
1998-1999	—	—	—	—	350

KM# 21   10000 KORUN
31.1035 g., 0.9999 Gold 1.0000 oz. AGW, 34 mm. **Subject:**
Historic Coins **Rev:** Lion holding Prague Groschen

Date	F	VF	XF	Unc	BU
1995-1997	—	—	—	—	975

Czechoslovakia

The Republic of Czechoslovakia, founded at the end of World War I, was part of the old Austrian-Hungarian Empire. It had an area of 49,371 sq. mi. (127,870 sq. km.) and a population of 15.6 million. Capital: Prague (Praha).

MONETARY SYSTEM
100 Haleru = 1 Koruna

REPUBLIC

DECIMAL COINAGE

KM# 5   2 HALERE
2.0000 g., Zinc, 17 mm. **Obv:** State emblem: Czech lion with Slovak shield **Rev:** Charles Bridge in Praha, value below **Edge:** Plain

Date	F	VF	XF	Unc	BU
1923-1925	2.25	3.50	5.00	9.00	—

KM# 41   10000 KORUN
31.1070 g., 0.9999 Gold 1.0000 oz. AGW, 34 mm. **Rev:** Karel IV and seals of Nove Mesto

Date	F	VF	XF	Unc	BU
1998-1999	—	—	—	—	700

KM# 45   10000 KORUN
31.1070 g., 0.9990 Gold 1.0000 oz. AGW **Subject:** Karl IV **Obv:** 3 coats of arms **Rev:** Karl IV with 3 coin designs **Edge Lettering:** *CESKA NARODNI BANKA8 31.107 g*

Date	F	VF	XF	Unc	BU
1999 Proof	Value: 675				

KM# 6   5 HALERU
1.6600 g., Bronze, 16 mm. **Obv:** State emblem: Czech lion with Slovak shield **Rev:** Charles Bridge in Praha, value below **Edge:** Plain

Date	F	VF	XF	Unc	BU
1923-1938	0.20	0.30	0.50	2.00	—

KM# 3   10 HALERU
Bronze, 18 mm. **Obv:** State emblem: Czech lion with Slovak shield **Rev:** Charles Bridge of Praha, value below **Edge:** Plain

Date	F	VF	XF	Unc	BU
1922-1938	0.25	0.35	0.60	2.00	—

KM# 1   20 HALERU
3.3300 g., Copper-Nickel, 20 mm. **Obv:** State emblem: Czech lion with Slovak shield, date **Rev:** Sheaf with sickle, lime spring **Edge:** Plain

Date	F	VF	XF	Unc	BU
1921-1938	0.25	0.35	0.60	2.50	—

KM# 16   25 HALERU
4.0000 g., Copper-Nickel, 21 mm. **Obv:** State emblem: Czech lion with Slovak shield **Rev:** 25 **Edge:** Milled

Date	F	VF	XF	Unc	BU
1932-1933	0.50	1.00	2.00	4.00	—

KM# 2   50 HALERU
5.0000 g., Copper-Nickel, 22 mm.   **Obv:** State emblem: Czech lion with Slovak shield, date **Rev:** Lime springs and ears, value **Edge:** Milled

Date	F	VF	XF	Unc	BU
1921-1931	0.20	0.40	0.60	2.50	—

KM# 4   KORUNA
6.6600 g., Copper-Nickel, 25 mm.   **Obv:** State emblem: Czech lion with Slovak shield, date **Rev:** Woman with sheaf and sickle **Edge:** Milled

Date	F	VF	XF	Unc	BU
1922-1938	0.30	0.50	0.75	2.00	—

KM# 10   5 KORUN
10.0000 g., Copper-Nickel, 30 mm.   **Obv:** State emblem: Czech lion with Slovak shield **Rev:** Industrial factory and large value

Date	F	VF	XF	Unc	BU
1925-1927	1.50	2.50	3.50	9.00	—

KM# 11   5 KORUN
7.0000 g., 0.5000 Silver .125 oz. ASW, 27 mm.   **Obv:** Czech lion with Slovak shield **Rev:** Industrial factory and large value **Edge:** Plain with crosses and waves

Date	F	VF	XF	Unc	BU
1928-1932	1.65	2.50	4.00	8.50	—

KM# 11a   5 KORUN
8.0000 g., Nickel, 27 mm.   **Obv:** Czech lion with Slovak shield **Rev:** Industrial factory and large value

Date	F	VF	XF	Unc	BU
1937-1938	1.25	2.50	4.00	6.50	—

KM# 12   10 KORUN
10.0000 g., 0.7000 Silver .2250 oz. ASW, 30 mm.   **Subject:** 10th Anniversary of Independence **Obv:** Value above state shield, date **Rev:** President Tomas G. Masaryk bust right **Edge:** Milled

Date	F	VF	XF	Unc	BU
ND(1928)	3.00	4.50	7.00	11.50	—

KM# 15   10 KORUN
10.0000 g., 0.7000 Silver .2250 oz. ASW, 30 mm.   **Obv:** State emblem, date **Rev:** Republic, lime tree, value, artist Jaroslav Horejc **Edge:** Milled

Date	F	VF	XF	Unc	BU
1930-1933	BV	3.50	5.00	9.00	—

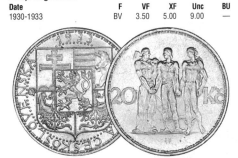

KM# 17   20 KORUN
12.0000 g., 0.7000 Silver .2700 oz. ASW, 34 mm.   **Obv:** State emblem, date **Rev:** Three figures: Industry, Agriculture, Business; value, artist Jaroslav Horejc **Edge:** Plain with crosses and waves

Date	F	VF	XF	Unc	BU
1933-1934	—	4.50	7.50	14.00	—

KM# 18   20 KORUN
12.0000 g., 0.7000 Silver .2700 oz. ASW, 34 mm.   **Subject:** Death of President Masaryk **Obv:** Value, state emblem **Rev:** President Tomas G. Masaryk bust right **Edge:** Plain with crosses and waves

Date	F	VF	XF	Unc	BU
ND(1937)	—	4.00	7.00	11.50	—

TRADE COINAGE

KM# 7 DUKAT
3.4900 g., 0.9860 Gold .1106 oz. AGW **Subject:** 5th Anniversary of the Republic **Obv:** Shield with Czech lion and Slovak shield **Rev:** Duke Wenceslas (Vaclav) half-length figure facing **Edge:** Milled **Note:** Serially numbered below the duke. The number is in the die.

Date	F	VF	XF	Unc	BU
1923	—	1,000	2,500	5,000	

KM# 8 DUKAT
3.4900 g., 0.9860 Gold .1106 oz. AGW **Obv:** Shield with Czech lion and Slovak shield **Rev:** Duke Wenceslas (Vaclav) half-length figure facing **Edge:** Milled **Note:** Similar to KM#7 but without serial numbers.

Date	F	VF	XF	Unc	BU
1923-1951	—	BV	80.00	125	—

KM# 9 2 DUKATY
6.9800 g., 0.9860 Gold .2212 oz. AGW, 25 mm. **Obv:** Shield with Czech lion and Slovak shield **Rev:** Duke Wenceslas (Vaclav) half-length figure facing **Edge:** Milled

Date	F	VF	XF	Unc	BU
1923-1951	—	160	300	400	—

KM# 13 5 DUKATU
17.4500 g., 0.9860 Gold .5532 oz. AGW, 34 mm. **Obv:** Value, state emblem, date **Rev:** Duke Wenceslas (Vaclav) on horseback right **Edge:** Milled

Date	F	VF	XF	Unc	BU
1929-1951	—	375	650	975	—

KM# 14 10 DUKATU
34.9000 g., 0.9860 Gold 1.1064 oz. AGW, 42 mm. **Obv:** State emblem, value, date **Rev:** Duke Wenceslas (Vaclav) on horseback right

Date	F	VF	XF	Unc	BU
1929-1951	—	750	1,700	2,250	—

POST WAR COINAGE

KM# 20 20 HALERU
Bronze, 18 mm. **Obv:** State emblem: Czech lion with Slovak shield, date **Rev:** Sheaf with sickle, lime spring **Edge:** Plain

Date	F	VF	XF	Unc	BU
1947-1950	0.10	0.15	0.40	1.50	

KM# 31 20 HALERU
Aluminum, 16 mm. **Obv:** Czech lion with Slovak shield **Rev:** Wheat ears, sickle, linden branch **Edge:** Plain

Date	F	VF	XF	Unc	BU
1951-1952	0.10	0.15	0.25	1.00	—

KM# 21 50 HALERU
Bronze, 20 mm. **Obv:** Czech lion with Slovak shield **Rev:** Value above linden branch and wheat wreath **Edge:** Plain

Date	F	VF	XF	Unc	BU
1947-1950	0.15	0.25	0.40	1.00	—

KM# 32 50 HALERU
Aluminum, 18 mm. **Obv:** Czech lion with Slovak shield **Rev:** Value above linden branch and wheat wreath **Edge:** Plain

Date	F	VF	XF	Unc	BU
1951-1953	0.15	0.35	0.50	0.75	—

KM# 19 KORUNA
Copper-Nickel, 21 mm. **Obv:** State emblem: Czech lion with Slovak shield, date **Rev:** Woman with sheaf and sickle **Edge:** Milled

Date	F	VF	XF	Unc	BU
1946-1947	0.15	0.25	0.50	1.00	—

KM# 22 KORUNA
Aluminum, 21 mm. **Obv:** Czech lion with Slovak shield **Rev:** Female harvesting wheat **Edge:** Milled

Date	F	VF	XF	Unc	BU
1947-1953	0.20	0.30	0.40	0.80	—

KM# 23 2 KORUNY
Copper-Nickel, 23.5 mm. **Obv:** Czech lion with Slovak shield **Rev:** Juraj Janosik bust right, wearing hat **Edge:** Milled

Date	F	VF	XF	Unc	BU
1947-1948	0.20	0.40	0.60	1.25	—

KM# 34 5 KORUN
Aluminum, 23 mm. **Obv:** Czech lion with Slovak shield **Rev:** Industrial factory and large value

Date	F	VF	XF	Unc	BU
1951-1952	25.00	50.00	90.00	140	—

KM# 24 50 KORUN
10.0000 g., 0.5000 Silver .1607 oz. ASW, 28 mm. **Subject:** 1944 Slovak Uprising **Obv:** Crowned lion, value **Rev:** Veiled female standing holding linden sprig **Edge:** Plain with stars and waves

Date	F	VF	XF	Unc	BU
ND(1947)	—	2.75	4.50	6.50	—

KM# 25 50 KORUN
10.0000 g., 0.5000 Silver .1607 oz. ASW, 28 mm. **Subject:** 3rd Anniverary - Prague Uprising **Obv:** Czech lion with Slovak shield **Rev:** Liberator, value **Edge:** Plain with stars and waves

Date	F	VF	XF	Unc	BU
ND(1948)	—	2.75	4.50	6.50	—

KM# 28 50 KORUN
10.0000 g., 0.5000 Silver .1607 oz. ASW, 28 mm. **Subject:** 70th Birthday - Josef Stalin **Obv:** Czech lion with Slovak shield, value **Rev:** Josef Stalin head left **Edge:** Plain with stars and waves

Date	F	VF	XF	Unc	BU
ND(1949)	—	2.75	4.50	7.00	—

KM# 26 100 KORUN
14.0000 g., 0.5000 Silver .2250 oz. ASW, 31 mm. **Subject:** 600th Anniversary - Charles University **Obv:** Shield of Czech lion with Slovak shield **Rev:** King Charles kneeling before Duke Wenceslas

Date	F	VF	XF	Unc	BU
1948	—	3.00	4.75	7.50	—

KM# 27 100 KORUN
14.0000 g., 0.5000 Silver .2250 oz. ASW, 31 mm. **Subject:** 30th Anniversary of Independence **Obv:** Shield of Czech lion with Slovak shield **Rev:** Man with flag and laurel branch **Edge:** Plain with stars and waves

Date	F	VF	XF	Unc	BU
ND(1948)	—	3.00	4.75	7.50	—

KM# 29 100 KORUN

14.0000 g., 0.5000 Silver .2250 oz. ASW, 31 mm. **Subject:** 700th Anniversary - Jihlava Mining Privileges **Obv:** Shield of Czech lion with Slovak shield, date **Rev:** King Karel I and St. Vaclav **Edge:** Plain with stars and waves

Date	F	VF	XF	Unc	BU
1949	—	3.00	4.75	7.50	—

KM# 30 100 KORUN

14.0000 g., 0.5000 Silver .2250 oz. ASW, 28 mm. **Subject:** 70th Birthday - Josef V. Stalin **Obv:** Shield of Czech lion with Slovak shield **Rev:** Josef Stalin bust left **Edge:** Plain with stars and waves

Date	F	VF	XF	Unc	BU
ND(1949)	—	3.00	4.75	7.50	—

KM# 33 100 KORUN

14.0000 g., 0.5000 Silver .2250 oz. ASW, 31 mm. **Subject:** 30th Anniversary - Communist party **Obv:** Shield of Czech lion with Slovak shield **Rev:** Klement Gottwald, Party Chairman, bust right **Edge:** Plain with stars and waves

Date	F	VF	XF	Unc	BU
ND(1951)	—	3.00	4.75	7.50	—

PEOPLES REPUBLIC

DECIMAL COINAGE

KM# 35 HALER

Aluminum, 16 mm. **Obv:** Czech lion with Slovak shield **Rev:** Value within linden wreath, star above **Edge:** Plain

Date	F	VF	XF	Unc	BU
1953-1960	0.10	0.25	0.10	0.25	—

KM# 36 3 HALERE

Aluminum, 18 mm. **Obv:** Czech lion with Slovak shield **Rev:** Value within linden wreath, star above **Edge:** Plain

Date	F	VF	XF	Unc	BU
1953-1954	—	0.10	0.15	0.30	—

KM# 37 5 HALERU

Aluminum, 20 mm. **Obv:** Czech lion with Slovak shield **Rev:** Value within linden wreath, star above **Edge:** Plain

Date	F	VF	XF	Unc	BU
1953-1955	0.10	0.15	0.25	0.50	—

KM# 38 10 HALERU

Aluminum, 22 mm. **Obv:** Czech lion with Slovak shield **Rev:** Value within linden wreath, star above

Date	F	VF	XF	Unc	BU
1953-1958	0.10	0.15	1.00	5.00	—

KM# 39 25 HALERU

Aluminum, 24 mm. **Obv:** Czech lion with Slovak shield **Rev:** Value within linden wreath, star above

Date	F	VF	XF	Unc	BU
1953-1954	0.10	0.20	0.30	4.00	—

KM# 46 KORUNA

Aluminum-Bronze, 23 mm. **Obv:** Czech lion with Slovak shield **Rev:** Female kneeling planting linden sprig, value **Edge:** Milled

Date	F	VF	XF	Unc	BU
1957-1960	0.15	0.25	0.35	4.50	—

KM# 40   10 KORUN
12.0000 g., 0.5000 Silver .1929 oz. ASW, 30 mm. **Subject:** 10th Anniversary - Slovak Uprising **Obv:** Shield with Czech lion and Slovak shield **Rev:** Soldier standing right, train and construction site in background **Edge:** Milled **Note:** 65,810 pieces, Unc and Proof, were melted by the Czech National Bank in 1999.

Date	F	VF	XF	Unc	BU
ND(1954)	—	2.50	3.50	6.00	—

KM# 42   10 KORUN
12.0000 g., 0.5000 Silver .1929 oz. ASW, 30 mm. **Subject:** 10th Anniversary - Liberation from Germany **Obv:** Czech lion with Slovak shield **Rev:** Soldier kneeling left holding child **Edge:** Milled **Note:** 95,552 pieces Unc and Proof, were melted by the Czech National Bank in 1999.

Date	F	VF	XF	Unc	BU
ND(1955)	—	2.75	3.75	6.50	—

KM# 47.1   10 KORUN
12.0000 g., 0.5000 Silver .1929 oz. ASW, 30 mm. **Subject:** 250th Anniversary - Technical College **Obv:** Czech lion with Slovak shield, value **Rev:** C. J. Willenberg bust left **Edge:** Plain with stars and waves **Note:** Raised designer initials.

Date	F	VF	XF	Unc	BU
1957	—	2.75	3.75	7.50	—

KM# 47.2   10 KORUN
12.0000 g., 0.5000 Silver .1929 oz. ASW, 30 mm. **Obv:** Czech lion with Slovak shield **Rev:** C. J. Willenberg bust left **Note:** Incuse designer initials.

Date	F	VF	XF	Unc	BU
1957 Proof	Value: 14.50				

KM# 48   10 KORUN
12.0000 g., 0.5000 Silver .1929 oz. ASW, 30 mm. **Obv:** Czech lion with Slovak shield **Rev:** Bust right of J. A. Komensky, Bishop of the Moravian Brotherhood **Edge:** Milled **Note:** 7,854 pieces Unc and Proof, were melted by the Czech National Bank in 1999.

Date	F	VF	XF	Unc	BU
1957	—	2.75	3.75	7.00	—

KM# 41   25 KORUN
16.0000 g., 0.5000 Silver .2572 oz. ASW, 34 mm. **Subject:** 10th Anniversary - Slovak Uprising **Obv:** Shield with Czech lion and Slovak shield **Rev:** Soldier standing right, train and construction site in background **Edge:** Milled **Note:** 110,933 Pieces, Unc and Proof, were melted by the Czech National Bank in 1999.

Date	F	VF	XF	Unc	BU
ND(1954)	—	—	5.00	8.00	—

KM# 43   25 KORUN
16.0000 g., 0.5000 Silver .2572 oz. ASW, 34 mm. **Subject:** 10th Anniversary - Liberation from Germany **Obv:** Czech lion with Slovak shield **Rev:** Mother and child greeting soldier **Edge:** Milled **Note:** 78,643 pieces, Unc and Proof, were melted by the Czech National Bank in 1999.

Date	F	VF	XF	Unc	BU
ND(1955)	—	—	5.00	8.00	—

KM# 44 50 KORUN

20.0000 g., 0.9000 Silver .5787 oz. ASW, 37 mm. **Subject:** 10th Anniversary - Liberation from Germany **Obv:** Czech lion with Slovak shield **Rev:** Soldier standing wearing cloak, raising rifle **Edge:** Milled **Note:** 36,650 pieces were melted by the Czech National Bank in 1999.

Date	F	VF	XF	Unc	BU
1955	—	7.50	10.00	17.50	—

KM# 45 100 KORUN

24.0000 g., 0.9000 Silver .6945 oz. ASW, 40 mm. **Subject:** 10th Anniversary - Liberation from Germany **Obv:** Czech lion with Slovak shield **Rev:** Father and young boy greeting two returning soldiers **Note:** 22,244 pieces were melted by the Czech National Bank in 1999.

Date	F	VF	XF	Unc	BU
ND(1955)	—	11.50	16.50	32.50	40.00

SOCIALIST REPUBLIC

DECIMAL COINAGE

KM# 51 HALER

Aluminum, 16 mm. **Obv:** Czech lion with socialist shield **Rev:** Value within linden wreath, star above **Edge:** Plain

Date	F	VF	XF	Unc	BU
1962-1986	—	—	0.10	0.15	—

KM# 52 3 HALERE

Aluminum, 18 mm. **Obv:** Czech lion with socialist shield **Rev:** Value within linden wreath, star above **Edge:** Plain

Date	F	VF	XF	Unc	BU
1962-1963	100	150	0.10	0.15	—

KM# 53 5 HALERU

Aluminum, 20 mm. **Obv:** Czech lion with socialist shield **Rev:** Value within linden wreath, star above **Edge:** Plain

Date	F	VF	XF	Unc	BU
1962-1976	—	0.10	0.15	0.20	—

KM# 53a 5 HALERU

2.0000 g., Brass **Obv:** Czech lion with socialist shield **Rev:** Value within linden wreath, star above

Date	F	VF	XF	Unc	BU
1967	—	—	300	500	—

KM# 86 5 HALERU

Aluminum, 16.2 mm. **Obv:** Czech lion with socialist shield **Rev:** Value, star above **Edge:** Plain

Date	F	VF	XF	Unc	BU
1977-1990	—	—	0.10	0.25	—

KM# 49.1 10 HALERU

Aluminum

Date	F	VF	XF	Unc	BU
1961-1971	—	0.10	0.15	0.35	—

KM# 49.2 10 HALERU

Aluminum, 22 mm. **Obv:** Czech lion with socialist shield, flat-top 3 in date **Rev:** Value within linden wreath, star above **Note:** Obverse muled from 50 Haleru, KM 55.1.

Date	F	VF	XF	Unc	BU
1963	12.50	25.00	60.00	150	—

KM# 49.1a 10 HALERU

2.4000 g., Brass

Date	F	VF	XF	Unc	BU
1968	—	—	300	500	—

KM# 80   10 HALERU
Aluminum, 18.2 mm.   **Obv:** Czech lion with socialist shield **Rev:**
Value, star above **Note:** Varieties exist.

Date	F	VF	XF	Unc	BU
1974-1990	—	—	0.10	0.25	—

KM# 74   20 HALERU
Brass, 19.5 mm.   **Obv:** Czech lion with socialist shield **Rev:** Value,
star above **Note:** Varieties exist.

Date	F	VF	XF	Unc	BU
1972-1990	—	0.10	0.15	0.30	—

KM# 54   25 HALERU
Aluminum, 24 mm.   **Obv:** Czech lion with socialist shield **Rev:**
Value within linden wreath, star above **Edge:** Milled **Note:** This
denomination ceased to be legal tender in 1972.

Date	F	VF	XF	Unc	BU
1962-1964	0.10	0.15	0.20	0.35	—

KM# 55.1   50 HALERU
Bronze, 21.5 mm.   **Obv:** Czech lion with socialist shield **Rev:**
Value within linden wreath, star above

Date	F	VF	XF	Unc	BU
1963-1971	0.10	0.20	0.30	0.40	—

KM# 55.2   50 HALERU
Bronze, 21.5 mm.   **Obv:** Czech lion with socialist shield, small
date, without dots **Rev:** Value within linden wreath, star above
Note: Obverse muled with 10 Haleru, KM 49.1.

Date	F	VF	XF	Unc	BU
1969	12.50	22.50	40.00	75.00	—

KM# 89   50 HALERU
Copper-Nickel, 20.8 mm.   **Obv:** Czech lion with socialist shield
Rev: Value, star above **Edge:** Milled **Note:** Date varieties exist.

Date	F	VF	XF	Unc	BU
1977-1990	—	—	0.10	0.50	—

KM# 50   KORUNA
Aluminum-Bronze, 23 mm.   **Obv:** Czech lion with socialist shield **Rev:**
Female planting linden sprig **Edge:** Milled **Note:** Date varieties exist.

Date	F	VF	XF	Unc	BU
1961-1990	0.40	0.15	0.30	0.60	—

KM# 75   2 KORUNY
Copper-Nickel, 24 mm.   **Obv:** Czech lion with socialist shield **Rev:**
Star above hammer and sickle, large value at right **Edge:** Plain
with crosses and waves

Date	F	VF	XF	Unc	BU
1972-1990	—	0.25	0.35	0.75	—

KM# 57   3 KORUNY
Copper-Nickel, 23.5 mm.   **Obv:** Czech lion with socialist shield
Rev: Branch of five linden leaves within banner, large value at
right **Edge:** Plain with lime leaves and waves

Date	F	VF	XF	Unc	BU
1965-1969	—	0.40	0.75	1.50	—

KM# 60   5 KORUN
Copper-Nickel, 26 mm.   **Obv:** Czech lion with socialist shield **Rev:**
Geometric design and large value **Edge:** Plain with rhombs and waves

Date	F	VF	XF	Unc	BU
1966-1990	0.75	0.75	0.75	1.25	—

KM# 56   10 KORUN
12.0000 g., 0.5000 Silver .1929 oz. ASW, 30 mm.   **Subject:** 20th
Anniversary - 1944 Slovak Uprising **Obv:** Czech lion with socialist

shield **Rev:** Three hands and linden sprig **Edge Lettering:** SLOVENSKE NARODNE POVSTANIE **Note:** 11,476 pieces were melted by the Czech National Bank in 1999.

Date	F	VF	XF	Unc	BU
ND(1964)	—	—	3.50	5.50	—

KM# 58   10 KORUN
12.0000 g., 0.5000 Silver .1929 oz. ASW, 30 mm. **Subject:** 550th Anniversary - Death of Jan Hus **Obv:** Czech lion with socialist shield, value **Rev:** Jan Hus bust right **Edge Lettering:** 550 LET UPALENI M, JANA HUSA **Note:** 380 pieces, Unc and Proof, were melted by the Czech National Bank in 1999.

Date	F	VF	XF	Unc	BU
ND(1965)	—	—	7.00	15.00	—

KM# 61   10 KORUN
12.0000 g., 0.5000 Silver .1929 oz. ASW, 30 mm. **Subject:** 1100th Anniversary of Great Moravia **Obv:** Czech lion with socialist shield **Rev:** Medal with horseman with falcon and plot of church **Edge:** Plain with ellipse and rings **Note:** 9,446 pieces, Unc and Proof, were melted by the Czech National Bank in 1999.

Date	F	VF	XF	Unc	BU
1966	—	—	4.00	6.50	—

KM# 62   10 KORUN
12.0000 g., 0.5000 Silver .1929 oz. ASW, 30 mm. **Subject:** 500th Anniversary - Bratislava University **Obv:** Czech lion with socialist shield above stylized three mountains and river **Rev:** University seal and building **Edge:** Plain with Rhombs and waves **Note:** 103 pieces, Unc and Proof, were melted by the Czech National Bank in 1999.

Date	F	VF	XF	Unc	BU
ND(1967)	—	—	10.00	20.00	—

KM# 63   10 KORUN
12.0000 g., 0.5000 Silver .1929 oz. ASW, 30 mm. **Subject:**

Centennial - Prague (Praha) National Theater **Obv:** Czech lion with socialist shield, value **Rev:** Female goddess in three-horse chariot **Edge:** Plain with crosses and waves **Note:** 50 pieces, Unc and Proof, were melted by the Czech National Bank in 1999.

Date	F	VF	XF	Unc	BU
ND(1968)	—	—	15.00	20.00	—

KM# 76   20 KORUN
9.0000 g., 0.5000 Silver .1446 oz. ASW, 29 mm. **Subject:** Centennial - Death of Andrej Sladkovic **Obv:** Czech lion with socialist shield **Rev:** Andrej Sladkovic head left **Note:** 3,842 pieces, Unc and Proof, were melted by the Czech National Bank in 1999.

Date	F	VF	XF	Unc	BU
ND(1972)	—	—	3.50	5.50	—

KM# 59   25 KORUN
16.0000 g., 0.5000 Silver .2572 oz. ASW, 34 mm. **Subject:** 20th Anniversary - Czechoslovakian Liberation **Obv:** Czech lion with socialist shield **Rev:** Female head, dove with linden branch **Edge Lettering:** 20 LET OSVOBOZENI CSSR **Note:** 18,114 pieces, Unc and Proof, were melted by the Czech National Bank in 1999.

Date	F	VF	XF	Unc	BU
ND(1965)	—	—	4.00	6.50	—

KM# 64   25 KORUN
16.0000 g., 0.5000 Silver .2572 oz. ASW, 34 mm. **Subject:** 150th Anniversary - Prague (Praha) National Museum **Obv:** Czech lion with socialist shield **Rev:** National Museum building **Edge:** Plain with crosses and waves **Note:** 151 pieces, Unc and Proof, were melted by the Czech National Bank in 1999.

Date	F	VF	XF	Unc	BU
ND(1968)	—	—	4.50	9.00	—

KM# 66   25 KORUN
16.0000 g., 0.5000 Silver .2572 oz. ASW, 34 mm.   **Subject:** 100th Anniversary - Death of J. E. Purkyne **Obv:** Czech lion with socialist shield **Rev:** Jan E. Purkyne head right **Edge Lettering:** FYSIOLOG, FILOSOF, BUDITEL, BASNIK **Note:** Edge varieties exist; 140 pieces, Unc and Proof, were melted by the Czech National Bank in 1999.

Date	F	VF	XF	Unc	BU
ND(1969)	—	—	4.00	8.00	—

KM# 67   25 KORUN
16.0000 g., 0.5000 Silver .2572 oz. ASW, 34 mm.   **Subject:** 25th Anniversary - 1944 Slovak Uprising **Obv:** Czech lion with socialist shield **Rev:** Three mountains and plant **Edge Lettering:** 25. VYROCIE SLOVENSKEHO NARODNEHO POVSTANIA **Note:** Edge varieties exist; 40 pieces, Unc and Proof, were melted by the Czech National Bank in 1999.

Date	F	VF	XF	Unc	BU
ND(1969)	—	—	45.00	75.00	—

KM# 68   25 KORUN
10.0000 g., 0.5000 Silver .1607 oz. ASW, 30 mm.   **Subject:** 50th Anniversary - Slovak National Theater **Obv:** Czech lion with socialist shield **Rev:** Stylized head of muse **Note:** 4,923 pieces, Unc and Proof, were melted by the Czech National Bank in 1999.

Date	F	VF	XF	Unc	BU
ND(1970)	—	—	5.00	10.00	—

KM# 69   25 KORUN
10.0000 g., 0.5000 Silver .1607 oz. ASW, 30 mm.   **Subject:** 25th

Anniversary of Liberation **Obv:** Czech lion with socialist shield **Rev:** Sun of Liberation, landscape **Edge:** - x - **Note:** 23,777 pieces, Unc and Proof, were melted by the Czech National Bank in 1999.

Date	F	VF	XF	Unc	BU
ND(1970)	—	—	4.00	6.00	—

KM# 65   50 KORUN
20.0000 g., 0.9000 Silver .5787 oz. ASW, 37 mm.   **Subject:** 50th Anniversary of Czechoslovakia 20th Anniversary - People's Republic **Obv:** Czech lion with socialist shield **Rev:** Female head left wearing linden and floral wreath **Note:** 650 pieces, Unc and Proof, were melted by the Czech National Bank in 1999.

Date	F	VF	XF	Unc	BU
ND(1968)	—	—	18.00	32.00	40.00

KM# 70   50 KORUN
13.0000 g., 0.7000 Silver .2926 oz. ASW, 31 mm.   **Subject:** Centennial - Birth of Lenin **Obv:** Czech lion with socialist shield **Rev:** V. I. Lenin head right **Note:** 451 pieces, Unc and Proof, were melted by the Czech National Bank in 1999.

Date	F	VF	XF	Unc	BU
ND(1970)	—	—	4.50	8.50	—

KM# 71   50 KORUN
13.0000 g., 0.7000 Silver .2926 oz. ASW, 31 mm.   **Subject:** 50th Anniversary - Czechoslovak Communist Party **Obv:** Czech lion with socialist shield **Rev:** Five figures standing within hammer and sickle, star above **Edge:** Wave, star, wave **Note:** 4,850 pieces, Unc and Proof, were melted by the Czech National Bank in 1999.

Date	F	VF	XF	Unc	BU
ND(1971)	—	—	4.50	8.50	—

KM# 72   50 KORUN

13.0000 g., 0.7000 Silver .2926 oz. ASW, 31 mm. **Subject:** 50th Anniversary - Death of Pavol Orsagh-Hviezdoslav **Obv:** Czech lion with socialist shield **Rev:** Pavol Orsagh-Hviezdoslav head left **Note:** 4,300 pieces, Unc and Proof, were melted by the Czech National Bank in 1999.

Date	F	VF	XF	Unc	BU
ND(1971)	—	—	4.00	7.00	—

KM# 77   50 KORUN

13.0000 g., 0.7000 Silver .2926 oz. ASW, 31 mm. **Subject:** 50th Anniversary - Death of J. V. Myslbek **Obv:** Czech lion with socialist shield **Rev:** J. V. Myslbek head left **Edge Lettering:** J. V. MYSLBEK *1922-1972* **Note:** 6,439 pieces, Unc and Proof, were melted by the Czech National Bank in 1999.

Date	F	VF	XF	Unc	BU
ND(1972)	—	—	4.00	7.00	—

KM# 78   50 KORUN

13.0000 g., 0.7000 Silver .2926 oz. ASW, 31 mm. **Subject:** 25th Anniversary - Victory of Communist Party **Obv:** Czech lion with socialist shield **Rev:** Soldier standing before large star, hammer and sickle at right **Edge Lettering:** 25. VYROCI VITEZNEHO UNORA* **Note:** 5,340 pieces, Unc and Proof, were melted by the Czech National Bank in 1999.

Date	F	VF	XF	Unc	BU
ND(1973)	—	—	4.00	7.00	—

KM# 79   50 KORUN

13.0000 g., 0.7000 Silver .2926 oz. ASW, 31 mm. **Subject:** 200th Anniversary - Birth of Josef Jungmann **Obv:** Czech lion with socialist shield **Rev:** J. Jungermann head right **Note:** 2,084 pieces, Unc and Proof, were melted by the Czech National Bank in 1999.

Date	F	VF	XF	Unc	BU
ND(1973)	—	—	4.00	7.00	—

KM# 81   50 KORUN

13.0000 g., 0.7000 Silver .2926 oz. ASW, 31 mm. **Subject:** Centennial - Birth of Janko Jesensky **Obv:** Czech lion with socialist shield **Rev:** Jan Jesensky head 3/4 facing right **Edge:** Plain with wave star wave **Note:** 112,038 pieces, Unc and Proof, were melted by the Czech National Bank in 1999.

Date	F	VF	XF	Unc	BU
ND(1974)	—	—	4.00	6.50	—

KM# 83   50 KORUN

13.0000 g., 0.7000 Silver .2926 oz. ASW, 31 mm. **Subject:** Centennial - Birth of S. K. Neumann **Obv:** Czech lion with socialist shield **Rev:** S. K. Neumann head right **Edge:** Milled **Note:** 11,537 pieces, Unc and Proof, were melted by the Czech National Bank in 1999.

Date	F	VF	XF	Unc	BU
ND(1975)	—	—	4.00	6.50	—

KM# 87   50 KORUN

13.0000 g., 0.7000 Silver .2926 oz. ASW, 31 mm. **Subject:** 125th Anniversary - Death of Jan Kollar **Obv:** Czech lion with socialist shield **Rev:** Jan Kollar head facing **Edge:** Milled **Note:** 19,743 pieces, Unc and Proof, were melted by the Czech National Bank in 1999.

Date	F	VF	XF	Unc	BU
ND(1977)	—	—	4.00	6.50	—

KM# 90   50 KORUN

13.0000 g., 0.7000 Silver .2926 oz. ASW, 31 mm. **Subject:** Centennial - Birth of Zdenek Nejedly **Obv:** Czech lion with socialist shield **Rev:** Z. Nejedly bust right **Edge:** Milled **Note:** 20,538 pieces, Unc and Proof, were melted by the Czech National Bank in 1999.

Date	F	VF	XF	Unc	BU
ND(1978)	—	—	4.00	6.50	—

KM# 91   50 KORUN
13.0000 g., 0.7000 Silver .2926 oz. ASW, 31 mm. **Subject:** 650th Anniversary of Kremnica Mint **Obv:** Czech lion with socialist shield **Rev:** Montage of five coin designs **Note:** 22,037 pieces, Unc and Proof, were melted by the Czech National Bank in 1999.

Date	F	VF	XF	Unc	BU
ND(1978)	—	—	4.00	6.50	—

KM# 98   50 KORUN
13.0000 g., 0.7000 Silver .2926 oz. ASW, 31 mm. **Subject:** 30th Anniversary of 9th Congress **Obv:** Czech lion with socialist shield, linden leaves flanking **Rev:** Hammer and sickle in gear at center, linden leaves at left **Edge:** Milled **Note:** 30,089 pieces, Unc and Proof, were melted by the Czech National Bank in 1999.

Date	F	VF	XF	Unc	BU
ND(1979)	—	—	4.00	6.50	—

KM# 121   50 KORUN
7.0000 g., 0.5000 Silver .1125 oz. ASW, 27 mm. **Obv:** Czech lion with socialist shield **Rev:** Prague (Praha) city view **Note:** 6,838 pieces, Unc and Proof, were melted by the Czech National Bank in 1999.

Date	F	VF	XF	Unc	BU
1986	—	—	—	6.00	—

KM# 122   50 KORUN
7.0000 g., 0.5000 Silver .1125 oz. ASW, 27 mm. **Obv:** Czech lion with socialist shield **Rev:** Levoca city view above three statues **Note:** 9,438 pieces, Unc and Proof, were melted by the Czech National Bank in 1999.

Date	F	VF	XF	Unc	BU
1986	—	—	—	6.00	—

KM# 124   50 KORUN
7.0000 g., 0.5000 Silver .1125 oz. ASW, 27 mm. **Obv:** Czech lion with socialist shield **Rev:** Three building facades in Telc **Note:** 13,438 pieces Unc and Proof, were melted by the Czech National Bank in 1999.

Date	F	VF	XF	Unc	BU
1986	—	—	—	6.00	—

KM# 125   50 KORUN
7.0000 g., 0.5000 Silver .1125 oz. ASW, 27 mm. **Obv:** Czech lion with socialist shield **Rev:** Bratislava city view **Note:** 12,188 pieces, Unc and Proof, were melted by the Czech National Bank in 1999.

Date	F	VF	XF	Unc	BU
1986	—	—	—	6.00	—

KM# 126   50 KORUN
7.0000 g., 0.5000 Silver .1125 oz. ASW, 27 mm. **Obv:** Czech lion with socialist shield **Rev:** Cesky Krumlov city view **Note:** 11,338 pieces Unc and Proof, were melted by the Czech National Bank in 1999.

Date	F	VF	XF	Unc	BU
1986	—	—	—	6.00	—

KM# 127   50 KORUN
7.0000 g., 0.5000 Silver .1125 oz. ASW, 27 mm. **Subject:** Environmental Protection **Obv:** Czech lion with socialist shield **Rev:** Two Przewalski's horses **Note:** 338 pieces Unc and Proof, were melted by the Czech National Bank in 1999.

Date	F	VF	XF	Unc	BU
1987	—	—	—	20.00	—

KM# 129 50 KORUN

7.0000 g., 0.5000 Silver .1125 oz. ASW, 27 mm. **Subject:** 300th Anniversary - Birth of Juraj Janosik **Obv:** Czech lion with socialist shield **Rev:** Caped male standing, bird at left **Note:** 735 pieces Unc and Proof, were melted by the Czech National Bank in 1999.

Date	F	VF	XF	Unc	BU
ND(1988)	—	—	—	7.00	—

KM# 133 50 KORUN

7.0000 g., 0.5000 Silver .1125 oz. ASW, 27 mm. **Subject:** 150th Anniversary - Breclav to Brno Railroad **Obv:** Czech lion with socialist shield **Rev:** Early steam locomotive **Note:** 1,835 pieces Unc and Proof, were melted by the Czech National Bank in 1999.

Date	F	VF	XF	Unc	BU
ND(1989)	—	—	—	7.00	—

KM# 73 100 KORUN

15.0000 g., 0.7000 Silver .3376 oz. ASW, 33 mm. **Subject:** Centennial - Death of Josef Manes **Obv:** Czech lion with socialist shield **Rev:** J. Manes bust right **Note:** 6,803 pieces, Unc and Proof, were melted by the Czech National Bank in 1999.

Date	F	VF	XF	Unc	BU
ND(1971)	—	—	10.00	13.50	—

KM# 82 100 KORUN

15.0000 g., 0.7000 Silver .3376 oz. ASW, 33 mm. **Subject:** Sesquicentennial - Birth of Bedrich Smetana **Obv:** Czech lion with socialist shield **Rev:** B. Smetana head right **Edge:** Plain with 150 LET OD NAROZENI **Note:** 6,201 pieces, Unc and Proof, were melted by the Czech National Bank in 1999.

Date	F	VF	XF	Unc	BU
ND(1974)	—	—	10.00	12.00	—

KM# 84 100 KORUN

15.0000 g., 0.7000 Silver .3376 oz. ASW, 33 mm. **Subject:** Centennial - Death of Janko Kral **Obv:** Czech lion with socialist shield **Rev:** J. Kral bust right **Edge Lettering:** BASNIK * REVOLUCIONAR **Note:** 19,839 pieces, Unc and Proof, were melted by the Czech National Bank in 1999.

Date	F	VF	XF	Unc	BU
ND(1976)	—	—	10.00	12.00	—

KM# 85 100 KORUN

15.0000 g., 0.7000 Silver .3376 oz. ASW, 33 mm. **Subject:** Centennial - Birth of Viktor Kaplan **Obv:** Czech lion with socialist shield **Rev:** V. Kaplan bust right **Edge:** - * - **Note:** 22,339 pieces, Unc and Proof, were melted by the Czech National Bank in 1999.

Date	F	VF	XF	Unc	BU
ND(1976)	—	—	10.00	12.00	—

KM# 88 100 KORUN

15.0000 g., 0.7000 Silver .3376 oz. ASW, 33 mm. **Subject:** 300th Anniversary - Death of Vaclav Hollar **Obv:** Czech lion with socialist shield **Rev:** V. Hollar bust left **Edge:** Plain with waves and dots **Note:** 32,789 pieces, Unc and Proof, were melted by the Czech National Bank in 1999.

Date	F	VF	XF	Unc	BU
ND(1977)	—	—	10.00	12.00	—

KM# 92 100 KORUN

15.0000 g., 0.7000 Silver .3376 oz. ASW, 33 mm. **Subject:** 75th Anniversary - Birth of Julius Fucik **Obv:** Czech lion with socialist shield **Rev:** J. Fucik head left **Edge Lettering:** LIDE, MEL JSEM VAS RAD, BDETE! **Note:** 24,840 pieces, Unc and Proof, were melted by the Czech National Bank in 1999.

Date	F	VF	XF	Unc	BU
ND(1978)	—	—	10.00	12.00	—

KM# 93   100 KORUN
15.0000 g., 0.7000 Silver .3376 oz. ASW, 33 mm. **Subject:** 600th Anniversary - Death of Charles IV **Obv:** Czech lion with socialist shield **Rev:** Charles IV bust right **Note:** 32,638 pieces, Unc and Proof, were melted by the Czech National Bank in 1999.

Date	F	VF	XF	Unc	BU
1978	—	—	10.00	12.00	—

KM# 99   100 KORUN
15.0000 g., 0.7000 Silver .3376 oz. ASW, 33 mm. **Subject:** 150th Anniversary - Birth of Jan Botto **Obv:** Czech lion with socialist shield **Rev:** J. Botto bust 3/4 facing left **Edge:** ooo star ooo **Note:** 26,740 pieces, Unc and Proof, were melted by the Czech National Bank in 1999.

Date	F	VF	XF	Unc	BU
ND(1979)	—	—	10.00	12.00	—

KM# 100   100 KORUN
15.0000 g., 0.7000 Silver .3376 oz. ASW, 33 mm. **Subject:** 150th Anniversary - Birth of Peter Parler **Obv:** Czech lion with socialist shield, medieval arches in background **Rev:** P. Parler bust facing, medieval arches in background **Edge:** Plain with waves and dots **Note:** 54,738 pieces, Unc and Proof, were melted by the Czech National Bank in 1999.

Date	F	VF	XF	Unc	BU
ND(1980)	—	—	10.00	12.00	—

KM# 101   100 KORUN
9.0000 g., 0.5000 Silver .1446 oz. ASW, 29 mm. **Subject:** Fifth Spartakiade Games **Obv:** Czech lion with socialist shield **Rev:** Seven female gymnastic figures **Note:** 50,391 pieces, Unc and Proof, were melted by the Czech National Bank in 1999.

Date	F	VF	XF	Unc	BU
1980	—	—	—	12.00	—

KM# 102   100 KORUN
9.0000 g., 0.5000 Silver .1446 oz. ASW, 29 mm. **Subject:** Centennial - Birth of Bohumir Smeral **Obv:** Czech lion with socialist shield **Rev:** B. Smeral bust 3/4 facing **Edge:** Milled **Note:** 29,943 pieces, Unc and Proof, were melted by the Czech National Bank in 1999.

Date	F	VF	XF	Unc	BU
ND(1980)	—	—	—	12.00	—

KM# 103   100 KORUN
9.0000 g., 0.5000 Silver .1446 oz. ASW, 29 mm. **Subject:** 20th Anniversary - Manned Space Flight **Obv:** Czech lion with socialist shield **Rev:** Cosmonaut Gagarin **Edge:** Milled **Note:** 31,639 pieces, Unc and Proof, were melted by the Czech National Bank in 1999.

Date	F	VF	XF	Unc	BU
ND(1981)	—	—	—	9.00	—

KM# 104   100 KORUN
9.0000 g., 0.5000 Silver .1446 oz. ASW, 29 mm. **Subject:** Centennial - Birth of Prof. Otakar Spaniel **Obv:** Czech lion with socialist shield **Rev:** O. Spaniel head left **Edge:** Milled **Note:** 56,189 pieces, Unc and Proof, were melted by the Czech National Bank in 1999.

Date	F	VF	XF	Unc	BU
ND(1981)	—	—	—	9.00	—

KM# 106   100 KORUN
9.0000 g., 0.5000 Silver .1446 oz. ASW, 29 mm. **Subject:**
Centennial - Birth of Ivan Olbracht **Obv:** Czech lion with socialist
shield **Rev:** I. Olbracht head left, wearing hat **Edge:** Milled **Note:**
24,140 pieces, Unc and Proof, were melted by the Czech National
Bank in 1999.

Date	F	VF	XF	Unc	BU
ND(1982)	—	—	—	12.00	—

KM# 107   100 KORUN
9.0000 g., 0.5000 Silver .1446 oz. ASW, 29 mm. **Subject:** 150th
Anniversary - Ceske Budejovice Horse Drawn Railway **Obv:**
Czech lion with socialist shield **Rev:** Horse-drawn train carriage
Note: 14,939 pieces, Unc and Proof, were melted by the Czech
National Bank in 1999.

Date	F	VF	XF	Unc	BU
ND(1982)	—	—	—	12.00	—

KM# 108   100 KORUN
9.0000 g., 0.5000 Silver .1446 oz. ASW, 29 mm. **Subject:** 100th
Anniversary - Death of Karl Marx **Obv:** Czech lion with socialist
shield **Rev:** K. Marx head facing **Edge:** Milled **Note:** 23,793 pieces,
Unc and Proof, were melted by the Czech National Bank in 1999.

Date	F	VF	XF	Unc	BU
ND(1983)	—	—	—	12.00	—

KM# 109   100 KORUN
9.0000 g., 0.5000 Silver .1446 oz. ASW, 29 mm. **Subject:**
Centennial - Birth of Jaroslav Hasek **Obv:** Czech lion with socialist
shield **Rev:** J. Hasek bust facing **Edge:** Milled **Note:** 21,538 pieces,
Unc and Proof, were melted by the Czech National Bank in 1999.

Date	F	VF	XF	Unc	BU
ND(1983)	—	—	—	12.00	—

KM# 110   100 KORUN
9.0000 g., 0.5000 Silver .1446 oz. ASW, 29 mm. **Subject:**
Centennial - Death of Samo Chalupka **Obv:** Czech lion with
socialist shield **Rev:** S. Chalupka bust 3/4 facing **Edge:** Milled
Note: 27,938 pieces, Unc and Proof, were melted by the Czech
National Bank in 1999.

Date	F	VF	XF	Unc	BU
ND(1983)	—	—	—	12.00	—

KM# 111   100 KORUN
9.0000 g., 0.5000 Silver .1446 oz. ASW, 29 mm. **Subject:** 100th
Anniversary of National Theater of Prague **Obv:** Czech lion with
socialist shield **Rev:** View of the National Theater in Prague **Edge:**
Milled **Note:** 23,538 pieces, Unc and Proof, were melted by the
Czech National Bank in 1999.

Date	F	VF	XF	Unc	BU
ND(1983)	—	—	—	9.00	—

KM# 113   100 KORUN
9.0000 g., 0.5000 Silver .1446 oz. ASW, 29 mm. **Subject:** 300th
Anniversary - Birth of Matej Bel **Obv:** Czech lion with socialist
shield **Rev:** Figure seated **Edge:** Milled **Note:** 5288 pieces, Unc
and Proof, were melted by the Czech National Bank in 1999.

Date	F	VF	XF	Unc	BU
ND(1984)	—	—	—	12.00	—

KM# 114   100 KORUN
9.0000 g., 0.5000 Silver .1446 oz. ASW, 29 mm. **Subject:** 150th
Anniversary - Birth of Jan Neruda **Obv:** Czech lion with socialist
shield **Rev:** J. Neruda head 3/4 facing left, house at left **Edge:**
Milled **Note:** 12,539 pieces, Unc and Proof, were melted by the
Czech National Bank in 1999.

Date	F	VF	XF	Unc	BU
ND(1984)	—	—	—	12.00	—

KM# 115   100 KORUN
9.0000 g., 0.5000 Silver .1446 oz. ASW, 29 mm. **Subject:**
Centennial - Birth of Antonin Zapotocky **Obv:** Czech lion with
socialist shield **Rev:** A. Zapocky head 3/4 facing right **Edge:** Milled
Note: 19,938 pieces, Unc and Proof, were melted by the Czech
National Bank in 1999.

Date	F	VF	XF	Unc	BU
ND(1984)	—	—	—	12.00	—

KM# 119   100 KORUN
9.0000 g., 0.5000 Silver .1446 oz. ASW, 29 mm. **Subject:** 10th
Anniversary of Helsinki Conference **Obv:** Czech lion with socialist
shield **Rev:** Stylized dove embracing European map **Edge:** Milled
Note: 18,838 pieces, Unc and Proof, were melted by the Czech
National Bank in 1999.

Date	F	VF	XF	Unc	BU
ND(1985)	—	—	—	10.00	—

KM# 116   100 KORUN
9.0000 g., 0.5000 Silver .1446 oz. ASW, 29 mm. **Subject:** 200th
Anniversary - Birth of Jan Holly **Obv:** Czech lion with socialist shield
Rev: J. Holly bust facing **Edge:** Milled **Note:** 9,338 pieces, Unc
and Proof, were melted by the Czech National Bank in 1999.

Date	F	VF	XF	Unc	BU
ND(1985)	—	—	—	12.00	—

KM# 120   100 KORUN
9.0000 g., 0.5000 Silver .1446 oz. ASW, 29 mm. **Subject:** 250th
Anniversary - Death of Petr Brandl **Obv:** Czech lion with socialist shield
Rev: P. Brandl bust facing **Edge:** Milled **Note:** 16,038 pieces, Unc
and Proof, were melted by the Czech National Bank in 1999.

Date	F	VF	XF	Unc	BU
ND(1985)	—	—	—	10.00	—

KM# 117   100 KORUN
9.0000 g., 0.5000 Silver .1446 oz. ASW, 29 mm. **Subject:** 1985
Ice Hockey Championships **Obv:** Czech lion with socialist shield
Rev: Hockey player skating left **Edge:** Milled **Note:** 2,788 pieces,
Unc and Proof, were melted by the Czech National Bank in 1999.

Date	F	VF	XF	Unc	BU
1985	—	—	—	12.00	—

KM# 123   100 KORUN
13.0000 g., 0.5000 Silver .2090 oz. ASW, 31 mm. **Subject:** 150th
Anniversary - Death of Karel Hynek Macha **Obv:** Czech lion with
socialist shield **Rev:** M. Macha bust facing 3/4 left **Edge:** Milled
Note: 10,288 pieces, Unc and Proof, were melted by the Czech
National Bank in 1999.

Date	F	VF	XF	Unc	BU
ND(1986)	—	—	—	10.00	—

KM# 118   100 KORUN
9.0000 g., 0.5000 Silver .1446 oz. ASW, 29 mm. **Subject:** 125th
Anniversary - Birth of Martin Kukucin **Obv:** Czech lion with socialist
shield **Rev:** M. Kukucin bust facing **Edge:** Milled **Note:** 11,838 pieces,
Unc and Proof, were melted by the Czech National Bank in 1999.

Date	F	VF	XF	Unc	BU
ND(1985)	—	—	—	12.00	—

KM# 128   100 KORUN
13.0000 g., 0.5000 Silver .2090 oz. ASW, 31 mm. **Subject:** 225th
Anniversary of Mining Academy **Obv:** Czech lion with socialist
shield **Rev:** Mining equipment **Edge:** Milled **Note:** 6,438 pieces,
Unc and Proof, were melted by the Czech National Bank in 1999.

Date	F	VF	XF	Unc	BU
ND(1987)	—	—	—	12.00	—

KM# 130   100 KORUN
13.0000 g., 0.5000 Silver .2090 oz. ASW, 31 mm. **Subject:**
Prague Philatelic Exposition **Obv:** Czech lion with socialist shield
Rev: City views of Prague presented as four stamps **Edge:** Milled
Note: 4,235 pieces, Unc and Proof, were melted by the Czech
National Bank in 1999.

Date	F	VF	XF	Unc	BU
1988	—	—	—	12.00	—

KM# 132   100 KORUN
13.0000 g., 0.5000 Silver .2090 oz. ASW, 31 mm. **Subject:**
Centennial - Birth of Martin Benka **Obv:** Czech lion with socialist shield
Rev: Young Slovak woman in national costume with dove, based on
painting by Martin Benko **Edge:** Milled **Note:** 8,635 pieces, Unc and
Proof, were melted by the Czech National Bank in 1999.

Date	F	VF	XF	Unc	BU
ND(1988)	—	—	—	12.00	—

KM# 135   100 KORUN
13.0000 g., 0.5000 Silver .2090 oz. ASW, 31 mm. **Subject:** 50th
Anniversary of Student Organization Against Occupation and
Fascism **Obv:** Czech lion with socialist shield **Rev:** Barbed wire
and medieval document seal **Edge:** Milled **Note:** 4,335 pieces,
Unc and Proof, were melted by the Czech National Bank in 1999.

Date	F	VF	XF	Unc	BU
ND(1989)	—	—	—	14.00	—

KM# 137   100 KORUN
13.0000 g., 0.5000 Silver .2090 oz. ASW, 31 mm. **Subject:** 100th
Anniversary - Birth of Karel Capek **Obv:** Czech lion with socialist

shield, value **Rev:** K. Capek bust left **Edge:** Milled **Note:** 7,920 pieces,
Unc and Proof, were melted by the Czech National Bank in 1999.

Date	F	VF	XF	Unc	BU
ND(1990)	—	—	—	14.00	—

KM# 138   100 KORUN
13.0000 g., 0.5000 Silver .2090 oz. ASW, 31 mm. **Subject:** 250th
Anniversary - Death of Jan Kupecky **Obv:** Czech lion with socialist
shield **Rev:** J. Kupecky half-length figure right **Edge:** Milled **Note:**
7,570 pieces, Unc and Proof, were melted by the Czech National
Bank in 1999.

Date	F	VF	XF	Unc	BU
ND(1990)	—	—	—	14.00	—

KM# 105   500 KORUN
24.0000 g., 0.9000 Silver .6944 oz. ASW, 40 mm. **Subject:** 125th
Anniversary - Death of Ludovit Stur **Obv:** Czech lion with socialist
shield, value **Rev:** L. Stur head facing **Edge Lettering:** 125
ROKOV OD SMRTI L' STURA **Note:** 7,057 pieces, Unc and Proof,
were melted by the Czech National Bank in 1999.

Date	F	VF	XF	Unc	BU
ND(1981)	—	—	—	35.00	—

KM# 112   500 KORUN
24.0000 g., 0.9000 Silver .6944 oz. ASW, 40 mm. **Subject:** 100th
Anniversary of National Theater in Prague **Obv:** Czech lion with
socialist shield, value **Rev:** Female with book, theater facade at
right **Edge Lettering:** NAROD SOBE **Note:** 4,740 pieces, Unc
and Proof, were melted by the Czech National Bank in 1999.

Date	F	VF	XF	Unc	BU
ND(1983)	—	—	—	40.00	—

KM# 136   500 KORUN
24.0000 g., 0.9000 Silver .6944 oz. ASW, 40 mm. **Subject:** 100th
Anniversary - Birth of Josef Lada **Obv:** Czech lion with socialist shield,
value **Rev:** Town view, children building snowman **Edge Lettering:**
CESKY MALIR   NARODNI UMELEC **Note:** 2,238 pieces, Unc and
Proof, were melted by the Czech National Bank in 1999.

Date	F	VF	XF	Unc	BU
ND(1987)	—	—	—	45.00	—

KM# 131   500 KORUN
24.0000 g., 0.9000 Silver .6944 oz. ASW, 40 mm. **Subject:** 20th
Anniversary of National Federation **Obv:** Czech lion with socialist
shield, value **Rev:** Stylized linden tree encircled by ribbon in shape

of country **Edge Lettering:** 20. VYROCIE CESKOSLOVENSKEJ
FEDERACIE oj **Note:** 6,435 pieces, Unc and Proof, were melted
by the Czech National Bank in 1999.

Date	F	VF	XF	Unc	BU
ND(1988)	—	—	—	40.00	—

KM# 134   500 KORUN
24.0000 g., 0.9000 Silver .6944 oz. ASW, 40 mm. **Subject:** 125th
Anniversary of Matica Slovenska Institute **Obv:** Czech lion with
socialist shield, value **Rev:** Female standing in national costume
holding book and linden sprig **Edge Lettering:** HOJ VLAST MOJA
TY ZEM DRAHA **Note:** 6,338 pieces, Unc and Proof, were melted
by the Czech National Bank in 1999.

Date	F	VF	XF	Unc	BU
ND(1988)	—	—	—	40.00	—

CZECH SLOVAK
FEDERAL REPUBLIC

DECIMAL COINAGE

KM# 149   HALER
Aluminum, 16 mm. **Obv:** CSFR above shield, linden leaves
flanking, date below **Rev:** Value within linden wreath **Edge:** Plain

Date	F	VF	XF	Unc	BU
1991-1992	—	—	—	2.50	—

KM# 150   5 HALERU
0.7500 g., Aluminum, 16.2 mm. **Obv:** CSFR above shield, linden
leaves flanking, date below **Rev:** Value **Edge:** Plain

Date	F	VF	XF	Unc	BU
1991-1992	—	—	0.10	0.25	—

KM# 146   10 HALERU
Aluminum, 18.2 mm. **Obv:** CSFR above shield, linden leaves
flanking, date below **Rev:** Value

Date	F	VF	XF	Unc	BU
1991-1992	—	—	—	0.50	—

KM# 143   20 HALERU

Aluminum-Bronze, 19.5 mm. **Obv:** CSFR above shield, linden leaves flanking, date below **Rev:** Value **Edge:** Milled

Date	F	VF	XF	Unc	BU
1991-1992	—	—	0.20	0.50	—

KM# 144   50 HALERU

Copper-Nickel, 20.8 mm. **Obv:** CSFR above shield, linden leaves flanking, date below **Rev:** Value **Edge:** Milled

Date	F	VF	XF	Unc	BU
1991-1992	—	—	0.35	0.75	—

KM# 151   KORUNA

Copper-Aluminum, 23 mm. **Obv:** CSFR above shield, linden leaves flanking, date below **Rev:** Female planting linden sprig **Edge:** Milled

Date	F	VF	XF	Unc	BU
1991-1992	—	—	0.50	1.00	—

KM# 148   2 KORUNY

Copper-Nickel, 24 mm. **Obv:** CSFR above shield, linden leaves flanking, date below **Rev:** Linden leaf, large value at right **Edge:** Plain with wave x wave

Date	F	VF	XF	Unc	BU
1991-1992	—	—	0.60	1.25	—

KM# 152   5 KORUN

Copper-Nickel, 26 mm. **Obv:** CSFR above shield, linden leaves flanking, date below **Rev:** Geometric design, large value **Edge:** Eight plain and eight milled areas

Date	F	VF	XF	Unc	BU
1991-1992	—	—	0.75	2.00	—

KM# 139.1   10 KORUN

Nickel-Bronze, 24.5 mm. **Obv:** CSFR above shield, date below **Rev:** Tomas G. Masaryk bust right **Edge:** Eight plain and eight milled areas **Note:** Designer initials (MR) below bust, four varieties exist.

Date	F	VF	XF	Unc	BU
1990-1993	—	—	2.00	6.00	—

KM# 139.2   10 KORUN

Nickel-Bronze, 24.5 mm. **Obv:** CSFR above shield, date below **Rev:** Tomas G. Masaryk bust right **Note:** Designer name below bust: RONAI.

Date	F	VF	XF	Unc	BU
1990	—	2.00	5.00	10.00	—

KM# 153   10 KORUN

Nickel-Bronze, 24.5 mm. **Obv:** CSFR above shield, date below **Rev:** M. R. Stefanik bust left

Date	F	VF	XF	Unc	BU
1991-1993	—	—	2.00	5.00	—

KM# 159   10 KORUN

Nickel-Bronze, 24.5 mm. **Obv:** Value, CSFR above shield, date below **Rev:** A. Rasin bust right **Edge:** Eight plain and eight milled areas

Date	F	VF	XF	Unc	BU
1992	—	—	2.00	5.00	—

KM# 140.1   50 KORUN

7.0000 g., 0.5000 Silver .1125 oz. ASW, 27 mm. **Obv:** CSFR shield with designer's initials (LK) below **Rev:** St. Agnes (Anezka) veiled head left **Edge:** Milled **Note:** See note with KM#140.2. Designer emblem exists with and without initials.

Date	F	VF	XF	Unc	BU
1990	—	—	—	7.00	—

KM# 140.2 50 KORUN

7.0000 g., 0.5000 Silver .1125 oz. ASW, 27 mm. **Obv:** CSFR shield, without designer's initials (LK) **Rev:** St. Agnes (Anezka) veiled head left **Note:** 12,070 pieces, Unc and Proof of either KM#140.1 or 140.2, were melted by the Czech National Bank in 1999.

Date	F	VF	XF	Unc	BU
1990	—	—	10.00	25.00	—

KM# 145 50 KORUN

7.0000 g., 0.5000 Silver .1125 oz. ASW, 27 mm. **Obv:** CSFR shield **Rev:** Steamship Bohemia **Edge:** Milled **Note:** 4,470 pieces, Unc and Proof, were melted by the Czech National Bank in 1999.

Date	F	VF	XF	Unc	BU
ND(1991)	—	—	—	7.00	—

KM# 155 50 KORUN

7.0000 g., 0.7000 Silver .1575 oz. ASW, 27 mm. **Obv:** CSFR shield **Rev:** Piestany Spa building **Edge:** Milled **Note:** 17,920 pieces, Unc and Proof, were melted by the Czech National Bank in 1999.

Date	F	VF	XF	Unc	BU
1991	—	—	—	7.50	—

KM# 156 50 KORUN

7.0000 g., 0.7000 Silver .1575 oz. ASW, 27 mm. **Obv:** CSFR shield, value, date **Rev:** Marianske Lazne Spa buildings **Edge:** Milled **Note:** 16,520 pieces, Unc and Proof, were melted by the Czech National Bank in 1999.

Date	F	VF	XF	Unc	BU
1991	—	—	—	7.50	—

KM# 157 50 KORUN

7.0000 g., 0.7000 Silver .1575 oz. ASW, 27 mm. **Obv:** CSFR shield, value, date **Rev:** Chamois on rock, Karlovy Vary Spa

buildings **Edge:** Milled **Note:** 15,920, pieces, Unc and Proof, were melted by the Czech National Bank in 1999.

Date	F	VF	XF	Unc	BU
1991	—	—	—	9.00	—

KM# 141 100 KORUN

13.0000 g., 0.5000 Silver .2090 oz. ASW, 31 mm. **Subject:** Two horsemen right **Obv:** CSFR shield, value **Edge:** Milled **Note:** 3,170 pieces, Unc and Proof, were melted by the Czech National Bank in 1999.

Date	F	VF	XF	Unc	BU
1990	—	—	—	15.00	—

KM# 142 100 KORUN

13.0000 g., 0.5000 Silver .2090 oz. ASW, 31 mm. **Subject:** 100th Anniversary - Birth of Bohuslav Martinu **Obv:** CSFR shield **Rev:** B. Martinu head facing **Edge:** Milled **Note:** 8,170 pieces, Unc and Proof, were melted by the Czech National Bank in 1999.

Date	F	VF	XF	Unc	BU
ND(1990)	—	—	—	15.00	—

KM# 147 100 KORUN

13.0000 g., 0.5000 Silver .2926 oz. ASW, 31 mm. **Subject:** 150th Anniversary - Birth of A. Dvorak **Obv:** State emblem, value **Rev:** A. Dvorak head right **Edge:** Milled **Note:** 16,220 pieces, Unc and Proof, were melted by the Czech National Bank in 1999.

Date	F	VF	XF	Unc	BU
1991	—	—	—	12.00	—

KM# 154 100 KORUN

13.0000 g., 0.7000 Silver .2926 oz. ASW, 31 mm. **Subject:** 200th Anniversary - Death of Wolfgang A. Mozart **Obv:** CSFR shield, value **Rev:** Mozart bust right **Edge:** Milled **Note:** 2,620 pieces, Unc and Proof, were melted by the Czech National Bank in 1999.

Date	F	VF	XF	Unc	BU
ND(1991)	—	—	—	12.00	—

KM# 160   100 KORUN
13.0000 g., 0.5000 Silver .2926 oz. ASW, 31 mm. **Subject:** 175th Anniversary - Moravian Museum **Obv:** CSFR shield, value **Rev:** Moravian Museum, Moravian eagle **Edge:** Milled **Note:** 226,977 pieces, Unc and Proof, were melted by the Czech National Bank in 1999.

Date	F	VF	XF	Unc	BU
1992	—	—	—	10.00	—

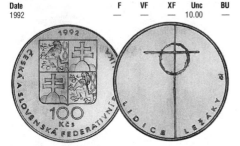

KM# 161   100 KORUN
13.0000 g., 0.5000 Silver .2926 oz. ASW, 31 mm. **Subject:** Nazi Massacres at Lidice and Lezaky **Obv:** CSFR shield, value **Rev:** Cross with barbed wire loop **Edge:** Milled **Note:** 24,620 pieces, Unc and Proof, were melted by the Czech National Bank in 1999.

Date	F	VF	XF	Unc	BU
1992	—	—	—	10.00	—

KM# 162   100 KORUN
13.0000 g., 0.5000 Silver .2926 oz. ASW, 31 mm. **Subject:** 1000 Years of Brevnov Monastery **Obv:** CSFR shield, value **Rev:** Church and cloiser columns **Edge:** Milled **Note:** 25,932 pieces, Unc and Proof, were melted by the Czech National Bank in 1999.

Date	F	VF	XF	Unc	BU
ND(1993)	—	—	—	8.00	—

KM# 163   100 KORUN
13.0000 g., 0.5000 Silver .2926 oz. ASW, 31 mm. **Subject:**

Slovak Museum Centennial **Obv:** CSFR shield, value **Rev:** Historic folk art designs **Edge:** Milled **Note:** 31,932 pieces, Unc and Proof, were melted by the Czech National Bank in 1999.

Date	F	VF	XF	Unc	BU
ND(1993)	—	—	—	8.00	—

KM# 158   500 KORUN
24.0000 g., 0.9000 Silver .6944 oz. ASW, 40 mm. **Subject:** 400th Anniversary - Birth of J. A. Komensky **Obv:** CSFR shield, value **Rev:** J. A. Komensky standing **Edge:** Milled **Note:** 14,820 pieces, Unc and Proof, were melted by the Czech National Bank in 1999.

Date	F	VF	XF	Unc	BU
1992	—	—	—	32.50	—

KM# 164   500 KORUN
24.0000 g., 0.9000 Silver .6944 oz. ASW, 40 mm. **Subject:** 100th Year of Czech Tennis **Obv:** CSFR shield, value **Rev:** Male tennis player, stadium at left **Edge:** Milled **Note:** 27,074 pieces, Unc and Proof, were melted by the Czech National Bank in 1999.

Date	F	VF	XF	Unc	BU
ND(1993)	—	—	—	35.00	—

Danzig

Danzig is an important seaport on the northern coast of Poland with access to the Baltic Sea. It has at different times belonged to the Teutonic Knights, Pomerania, Russia, and Prussia. It was part of the Polish Kingdom from 1587-1772.

Danzig (Gdansk) was a free city from 1919 to 1939 during which most of its modern coinage was made.

MONETARY SYSTEM

Until 1923
100 Pfennig = 1 Mark

Commencing 1923
100 Pfennig = 1 Gulden

FREE CITY

STANDARD COINAGE

KM# 140   PFENNIG
Bronze

Date	F	VF	XF	Unc	BU
1923-1937	1.00	3.00	5.00	10.00	18.00

KM# 141   2 PFENNIG
Bronze

Date	F	VF	XF	Unc	BU
1923-1937	1.75	4.50	7.50	15.00	35.00

KM# 142   5 PFENNIG
Copper-Nickel

Date	F	VF	XF	Unc	BU
1923-1928	1.25	2.75	6.00	12.50	22.00

KM# 151   5 PFENNIG
Aluminum-Bronze   **Rev:** Turbot

Date	F	VF	XF	Unc	BU
1932	1.50	2.50	7.00	16.00	35.00

KM# 143   10 PFENNIG
Copper-Nickel

Date	F	VF	XF	Unc	BU
1923	2.50	3.50	9.00	18.00	35.00

KM# 152   10 PFENNIG
Aluminum-Bronze   **Rev:** Codfish (godus morrhua)

Date	F	VF	XF	Unc	BU
1932	1.75	2.75	8.00	17.00	35.00

KM# 144   1/2 GULDEN
2.5000 g., 0.7500 Silver .0603 oz. ASW

Date	F	VF	XF	Unc	BU
1923-1927	7.50	20.00	35.00	75.00	—

KM# 153   1/2 GULDEN
Nickel

Date	F	VF	XF	Unc	BU
1932	8.00	25.00	37.50	70.00	—

KM# 145   GULDEN
5.0000 g., 0.7500 Silver .1206 oz. ASW

Date	F	VF	XF	Unc	BU
1923	12.50	27.50	40.00	95.00	—

KM# 154   GULDEN
Nickel

Date	F	VF	XF	Unc	BU
1932	8.00	25.00	35.00	60.00	90.00

KM# 146   2 GULDEN
10.0000 g., 0.7500 Silver .2411 oz. ASW

Date	F	VF	XF	Unc	BU
1923	30.00	70.00	125	235	—

Danzig

KM# 155   2 GULDEN
10.0000 g., 0.5000 Silver .1608 oz. ASW

Date	F	VF	XF	Unc	BU
1932	100	150	200	375	—

KM# 147   5 GULDEN
25.0000 g., 0.7500 Silver .6028 oz. ASW   **Obv:** Marienkirche

Date	F	VF	XF	Unc	BU
1923-1927	65.00	135	225	465	—

KM# 156   5 GULDEN
14.8200 g., 0.5000 Silver .2382 oz. ASW   **Obv:** Marienkirche

Date	F	VF	XF	Unc	BU
1932	125	225	350	950	—

KM# 157   5 GULDEN
14.8200 g., 0.5000 Silver .2382 oz. ASW   **Obv:** Grain elevator by harbor

Date	F	VF	XF	Unc	BU
1932	150	350	850	1,500	—

KM# 158   5 GULDEN
Nickel

Date	F	VF	XF	Unc	BU
1935	120	180	250	485	—

KM# 159   10 GULDEN
Nickel   **Obv:** Town hall tower

Date	F	VF	XF	Unc	BU
1935	300	500	700	1,350	—

KM# 148   25 GULDEN
7.9881 g., 0.9170 Gold .2354 oz. AGW   **Rev:** Statue from the Nepture fountain **Note:** Presented to senate members.

Date	F	VF	XF	Unc	BU
1923	—	1,600	1,900	2,800	—

KM# 150   25 GULDEN
7.9881 g., 0.9170 Gold .2354 oz. AGW   **Rev:** Statue from the Nepture fountain **Note:** Not released for circulation. A few were distributed on Sept. 1, 1939, in VIP presentation cases.

Date	F	VF	XF	Unc	BU
1930	—	—	7,000	—	—

TOKEN COINAGE

KM# Tn1   10 PFENNIG
Zinc   **Note:** Small "10" in cartouche.

Date	F	VF	XF	Unc	BU
1920	12.00	18.00	35.00	75.00	—

KM# Tn2   10 PFENNIG
Zinc   **Note:** Large "10".

Date	F	VF	XF	Unc	BU
1920	100	150	225	350	—

Denmark

The Kingdom of Denmark (Danmark), a constitutional monarchy located at the mouth of the Baltic Sea, has an area of 16,639 sq. mi. (43,070 sq. km.) and a population of 5.2 million. Capital: Copenhagen. Most of the country is arable. Agriculture is conducted by large farms served by cooperatives. The largest industries are food processing, iron and metal, and shipping. Machinery, meats (chiefly bacon), dairy products and chemicals are exported.

MONETARY SYSTEM
100 Øre = 1 Krone

KINGDOM
REFORM COINAGE
1813-1854

MONETARY SYSTEM
96 Rigsbankskilling = 1 Rigsbankdaler
30 Schilling Courant = 1 Rigsbankdaler
2 Rigsbankdaler = 1 Speciedaler
5 Speciedaler = 1 D'Or

KM# 723   1/5 RIGSBANKSKILLING
1.4620 g., Copper **Ruler:** Christian VIII **Obv:** Head right **Rev:** Crown above crossed sword and scepter **Note:** Value spelled out in full.

Date	VG	F	VF	XF	Unc
1842	5.50	11.00	22.50	60.00	100

KM# 724   1/5 RIGSBANKSKILLING
1.4620 g., Copper **Ruler:** Christian VIII **Obv:** Head right **Rev:** Crown above crossed sword and scepter **Note:** Value as 1/5 R.B.S.

Date	VG	F	VF	XF	Unc
1842	1.75	4.50	10.00	20.00	40.00

KM# 725   1/2 RIGSBANKSKILLING
3.6540 g., Copper **Ruler:** Christian VIII **Obv:** Head right **Rev:** Crown above crossed sword and scepter

Date	VG	F	VF	XF	Unc
1842	3.00	6.00	14.00	50.00	120

KM# 753   1/2 RIGSBANKSKILLING
3.6540 g., Copper **Ruler:** Frederik VII **Obv:** Crowned CVII within oak branches **Rev:** Large value

Date	VG	F	VF	XF	Unc
1852	2.25	5.00	10.00	27.50	75.00

KM# 726.1   RIGSBANKSKILLING
7.3080 g., Copper **Ruler:** Christian VIII **Obv:** Bust right **Rev:** Crown above crossed sword and sceptre, value and date below

Date	VG	F	VF	XF	Unc
1842	3.25	7.00	15.00	40.00	75.00

KM# 726.2   RIGSBANKSKILLING
7.3080 g., Copper **Ruler:** Christian VIII **Obv:** Bust right **Rev:** Crown above crossed sword and sceptre, value and date below

Date	VG	F	VF	XF	Unc
1842	3.25	7.00	15.00	40.00	75.00

KM# 754   RIGSBANKSKILLING
7.3080 g., Copper **Ruler:** Frederik VII **Obv:** Large bust right **Rev:** Crown above crossed sword and sceptre, value and date below

Date	VG	F	VF	XF	Unc
1852	3.00	9.00	30.00	85.00	175

KM# 756   RIGSBANKSKILLING
Copper **Ruler:** Frederik VII **Obv:** Medium bust right **Rev:** Crown above crossed sword and sceptre, value and date below

Date	VG	F	VF	XF	Unc
1853	2.75	6.50	12.50	27.50	55.00

KM# 728   2 RIGSBANKSKILLING
14.6160 g., Copper **Ruler:** Christian VIII **Obv:** Head right **Rev:** Large crown above crossed sword and scepter

Date	VG	F	VF	XF	Unc
1842	16.00	45.00	125	225	500

KM# 729   3 RIGSBANKSKILLING
1.5190 g., 0.2290 Silver .0112 oz. ASW **Ruler:** Christian VIII

Date	VG	F	VF	XF	Unc
1842	3.50	7.00	17.50	45.00	75.00

KM# A730   3 RIGSBANKSKILLING
1.5190 g., 0.2290 Silver .0112 oz. ASW **Ruler:** Christian VIII **Obv:** Head right **Rev:** Large crown above crossed sword and scepter **Note:** Prev. KM#730.

Date	VG	F	VF	XF	Unc
1842	3.50	7.00	20.00	50.00	100

KM# 721.1   4 RIGSBANKSKILLING
1.8560 g., 0.2500 Silver .0149 oz. ASW   **Obv:** Head right **Rev:** Large crown with crossed sword and scepter **Note:** Dual denominated in consideration of Schleswig-Holstein.

Date	VG	F	VF	XF	Unc
1841	2.25	5.50	12.50	32.50	85.00

KM# 721.2   4 RIGSBANKSKILLING
1.8560 g., 0.2500 Silver .0149 oz. ASW   **Ruler:** Christian VIII **Obv:** Head right **Rev:** Large crown with crossed sword and scepter **Note:** Dual denominated in consideration of Schleswig-Holstein.

Date	VG	F	VF	XF	Unc
1842	2.25	5.50	11.00	30.00	85.00

KM# 737   8 RIGSBANKSKILLING
2.8090 g., 0.3750 Silver .0339 oz. ASW   **Ruler:** Christian VIII **Obv:** Head right **Rev:** Crowned and draped arms **Note:** Dual denominated in consideration of use in Schleswig-Holstein.

Date	VG	F	VF	XF	Unc
1843	12.50	30.00	80.00	165	275

KM# 733   16 RIGSBANKSKILLING
4.2140 g., 0.5000 Silver .0677 oz. ASW   **Ruler:** Christian VIII **Obv:** Head right **Rev:** Crowned draped arms **Note:** Dual denominated in consideration of Schleswig-Holstein.

Date	VG	F	VF	XF	Unc
1842-1844	22.50	45.00	85.00	165	—

KM# 734   32 RIGSBANKSKILLING
6.1290 g., 0.6870 Silver .1354 oz. ASW   **Ruler:** Christian VIII **Obv:** Head right **Rev:** Crowned draped arms **Note:** Dual denominated in consideration of Schleswig-Holstein.

Date	VG	F	VF	XF	Unc
1842-1843	22.50	45.00	90.00	200	360

KM# 735.1   RIGSBANKDALER
14.4470 g., 0.8750 Silver .4064 oz. ASW   **Ruler:** Christian VIII **Obv:** Head right **Rev:** Large crown above crossed sword and sceptre **Note:** Dual denominated in consideration of Schleswig-Holstein.

Date	VG	F	VF	XF	Unc
1842-1848	25.00	60.00	85.00	175	300

KM# 735.2   RIGSBANKDALER
14.4470 g., 0.8750 Silver .4064 oz. ASW   **Ruler:** Christian VIII **Obv:** Head right **Rev:** Large crown above crossed sword and scepter **Note:** Dual denominated in consideration of Schleswig-Holstein.

Date	VG	F	VF	XF	Unc
1844-1847	25.00	60.00	100	200	350

KM# 743   RIGSBANKDALER
14.4470 g., 0.8750 Silver .4064 oz. ASW   **Ruler:** Frederik VII **Obv:** Head right **Rev:** Crowned draped arms **Note:** Dual denominated in consideration of Schleswig-Holstein.

Date	VG	F	VF	XF	Unc
1849-1851	40.00	100	200	425	850

KM# 720.1   SPECIEDALER
28.8930 g., 0.8750 Silver .8128 oz. ASW   **Ruler:** Christian VIII **Obv:** Head right **Rev:** Crowned supported and draped arms

Date	VG	F	VF	XF	Unc
1840-1847	40.00	80.00	165	300	475

KM# 720.2   SPECIEDALER
28.8930 g., 0.8750 Silver .8128 oz. ASW   **Ruler:** Christian VIII **Obv:** Head right **Rev:** Crowned supported and draped arms

Date	VG	F	VF	XF	Unc
1840-1841	42.50	95.00	180	300	—

KM# 720.3   SPECIEDALER
28.8930 g., 0.8750 Silver .8128 oz. ASW   **Ruler:** Christian VIII **Obv:** Head right **Rev:** Crowned supported and draped arms

Date	VG	F	VF	XF	Unc
1843-1846	40.00	80.00	140	300	450

KM# 741   SPECIEDALER
28.8930 g., 0.8750 Silver .8128 oz. ASW   **Ruler:** Christian VIII
Obv: Head right **Rev:** Crowned supported and draped arms

Date	VG	F	VF	XF	Unc
1846-1848	42.50	95.00	180	325	525

KM# 742   SPECIEDALER
28.8930 g., 0.8750 Silver .8128 oz. ASW   **Ruler:** Frederik VII
Subject: Christian VIII Death and Accession of Frederik VII

Date	VG	F	VF	XF	Unc
1848	42.50	90.00	180	325	700

KM# 744.1   SPECIEDALER
28.8930 g., 0.8750 Silver .8128 oz. ASW   **Ruler:** Frederik VII
Obv: Head right **Rev:** Crowned arms within oak wreath

Date	VG	F	VF	XF	Unc
1849-1854	50.00	100	225	450	700

KM# 744.2   SPECIEDALER
28.8930 g., 0.8750 Silver .8128 oz. ASW   **Ruler:** Frederik VII
Obv: Head right **Rev:** Crowned arms within oak wreath

Date	VG	F	VF	XF	Unc
1851-1853	75.00	125	325	575	—

REFORM COINAGE
1854-1874

MONETARY SYSTEM
    96 Skilling Rigsmont = 1 Rigsdaler Rigsmont
    1 (old) Speciedaler = 2 Rigsdaler Rigsmont
    10 Rigsdaler Rigsmont = 1 D'Or

KM# 767   1/2 SKILLING RIGSMONT
Bronze **Ruler:** Frederik VII **Obv:** Crowned FVII monogram above
oak branches **Rev:** Value

Date	VG	F	VF	XF	Unc
1857	1.25	2.25	4.50	11.00	20.00

KM# 776   1/2 SKILLING RIGSMONT
Bronze **Ruler:** Christian IX **Obv:** Crowned CIX monogram above
oak branches **Rev:** Value

Date	VG	F	VF	XF	Unc
1868	1.25	3.50	7.00	11.50	24.00

KM# 763   SKILLING RIGSMONT
Bronze **Ruler:** Frederik VII **Obv:** Crowned FVII monogram above
oak branches **Rev:** Value

Date	VG	F	VF	XF	Unc
1856-1863	0.75	1.50	5.50	11.00	20.00

KM# 774   SKILLING RIGSMONT
Bronze **Ruler:** Christian IX **Obv:** Crowned CIX monogram above
oak branches **Rev:** Value

Date	VG	F	VF	XF	Unc
1867-1872	0.75	1.75	6.00	11.00	24.00

KM# 758.1   4 SKILLING RIGSMONT
1.8560 g., 0.2500 Silver .0149 oz. ASW   **Ruler:** Frederik VII **Obv:**
Head right **Rev:** Value within oak wreath

Date	VG	F	VF	XF	Unc
1854	1.25	6.00	17.50	50.00	100

KM# 758.2   4 SKILLING RIGSMONT
1.8560 g., 0.2500 Silver .0149 oz. ASW   **Ruler:** Frederik VII **Obv:**
Head right **Rev:** Value within oak wreath

Date	VG	F	VF	XF	Unc
1856	1.25	4.50	10.00	27.50	65.00

Denmark

KM# 775.1   4 SKILLING RIGSMONT
1.8560 g., 0.2500 Silver .0149 oz. ASW **Ruler:** Christian IX **Obv:**
Head right **Rev:** Value within oak wreath

Date	VG	F	VF	XF	Unc
1867	1.25	6.50	12.50	30.00	65.00

KM# 775.2   4 SKILLING RIGSMONT
1.8560 g., 0.2500 Silver .0149 oz. ASW **Ruler:** Christian IX **Obv:**
Head right **Rev:** Value within oak wreath

Date	VG	F	VF	XF	Unc
1869-1874	2.25	6.50	12.00	27.50	62.50

KM# 765   16 SKILLING RIGSMONT
3.8980 g., 0.5000 Silver .0626 oz. ASW **Ruler:** Frederik VII

Date	VG	F	VF	XF	Unc
1856-1858	1.75	5.00	12.00	32.50	57.50

KM# 759   1/2 RIGSDALER
7.2240 g., 0.8750 Silver .2032 oz. ASW **Ruler:** Frederik VII **Obv:**
Head right **Rev:** Value within oak wreath

Date	VG	F	VF	XF	Unc
1854-1855	8.00	22.00	50.00	75.00	150

KM# 760.1   RIGSDALER
14.4470 g., 0.8750 Silver .4064 oz. ASW **Ruler:** Frederik VII
Obv: Head right **Rev:** Value within oak wreath

Date	VG	F	VF	XF	Unc
1854-1855	17.50	37.50	70.00	125	300

KM# 760.2   RIGSDALER
14.4470 g., 0.8750 Silver .4064 oz. ASW **Ruler:** Frederik VII
Obv: Head right **Rev:** Value within oak wreath

Date	VG	F	VF	XF	Unc
1855	17.50	37.50	70.00	125	300

KM# 761.1   2 RIGSDALER
28.8930 g., 0.8750 Silver .8128 oz. ASW **Ruler:** Frederik VII
Obv: Head right **Rev:** Value within oak wreath

Date	VG	F	VF	XF	Unc
1854-1856	42.50	80.00	175	285	525

KM# 761.2   2 RIGSDALER
28.8930 g., 0.8750 Silver .8128 oz. ASW **Ruler:** Frederik VII

Date	VG	F	VF	XF	Unc
1854-1855	47.50	95.00	190	300	550

KM# 761.3   2 RIGSDALER
28.8930 g., 0.8750 Silver .8128 oz. ASW **Ruler:** Frederik VII
Obv: Head right **Rev:** Value within oak wreath

Date	VG	F	VF	XF	Unc
1863-1863/53	57.50	125	300	525	850

KM# 770   2 RIGSDALER
28.8930 g., 0.8750 Silver .8128 oz. ASW **Ruler:** Christian IX
Subject: Frederik VII Death and Accession of Christian IX

Date	VG	F	VF	XF	Unc
1863	42.50	95.00	200	360	525

KM# 772.1 2 RIGSDALER
28.8930 g., 0.8750 Silver .8128 oz. ASW **Ruler:** Christian IX
Obv: Head right **Rev:** Value within oak wreath

Date	VG	F	VF	XF	Unc
1864-1868	100	200	340	625	975

KM# 772.2 2 RIGSDALER
28.8930 g., 0.8750 Silver .8128 oz. ASW **Ruler:** Christian IX
Obv: Head right **Rev:** Value within oak wreath

Date	VG	F	VF	XF	Unc
1871-1872	125	225	400	700	975

GOLD COINAGE
1840-1874

KM# 757 FR(EDERIKS) D'OR
6.6420 g., 0.8960 Gold .1913 oz. AGW **Ruler:** Frederik VII **Obv:**
Head right **Rev:** Crowned supported draped arms

Date	VG	F	VF	XF	Unc
1853	400	775	2,450	3,800	—

KM# 730 CHR(ISTIANS) D'OR
6.6420 g., 0.8960 Gold .1913 oz. AGW **Ruler:** Christian VIII **Obv:**
Head right **Rev:** Crowned supported and draped arms

Date	VG	F	VF	XF	Unc
1843-1847	235	475	1,200	2,250	—

KM# 778 CHR(ISTIANS) D'OR
6.6420 g., 0.8960 Gold .1913 oz. AGW **Ruler:** Christian IX **Obv:**
Head right **Rev:** Crowned supported and draped arms

Date	VG	F	VF	XF	Unc
1869	800	1,500	3,250	6,000	—

KM# 750.1 2 FR(EDERIKS) D'OR
13.2840 g., 0.8960 Gold .3827 oz. AGW **Ruler:** Frederik VII **Obv:**
Head right **Rev:** Crowned supported and draped arms **Note:** Total
mintage 1850VS and 1863RH 31,000.

Date	VG	F	VF	XF	Unc
1850	275	600	2,000	3,000	—

KM# 750.2 2 FR(EDERIKS) D'OR
13.2840 g., 0.8960 Gold .3827 oz. AGW **Ruler:** Frederik VII **Obv:**
Head right **Rev:** Crowned supported and draped arms

Date	VG	F	VF	XF	Unc
1851-1855	300	600	1,650	2,700	—

KM# 750.3 2 FR(EDERIKS) D'OR
13.2840 g., 0.8960 Gold .3827 oz. AGW **Ruler:** Frederik VII **Obv:**
Head right **Rev:** Crowned supported and draped arms

Date	VG	F	VF	XF	Unc
1856-1859	300	600	1,650	2,700	—

KM# 750.4 2 FR(EDERIKS) D'OR
13.2840 g., 0.8960 Gold .3827 oz. AGW **Ruler:** Frederik VII **Obv:**
Head right **Rev:** Crowned supported and draped arms **Note:** Total
mintage 1850VS and 1863RH 31,000.

Date	VG	F	VF	XF	Unc
1863	350	700	2,000	3,000	—

KM# 722.1 2 CHR(ISTIANS) D'OR
13.2840 g., 0.8960 Gold .3827 oz. AGW **Ruler:** Christian VIII
Obv: Head right **Rev:** Crowned supported and draped arms

Date	VG	F	VF	XF	Unc
1841	350	700	1,200	2,500	—

KM# 722.2 2 CHR(ISTIANS) D'OR
13.2840 g., 0.8960 Gold .3827 oz. AGW **Ruler:** Christian VIII

Date	VG	F	VF	XF	Unc
1842-1847	300	525	1,350	2,350	—

KM# 722.3 2 CHR(ISTIANS) D'OR
13.2840 g., 0.8960 Gold .3827 oz. AGW **Ruler:** Christian VIII
Obv: Head right

Date	VG	F	VF	XF	Unc
1844	300	600	1,400	2,400	3,600

KM# 773.1 2 CHR(ISTIANS) D'OR
13.2840 g., 0.8960 Gold .3827 oz. AGW **Ruler:** Christian IX **Obv:**
Head right **Rev:** Crowned supported and draped arms

Date	VG	F	VF	XF	Unc
1866	400	800	2,400	4,500	—

KM# 773.2 2 CHR(ISTIANS) D'OR
13.2840 g., 0.8960 Gold .3827 oz. AGW **Ruler:** Christian IX **Obv:** Head right **Rev:** Crowned supported and draped arms

Date	VG	F	VF	XF	Unc
1869	400	800	2,250	4,400	—

DECIMAL COINAGE
100 Øre = 1 Krone; 1874-present

KM# 792.1 ORE
2.0000 g., Bronze **Ruler:** Christian IX **Obv:** Crowned CIX monogram **Rev:** Value above porpoise and barley ear

Date	F	VF	XF	Unc	BU
1874-1892	2.75	5.00	8.00	37.50	—

KM# 792.2 ORE
2.0000 g., Bronze **Ruler:** Christian IX **Obv:** Crowned CIX monogram, date at lower left, initials VBP at lower right **Rev:** Value above porpoise and barley ear

Date	F	VF	XF	Unc	BU
1894-1904/804	1.25	2.25	4.50	15.00	—

KM# 804 ORE
2.0000 g., Bronze **Ruler:** Frederik VIII **Obv:** Value within legend, date and initials VBP **Rev:** Crowned F8F monogram, initials GJ at lower right

Date	F	VF	XF	Unc	BU
1907-1912	1.25	2.75	5.50	16.00	—

KM# 812.1 ORE
2.0000 g., Bronze **Ruler:** Christian X **Obv:** Crowned CX monogram, initials VBP and mint mark at lower left, date and initials GJ at lower right **Rev:** Value, ornaments flanking

Date	F	VF	XF	Unc	BU
1913-1917	1.00	1.50	2.00	6.00	—

KM# 812.1a ORE
1.7400 g., Iron **Ruler:** Christian X **Obv:** Crowned CX monogram, initials VBP and mint mark at lower left, date and initials GJ at lower right **Rev:** Value, ornaments flanking

Date	F	VF	XF	Unc	BU
1918	1.75	4.50	17.50	50.00	—

KM# 812.2 ORE
2.0000 g., Bronze **Ruler:** Christian X **Obv:** Crowned CX monogram, initials HCN and mint mark at lower left, date and initials GJ at lower right **Rev:** Value, ornaments flanking

Date	F	VF	XF	Unc	BU
1919-1923	1.00	1.50	3.25	8.50	—

KM# 812.2a ORE
1.7400 g., Iron **Ruler:** Christian X **Obv:** Crowned CX monogram, initials HCN and mint mark at lower left, date and initials GJ at lower right **Rev:** Value, ornaments flanking

Date	F	VF	XF	Unc	BU
1919	5.00	15.00	37.50	75.00	—

KM# 826.1 ORE
1.9000 g., Bronze **Ruler:** Christian X **Obv:** Crowned CXC monogram within title "KING OF DENMARK", initials GJ below **Rev:** Country name and date above center hole, denomination, mint mark, and initials HCN below

Date	F	VF	XF	Unc	BU
1926-1927	0.10	0.30	4.50	25.00	—

KM# 826.2 ORE
1.9000 g., Bronze **Ruler:** Christian X **Obv:** Crowned CXC monogram within title "KING OF DENMARK", initials GJ belokmw **Rev:** Country name and date above center hole, denomination, mint mark, and initial N below **Note:** For coins dated 1941 refer to Faeroe Islands listings.

Date	F	VF	XF	Unc	BU
1927-1940	0.10	0.10	0.30	2.00	—

KM# 832 ORE
1.6000 g., Zinc **Ruler:** Christian X **Obv:** Crowned CX monogram and date within title: "KING OF DENMARK"; mint mark and initials N-S below **Rev:** Value between oak and beech leaves, denomination below

Date	F	VF	XF	Unc	BU
1941-1946	0.10	0.30	9.00	40.00	—

KM# 839.1 ORE
1.6000 g., Zinc **Ruler:** Frederik IX **Obv:** Crowned F IX R monogram and date **Rev:** Mint mark, initials N-S below value

Date	F	VF	XF	Unc	BU
1948-1955	0.10	0.20	1.75	25.00	—

KM# 839.2 ORE
1.6000 g., Zinc **Ruler:** Frederik IX **Obv:** Crowned F IX R monogram and date **Rev:** Mint mark, initials C-S below value

Date	F	VF	XF	Unc	BU
1956-1971	0.10	0.10	0.10	0.50	—

KM# 839.3 ORE
1.6000 g., Zinc **Ruler:** Frederik IX **Obv:** Crowned F IX R monogram and date **Rev:** Mint mark, initials C-S below value

Date	F	VF	XF	Unc	BU
1972	—	—	0.10	0.60	—

KM# 846 ORE
1.8000 g., Bronze **Ruler:** Frederik IX **Obv:** Crowned F IX R monogram, date **Rev:** Two barley stalks around value, initials below **Note:** Never released for circulation, see note at 2 Ore, KM#847.

Date	F	VF	XF	Unc	BU
1960-1964	—	—	1.00	1.50	—

KM# 793.1 2 ORE
4.0000 g., Bronze **Ruler:** Christian IX **Obv:** Crowned CIX
monogram **Rev:** Value above porpoise and barley ear

Date	F	VF	XF	Unc	BU
1874-1892	4.00	7.25	15.00	47.50	—

KM# 793.2 2 ORE
4.0000 g., Bronze **Ruler:** Christian IX **Obv:** Crowned CIX
monogram, date at lower left, initials VBP at lower right **Rev:** Value
above porpoise and barley ear

Date	F	VF	XF	Unc	BU
1894-1906	1.50	3.00	6.00	32.50	—

KM# 805 2 ORE
4.0000 g., Bronze **Ruler:** Frederik VIII **Obv:** Value within legend,
date and initials VBP **Rev:** Crowned F8F monogram, initials GJ at
lower right

Date	F	VF	XF	Unc	BU
1907-1912	1.50	3.00	10.00	27.50	—

KM# 813.1 2 ORE
4.0000 g., Bronze **Ruler:** Christian X **Obv:** Crowned CX
monogram, initials VBP and mint mark at lower left, date and initials
GJ at lower right **Rev:** Value, ornament flanking

Date	F	VF	XF	Unc	BU
1913-1917	1.75	4.00	6.50	22.50	—

KM# 813.1a 2 ORE
3.4700 g., Iron **Ruler:** Christian X **Obv:** Crowned CX monogram,
initials VBP and mint mark at lower left, date and initials GJ at
lower right **Rev:** Value, ornament flanking

Date	F	VF	XF	Unc	BU
1918	2.25	7.50	25.00	80.00	—

KM# 813.2 2 ORE
4.0000 g., Bronze **Ruler:** Christian X **Obv:** Crowned F VIII
monogram, initials HCN and mint mark at lower left, date and
initials GJ at lower right **Rev:** Value, ornament flanking

Date	F	VF	XF	Unc	BU
1919-1923	1.00	1.50	3.50	20.00	—

KM# 813.2a 2 ORE
3.4700 g., Iron **Ruler:** Christian X **Obv:** Crowned CX monogram,
initials HCN and mint mark at lower left, date and initials GJ at
lower right **Rev:** Value, ornament flanking

Date	F	VF	XF	Unc	BU
1919	20.00	45.00	90.00	250	—

KM# 827.1 2 ORE
3.8000 g., Bronze **Ruler:** Christian X **Obv:** Crowned CXC
monogram within title "KING OF DENMARK", initials GJ below
Rev: Country name and date above center hole, denomination,
mint mark, and initials HCN below

Date	F	VF	XF	Unc	BU
1926-1927	0.10	0.20	3.25	25.00	—

KM# 827.2 2 ORE
3.8000 g., Bronze **Ruler:** Christian X **Obv:** Crowned CXC
monogram within title "KING OF DENMARK", initials GJ below
Rev: Country name and date above center hole, denomination,
mint mark, and initial N below **Note:** For coins dated 1941 refer
to Faeroe Islands listings.

Date	F	VF	XF	Unc	BU
1927-1940	0.10	0.10	0.50	2.25	—

KM# 833 2 ORE
1.2000 g., Aluminum **Ruler:** Christian X **Obv:** Crowned CX
monogram and date within title: "KING OF DENMARK"; mint mark
and initials N-S below **Rev:** Value between oak and beach leaves

Date	F	VF	XF	Unc	BU
1941	0.10	0.60	2.25	14.00	—

KM# 833a 2 ORE
3.2000 g., Zinc **Ruler:** Christian X **Obv:** Crowned CX monogram
and date within title: "KING OF DENMARK"; mint mark and initials
N-S below **Rev:** Value between oak and beach leaves

Date	F	VF	XF	Unc	BU
1942-1947	0.10	0.40	10.00	55.00	—

KM# 840.1 2 ORE
3.2000 g., Zinc **Ruler:** Frederik IX **Obv:** Crowned F IX R
monogram and date **Rev:** Mint mark, initials N-S below value

Date	F	VF	XF	Unc	BU
1948-1955	0.10	0.10	1.50	15.00	—

KM# 840.2 2 ORE
3.2000 g., Zinc **Ruler:** Frederik IX **Obv:** Crowned F IX R
monogram and date **Rev:** Mint mark, initials C-S below value

Date	F	VF	XF	Unc	BU
1956-1971	—	0.10	0.10	0.50	—

KM# 847 2 ORE

3.6000 g., Bronze **Ruler:** Frederik IX **Obv:** Crowned F IX R monogram, date **Rev:** Two barley stalks around value, mint mark and initials C-S below **Note:** KM#847 was never released for circulation. Together with the 4 dates of 1 Øre, KM#846, they were sold as a 10 coin set to collectors by the mint. Approximately 100,000 sets were sold, remaining coins were melted.

Date	F	VF	XF	Unc	BU
1960-1966	—	—	1.00	1.50	—

KM# 840.3 2 ORE

3.2000 g., Zinc **Ruler:** Frederik IX **Obv:** Crowned F IX R monogram and date **Rev:** Mint mark, initials S-S below value

Date	F	VF	XF	Unc	BU
1972	—	0.15	0.30	0.85	—

KM# 794.1 5 ORE

8.0000 g., Bronze **Ruler:** Christian IX **Obv:** Crowned CIX monogram **Rev:** Value above porpoise and barley ear

Date	F	VF	XF	Unc	BU
1874-1891	7.50	15.00	70.00	220	—

KM# 794.2 5 ORE

8.0000 g., Bronze **Ruler:** Christian IX **Obv:** Crowned CIX monogram, date at lower left, initials VBP at lower right **Rev:** Value above porpoise and barley ear

Date	F	VF	XF	Unc	BU
1894-1906	12.50	25.00	47.50	140	—

KM# 806 5 ORE

8.0000 g., Bronze **Ruler:** Frederik VIII **Obv:** Crowned F VIII F monogram, initials VBP at lower right **Rev:** Value within legend, date and initials GJ

Date	F	VF	XF	Unc	BU
1907-1912	5.50	10.00	25.00	70.00	—

KM# 814.1 5 ORE

8.0000 g., Bronze **Ruler:** Christian X **Obv:** Crowned CX monogram, initials VBP and mint mark lower at left, date and initials GJ at lower right **Rev:** Value, ornament flanking

Date	F	VF	XF	Unc	BU
1913-1917	8.00	16.00	20.00	45.00	—

KM# 814.1a 5 ORE

6.9400 g., Iron **Ruler:** Christian X **Obv:** Crowned CX monogram, initials VBP and mint mark at lower left, date and initials GJ at lower right **Rev:** Value, ornament flanking

Date	F	VF	XF	Unc	BU
1918	6.50	11.00	27.50	85.00	—

KM# 814.2 5 ORE

8.0000 g., Bronze **Ruler:** Christian X **Obv:** Crowned CX monogram, initials HCN and mint mark at lower left, date and initials GJ at lower right **Rev:** Value, ornament flanking

Date	F	VF	XF	Unc	BU
1919-1923	3.25	5.50	8.50	20.00	—

KM# 814.2a 5 ORE

6.9400 g., Iron **Ruler:** Christian X **Obv:** Crowned CX monogram, initials HCN and mint mark at lower left, date and initials GJ at lower right **Rev:** Value, ornament flanking

Date	F	VF	XF	Unc	BU
1919	15.00	45.00	80.00	225	—

KM# 828.1 5 ORE

7.6000 g., Bronze **Ruler:** Christian X **Obv:** Crowned CXC monogram within title "KING OF DENMARK", initials GJ below **Rev:** Country name and date above center hole, denomination, mint mark, and initials HCN below

Date	F	VF	XF	Unc	BU
1927	0.10	0.20	3.50	30.00	—

KM# 828.2 5 ORE

7.6000 g., Bronze **Ruler:** Christian X **Obv:** Crowned CXC monogram within title "KING OF DENMARK", initials GJ below **Rev:** Country name and date above center hole, denomination, mint mark, and initial N below **Note:** For coins dated 1941 refer to Faeroe Islands.

Date	F	VF	XF	Unc	BU
1927-1940	0.10	0.20	0.50	4.25	—

KM# 834 5 ORE

2.4000 g., Aluminum **Ruler:** Christian X **Obv:** Crowned CX monogram and date within title: "KING OF DENMARK"; mint mark and initials N-S below **Rev:** Value between oak and beech leaves

Date	F	VF	XF	Unc	BU
1941	0.10	1.00	3.75	20.00	—

KM# 834a 5 ORE
6.4000 g., Zinc **Ruler:** Christian X **Obv:** Crowned CX monogram and date within title: "KING OF DENMARK"; mint mark and initials N-S below **Rev:** Value between oak and beech leaves

Date	F	VF	XF	Unc	BU
1942-1945	0.50	1.75	22.50	75.00	—

KM# 843.1 5 ORE
6.4000 g., Zinc **Ruler:** Frederik IX **Obv:** Crowned F IX R monogram and date **Rev:** Mint mark, initials N-S below value

Date	F	VF	XF	Unc	BU
1950-1955	0.40	1.00	4.00	25.00	—

KM# 843.2 5 ORE
6.4000 g., Zinc **Ruler:** Frederik IX **Obv:** Crowned F IX R monogram and date **Rev:** Mint mark, initials C-S below value

Date	F	VF	XF	Unc	BU
1956-1964	0.10	0.20	0.80	2.50	—

KM# 848.1 5 ORE
6.0000 g., Bronze **Ruler:** Frederik IX **Obv:** Crowned F IX R monogram, date **Rev:** Two barley stalks around value, initials C-S below

Date	F	VF	XF	Unc	BU
1960-1971	0.10	0.10	0.10	1.00	—

KM# 848.2 5 ORE
6.0000 g., Bronze **Ruler:** Frederik IX **Obv:** Crowned F IX R monogram, date **Rev:** Two barley stalks around value, initials S-S below

Date	F	VF	XF	Unc	BU
1972	—	—	0.10	1.00	—

KM# 859.1 5 ORE
1.6000 g., Copper Clad Iron **Ruler:** Margrethe II **Obv:** Crowned MIIR monogram divides date; mint mark, initials S-B **Rev:** "DANMARK" above value

Date	F	VF	XF	Unc	BU
1973-1978	—	—	0.10	0.70	—

KM# 859.2 5 ORE
1.6000 g., Copper Clad Iron **Ruler:** Margrethe II **Obv:** Crowned MIIR monogram divides date; mint mark, initials B-B **Rev:** "DANMARK" above value

Date	F	VF	XF	Unc	BU
1979-1981	—	—	0.10	0.35	—

KM# 859.3 5 ORE
1.6000 g., Copper Clad Iron **Ruler:** Margrethe II **Obv:** Crowned MIIR monogram divides date; mint mark, initials R-B **Rev:** "DANMARK" above value

Date	F	VF	XF	Unc	BU
1982-1988	—	—	0.10	0.30	—

KM# 795.1 10 ORE
1.4500 g., Bronze **Ruler:** Christian IX **Obv:** Head right **Rev:** Value above porpoise and barley ear, star at top

Date	F	VF	XF	Unc	BU
1874-1891	9.00	20.00	37.50	75.00	—

KM# 795.2 10 ORE
1.4500 g., 0.4000 Silver .0186 oz. ASW **Ruler:** Christian IX **Obv:** Head of Christian IX, date, mint mark and initials VBP **Rev:** Value above porpoise and barley ear, star at top

Date	F	VF	XF	Unc	BU
1894-1905	2.25	4.50	9.00	20.00	—

KM# 807 10 ORE
1.4500 g., 0.4000 Silver .0186 oz. ASW **Ruler:** Frederik VIII **Obv:** Head of Frederik VIII, initials GJ below **Rev:** Value, date, mint mark, initials VBP within lily ornamentation

Date	F	VF	XF	Unc	BU
1907-1912	2.75	4.50	9.00	22.50	—

KM# 818.1 10 ORE
1.4500 g., 0.4000 Silver .0186 oz. ASW **Ruler:** Christian X **Obv:** Crowned CX monogram, initials VBP and mint mark at lower left, date and initials GJ at lower right **Rev:** Value, ornament flanking

Date	F	VF	XF	Unc	BU
1914-1918	1.35	2.50	4.25	7.00	—

KM# 818.2 10 ORE
1.4500 g., 0.4000 Silver .0186 oz. ASW **Ruler:** Christian X **Obv:** Crowned CX monogram, initials HCN and mint mark at lower left, date and initials GJ at lower right **Rev:** Value, ornament flanking

Date	F	VF	XF	Unc	BU
1919	1.00	1.50	2.75	4.00	—

KM# 818.2a 10 ORE
1.5000 g., Copper-Nickel **Ruler:** Christian X **Obv:** Crowned CX monogram, initials HCN and mint mark at lower left, date and initials GJ at lower right **Rev:** Value, ornament flanking

Date	F	VF	XF	Unc	BU
1920-1923	2.75	3.75	8.00	32.50	—

KM# 822.1   10 ORE

3.0000 g., Copper-Nickel **Ruler:** Christian X **Obv:** Crowned CXR monogram around center hole, date, mint mark and initials HCN-GJ below hole **Rev:** Value above, ornaments flanking center hole

Date	F	VF	XF	Unc	BU
1924-1926	0.25	1.50	3.00	20.00	—

KM# 822.2   10 ORE

3.0000 g., Copper-Nickel **Ruler:** Christian X **Obv:** Crowned CXR monogram around center hole, date, mint mark and initial N-GJ below hole **Rev:** Value above, ornaments flanking center hole
Note: For coins dated 1941 without mint mark or initials refer to Faeroe Islands listings.

Date	F	VF	XF	Unc	BU
1929-1947	0.50	1.00	2.00	9.00	—

KM# 822.2a   10 ORE

2.4000 g., Zinc **Ruler:** Christian X **Obv:** Crowned CXR monogram around center hole, date, mint mark and initials N-GJ below hole **Rev:** Value above, ornaments flanking center hole

Date	F	VF	XF	Unc	BU
1941-1945	1.00	2.00	10.00	27.50	—

KM# 841.1   10 ORE

3.0000 g., Copper-Nickel **Ruler:** Frederik IX **Obv:** Crowned FIXR above oak and beech branches separating date **Rev:** Value, country name, mint mark, initials N-S

Date	F	VF	XF	Unc	BU
1948-1955	0.10	0.10	1.50	10.00	—

KM# 841.2   10 ORE

3.0000 g., Copper-Nickel **Ruler:** Frederik IX **Obv:** Crowned FIXR above oak and beech branches separating date **Rev:** Value, country name, mint mark, initials C-S

Date	F	VF	XF	Unc	BU
1956-1960	0.10	0.10	1.00	3.75	—

KM# 849.1   10 ORE

3.0000 g., Copper-Nickel **Ruler:** Frederik IX **Obv:** Crowned FIXR above mint mark and initials C-S **Rev:** Value, country name above oak branches

Date	F	VF	XF	Unc	BU
1960-1971	0.10	0.15	0.10	0.30	—

KM# 849.2   10 ORE

3.0000 g., Copper-Nickel **Ruler:** Frederik IX **Obv:** Crowned FIXR above mint mark and initials S-S **Rev:** Value, country name above oak branches

Date	F	VF	XF	Unc	BU
1972	—	—	0.10	0.30	—

KM# 860.1   10 ORE

3.0000 g., Copper-Nickel **Ruler:** Margrethe II **Obv:** Crowned MIIR monogram divides date, mint mark and initials S-B below **Rev:** Value flanked by oak leaves

Date	F	VF	XF	Unc	BU
1973-1978	—	—	0.10	0.30	—

KM# 860.2   10 ORE

3.0000 g., Copper-Nickel **Ruler:** Margrethe II **Obv:** Crowned MIIR monogram divides date, mint mark and initials B-B below **Rev:** Value flanked by oak leaves

Date	F	VF	XF	Unc	BU
1979-1981	—	—	0.10	0.20	—

KM# 860.3   10 ORE

3.0000 g., Copper-Nickel **Ruler:** Margrethe II **Obv:** Crowned MIIR monogram divides date, mint mark and initials R-B below **Rev:** Value flanked by oak leaves

Date	F	VF	XF	Unc	BU
1982-1988	—	—	0.10	0.20	—

KM# 796.1   25 ORE

2.4200 g., 0.6000 Silver .0467 oz. ASW **Ruler:** Christian IX **Obv:** Head right **Rev:** Value above porpoise and barley ear, star at top

Date	F	VF	XF	Unc	BU
1874-1891	14.00	45.00	75.00	150	—

KM# 796.2   25 ORE

2.4200 g., 0.6000 Silver .0467 oz. ASW **Ruler:** Christian IX **Obv:** Head of Christian IX, date, mint mark and initials VBP **Rev:** Value above porpoise and barley ear, star at top

Date	F	VF	XF	Unc	BU
1894-1905/805	5.50	10.00	25.00	50.00	—

KM# 808   25 ORE

2.4200 g., 0.6000 Silver .0467 oz. ASW **Ruler:** Frederik VIII **Obv:** Head of Frederik VIII, initials GJ below **Rev:** Value, date, mint mark, initials VBP within lily ornamentation

Date	F	VF	XF	Unc	BU
1907-1911	6.00	11.00	20.00	45.00	—

KM# 815.1　25 ORE
2.4200 g., 0.6000 Silver .0467 oz. ASW **Ruler:** Christian X **Obv:**
Crowned CX monogram, initials VBP and mint mark lower left,
date and initials GJ lower right **Rev:** Value, ornament flanking

Date	F	VF	XF	Unc	BU
1913-1918	3.25	6.00	10.00	20.00	—

KM# 815.2　25 ORE
2.4200 g., 0.6000 Silver .0467 oz. ASW **Ruler:** Christian X **Obv:**
Crowned CX monogram, initials HCN and mint mark lower left,
date and initials GJ lower right **Rev:** Value, ornament flanking

Date	F	VF	XF	Unc	BU
1919	1.25	2.00	3.00	6.00	—

KM# 815.2a　25 ORE
2.4000 g., Copper-Nickel **Ruler:** Christian X **Obv:** Crowned CX
monogram, initials HCN and mint mark lower left, date and initials
GJ lower right **Rev:** Value, ornament flanking

Date	F	VF	XF	Unc	BU
1920-1922	2.50	4.00	16.00	50.00	—

KM# 823.1　25 ORE
4.5000 g., Copper-Nickel **Ruler:** Christian X **Obv:** Crowned CXR
monogram around center hole, date, mint mark and initials HCN-
GJ below hole **Rev:** Value above, ornaments flanking center hole

Date	F	VF	XF	Unc	BU
1924-1926	0.30	1.75	4.50	17.50	—

KM# 823.2　25 ORE
4.5000 g., Copper-Nickel **Ruler:** Christian X **Obv:** Crowned CXR
monogram around center hole, date, mint mark and initials N-GJ
below hole **Rev:** Value above, ornaments flanking center hole
Note: For coins dated 1941 refer to Faeroe Islands listings.

Date	F	VF	XF	Unc	BU
1929-1947	1.25	2.25	4.00	10.00	—

KM# 823.2a　25 ORE
3.6000 g., Zinc **Ruler:** Christian X **Obv:** Crowned CXR
monogram around center hole, date, mint mark and initials N-GJ
below hole **Rev:** Value above, ornaments flanking center hole

Date	F	VF	XF	Unc	BU
1941-1945	1.50	3.50	12.50	40.00	—

KM# 842.1　25 ORE
4.5000 g., Copper-Nickel **Ruler:** Frederik IX **Obv:** Crowned FIXR
above oak and beech branches **Rev:** Value, country name, mint
mark, initials N-S

Date	F	VF	XF	Unc	BU
1948-1955	0.10	0.20	1.50	6.50	—

KM# 842.2　25 ORE
4.5000 g., Copper-Nickel **Ruler:** Frederik IX **Obv:** Crowned FIXR
above oak and beech branches **Rev:** Value, country name, mint
mark, initials C-S

Date	F	VF	XF	Unc	BU
1956-1960	0.20	0.25	0.75	4.50	—

KM# 850　25 ORE
4.5000 g., Copper-Nickel **Ruler:** Frederik IX **Obv:** Crowned FIXR
above oak and beech branches **Rev:** Value, country name, mint
mark, initials C-S

Date	F	VF	XF	Unc	BU
1960-1967	0.10	0.20	0.75	4.50	—

KM# 855.1　25 ORE
4.3000 g., Copper-Nickel **Ruler:** Frederik IX **Obv:** Crowned F IX
R monogram and date to left of center hole, beech branch to right,
initials C-S and mint mark at bottom **Rev:** Value, country name
and 2 stalks of barley around center hole

Date	F	VF	XF	Unc	BU
1966-1971	—	0.10	0.15	0.70	—

KM# 855.2　25 ORE
4.3000 g., Copper-Nickel **Ruler:** Frederik IX **Obv:** Crowned F IX
R monogram and date to left of center hole, beech branch to right,
initial S-S and mint mark at bottom **Rev:** Value, country name and
2 stalks of barley around center hole

Date	F	VF	XF	Unc	BU
1972	—	—	0.10	0.50	—

Denmark

KM# 861.1   25 ORE
4.3000 g., Copper-Nickel **Ruler:** Margrethe II **Obv:** Crowned MIIR monogram to left, oak branch to right of center hole, date above, mint mark and initials S-B below **Rev:** Value above center hole, denomination and country name below, stylized stalks to left and right of hole

Date	F	VF	XF	Unc	BU
1973-1978	—	—	0.10	0.50	—

KM# 861.2   25 ORE
4.3000 g., Copper-Nickel **Ruler:** Margrethe II **Obv:** Crowned MIIR monogram to left, oak branch to right of center hole, date above, mint mark and initials B-B below **Rev:** Value above center hole. Denomination and country name below, stylized stalks left and right of hole

Date	F	VF	XF	Unc	BU
1979-1981	—	—	0.10	0.50	—

KM# 861.3   25 ORE
4.3000 g., Copper-Nickel **Ruler:** Margrethe II **Obv:** Crowned MIIR monogram to left, oak branch to right of center hole, date above, mint mark and initials R-B below **Rev:** Value above center hole; denomination and country name below, stylized stalks left and right of hole

Date	F	VF	XF	Unc	BU
1982-1988	—	—	0.10	0.50	—

KM# 868.1   25 ORE
2.8000 g., Bronze **Ruler:** Margrethe II **Obv:** Date above large crown, country name below, initial A to right **Rev:** Large heart above value, mint mark and initials LG-JP below **Note:** Beginning in 1996 and ending with 1998, the words "DANMARK" and "ØRE" have raised edges. Heart mint mark under "ØRE"; Prev. KM#868.

Date	F	VF	XF	Unc	BU
1990-2001	—	—	—	0.15	—

KM# 868.2   25 ORE
2.8000 g., Bronze, 17.5 mm. **Ruler:** Margrethe II **Obv:** Crown **Rev:** Value **Edge:** Plain **Note:** Without initials

Date	F	VF	XF	Unc	BU
2002-2006	—	—	—	0.15	—

KM# 866.1   50 ORE
4.3000 g., Bronze **Ruler:** Margrethe II **Obv:** Date above large crown, country name below, initial A to right **Rev:** Large heart above value, mint mark and initials NR-JP below **Note:** Heart mint mark under the word "Øre".

Date	F	VF	XF	Unc	BU
1989	—	—	—	0.15	—

KM# 866.2   50 ORE
4.3000 g., Bronze **Ruler:** Margrethe II **Obv:** Date above large crown, country name below, initial A to right **Rev:** Large heart above value, mint mark and initials LG-JP below **Note:** Beginning in 1996 and ending with 1998, the words "DANMARK" and "ØRE" have raised edges. Heart mint mark under the word "ØRE".

Date	F	VF	XF	Unc	BU
1990-2001	—	—	—	0.20	—

KM# 866.3   50 ORE
4.3000 g., Bronze **Ruler:** Margrethe II **Note:** No initials

Date	F	VF	XF	Unc	BU
2002-2006	—	—	—	0.20	—

KM# 831.1   1/2 KRONE
3.0000 g., Aluminum-Bronze **Ruler:** Christian X **Obv:** Crowned CXC monogram, date, mint mark, and initials HCN-GJ **Rev:** Value above, country name below large crown

Date	F	VF	XF	Unc	BU
1924-1926	4.00	9.00	17.50	60.00	—

KM# 831.2   1/2 KRONE
3.0000 g., Aluminum-Bronze **Ruler:** Christian X **Obv:** Crowned CXC monogram, date, mint mark, and initial N-GJ **Rev:** Value above, country name below large crown

Date	F	VF	XF	Unc	BU
1939-1940	4.00	8.00	12.00	20.00	—

KM# 797.1   KRONE
7.5000 g., 0.8000 Silver .1929 oz. ASW **Ruler:** Christian IX **Obv:** Head right **Rev:** Crowned arms, porpoise and barley ear flanking

Date	F	VF	XF	Unc	BU
1875-1892	7.50	42.50	65.00	140	—

KM# 797.2   KRONE
7.5000 g., 0.8000 Silver .1929 oz. ASW **Ruler:** Christian IX **Obv:** Head right **Rev:** Crowned arms, porpoise and barley ear flanking

Date	F	VF	XF	Unc	BU
1898	60.00	100	150	235	—

KM# 819   KRONE
7.5000 g., 0.8000 Silver .1929 oz. ASW **Ruler:** Christian X **Obv:** Head of Christian X with titles, date, mint mark and initials AH at neck, and VBP at date **Rev:** Crowned royal arms with porpoise to left, barley stalk to right, value below

Date	F	VF	XF	Unc	BU
1915-1916	2.75	5.00	8.00	20.00	—

Denmark

KM# 824.1 KRONE
6.5000 g., Aluminum-Bronze **Ruler:** Christian X **Obv:** Crowned CXC monogram, date, mint mark, and initials HCN-GJ **Rev:** Value above, country name below large crown

Date	F	VF	XF	Unc	BU
1924-1926	1.50	8.00	35.00	100	—

KM# 824.2 KRONE
6.5000 g., Aluminum-Bronze **Ruler:** Christian X **Obv:** Crowned CXC monogram, date, mint mark, and initials N-GJ **Rev:** Value above, country name below large crown

Date	F	VF	XF	Unc	BU
1929-1941	1.75	2.75	8.00	45.00	—

KM# 835 KRONE
6.5000 g., Aluminum-Bronze **Ruler:** Christian X **Obv:** Head of Christian X with titles, mint mark, initials N-S **Rev:** Value divided by stalk of wheat and stalk of oats, date

Date	F	VF	XF	Unc	BU
1942-1947	1.00	2.25	3.00	11.50	—

KM# 837.1 KRONE
6.5000 g., Aluminum-Bronze **Ruler:** Frederik IX **Obv:** Head of Frederic IX, titles, mint mark, initials N-S **Rev:** Crowned royal arms dividing date, value above

Date	F	VF	XF	Unc	BU
1947-1955	1.00	2.00	5.00	12.50	—

KM# 837.2 KRONE
6.5000 g., Aluminum-Bronze **Ruler:** Frederik IX **Obv:** Head of Frederic IX, titles, mint mark, initials C-S **Rev:** Crowned royal arms dividing date, value above

Date	F	VF	XF	Unc	BU
1956-1960	0.60	1.00	1.50	3.75	—

KM# 851.1 KRONE
6.8000 g., Copper-Nickel **Ruler:** Frederik IX **Obv:** Older head of Frederik IX, titles, mint mark, initials C-S **Rev:** Crowned royal arms dividing date, value at top

Date	F	VF	XF	Unc	BU
1960-1971	0.75	0.20	0.45	1.35	—

KM# 851.2 KRONE
6.8000 g., Copper-Nickel **Ruler:** Frederik IX **Obv:** Older head of Frederik IX, titles, mint mark, initials S-S **Rev:** Crowned royal arms dividing date, value at top

Date	F	VF	XF	Unc	BU
1972	—	—	0.40	1.25	—

KM# 862.1 KRONE
6.8000 g., Copper-Nickel **Ruler:** Margrethe II **Obv:** Head of Margrethe II with titles, mint mark, initials S-B **Rev:** Crowned royal arms dividing date, value at bottom

Date	F	VF	XF	Unc	BU
1973-1978	—	—	0.20	0.75	—

KM# 862.2 KRONE
6.8000 g., Copper-Nickel **Ruler:** Margrethe II **Obv:** Head of Margrethe II with titles, mint mark, initials S-B **Rev:** Crowned royal arms dividing date, value at bottom

Date	F	VF	XF	Unc	BU
1979-1981	—	—	0.25	0.75	—

KM# 862.3 KRONE
6.8000 g., Copper-Nickel **Ruler:** Margrethe II **Obv:** Head of Margrethe II with titles, mint mark, initials **Rev:** Crowned royal arms dividing date, value at bottom

Date	F	VF	XF	Unc	BU
1982-1989	—	—	0.20	0.45	—

KM# 873.1 KRONE
3.6000 g., Copper-Nickel **Ruler:** Margrethe II **Obv:** 3 crowned MII monograms, date, mint mark and initials LG-JP-A below **Rev:** Value, country name, ornaments around center hole **Note:** Prev. KM#873.

Date	F	VF	XF	Unc	BU
1992-2001	—	—	—	0.30	—

KM# 873.2 KRONE
3.6000 g., Copper-Nickel, 20.2 mm. **Ruler:** Margrethe II **Obv:** 3 crowns and MII monograms, date and mint mark **Rev:** Value and country name **Edge:** Reeded **Note:** Without initials

Date	F	VF	XF	Unc	BU
2002-2006	—	—	—	0.30	—

KM# 798.1 2 KRONER
15.0000 g., 0.8000 Silver .3858 oz. ASW **Ruler:** Christian IX **Obv:** Head right **Rev:** Crowned arms, porpoise and barley ear flanking

Date	F	VF	XF	Unc	BU
1875-1876	8.00	62.50	115	280	—

KM# 799   2 KRONER

15.0000 g., 0.8000 Silver .3858 oz. ASW   **Ruler:** Christian IX
Subject: 25th Anniversary of Reign **Obv:** Head right **Rev:** King's
motto in center

Date	F	VF	XF	Unc	BU
1888	8.00	24.00	42.50	70.00	135

KM# 800   2 KRONER

15.0000 g., 0.8000 Silver .3858 oz. ASW   **Ruler:** Christian IX
Subject: Golden Wedding Anniversary **Obv:** Heads of Christian
IX and Queen Louise **Rev:** Wedding date with myrtle wreath

Date	F	VF	XF	Unc	BU
1892	8.00	24.00	42.50	75.00	135

KM# 798.2   2 KRONER

15.0000 g., 0.8000 Silver .3858 oz. ASW

Date	F	VF	XF	Unc	BU
1897-1899	70.00	130	175	250	—

KM# 802   2 KRONER

15.0000 g., 0.8000 Silver .3858 oz. ASW   **Ruler:** Christian IX
Subject: 40th Anniversary of Reign **Obv:** Christian IX with titles
and anniversary dates, date below bust **Rev:** Seated woman
holding royal shield; flying dove to the left; Motto: "With God for
honor and justice"; denomination in exergue

Date	F	VF	XF	Unc	BU
1903	6.50	15.00	35.00	60.00	120

KM# 803   2 KRONER

15.0000 g., 0.8000 Silver .3858 oz. ASW   **Ruler:** Frederik VIII
Subject: Death of Christian IX and Accession of Frederik VIII **Obv:**
Frederik VIII with titles, motto, date, initials VBP **Rev:** Christian IX,
titles, date of death, value, initials GJ

Date	F	VF	XF	Unc	BU
1906	5.00	9.00	30.00	50.00	105

KM# 811   2 KRONER

15.0000 g., 0.8000 Silver .3858 oz. ASW   **Ruler:** Christian X
Subject: Death of Frederik VIII and Accession of Christian X **Obv:**
Head of Christian X right with initials AH at neck, date, mint mark
and initials VBP below **Rev:** Head of Frederik VIII right with initials
AH, value below, date of death **Note:** Coin rotation.

Date	F	VF	XF	Unc	BU
1912	6.50	14.00	35.00	65.00	120

KM# 820   2 KRONER

15.0000 g., 0.8000 Silver .3858 oz. ASW   **Ruler:** Christian X **Obv:**
Head of Christian X right with initials AH at neck, date, mint mark
and initial VBP below **Rev:** Crowned royal arms, porpoise and
barley stalk flanking, value below

Date	F	VF	XF	Unc	BU
1915-1916	6.00	12.50	17.50	37.50	—

KM# 821   2 KRONER

15.0000 g., 0.8000 Silver .3858 oz. ASW   **Ruler:** Christian X
Subject: Silver Wedding Anniversary **Obv:** Heads of Christian X
and Queen Alexandrine right, initials GJ **Rev:** Crowned arms within
anniversary dates, initials HCN

Date	F	VF	XF	Unc	BU
1923	—	—	15.00	30.00	55.00

KM# 825.1 2 KRONER
13.0000 g., Aluminum-Bronze **Ruler:** Christian X **Obv:** Crowned CXC monogram, date, mint mark, and initials HCN-GJ **Rev:** Value above, country name below large crown

Date	F	VF	XF	Unc	BU
1924-1926	1.50	10.00	30.00	100	—

KM# 825.2 2 KRONER
13.0000 g., Aluminum-Bronze **Ruler:** Christian X **Obv:** Crowned CX monogram, date, mint mark, and initials N-GJ **Rev:** Value above, country name below large crown

Date	F	VF	XF	Unc	BU
1936-1941	2.00	3.75	10.00	45.00	—

KM# 829 2 KRONER
15.0000 g., 0.8000 Silver .3858 oz. ASW **Ruler:** Christian X **Subject:** King's 60th Birthday **Obv:** Head of Christian X right, date, mint mark, initials AH at neck, N below **Rev:** Draped and supported national arms, value below, initials HS

Date	F	VF	XF	Unc	BU
1930	—	—	6.00	12.00	27.50

KM# 830 2 KRONER
15.0000 g., 0.8000 Silver .3858 oz. ASW **Ruler:** Christian X **Subject:** 25th Anniversary of Reign **Obv:** Head of Christian X right, mint mark and initials N-S below **Rev:** Crowned royal arms, value below

Date	F	VF	XF	Unc	BU
ND(1937)	—	—	7.00	16.00	30.00

KM# 836 2 KRONER
15.0000 g., 0.8000 Silver .3858 oz. ASW **Ruler:** Christian X **Subject:** King's 75th Birthday **Obv:** Head of Christian X right, mint mark and initials N-S below **Rev:** Dates of birth and 75th birthday year within wreath, legend around

Date	F	VF	XF	Unc	BU
ND(1945)	—	—	10.00	22.50	55.00

KM# 838.1 2 KRONER
13.0000 g., Aluminum-Bronze **Ruler:** Frederik IX **Obv:** Head of Frederik IX right, mint mark and initials N-S below **Rev:** Crowned royal arms divide date, value above

Date	F	VF	XF	Unc	BU
1947-1955	1.00	2.00	4.50	20.00	—

KM# 838.2 2 KRONER
13.0000 g., Aluminum-Bronze **Ruler:** Frederik IX **Obv:** Head of Frederik IX right, mint mark and initials C-S below **Rev:** Crowned royal arms divide date, value above

Date	F	VF	XF	Unc	BU
1956-1959	1.00	1.65	2.25	5.50	—

KM# 844 2 KRONER
15.0000 g., 0.8000 Silver .3858 oz. ASW **Ruler:** Frederik IX **Subject:** Foundation for the Campaign against Tuberculosis in Greenland **Obv:** Heads of Frederik IX and Queen Ingrid right. Date, mint mark and initials N-S below **Rev:** Map of Greenland, country name in Greenlandic language, value **Note:** Greenland Commemorative.

Date	F	VF	XF	Unc	BU
1953	—	5.50	17.50	40.00	200

KM# 845 2 KRONER
15.0000 g., 0.8000 Silver .3858 oz. ASW **Ruler:** Frederik IX **Subject:** Princess Margrethe's 18th Birthday **Obv:** Head of Frederik IX right with titles, mint mark and initials C-S below **Rev:** Head of Princess Margrethe left, date of 18th birthday, value below

Date	F	VF	XF	Unc	BU
ND(1958)	—	—	8.50	17.50	30.00

KM# 874.1 2 KRONER
Copper-Nickel **Ruler:** Margrethe II **Obv:** Value, country name, ornaments around center hole **Rev:** 3 crowned MII monograms around center hole, date and initials LG-JP-A below **Note:** Prev. KM#874.

Date	F	VF	XF	Unc	BU
1992-2001	—	—	—	0.50	—

KM# 874.2 2 KRONER
5.9400 g., Copper-Nickel, 24.5 mm. **Ruler:** Margrethe II **Obv:** 3 crowned MII monograms around center hole, date below **Rev:** Value, country name, ornaments around center hole **Edge:** Reeded and plain sections **Note:** Without initials

Date	F	VF	XF	Unc	BU
2002-2006	—	—	—	0.50	—

KM# 852 5 KRONER
17.0000 g., 0.8000 Silver .4372 oz. ASW **Ruler:** Frederik IX **Subject:** Silver Wedding Anniversary **Obv:** Heads of Frederik IX and Queen Ingrid right within titles **Rev:** Crowned double FI monogram, Silver anniversary dates above. 2 barley ears, denomination, mint mark and initials C-S below

Date	F	VF	XF	Unc	BU
ND(1960)	—	5.50	7.00	10.00	27.50

KM# 853.1 5 KRONER
15.0000 g., Copper-Nickel **Ruler:** Frederik IX **Obv:** Head of Frederik IX right, titles, mint mark and initials C-S **Rev:** Crowned arms divide date within two oak branches, value above

Date	F	VF	XF	Unc	BU
1960-1971	2.00	1.35	1.50	3.25	—

KM# 853.2 5 KRONER
15.0000 g., Copper-Nickel **Ruler:** Frederik IX **Obv:** Head of Frederik IX right, mint mark and initials S-S **Rev:** Crowned arms divide date within two oak branches, value above

Date	F	VF	XF	Unc	BU
1972	—	—	1.50	2.50	—

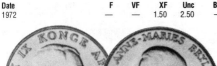

KM# 854 5 KRONER
17.0000 g., 0.8000 Silver .4372 oz. ASW **Ruler:** Frederik IX **Subject:** Wedding of Princess Anne Marie **Obv:** Head of Frederik IX right, mint mark and initials C-S **Rev:** Head of Princess Anne-Marie within title and wedding date

Date	F	VF	XF	Unc	BU
1964	—	—	6.50	14.00	—

KM# 863.1 5 KRONER
15.0000 g., Copper-Nickel **Ruler:** Margrethe II **Obv:** Head of Margrethe right, mint mark and initial S-B below **Rev:** Crowned national arms divide date and oak leaves, value below

Date	F	VF	XF	Unc	BU
1973-1978	—	—	1.35	3.50	—

KM# 863.2 5 KRONER
15.0000 g., Copper-Nickel **Ruler:** Margrethe II **Obv:** Head of Margrethe right, mint mark and initials B-B below **Rev:** Crowned national arms divide date and oak leaves, value below

Date	F	VF	XF	Unc	BU
1979-1981	—	—	1.35	3.00	—

KM# 863.3 5 KRONER
15.0000 g., Copper-Nickel **Ruler:** Margrethe II **Obv:** Head of Margrethe right, mint mark and initials R-B below **Rev:** Crowned national arms divide date and oak leaves, value below

Date	F	VF	XF	Unc	BU
1982-1988	—	—	1.25	3.00	—

KM# 869.1 5 KRONER
9.2000 g., Copper-Nickel **Ruler:** Margrethe II **Obv:** 3 crowned MII monograms around center hole, dates and initials LG-JP-A below **Rev:** Value, country name, ornaments around center hole **Note:** Large and small date varieties exist.

Date	F	VF	XF	Unc	BU
1990-2001	—	—	—	1.40	—

KM# 869.2 5 KRONER
9.2000 g., Copper Nickel, 28.5 mm. **Ruler:** Margrethe II **Obv:** 3 crowned MII monograms around center hole, dates below **Rev:** Value, country name, ornaments around center hole **Edge:** Reeded **Note:** Without initials

Date	F	VF	XF	Unc	BU
2002-2006	—	—	—	1.40	—

KM# 790.1 10 KRONER
4.4803 g., 0.9000 Gold .1296 oz. AGW

Date	F	VF	XF	Unc	BU
1873-1890	BV	90.00	155	250	—

Denmark

KM# 790.2   10 KRONER
4.4803 g., 0.9000 Gold .1296 oz. AGW **Ruler:** Christian IX

Date	F	VF	XF	Unc	BU
1898-1900	BV	85.00	110	200	—

KM# 809   10 KRONER
4.4803 g., 0.9000 Gold .1296 oz. AGW **Ruler:** Frederik VIII **Obv:**
Head of Frederik VIII with titles **Rev:** Draped crowned national
arms above date, value, mint mark and initials VBP

Date	F	VF	XF	Unc	BU
1908-1909	—	—	BV	100	—

KM# 816   10 KRONER
4.4803 g., 0.9000 Gold .1296 oz. AGW **Ruler:** Christian X **Obv:**
Head of Christian X with title, date, mint mark, initials VBP. Initials
AH at neck **Rev:** Draped crowned national arms above date, value,
mint mark and initials VBP

Date	F	VF	XF	Unc	BU
1913-1917	—	—	BV	100	—

KM# 856   10 KRONER
20.4000 g., 0.8000 Silver .5247 oz. ASW **Ruler:** Frederik IX
Subject: Wedding of Princess Margrethe **Obv:** Head of Frederik
IX with titles, mint mark, initials C-S **Rev:** Head of Princess
Margrethe and Prince Henrik right, value below

Date	F	VF	XF	Unc	BU
ND(1967)	—	—	7.00	12.50	45.00

KM# 857   10 KRONER
20.4000 g., 0.8000 Silver .5247 oz. ASW **Ruler:** Frederik IX
Subject: Wedding of Princess Benedikte **Obv:** Head of Frederik
IX right, mint mark and initials C-S below **Rev:** Head of Princess
Benedikte left, value below

Date	F	VF	XF	Unc	BU
ND(1968)	—	—	7.50	16.00	50.00

KM# 858   10 KRONER
20.4000 g., 0.8000 Silver .5247 oz. ASW **Ruler:** Margrethe II
Subject: Death of Frederik IX and Accession of Margrethe II **Obv:**
Head of Margrethe right, motto, titles, mint mark and initials S-B
Rev: Head of Frederik IX with titles, date of death, value below

Date	F	VF	XF	Unc	BU
1972	—	—	6.75	8.00	15.00

KM# 864.1   10 KRONER
12.5000 g., Copper-Nickel **Ruler:** Margrethe II **Obv:** Head of
Margrethe II right, mint mark and initials B-B below **Rev:** Large 10
on horizontal grid, two rye stalks flanking, date above

Date	F	VF	XF	Unc	BU
1979-1981	—	2.00	1.35	4.50	—

KM# 864.2   10 KRONER
12.5000 g., Copper-Nickel **Ruler:** Margrethe II **Obv:** Head of
Margarethe II right, mint mark and initials R-B below **Rev:** Large
10 on horizontal grid, two rye stalks flanking, date above

Date	F	VF	XF	Unc	BU
1982-1988	—	2.00	3.25	11.00	—

KM# 865   10 KRONER
12.5000 g., Copper-Nickel **Ruler:** Margrethe II **Subject:** Crown
Prince's 18th Birthday **Obv:** Head of Margrethe II with crown right,
mint mark and initials R-A below **Rev:** Head of Crown Prince
Frederik left, date of 18th birthday, value below **Edge:** Plain

Date	F	VF	XF	Unc	BU
ND(1986)	—	—	—	12.50	—

KM# 865a   10 KRONER
14.3000 g., 0.8000 Silver .3678 oz. ASW **Ruler:** Margrethe II
Obv: Head of Margrethe II with crown right, mint mark and initials
R-A below **Rev:** Head of Crown Prince Frederik left, date of 18th
birthday, value below

Date	F	VF	XF	Unc	BU
1986 Proof	Value: 75.00				

KM# 867.1 10 KRONER
7.0000 g., Aluminum-Bronze, 23.4 mm. **Ruler:** Margrethe II **Obv:** Head of Margrethe II, titles, date, initials NR-JP-A **Rev:** Crowned arms within ornaments, value below **Edge:** Plain

Date	F	VF	XF	Unc	BU
1989	—	—	—	3.00	—

KM# 867.2 10 KRONER
7.0000 g., Aluminum-Bronze, 23.4 mm. **Ruler:** Margrethe II **Obv:** Head of Margrethe II, titles, date, initials LG-JP-A **Rev:** Crowned arms within ornaments, value below **Edge:** Plain

Date	F	VF	XF	Unc	BU
1990-1993	—	—	—	3.00	—

KM# 877 10 KRONER
7.0000 g., Aluminum-Bronze, 23.4 mm. **Ruler:** Margrethe II **Obv:** New portrait of Queen Margrethe **Rev:** Crowned arms within ornaments, value below **Edge:** Plain **Note:** Beginning with strikes in 1995 and ending in 1998, letters and numbers on reverse have raised edges.

Date	F	VF	XF	Unc	BU
1994-1999	—	—	—	3.00	—

KM# 887.1 10 KRONER
7.0000 g., Aluminum-Bronze, 23.4 mm. **Ruler:** Margrethe II **Obv:** Crowned head of Queen Margrethe II right within inner circle, date, initials LG-JP-A below, mint mark after II in title **Rev:** Crowned arms above denomination **Edge:** Plain

Date	F	VF	XF	Unc	BU
2001	—	—	—	2.75	—

KM# 887.2 10 KRONER
7.0000 g., Aluminum-Bronze, 23.4 mm. **Ruler:** Margrethe II **Obv:** Crowned head of Queen Margrethe II right, mint mark after II in title **Rev:** Crowned arms and value **Edge:** Plain **Note:** Without initials

Date	F	VF	XF	Unc	BU
2002	—	—	—	2.75	—

KM# 896 10 KRONER
Aluminum-Bronze **Ruler:** Margrethe II **Obv:** Queen's portrait **Rev:** Similar to KM#891.

Date	F	VF	XF	Unc	BU
2004-2006	—	—	—	2.50	—

KM# 898 10 KRONER
7.0000 g., Copper-Aluminum-Nickel, 23.4 mm. **Ruler:** Margrethe II **Subject:** Hans Christian Andersen's Ugly duckling story **Obv:** Margrethe II **Rev:** Swan and reflection on water **Edge:** Plain

Date	F	VF	XF	Unc	BU
2005	—	—	—	4.50	—

KM# 900 10 KRONER
7.0000 g., Aluminum-Bronze, 23.4 mm. **Ruler:** Margrethe II **Subject:** Hans Christian Andersen's Little Mermaid **Obv:** Queen **Rev:** Little Mermaid **Edge:** Plain

Date	F	VF	XF	Unc	BU
2005	—	—	—	—	4.25

KM# 906 10 KRONER
31.1000 g., 0.9990 Silver 0.9989 oz. ASW, 38 mm. **Ruler:** Margrethe II **Subject:** Hans Christian Andersen's The Ugly Duckling **Obv:** Queen **Rev:** Swan and reflection on water

Date	F	VF	XF	Unc	BU
2005	—	—	—	—	35.00

KM# 907 10 KRONER
8.6500 g., 0.9000 Gold 0.2503 oz. AGW **Ruler:** Margrethe II **Subject:** Hans Christian Andersen's The Ugly Duckling **Obv:** Queen **Rev:** Swan and reflection on water

Date	F	VF	XF	Unc	BU
2005	—	—	—	—	340

KM# 908 10 KRONER
31.1000 g., 0.9990 Silver 0.9989 oz. ASW **Ruler:** Margrethe II **Subject:** Hans Christian Andersen's Little Mermaid **Obv:** Queen **Rev:** Little Mermaid

Date	F	VF	XF	Unc	BU
2005	—	—	—	—	35.00

KM# 911 (KM900b) 10 KRONER
8.6500 g., 0.9000 Gold 0.2214 oz. AGW **Ruler:** Margrethe II **Subject:** Hans Christian Andersen's Little Mermaid **Obv:** Queen **Rev:** Little Mermaid

Date	F	VF	XF	Unc	BU
2005	—	—	—	—	340

KM# 911 (KM900b) 10 KRONER
8.6500 g., 0.9000 Gold 0.2214 oz. AGW **Ruler:** Margrethe II **Subject:** Hans Christian Andersen's Little Mermaid **Obv:** Queen **Rev:** Little Mermaid

Date	F	VF	XF	Unc	BU
2005	—	—	—	—	340

KM# 903 10 KRONER
7.0000 g., Aluminum-Bronze, 23.4 mm. **Ruler:** Margrethe II **Subject:** H.C. Andersen's "Skyggen" (The Shadow) **Obv:** Queen **Rev:** Stylized figures **Note:** 3rd H.C. Andersen coin

Date	F	VF	XF	Unc	BU
2006	—	—	—	4.50	—

KM# 909 10 KRONER
31.1000 g., 0.9990 Silver, 38 mm. **Ruler:** Margrethe II **Subject:** H.C. Andersen's "Skyggen (The Shadow)" **Obv:** Queen **Rev:** Stylized figures

Date	F	VF	XF	Unc	BU
2006	—	—	—	35.00	—

KM# 910 10 KRONER
8.6500 g., 0.9000 Gold, 22 mm. **Ruler:** Margrethe II **Subject:** H.C. Andersen's "Skyggen" (The Shadow) **Obv:** Queen **Rev:** Stylized figures

Date	F	VF	XF	Unc	BU
2006	—	—	—	340	—

KM# 791.1 20 KRONER
8.9606 g., 0.9000 Gold .2592 oz. AGW

Date	F	VF	XF	Unc	BU
1873-1890	—	BV	180	230	—

KM# 791.2   20 KRONER
8.9606 g., 0.9000 Gold .2592 oz. AGW   **Ruler:** Christian IX

Date	F	VF	XF	Unc	BU
1900	—	BV	230	340	—

KM# 810   20 KRONER
8.9606 g., 0.9000 Gold .2592 oz. AGW   **Ruler:** Frederik VIII **Obv:** Head of Frederik VIII with titles **Rev:** Draped crowned national arms above date, value, mint mark and initials VBP

Date	F	VF	XF	Unc	BU
1908-1912	—	—	BV	200	—

KM# 817.1   20 KRONER
8.9606 g., 0.9000 Gold .2592 oz. AGW   **Ruler:** Christian X **Obv:** Head of Christian X with title, date, mint mark, initials VBP, initials AH at neck **Rev:** Draped crowned national arms above date, value, mint mark and initials VBP

Date	F	VF	XF	Unc	BU
1913-1917	—	—	BV	175	—

KM# 817.2   20 KRONER
8.9606 g., 0.9000 Gold .2592 oz. AGW   **Ruler:** Christian X **Obv:** Head of Christian X with title, date, mint mark, and initials HCN, initials AH at neck **Rev:** Draped crowned national arms above date, value, mint mark, and initials HCN **Note:** 1926-1927 dated 20 Kroners were not released for circulation.

Date	F	VF	XF	Unc	BU
1926-1927	—	—	3,000	5,500	—

KM# 817.3   20 KRONER
8.9606 g., 0.9000 Gold .2592 oz. AGW   **Ruler:** Christian X **Obv:** Head of Christian X with title, date, mint mark, and initials HCN. Initials AH at neck **Rev:** Draped crowned national arms above date, value, mint mark and initials HCN **Note:** The 1930-1931 dated 20 Kroners were not released for circulation.

Date	F	VF	XF	Unc	BU
1930-1931	—	—	3,000	5,500	—

KM# 870   20 KRONER
9.3000 g., Aluminum-Bronze **Ruler:** Margrethe II **Subject:** 50th Birthday of Queen Margrethe **Obv:** Head of Margrethe II with hat, mint mark after 2 in legend, initials LG left of shoulder **Rev:** Large crown above daisy flower, value below **Edge:** Alternate reeded and plain sections

Date	F	VF	XF	Unc	BU
ND(1990)	—	—	—	5.50	—

KM# 871   20 KRONER
9.3000 g., Aluminum-Bronze **Ruler:** Margrethe II **Obv:** Head of Margrethe II, titles, date, initials LG-JP-A, mint mark after II in legend **Rev:** Crowned arms within ornaments and value **Edge:** Alternate reeded and plain sections **Note:** Large and small date varieties exist.

Date	F	VF	XF	Unc	BU
1990-1993	—	—	—	6.00	—

KM# 875   20 KRONER
9.3000 g., Aluminum-Bronze **Ruler:** Margrethe II **Subject:** Silver Wedding Anniversary **Obv:** Heads of Prince Henrik and Margrethe II facing each other, anniversary dates below **Rev:** Fairy tale house, mint mark and initials LG at lower left **Edge:** Alternate reeded and plain sections

Date	F	VF	XF	Unc	BU
ND(1992)	—	—	—	5.00	—

KM# 878   20 KRONER
9.3000 g., Aluminum-Bronze **Ruler:** Margrethe II **Obv:** New portrait of Queen Margrethe, date, mint mark and initials LG-JP-A below **Rev:** Crowned arms within ornament and value **Edge:** Alternating reeded and plain sections **Note:** Strikes dated 1996 and 1998 have letters and numbers on reverse with raised edges.

Date	F	VF	XF	Unc	BU
1994-1999	—	—	—	5.00	—

KM# 879   20 KRONER
9.3000 g., Aluminum-Bronze **Ruler:** Margrethe II **Subject:** 1000 Years of Danish Coinage **Obv:** Head of Margrethe II left, inner legend in runic letters **Rev:** Large crown on cross, mint mark and initials LG **Edge:** Alternate reeded and plain sections

Date	F	VF	XF	Unc	BU
ND(1995)	—	—	—	5.50	—

KM# 881   20 KRONER
9.3000 g., Aluminum-Bronze **Ruler:** Margrethe II **Subject:**
Wedding of Prince Joachim **Obv:** Crowned head of Queen
Margrethe II right, mint mark after II in legend, initials LG below at
date **Rev:** Schackenborg castle at center, value below **Edge:**
Alternate reeded and plain sections

Date	F	VF	XF	Unc	BU
1995	—	—	—	5.00	—

KM# 883   20 KRONER
9.3000 g., Aluminum-Bronze **Ruler:** Margrethe II **Subject:** 25th
Anniversary - Queen's Reign **Obv:** Full-length portrait, mint mark
and initials LG **Rev:** Crowned arms within anniversary date and
value **Edge:** Alternate reeded and plain sections

Date	F	VF	XF	Unc	BU
ND(1997)	—	—	—	5.50	—

KM# 885   20 KRONER
9.3600 g., Aluminum-Bronze **Ruler:** Margrethe II **Subject:** 60th
Birthday of Queen Margrethe II **Obv:** Bust of Queen Margrethe II
right **Rev:** Crown above daisy flowers **Edge:** Alternating reeded
and plain sections

Date	F	VF	XF	Unc	BU
ND(2000)	—	—	—	5.00	—

KM# 888.1   20 KRONER
9.3000 g., Aluminum-Bronze **Ruler:** Margrethe II **Obv:** Crowned
head of Queen Margrethe II right within inner circle, date and initials
LG-JP-A below, mint mark after II in legend **Rev:** Crowned arms within
ornaments and value **Edge:** Alternate reeded and plain sections

Date	F	VF	XF	Unc	BU
2001	—	—	—	4.50	—

KM# 888.2   20 KRONER
9.3000 g., Aluminum-Bronze, 26.9 mm. **Ruler:** Margrethe II **Obv:**
Crowned head of Queen Margrethe II right within inner circle, mint
mark after II in legend **Rev:** Crowned arms within ornaments and
value **Edge:** Alternate reeded and plain sections **Note:** Without
initials.

Date	F	VF	XF	Unc	BU
2002	—	—	—	4.50	—

KM# 889   20 KRONER
9.3000 g., Aluminum-Bronze **Ruler:** Margrethe II **Subject:** Arhus
City Hall **Obv:** Queen's portrait, mint mark after II in legend **Rev:**
Tower, without initials **Edge:** Reeded and plain sections

Date	F	VF	XF	Unc	BU
2002	—	—	—	4.50	—

KM# 890   20 KRONER
9.3000 g., Aluminum-Bronze, 26.8 mm. **Ruler:** Margrethe II
Subject: Danish towers **Obv:** Queen's portrait, mint mark and date
Rev: Copenhagen Old Stock Exchange spire with four intertwined
dragon tails **Edge:** Alternate reeded and plain sections

Date	F	VF	XF	Unc	BU
2003	—	—	—	4.50	—

KM# 891   20 KRONER
9.3000 g., Aluminum-Bronze, 26.8 mm. **Ruler:** Margrethe II **Obv:**
Queen's portrait, mint mark and date **Rev:** Crowned arms above
denomination **Edge:** Alternate reeded and plain sections

Date	F	VF	XF	Unc	BU
2003-2006	—	—	—	4.50	—

KM# 892   20 KRONER
9.3100 g., Aluminum-Bronze, 26.8 mm. **Ruler:** Margrethe II
Subject: Danish towers **Obv:** Queen Margrethe II, mint mark and
date **Rev:** Christiansborg Castle (parliament) tower and Danish
flag **Edge:** Alternate reeded and plain sections

Date	F	VF	XF	Unc	BU
2003	—	—	—	4.50	—

KM# 893 20 KRONER
9.3100 g., Aluminum-Bronze, 26.8 mm. **Ruler:** Margrethe II
Subject: Danish towers **Obv:** Queen Margrethe II **Rev:**
Gåsetårnet tower **Edge:** Alternate reeded and plain sections

Date	F	VF	XF	Unc	BU
2004	—	—	—	4.50	—

KM# 894 20 KRONER
9.3100 g., Aluminum-Bronze, 26.8 mm. **Ruler:** Margrethe II
Subject: Crown Prince's Wedding **Obv:** Queen Margrethe II **Rev:**
Crown Prince Frederik and Crown Princess Mary **Edge:** Alternate
reeded and plain sections

Date	F	VF	XF	Unc	BU
2004	—	—	—	4.50	—

KM# 897 20 KRONER
Aluminum-Bronze, 26.8 mm. **Ruler:** Margrethe II **Subject:**
Danish towers **Obv:** Queen Margrethe II **Rev:** Svaneke water
tower, Bornholm **Edge:** Alternate reeded and plain sections

Date	F	VF	XF	Unc	BU
2004	—	—	—	4.50	—

KM# 904 20 KRONER
9.7300 g., Nickel-Brass, 27.4 mm. **Ruler:** Margrethe II **Subject:**
150 Years of Railway

Date	F	VF	XF	Unc	BU
2004	—	—	—	10.00	—

KM# 899 20 KRONER
9.3000 g., Copper-Aluminum-Nickel, 26.8 mm. **Ruler:** Margrethe II
Obv: Margrethe II **Rev:** Landet Kirke, with elements from the story of
Elvira Madigan and Sixten Sparre, including a revolver among leaves
of chestnut-trees **Edge:** Segmented reeding

Date	F	VF	XF	Unc	BU
2005	—	—	—	8.00	—

KM# 901 20 KRONER
9.3000 g., Aluminum-Bronze, 26.8 mm. **Ruler:** Margrethe II **Rev:**
Lighthouse of Nolsoy (Faeroe Islands)

Date	F	VF	XF	Unc	BU
2005	—	—	—	8.00	—

KM# 902 20 KRONER
9.3300 g., Brass, 26.9 mm. **Ruler:** Margrethe II **Obv:** Queen **Rev:**
Grasten Slut Bell Tower **Edge:** Segmented reeding

Date	F	VF	XF	Unc	BU
2006	—	—	—	—	7.50

KM# 905 20 KRONER
9.7300 g., Nickel-Brass, 27.4 mm. **Ruler:** Margrethe II **Subject:**
Henrik Ibsen

Date	F	VF	XF	Unc	BU
2006	—	—	—	10.00	—

KM# 872 200 KRONER
31.1000 g., 0.8000 Silver .8000 oz. ASW, 38 mm. **Ruler:**
Margrethe II **Subject:** 50th Birthday of Queen Margrethe **Obv:**
Head of Margrethe 2, with hat, mintmark after 2 in legend, initials
LG and Fox mark above shoulder **Rev:** Large crown above daisy
flower, value below **Edge:** Plain

Date	F	VF	XF	Unc	BU
ND(1990)	—	—	—	37.50	—

KM# 876 200 KRONER
31.1000 g., 0.9990 Silver 1.0000 oz. ASW, 38 mm. **Ruler:**
Margrethe II **Subject:** Silver Wedding Anniversary **Obv:** Heads of
Prince Henrik and Queen Margrethe II facing each other,
anniversary dates below **Rev:** Fairy tale house, mintmark and
initials LG at lower left **Edge:** Plain

Date	F	VF	XF	Unc	BU
ND(1992)	—	—	—	37.50	—

KM# 880   200 KRONER
31.1000 g., 0.9990 Silver 1.0000 oz. ASW, 38 mm. **Ruler:**
Margrethe II **Subject:** 1000 Year of Danish Coinage **Obv:** Head
of Margrethe II left. Runic lettering within legend **Rev:** Large crown
on cross, mintmark at left, initials LG at bottom **Edge:** Plain

Date	F	VF	XF	Unc	BU
ND(1995)	—	—	—	60.00	—

KM# 886   200 KRONER
31.1000 g., 0.9990 Silver 1.0000 oz. ASW, 38 mm. **Ruler:**
Margrethe II **Subject:** 60th Birthday of Queen Margrethe II **Obv:**
Bust of Queen Margrethe II right **Rev:** Crown above flowers **Edge:**
Plain

Date	F	VF	XF	Unc	BU
ND(2000)	—	—	—	50.00	—

KM# 895   200 KRONER
31.1000 g., 0.9990 Silver 0.9989 oz. ASW, 38.3 mm. **Ruler:**
Margrethe II **Subject:** Wedding of Crown Prince **Obv:** Queen
Margrethe II **Rev:** Crown Prince Frederik and Crown Princess
Mary **Edge:** Plain **Note:** No initials.

Date	F	VF	XF	Unc	BU
2004	—	—	—	50.00	—

KM# 882   200 KRONER
31.1000 g., 0.9990 Silver 1.0000 oz. ASW, 38 mm. **Ruler:**
Margrethe II **Subject:** Wedding of Prince Joachim **Obv:** Queen
Margrethe II **Rev:** Schackenburg Castle **Edge:** Plain

Date	F	VF	XF	Unc	BU
1995	—	—	—	50.00	—

KM# 884   200 KRONER
31.1000 g., 0.9990 Silver 1.0000 oz. ASW, 38 mm. **Ruler:**
Margrethe II **Subject:** 25th Anniversary - Queen's Reign **Obv:**
Full-length portrait **Rev:** National arms and date of 25th
anniversary **Edge:** Plain

Date	F	VF	XF	Unc	BU
ND(1997)	—	—	—	50.00	—

Estonia

The Republic of Estonia (formerly the Estonian Soviet Socialist Republic of the U.S.S.R.) is the northernmost of the three Baltic States in Eastern Europe. It has an area of 17,462 sq. mi. (45,100 sq. km.) and a population of 1.6 million. Capital: Tallinn. Agriculture and dairy farming are the principal industries. Butter, eggs, bacon, timber and petroleum are exported.

REPUBLIC
1918 - 1941

REPUBLIC COINAGE

KM# 1   MARK
Copper-Nickel, 18 mm.   **Edge:** Milled

Date	F	VF	XF	Unc	BU
1922	3.00	4.00	7.00	12.50	—

KM# 1a   MARK
2.6000 g., Nickel-Bronze, 18 mm.   **Edge:** Milled

Date	F	VF	XF	Unc	BU
1924	3.00	6.00	8.00	15.00	—

KM# 5   MARK
Nickel-Bronze

Date	F	VF	XF	Unc	BU
1926	5.00	8.00	15.00	30.00	—

KM# 2   3 MARKA
Copper-Nickel

Date	F	VF	XF	Unc	BU
1922	3.00	6.00	8.00	14.00	—

KM# 2a   3 MARKA
Nickel-Bronze

Date	F	VF	XF	Unc	BU
1925	5.00	8.00	15.00	30.00	—

KM# 6   3 MARKA
Nickel-Bronze

Date	F	VF	XF	Unc	BU
1926	25.00	50.00	80.00	150	—

KM# 3   5 MARKA
5.0000 g., Copper-Nickel, 23 mm.   **Edge:** Milled

Date	F	VF	XF	Unc	BU
1922	5.00	8.00	10.00	20.00	—

KM# 3a   5 MARKA
5.0000 g., Nickel-Bronze, 23 mm.   **Edge:** Milled

Date	F	VF	XF	Unc	BU
1924	5.00	8.00	11.00	25.00	—

KM# 7   5 MARKA
Nickel-Bronze

Date	F	VF	XF	Unc	BU
1926	75.00	150	200	350	—

KM# 4   10 MARKA
6.0000 g., Nickel-Bronze, 26 mm.   **Edge:** Milled

Date	F	VF	XF	Unc	BU
1925	7.00	12.00	20.00	40.00	—

KM# 8   10 MARKA
Nickel-Bronze

Date	F	VF	XF	Unc	BU
1926	650	1,000	1,500	2,000	—

REFORM COINAGE
100 Senti = 1 Kroon

KM# 10   SENT
2.0000 g., Bronze, 17 mm.   **Edge:** Plain

Date	F	VF	XF	Unc	BU
1929	1.00	2.00	3.00	4.00	—

KM# 19.1   SENT
2.0000 g., Bronze, 16 mm. **Edge:** Plain **Note:** 1 mm thick planchet.

Date	F	VF	XF	Unc	BU
1939	4.00	8.00	15.00	35.00	—

KM# 19.2   SENT
Bronze **Note:** 0.9mm thick planchet.

Date	F	VF	XF	Unc	BU
1939	6.00	10.00	15.00	35.00	—

KM# 15   2 SENTI
3.5000 g., Bronze, 19 mm. **Edge:** Plain

Date	F	VF	XF	Unc	BU
1934	2.00	3.00	6.00	10.00	—

KM# 11   5 SENTI
3.5000 g., Bronze, 23.3 mm. **Edge:** Plain

Date	F	VF	XF	Unc	BU
1931	2.00	3.00	6.00	10.00	—

KM# 12   10 SENTI
Nickel-Bronze, 18 mm. **Edge:** Plain

Date	F	VF	XF	Unc	BU
1931	2.00	3.00	6.00	12.00	—

KM# 17   20 SENTI
Nickel-Bronze, 21 mm. **Edge:** Plain

Date	F	VF	XF	Unc	BU
1935	4.00	6.00	8.00	15.00	—

KM# 9   25 SENTI
Nickel-Bronze

Date	F	VF	XF	Unc	BU
1928	6.00	9.00	20.00	35.00	—

KM# 18   50 SENTI
7.5000 g., Nickel-Bronze, 27.5 mm. **Edge:** Plain

Date	F	VF	XF	Unc	BU
1936	6.00	9.00	17.00	35.00	—

KM# 14   KROON
6.0000 g., 0.5000 Silver .0965 oz. ASW **Subject:** 10th Singing Festival

Date	F	VF	XF	Unc	BU
1933	15.00	25.00	40.00	55.00	75.00

KM# 16   KROON
Aluminum-Bronze, 25 mm. **Obv:** State emblem **Rev:** Ship of Vikings **Edge:** Plain **Note:** 1990 restrikes which exist are private issues.

Date	F	VF	XF	Unc	BU
1934	5.00	8.00	14.00	40.00	60.00

KM# 20   2 KROONI
12.0000 g., 0.5000 Silver .1929 oz. ASW, 30 mm. **Subject:** Toompea Fortress at Tallinn **Obv:** State emblem **Rev:** Castle, value **Edge:** Milled

Date	F	VF	XF	Unc	BU
1930	4.50	9.00	16.00	35.00	55.00

KM# 13   2 KROONI
12.0000 g., 0.5000 Silver .1929 oz. ASW, 30 mm. **Subject:** Tercentenary - University of Tartu **Obv:** State emblem **Edge:** Plain

Date	F	VF	XF	Unc	BU
1932	15.00	25.00	35.00	50.00	70.00

Estonia

MODERN REPUBLIC
1991 - present
STANDARD COINAGE

KM# 21   5 SENTI
1.2900 g., Brass, 15.9 mm.   **Edge:** Plain

Date	F	VF	XF	Unc	BU
1991-1995	—	—	—	0.25	—

KM# 22   10 SENTI
Copper-Aluminum-Nickel, 17.2 mm.   **Edge:** Plain

Date	F	VF	XF	Unc	BU
1991-2002	—	—	—	0.34	—

KM# 23   20 SENTI
2.2700 g., Brass, 18.9 mm.   **Edge:** Plain

Date	F	VF	XF	Unc	BU
1992-1999	—	—	—	0.65	—

KM# 23a   20 SENTI
2.0000 g., Nickel Plated Steel, 18.9 mm.   **Edge:** Plain

Date	F	VF	XF	Unc	BU
1997-2004	—	—	—	0.65	—

KM# 24   50 SENTI
3.0000 g., Brass, 19.5 mm.   **Edge:** Plain

Date	F	VF	XF	Unc	BU
1992-2004	—	—	—	1.00	—

KM# 28   KROON
5.4400 g., Copper-Nickel, 23.5 mm.   **Edge:** Plain

Date	F	VF	XF	Unc	BU
1993-1995	—	—	—	1.50	—

KM# 35   KROON
5.0000 g., Brass, 23.25 mm.   **Edge:** Three reeded and plain sections

Date	F	VF	XF	Unc	BU
1998-2003	—	—	—	1.25	—

KM# 36   KROON
Brass   **Obv:** Bird above date **Rev:** Festival building and denomination

Date	F	VF	XF	Unc	BU
1999	—	—	—	5.00	—

KM# 29   5 KROONI
7.1000 g., Brass, 26.2 mm.   **Subject:** 75th Anniversary - Declaration of Independence **Edge:** Plain

Date	F	VF	XF	Unc	BU
1993	—	—	—	4.00	6.00

KM# 30   5 KROONI
7.1000 g., Brass, 26.1 mm.   **Subject:** 75th Anniversary - Estonian National Bank **Edge:** Plain

Date	F	VF	XF	Unc	BU
1994	—	—	—	3.00	—

KM# 25   10 KROONI
28.2800 g., 0.9250 Silver .8411 oz. ASW   **Series:** Olympics **Rev:** Two sail boats

Date	F	VF	XF	Unc	BU
1992 Proof	Value: 50.00				

KM# 26 10 KROONI
28.2800 g., 0.9250 Silver .8411 oz. ASW **Rev:** Barn Swallow

Date	F	VF	XF	Unc	BU
1992 Proof		Value: 50.00			

KM# 32 10 KROONI
16.0000 g., 0.9250 Silver .4758 oz. ASW **Subject:** 80th Anniversary of Nation **Obv:** Framed dates **Rev:** Farmer plowing field

Date	F	VF	XF	Unc	BU
ND(1998)	—	—	—	22.50	—

KM# 37 15.65 KROONI
1.7300 g., 0.9000 Gold .0501 oz. AGW **Subject:** Estonia's Euro Equivalent **Obv:** National arms **Rev:** Cross and stars design

Date	F	VF	XF	Unc	BU
1999 Proof		Value: 40.00			

KM# 27 100 KROONI
24.0000 g., 0.9250 Silver .7135 oz. ASW **Rev:** Barn Swallows

Date	F	VF	XF	Unc	BU
1992 Proof		Value: 30.00			

KM# 31 100 KROONI
28.2800 g., 0.9250 Silver .8411 oz. ASW **Rev:** Olympics - Nike crowning Wrestler

Date	F	VF	XF	Unc	BU
1996	—	—	—	30.00	—

KM# 33 100 KROONI
27.0000 g., 0.9250 Silver .8030 oz. ASW **Subject:** 80th Anniversary of Nation **Obv:** Framed dates **Rev:** Male figure and stylized eagle head

Date	F	VF	XF	Unc	BU
ND(1998)	—	—	—	35.00	—

KM# 34 500 KROONI
8.6400 g., 0.9000 Gold .2500 oz. AGW **Subject:** 80th Anniversary of Nation **Obv:** Framed dates **Rev:** Male figure on horse

Date	F	VF	XF	Unc	BU
ND(1998) Proof		Value: 185			

Faeroe Islands

The Faeroe Islands, a self-governing community within the kingdom of Denmark, are situated in the North Atlantic between Iceland and the Shetland Islands. The 17 inhabited islands and numerous islets and reefs have an area of 540 sq. mi. (1,400 sq. km.) and a population of 46,000. Capital: Thorshavn. The principal industries are fishing and livestock. Fish and fish products are exported.

The islands were occupied by British troops during World War II, after the German occupation of Denmark. The Faeroe island coinage was struck in London during World War II.

MONETARY SYSTEM
100 Øre = 1 Krone

DANISH STATE
DECIMAL COINAGE

KM# 1   ORE
Bronze

Date	F	VF	XF	Unc	BU
1941	20.00	40.00	60.00	92.50	—

KM# 2   2 ORE
Bronze

Date	F	VF	XF	Unc	BU
1941	5.00	10.00	22.50	55.00	—

KM# 3   5 ORE
Bronze

Date	F	VF	XF	Unc	BU
1941	4.00	8.00	18.50	55.00	—

KM# 4   10 ORE
Copper-Nickel

Date	F	VF	XF	Unc	BU
1941	5.50	11.00	27.50	83.50	—

KM# 5   25 ORE
Copper-Nickel

Date	F	VF	XF	Unc	BU
1941	7.00	12.50	30.00	95.00	—

Finland

The Republic of Finland, the third northernmost state of the European continent, has an area of 130,559 sq. mi. (338,127 sq. km.) and a population of 5.1 million. Capital: Helsinki. Lumbering, shipbuilding, metal and woodworking are the leading industries. Paper, timber, wood pulp, plywood and metal products are exported.

MONETARY SYSTEM
100 Pennia = 1 Markka

Commencing 1963
100 Old Markka = 1 New Markka

GRAND DUCHY
DECIMAL COINAGE

KM# 1.1   PENNI
Copper   **Note:** Dotted border; varieties exist.

Date	F	VF	XF	Unc	BU
1864-1871	10.00	15.00	35.00	75.00	—

KM# 1.2   PENNI
Copper   **Note:** Dentilated border.

Date	F	VF	XF	Unc	BU
1872-1876	7.00	10.00	30.00	60.00	—

KM# 10   PENNI
Copper

Date	F	VF	XF	Unc	BU
1881-1894	0.75	1.50	4.00	10.00	—

KM# 13   PENNI
1.2800 g., Copper, 15 mm.   **Obv:** Monogram of Nicholas II **Rev:** Value, date

Date	F	VF	XF	Unc	BU
1895-1916	0.25	0.50	1.00	2.00	—

KM# 4.1   5 PENNIA
Copper   **Note:** Dotted border; varieties exist.

Date	F	VF	XF	Unc	BU
1865-1870	1.00	7.00	50.00	125	—

KM# 4.2   5 PENNIA
Copper   **Note:** Dentilated border.

Date	F	VF	XF	Unc	BU
1872-1875	1.00	10.00	50.00	150	—

KM# 11   5 PENNIA
Copper

Date	F	VF	XF	Unc	BU
1888-1892	1.00	7.00	50.00	120	—

KM# 15   5 PENNIA
6.4000 g., Copper, 25 mm. **Obv:** Monogram of Nicholas II **Rev:** Value, date

Date	F	VF	XF	Unc	BU
1896-1917	0.30	0.75	3.00	10.00	—

KM# 5.1   10 PENNIA
Copper **Note:** Dotted border.

Date	F	VF	XF	Unc	BU
1865-1867	3.00	20.00	75.00	200	—

KM# 5.2   10 PENNIA
Copper **Note:** Dentilated border; varieties exist.

Date	F	VF	XF	Unc	BU
1875-1876	5.00	35.00	250	—	—

KM# 12   10 PENNIA
Copper

Date	F	VF	XF	Unc	BU
1889-1891	5.00	15.00	75.00	250	—

KM# 14   10 PENNIA
12.8000 g., Copper, 30 mm. **Obv:** Monogram of Nicholas II **Rev:** Value and date in wreath

Date	F	VF	XF	Unc	BU
1895-1917	0.50	1.00	3.00	10.00	—

KM# 6.1   25 PENNIA
1.2747 g., 0.7500 Silver .0307 oz. ASW **Note:** Dotted border; varieties exist.

Date	F	VF	XF	Unc	BU
1865-1871	10.00	30.00	75.00	150	—

KM# 6.2   25 PENNIA
1.2747 g., 0.7500 Silver .0307 oz. ASW, 16 mm. **Obv:** Coat of arms **Rev:** Value and date in wreath **Note:** Dentilated border.

Date	F	VF	XF	Unc	BU
1872-1917	0.50	0.75	1.00	1.50	—

KM# 2.1   50 PENNIA
2.5495 g., 0.7500 Silver .0615 oz. ASW **Note:** Dotted border.

Date	F	VF	XF	Unc	BU
1864-1871	3.00	15.00	100	200	—

KM# 2.2   50 PENNIA
2.5494 g., 0.7500 Silver .0615 oz. ASW, 18.6 mm. **Obv:** Coat of arms **Rev:** Value and date in wreath **Note:** Dentilated border.

Date	F	VF	XF	Unc	BU
1872-1917	0.80	1.00	1.50	2.50	—

KM# 3.1   MARKKA
5.1828 g., 0.8680 Silver .1446 oz. ASW **Note:** Dotted border; varieties exist.

Date	F	VF	XF	Unc	BU
1864-1867	7.00	12.00	35.00	100	—

KM# 3.2   MARKKA
5.1828 g., 0.8680 Silver .1446 oz. ASW, 24 mm. **Obv:** Coat of arms, fineness around (text in Finnish) **Note:** Obverse text translates to: "94.48 pieces from one pound of fine silver." Dentilated border.

Date	F	VF	XF	Unc	BU
1872-1915	5.00	7.00	10.00	12.00	—

KM# 7.1   2 MARKKAA
10.3657 g., 0.8680 Silver .2893 oz. ASW **Note:** Dotted border.

Date	F	VF	XF	Unc	BU
1865-1870	15.00	20.00	75.00	250	—

KM# 7.2   2 MARKKAA
10.3657 g., 0.8680 Silver .2893 oz. ASW, 27.5 mm. **Obv:** Coat of arms, fineness around (Finnish text) **Note:** Obverse text translates to: "47.24 pieces from one pound of fine silver." Dentilated border.

Date	F	VF	XF	Unc	BU
1872-1908	12.00	17.00	50.00	75.00	—

KM# 8.1 10 MARKKAA
3.2258 g., 0.9000 Gold .0933 oz. AGW **Obv:** Narrow eagle **Note:** Regal issues; similar to 20 Markkaa, KM#9.2.

Date	F	VF	XF	Unc	BU
1878	100	150	175	200	—

KM# 8.2 10 MARKKAA
3.2258 g., 0.9000 Gold .0933 oz. AGW, 18.9 mm. **Obv:** Wide eagle coat of arms **Rev:** Value and date, fineness around **Note:** Regal issues; similar to 20 Markkaa, KM#9.2.

Date	F	VF	XF	Unc	BU
1879-1913	100	150	175	200	—

KM# 9.1 20 MARKKAA
6.4516 g., 0.9000 Gold .1867 oz. AGW **Obv:** Narrow eagle **Note:** Regal issues; similar to 10 Markkaa, KM#8.1.

Date	F	VF	XF	Unc	BU
1878	150	180	220	270	—

KM# 9.2 20 MARKKAA
6.4516 g., 0.9000 Gold .1867 oz. AGW, 21.3 mm. **Obv:** Wide eagle coat of arms **Rev:** Value and date, fineness around **Note:** Regal issues.

Date	F	VF	XF	Unc	BU
1879-1913	150	180	200	220	—

CIVIL WAR COINAGE
Kerenski Government Issue
KM# 16 PENNI
1.2800 g., Copper, 15 mm.

Date	F	VF	XF	Unc	BU
1917	0.25	0.75	1.00	1.50	—

KM# 17 5 PENNIA
6.4000 g., Copper, 25 mm.

Date	F	VF	XF	Unc	BU
1917	0.30	0.75	3.00	7.00	—

KM# 18 10 PENNIA
12.8000 g., Copper, 30 mm.

Date	F	VF	XF	Unc	BU
1917	0.50	1.00	4.00	10.00	—

KM# 19 25 PENNIA
1.2747 g., 0.7500 Silver .0307 oz. ASW, 16 mm. **Obv:** Crown above eagle removed

Date	F	VF	XF	Unc	BU
1917	—	BV	1.00	1.50	—

KM# 20 50 PENNIA
2.5494 g., 0.7500 Silver .0615 oz. ASW, 18.6 mm. **Obv:** Crown above eagle removed

Date	F	VF	XF	Unc	BU
1917	—	BV	1.25	2.00	—

CIVIL WAR COINAGE
Liberated Finnish Government Issue

KM# 21.1 5 PENNIA
2.5000 g., Copper **Obv:** Wreath knot centered between 9 and 1 of date

Date	F	VF	XF	Unc	BU
1918	20.00	30.00	45.00	60.00	—

KM# 21.2 5 PENNIA
2.5000 g., Copper **Obv:** Wreath knot above second 1 in 1918

Date	F	VF	XF	Unc	BU
1918	50.00	100	175	350	—

REPUBLIC
DECIMAL COINAGE

KM# 23 PENNI
1.0000 g., Copper, 14 mm.

Date	F	VF	XF	Unc	BU
1919-1924	0.25	0.65	1.75	3.00	—

KM# 22 5 PENNIA
2.5000 g., Copper, 18 mm.

Date	F	VF	XF	Unc	BU
1918-1940	0.10	0.25	1.00	3.00	—

KM# 64.1 5 PENNIA
1.2700 g., Copper, 16 mm. **Note:** Punched center hole.

Date	F	VF	XF	Unc	BU
1941-1943	0.10	0.20	0.50	1.25	—

KM# 64.2   5 PENNIA

Copper, 16 mm.   **Note:** Without punched center hole. These issues were not authorized by the government and any that exist were illegally removed from the mint.

Date	F	VF	XF	Unc	BU
1941-1943	25.00	30.00	70.00	100	—

KM# 24   10 PENNIA

5.0000 g., Copper, 22 mm.

Date	F	VF	XF	Unc	BU
1919-1940	0.10	0.25	0.50	3.50	—

KM# 33.1   10 PENNIA

2.5500 g., Copper, 18.5 mm.

Date	F	VF	XF	Unc	BU
1941-1943	0.10	0.25	0.50	1.25	—

KM# 33.2   10 PENNIA

2.6000 g., Copper, 18.5 mm.   **Note:** Without punched center hole. These issues were not authorized by the government and any that exist were illegally removed from the mint.

Date	F	VF	XF	Unc	BU
1941-1943	20.00	30.00	50.00	75.00	—

KM# 34.1   10 PENNIA

1.1200 g., Iron, 16 mm.   **Note:** Reduced planchet size.

Date	F	VF	XF	Unc	BU
1943-1945	0.10	0.25	1.00	5.00	—

KM# 34.2   10 PENNIA

Iron   **Note:** Without punched center hole. These issues were not authorized by the government and any that exist were illegally removed from the mint.

Date	F	VF	XF	Unc	BU
1943-1945	30.00	50.00	70.00	100	—

KM# 25   25 PENNIA

1.2700 g., Copper-Nickel, 16 mm.

Date	F	VF	XF	Unc	BU
1921-1940	0.10	0.25	0.75	2.00	—

KM# 25a   25 PENNIA

1.2700 g., Copper, 16 mm.

Date	F	VF	XF	Unc	BU
1940-1943	0.10	0.35	2.00	5.00	—

KM# 25b   25 PENNIA

Iron, 16 mm.

Date	F	VF	XF	Unc	BU
1943-1945	0.15	0.50	2.00	8.00	—

KM# 26   50 PENNIA

2.5500 g., Copper-Nickel, 18.5 mm.

Date	F	VF	XF	Unc	BU
1921-1940	0.15	0.25	1.00	3.00	—

KM# 26a   50 PENNIA

2.5500 g., Copper, 18.5 mm.

Date	F	VF	XF	Unc	BU
1940-1943	0.15	0.40	3.00	8.00	—

KM# 26b   50 PENNIA

2.2500 g., Iron, 18.5 mm.

Date	F	VF	XF	Unc	BU
1943-1948	0.15	0.40	3.00	12.00	—

KM# 27   MARKKA

5.1000 g., Copper-Nickel, 24 mm.

Date	F	VF	XF	Unc	BU
1921-1924	1.00	2.00	3.00	10.00	—

KM# 30   MARKKA

4.0000 g., Copper-Nickel, 21 mm.   **Note:** Reduced size.

Date	F	VF	XF	Unc	BU
1928-1940	0.15	1.00	3.00	6.00	—

KM# 30a   MARKKA

4.0000 g., Copper, 21 mm.

Date	F	VF	XF	Unc	BU
1940-1951	0.15	0.50	2.00	8.00	—

KM# 30b   MARKKA

3.5000 g., Iron, 21 mm.

Date	F	VF	XF	Unc	BU
1943-1952	0.15	0.25	2.00	7.00	—

KM# 36   MARKKA

1.1500 g., Iron, 16 mm.

Date	F	VF	XF	Unc	BU
1952-1953	0.15	0.35	1.00	7.00	—

KM# 36a   MARKKA

1.1500 g., Nickel Plated Iron, 16 mm.

Date	F	VF	XF	Unc	BU
1953-1962	0.10	0.10	0.25	0.50	—

KM# 31   5 MARKKAA

4.5000 g., Aluminum-Bronze, 23 mm.

Date	F	VF	XF	Unc	BU
1928-1946	1.00	2.00	10.00	20.00	—

KM# 31a 5 MARKKAA
4.5500 g., Brass, 23 mm.

Date	F	VF	XF	Unc	BU
1946-1952	0.50	1.00	2.00	5.00	—

KM# 39 20 MARKKAA
4.5000 g., Aluminum-Bronze, 25.5 mm.

Date	F	VF	XF	Unc	BU
1952-1962	0.15	0.50	2.00	8.00	—

KM# 37 5 MARKKAA
2.5500 g., Iron, 18 mm.

Date	F	VF	XF	Unc	BU
1952-1953	0.20	0.35	2.00	8.00	—

KM# 37a 5 MARKKAA
2.5500 g., Nickel Plated Iron, 18 mm.

Date	F	VF	XF	Unc	BU
1953-1962	0.10	0.20	0.50	3.00	—

KM# 40 50 MARKKAA
5.5000 g., Aluminum-Bronze, 25 mm.

Date	F	VF	XF	Unc	BU
1952-1962	0.25	0.50	3.00	10.00	—

KM# 63 10 MARKKAA
8.0000 g., Aluminum-Bronze, 27 mm.

Date	F	VF	XF	Unc	BU
1928-1939	1.00	2.50	10.00	60.00	—

KM# 28 100 MARKKAA
4.2105 g., 0.9000 Gold .1218 oz. AGW, 18.5 mm.

Date	F	VF	XF	Unc	BU
1926	—	950	1,150	1,300	—

KM# 38 10 MARKKAA
3.0000 g., Aluminum-Bronze, 20 mm.

Date	F	VF	XF	Unc	BU
1952-1962	0.15	0.35	1.00	5.00	—

KM# 41 100 MARKKAA
5.2000 g., 0.5000 Silver .0836 oz. ASW, 24 mm.

Date	F	VF	XF	Unc	BU
1956-1960	—	BV	1.50	3.00	—

KM# 32 20 MARKKAA
13.0000 g., Aluminum-Bronze, 31 mm.

Date	F	VF	XF	Unc	BU
1931-1939	1.00	2.00	6.00	20.00	—

KM# 29 200 MARKKAA
8.4210 g., 0.9000 Gold .2436 oz. AGW, 22.5 mm.

Date	F	VF	XF	Unc	BU
1926	—	1,300	1,800	2,000	—

KM# 42 200 MARKKAA
8.3000 g., 0.5000 Silver .1334 oz. ASW, 27.5 mm.

Date	F	VF	XF	Unc	BU
1956-1959	—	BV	3.00	7.00	—

KM# 35 500 MARKKAA
12.0000 g., 0.5000 Silver .1929 oz. ASW, 32 mm.

Date	F	VF	XF	Unc	BU
1951-1952	20.00	28.00	40.00	50.00	—

KM# 43 1000 MARKKAA
14.0000 g., 0.8750 Silver .3938 oz. ASW, 30 mm. **Subject:** Markka Currency System Centennial - Snellman

Date	F	VF	XF	Unc	BU
1960	7.00	10.00	20.00	30.00	—

REFORM COINAGE
100 Old Markka = 1 New Markka 1963

KM# 44 PENNI
1.6000 g., Copper, 15.8 mm.

Date	F	VF	XF	Unc	BU
1963-1969	—	0.15	0.25	1.50	—

KM# 44a PENNI
0.4500 g., Aluminum, 15.8 mm.

Date	F	VF	XF	Unc	BU
1969-1979	—	—	0.20	0.50	—

KM# 45 5 PENNIA
2.6000 g., Copper, 18.5 mm.

Date	F	VF	XF	Unc	BU
1963-1977	0.50	0.10	0.25	1.00	—

KM# 45a 5 PENNIA
0.8000 g., Aluminum, 18 mm.

Date	F	VF	XF	Unc	BU
1977-1990	—	0.20	0.15	0.15	—

KM# 46 10 PENNIA
3.0000 g., Aluminum-Bronze, 20 mm.

Date	F	VF	XF	Unc	BU
1963-1982	0.15	0.15	0.10	0.50	—

KM# 46a 10 PENNIA
1.0000 g., Aluminum, 20 mm.

Date	F	VF	XF	Unc	BU
1983-1990	—	—	0.10	0.50	—

KM# 65 10 PENNIA
1.8000 g., Copper-Nickel, 16.3 mm. **Obv:** Flower pods and stems

Date	F	VF	XF	Unc	BU
1990-2001	—	—	0.10	0.15	—

KM# 47 20 PENNIA
4.5000 g., Aluminum-Bronze, 22.5 mm.

Date	F	VF	XF	Unc	BU
1963-1990	0.10	0.15	0.20	0.50	—

KM# 48 50 PENNIA
5.5000 g., Aluminum-Bronze, 25.0 mm.

Date	F	VF	XF	Unc	BU
1963-1990	0.25	0.20	0.25	1.00	—

KM# 66   50 PENNIA
3.3000 g., Copper-Nickel, 19.7 mm.   **Obv:** Polar bear

Date	F	VF	XF	Unc	BU
1990-2001	—	—	0.20	0.75	—

KM# 49   MARKKA
6.4000 g., 0.3500 Silver .0720 oz. ASW, 24 mm.   **Edge Lettering:** SUOMI FINLAND

Date	F	VF	XF	Unc	BU
1964-1968	—	BV	1.50	3.00	—

KM# 49a   MARKKA
6.1000 g., Copper-Nickel, 24 mm.   **Edge Lettering:** SUOMI FINLAND

Date	F	VF	XF	Unc	BU
1969-1993	0.25	0.35	0.35	0.75	—

KM# 76   MARKKA
4.9000 g., Aluminum-Bronze, 22 mm.

Date	F	VF	XF	Unc	BU
1993-2001	—	—	0.35	0.75	—

KM# 106   MARKKA
6.1000 g., Copper-Nickel, 24 mm.   **Subject:** Remembrance Markka   **Obv:** National arms   **Rev:** Denomination and pine tree   **Edge:** Plain   **Note:** This coin is encased in acrylic resin and sealed in a display card.

Date	F	VF	XF	Unc	BU
2001	—	—	—	5.00	6.50

KM# 95   MARKKA
8.6400 g., 0.7500 Gold .2083 oz. AGW, 22 mm.   **Subject:** Last Markka Coin   **Obv:** National arms   **Rev:** Stylized tree with roots   **Edge:** Reeded

Date	F	VF	XF	Unc	BU
2001 Proof	Value: 200				

KM# 53   5 MARKKAA
8.0000 g., Aluminum-Bronze, 26.3 mm.   **Obv:** Icebreaker "Varma"   **Edge Lettering:** REPUBLIKEN FINLAND SUOMEN TASAVALTA

Date	F	VF	XF	Unc	BU
1972-1978	1.50	1.25	2.00	3.00	—

KM# 57   5 MARKKAA
8.0000 g., Aluminum-Bronze, 26.3 mm.   **Obv:** Icebreaker "Urho"

Date	F	VF	XF	Unc	BU
1979-1993	—	1.50	1.50	2.25	—

KM# 73   5 MARKKAA
5.5000 g., Copper-Aluminum-Nickel, 24.5 mm.   **Obv:** Lake Saimaa ringed seal

Date	F	VF	XF	Unc	BU
1992-2001	—	—	2.00	2.00	4.00

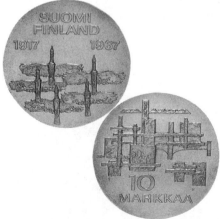

KM# 50   10 MARKKAA
23.7500 g., 0.9000 Silver .6872 oz. ASW, 35 mm.   **Subject:** 50th Anniversary of Independence   **Obv:** Five Whooper swans in flight   **Edge Lettering:** ITSENAINEN SUOMI 50 FINLAND SJALVSTANDIGT 50

Date	F	VF	XF	Unc	BU
1967	—	—	BV	8.00	9.00

KM# 51   10 MARKKAA

22.7500 g., 0.5000 Silver .3657 oz. ASW, 35 mm. **Subject:** Centennial - Birth of President Paasikivi

Date	F	VF	XF	Unc	BU
1970	—	—	BV	5.00	6.00

KM# 52   10 MARKKAA

24.2000 g., 0.5000 Silver .3890 oz. ASW, 35 mm. **Subject:** 10th European Athletic Championships

Date	F	VF	XF	Unc	BU
1971	—	—	BV	5.00	6.00

KM# 54   10 MARKKAA

23.5000 g., 0.5000 Silver .3778 oz. ASW, 35 mm. **Subject:** 75th Birthday of President Kekkonen

Date	F	VF	XF	Unc	BU
1975	—	—	BV	5.00	6.00

KM# 55   10 MARKKAA

21.7800 g., 0.5000 Silver .3501 oz. ASW, 35 mm. **Subject:** 60th Anniversary of Independence

Date	F	VF	XF	Unc	BU
1977	—	—	BV	5.00	6.00

KM# 77   10 MARKKAA

8.8000 g., Bi-Metallic Brass center in Copper-Nickel ring, 27.25 mm. **Obv:** Capercaillie bird

Date	F	VF	XF	Unc	BU
1993-2001	—	—	2.00	3.50	4.50

KM# 82   10 MARKKAA

8.0000 g., Bi-Metallic Brass center in Copper-Nickel ring, 27.25 mm. **Subject:** European Unity **Obv:** Swan in flight

Date	F	VF	XF	Unc	BU
1995	—	—	2.50	4.50	6.00

KM# 82a   10 MARKKAA

Bi-Metallic Gold center in Silver ring, 27.25 mm. **Subject:** European Unity **Obv:** Swan in flight **Note:** Total weight 12.200 grams.

Date	F	VF	XF	Unc	BU
1995 Proof		Value: 2,500			

KM# 91   10 MARKKAA

8.8200 g., Bi-Metallic Copper-Nickel center in Brass ring, 27.25 mm. **Obv:** Fire breathing face **Rev:** Denomination, pine branch **Note:** Finnish Presidency of the EU.

Date	F	VF	XF	Unc	BU
1999	—	—	7.50	10.00	—

KM# 91a   10 MARKKAA

13.2000 g., Bi-Metallic Gold And Silver **Ring Composition:** 0.7500 Gold **Center Composition:** 0.9250 Silver, 27.25 mm. **Edge:** Lettered **Note:** Total weight 13.200 grams.

Date	F	VF	XF	Unc	BU
1999	—	—	—	1,000	1,150

KM# 56   25 MARKKAA

26.3000 g., 0.5000 Silver .4228 oz. ASW, 37 mm. **Subject:** Winter Games in Lahti

Date	F	VF	XF	Unc	BU
1978	—	—	6.00	7.00	—

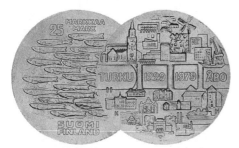

KM# 58   25 MARKKAA
26.3000 g., 0.5000 Silver .4228 oz. ASW, 37 mm. **Subject:** 750th Anniversary of Turku

Date	F	VF	XF	Unc	BU
1979	—	—	6.00	7.00	10.00

KM# 85   25 MARKKAA
20.2000 g., Bi-Metallic Brass center in Copper-Nickel ring, 35 mm. **Subject:** 80th Anniversary of Independence **Obv:** Stylized landscape **Rev:** Stylized city view

Date	F	VF	XF	Unc	BU
ND(1997)	—	—	10.00	12.00	—

KM# 96   25 MARKKAA
20.2000 g., Bi-Metallic Brass center in Copper-Nickel ring, 35 mm. **Subject:** First Nordic Ski Championship, "Lahti 2001" **Obv:** Stylized woman's face **Rev:** Female torso, landscape **Edge:** Plain

Date	F	VF	XF	Unc	BU
2001	—	—	—	—	25.00

KM# 59   50 MARKKAA
20.0000 g., 0.5000 Silver .3216 oz. ASW, 30 mm. **Subject:** 80th Birthday of President Kekkonen

Date	F	VF	XF	Unc	BU
1981	—	—	8.50	10.00	12.00

KM# 60   50 MARKKAA
23.1000 g., 0.5000 Silver .3698 oz. ASW, 35 mm. **Subject:** World Ice Hockey Championship Games

Date	F	VF	XF	Unc	BU
1982	—	—	10.00	12.00	15.00

KM# 61   50 MARKKAA
21.8000 g., 0.5000 Silver .3537 oz. ASW, 35 mm. **Subject:** 1st World Athletics Championships

Date	F	VF	XF	Unc	BU
1983	—	—	10.00	12.00	15.00

KM# 62   50 MARKKAA
19.9000 g., 0.5000 Silver .3216 oz. ASW, 35 mm. **Subject:** National Epic - The Kalevala

Date	F	VF	XF	Unc	BU
1985	—	—	13.00	15.00	18.00

KM# 75   100 MARKKAA
24.0000 g., 0.8300 Silver .6405 oz. ASW **Subject:** Pictorial Arts of Finland

Date	F	VF	XF	Unc	BU
1989	—	—	25.00	35.00	42.50

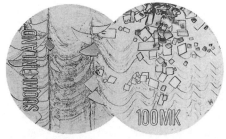

KM# 67 100 MARKKAA
24.0000 g., 0.8300 Silver .6405 oz. ASW **Subject:** 50th
Anniversary of Disabled War Veterans Association

Date	F	VF	XF	Unc	BU
1990	—	—	25.00	35.00	40.00

KM# 71 100 MARKKAA
24.0000 g., 0.9250 Silver .7137 oz. ASW **Subject:** 75th
Anniversary of Independence

Date	F	VF	XF	Unc	BU
1992	—	—	20.00	22.50	25.00

KM# 68 100 MARKKAA
24.0000 g., 0.8300 Silver .6405 oz. ASW **Subject:** 350th
Anniversary - University of Helsinki

Date	F	VF	XF	Unc	BU
1990	—	—	25.00	45.00	60.00

KM# 78 100 MARKKAA
24.0000 g., 0.9250 Silver .7137 oz. ASW **Subject:** Stadium of
Friendship

Date	F	VF	XF	Unc	BU
1994	—	—	—	22.50	25.00

KM# 69 100 MARKKAA
24.0000 g., 0.8300 Silver .6405 oz. ASW **Subject:** Ice Hockey
World Championship Games

Date	F	VF	XF	Unc	BU
1991	—	—	25.00	35.00	40.00

KM# 80 100 MARKKAA
24.0000 g., 0.9250 Silver .7137 oz. ASW **Subject:** 100th Birthday
- Artturi Ilmari Virtanen

Date	F	VF	XF	Unc	BU
1995	—	—	30.00	35.00	40.00

KM# 70 100 MARKKAA
24.0000 g., 0.9250 Silver .7137 oz. ASW **Subject:** 70th
Anniversary - Autonomy of Aland

Date	F	VF	XF	Unc	BU
1991	—	—	25.00	35.00	40.00

KM# 81 100 MARKKAA
24.0000 g., 0.9250 Silver .7137 oz. ASW **Subject:** 50th
Anniversary - United Nations

Date	F	VF	XF	Unc	BU
1995	—	—	—	35.00	40.00

KM# 83   100 MARKKAA
24.0000 g., 0.9250 Silver .7137 oz. ASW **Subject:** Helene
Schjerfbeck - Painter - 50th Anniversary of Her Death

Date	F	VF	XF	Unc	BU
1996	—	—	—	60.00	75.00

KM# 89   100 MARKKAA
22.0000 g., 0.9250 Silver .6543 oz. ASW **Subject:** Jean Sibelius
- Composer **Obv:** Finlandia musical score **Rev:** Sibelius head left

Date	F	VF	XF	Unc	BU
1999	—	—	30.00	35.00	40.00

KM# 84   100 MARKKAA
22.0000 g., 0.9250 Silver .6543 oz. ASW **Subject:** 100th Birthday
- Paavo Nurmi **Obv:** Two gymnasts **Rev:** Facial portrait and
running Paavo Nurmi

Date	F	VF	XF	Unc	BU
1997	—	—	30.00	35.00	40.00

KM# 92   100 MARKKAA
22.0000 g., 0.9250 Silver .6543 oz. ASW **Subject:** Jubilee Year
2000 **Obv:** Turku Cathedral vault ceiling design **Rev:** Leaf **Edge:**
Plain

Date	F	VF	XF	Unc	BU
2000	—	—	35.00	50.00	60.00

KM# 87   100 MARKKAA
22.0000 g., 0.9250 Silver .6543 oz. ASW **Subject:** 100th Birthday
- Alvar Aalto **Obv:** Walls above cliffs and denominations **Rev:**
Mature rye plants

Date	F	VF	XF	Unc	BU
1998	—	—	—	25.00	30.00

KM# 93   100 MARKKAA
22.0000 g., 0.9250 Silver .6543 oz. ASW **Subject:** 450th
Anniversary - Helsinki Cultural Capital **Obv:** Symbolic column
design **Rev:** Carved city view **Edge:** Plain

Date	F	VF	XF	Unc	BU
2000	—	—	35.00	50.00	60.00

KM# 88   100 MARKKAA
22.0000 g., 0.9250 Silver .6543 oz. ASW **Subject:** Suomenlinna
Fortress **Obv:** Stylized island view **Rev:** Sailship and fortress gate

Date	F	VF	XF	Unc	BU
1998	—	—	25.00	30.00	35.00

KM# 94   100 MARKKAA
22.0000 g., 0.9250 Silver .6543 oz. ASW, 35 mm. **Subject:**
Aleksis Kivi **Obv:** Books on shelves **Rev:** Portrait on partial disc
Edge: Plain

Date	F	VF	XF	Unc	BU
2000	—	—	—	35.00	50.00

Finland

KM# 97   100 MARKKAA
31.0000 g., 0.9250 Silver 0.9219 oz. ASW, 35 mm. **Subject:** Aino Ackte **Obv:** Partial portrait **Rev:** High heel shoe and trouser bottom **Edge:** Plain

Date	F	VF	XF	Unc	BU
2001	—	—	—	35.00	40.00

KM# 72   1000 MARKKAA
9.0000 g., 0.9000 Gold .2604 oz. AGW, 22.1 mm. **Subject:** 75th Anniversary of Independence

Date	F	VF	XF	Unc	BU
1992	—	—	—	200	250

KM# 86   1000 MARKKAA
8.6400 g., 0.9000 Gold .2500 oz. AGW **Subject:** 80th Anniversary of Independence **Obv:** New shoot growing from tree stump **Rev:** Symbolic design separating dates

Date	F	VF	XF	Unc	BU
ND (1997) Proof		Value: 330			

KM# 90   1000 MARKKAA
8.6400 g., 0.9000 Gold .2500 oz. AGW **Subject:** Jean Sibelius - Composer **Obv:** Sibelius head left **Rev:** Finlandia musical score, denomination above, date below

Date	F	VF	XF	Unc	BU
1999 Proof		Value: 350			

KM# 79   2000 MARKKAA
16.9700 g., 0.9000 Gold .4910 oz. AGW, 28 mm. **Subject:** 50 Years of Peace

Date	F	VF	XF	Unc	BU
1995 Proof		Value: 700			

EURO COINAGE
European Economic Community Issues

KM# 98   EURO CENT
2.2700 g., Copper Plated Steel, 16.3 mm. **Obv:** Rampant lion surrounded by stars **Rev:** Value and globe **Edge:** Plain

Date	F	VF	XF	Unc	BU
1999-2005	—	—	—	1.25	—

KM# 99   2 EURO CENTS
3.0000 g., Copper Plated Steel, 18.7 mm. **Obv:** Rampant lion surrounded by stars **Rev:** Value and globe **Edge:** Grooved

Date	F	VF	XF	Unc	BU
1999-2005	—	—	—	1.25	—

KM# 100   5 EURO CENTS
3.8600 g., Copper Plated Steel, 21.2 mm. **Obv:** Rampant lion surrounded by stars **Rev:** Value and globe **Edge:** Plain

Date	F	VF	XF	Unc	BU
1999-2005	—	—	—	0.50	—

KM# 101   10 EURO CENTS
4.0000 g., Brass, 19.7 mm. **Obv:** Rampant lion surrounded by stars **Rev:** Value and map **Edge:** Reeded

Date	F	VF	XF	Unc	BU
1999-2005	—	—	—	1.25	—

KM# 102   20 EURO CENTS
5.7300 g., Brass, 22.2 mm. **Obv:** Rampant lion surrounded by stars **Rev:** Value and map **Edge:** Notched

Date	F	VF	XF	Unc	BU
1999-2005	—	—	—	1.25	—

Finland

KM# 103 50 EURO CENTS
7.8100 g., Brass, 24.2 mm. **Obv:** Rampant lion surrounded by stars **Rev:** Value and map **Edge:** Reeded

Date	F	VF	XF	Unc	BU
1999-2005	—	—	—	1.50	—

KM# 104 EURO
7.5000 g., Bi-Metallic Copper-nickel center in Brass ring, 23.2 mm. **Obv:** 2 flying swans surrounded by stars on outer ring **Rev:** Value and map **Edge:** Reeded and plain sections

Date	F	VF	XF	Unc	BU
1999-2005	—	—	—	3.00	—

KM# 105 2 EURO
8.5200 g., Bi-Metallic Brass center in Copper-nickel ring, 25.6 mm. **Obv:** 2 cloudberry flowers surrounded by stars on outer ring **Rev:** Value and map **Edge:** Reeded and lettered **Edge Lettering:** SUOMI FINLAND

Date	F	VF	XF	Unc	BU
1999-2005	—	—	—	4.00	—

KM# 114 2 EURO
8.5200 g., Bi-Metallic, 25.6 mm. **Obv:** Stylized flower **Rev:** Value and map **Edge:** Reeded and lettered

Date	F	VF	XF	Unc	BU
2004	—	—	—	10.00	11.50

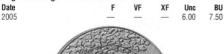

KM# 119 2 EURO
8.5200 g., Bi-Metallic Brass center in Copper-Nickel ring, 25.6 mm. **Subject:** 60th Anniversary - Finland - UN **Obv:** Dove on a puzzle **Rev:** Value over map **Edge:** Reeded and lettered **Edge Lettering:** "YK 1945-2005 FN"

Date	F	VF	XF	Unc	BU
2005	—	—	—	6.00	7.50

KM# 111 5 EURO
20.1000 g., Bi-Metallic Copper-Nickel center in Brass ring, 34.9 mm. **Subject:** Ice Hockey World Championships **Obv:** Summer landscape **Rev:** Three hockey sticks and a puck **Edge:** Plain

Date	F	VF	XF	Unc	BU
2003	—	—	—	15.00	20.00

KM# 118 5 EURO
19.8000 g., Bi-Metallic Brass center in Copper-Nickel ring, 35 mm. **Obv:** Female javelin thrower **Rev:** Running feet **Edge:** Plain

Date	F	VF	XF	Unc	BU
2005	—	—	—	15.00	20.00

KM# 123 5 EURO
18.7000 g., Copper, 35 mm. **Subject:** 150th Anniversary - Demilitarization of Aland **Obv:** Boat, Dove of Peace on the helm **Rev:** Tree **Edge Lettering:** AHVENANMAAN DEMILITARISOINTI 150 VUOTTA*

Date	F	VF	XF	Unc	BU
2006	—	—	—	20.00	25.00

KM# 107 10 EURO
27.4000 g., 0.9250 Silver 0.8149 oz. ASW, 38.6 mm. **Subject:** 50th Anniversary - Helsinki Olympics **Obv:** Flames and denomination above globe with map of Finland **Rev:** Tower and partial coin design **Edge:** Plain

Date	F	VF	XF	Unc	BU
2002	—	—	—	28.00	30.00

KM# 108   10 EURO

27.4000 g., 0.9250 Silver 0.803 oz. ASW, 38.6 mm. **Subject:**
Elias Lönnrot **Obv:** Ribbon with stars **Rev:** Quill and signature
Edge: Plain

Date	F	VF	XF	Unc	BU
2002	—	—	—	28.00	30.00

KM# 110   10 EURO

27.4000 g., 0.9250 Silver 0.8327 oz. ASW, 38.6 mm. **Subject:**
Anders Chydenius **Obv:** Stylized design **Rev:** Name and book
Edge: Plain

Date	F	VF	XF	Unc	BU
2003	—	—	—	32.00	35.00

KM# 112   10 EURO

27.4000 g., 0.9250 Silver 0.8149 oz. ASW, 38.6 mm. **Subject:**
Mannerheim and St. Petersburg **Obv:** Fortress **Rev:** Carl Gustaf
Emil Mannerheim

Date	F	VF	XF	Unc	BU
2003	—	—	—	35.00	37.50

KM# 115   10 EURO

27.4000 g., 0.9250 Silver 0.8149 oz. ASW, 38.6 mm. **Subject:**
200th Birthday of Johan Ludwig Runeberg **Obv:** Head of Runeberg
Rev: Text of 1831 Helsingfors Tidningar newspaper

Date	F	VF	XF	Unc	BU
2004	—	—	—	32.00	35.00

KM# 116   10 EURO

27.4000 g., 0.9250 Silver 0.8149 oz. ASW, 38.6 mm. **Subject:** Tove
Jansson **Obv:** Three "muumi" figures **Rev:** Head of Tove Jansson

Date	F	VF	XF	Unc	BU
2004	—	—	—	32.00	35.00

KM# 120   10 EURO

25.5000 g., 0.9250 Silver 0.7584 oz. ASW **Subject:** 60 years of
Peace **Obv:** Dove of peace **Rev:** Flowering plant

Date	F	VF	XF	Unc	BU
2005	—	—	—	32.00	35.00

KM# 122   10 EURO

25.5000 g., 0.9250 Silver 0.7584 oz. ASW **Subject:** Unknown
Soldier and Finnish Film Art **Obv:** Trench **Rev:** Soldier with helmet
on top of a film

Date	F	VF	XF	Unc	BU
2005	—	—	—	35.00	37.50

KM# 124   10 EURO

25.5000 g., 0.9250 Silver 0.7584 oz. ASW **Subject:** 200th
Birthday - Johan Vilhelm Snellman **Obv:** Sun rising over the lake
Rev: Snellman

Date	F	VF	XF	Unc	BU
2006	—	—	—	32.00	35.00

KM# 121   20 EURO

1.7300 g., 0.9000 Gold 0.0501 oz. AGW **Subject:** 10th
Anniversary - IAAF World Championships in Athletics **Obv:**
Helsinki Stadium **Rev:** Two faces

Date	F	VF	XF	Unc	BU
2005 Proof		Value: 100			

KM# 113   50 EURO

13.2000 g., Bi-Metallic Gold And Silver **Ring Composition:**
0.9250 Silver **Center Composition:** 0.7500 Gold, 27.25 mm.
Subject: Finnish art and design

Date	F	VF	XF	Unc	BU
2003 Proof		Value: 300			

KM# 109   100 EURO

8.6400 g., 0.9000 Gold 0.25 oz. AGW, 22 mm. **Subject:** Lapland
Obv: Small tree and mountain stream **Rev:** Lake landscape
beneath the midnight sun **Edge:** Plain with serial number

Date	F	VF	XF	Unc	BU
2002 Proof		Value: 225			

KM# 117   100 EURO

8.6400 g., 0.9000 Gold 0.25 oz. AGW, 22 mm. **Subject:** 150th
Birthday of Albert Edelfelt **Obv:** Flower **Rev:** Head of Edelfelt

Date	F	VF	XF	Unc	BU
2004 Proof		Value: 280			

German States

ANHALT-BERNBURG

Located in north-central Germany. Appeared as part of the patrimony of Albrecht the Bear of Brandenburg in 1170. Bracteates were first made in the 12th century. It was originally in the inheritance of Heinrich the Fat in 1252 and became extinct in 1468. The division of 1603, among the sons of Joachim Ernst, revitalized Anhalt-Bernburg. Bernburg passed to Dessau after the death of Alexander Carl in 1863.

DUCHY
REGULAR COINAGE

KM# 85   1/6 THALER
5.3400 g., 0.5200 Silver .0892 oz. ASW **Ruler:** Alexander Carl
Obv: Crowned bear walking right on wall **Rev. Inscription:**
6/EINEN/THALER in sprays

Date	F	VF	XF	Unc	BU
1856	10.00	15.00	30.00	50.00	75.00

KM# 87   1/6 THALER
5.3400 g., 0.5200 Silver .0892 oz. ASW **Ruler:** Alexander Carl
Obv: Crowned bear walking right on wall

Date	F	VF	XF	Unc	BU
1861-1862	5.00	10.00	25.00	40.00	55.00

KM# 84   THALER
22.2700 g., 0.7500 Silver .5370 oz. ASW **Ruler:** Alexander Carl
Rev: Crowned bear walking right on wall **Note:** Dav. #504.

Date	F	VF	XF	Unc	BU
1846-1855	20.00	40.00	70.00	130	165

KM# 86   THALER
18.5200 g., 0.9000 Silver .5358 oz. ASW **Ruler:** Alexander Carl
Obv: Head of Alexander Carl left **Rev:** Crowned arms with bear supporters **Note:** Vereins Thaler. Dav. #505.

Date	F	VF	XF	Unc	BU
1859	35.00	60.00	140	350	600

KM# 88   THALER
18.5200 g., 0.9000 Silver .5358 oz. ASW **Ruler:** Alexander Carl
Rev: Crowned bear walking right on wall **Note:** Mining Thaler. Dav. #506.

Date	F	VF	XF	Unc	BU
1861-1862	25.00	40.00	70.00	130	180

KM# 83   2 THALER (3-1/2 Gulden)
37.1200 g., 0.9000 Silver 1.0741 oz. ASW **Ruler:** Alexander Carl
Obv: Bust of Alexander Carl right **Rev:** Crowned and mantled arms **Note:** Dav. #503.

Date	F	VF	XF	Unc	BU
1840-1855	350	600	800	1,200	1,600

JOINT COINAGE
Under Alexander Carl for Anhalt-Cothen and Anhalt-Dessau

KM# 96   PFENNIG
Copper **Ruler:** Alexander Carl **Obv:** Crowned arms

Date	F	VF	XF	Unc	BU
1856-1867	5.00	8.00	12.00	30.00	50.00

KM# 98   3 PFENNIGE
Copper **Ruler:** Alexander Carl **Obv:** Crowned arms

Date	F	VF	XF	Unc	BU
1861-1867	4.00	6.00	15.00	27.00	40.00

KM# 95   SILBERGROSCHEN
2.1900 g., 0.2220 Silver .0156 oz. ASW **Ruler:** Alexander Carl
Obv: Crowned arms

Date	F	VF	XF	Unc	BU
1851-1862	3.00	6.00	14.00	25.00	45.00

KM# 97   2-1/2 SILBERGROSCHEN
3.2400 g., 0.3750 Silver .0390 oz. ASW **Ruler:** Alexander Carl
Obv: Crowned arms

Date	F	VF	XF	Unc	BU
1856-1864	5.00	8.00	20.00	45.00	75.00

ANHALT-DESSAU
DUCHY
REGULAR COINAGE

KM# 19   1/6 THALER
5.3400 g., 0.5200 Silver .0892 oz. ASW **Obv:** Head of Leopold
Friedrich left **Rev:** Crowned arms

Date	F	VF	XF	Unc	BU
1865	10.00	20.00	35.00	65.00	90.00

KM# 14   THALER (Vereinsthaler)
18.5200 g., 0.9000 Silver .5359 oz. ASW **Ruler:** Leopold Friedrich
Obv: Bust of Leopold Friedrich left **Rev:** Crowned arms supported
by bears **Edge Lettering:** GOTT SEGNE ANHALT **Note:** Dav. #509.

Date	F	VF	XF	Unc	BU
1858	25.00	50.00	110	200	265

KM# 15   THALER (Vereinsthaler)
18.5200 g., 0.9000 Silver .5359 oz. ASW **Subject:** Separation of
Anhalt Duchies - 1603, Reunion of Anhalt Duchies - 1863 **Obv:**
Bust of Leopold Friedrich left **Rev:** Crowned arms in sprays **Edge
Lettering:** GOTT SEGNE ANHALT

Date	F	VF	XF	Unc	BU
1863	25.00	45.00	75.00	125	175

KM# 20   THALER (Vereinsthaler)
18.5200 g., 0.9000 Silver .5359 oz. ASW **Obv:** Bust of Leopold
Friedrich left **Rev:** Crowned arms supported by bears

Date	F	VF	XF	Unc	BU
1866-1869	30.00	50.00	100	180	230

REFOVORM COINAGE

KM# 22   2 MARK
11.1110 g., 0.9000 Silver .3215 oz. ASW **Ruler:** Friedrich I **Obv:**
Large head of Friedrich I right **Rev:** Crowned German eagle

Date	F	VF	XF	Unc	BU
1876	125	225	700	1,400	1,750

KM# 23   2 MARK
11.1110 g., 0.9000 Silver .3215 oz. ASW   **Ruler:** Friedrich I
Subject: 25th Year of Reign of Friedrich I **Obv:** Small head of
Friedrich I right **Rev:** Crowned imperial German eagle

Date	F	VF	XF	Unc	BU
1896	200	350	500	800	900

KM# 24   5 MARK
27.7770 g., 0.9000 Silver .8038 oz. ASW   **Ruler:** Friedrich I
Subject: 25th Year of Reign of Friedrich I **Obv:** Head of Friedrich
I right **Rev:** Crowned imperial German eagle

Date	F	VF	XF	Unc	BU
1896	600	1,000	1,800	2,250	3,000

KM# 27   2 MARK
11.1110 g., 0.9000 Silver .3215 oz. ASW   **Ruler:** Friedrich II **Obv:**
Head of Friedrich II left **Rev:** Crowned imperial German eagle

Date	F	VF	XF	Unc	BU
1904	150	320	550	750	1,000

KM# 29   3 MARK
16.6670 g., 0.9000 Silver .4823 oz. ASW   **Ruler:** Friedrich II **Obv:**
Head of Friedrich II left **Rev:** Crowned imperial German eagle

Date	F	VF	XF	Unc	BU
1909-1911	35.00	75.00	150	275	320

KM# 31   5 MARK
27.7770 g., 0.9000 Silver .8038 oz. ASW   **Ruler:** Friedrich II
Subject: Silver Wedding Anniversary **Obv:** Jugate heads of
Friedrich II and Marie left **Rev:** Crowned imperial German eagle

Date	F	VF	XF	Unc	BU
1914	65.00	180	285	450	500

KM# 25   10 MARK
3.9820 g., 0.9000 Gold .1152 oz. AGW   **Ruler:** Friedrich I **Obv:**
Head of Friedrich I right **Rev:** Crowned imperial German eagle

Date	F	VF	XF	Unc	BU
1896-1901	500	900	1,500	2,250	2,800

KM# 30   3 MARK
16.6670 g., 0.9000 Silver .4823 oz. ASW   **Ruler:** Friedrich II
Subject: Silver Wedding Anniversary **Obv:** Jugate heads of
Friedrich II and Marie left **Rev:** Crowned imperial German eagle

Date	F	VF	XF	Unc	BU
1914	25.00	60.00	85.00	100	130

KM# 21   20 MARK
7.9650 g., 0.9000 Gold .2304 oz. AGW   **Ruler:** Friedrich I **Obv:** Large
head of Friedrich I right **Rev:** Crowned imperial German eagle

Date	F	VF	XF	Unc	BU
1875	500	900	1,350	2,500	3,500

KM# 26 20 MARK
7.9650 g., 0.9000 Gold .2304 oz. AGW **Ruler:** Friedrich I **Obv:** Small
head of Friedrich I right **Rev:** Crowned imperial German eagle

Date	F	VF	XF	Unc	BU
1896-1901	600	900	1,600	2,000	3,000

KM# 28 20 MARK
7.9650 g., 0.9000 Gold .2304 oz. AGW **Ruler:** Friedrich II **Obv:**
Head of Friedrich II left **Rev:** Crowned imperial German eagle

Date	F	VF	XF	Unc	BU
1904	450	850	1,250	2,200	3,000

BADEN

The earliest rulers of Baden, in the southwestern part of Germany along the Rhine, descended from the dukes of Zähringen in the late 11th century. In 1515, the most significant division of the patrimony took place, in which the Baden-Baden and Baden-(Pforzheim) Durlach lines were established.

After the male line of Baden-Baden failed in 1771 and the two parts of Baden were reunited, the fortunes of the margraviate continued to grow. The ruler was given the rank of elector in 1803, only to be raised to grand duke three years later. The grand duchy came to an end in 1918, but had by this time become one of the largest states in Germany.

UNITED BADEN LINE
REGULAR COINAGE

KM# 213 1/2 KREUZER
Copper

Date	F	VF	XF	Unc	BU
1842-1852	4.00	8.00	20.00	35.00	50.00

KM# 230 1/2 KREUZER
Copper   **Ruler:** Friedrich I as Grand Duke **Obv:** Bust right

Date	F	VF	XF	Unc	BU
1856	4.00	8.00	20.00	40.00	60.00

KM# 241 1/2 KREUZER
Copper

Date	F	VF	XF	Unc	BU
1859-1871	3.00	6.00	15.00	22.00	30.00

KM# 218.2 KREUZER
Copper   **Obv:** Period after Baden

Date	F	VF	XF	Unc	BU
1847-1852	2.00	4.00	7.00	15.00	25.00

KM# 231 KREUZER
Copper   **Ruler:** Friedrich I as Prince Regent **Obv:** Bust right

Date	F	VF	XF	Unc	BU
1856	10.00	20.00	40.00	55.00	75.00

KM# 232 KREUZER
Copper   **Ruler:** Friedrich I as Grand Duke

Date	F	VF	XF	Unc	BU
1856	5.00	10.00	25.00	45.00	70.00

KM# 238 KREUZER
Copper   **Subject:** Birth of Heir

Date	F	VF	XF	Unc	BU
1857	5.00	15.00	25.00	40.00	65.00

KM# 242 KREUZER
Copper

Date	F	VF	XF	Unc	BU
1859-1871	3.00	5.00	8.00	15.00	24.00

KM# 244 KREUZER
Copper   **Subject:** Leopold Memorial

Date	F	VF	XF	Unc	BU
1861	5.00	20.00	40.00	55.00	75.00

KM# 250 KREUZER
Copper **Subject:** 50th Anniversary of Baden's Constitution

Date	F	VF	XF	Unc	BU
1868	5.00	10.00	25.00	35.00	55.00

KM# 251 KREUZER
Copper **Subject:** Church at Seckenheim

Date	F	VF	XF	Unc	BU
1869	30.00	50.00	100	160	240

KM# 252 KREUZER
Copper **Subject:** Victory in War with France

Date	F	VF	XF	Unc	BU
1871	3.00	5.00	10.00	18.00	—

KM# 253 KREUZER
Copper **Obv:** SCHEIDE MUNZE below shield

Date	F	VF	XF	Unc	BU
1871	5.00	10.00	20.00	30.00	45.00

KM# 254 KREUZER
Copper **Subject:** Buehl Commemorating Victory Over France

Date	F	VF	XF	Unc	BU
1871	45.00	75.00	125	160	220

KM# 255 KREUZER
Copper **Subject:** Karlsruhe Commemorating Victory Over France
Obv: Arms **Rev:** Legend

Date	F	VF	XF	Unc	BU
1871	7.00	15.00	20.00	50.00	75.00

KM# 256 KREUZER
Copper **Subject:** Offenburg Commemorating Victory Over France

Date	F	VF	XF	Unc	BU
1871	20.00	45.00	90.00	145	210

KM# 211 3 KREUZER
1.2990 g., 0.3330 Silver .0139 oz. ASW

Date	F	VF	XF	Unc	BU
1841-1856	3.00	6.00	15.00	40.00	65.00

KM# 246 3 KREUZER
1.2320 g., 0.3500 Silver .0138 oz. ASW **Obv:** SCHEIDE/MUNZE
below arms

Date	F	VF	XF	Unc	BU
1866-1871	3.00	7.00	12.00	20.00	30.00

KM# 210 6 KREUZER
2.5980 g., 0.3330 Silver .0278 oz. ASW

Date	F	VF	XF	Unc	BU
1839-1856	4.00	8.00	25.00	40.00	65.00

KM# 221 1/2 GULDEN
5.3030 g., 0.9000 Silver .1534 oz. ASW **Obv:** Without D on
truncation, larger head`

Date	F	VF	XF	Unc	BU
1845-1852	8.00	35.00	65.00	90.00	150

KM# 233 1/2 GULDEN
5.3030 g., 0.9000 Silver .1534 oz. ASW **Obv:** Head of Friedrich I right

Date	F	VF	XF	Unc	BU
1856	35.00	65.00	125	250	420

KM# 234 1/2 GULDEN
5.3030 g., 0.9000 Silver .1534 oz. ASW **Obv:** VOIGHT below head

Date	F	VF	XF	Unc	BU
1856-1860	20.00	45.00	100	160	210

KM# 243   1/2 GULDEN
5.2910 g., 0.9000 Silver .0850 oz. ASW

Date	F	VF	XF	Unc	BU
1860-1865	20.00	45.00	80.00	140	180

KM# 248   1/2 GULDEN
5.2910 g., 0.9000 Silver .0850 oz. ASW

Date	F	VF	XF	Unc	BU
1867-1869	15.00	30.00	75.00	150	210

KM# 219   GULDEN
10.6060 g., 0.9000 Silver .3069 oz. ASW

Date	F	VF	XF	Unc	BU
1845-1852	25.00	35.00	75.00	100	150

KM# 224   GULDEN
10.6060 g., 0.9000 Silver .3069 oz. ASW **Subject:** Blessing on the Baden Mines

Date	F	VF	XF	Unc	BU
1852	35.00	55.00	100	150	220

KM# 235   GULDEN
10.5820 g., 0.9000 Silver .3062 oz. ASW

Date	F	VF	XF	Unc	BU
1856	60.00	110	250	450	600

KM# 236   GULDEN
10.5820 g., 0.9000 Silver .3062 oz. ASW **Rev:** Similar to KM#235

Date	F	VF	XF	Unc	BU
1856-1860	25.00	45.00	70.00	170	240

KM# 239   GULDEN
10.5820 g., 0.9000 Silver .3062 oz. ASW **Subject:** Mint Visit

Date	F	VF	XF	Unc	BU
1857	75.00	175	250	325	425

KM# 247   GULDEN
10.5820 g., 0.9000 Silver .3062 oz. ASW **Subject:** First Shooting Festival at Mannheim

Date	F	VF	XF	Unc	BU
1863	20.00	35.00	70.00	110	150

KM# 249   GULDEN
10.5820 g., 0.9000 Silver .3062 oz. ASW **Subject:** Second Shooting Festival at Karlsruhe

Date	F	VF	XF	Unc	BU
1867	45.00	90.00	175	250	—

KM# 222   2 GULDEN
21.2100 g., 0.9000 Silver .6138 oz. ASW **Ruler:** Leopold I

Date	F	VF	XF	Unc	BU
1846-1852	35.00	60.00	100	190	300

KM# 237   2 GULDEN
21.2100 g., 0.9000 Silver .6138 oz. ASW **Ruler:** Friedrich I as Prince Regent **Rev:** Similar to KM#222

Date	F	VF	XF	Unc	BU
1856	125	250	400	750	1,050

KM# 240 THALER (Vereinsthaler)
18.1590 g., 0.9000 Silver .5359 oz. ASW **Ruler:** Friedrich I as
Grand Duke **Obv:** Head right

Date	F	VF	XF	Unc	BU
1857-1865	35.00	60.00	90.00	150	270

KM# 245 THALER (Vereinsthaler)
18.1590 g., 0.9000 Silver .5359 oz. ASW

Date	F	VF	XF	Unc	BU
1865-1871	45.00	65.00	90.00	190	300

KM# 220 2 THALER (3-1/2 Gulden)
37.1200 g., 0.9000 Silver 1.0743 oz. ASW

Date	F	VF	XF	Unc	BU
1845-1852	75.00	100	200	375	550

KM# 225 2 THALER (3-1/2 Gulden)
37.1200 g., 0.9000 Silver 1.0743 oz. ASW **Ruler:** Friedrich I as
Prince Regent **Obv:** BALBACH below truncation

Date	F	VF	XF	Unc	BU
1854	450	750	1,500	3,000	4,200

TRADE COINAGE

KM# 223.1 DUCAT
3.6600 g., 0.9380 Gold .1103 oz. AGW **Obv:** Larger head

Date	F	VF	XF	Unc	BU
1847-1852	—	1,200	1,600	2,350	—

KM# 223.2 DUCAT
3.6600 g., 0.9380 Gold .1103 oz. AGW **Obv:** Star below head
Note: Posthumous issue.

Date	F	VF	XF	Unc	BU
1852	—	1,350	1,750	2,550	—

KM# 227 DUCAT
3.6600 g., 0.9380 Gold .1103 oz. AGW **Ruler:** Friedrich I as
Prince Regent **Obv:** Head right

Date	F	VF	XF	Unc	BU
1854	—	1,500	3,000	4,750	—

REFORM COINAGE

KM# 265 2 MARK
11.1110 g., 0.9000 Silver .3215 oz. ASW **Ruler:** Friedrich I as
Grand Duke **Obv:** Head left

Date	F	VF	XF	Unc	BU
1876-1888	35.00	100	700	1,600	2,000

German States • Baden

KM# 269   2 MARK

11.1110 g., 0.9000 Silver .3215 oz. ASW   **Ruler:** Friedrich I as Grand Duke **Obv:** Head left

Date	F	VF	XF	Unc	BU
1892-1902	35.00	95.00	300	950	1,100

KM# 271   2 MARK

11.1110 g., 0.9000 Silver .3215 oz. ASW   **Ruler:** Friedrich I as Grand Duke **Subject:** 50th Year of Reign

Date	F	VF	XF	Unc	BU
1902	12.00	28.00	40.00	50.00	60.00

KM# 272   2 MARK

11.1110 g., 0.9000 Silver .3215 oz. ASW   **Ruler:** Friedrich I as Grand Duke

Date	F	VF	XF	Unc	BU
1902-1907	20.00	40.00	65.00	150	180

KM# 276   2 MARK

11.1110 g., 0.9000 Silver .3215 oz. ASW   **Ruler:** Friedrich I as Grand Duke **Subject:** Golden Wedding Anniversary

Date	F	VF	XF	Unc	BU
1906	15.00	30.00	40.00	60.00	70.00

KM# 278   2 MARK

11.1110 g., 0.9000 Silver .3215 oz. ASW   **Ruler:** Friedrich I as Grand Duke **Subject:** Death of Friedrich

Date	F	VF	XF	Unc	BU
1907	20.00	50.00	70.00	90.00	100

KM# 283   2 MARK

11.1110 g., 0.9000 Silver .3215 oz. ASW   **Ruler:** Friedrich II **Obv:** Head left

Date	F	VF	XF	Unc	BU
1911-1913	100	250	400	650	750

KM# 280   3 MARK

16.6670 g., 0.9000 Silver .4823 oz. ASW   **Ruler:** Friedrich II **Obv:** Head left

Date	F	VF	XF	Unc	BU
1908-1915	12.00	25.00	35.00	70.00	100

KM# 263.1   5 MARK

27.7770 g., 0.9000 Silver .8038 oz. ASW   **Ruler:** Friedrich I as Grand Duke **Obv:** Head left

Date	F	VF	XF	Unc	BU
1875-1888	35.00	75.00	900	4,000	6,500

KM# 263.2   5 MARK

27.7770 g., 0.9000 Silver .8038 oz. ASW   **Obv:** Inverted "V" for "A" of BADEN in legend

Date	F	VF	XF	Unc	BU
1875-1888	35.00	75.00	1,000	4,000	6,000

KM# 266 5 MARK
1.9910 g., 0.9000 Gold .0576 oz. AGW

Date	F	VF	XF	Unc	BU
1877	200	300	450	800	1,200

KM# 268 5 MARK
27.7770 g., 0.9000 Silver .8038 oz. ASW **Ruler:** Friedrich I as Grand Duke

Date	F	VF	XF	Unc	BU
1891-1902	30.00	70.00	300	2,000	2,800

KM# 273 5 MARK
27.7770 g., 0.9000 Silver .8038 oz. ASW **Ruler:** Friedrich I as Grand Duke **Subject:** 50th Year of Reign

Date	F	VF	XF	Unc	BU
1902	45.00	90.00	150	225	300

KM# 274 5 MARK
27.7770 g., 0.9000 Silver .8038 oz. ASW **Ruler:** Friedrich I as Grand Duke

Date	F	VF	XF	Unc	BU
1902-1907	20.00	50.00	165	585	650

KM# 277 5 MARK
27.7770 g., 0.9000 Silver .8038 oz. ASW **Ruler:** Friedrich I as Grand Duke **Subject:** Golden Wedding Anniversary **Obv:** Conjoined busts of Friedrich and Luise right

Date	F	VF	XF	Unc	BU
1906	40.00	80.00	145	220	275

KM# 279 5 MARK
27.7770 g., 0.9000 Silver .8038 oz. ASW **Ruler:** Friedrich I as Grand Duke **Subject:** Death of Friedrich

Date	F	VF	XF	Unc	BU
1907	60.00	125	175	250	300

KM# 281 5 MARK
27.7770 g., 0.9000 Silver .8038 oz. ASW **Ruler:** Friedrich II **Obv:** Head left

Date	F	VF	XF	Unc	BU
(1908-1913)-1913	30.00	50.00	165	400	500

KM# 260 10 MARK
3.9820 g., 0.9000 Gold .1152 oz. AGW **Ruler:** Friedrich I as Grand Duke **Obv:** Head left **Rev:** Type I

Date	F	VF	XF	Unc	BU
1872-1873	85.00	200	300	600	1,000

KM# 264 10 MARK
3.9820 g., 0.9000 Gold .1152 oz. AGW **Rev:** Type II

Date	F	VF	XF	Unc	BU
(1876-88)-1888	80.00	125	225	400	750

KM# 267 10 MARK
3.9820 g., 0.9000 Gold .1152 oz. AGW **Ruler:** Friedrich I as Grand Duke **Obv:** Head left

Date	F	VF	XF	Unc	BU
1890-1901	115	175	250	400	500

KM# 275 10 MARK
3.9820 g., 0.9000 Gold .1152 oz. AGW **Ruler:** Friedrich I as Grand Duke

Date	F	VF	XF	Unc	BU
(1902-1907)-1907	110	170	245	400	550

KM# 282 10 MARK
3.9820 g., 0.9000 Gold .1152 oz. AGW **Ruler:** Friedrich II **Obv:** Head right

Date	F	VF	XF	Unc	BU
(1909-1913)-1913	225	500	650	950	1,200

KM# 261 20 MARK
7.9650 g., 0.9000 Gold .2304 oz. AGW **Ruler:** Friedrich I as Grand Duke **Obv:** Head left **Rev:** Type I

Date	F	VF	XF	Unc	BU
(1872-73)-1873	125	150	250	500	800

KM# 262 20 MARK
7.9650 g., 0.9000 Gold .2304 oz. AGW **Ruler:** Friedrich I as Grand Duke **Rev:** Type II

Date	F	VF	XF	Unc	BU
1874	225	375	600	1,250	1,600

KM# 270 20 MARK
7.9650 g., 0.9000 Gold .2304 oz. AGW **Ruler:** Friedrich I as Grand Duke **Rev:** Type III

Date	F	VF	XF	Unc	BU
(1894-95)-1895	135	160	250	400	500

KM# 284 20 MARK
7.9650 g., 0.9000 Gold .2304 oz. AGW **Ruler:** Friedrich II **Obv:** Head left

Date	F	VF	XF	Unc	BU
(1911-1914)-1914	BV	165	220	300	400

BAVARIA

(Bayern)

Located in south Germany. In 1180 the Duchy of Bavaria was given to the Count of Wittelsbach by the emperor. He is the ancestor of all who ruled in Bavaria until 1918. Primogeniture was proclaimed in 1506 and in 1623 the dukes of Bavaria were given the electoral right. Bavaria, which had been divided for the various heirs, was reunited in 1799. The title of king was granted to Bavaria in 1805.

KINGDOM

REGULAR COINAGE

KM# 419 HELLER
Copper

Date	F	VF	XF	Unc	BU
1839-1856	4.00	8.00	10.00	20.00	30.00

KM# 420 PFENNIG
Copper

Date	F	VF	XF	Unc	BU
1839-1856	4.00	8.00	15.00	30.00	45.00

KM# 471 PFENNIG
Copper

Date	F	VF	XF	Unc	BU
1858-1871	3.00	5.00	9.00	20.00	30.00

KM# 421   2 PFENNIG
Copper

Date	F	VF	XF	Unc	BU
1839-1850	4.00	8.00	25.00	50.00	75.00

KM# 472   2 PFENNIG
Copper

Date	F	VF	XF	Unc	BU
1858-1871	4.00	8.00	14.00	20.00	30.00

KM# 463   1/2 KREUZER
Copper

Date	F	VF	XF	Unc	BU
1851-1856	4.00	8.00	12.00	28.00	45.00

KM# 422   KREUZER
0.8400 g., 0.1660 Silver .0044 oz. ASW

Date	F	VF	XF	Unc	BU
1839-1856	2.00	5.00	10.00	15.00	24.00

KM# 473   KREUZER
0.8400 g., 0.1660 Silver .0044 oz. ASW

Date	F	VF	XF	Unc	BU
1858-1864	3.00	5.00	8.00	12.00	18.00

KM# 487   KREUZER
0.8400 g., 0.1660 Silver .0044 oz. ASW

Date	F	VF	XF	Unc	BU
1865-1871	3.00	5.00	8.00	10.00	18.00

KM# 423   3 KREUZER (Groschen)
1.3000 g., 0.3330 Silver .0139 oz. ASW

Date	F	VF	XF	Unc	BU
1839-1856	5.00	10.00	15.00	20.00	35.00

KM# 488   3 KREUZER (Groschen)
1.2300 g., 0.3500 Silver .0138 oz. ASW

Date	F	VF	XF	Unc	BU
1865-1868	4.00	8.00	15.00	40.00	60.00

KM# 424   6 KREUZER
2.6000 g., 0.3330 Silver .0278 oz. ASW

Date	F	VF	XF	Unc	BU
1839-1856	5.00	8.00	20.00	35.00	55.00

KM# 491   6 KREUZER
2.4600 g., 0.3500 Silver .0276 oz. ASW

Date	F	VF	XF	Unc	BU
1866-1867	7.50	40.00	80.00	175	240

KM# 417   1/2 GULDEN
5.3000 g., 0.9000 Silver .1533 oz. ASW   **Obv:** Head of Ludwig I right

Date	F	VF	XF	Unc	BU
1838-1848	10.00	20.00	35.00	60.00	90.00

KM# 444   1/2 GULDEN
5.3000 g., 0.9000 Silver .1533 oz. ASW   **Obv:** Head of Maximilian II right

Date	F	VF	XF	Unc	BU
1848-1864	8.00	15.00	35.00	65.00	90.00

KM# 479   1/2 GULDEN
5.3000 g., 0.9000 Silver .1533 oz. ASW   **Obv:** Ludwig II with part in hair

Date	F	VF	XF	Unc	BU
1864-1866	25.00	50.00	20.00	200	275

KM# 492   1/2 GULDEN
5.3000 g., 0.9000 Silver .1533 oz. ASW **Obv:** Without part in hair

Date	F	VF	XF	Unc	BU
1866-1871	17.00	35.00	85.00	150	210

KM# 414   GULDEN
10.6000 g., 0.9000 Silver .3067 oz. ASW **Obv:** Head of Ludwig I right

Date	F	VF	XF	Unc	BU
1837-1848	15.00	30.00	40.00	60.00	90.00

KM# 445   GULDEN
10.6000 g., 0.9000 Silver .3067 oz. ASW **Obv:** Head of Maximilian I right

Date	F	VF	XF	Unc	BU
1848-1864	8.00	15.00	50.00	110	135

KM# 480   GULDEN
10.6000 g., 0.9000 Silver .3067 oz. ASW **Obv:** Ludwig II with part in hair

Date	F	VF	XF	Unc	BU
1864-1866	35.00	60.00	150	250	350

KM# 493   GULDEN
10.6000 g., 0.9000 Silver .3067 oz. ASW **Obv:** Without part in hair

Date	F	VF	XF	Unc	BU
1866-1871	30.00	50.00	115	160	195

KM# 438   2 GULDEN
21.2100 g., 0.9000 Silver .6138 oz. ASW

Date	F	VF	XF	Unc	BU
1845-1848	30.00	50.00	65.00	95.00	145

KM# 446   2 GULDEN
21.2100 g., 0.9000 Silver .6138 oz. ASW **Rev:** Similar to KM#438.

Date	F	VF	XF	Unc	BU
1848-1856	20.00	40.00	55.00	75.00	115

KM# 465   2 GULDEN
21.2100 g., 0.9000 Silver .6138 oz. ASW **Subject:** Restoration of Madonna Column in Munich

Date	F	VF	XF	Unc	BU
1855	15.00	25.00	45.00	70.00	90.00

KM# 481 THALER
18.5200 g., 0.9000 Silver .5360 oz. ASW **Obv:** Ludwig II with part
in hair

Date	F	VF	XF	Unc	BU
1864-1866	30.00	50.00	150	250	310

KM# 489 THALER
18.5200 g., 0.9000 Silver .5360 oz. ASW **Obv:** No part in hair
Rev: Madonna with child, J. Reis below truncation

Date	F	VF	XF	Unc	BU
ND(1865)-1871	17.00	25.00	45.00	65.00	80.00

KM# 494.1 THALER
18.5200 g., 0.9000 Silver .5360 oz. ASW **Rev:** Arms

Date	F	VF	XF	Unc	BU
1866-1871	35.00	55.00	100	140	195

KM# 494.2 THALER
18.5200 g., 0.9000 Silver .5360 oz. ASW **Rev:** New arabesques
below arms

Date	F	VF	XF	Unc	BU
1871	150	300	475	900	1,200

KM# 495 THALER
18.5200 g., 0.9000 Silver .5360 oz. ASW **Obv:** J. REIS below
truncation

Date	F	VF	XF	Unc	BU
1871	85.00	160	300	750	1,000

KM# 496 THALER
18.5200 g., 0.9000 Silver .5360 oz. ASW **Subject:** German
Victory in Franco-Prussian War

Date	F	VF	XF	Unc	BU
1871	18.00	25.00	60.00	90.00	120

KM# 468 THALER (Vereins)
18.5200 g., 0.9000 Silver .5360 oz. ASW **Obv:** Head of
Maximilian II right

Date	F	VF	XF	Unc	BU
1857-1864	12.00	20.00	50.00	90.00	120

KM# 432 2 THALER (3-1/2 Gulden)
37.1200 g., 0.9000 Silver 1.0743 oz. ASW

Date	F	VF	XF	Unc	BU
1842-1848	50.00	125	250	500	650

KM# 443 2 THALER (3-1/2 Gulden)
37.1200 g., 0.9000 Silver 1.0743 oz. ASW **Subject:** Abdication
of Ludwig I for Maximilian

Date	F	VF	XF	Unc	BU
1848	400	100	1,600	2,800	3,600

KM# 447.1   2 THALER (3-1/2 Gulden)
37.1200 g., 0.9000 Silver 1.0743 oz. ASW   **Subject:** New Constitution **Obv:** Maximilian II head right **Edge Lettering:** VEREINSMUNZE

Date	F	VF	XF	Unc	BU
1848	175	245	400	850	1,200

KM# 447.2   2 THALER (3-1/2 Gulden)
37.1200 g., 0.9000 Silver 1.0743 oz. ASW   **Edge Lettering:** CONVENTION-VOM

Date	F	VF	XF	Unc	BU
1848	175	275	400	775	1,025

KM# 447.3   2 THALER (3-1/2 Gulden)
37.1200 g., 0.9000 Silver 1.0743 oz. ASW   **Edge Lettering:** DREY EIN HALB GULDEN **Note:** Restrike post 1857.

Date	F	VF	XF	Unc	BU
1848	150	245	500	700	1,025

KM# 448.1   2 THALER (3-1/2 Gulden)
37.1200 g., 0.9000 Silver 1.0743 oz. ASW   **Subject:** Johann Christoph von Gluck **Edge Lettering:** VEREINSMUNZE

Date	F	VF	XF	Unc	BU
1848	500	1,150	1,750	2,500	3,350

KM# 448.2   2 THALER (3-1/2 Gulden)
37.1200 g., 0.9000 Silver 1.0743 oz. ASW   **Edge Lettering:** DREY EIN HALB GULDEN **Note:** Restrike post 1857.

Date	F	VF	XF	Unc	BU
1848	500	1,250	1,700	3,000	3,600

KM# 455.1   2 THALER (3-1/2 Gulden)
37.1200 g., 0.9000 Silver 1.0743 oz. ASW   **Subject:** Orlando Di Lasso **Edge Lettering:** VEREINSMUNZE

Date	F	VF	XF	Unc	BU
1849	700	1,250	1,750	3,000	3,700

KM# 455.2   2 THALER (3-1/2 Gulden)
37.1200 g., 0.9000 Silver 1.0743 oz. ASW   **Edge Lettering:** DREY EIN HALB GULDEN **Note:** Restrike post 1857.

Date	F	VF	XF	Unc	BU
1849	700	1,250	2,100	3,200	4,200

KM# 456   2 THALER (3-1/2 Gulden)
37.1200 g., 0.9000 Silver 1.0743 oz. ASW

Date	F	VF	XF	Unc	BU
1849-1856	75.00	140	220	450	550

KM# 464.1   2 THALER (3-1/2 Gulden)
37.1200 g., 0.9000 Silver 1.0743 oz. ASW   **Subject:** Exibition of German Products in Crystal Palace **Edge Lettering:** VEREINS MUNZE

Date	F	VF	XF	Unc	BU
1854	90.00	125	250	350	420

KM# 464.2   2 THALER (3-1/2 Gulden)
37.1200 g., 0.9000 Silver 1.0743 oz. ASW   **Edge Lettering:**
CONVENTION-BOM

Date	F	VF	XF	Unc	BU
1854	100	150	275	450	625

KM# 467   2 THALER (3-1/2 Gulden)
37.1200 g., 0.9000 Silver 1.0743 oz. ASW   **Subject:** Erection of
Monument to King Maximilian II

Date	F	VF	XF	Unc	BU
1856	300	350	600	900	1,200

KM# 474   2 THALER (Vereins)
37.0400 g., 0.9000 Silver 1.0717 oz. ASW

Date	F	VF	XF	Unc	BU
1859-1860	200	300	600	1,250	1,800

KM# 475   2 THALER (Vereins)
37.0400 g., 0.9000 Silver 1.0717 oz. ASW   **Obv:** Different hair style

Date	F	VF	XF	Unc	BU
1861-1864	175	300	700	1,100	1,450

KM# 490   2 THALER (Vereins)
37.0400 g., 0.9000 Silver 1.0717 oz. ASW   **Obv:** Ludwig II head right

Date	F	VF	XF	Unc	BU
1865-1869	2,000	3,500	5,000	7,000	—

KM# 469   1/2 KRONE
5.5550 g., 0.9000 Gold .1607 oz. AGW   **Obv:** Maximilian II head right

Date	F	VF	XF	Unc	BU
1857-1864	—	2,500	4,000	—	—

KM# 470   KRONE
11.1110 g., 0.9000 Gold .3215 oz. AGW   **Obv:** Maximilian II head right

Date	F	VF	XF	Unc	BU
1857-1864	—	5,000	8,000	—	—

KM# 483   KRONE
10.0000 g., 0.9000 Gold .2892 oz. AGW   **Obv:** Ludwig II head right

Date	F	VF	XF	Unc	BU
1864-1869	—	—	—	—	—

TRADE COINAGE

KM# 428   DUCAT
3.4900 g., 0.9370 Gold .1051 oz. AGW   **Note:** Fr. #271.

Date	F	VF	XF	Unc	BU
1840-1848	600	1,000	1,500	2,150	—

KM# 457 DUCAT
3.4900 g., 0.9370 Gold .1051 oz. AGW **Obv:** Maximilian II head right **Note:** Fr. #277.

Date	F	VF	XF	Unc	BU
1849-1856	400	600	900	1,200	—

KM# 461 DUCAT
3.4900 g., 0.9370 Gold .1051 oz. AGW

Date	F	VF	XF	Unc	BU
1850	1,750	2,250	3,500	5,250	—

KM# 462 DUCAT
3.4900 g., 0.9370 Gold .1051 oz. AGW **Subject:** Rhine **Note:** Fr. #278.

Date	F	VF	XF	Unc	BU
1850-1856	425	900	1,500	1,800	—

KM# 466 DUCAT
3.4900 g., 0.9370 Gold .1051 oz. AGW **Note:** Fr. #279.

Date	F	VF	XF	Unc	BU

KM# 477 DUCAT
3.4900 g., 0.9370 Gold .1051 oz. AGW **Note:** Reduced size. Fr. #278.

Date	F	VF	XF	Unc	BU
1863	1,500	2,500	4,000	5,000	—

REFORM COINAGE

KM# 505 2 MARK
11.1110 g., 0.9000 Silver .3215 oz. ASW **Obv:** Ludwig II head right

Date	F	VF	XF	Unc	BU
1876-1883	35.00	70.00	225	550	650

KM# 507 2 MARK
11.1110 g., 0.9000 Silver .3215 oz. ASW **Obv:** Otto head left

Date	F	VF	XF	Unc	BU
1888	150	300	700	1,200	1,500

KM# 511 2 MARK
11.1110 g., 0.9000 Silver .3215 oz. ASW **Ruler:** Otto Prince Regent Luitpold **Note:** Open and closed curl varieties exist.

Date	F	VF	XF	Unc	BU
1891-1913	9.00	20.00	35.00	85.00	150

KM# 516 2 MARK
11.1110 g., 0.9000 Silver .3215 oz. ASW **Ruler:** Otto Prince Regent Luitpold **Subject:** 90th Birthday of Prince Regent Luitpold

Date	F	VF	XF	Unc	BU
1911	12.00	22.00	35.00	45.00	55.00

KM# 519 2 MARK
11.1110 g., 0.9000 Silver .3215 oz. ASW **Ruler:** Ludwig III **Obv:** Head left

Date	F	VF	XF	Unc	BU
1914	30.00	65.00	100	165	185

KM# 515 3 MARK
16.6670 g., 0.9000 Silver .4823 oz. ASW **Ruler:** Otto Prince Regent Luitpold **Obv:** Head left

Date	F	VF	XF	Unc	BU
1908-1913	10.00	18.00	30.00	50.00	65.00

KM# 517   3 MARK
16.6670 g., 0.9000 Silver .4823 oz. ASW **Ruler:** Otto Prince
Regent Luitpold **Subject:** 90th Birthday of Prince Regent Luitpold

Date	F	VF	XF	Unc	BU
1911	12.00	22.00	35.00	50.00	65.00

KM# 520   3 MARK
16.6670 g., 0.9000 Silver .4823 oz. ASW **Ruler:** Ludwig III **Obv:**
Head left

Date	F	VF	XF	Unc	BU
1914	17.50	32.50	50.00	75.00	90.00

KM# 523   3 MARK
16.6670 g., 0.9000 Silver .4823 oz. ASW **Ruler:** Ludwig III
Subject: Golden Wedding Anniversary

Date	F	VF	XF	Unc	BU
1918D	—	'16,000	26,000	32,000	40,000

KM# 502   5 MARK
27.7770 g., 0.9000 Silver .8038 oz. ASW **Obv:** Ludwig II head right

Date	F	VF	XF	Unc	BU
1874-1876	35.00	65.00	225	600	800

KM# 506   5 MARK
1.9910 g., 0.9000 Gold .0576 oz. AGW

Date	F	VF	XF	Unc	BU
1877-1878	200	350	450	700	1,000

KM# 508   5 MARK
27.7770 g., 0.9000 Silver .8038 oz. ASW **Obv:** Otto

Date	F	VF	XF	Unc	BU
1888	200	300	800	1,000	1,250

KM# 512   5 MARK
27.7770 g., 0.9000 Silver .8038 oz. ASW **Ruler:** Otto **Note:**
Varieties in the hair locks and curls exist.

Date	F	VF	XF	Unc	BU
(1891-1900)-1913	14.00	20.00	40.00	150	225

KM# 518   5 MARK
27.7770 g., 0.9000 Silver .8038 oz. ASW **Ruler:** Otto Prince
Regent Luitpold **Subject:** 90th Birthday of Prince Regent Luitpold

Date	F	VF	XF	Unc	BU
1911	25.00	65.00	95.00	170	200

KM# 521   5 MARK
27.7770 g., 0.9000 Silver .8038 oz. ASW **Ruler:** Ludwig III **Obv:** Head left

Date	F	VF	XF	Unc	BU
1914	40.00	90.00	175	225	275

KM# 500   10 MARK
3.9820 g., 0.9000 Gold .1152 oz. AGW **Obv:** Ludwig II head right; J. REIS below truncation **Rev:** Type I

Date	F	VF	XF	Unc	BU
1872-1873	85.00	150	250	450	650

KM# 503   10 MARK
3.9820 g., 0.9000 Gold .1152 oz. AGW **Rev:** Type II

Date	F	VF	XF	Unc	BU
1874-1881	80.00	130	200	325	450

KM# 509   10 MARK
3.9820 g., 0.9000 Gold .1152 oz. AGW **Obv:** Otto head left **Rev:** Type II

Date	F	VF	XF	Unc	BU
1888	150	275	375	550	800

KM# 510   10 MARK
3.9820 g., 0.9000 Gold .1152 oz. AGW **Rev:** Type III

Date	F	VF	XF	Unc	BU
1890-1900	85.00	150	200	250	350

KM# 514   10 MARK
3.9820 g., 0.9000 Gold .1152 oz. AGW **Ruler:** Otto

Date	F	VF	XF	Unc	BU
1901-1912	90.00	130	185	275	300

KM# 501   20 MARK
7.9650 g., 0.9000 Gold .2304 oz. AGW **Obv:** Ludwig II head right **Rev:** Type I

Date	F	VF	XF	Unc	BU
1872-1873	155	170	250	500	700

KM# 504   20 MARK
7.9650 g., 0.9000 Gold .2304 oz. AGW **Rev:** Type II

Date	F	VF	XF	Unc	BU
1874-1878	155	170	225	300	450

KM# 513   20 MARK
7.9650 g., 0.9000 Gold .2304 oz. AGW **Ruler:** Otto **Obv:** Head left **Rev:** Type III

Date	F	VF	XF	Unc	BU
1895-1913	BV	155	200	275	325

KM# 522   20 MARK
7.9650 g., 0.9000 Gold .2304 oz. AGW **Ruler:** Ludwig III **Obv:** Head left **Note:** Never officially released.

Date	F	VF	XF	Unc	BU
1914	—	2,000	2,500	3,000	3,500

BIRKENFELD

Located in southwest Germany. For most of the time prior to 1801, Birkenfeld was in the possession of the Counts Palatine. It was a part of France from 1801-1814, Prussia from 1814-1817 and was made a principality in 1817 and given to the Duke of Oldenburg.

COUNTSHIP
REGULAR COINAGE

KM# 6   PFENNIG
Copper **Ruler:** Paul Friedrich August of Oldenburg

Date	F	VF	XF	Unc	BU
1848	7.00	15.00	50.00	125	180

KM# 20 PFENNIG
Copper **Ruler:** Paul Friedrich August of Oldenburg

Date	F	VF	XF	Unc	BU
1859	25.00	55.00	70.00	110	150

KM# 7 2 PFENNIGE
Copper **Ruler:** Paul Friedrich August of Oldenburg

Date	F	VF	XF	Unc	BU
1848	8.00	15.00	40.00	100	135

KM# 15 2 PFENNIGE
Copper **Ruler:** Paul Friedrich August of Oldenburg

Date	F	VF	XF	Unc	BU
1858	10.00	20.00	60.00	100	140

KM# 8 3 PFENNIGE
Copper **Ruler:** Paul Friedrich August of Oldenburg

Date	F	VF	XF	Unc	BU
1848	8.00	15.00	40.00	100	135

KM# 16 3 PFENNIGE
Copper **Ruler:** Paul Friedrich August of Oldenburg **Obv:** Crowned NFP monogram

Date	F	VF	XF	Unc	BU
1858	10.00	20.00	55.00	90.00	135

KM# 2 ALBUS
Silver **Ruler:** Paul Friedrich August of Oldenburg **Obv:** Small shield of three-fold arms on larger shield of Sponheim arms **Rev:** I/ALB in center

Date	VG	F	VF	XF	Unc
ND	45.00	75.00	110	180	—

KM# 17 1/2 SILBER GROSCHEN
1.0900 g., 0.2200 Silver .0077 oz. ASW **Ruler:** Paul Friedrich August of Oldenburg

Date	F	VF	XF	Unc	BU
1858	25.00	55.00	135	220	300

KM# 9 SILBER GROSCHEN
2.1900 g., 0.2200 Silver .0154 oz. ASW **Ruler:** Paul Friedrich August of Oldenburg **Obv:** Crowned arms **Rev:** Value

Date	F	VF	XF	Unc	BU
1848	10.00	20.00	60.00	110	150

KM# 18 SILBER GROSCHEN
2.1900 g., 0.2200 Silver .0154 oz. ASW **Ruler:** Paul Friedrich August of Oldenburg **Obv:** Different arms

Date	F	VF	XF	Unc	BU
1858	25.00	60.00	140	225	330

KM# 10 2-1/2 SILBER GROSCHEN (1/12 Thaler)
3.2200 g., 0.3750 Silver .0388 oz. ASW **Ruler:** Paul Friedrich August of Oldenburg **Obv:** Crowned arms **Rev:** Value

Date	F	VF	XF	Unc	BU
1848	25.00	55.00	110	225	300

KM# 19 2-1/2 SILBER GROSCHEN (1/12 Thaler)
3.2200 g., 0.3750 Silver .0388 oz. ASW **Ruler:** Paul Friedrich August of Oldenburg **Obv:** Different arms

Date	F	VF	XF	Unc	BU
1858	25.00	60.00	140	225	330

BREMEN

FREE CITY

Established at about the same time as the bishopric in 787, Bremen was under the control of the bishops and archbishops until joining the Hanseatic League in 1276. Archbishop Albrecht II granted the mint right to the city in 1369, but this was not formalized by imperial decree until 1541. In 1646, Bremen was raised to free imperial status and continued to strike its own coins into the early 20th century. The city lost its free imperial status in 1803 and was controlled by France from 1806 until 1813. Regaining it independence in 1815, Bremen joined the North German Confederation in 1867 and the German Empire in 1871.

REGULAR COINAGE

KM# 241 SCHWAREN
Copper

Date	F	VF	XF	Unc	BU
1859	4.00	8.00	12.00	40.00	60.00

KM# 234 2-1/2 SCHWAREN
Copper

Date	F	VF	XF	Unc	BU
1841-1866	4.00	8.00	25.00	45.00	65.00

KM# 240 6 GROTE / 1/12 THALER
2.9200 g., 0.4940 Silver .0463 oz. ASW

Date	F	VF	XF	Unc	BU
1857	5.00	15.00	40.00	65.00	90.00

KM# 245   6 GROTE / 1/12 THALER
2.9200 g., 0.4940 Silver .0463 oz. ASW

Date	F	VF	XF	Unc	BU
1861	5.00	15.00	50.00	60.00	85.00

KM# 242   12 GROTE (1/6 Thaler)
3.8890 g., 0.7400 Silver .0925 oz. ASW **Obv:** Crowned cornered arms

Date	F	VF	XF	Unc	BU
1859-1860	5.00	15.00	30.00	60.00	80.00

KM# 233   36 GROTE (1/2 Thaler)
8.7700 g., 0.9860 Silver .2780 oz. ASW

Date	F	VF	XF	Unc	BU
1840-1859	10.00	35.00	60.00	120	150

KM# 243   36 GROTE (1/2 Thaler)
8.7700 g., 0.9860 Silver .2780 oz. ASW

Date	F	VF	XF	Unc	BU
1859-1864	8.00	20.00	65.00	95.00	125

KM# 246   THALER (Vereins)
17.5390 g., 0.9860 Silver .5560 oz. ASW **Subject:** 50th Anniversary - Liberation of Germany

Date	F	VF	XF	Unc	BU
1863	20.00	35.00	60.00	125	150

KM# 248   THALER (Vereins)
17.5390 g., 0.9860 Silver .5560 oz. ASW **Subject:** 2nd German Shooting Festival

Date	F	VF	XF	Unc	BU
1865	20.00	35.00	55.00	75.00	90.00

KM# 249   THALER (Vereins)
17.5390 g., 0.9860 Silver .5560 oz. ASW **Subject:** Victory Over France

Date	F	VF	XF	Unc	BU
1871	20.00	35.00	60.00	90.00	120

KM# 250   2 MARK
11.1110 g., 0.9000 Silver .3215 oz. ASW

Date	F	VF	XF	Unc	BU
1904	30.00	60.00	90.00	150	175

KM# 251   5 MARK
27.7770 g., 0.9000 Silver .8038 oz. ASW

Date	F	VF	XF	Unc	BU
1906	85.00	200	300	450	500

KM# 253   10 MARK
3.9820 g., 0.9000 Gold .1152 oz. AGW

Date	F	VF	XF	Unc	BU
1907	425	800	1,250	1,700	2,100

KM# 252   20 MARK
7.9650 g., 0.9000 Gold .2304 oz. AGW

Date	F	VF	XF	Unc	BU
1906	425	725	1,150	1,750	—

TOKEN COINAGE
Reckoning Tokens

These vouchers, issued March 18, 1924, were based on the American dollar. Issued in conjunction with Bremens issue of treasury. Due to monies being held to purchase Bremens 5% Dollar Bond, they rarely circulated. The tokens were withdrawn September 30 of that same year.

KM# Tn1   2 VERRECHNUNGS-PFENNIG
Brass **Obv:** State arms **Rev:** Denomination **Note:** Struck at Nurnberg.

Date	F	VF	XF	Unc	BU
ND(1924)	10.00	25.00	45.00	85.00	—

KM# Tn2   5 VERRECHNUNGS-PFENNIG
Aluminum **Obv:** State arms **Rev:** Denomination **Note:** Struck at Nurnberg.

Date	F	VF	XF	Unc	BU
ND(1924)	9.00	18.00	30.00	70.00	—

KM# Tn3   10 VERRECHNUNGS-PFENNIG
Aluminum **Obv:** State arms **Rev:** Denomination **Note:** Struck at Nurnberg.

Date	F	VF	XF	Unc	BU
ND(1924)	10.00	20.00	35.00	75.00	—

KM# Tn4   20 VERRECHNUNGS-PFENNIG
Aluminum **Obv:** State arms **Rev:** Denomination **Note:** Struck at Nurnberg.

Date	F	VF	XF	Unc	BU
ND(1924)	17.00	35.00	60.00	120	—

KM# Tn5   50 VERRECHNUNGS-PFENNIG
Aluminum **Obv:** Lions supporting crowned arms **Rev:** Denomination **Note:** Struck at Hamburg.

Date	F	VF	XF	Unc	BU
ND(1924)	30.00	55.00	100	200	—

KM# Tn6   VERRECHNUNGSMARK
Aluminum **Obv:** Lions support crowned arms on pedestal **Rev:** Denomination **Note:** Struck at Menden. This coin is listed in Jaeger & Funck as struck in aluminum. Kunker has listed it as having an iron core but doesn't indicate what metal clads or plates the piece.

Date	F	VF	XF	Unc	BU
ND(1924)	75.00	150	275	500	—

BRUNSWICK-WOLFENBUTTEL

(Braunschweig-Wolfenbüttel)

From 1884 until 1913, Brunswick-Wolfenbüttel was governed by Prussia and then turned over to a younger prince of Brunswick who married a daughter of Kaiser Wilhelm II. His reign was short, however, as he was forced to abdicate at the end of World War I.

DUCHY
REGULAR COINAGE

KM# 1142   PFENNIG
Copper **Ruler:** Wilhelm

Date	F	VF	XF	Unc	BU
1851-1856	5.00	10.00	18.00	40.00	60.00

KM# 1148   PFENNIG
Copper **Ruler:** Wilhelm **Rev:** Without B below date

Date	F	VF	XF	Unc	BU
1854-1856	4.00	8.00	20.00	40.00	55.00

KM# 1154   PFENNIG
Copper **Ruler:** Wilhelm

Date	F	VF	XF	Unc	BU
1859-1860	4.00	8.00	20.00	30.00	54.00

KM# 1143   2 PFENNIGE
Copper **Ruler:** Wilhelm

Date	F	VF	XF	Unc	BU
1851-1856	4.00	8.00	15.00	30.00	55.00

KM# 1155   2 PFENNIGE
Copper   **Ruler:** Wilhelm

Date	F	VF	XF	Unc	BU
1859-1860	5.00	10.00	13.00	32.00	55.00

KM# 1151   1/2 GROSCHEN (1/60 Thaler; Vereins)
1.0900 g., 0.2200 Silver .0077 oz. ASW

Date	F	VF	XF	Unc	BU
1858-1860	4.00	8.00	20.00	55.00	—

KM# 1150   GROSCHEN (1/30 Thaler; Vereins)
2.1900 g., 0.2200 Silver .0154 oz. ASW

Date	F	VF	XF	Unc	BU
1857-1860	4.00	8.00	15.00	30.00	45.00

KM# 1131   THALER
22.2700 g., 0.7500 Silver .5371 oz. ASW   **Obv:** Smaller head, without name at truncation

Date	F	VF	XF	Unc	BU
1839-1850	15.00	30.00	85.00	300	510

KM# 1144   THALER
22.2700 g., 0.7500 Silver .5371 oz. ASW   **Rev:** Similar to KM#1129

Date	F	VF	XF	Unc	BU
1851	60.00	110	325	1,000	2,400

KM# 1146   THALER
22.2700 g., 0.7500 Silver .5371 oz. ASW

Date	F	VF	XF	Unc	BU
1853-1855	20.00	55.00	140	400	600

KM# 1152   THALER
18.5200 g., 0.9000 Silver .5360 oz. ASW   **Note:** Vereins Thaler.

Date	F	VF	XF	Unc	BU
1858-1871	25.00	40.00	100	175	240

KM# 1136   2 THALER (3 1/2 Gulden)
37.1200 g., 0.9000 Silver 1.0743 oz. ASW   **Obv:** Wilhelm head right

Date	F	VF	XF	Unc	BU
1842-1850	75.00	175	300	600	1,325

KM# 1140   2 THALER (3 1/2 Gulden)
37.1200 g., 0.9000 Silver 1.0743 oz. ASW

Date	F	VF	XF	Unc	BU
1850-1855	35.00	90.00	150	325	450

KM# 1149   2 THALER (3 1/2 Gulden)
37.1200 g., 0.9000 Silver 1.0743 oz. ASW   Subject: 25th Anniversary of Reign

Date	F	VF	XF	Unc	BU
1856	65.00	110	175	250	305

KM# 1145   2-1/2 THALER
3.3200 g., 0.9000 Gold .0961 oz. AGW   Obv: William head right

Date	F	VF	XF	Unc	BU
1851	350	500	750	1,100	—

KM# 1141   10 THALER
13.3000 g., 0.9000 Gold .3848 oz. AGW

Date	F	VF	XF	Unc	BU
1850	975	1,650	2,150	2,750	—

KM# 1147   10 THALER
13.3000 g., 0.9000 Gold .3848 oz. AGW

Date	F	VF	XF	Unc	BU
1853-1857	400	650	1,000	2,000	—

KM# 1153   KRONE
11.1110 g., 0.9000 Gold .3215 oz. AGW   Obv: Wilhelm head right

Date	F	VF	XF	Unc	BU
1858-1859	500	950	1,450	2,500	—

KM# 1160   20 MARK
7.9650 g., 0.9000 Gold .2304 oz. AGW   Obv: Wilhelm head left   Rev: Type II

Date	F	VF	XF	Unc	BU
1875	350	700	1,000	1,750	2,500

REFORM COINAGE

KM# 1161   3 MARK
16.6670 g., 0.9000 Silver .4823 oz. ASW   Ruler: Ernst August   Subject: Ernst August Wedding and Accession

Date	F	VF	XF	Unc	BU
1915	600	1,150	1,850	2,500	3,000

KM# 1162   3 MARK
16.6670 g., 0.9000 Silver .4823 oz. ASW   Ruler: Ernst August   Subject: Ernst August Wedding and Accession

Date	F	VF	XF	Unc	BU
1915	50.00	120	200	250	300

KM# 1163 5 MARK
27.7770 g., 0.9000 Silver .8038 oz. ASW **Ruler:** Ernst August
Subject: Ernst August Wedding and Accession

Date	F	VF	XF	Unc	BU
1915	800	1,650	2,750	3,500	4,000

KM# 1164 5 MARK
27.7770 g., 0.9000 Silver .8038 oz. ASW **Ruler:** Ernst August
Subject: Ernst August Wedding and Accession **Rev:** Similar to
KM#1163

Date	F	VF	XF	Unc	BU
1915	185	400	700	1,150	1,400

FRANKFURT AM MAIN

One of the largest cities of modern Germany, Frankfurt is
located on the north bank of the Main River about 25 miles (42 kilometers) upstream from where it joins the Rhine at Mainz. Frankfurt
was a commercial center from the early Middle Ages and became
a favored location for imperial councils during the Carolingian
period because of its central location. Frankfurt remained a free city
until 1806 and then was the capital of the Grand Duchy of Frankfurt
from 1810 until 1814, only to regain its free status in 1815. The city
chose the wrong side in the Austro-Prussian War of 1866 and thus
was absorbed by victorious Prussia in the latter year.

NOTE: In some instances old dies were used with initials
beyond the date range of the man that held the position.

ARMS: Crowned eagle, usually in circle.

FREE CITY
REGULAR COINAGE

KM# 327 HELLER
Copper **Obv:** Eagle with wide streched wings **Rev:** 1 / HELLER / date

Date	F	VF	XF	Unc	BU
1841-1852	4.00	8.00	16.00	30.00	—

KM# 351 HELLER
Copper **Obv:** Round eagle, legend at sides

Date	F	VF	XF	Unc	BU
1853-1858	4.00	8.00	18.00	32.00	—

KM# 356 HELLER
Copper **Obv:** Small round eagle within legend

Date	F	VF	XF	Unc	BU
1859-1865	3.00	5.00	8.00	20.00	—

KM# 312 KREUZER
0.8350 g., 0.1670 Silver .0044 oz. ASW **Obv:** Eagle with wide
spread wings **Rev:** Value and date within oak wreath

Date	F	VF	XF	Unc	BU
1838-1857	3.00	7.00	12.00	25.00	—

KM# 357 KREUZER
0.8350 g., 0.1670 Silver .0044 oz. ASW **Obv:** Eagle with long
body **Rev:** Value and date within oak wreath

Date	F	VF	XF	Unc	BU
1859-1862	4.00	7.00	15.00	25.00	—

KM# 367 KREUZER
0.8350 g., 0.1670 Silver .0044 oz. ASW **Obv:** Eagle with heart-
shaped body **Rev:** Value and date within oak wreath

Date	F	VF	XF	Unc	BU
1862-1866	2.50	4.00	8.00	16.00	—

KM# 334 3 KREUZER
1.2990 g., 0.3330 Silver .0139 oz. ASW

Date	F	VF	XF	Unc	BU
1846-1856	6.00	12.00	22.00	45.00	—

KM# 373 3 KREUZER
1.2990 g., 0.3330 Silver .0139 oz. ASW

Date	F	VF	XF	Unc	BU
1866	2.00	4.00	9.00	20.00	—

KM# 335   6 KREUZER
2.5980 g., 0.3330 Silver .0277 oz. ASW

Date	F	VF	XF	Unc	BU
1846-1856	6.00	12.00	25.00	50.00	—

KM# 350   6 KREUZER
2.5980 g., 0.3330 Silver .0277 oz. ASW

Date	F	VF	XF	Unc	BU
1852-1856	3.50	10.00	25.00	65.00	—

KM# 374   6 KREUZER
2.4630 g., 0.3500 Silver 0.0276 oz. ASW

Date	F	VF	XF	Unc	BU
1866	4.00	8.00	15.00	25.00	—

KM# 330   1/2 GULDEN
5.3030 g., 0.9000 Silver .1533 oz. ASW

Date	F	VF	XF	Unc	BU
1842-1849	20.00	35.00	75.00	150	—

KM# 368   1/2 GULDEN
5.2910 g., 0.9000 Silver .1533 oz. ASW

Date	F	VF	XF	Unc	BU
1862	120	260	520	980	—

KM# 331   GULDEN
10.6060 g., 0.9000 Silver .3067 oz. ASW **Obv:** Eagle with large arabesques

Date	F	VF	XF	Unc	BU
1842-1855	18.00	40.00	80.00	170	—

KM# 358   GULDEN
10.5820 g., 0.9000 Silver .3069 oz. ASW **Obv:** Eagle with small arabesques

Date	F	VF	XF	Unc	BU
1859-1861	16.00	35.00	80.00	150	—

KM# 369   GULDEN
10.5820 g., 0.9000 Silver .3069 oz. ASW **Obv:** Eagle without arabesques

Date	F	VF	XF	Unc	BU
1862-1863	50.00	90.00	180	360	—

KM# 333   2 GULDEN
21.2110 g., 0.9000 Silver .6138 oz. ASW

Date	F	VF	XF	Unc	BU
1845-1856	40.00	70.00	200	300	—

KM# 337   2 GULDEN
21.2110 g., 0.9000 Silver .6138 oz. ASW **Subject:** Constitutional Convention, May 18, 1848

Date	F	VF	XF	Unc	BU
1848	60.00	125	240	400	—

KM# 338   2 GULDEN
21.2110 g., 0.9000 Silver .6138 oz. ASW **Subject:** Archduke Johann of Austria Elected as Vicar

Date	F	VF	XF	Unc	BU
1848	35.00	70.00	125	200	—

KM# 339 2 GULDEN
21.2110 g., 0.9000 Silver .6138 oz. ASW **Subject:** Archduke Johann of Austria Elected as Vicar

Date	F	VF	XF	Unc	BU
1848 Rare	—	—	—	—	—

KM# 340 2 GULDEN
21.2110 g., 0.9000 Silver .6138 oz. ASW **Subject:** Opening of German Parliament **Obv:** KM#337 **Rev:** KM#333 **Note:** Mule.

Date	F	VF	XF	Unc	BU
1848 Rare	—	—	—	—	—

KM# 341.1 2 GULDEN
21.2110 g., 0.9000 Silver .6138 oz. ASW **Subject:** Friedrich Wilhelm IV of Prussia Elected as Emperor of Germany

Date	F	VF	XF	Unc	BU
1849	—	3,000	4,800	6,800	—

KM# 341.2 2 GULDEN
21.2110 g., 0.9000 Silver .6138 oz. ASW **Subject:** Friedrich Wilhelm IV of Prussia Elected as Emperor of Germany **Edge:** Plain

Date	F	VF	XF	Unc	BU
1849(1890) Restrike	—	—	—	—	—

KM# 342 2 GULDEN
21.2110 g., 0.9000 Silver .6138 oz. ASW **Obv:** Similar to KM#333

Date	F	VF	XF	Unc	BU
1849 Rare	—	—	—	—	—

KM# 343 2 GULDEN
21.2110 g., 0.9000 Silver .6138 oz. ASW **Subject:** Centenary of Goethe's Birth

Date	F	VF	XF	Unc	BU
1849	40.00	80.00	120	220	—

KM# 353 2 GULDEN
21.2110 g., 0.9000 Silver .6138 oz. ASW **Subject:** 300th Anniversary of Religious Peace

Date	F	VF	XF	Unc	BU
1855	40.00	70.00	100	150	—

KM# 354 THALER
18.5200 g., 0.9000 Silver .5360 oz. ASW **Note:** Veriens Thaler.

Date	F	VF	XF	Unc	BU
1857	190	330	750	1,600	—

KM# 355 THALER
18.5200 g., 0.9000 Silver .5360 oz. ASW **Obv:** House roofs visible around tower at left

Date	F	VF	XF	Unc	BU
1857-1858	40.00	90.00	200	400	—

KM# 359 THALER
18.5200 g., 0.9000 Silver .5360 oz. ASW **Subject:** Schiller Centennial **Note:** Gedenk Thaler.

Date	F	VF	XF	Unc	BU
1859	20.00	40.00	70.00	120	—

KM# 360 THALER
18.5200 g., 0.9000 Silver .5360 oz. ASW **Note:** Vereins Thaler.

Date	F	VF	XF	Unc	BU
1859-1860	20.00	35.00	60.00	100	—

KM# 366 THALER
18.5200 g., 0.9000 Silver .5360 oz. ASW **Obv:** Different hair knot

Date	F	VF	XF	Unc	BU
1861	120	200	420	800	—

KM# 370 THALER
18.5200 g., 0.9000 Silver .5360 oz. ASW **Obv:** Different dress

Date	F	VF	XF	Unc	BU
1862-1865	20.00	40.00	65.00	130	—

KM# 371 THALER
18.5200 g., 0.9000 Silver .5360 oz. ASW **Subject:** German
Shooting Festival **Obv:** Similar to KM#359 **Note:** Gedenk Thaler.

Date	F	VF	XF	Unc	BU
1862	20.00	40.00	65.00	110	—

KM# 372 THALER
18.5200 g., 0.9000 Silver .5360 oz. ASW **Subject:** Assembly of
Princes

Date	F	VF	XF	Unc	BU
1863	35.00	70.00	135	220	—

KM# 329 2 THALER (3-1/2 Gulden)
37.1000 g., 0.9000 Silver 1.0743 oz. ASW **Rev:** Value

Date	F	VF	XF	Unc	BU
1841-1855	60.00	110	180	400	—

KM# 365 2 THALER (3-1/2 Gulden)
37.0400 g., 0.9000 Silver 1.0717 oz. ASW

Date	F	VF	XF	Unc	BU
1860-1866	20.00	38.00	70.00	110	—

TRADE COINAGE

KM# 352 DUCAT
3.5000 g., 0.9860 Gold .1109 oz. AGW

Date	F	VF	XF	Unc	BU
1853-1856	300	450	900	1,600	—

HAMBURG

The city of Hamburg is located on the Elbe River about 75 miles
(125 kilometers) from the North Sea. In 1510, Hamburg was granted
the status of a Free City of the Empire, although it had actually been
free for about 250 years. It was occupied by the French during the
period of the Napoleonic Wars. In 1866, Hamburg joined the North German Confederation and became a part of the German Empire in 1871.

FREE CITY
REGULAR COINAGE

KM# 270   DREILING (3 Pfennig; 1/4 Schilling; 1/128 Thaler)
0.5100 g., 0.1870 Silver .0030 oz. ASW   **Rev:** "I" between six-pointed stars

Date	F	VF	XF	Unc	BU
1851	3.00	7.00	12.00	18.00	25.00

KM# 275   DREILING (3 Pfennig; 1/4 Schilling; 1/128 Thaler)
0.5100 g., 0.1870 Silver .0030 oz. ASW   **Note:** Beaded borders.

Date	F	VF	XF	Unc	BU
1855	3.00	7.00	10.00	18.00	25.00

KM# 271   SECHSLING (6 Pfennig; 1/2 Schilling; 1/64 Thaler)
0.7600 g., 0.2500 Silver .0061 oz. ASW   **Rev:** "I" between six-pointed stars

Date	F	VF	XF	Unc	BU
1851	3.00	7.00	11.00	16.00	20.00

KM# 276   SECHSLING (6 Pfennig; 1/2 Schilling; 1/64 Thaler)
0.7600 g., 0.2500 Silver .0061 oz. ASW   **Note:** Beaded borders

Date	F	VF	XF	Unc	BU
1855	3.00	7.00	12.00	18.00	25.00

KM# 272   SCHILLING
1.0800 g., 0.3750 Silver .0130 oz. ASW   **Rev:** "I" between six-pointed stars

Date	F	VF	XF	Unc	BU
1851	4.00	8.00	12.00	22.00	30.00

KM# 277   SCHILLING
1.0800 g., 0.3750 Silver .0130 oz. ASW   **Note:** Beaded borders.

Date	F	VF	XF	Unc	BU
1855	3.00	7.00	12.00	18.00	25.00

TRADE COINAGE

KM# 263   DUCAT
3.4900 g., 0.9790 Gold .1099 oz. AGW   **Note:** Struck in a collar.

Date	F	VF	XF	Unc	BU
1843-1850	200	325	550	875	—

KM# 273   DUCAT
3.4900 g., 0.9790 Gold .1099 oz. AGW   **Obv:** Knights' shield redesigned

Date	F	VF	XF	Unc	BU
1851-1853	225	375	750	1,000	—

KM# 274   DUCAT
3.4900 g., 0.9790 Gold .1099 oz. AGW

Date	F	VF	XF	Unc	BU
1854-1867	150	200	350	700	—

KM# 280   DUCAT
3.4900 g., 0.0700 Gold .1099 oz. AGW   **Rev:** Mint mark B below shell

Date	F	VF	XF	Unc	BU
1868-1872	135	175	300	600	—

REFORM COINAGE

KM# 290   2 MARK
11.1110 g., 0.9000 Silver .3215 oz. ASW

Date	F	VF	XF	Unc	BU
1876-1888	20.00	45.00	225	500	600

KM# 294   2 MARK
11.1110 g., 0.9000 Silver .3215 oz. ASW

Date	F	VF	XF	Unc	BU
1901-1914	10.00	25.00	50.00	140	160

KM# 296   3 MARK
16.6670 g., 0.9000 Silver .4823 oz. ASW

Date	F	VF	XF	Unc	BU
1908-1914	12.50	25.00	40.00	80.00	100

KM# 287 5 MARK
27.7770 g., 0.9000 Silver .8038 oz. ASW **Rev:** Type I

Date	F	VF	XF	Unc	BU
1875-1888	30.00	50.00	350	1,250	1,750

KM# 291 5 MARK
1.9910 g., 0.9000 Gold .0576 oz. AGW

Date	F	VF	XF	Unc	BU
1877	200	300	400	600	800

KM# 293 5 MARK
27.7770 g., 0.9000 Silver .8038 oz. ASW

Date	F	VF	XF	Unc	BU
(1901-1913)-1913	16.00	32.00	60.00	165	250

KM# 285 10 MARK
3.9820 g., 0.9000 Gold .1152 oz. AGW **Rev:** Type I

Date	F	VF	XF	Unc	BU
1873	600	1,300	2,000	3,500	4,500

KM# 286 10 MARK
3.9820 g., 0.9000 Gold .1152 oz. AGW **Rev:** Type II

Date	F	VF	XF	Unc	BU
1874	450	800	1,500	2,500	3,000

KM# 288 10 MARK
3.9820 g., 0.9000 Gold .1152 oz. AGW

Date	F	VF	XF	Unc	BU
1875-1888	85.00	125	200	350	450

KM# 292 10 MARK
3.9820 g., 0.9000 Gold .1152 oz. AGW **Rev:** Type II

Date	F	VF	XF	Unc	BU
1890-1913	90.00	150	225	300	375

KM# 289 20 MARK
7.9650 g., 0.9000 Gold .2304 oz. AGW **Rev:** Type II

Date	F	VF	XF	Unc	BU
1875-1889	—	BV	155	250	325

KM# 295 20 MARK
7.9650 g., 0.9000 Gold .2304 oz. AGW **Rev:** Type III

Date	F	VF	XF	Unc	BU
1893-1913	—	BV	160	200	275

TOKEN COINAGE
Reckoning Tokens

KM# Tn1 1/100 VERRECHNUNGSMARKE
Aluminum, 20.5 mm. **Issuer:** Hamburg Bank **Obv:** City arms **Rev:** Denomination

Date	F	VF	XF	Unc	BU
1923	3.00	6.00	12.50	25.00	—

KM# Tn2 5/100 VERRECHNUNGSMARKE
Aluminum, 23 mm. **Issuer:** Hamburg Bank **Obv:** City arms **Rev:** Denomination

Date	F	VF	XF	Unc	BU
1923	2.75	4.50	9.00	18.00	—

KM# Tn3   1/10 VERRECHNUNGSMARKE
Aluminum, 26.5 mm. **Issuer:** Hamburg Bank **Obv:** City arms **Rev:**
Denomination

Date	F	VF	XF	Unc	BU
1923	2.75	4.50	10.00	20.00	—

HANNOVER

PROVINCIAL CITY

Located in North Central Germany, Hannover had its beginnings as early as the 12th century. The city obtained the mint right
in 1331, but fell under the control of the dukes of Brunswick who
later made it their residence. Hannover eventually became the capitol of the Kingdom of the same name. The city coinage lasted until
1674.

ARMS
3-petaled cloverleaf or complex arms consisting of twin-towered city gate, 3-petaled cloverleaf in portal and rampant lion left
between towers.

REGULAR COINAGE

KM# 201.1   PFENNIG
Copper   **Rev:** B below value

Date	F	VF	XF	Unc	BU
1845-1851	4.00	9.00	15.00	25.00	35.00

KM# 201.2   PFENNIG
Copper   **Rev:** A below value

Date	F	VF	XF	Unc	BU
1846-1849	4.00	9.00	15.00	25.00	35.00

KM# 216   PFENNIG
Copper   **Obv:** V below monogram

Date	F	VF	XF	Unc	BU
1852	12.00	25.00	40.00	90.00	120

KM# 221   PFENNIG
Copper

Date	F	VF	XF	Unc	BU
1853-1856	2.00	5.00	12.00	30.00	40.00

KM# 233   PFENNIG
Copper

Date	F	VF	XF	Unc	BU
1858-1864	2.00	5.00	11.00	20.00	30.00

KM# 202.1   2 PFENNIG
Copper   **Rev:** B below date, struck in a ring

Date	F	VF	XF	Unc	BU
1845-1851	5.00	10.00	15.00	40.00	60.00

KM# 202.2   2 PFENNIG
Copper   **Rev:** A below date

Date	F	VF	XF	Unc	BU
1846-1849	5.00	10.00	15.00	40.00	60.00

KM# 217   2 PFENNIG
Copper   **Rev:** B below date

Date	F	VF	XF	Unc	BU
1852-1856	2.00	5.00	8.00	30.00	40.00

KM# 234   2 PFENNIG
Copper

Date	F	VF	XF	Unc	BU
1858-1864	2.00	5.00	11.00	20.00	30.00

KM# 205   6 PFENNIG
1.3900 g., 0.2180 Silver .0097 oz. ASW

Date	F	VF	XF	Unc	BU
1846-1851	5.00	10.00	15.00	30.00	45.00

KM# 218   6 PFENNIG
1.3900 g., 0.2180 Silver .0097 oz. ASW

Date	F	VF	XF	Unc	BU
1852-1855	5.00	10.00	15.00	32.00	45.00

KM# 235 1/2 GROSCHEN
1.0900 g., 0.2200 Silver .0077 oz. ASW

Date	F	VF	XF	Unc	BU
1858-1865	2.00	5.00	10.00	20.00	30.00

KM# 236 GROSCHEN
2.1900 g., 0.2200 Silver .0154 oz. ASW

Date	F	VF	XF	Unc	BU
1858-1866	2.00	4.00	7.50	18.00	24.00

KINGDOM

Located in North Central Germany, Hannover had its beginnings as early as the 12th century. The city obtained the mint right in 1331, but fell under the control of the dukes of Brunswick who later made it their residence. Hannover eventually became the capitol of the Kingdom of the same name. The city coinage lasted until 1674.

ARMS
3-petaled cloverleaf or complex arms consisting of twin-towered city gate, 3-petaled cloverleaf in portal and rampant lion left between towers.

REGULAR COINAGE

KM# 227 1/24 THALER
1.9400 g., 0.3120 Silver .0194 oz. ASW

Date	F	VF	XF	Unc	BU
1854-1856	8.00	15.00	18.00	40.00	60.00

KM# 206 1/12 THALER (3 Mariengroschen)
2.6700 g., 0.5200 Silver .0446 oz. ASW **Obv:** Larger head

Date	F	VF	XF	Unc	BU
1848-1851	5.00	10.00	15.00	40.00	55.00

KM# 219 1/12 THALER (3 Mariengroschen)
2.67 g., 0.52 Silver .0446 oz. ASW **Obv:** BREHMER F at truncation

Date	F	VF	XF	Unc	BU
1852-1853	4.00	10.00	24.00	45.00	60.00

KM# 237 1/12 THALER (3 Mariengroschen)
3.2200 g., 0.3750 Silver .0388 oz. ASW **Obv:** Without name at truncation **Rev:** Value: SCHEIDEMUNZE

Date	F	VF	XF	Unc	BU
1859-1862	3.00	8.00	15.00	85.00	120

KM# 238 1/6 THALER
5.3400 g., 0.5200 Silver .0893 oz. ASW

Date	F	VF	XF	Unc	BU
1859-1866	2.00	5.00	10.00	45.00	60.00

KM# 197.1 THALER
16.8200 g., 0.9930 Silver .5370 oz. ASW **Obv:** A below head

Date	F	VF	XF	Unc	BU
1842-1849	20.00	40.00	80.00	200	300

KM# 208 THALER
16.8200 g., 0.9930 Silver .5370 oz. ASW **Obv:** BREHMER F. at truncation

Date	F	VF	XF	Unc	BU
1848-1849	20.00	45.00	70.00	160	220

KM# 209.1 THALER
16.8200 g., 0.9930 Silver .5370 oz. ASW **Rev:** HARZ SEGEN above crown

Date	F	VF	XF	Unc	BU
1849	60.00	100	300	1,000	1,500

KM# 209.2 THALER
16.8200 g., 0.9930 Silver .5370 oz. ASW **Rev:** BERGSEGEN DES HARZES above crown

Date	F	VF	XF	Unc	BU
1850-1851	20.00	45.00	70.00	175	220

KM# 220 THALER
16.8200 g., 0.9930 Silver .5370 oz. ASW

Date	F	VF	XF	Unc	BU
1852-1856	10.00	25.00	60.00	125	175

KM# 230 THALER
18.5200 g., 0.9000 Silver .5360 oz. ASW

Date	F	VF	XF	Unc	BU
1857-1866	15.00	25.00	35.00	75.00	100

KM# 241 THALER
18.5200 g., 0.9000 Silver .5360 oz. ASW **Subject:** 50th Anniversary - Battle of Waterloo

Date	F	VF	XF	Unc	BU
1865	30.00	50.00	70.00	140	175

KM# 242 THALER
18.5200 g., 0.9000 Silver .5360 oz. ASW **Subject:** 50th Anniversary Union East Friesia and Hannover

Date	F	VF	XF	Unc	BU
1865	100	165	225	325	475

KM# 243 THALER
18.5200 g., 0.9000 Silver .5360 oz. ASW **Subject:** Frisian Oath Commemorative

Date	F	VF	XF	Unc	BU
1865	70.00	165	240	300	425

KM# 229 2 THALER (3-1/2 Gulden)
37.1200 g., 0.9000 Silver 1.0742 oz. ASW

Date	F	VF	XF	Unc	BU
1854-1855	50.00	90.00	135	275	350

KM# 240 2 THALER (3-1/2 Gulden)
37.0400 g., 0.9000 Silver 1.0719 oz. ASW

Date	F	VF	XF	Unc	BU
1862-1866	65.00	100	150	250	325

KM# 185.2   2-1/2 THALER
3.3200 g., 0.8960 Gold .0956 oz. AGW

Date	F	VF	XF	Unc	BU
1845-1848	225	400	600	1,000	—

KM# 215   2-1/2 THALER
3.3200 g., 0.8960 Gold .0956 oz. AGW

Date	F	VF	XF	Unc	BU
1850	200	300	500	900	—

KM# 223   2-1/2 THALER
3.3200 g., 0.8960 Gold .0956 oz. AGW   **Obv:** BREHMER F. at truncation, B below

Date	F	VF	XF	Unc	BU
1853-1855	175	350	700	1,000	—

KM# 204   5 THALER
6.6500 g., 0.8960 Gold .1916 oz. AGW   **Obv:** B below head

Date	F	VF	XF	Unc	BU
1845-1848	300	500	800	1,350	—

KM# 210   5 THALER
6.6500 g., 0.8960 Gold .1916 oz. AGW

Date	F	VF	XF	Unc	BU
1849-1851	300	500	750	1,350	—

KM# 211   5 THALER
6.6500 g., 0.8960 Gold .1916 oz. AGW   **Rev:** HARZ GOLD added to legend

Date	F	VF	XF	Unc	BU
1849-1850	300	500	750	1,300	—

KM# 224   5 THALER
6.6500 g., 0.8960 Gold .1916 oz. AGW   **Obv:** BREHMER F. at truncation, B below

Date	F	VF	XF	Unc	BU
1853-1856	300	500	750	1,200	—

KM# 225   5 THALER
6.6500 g., 0.8960 Gold .1916 oz. AGW   **Rev:** HARZ GOLD added to legend

Date	F	VF	XF	Unc	BU
1853-1856	500	875	1,200	2,250	—

KM# 200.3   10 THALER
13.3000 g., 0.8960 Gold .3832 oz. AGW   **Obv:** Without markings on truncation

Date	F	VF	XF	Unc	BU
1846-1848	300	600	900	1,500	—

KM# 212   10 THALER
13.3000 g., 0.8960 Gold .3832 oz. AGW

Date	F	VF	XF	Unc	BU
1849-1851	350	600	1,000	1,500	—

KM# 226   10 THALER
13.3000 g., 0.8960 Gold .3832 oz. AGW

Date	F	VF	XF	Unc	BU
1853-1856	300	500	900	1,250	—

TRADE COINAGE

KM# 231   1/2 KRONE
5.5500 g., 0.9000 Gold .1606 oz. AGW

Date	F	VF	XF	Unc	BU
1857-1866	300	600	950	1,500	—

KM# 232   KRONE
11.1100 g., 0.9000 Gold .3215 oz. AGW

Date	F	VF	XF	Unc	BU
1857-1866	350	500	900	1,500	—

HESSE-CASSEL

(Hessen-Kassel)

The Hesse principalities were located for the most part north of the Main River, bounded by Westphalia on the west, the Brunswick duchies on the north, the Saxon-Thuringian duchies on the east and Rhine Palatinate and the bishoprics of Mainz and Fulda on the south.

ARMS
Hessian lion rampant left.
Diez – 2 leopards passant to left, one above the other.
Katzenelnbogen – Crowned lion springing to left.
Nidda – 2-fold divided horizontally, two 8-pointed stars in upper half, lower half shaded.
Ziegenhain – 2-fold divided horizontally, 6-pointed star in upper half, lower half shaded.

PRINCIPALITY
REGULAR COINAGE

KM# 613   HELLER
Copper   **Note:** Issued under Friedrich Wilhelm.

Date	F	VF	XF	Unc	BU
1849-1866	5.00	10.00	20.00	30.00	—

KM# 612   3 HELLER
Copper   **Ruler:** Friedrich Wilhelm

Date	F	VF	XF	Unc	BU
1848-1866	4.00	6.00	12.00	18.00	—

KM# 615   SILBER GROSCHEN
2.0000 g., 0.3120 Silver .0156 oz. ASW

Date	F	VF	XF	Unc	BU
1851-1866	6.00	12.00	25.00	50.00	—

KM# 620   2-1/2 SILBER GROSCHEN
3.2500 g., 0.3750 Silver .0391 oz. ASW

Date	F	VF	XF	Unc	BU
1852-1865	6.00	12.00	24.00	50.00	—

KM# 616   1/6 THALER
5.3500 g., 0.5200 Silver .0894 oz. ASW   **Obv:** C.P. at truncation

Date	F	VF	XF	Unc	BU
1851-1856	12.00	25.00	90.00	130	—

KM# 617   THALER
22.2700 g., 0.7500 Silver .5371 oz. ASW   **Obv:** C. PFEUFFER F. at truncation

Date	F	VF	XF	Unc	BU
1851-1855	40.00	100	280	1,200	—

KM# 621.1   THALER
18.5200 g., 0.9000 Silver .5360 oz. ASW   **Obv:** With C.P. at truncation

Date	F	VF	XF	Unc	BU
1858-1865	33.00	55.00	160	250	—

KM# 621.2 THALER
18.5200 g., 0.9000 Silver .5360 oz. ASW **Obv:** Without C.P. at truncation

Date	F	VF	XF	Unc	BU
1858-1865	40.00	70.00	150	260	—

KM# 618.1 2 THALER (3-1/2 Gulden)
37.1200 g., 0.9000 Silver 1.0742 oz. ASW **Obv:** CP on truncation

Date	F	VF	XF	Unc	BU
1851-1855	60.00	100	250	500	—

KM# 618.2 2 THALER (3-1/2 Gulden)
37.1200 g., 0.9000 Silver 1.0741 oz. ASW **Ruler:** Friedrich Wilhelm **Obv:** Without CP on truncation

Date	F	VF	XF	Unc	BU
1854-1855	70.00	120	280	550	—

KM# 619 5 THALER (1 Pistole or Friedrich d'or)
6.6500 g., 0.9000 Gold .1924 oz. AGW **Obv:** CP on truncation

Date	F	VF	XF	Unc	BU
1851	1,400	1,900	2,800	3,800	—

HESSE-DARMSTADT
(Hessen-Darmstadt)

Founded by the youngest of Philipp I's four sons upon the death of their father in 1567, Hesse-Darmstadt was one of the two main branches of the family which survived past the beginning of the 17th century. The Landgrave was elevated to the status of Grand Duke in 1806 and reacquired Hesse-Homburg, which got its souveranity back in 1816. In 1815 the Congress of Vienna awarded Hesse-Darmstadt the city of Worms and all of Mainz. These were relinquished, along with Hesse-Homburg, to Prussia in 1866 and Hesse-Darmstadt was called just Hesse from 1867 onwards. Hesse became part of the German Empire in 1871, but ceased to exist as a semi-sovereign state at the end of World War I.

GRAND DUCHY
REGULAR COINAGE

KM# 323 HELLER (Pfennig)
Copper **Ruler:** Ludwig III

Date	F	VF	XF	Unc	BU
1848-1855	4.00	7.00	23.00	50.00	—

KM# 337 PFENNIG (Heller)
Copper **Ruler:** Ludwig III

Date	F	VF	XF	Unc	BU
1857-1872	4.00	9.00	14.00	45.00	—

KM# 324 KREUZER
0.8300 g., 0.1660 Silver .0044 oz. ASW **Ruler:** Ludwig III

Date	F	VF	XF	Unc	BU
1848-1856	4.00	8.00	18.00	35.00	—

KM# 339 KREUZER
0.8300 g., 0.1660 Silver .0044 oz. ASW **Ruler:** Ludwig III

Date	F	VF	XF	Unc	BU
1858-1872	4.00	9.00	20.00	30.00	—

KM# 325 3 KREUZER
1.3900 g., 0.2810 Silver .0125 oz. ASW **Ruler:** Ludwig III

Date	F	VF	XF	Unc	BU
1848-1856	6.00	10.00	25.00	60.00	—

KM# 345   3 KREUZER
1.2300 g., 0.2500 Silver .0138 oz. ASW   **Ruler:** Ludwig III

Date	F	VF	XF	Unc	BU
1864-1867	5.00	12.00	25.00	50.00	—

KM# 326   6 KREUZER
2.4600 g., 0.3500 Silver .0276 oz. ASW   **Ruler:** Ludwig III

Date	F	VF	XF	Unc	BU
1848-1856	6.00	14.00	25.00	50.00	—

KM# 346   6 KREUZER
2.4600 g., 0.3500 Silver .0276 oz. ASW   **Ruler:** Ludwig III

Date	F	VF	XF	Unc	BU
1864-1867	6.00	12.00	45.00	75.00	—

KM# 336   1/2 GULDEN
5.3000 g., 0.9000 Silver .1533 oz. ASW   **Ruler:** Ludwig III **Obv:** VOIGHT below head

Date	F	VF	XF	Unc	BU
1855	50.00	125	320	700	—

KM# 327   GULDEN
10.6000 g., 0.9000 Silver .3067 oz. ASW   **Ruler:** Ludwig II **Subject:** Public Freedom Through German Parliament

Date	F	VF	XF	Unc	BU
1848	—	250	400	600	—

KM# 328   GULDEN
10.5800 g., 0.9000 Silver .3061 oz. ASW   **Ruler:** Ludwig III

Date	F	VF	XF	Unc	BU
1848-1856	40.00	80.00	130	270	—

KM# 329   2 GULDEN
21.2100 g., 0.9000 Silver .6138 oz. ASW   **Ruler:** Ludwig III **Obv:** VOIGHT below head

Date	F	VF	XF	Unc	BU
1849-1856	40.00	90.00	230	400	—

KM# 338   THALER
18.5200 g., 0.9000 Silver .5360 oz. ASW   **Ruler:** Ludwig III **Note:** Vereins Thaler.

Date	F	VF	XF	Unc	BU
1857-1871	35.00	70.00	150	330	—

KM# 335   2 THALER (3-1/2 Gulden)
37.1200 g., 0.9000 Silver 1.0742 oz. ASW   **Ruler:** Ludwig III **Rev:** Similar to KM#320

Date	F	VF	XF	Unc	BU
1854	300	750	1,100	2,300	—

REFORM COINAGE
Grossherzogtum within the German Empire

KM# 355   2 MARK
11.1110 g., 0.9000 Silver .3215 oz. ASW   **Ruler:** Ludwig III

Date	F	VF	XF	Unc	BU
1876-1877	120	350	3,000	—	—

KM# 359   2 MARK
11.1110 g., 0.9000 Silver .3215 oz. ASW   **Ruler:** Ludwig IV

Date	F	VF	XF	Unc	BU
1888	500	1,900	3,800	7,000	—

KM# 363   2 MARK
11.1110 g., 0.9 Silver .3215 oz. ASW   **Ruler:** Ludwig IV **Rev:** Type III

Date	F	VF	XF	Unc	BU
1891	400	700	1,500	4,000	5,000

KM# 368   2 MARK
11.1110 g., 0.9000 Silver .3215 oz. ASW   **Ruler:** Ernst Ludwig

Date	F	VF	XF	Unc	BU
1895-1900	190	400	1,000	2,500	3,000

KM# 372   2 MARK
11.1110 g., 0.9000 Silver .3215 oz. ASW   **Ruler:** Ernst Ludwig
Subject: 400th Birthday of Philipp the Magnanimous

Date	F	VF	XF	Unc	BU
1904	30.00	60.00	90.00	140	200

KM# 375   3 MARK
16.6670 g., 0.9000 Silver .4823 oz. ASW   **Ruler:** Ernst Ludwig

Date	F	VF	XF	Unc	BU
1910	50.00	100	150	400	550

KM# 376   3 MARK
16.6670 g., 0.9000 Silver .4823 oz. ASW   **Ruler:** Ernst Ludwig
Subject: 25-Year Jubilee **Note:** All minted pieces are proof.
Values in circulated grades are for impaired proofs.

Date	F	VF	XF	Unc	BU
1917	—	3,000	4,600	6,000	8,000

KM# 353   5 MARK
27.7770 g., 0.9000 Silver .8038 oz. ASW   **Ruler:** Ludwig III **Rev:** Type II

Date	F	VF	XF	Unc	BU
1875-1876	60.00	150	2,200	8,000	—

KM# 356   5 MARK
1.9910 g., 0.9000 Gold .0576 oz. AGW   **Ruler:** Ludwig III

Date	F	VF	XF	Unc	BU
1877	800	1,300	1,800	3,000	4,000

KM# 357   5 MARK
1.9910 g., 0.9000 Gold .0576 oz. AGW   **Ruler:** Ludwig IV **Rev:** Type II

Date	F	VF	XF	Unc	BU
1877	800	1,400	2,000	3,200	4,000

KM# 360   5 MARK
27.7770 g., 0.9000 Silver .8038 oz. ASW   **Ruler:** Ludwig IV **Rev:** Type II

Date	F	VF	XF	Unc	BU
1888	650	1,800	3,800	9,000	—

KM# 364   5 MARK
27.7770 g., 0.9000 Silver .8038 oz. ASW   **Ruler:** Ludwig IV **Rev:** Type III

Date	F	VF	XF	Unc	BU
1891	300	800	3,200	8,000	—

KM# 369   5 MARK
27.7770 g., 0.9000 Silver .8038 oz. ASW   **Ruler:** Ernst Ludwig

Date	F	VF	XF	Unc	BU
1895-1900	90.00	200	950	2,500	—

KM# 373   5 MARK
27.7770 g., 0.9000 Silver .8038 oz. ASW   **Ruler:** Ernst Ludwig
Subject: 400th birthday of Philipp the Magnanimous

Date	F	VF	XF	Unc	BU
1904	70.00	130	200	350	—

KM# 350   10 MARK
3.9820 g., 0.9000 Gold .1152 oz. AGW   **Ruler:** Ludwig III

Date	F	VF	XF	Unc	BU
1872-1873	180	300	450	1,300	2,000

KM# 354   10 MARK
3.9820 g., 0.9000 Gold .1152 oz. AGW   **Ruler:** Ludwig III **Rev:** Type II

Date	F	VF	XF	Unc	BU
1875-1877	150	300	450	2,200	4,000

KM# 358   10 MARK
3.9820 g., 0.9000 Gold .1152 oz. AGW   **Ruler:** Ludwig IV

Date	F	VF	XF	Unc	BU
1878-1880	250	500	650	1,700	2,000

KM# 361   10 MARK
3.9820 g., 0.9000 Gold .1152 oz. AGW   **Ruler:** Ludwig IV

Date	F	VF	XF	Unc	BU
1888	350	750	1,200	2,400	3,000

KM# 362   10 MARK
3.9820 g., 0.9000 Gold .1152 oz. AGW   **Ruler:** Ludwig IV **Edge:** Vines and stars

Date	F	VF	XF	Unc	BU
1890	400	650	1,000	2,000	2,600

KM# 366   10 MARK
3.9820 g., 0.9000 Gold .1152 oz. AGW   **Ruler:** Ernst Ludwig **Rev:** Type III

Date	F	VF	XF	Unc	BU
1893	550	1,000	1,500	3,000	3,500

KM# 370   10 MARK
3.9820 g., 0.9000 Gold .1152 oz. AGW   **Ruler:** Ernst Ludwig

Date	F	VF	XF	Unc	BU
1896-1898	240	500	900	1,800	2,400

KM# 351   20 MARK
7.9650 g., 0.9000 Gold .2304 oz. AGW   **Ruler:** Ludwig III **Rev:** Type I

Date	F	VF	XF	Unc	BU
1872-1873	130	280	550	1,500	2,000

KM# 352   20 MARK
7.9650 g., 0.9000 Gold .2304 oz. AGW   **Ruler:** Ludwig III **Rev:** Type II

Date	F	VF	XF	Unc	BU
1874	350	600	800	2,800	4,000

KM# 365   20 MARK
7.9650 g., 0.9000 Gold .2304 oz. AGW   **Ruler:** Ludwig IV

Date	F	VF	XF	Unc	BU
1892	800	1,500	2,100	4,500	5,000

KM# 367   20 MARK
7.9650 g., 0.9000 Gold .2304 oz. AGW   **Ruler:** Ernst Ludwig **Rev:** Type III

Date	F	VF	XF	Unc	BU
1893	700	1,400	1,900	3,500	4,000

KM# 371   20 MARK
7.9650 g., 0.9000 Gold .2304 oz. AGW   **Ruler:** Ernst Ludwig

Date	F	VF	XF	Unc	BU
1896-1903	200	350	600	1,250	2,000

KM# 374   20 MARK
7.9650 g., 0.9000 Gold .2304 oz. AGW   **Ruler:** Ernst Ludwig

Date	F	VF	XF	Unc	BU
1905-1911	155	310	400	900	900

HESSE-HOMBURG

Located in west central Germany, Hesse-Homburg was created from part of Hesse-Darmstadt in 1622. It had six villages along with Homburg (today Bad Homburg) and is mostly known for its famous landgrave, Friedrich II. Commander of the Brandenburg cavalry, Friedrich II (with the silver leg) won the Battle of Fehrbellin in 1675. Hesse-Homburg was mediatized to Hesse-Darmstadt in 1806 and by 1816 had acquired full sovereignty and the lordship of Meisenheim. The Homburg line became extinct in 1866, and along with Hesse-Darmstadt, was annexed by Prussia.

PRINCIPALITY

REGULAR COINAGE

KM# 20   THALER (Vereins)
18.5200 g., 0.9000 Silver .5358 oz. ASW   **Ruler:** Philipp August

Date	F	VF	XF	Unc	BU
1858-1863	60.00	120	220	400	—

HOHENZOLLERN, UNDER PRUSSIA

In 1849, Prussia obtained the Hohenzollern lands due to the 1848 revolutions and political unrest. One series of coins was issued by Prussia for their Hohenzollern holdings.

PRINCIPALITY
REGULAR COINAGE

KM# 1 KREUZER
Copper **Ruler:** Friedrich Wilhelm IV (of Prussia)

Date	F	VF	XF	Unc	BU
1852	15.00	25.00	50.00	90.00	115

KM# 2 3 KREUZER
1.2900 g., 0.3330 Silver .0138 oz. ASW **Ruler:** Friedrich Wilhelm IV (of Prussia)

Date	F	VF	XF	Unc	BU
1852	15.00	50.00	75.00	140	180

KM# 3 6 KREUZER
2.5900 g., 0.3330 Silver .0277 oz. ASW **Ruler:** Friedrich Wilhelm IV (of Prussia)

Date	F	VF	XF	Unc	BU
1852	15.00	45.00	70.00	160	200

KM# 4 1/2 GULDEN
5.3000 g., 0.9000 Silver .1537 oz. ASW **Ruler:** Friedrich Wilhelm IV (of Prussia)

Date	F	VF	XF	Unc	BU
1852	25.00	45.00	60.00	150	185

KM# 5 GULDEN
10.6000 g., 0.9000 Silver .3067 oz. ASW **Ruler:** Friedrich Wilhelm IV (of Prussia)

Date	F	VF	XF	Unc	BU
1852	30.00	60.00	90.00	160	210

HOHENZOLLERN-SIGMARINGEN
PRINCIPALITY
REGULAR COINAGE

KM# 15 1/2 GULDEN
5.3000 g., 0.9000 Silver .1533 oz. ASW

Date	F	VF	XF	Unc	BU
1838-1848	35.00	60.00	135	250	325

KM# 16.2 GULDEN
10.6000 g., 0.9000 Silver .3067 oz. ASW **Obv:** DOELL below head

Date	F	VF	XF	Unc	BU
1839-1848	40.00	90.00	200	350	450

KM# 25 GULDEN
10.6000 g., 0.9000 Silver .3067 oz. ASW **Obv:** BALBACH below head

Date	F	VF	XF	Unc	BU
1849	75.00	175	450	725	925

KM# 24 2 GULDEN
21.2100 g., 0.9000 Silver .6138 oz. ASW

Date	F	VF	XF	Unc	BU
1845-1848	175	400	525	750	950

KM# 26 2 GULDEN
21.2100 g., 0.9000 Silver .6138 oz. ASW **Obv:** BALBACH below bust

Date	F	VF	XF	Unc	BU
1849	325	750	1,000	1,900	2,400

LIPPE-DETMOLD

After the division of 1613, the Counts of Lippe-Detmold, as the senior branch of the family, ruled over the largest portion of Lippe (see), a small patrimony in northwestern Germany. The younger brother of Hermann Adolf founded the line of Lippe-Sternberg-Schwalenberg (Biesterfeld) in 1652, which lasted into the 20th century. In 1720, the count was raised to the rank of prince, but did not use the title until 1789. Lippe joined the North German Confederation in 1866 and became part of the German Empire in 1871. Prince Alexander was declared insane and placed under a regency during his entire reign. There ensued a ten-year testamentary dispute between the Lippe-Biesterfeld and the Schaumburg-Lippe lines over the succession to the childless Alexander - a Wilhelmine cause célèbre. Leopold (V) of the Biesterfeld line gained the principality in 1905, but was forced to abdicate in 1918, at the end of World War I. In 1947, Lippe was absorbed by the German state of North Rhine-Westphalia.

PRINCIPALITY
REGULAR COINAGE

KM# 260 PFENNING
Copper **Ruler:** Paul Friedrich Emil Leopold III

Date	F	VF	XF	Unc	BU
1851-1858	4.00	8.00	12.00	25.00	35.00

KM# 261 3 PFENNINGE
Copper **Ruler:** Paul Friedrich Emil Leopold III

Date	F	VF	XF	Unc	BU
1858	8.00	15.00	25.00	50.00	70.00

KM# 265 SILBER GROSCHEN
2.1900 g., 0.2200 Silver .0154 oz. ASW **Ruler:** Paul Friedrich Emil Leopold III

Date	F	VF	XF	Unc	BU
1860	10.00	20.00	35.00	45.00	60.00

KM# 266 2-1/2 SILBER GROSCHEN
3.2200 g., 0.3750 Silver .0388 oz. ASW **Ruler:** Paul Friedrich Emil Leopold III

Date	F	VF	XF	Unc	BU
1860	8.00	15.00	30.00	65.00	90.00

KM# 267 THALER
18.5200 g., 0.9000 Silver .5360 oz. ASW **Ruler:** Paul Friedrich Emil Leopold III

Date	F	VF	XF	Unc	BU
1860-1866	30.00	65.00	125	200	270

REFORM COINAGE

KM# 270 2 MARK
11.1110 g., 0.9000 Silver .3215 oz. ASW **Ruler:** Leopold IV

Date	F	VF	XF	Unc	BU
1906	125	250	350	475	575

KM# 275 3 MARK
16.6670 g., 0.9000 Silver .4823 oz. ASW **Ruler:** Leopold IV

Date	F	VF	XF	Unc	BU
1913	150	300	425	550	700

LUBECK

The original settlement was called Liubice, the capital of a Slavic principality. It was located at the confluence of the Schwartau with the Trave Rivers and contained a castle with a merchant town on a harbor. After 1815, the city was a member of the German Confederation and joined the North German Confederation in 1866. It remained a free city as part of the German Empire from 1871 until the end of World War I in 1918. However, its status as a self-governing entity, which had begun in 1226, did not end until 1937, when it was made a part of the province of Schleswig-Holstein.

FREE CITY
REFORM COINAGE

KM# 210 2 MARK
11.1110 g., 0.9000 Silver .3215 oz. ASW

Date	F	VF	XF	Unc	BU
1901	100	200	300	475	525

KM# 212 2 MARK
11.1110 g., 0.9000 Silver .3215 oz. ASW

Date	F	VF	XF	Unc	BU
1904-1912	45.00	85.00	135	220	275

KM# 215 3 MARK
16.6670 g., 0.9000 Silver .4823 oz. ASW

Date	F	VF	XF	Unc	BU
(1908-1914)-1914	25.00	70.00	125	200	225

KM# 213 5 MARK
27.7770 g., 0.9000 Silver .8038 oz. ASW

Date	F	VF	XF	Unc	BU
1904-1913	120	275	400	550	650

KM# 211 10 MARK
3.9820 g., 0.9000 Gold .1152 oz. AGW

Date	F	VF	XF	Unc	BU
1901-1904	375	800	1,200	1,650	2,000

KM# 214 10 MARK
3.9820 g., 0.9000 Gold .1152 oz. AGW

Date	F	VF	XF	Unc	BU
1905-1910	300	550	1,100	1,350	1,800

MECKLENBURG-SCHWERIN

The Duchy of Mecklenburg was divided in 1592 to form the branches of Mecklenburg-Schwerin and Mecklenburg-Güstrow. During the Thirty Years' War, the several dukes of the Mecklenburg states sided with the Protestant forces against the emperor. No coinage was produced for Mecklenburg-Schwerin from 1708 until 1750. In 1815, the Congress of Vienna elevated the ruler to the rank of Grand Duke. Mecklenburg-Schwerin became a part of the German Empire in 1871. The last grand duke abdicated at the end of World War I in 1918.

GRAND DUCHY
REGULAR COINAGE

KM# 315   PFENNIG
Copper   **Ruler:** Friedrich Franz II

Date	F	VF	XF	Unc	BU
1872	3.00	6.00	8.00	14.00	18.00

KM# 316   2 PFENNIG (Zweier)
Copper   **Ruler:** Friedrich Franz II

Date	F	VF	XF	Unc	BU
1872	3.00	6.00	8.00	13.00	20.00

KM# 299   3 PFENNIG (Dreiling)
Copper   **Ruler:** Friedrich Franz II

Date	F	VF	XF	Unc	BU
1843-1848	4.00	8.00	14.00	30.00	40.00

KM# 310   3 PFENNIG (Dreiling)
Copper   **Ruler:** Friedrich Franz II

Date	F	VF	XF	Unc	BU
1852-1864	3.00	6.00	10.00	25.00	35.00

KM# 317   5 PFENNIG
Copper   **Ruler:** Friedrich Franz II

Date	F	VF	XF	Unc	BU
1872	3.00	6.00	9.00	17.00	25.00

KM# 301   1/48 THALER (Schilling)
1.3000 g., 0.2080 Silver .0086 oz. ASW   **Ruler:** Friedrich Franz II

Date	F	VF	XF	Unc	BU
1848	4.00	8.00	15.00	40.00	55.00

KM# 311   1/48 THALER (Schilling)
1.3000 g., 0.2080 Silver .0086 oz. ASW   **Ruler:** Friedrich Franz II

Date	F	VF	XF	Unc	BU
1852-1866	4.00	8.00	11.00	22.00	30.00

KM# 302   1/12 THALER
2.4400 g., 0.5000 Silver .0392 oz. ASW   **Ruler:** Friedrich Franz II
Note: Varieties exist.

Date	F	VF	XF	Unc	BU
1848	5.00	10.00	20.00	50.00	65.00

KM# 303   1/6 THALER
5.3500 g., 0.5200 Silver .0894 oz. ASW   **Ruler:** Friedrich Franz II

Date	F	VF	XF	Unc	BU
1848	10.00	25.00	50.00	75.00	100

KM# 304   THALER
22.2700 g., 0.7500 Silver .5370 oz. ASW   **Ruler:** Friedrich Franz II

Date	F	VF	XF	Unc	BU
1848	35.00	60.00	115	225	270

KM# A310 THALER

18.5200 g., 0.9000 Silver .5360 oz. ASW **Ruler:** Friedrich II **Note:** Prev. KM#310.

Date	F	VF	XF	Unc	BU
1864	35.00	65.00	120	225	300

KM# A311 THALER

18.5200 g., 0.9000 Silver .5360 oz. ASW **Ruler:** Friedrich II **Subject:** 25th Anniversary of Reign **Note:** Prev. KM#311.

Date	F	VF	XF	Unc	BU
1867	30.00	60.00	100	175	240

REFORM COINAGE

KM# 320 2 MARK

11.1110 g., 0.9000 Silver .3215 oz. ASW **Ruler:** Friedrich Franz II

Date	F	VF	XF	Unc	BU
1876	110	250	775	2,750	3,500

KM# 330 2 MARK

11.1110 g., 0.9000 Silver .3215 oz. ASW **Ruler:** Friedrich Franz IV **Subject:** Grand Duke Coming of Age

Date	F	VF	XF	Unc	BU
1901	125	300	465	1,100	1,250

KM# 333 2 MARK

11.1110 g., 0.9000 Silver .3215 oz. ASW **Ruler:** Friedrich Franz IV **Subject:** Friedrich Franz IV Wedding

Date	F	VF	XF	Unc	BU
1904	18.00	40.00	65.00	100	120

KM# 340 3 MARK

16.6670 g., 0.9000 Silver .4823 oz. ASW **Ruler:** Friedrich Franz IV **Subject:** 100 Years as Grand Duchy

Date	F	VF	XF	Unc.	BU
1915	50.00	100	175	250	300

KM# 334 5 MARK

27.7770 g., 0.9000 Silver .8038 oz. ASW **Ruler:** Friedrich Franz IV **Subject:** Friedrich Franz IV Wedding

Date	F	VF	XF	Unc	BU
1904	45.00	100	175	250	325

KM# 341 5 MARK
27.7770 g., 0.9000 Silver .8038 oz. ASW **Ruler:**
Friedrich Franz IV **Subject:** 100 Years as Grand Duchy

Date	F	VF	XF	Unc	BU
1915	135	375	500	900	1,200

KM# 318 10 MARK
3.9820 g., 0.9000 Gold .1152 oz. AGW **Ruler:** Friedrich Franz II
Rev: Type I

Date	F	VF	XF	Unc	BU
1872	1,500	2,000	3,000	6,000	9,000

KM# 321 10 MARK
3.9820 g., 0.9000 Gold .1152 oz. AGW **Ruler:** Friedrich Franz II
Rev: Type II

Date	F	VF	XF	Unc	BU
1878	500	1,000	1,500	2,000	2,500

KM# 325 10 MARK
3.9820 g., 0.9000 Gold .1152 oz. AGW **Ruler:** Friedrich Franz III

Date	F	VF	XF	Unc	BU
1890	250	600	900	1,400	1,800

KM# 331 10 MARK
3.9820 g., 0.9000 Gold .1152 oz. AGW **Ruler:** Friedrich Franz IV
Subject: Grand Duke Coming of Age **Rev:** Type III

Date	F	VF	XF	Unc	BU
1901	750	1,600	2,500	3,250	4,000

KM# 319 20 MARK
7.9650 g., 0.9000 Gold .2304 oz. AGW **Ruler:** Friedrich Franz II
Rev: Type I

Date	F	VF	XF	Unc	BU
1872	450	1,000	1,750	2,500	3,000

KM# 332 20 MARK
7.9650 g., 0.9000 Gold .2304 oz. AGW **Ruler:** Friedrich Franz IV
Subject: Grand Duke Coming of Age **Rev:** Type III

Date	F	VF	XF	Unc	BU
1901	1,000	2,250	3,500	5,000	6,000

MECKLENBURG-STRELITZ

The Duchy of Mecklenburg-Strelitz was the youngest branch of
the dynasty established when Mecklenburg-Schwerin was divided in
1658. Like its parent senior line, Mecklenburg-Strelitz became a grand
duchy in 1815 as enacted by the Congress of Vienna. It became a con-
stituent part of the German Empire in 1871, but all sovereignty ended
with the conclusion of World War I in 1918.

GRAND DUCHY
REGULAR COINAGE

KM# 101 PFENNIG
Copper **Note:** Prev. C#46.

Date	F	VF	XF	Unc	BU
1872	3.00	6.00	10.00	30.00	40.00

KM# 102 2 PFENNIG
Copper

Date	F	VF	XF	Unc	BU
1872	3.00	6.00	10.00	30.00	40.00

KM# 90 3 PFENNIG
Copper

Date	F	VF	XF	Unc	BU
1855-1859	4.00	8.00	14.00	25.00	36.00

KM# 95   3 PFENNIG
Copper

Date	F	VF	XF	Unc	BU
1862-1864	4.00	8.00	12.00	25.00	35.00

KM# 103   5 PFENNIG
Copper

Date	F	VF	XF	Unc	BU
1872	4.00	7.00	12.00	40.00	55.00

KM# 85   4 SCHILLINGE
3.2500 g., 0.3750 Silver .0392 oz. ASW

Date	F	VF	XF	Unc	BU
1846-1849	5.00	10.00	30.00	50.00	65.00

KM# 91   1/48 THALER (Schilling)
1.3300 g., 0.2080 Silver .0086 oz. ASW

Date	F	VF	XF	Unc	BU
1855-1859	4.00	8.00	12.00	30.00	40.00

KM# 96   1/48 THALER (Schilling)
1.3300 g., 0.2080 Silver .0086 oz. ASW

Date	F	VF	XF	Unc	BU
1862-1864	4.00	8.00	12.00	30.00	40.00

KM# 100   THALER
18.5200 g., 0.9000 Gold .5360 oz. AGW

Date	F	VF	XF	Unc	BU
1870	25.00	45.00	80.00	160	210

REFORM COINAGE

KM# 108   2 MARK
11.1110 g., 0.9000 Silver .3215 oz. ASW

Date	F	VF	XF	Unc	BU
1877	175	300	1,600	3,000	4,000

KM# 115   2 MARK
11.1110 g., 0.9000 Silver .3215 oz. ASW   **Ruler:** Adolph Friedrich V

Date	F	VF	XF	Unc	BU
1905	150	350	575	800	1,200

KM# 120   3 MARK
16.6670 g., 0.9000 Silver .4823 oz. ASW   **Ruler:** Adolph Friedrich V

Date	F	VF	XF	Unc	BU
1913	250	500	950	1,600	2,000

KM# 104   10 MARK
3.9820 g., 0.9000 Gold .1152 oz. AGW   **Rev:** Type I

Date	F	VF	XF	Unc	BU
1873	5,000	—	—	—	—

KM# 106   10 MARK
3.9820 g., 0.9000 Gold .1152 oz. AGW

Date	F	VF	XF	Unc	BU
1874-1880	2,250	4,000	6,500	8,500	—

KM# 116   10 MARK
3.9820 g., 0.9000 Gold .1152 oz. AGW **Ruler:** Adolph Friedrich V

Date	F	VF	XF	Unc	BU
1905	1,750	3,000	4,500	6,500	7,000

KM# 105   20 MARK
7.9650 g., 0.9000 Gold .2304 oz. AGW

Date	F	VF	XF	Unc	BU
1873	1,750	3,500	6,000	8,000	—

KM# 107   20 MARK
7.9650 g., 0.9000 Gold .2304 oz. AGW **Rev:** Type II

Date	F	VF	XF	Unc	BU
1874	1,750	3,500	5,000	7,500	—

KM# 117   20 MARK
7.9650 g., 0.9000 Gold .2304 oz. AGW **Ruler:** Adolph Friedrich V
Rev: Type III

Date	F	VF	XF	Unc	BU
1905	2,000	4,000	5,500	8,000	—

NASSAU

The Countship of Nassau had its origins in the area of the Lahn of the central Rhineland, with territory on both sides of that river.

Several times, various branches of the family issued joint coinage, notably in the late 17th and again in the early 19th centuries. Eventually, through extinction of the various lines and the elevation of one ruler to the throne of the Netherlands, all Nassau was reunited under the house of Nassau-Weilburg.

ARMS:
Nassau – lion rampant left on field of billets (small vertical rectangles)
Holzappel – griffin rampant left holding apple

UNITED DUCHIES OF NASSAU

STANDARD COINAGE

C# 52   PFENNIG
Copper

Date	F	VF	XF	Unc	BU
1859-1862	3.00	6.00	8.00	35.00	48.00

C# 53   KREUZER
Copper

Date	F	VF	XF	Unc	BU
1842-1856	3.00	5.00	14.00	35.00	55.00

C# 54   KREUZER
Copper

Date	F	VF	XF	Unc	BU
1859-1863	3.00	6.00	8.00	20.00	30.00

C# 55   KREUZER
0.5300 g., 0.2290 Silver .0039 oz. ASW

Date	F	VF	XF	Unc	BU
1861	4.00	8.00	10.00	30.00	40.00

C# 56   3 KREUZER
1.2900 g., 0.3330 Silver .0138 oz. ASW

Date	F	VF	XF	Unc	BU
1841-1855	5.00	10.00	14.00	25.00	35.00

C# 57   6 KREUZER
2.5900 g., 0.3330 Silver .0277 oz. ASW

Date	F	VF	XF	Unc	BU
1840-1855	5.00	10.00	16.00	40.00	60.00

C# 59   1/2 GULDEN
5.3000 g., 0.9000 Silver .1533 oz. ASW   **Obv:** Head left

Date	F	VF	XF	Unc	BU
1856-1860	15.00	25.00	55.00	115	150

C# 60   GULDEN
10.6000 g., 0.9000 Silver .3067 oz. ASW   **Obv:** ZOLLMANN on truncation

Date	F	VF	XF	Unc	BU
1840-1855	15.00	30.00	70.00	140	180

C# 61   GULDEN
10.6000 g., 0.9000 Silver .3067 oz. ASW

Date	F	VF	XF	Unc	BU
1855-1856	25.00	45.00	70.00	160	210

C# 62   THALER (Krone)
18.5200 g., 0.9000 Silver .5360 oz. ASW   **Obv:** Z on truncation
Note: Vereins Thaler.

Date	F	VF	XF	Unc	BU
1859-1860	30.00	55.00	90.00	175	240

C# 63   THALER (Krone)
18.5200 g., 0.9000 Silver .5360 oz. ASW   **Subject:** Duke's Visit to the Mint

Date	F	VF	XF	Unc	BU
ND(1861) Proof	Value: 12,000				

C# 62a   THALER (Krone)
18.5200 g., 0.9000 Silver .5360 oz. ASW   **Obv:** F. KORN on truncation

Date	F	VF	XF	Unc	BU
1863	25.00	60.00	140	550	780

C# 64   THALER (Krone)
18.5200 g., 0.9000 Silver .5360 oz. ASW   **Subject:** 25th Anniversary of Reign

Date	F	VF	XF	Unc	BU
1864	30.00	45.00	70.00	95.00	120

C# 67 2 THALER (3-1/2 Gulden)
37.1200 g., 0.9000 Silver 1.0742 oz. ASW **Obv:** Truncation bare

Date	F	VF	XF	Unc	BU
1844-1854	80.00	225	500	900	1,200

C# 68 2 THALER (3-1/2 Gulden)
37.0400 g., 0.9000 Silver 1.0719 oz. ASW **Obv:** C ZOLLMANN on truncation

Date	F	VF	XF	Unc	BU
1860	95.00	185	350	750	960

OLDENBURG

The county of Oldenburg was situated on the North Seacoast, to the east of the principality of East Friesland. It was originally part of the old duchy of Saxony and the first recorded lord ruled from the beginning of the 11th century. Oldenburg acquired the principality of Birkenfeld from Prussia and struck coins in denominations used there. World War I spelled the end of temporal power for the Grand Duke in 1918, but the title has continued up to the present time. Grand Duke Anton Günther was born in 1923.

DUCHY
REGULAR COINAGE

KM# 185 SCHWAREN (= 3 Light Pfennig)
Copper **Ruler:** Paul Friedrich August **Rev:** B below date

Date	F	VF	XF	Unc	BU
1852	4.00	8.00	16.00	35.00	48.00

KM# 188 SCHWAREN (= 3 Light Pfennig)
Copper **Ruler:** Nicolaus Friedrich Peter

Date	F	VF	XF	Unc	BU
1854-1856	3.00	6.00	10.00	25.00	35.00

KM# 190 SCHWAREN (= 3 Light Pfennig)
Copper **Ruler:** Nicolaus Friedrich Peter

Date	F	VF	XF	Unc	BU
1858-1869	3.00	6.00	11.00	25.00	35.00

KM# 191 3 SCHWAREN (3 Pfennig)
Copper **Ruler:** Nicolaus Friedrich Peter

Date	F	VF	XF	Unc	BU
1858-1869	4.00	8.00	12.00	20.00	30.00

KM# 186 1/2 GROTEN
Copper **Ruler:** Nicolaus Friedrich Peter

Date	F	VF	XF	Unc	BU
1853-1856	4.00	8.00	16.00	40.00	55.00

KM# 179   GROTEN (1/144 Thaler)
0.92 g., 0.2180 Silver .0064 oz. ASW **Ruler:** Peter Friedrich Wilhelm

Date	F	VF	XF	Unc	BU
1849-1850	5.00	10.00	20.00	40.00	55.00

KM# 187   GROTEN (1/144 Thaler)
0.92 g., 0.2180 Silver .0064 oz. ASW **Ruler:** Peter Friedrich Wilhelm

Date	F	VF	XF	Unc	BU
1853-1857	5.00	10.00	20.00	40.00	55.00

KM# 189   3 GROTE (1/24 Thaler)
1.94 g., 0.3120 Silver .0194 oz. ASW   **Ruler:** Nicolaus Friedrich Peter

Date	F	VF	XF	Unc	BU
1856	5.00	10.00	20.00	40.00	55.00

KM# 192   1/2 GROSCHEN
1.09 g., 0.22 Silver .0077 oz. ASW **Ruler:** Nicolaus Friedrich Peter

Date	F	VF	XF	Unc	BU
1858-1869	4.00	7.00	12.00	20.00	30.00

KM# 193   GROSCHEN
2.19 g., 0.22 Silver .0154 oz. ASW **Ruler:** Nicolaus Friedrich Peter

Date	F	VF	XF	Unc	BU
1858	4.00	7.00	15.00	35.00	48.00

KM# 194   GROSCHEN
2.1900 g., 0.2200 Silver .0154 oz. ASW **Ruler:** Nicolaus Friedrich Peter

Date	F	VF	XF	Unc	BU
1858-1869	3.00	8.00	12.00	20.00	30.00

KM# 195   2-1/2 GROSCHEN (1/12 Thaler)
3.2200 g., 0.3750 Silver .0388 oz. ASW   **Ruler:** Nicolaus Friedrich Peter

Date	F	VF	XF	Unc	BU
1858	5.00	10.00	20.00	40.00	55.00

KM# 196   THALER
18.5200 g., 0.9000 Silver .5360 oz. ASW   **Ruler:** Nicolaus Friedrich Peter

Date	F	VF	XF	Unc	BU
1858-1866	30.00	60.00	110	175	240

REFORM COINAGE

KM# 201   2 MARK
11.1110 g., 0.9000 Silver .3215 oz. ASW   **Ruler:** Nicolaus Friedrich Peter

Date	F	VF	XF	Unc	BU
1891	BV	250	400	750	900

KM# 202   2 MARK
11.1110 g., 0.9000 Silver .3215 oz. ASW   **Ruler:** Friedrich August

Date	F	VF	XF	Unc	BU
1900-1901	BV	225	400	900	1,100

KM# 203   5 MARK
27.7770 g., 0.9000 Silver .8038 oz. ASW **Ruler:** Friedrich August

Date	F	VF	XF	Unc	BU
1900-1901	300	550	1,500	2,750	3,250

KM# 200   10 MARK
3.9820 g., 0.9000 Gold .1152 oz. AGW **Ruler:** Nicolaus Friedrich Peter

Date	F	VF	XF	Unc	BU
1874	1,000	2,500	4,500	7,000	—

PRUSSIA

(Preussen)

Under successive strong leaders, Prussia gained increasing importance and added to its territories to become one of the leading countries of Europe in the course of the 18th century. As part of the reforms instituted by Friedrich II, the system of single letter mintmarks representing specific mints replaced the traditional incorporation of mint officials' symbols and/or initials as part of coin designs. Some of these very same mintmarks are still in use on modern German coins up to the present day. During the Napoleonic Wars (1792-1815), Prussia was allied with Saxony and they were soundly defeated at Jena in 1806. Prussia was forced to cede large portions of its territory at the time, but played a large part in the final defeat of Napoleon. The Congress of Vienna awarded Prussia part of Pomerania, the northern half of Saxony, much of Westphalia and the Rhineland, thus making it the largest state in Germany and a major power in European affairs. After defeating Denmark in 1864 and Austria in 1866, Prussia acquired Schleswig-Holstein, Hannover, Hesse-Cassel, Nassau and Frankfurt am Main. By this time, Prussia encompassed a large part of German territory and its population included two-thirds of all the German people. By winning the Franco-Prussian War (1870-71), Prussia became the pivotal state in the unification of Germany in 1871. King Wilhelm I was proclaimed Kaiser (Emperor) of all Germany, but World War I brought an end to both the Empire and the Kingdom of Prussia in 1918.

KINGDOM

REGULAR COINAGE

A series of counterfeit Prussian 5, 10 and 20 Mark gold pieces all dated 1887A were being marketed in the early 1970's. They were created by a dentist in Bonn, West Germany and the previously unknown date listed above aroused the curiosity of the numismatic community and eventually exposed the scam.

KM# 451   PFENNIG
Copper **Ruler:** Friedrich Wilhelm IV

Date	F	VF	XF	Unc	BU
1846-1860	3.00	7.00	12.00	17.00	24.00

KM# 480   PFENNIG
Copper **Ruler:** Wilhelm I

Date	F	VF	XF	Unc	BU
1861-1873	3.00	7.00	12.00	17.00	24.00

KM# 452   2 PFENNIG
Copper **Ruler:** Friedrich Wilhelm IV

Date	F	VF	XF	Unc	BU
1846-1860	3.00	6.00	8.00	20.00	30.00

KM# 481   2 PFENNIG
Copper **Ruler:** Wilhelm I

Date	F	VF	XF	Unc	BU
1861-1873	3.00	6.00	8.00	17.00	24.00

KM# 453   3 PFENNIG
Copper **Ruler:** Friedrich Wilhelm IV **Note:** Struck in collared dies.

Date	F	VF	XF	Unc	BU
1846-1860	4.00	8.00	12.00	25.00	36.00

KM# 460   3 PFENNIG
Copper **Ruler:** Friedrich Wilhelm IV **Rev:** Reuss-Schleiz 3 PFENNIGE **Note:** Mule.

Date	F	VF	XF	Unc	BU
1850	90.00	150	225	475	660

KM# 482   3 PFENNIG
Copper **Ruler:** Wilhelm I

Date	F	VF	XF	Unc	BU
1861-1873	4.00	8.00	12.00	20.00	30.00

KM# 454   4 PFENNIG
Copper **Ruler:** Friedrich Wilhelm IV **Note:** Struck in collared dies.

Date	F	VF	XF	Unc	BU
1846-1860	5.00	10.00	15.00	40.00	60.00

KM# 483   4 PFENNIG
Copper **Ruler:** Wilhelm I

Date	F	VF	XF	Unc	BU
1861-1871	5.00	10.00	15.00	40.00	60.00

KM# 434   1/2 SILBER GROSCHEN
1.0900 g., 0.2220 Silver .0077 oz. ASW **Ruler:** Friedrich Wilhelm IV

Date	F	VF	XF	Unc	BU
1841-1852	4.00	8.00	15.00	35.00	48.00

KM# 461   1/2 SILBER GROSCHEN
1.0900 g., 0.2220 Silver .0077 oz. ASW **Ruler:** Friedrich Wilhelm IV
Obv: Older head

Date	F	VF	XF	Unc	BU
1853-1860	20.00	40.00	45.00	100	145

KM# 484   1/2 SILBER GROSCHEN
1.0900 g., 0.2220 Silver .0077 oz. ASW **Ruler:** Wilhelm I

Date	F	VF	XF	Unc	BU
1861-1873	3.00	8.00	10.00	17.00	24.00

KM# 435   GROSCHEN (Silber)
2.1900 g., 0.2220 Silver .0156 oz. ASW **Ruler:** Friedrich Wilhelm IV

Date	F	VF	XF	Unc	BU
1841-1852	4.00	8.00	13.00	30.00	42.00

KM# 462   GROSCHEN (Silber)
2.1900 g., 0.2220 Silver .0156 oz. ASW **Ruler:** Friedrich Wilhelm IV
Obv: Older head

Date	F	VF	XF	Unc	BU
1853-1860	5.00	10.00	16.00	30.00	42.00

KM# 485   GROSCHEN (Silber)
2.1900 g., 0.2220 Silver .0156 oz. ASW **Ruler:** Wilhelm I

Date	F	VF	XF	Unc	BU
1861-1873	3.00	6.00	10.00	17.00	24.00

KM# 444   2-1/2 SILBER GROSCHEN
3.2400 g., 0.3750 Silver .0390 oz. ASW **Ruler:** Friedrich Wilhelm IV

Date	F	VF	XF	Unc	BU
1842-1852	5.00	10.00	13.00	25.00	36.00

KM# 463   2-1/2 SILBER GROSCHEN
3.2400 g., 0.3750 Silver .0390 oz. ASW **Ruler:** Friedrich Wilhelm IV

Date	F	VF	XF	Unc	BU
1853-1860	5.00	10.00	15.00	40.00	55.00

KM# 486   2-1/2 SILBER GROSCHEN
3.2400 g., 0.3750 Silver .0390 oz. ASW **Ruler:** Wilhelm I

Date	F	VF	XF	Unc	BU
1861-1873	3.00	7.00	12.00	20.00	30.00

KM# 436.2   1/6 THALER
5.3450 g., 0.5210 Silver .0895 oz. ASW **Ruler:** Friedrich Wilhelm IV
Rev: Different crown above shield

Date	F	VF	XF	Unc	BU
1843-1852	10.00	20.00	45.00	80.00	115

KM# 464 1/6 THALER
5.3450 g., 0.5210 Silver .0895 oz. ASW **Ruler:** Friedrich Wilhelm IV
Obv: Older head

Date	F	VF	XF	Unc	BU
1853-1856	45.00	100	190	375	510

KM# 473 1/6 THALER
5.3450 g., 0.5210 Silver .0895 oz. ASW **Ruler:**
Friedrich Wilhelm IV **Rev:** Crowned eagle with scepter and orb

Date	F	VF	XF	Unc	BU
1858-1860	65.00	130	220	295	390

KM# 487 1/6 THALER
5.3450 g., 0.5210 Silver .0895 oz. ASW **Ruler:** Friedrich Wilhelm IV

Date	F	VF	XF	Unc	BU
1861-1864	15.00	35.00	55.00	95.00	130

KM# 495 1/6 THALER
5.3450 g., 0.5210 Silver .0895 oz. ASW **Ruler:** Friedrich Wilhelm IV
Rev: Eagle with larger head

Date	F	VF	XF	Unc	BU
1865-1868	20.00	45.00	80.00	150	210

KM# 445 THALER
22.2720 g., 0.7500 Silver .5371 oz. ASW **Ruler:** Friedrich Wilhelm IV
Note: Reichs Thaler.

Date	F	VF	XF	Unc	BU
1842-1852	15.00	40.00	65.00	100	150

KM# 455 THALER
22.2720 g., 0.7500 Silver .5371 oz. ASW **Ruler:** Friedrich Wilhelm IV
Rev: Without dot after THALER **Note:** Mining Thaler

Date	F	VF	XF	Unc	BU
1847-1852	20.00	45.00	80.00	150	210

KM# 465 THALER
22.2720 g., 0.7500 Silver .5371 oz. ASW **Ruler:** Friedrich Wilhelm IV
Obv: Older head **Note:** Reichtaler

Date	F	VF	XF	Unc	BU
1853-1856	25.00	55.00	60.00	115	160

KM# 466 THALER
22.2720 g., 0.7500 Silver .5371 oz. ASW **Ruler:** Friedrich Wilhelm IV
Obv: Older head **Note:** Mining Thaler

Date	F	VF	XF	Unc	BU
1853-1856	20.00	40.00	70.00	140	210

KM# 471 THALER
18.5200 g., 0.9000 Silver .5360 oz. ASW **Ruler:** Friedrich Wilhelm IV
Note: Vereins Thaler.

Date	F	VF	XF	Unc	BU
1857-1861	20.00	35.00	65.00	90.00	120

KM# 472 THALER
18.5200 g., 0.9000 Silver .5360 oz. ASW **Ruler:** Friedrich Wilhelm IV
Obv: Similar to KM#471 **Note:** Mining Thaler.

Date	F	VF	XF	Unc	BU
1857-1860	30.00	65.00	80.00	125	180

KM# 488 THALER
18.5200 g., 0.9000 Silver .5360 oz. ASW **Ruler:** Friedrich Wilhelm IV
Subject: Coronation of Wilhelm and Augusta **Note:** Vereins Thaler.

Date	F	VF	XF	Unc	BU
1861	10.00	12.00	18.00	40.00	55.00

KM# 489 THALER
18.5200 g., 0.9000 Silver .5360 oz. ASW **Ruler:** Friedrich Wilhelm IV
Obv: Similar to KM#494 **Rev:** Similar to KM#471

Date	F	VF	XF	Unc	BU
1861-1863	20.00	35.00	45.00	110	150

KM# 490 THALER
18.5200 g., 0.9000 Silver .5360 oz. ASW **Ruler:** Wilhelm I **Note:** Mining Thaler.

Date	F	VF	XF	Unc	BU
1861-1862	20.00	40.00	65.00	150	210

KM# 494 THALER
18.5200 g., 0.9000 Silver .5360 oz. ASW **Ruler:** Wilhelm I

Date	F	VF	XF	Unc	BU
1864-1871	12.00	24.00	40.00	85.00	120

KM# 497 THALER
18.5200 g., 0.9000 Silver .5360 oz. ASW **Ruler:** Wilhelm I
Subject: Victory of Austria **Note:** Vereins Thaler.

Date	F	VF	XF	Unc	BU
1866	8.00	15.00	35.00	65.00	90.00

KM# 500 THALER
18.5200 g., 0.9000 Silver .5360 oz. ASW **Ruler:** Wilhelm I
Subject: Victory of France

Date	F	VF	XF	Unc	BU
1871	8.00	15.00	22.00	55.00	80.00

KM# 440.2 2 THALER (3-1/2 Gulden)
37.1190 g., 0.9000 Silver 1.0742 oz. ASW **Ruler:** Friedrich Wilhelm IV **Rev:** Different crown above shield

Date	F	VF	XF	Unc	BU
1843-1851	25.00	50.00	130	265	350

KM# 467   2 THALER (3-1/2 Gulden)
37.1190 g., 0.9000 Silver 1.0742 oz. ASW   **Ruler:** Friedrich Wilhelm IV

Date	F	VF	XF	Unc	BU
1853-1856	65.00	125	145	230	330

KM# 474   2 THALER (3-1/2 Gulden)
37.0370 g., 0.9000 Silver 1.0718 oz. ASW   **Ruler:** Friedrich Wilhelm IV **Obv:** Similar to KM#467

Date	F	VF	XF	Unc	BU
1858-1859	250	550	800	1,325	1,800

KM# 491   2 THALER (3-1/2 Gulden)
37.0370 g., 0.9000 Silver 1.0718 oz. ASW   **Ruler:** Friedrich Wilhelm IV **Rev:** Similar to KM#474

Date	F	VF	XF	Unc	BU
1861-1863	350	600	950	1,650	2,400

KM# 496   2 THALER (3-1/2 Gulden)
37.0370 g., 0.9000 Silver 1.0718 oz. ASW   **Ruler:** Wilhelm I

Date	F	VF	XF	Unc	BU
1865-1871	125	225	425	750	1,075

KM# 475   1/2 KRONE
5.5550 g., 0.9000 Gold .1607 oz. AGW   **Ruler:** Friedrich Wilhelm IV

Date	F	VF	XF	Unc	BU
1858	800	1,500	2,000	3,250	—

KM# 493   1/2 KRONE
5.5550 g., 0.9000 Gold .1607 oz. AGW   **Ruler:** Wilhelm I

Date	F	VF	XF	Unc	BU
1862-1869	400	800	1,200	1,600	—

KM# 476   KRONE
11.1110 g., 0.9000 Gold .3272 oz. AGW   **Ruler:** Wilhelm I

Date	F	VF	XF	Unc	BU
1858-1860	500	1,200	1,600	2,600	—

KM# 492   KRONE
11.1110 g., 0.9160 Gold .3272 oz. AGW   **Ruler:** Wilhelm I

Date	F	VF	XF	Unc	BU
1861-1870	400	800	1,200	2,000	—

TRADE COINAGE

KM# 441   1/2 FREDERICK D'OR
3.3410 g., 0.9030 Gold .0970 oz. AGW   **Ruler:** Friedrich Wilhelm IV

Date	F	VF	XF	Unc	BU
1841-1849	300	500	750	1,000	—

KM# 468　1/2 FREDERICK D'OR
3.3410 g., 0.9030 Gold .0970 oz. AGW　**Ruler:** Friedrich Wilhelm IV

Date	F	VF	XF	Unc	BU
1853	500	900	1,250	1,600	—

KM# 442　FREDERICK D'OR
6.6820 g., 0.9030 Gold .1940 oz. AGW　**Ruler:** Friedrich Wilhelm IV

Date	F	VF	XF	Unc	BU
1841-1852	300	550	800	1,400	—

KM# 469　FREDERICK D'OR
6.6820 g., 0.9030 Gold .1940 oz. AGW　**Ruler:** Friedrich Wilhelm IV

Date	F	VF	XF	Unc	BU
1853-1855	300	750	1,200	1,750	—

KM# 443　2 FREDERICK D'OR
13.3630 g., 0.9030 Gold .3880 oz. AGW　**Ruler:** Friedrich Wilhelm IV

Date	F	VF	XF	Unc	BU
1841-1852	500	800	1,200	1,500	—

KM# 470　2 FREDERICK D'OR
13.3630 g., 0.9030 Gold .3880 oz. AGW　**Ruler:** Friedrich Wilhelm IV

Date	F	VF	XF	Unc	BU
1853-1855	500	800	1,200	2,000	—

REFORM COINAGE

KM# 506　2 MARK
11.1110 g., 0.9000 Silver .3215 oz. ASW　**Ruler:** Wilhelm I

Date	F	VF	XF	Unc	BU
1876-1884	10.00	30.00	180	450	600

KM# 510　2 MARK
11.1110 g., 0.9000 Silver .3215 oz. ASW　**Ruler:** Wilhelm I

Date	F	VF	XF	Unc	BU
1888	12.50	25.00	45.00	75.00	90.00

KM# 511　2 MARK
11.1110 g., 0.9000 Silver .3215 oz. ASW　**Ruler:** Wilhelm II

Date	F	VF	XF	Unc	BU
1888	120	250	400	500	600

KM# 522　2 MARK
11.1110 g., 0.9000 Silver .2215 oz. ASW　**Ruler:** Wilhelm II

Date	F	VF	XF	Unc	BU
1891-1912	7.00	15.00	40.00	100	125

KM# 525　2 MARK
11.1110 g., 0.9000 Silver .3215 oz. ASW　**Ruler:** Wilhelm II
Subject: 200 Years - Kingdom of Prussia

Date	F	VF	XF	Unc	BU
1901	7.50	17.50	24.00	30.00	40.00

KM# 532   2 MARK
11.1110 g., 0.9000 Silver .3215 oz. ASW   **Ruler:** Wilhelm II
Subject: 100 Years - Defeat of Napoleon

Date	F	VF	XF	Unc	BU
1913	7.50	17.50	25.00	30.00	35.00

KM# 533   2 MARK
11.1110 g., 0.9000 Silver .3215 oz. ASW   **Ruler:** Wilhelm II
Subject: 25th Year of Reign

Date	F	VF	XF	Unc	BU
1913	7.50	17.50	24.00	30.00	35.00

KM# 527   3 MARK
16.6670 g., 0.9000 Silver .4823 oz. ASW   **Ruler:** Wilhelm II

Date	F	VF	XF	Unc	BU
(1908-1912)-1912	7.00	14.00	24.00	45.00	60.00

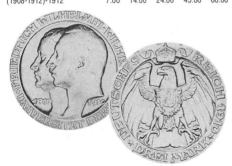

KM# 530   3 MARK
16.6670 g., 0.9000 Silver .4823 oz. ASW   **Ruler:** Wilhelm II
Subject: Berlin University

Date	F	VF	XF	Unc	BU
1910	22.00	55.00	85.00	125	150

KM# 531   3 MARK
16.6670 g., 0.9000 Silver .4823 oz. ASW   **Ruler:** Wilhelm II
Subject: Breslau University

Date	F	VF	XF	Unc	BU
1911	18.00	45.00	70.00	85.00	110

KM# 534   3 MARK
16.6670 g., 0.9000 Silver .4823 oz. ASW   **Ruler:** Wilhelm II
Subject: 100 Years - Defeat of Napoleon

Date	F	VF	XF	Unc	BU
1913	8.00	20.00	25.00	30.00	35.00

KM# 535   3 MARK
16.6670 g., 0.9000 Silver .4823 oz. ASW   **Ruler:** Wilhelm II
Subject: 25th Year of Reign

Date	F	VF	XF	Unc	BU
1913	8.00	20.00	25.00	30.00	35.00

KM# 538   3 MARK
16.6670 g., 0.9000 Silver .4823 oz. ASW   **Ruler:** Wilhelm II

Date	F	VF	XF	Unc	BU
1914	10.00	20.00	25.00	70.00	90.00

KM# 539   3 MARK
16.6670 g., 0.9000 Silver .4823 oz. ASW   **Ruler:** Wilhelm II
Subject: Centenary - Absorption of Mansfeld

Date	F	VF	XF	Unc	BU
1915	220	580	800	1,000	1,200

KM# 513   5 MARK
27.7770 g., 0.9000 Silver .8038 oz. ASW   **Ruler:** Wilhelm II **Rev:** Type II

Date	F	VF	XF	Unc	BU
1888	200	450	700	1,100	1,500

KM# 503   5 MARK
27.7770 g., 0.9000 Silver .8038 oz. ASW   **Ruler:** Wilhelm I

Date	F	VF	XF	Unc	BU
1874-1876	15.00	35.00	200	600	800

KM# 507   5 MARK
1.9910 g., 0.9000 Gold .0576 oz. AGW   **Ruler:** Wilhelm I

Date	F	VF	XF	Unc	BU
1877-1878	125	200	300	500	650

KM# 523   5 MARK
27.7770 g., 0.9000 Silver .8038 oz. ASW   **Ruler:** Wilhelm II **Rev:** Type III

Date	F	VF	XF	Unc	BU
(1891-1908)-1908	8.00	16.00	60.00	200	275

KM# 512   5 MARK
27.7770 g., 0.9000 Silver .8038 oz. ASW   **Ruler:** Friedrich III
March - June

Date	F	VF	XF	Unc	BU
1888	40.00	75.00	125	175	225

KM# 526   5 MARK
27.7770 g., 0.9000 Silver .8038 oz. ASW   **Ruler:** Wilhelm II
Subject: 200 Years - Kingdom of Prussia

Date	F	VF	XF	Unc	BU
1901	30.00	50.00	80.00	110	140

KM# 536   5 MARK
27.7770 g., 0.9000 Silver .8038 oz. ASW   **Ruler:** Wilhelm II

Date	F	VF	XF	Unc	BU
(1913-1914)-1914	13.00	24.00	35.00	150	200

KM# 502   10 MARK
3.9820 g., 0.9000 Gold .1152 oz. AGW   **Ruler:** Wilhelm I

Date	F	VF	XF	Unc	BU
1872-1873	—	BV	90.00	200	250

KM# 504   10 MARK
3.9820 g., 0.9000 Gold .1152 oz. AGW   **Ruler:** Wilhelm I   **Rev:** Type II

Date	F	VF	XF	Unc	BU
1874-1888	BV	85.00	110	225	275

KM# 514   10 MARK
3.9820 g., 0.9000 Gold .1152 oz. AGW   **Ruler:** Friedrich III March - June

Date	F	VF	XF	Unc	BU
1888	BV	95.00	120	175	225

KM# 517   10 MARK
3.9820 g., 0.9000 Gold .1152 oz. AGW   **Ruler:** Wilhelm II   **Rev:** Type II

Date	F	VF	XF	Unc	BU
1889	1,600	3,000	3,500	4,500	6,500

KM# 520   10 MARK
3.9820 g., 0.9 Gold .1152 oz. AGW   **Ruler:** Wilhelm II   **Rev:** Type III

Date	F	VF	XF	Unc	BU
1890-1912	BV	95.00	120	250	275

KM# 501   20 MARK
7.9650 g., 0.9000 Gold .2304 oz. AGW   **Ruler:** Wilhelm I

Date	F	VF	XF	Unc	BU
1871-1873	—	BV	170	200	250

KM# 505   20 MARK
7.9650 g., 0.9000 Gold .2304 oz. AGW   **Ruler:** Wilhelm I   **Rev:** Type II

Date	F	VF	XF	Unc	BU
1874-1888	—	BV	155	200	250

KM# 515   20 MARK
7.9650 g., 0.9 Gold .2304 oz. AGW   **Ruler:** Friedrich III March - June

Date	F	VF	XF	Unc	BU
1888	—	BV	155	225	300

KM# 516   20 MARK
7.9650 g., 0.9000 Gold .2304 oz. AGW   **Ruler:** Wilhelm II

Date	F	VF	XF	Unc	BU
1888-1889	—	BV	155	200	275

KM# 521   20 MARK
7.9650 g., 0.9 Gold .2304 oz. AGW   **Ruler:** Wilhelm II   **Rev:** Type III

Date	F	VF	XF	Unc	BU
1890-1913	—+5%	BV+5%	160+10%	225	275

KM# 537 20 MARK
7.9650 g., 0.9000 Gold .2304 oz. AGW **Ruler:** Wilhelm II

Date	F	VF	XF	Unc	BU
1913-1915	—	BV+5%	180	250	300

REUSS-OBERGREIZ
PRINCIPALITY
REGULAR COINAGE

KM# 115 PFENNIG
Copper **Ruler:** Heinrich XXII **Obv:** King's crown

Date	F	VF	XF	Unc	BU
1864	2.00	4.00	8.00	40.00	—

KM# 117 PFENNIG
Copper **Ruler:** Heinrich XXII **Obv:** Prince's crown

Date	F	VF	XF	Unc	BU
1868	2.00	4.00	8.00	38.00	—

KM# 116 3 PFENNIG
Copper **Ruler:** Heinrich XXII **Obv:** King's crown

Date	F	VF	XF	Unc	BU
1864	2.50	5.00	10.00	38.00	—

KM# 118 3 PFENNIG
Copper **Ruler:** Heinrich XXII **Obv:** Prince's crown

Date	F	VF	XF	Unc	BU
1868	2.50	5.00	10.00	38.00	—

KM# 119 GROSCHEN
2.1900 g., 0.2200 Silver .0154 oz. ASW **Ruler:** Heinrich XXII

Date	F	VF	XF	Unc	BU
1868	4.00	8.00	20.00	70.00	—

KM# 110 THALER
18.5200 g., 0.9000 Silver .5360 oz. ASW **Ruler:** Heinrich XX

Date	F	VF	XF	Unc	BU
1858	60.00	100	200	450	—

KM# 120 THALER
18.5200 g., 0.9000 Silver .5360 oz. ASW **Ruler:** Heinrich XXII

Date	F	VF	XF	Unc	BU
1868	60.00	100	200	450	—

KM# 105 2 THALER (3-1/2 Gulden)
37.1200 g., 0.9000 Silver 1.0742 oz. ASW **Ruler:** Heinrich XX

Date	F	VF	XF	Unc	BU
1841-1851	200	375	750	1,500	—

REFORM COINAGE

KM# 126 2 MARK
11.1110 g., 0.9000 Silver .3215 oz. ASW **Ruler:** Heinrich XXII
Rev: Type II

Date	F	VF	XF	Unc	BU
1877	175	325	1,200	2,750	3,250

KM# 127 2 MARK
11.1110 g., 0.9000 Silver .3215 oz. ASW **Ruler:** Heinrich XXII
Rev: Type III

Date	F	VF	XF	Unc	BU
1892	150	350	650	950	1,250

KM# 128 2 MARK
11.1110 g., 0.9000 Silver .3215 oz. ASW **Ruler:** Heinrich XXII

Date	F	VF	XF	Unc	BU
1899-1901	125	225	375	625	750

KM# 130 3 MARK
16.6670 g., 0.9000 Silver .4823 oz. ASW **Ruler:** Heinrich XXIV

Date	F	VF	XF	Unc	BU
1909	120	285	450	800	900

KM# 125 20 MARK
7.965 g., 0.9 Gold .2304 oz. AGW **Ruler:** Heinrich XXII **Rev:** Type II

Date	F	VF	XF	Unc	BU
1875	6,500	—	—	—	—

REUSS-SCHLEIZ

Originally part of the holdings of Reuss-Gera, Schleiz was ruled separately on and off during the first half of the 16th century. When the Gera line died out in 1550, Schleiz passed to Obergreiz. Schleiz was reintegrated into a new line of Gera and a separate countship at Schleiz was founded in 1635, only to last one generation. At its extinction in 1666, Schleiz passed to Reuss-Saalburg which thereafter took the name of Reuss-Schleiz.

PRINCIPALITY
REGULAR COINAGE

KM# 65 PFENNIG
Copper

Date	F	VF	XF	Unc	BU
1850	2.00	4.00	12.00	50.00	—

KM# 69 PFENNIG
Copper

Date	F	VF	XF	Unc	BU
1855-1864	2.00	4.00	12.00	50.00	—

KM# 75 PFENNIG
Copper

Date	F	VF	XF	Unc	BU
1868	2.00	4.00	12.00	50.00	—

KM# 66 3 PFENNIG
Copper

Date	F	VF	XF	Unc	BU
1850	3.00	7.00	20.00	70.00	—

KM# 70 3 PFENNIG
Copper

Date	F	VF	XF	Unc	BU
1855-1864	3.00	7.00	20.00	70.00	—

KM# 76 3 PFENNIG
Copper

Date	F	VF	XF	Unc	BU
1868	3.00	7.00	20.00	70.00	—

KM# 67 SILBER GROSCHEN
2.1900 g., 0.2220 Silver .0156 oz. ASW

Date	F	VF	XF	Unc	BU
1850	5.00	10.00	25.00	110	—

KM# 71 SILBER GROSCHEN
2.1900 g., 0.2220 Silver .0156 oz. ASW

Date	F	VF	XF	Unc	BU
1855	6.00	12.00	30.00	125	—

KM# 68 2 SILBER GROSCHEN (1/12 Thaler)
3.1100 g., 0.3120 Silver .0311 oz. ASW **Obv:** Crowned shield with crowned lion **Rev:** Value

Date	F	VF	XF	Unc	BU
1850	6.00	15.00	30.00	150	—

KM# 72 2 SILBER GROSCHEN (1/12 Thaler)
3.1100 g., 0.3120 Silver .0311 oz. ASW

Date	F	VF	XF	Unc	BU
1855	10.00	20.00	40.00	150	—

KM# 73 THALER
18.5200 g., 0.9000 Silver .5360 oz. ASW

Date	F	VF	XF	Unc	BU
1858-1862	45.00	75.00	140	350	—

KM# 77 THALER
18.5200 g., 0.9000 Silver .5360 oz. ASW **Rev:** Similar to KM#73

Date	F	VF	XF	Unc	BU
1868	40.00	65.00	125	325	—

KM# 55 2 THALER (3-1/2 Gulden)
37.1200 g., 0.9000 Silver 1.0742 oz. ASW

Date	F	VF	XF	Unc	BU
1840-1854	225	400	800	1,500	—

REFORM COINAGE

KM# 82 2 MARK
11.1110 g., 0.9000 Silver .3215 oz. ASW

Date	F	VF	XF	Unc	BU
1884	160	300	750	1,750	2,750

KM# 81 10 MARK
3.9820 g., 0.9000 Gold .1152 oz. AGW

Date	F	VF	XF	Unc	BU
1882	1,500	3,500	5,500	7,500	—

KM# 80 20 MARK
7.9650 g., 0.9000 Gold .2304 oz. AGW

Date	F	VF	XF	Unc	BU
1881	1,250	2,250	3,500	5,000	6,500

ROSTOCK

A city, near the Baltic Sea in Mecklenburg, has a history from the 12th century. The first municipal charter dates from 1218. In 1325, Rostock obtained the mint right and not long after, joined the Hanseatic League. The city coinage extends to 1864.

FREE CITY
REGULAR COINAGE
KM# 138 PFENNIG
Copper **Note:** Previous C#7a.

Date	F	VF	XF	Unc	BU
1848	6.00	12.00	30.00	100	—

C# 5 PFENNIG
Copper

Date	VG	F	VF	XF	Unc
1848	9,876	6.00	12.00	30.00	80.00

C# 11 3 PFENNIG
Copper

Date	VG	F	VF	XF	Unc
1855	9,876	5.00	10.00	25.00	75.00

C# 12 3 PFENNIG
Copper

Date	VG	F	VF	XF	Unc
1855	9,876	5.00	10.00	25.00	75.00

KM# 139 3 PFENNIG
Copper **Note:** Prev. C#11.

Date	F	VF	XF	Unc	BU
1855	5.00	10.00	27.00	100	—

KM# 140 3 PFENNIG
Copper **Note:** Prev. C#12.

Date	F	VF	XF	Unc	BU
1859	5.00	10.00	27.00	100	—

C# 12a 3 PFENNIG
Copper

Date	VG	F	VF	XF	Unc
1862-1864	9,876	5.00	10.00	25.00	75.00

KM# 141 3 PFENNIG
Copper **Note:** Prev. C#12a.

Date	F	VF	XF	Unc	BU
1862-1864	5.00	10.00	27.00	100	—

SAXE-ALTENBURG

DUCHY
REGULAR COINAGE

C# 11 PFENNIG
Copper **Ruler:** Joseph **Rev:** "F" below date

Date	F	VF	XF	Unc	BU
1852	1.50	3.00	6.00	40.00	—

C# 14 PFENNIG
Copper **Ruler:** Joseph **Rev:** "F" below date

Date	F	VF	XF	Unc	BU
1856-1858	1.50	3.00	6.00	40.00	—

C# 14a PFENNIG
Copper **Ruler:** Joseph **Rev:** Without initial

Date	F	VF	XF	Unc	BU
1857	1.50	3.00	6.00	40.00	—

C# 14b PFENNIG
Copper **Ruler:** Joseph **Rev:** "B" below date

Date	F	VF	XF	Unc	BU
1861-1865	1.50	3.00	6.00	40.00	—

C# 12 2 PFENNIG
Copper **Ruler:** Joseph

Date	F	VF	XF	Unc	BU
1852	2.50	5.00	10.00	50.00	—

C# 15 2 PFENNIG
Copper **Ruler:** Joseph

Date	F	VF	XF	Unc	BU
1856	2.50	5.00	10.00	50.00	—

C# 16 THALER
18.5200 g., 0.9000 Silver .5360 oz. ASW **Ruler:** Ernst I **Note:** Vereins Thaler.

Date	F	VF	XF	Unc	BU
1858-1869	30.00	60.00	125	400	—

C# 13 2 THALER (3-1/2 Gulden)
37.1190 g., 0.9000 Silver 1.0742 oz. ASW **Ruler:** Georg **Rev:** Similar to 1 Thaler, C#16

Date	F	VF	XF	Unc	BU
1852	250	450	900	1,900	—

REFORM COINAGE

KM# 144 2 MARK
11.1110 g., 0.9000 Silver .3215 oz. ASW **Ruler:** Ernst I **Subject:** Ernst 75th Birthday

Date	F	VF	XF	Unc	BU
1901	120	250	450	675	800

KM# 145 5 MARK
27.7770 g., 0.9000 Silver .8038 oz. ASW **Ruler:** Ernst I **Subject:** Ernst 75th Birthday

Date	F	VF	XF	Unc	BU
1901	200	425	800	1,400	1,750

KM# 147   5 MARK
27.7770 g., 0.9000 Silver .8038 oz. ASW   **Ruler:** Ernst I **Subject:** Ernst's 50th Year of Reign

Date	F	VF	XF	Unc	BU
1903	100	200	325	500	700

Y# 146   20 MARK
7.9650 g., 0.9000 Gold .2304 oz. AGW   **Ruler:** Ernst I

Date	F	VF	XF	Unc	BU
1887	900	1,600	2,250	3,500	4,500

SAXE-COBURG-GOTHA

(Sachsen-Coburg-Gotha)

Upon the extinction of the ducal line in Saxe-Gotha-Altenburg in 1826, Gotha was assigned to Saxe-Coburg-Saalfeld and Saxe-Meiningen received Saalfeld. The resulting duchy became called Saxe-Coburg-Gotha. Albert, the son of Ernst I and younger brother of Ernst II, married Queen Victoria of Great Britain and the British royal dynastic name was that of Saxe-Coburg-Gotha. Their son, Alfred was made the Duke of Edinburgh and succeeded his uncle, Ernst II, as Duke of Saxe-Coburg-Gotha. Alfred's older brother, Eduard Albert, followed their mother as King Edward VII (1901-1910). The last duke of Saxe-Coburg-Gotha was Alfred's nephew, Karl Eduard, forced to abdicate in 1918 as a result of World War I, which was fought in part against his cousin, King George V.

DUCHY
REGULAR COINAGE

C# 109   PFENNIG
Copper   **Ruler:** Ernst I **Obv:** "F" above crowned arms

Date	F	VF	XF	Unc	BU
1847-1856	1.50	3.00	6.00	50.00	—

C# 109a   PFENNIG
Copper   **Ruler:** Ernst II **Obv:** "B" above arms

Date	F	VF	XF	Unc	BU
1865	1.50	3.00	6.00	50.00	—

C# 109b   PFENNIG
Copper   **Ruler:** Ernst II

Date	F	VF	XF	Unc	BU
1868-1870	1.50	3.00	6.00	50.00	—

C# 110   2 PFENNIG
Copper   **Ruler:** Ernst II **Obv:** "F" and date below bow

Date	F	VF	XF	Unc	BU
1847-1856	1.50	3.00	6.00	50.00	—

C# 110a   2 PFENNIG
Copper   **Ruler:** Ernst II **Obv:** "B" and date below bow

Date	F	VF	XF	Unc	BU
1868-1870	1.50	3.00	6.00	50.00	—

C# 111   1/2 GROSCHEN
1.0600 g., 0.2290 Silver .0078 oz. ASW   **Ruler:** Ernst II

Date	F	VF	XF	Unc	BU
1851-1858	2.00	4.00	8.00	50.00	—

C# 114   1/2 GROSCHEN
1.0600 g., 0.2290 Silver .0078 oz. ASW   **Ruler:** Ernst II **Obv:** "B" below arms

Date	F	VF	XF	Unc	BU
1868-1870	2.00	4.00	8.00	50.00	—

C# 112   GROSCHEN
2.1200 g., 0.2290 Silver .0156 oz. ASW   **Ruler:** Ernst II

Date	F	VF	XF	Unc	BU
1847-1858	2.00	4.00	8.00	50.00	—

C# 115   GROSCHEN
2.1200 g., 0.2290 Silver .0156 oz. ASW   **Ruler:** Ernst II

Date	F	VF	XF	Unc	BU
1865-1870	2.00	4.00	10.00	60.00	—

C# 113   2 GROSCHEN
3.1100 g., 0.3120 Silver .0311 oz. ASW   **Ruler:** Ernst II

Date	F	VF	XF	Unc	BU
1847-1858	6.00	12.00	20.00	60.00	—

C# 116   2 GROSCHEN
3.2200 g., 0.3000 Silver .0310 oz. ASW   **Ruler:** Ernst II

Date	F	VF	XF	Unc	BU
1865-1870	5.00	10.00	20.00	50.00	—

C# 117a   1/6 THALER
5.3450 g., 0.5210 Silver .0895 oz. ASW   **Ruler:** Ernst II

Date	F	VF	XF	Unc	BU
1848	10.00	30.00	60.00	200	—

C# 117b   1/6 THALER
5.3450 g., 0.5210 Silver .0895 oz. ASW **Ruler:** Ernst II **Obv:** Head with beard

Date	F	VF	XF	Unc	BU
1852-1855	15.00	35.00	75.00	250	—

C# 118   1/6 THALER
5.3400 g., 0.5200 Silver .0892 oz. ASW   **Ruler:** Ernst II

Date	F	VF	XF	Unc	BU
1864	10.00	30.00	60.00	150	—

C# 119   1/6 THALER
5.3400 g., 0.5200 Silver .0892 oz. ASW   **Ruler:** Ernst II **Subject:** 25th Anniversary of Reign

Date	F	VF	XF	Unc	BU
1869	10.00	30.00	50.00	125	—

C# 120a   THALER (Krone)
22.2700 g., 0.7500 Silver .5371 oz. ASW   **Ruler:** Ernst II

Date	F	VF	XF	Unc	BU
1848	75.00	150	300	1,000	—

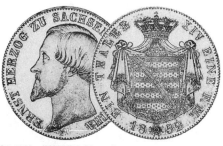

C# 120b   THALER (Krone)
22.2700 g., 0.7500 Silver .5371 oz. ASW   **Ruler:** Ernst II

Date	F	VF	XF	Unc	BU
1851-1852	75.00	150	300	1,000	—

C# 121   THALER (Krone)
18.5200 g., 0.9000 Silver .5360 oz. ASW   **Ruler:** Ernst II

Date	F	VF	XF	Unc	BU
1862-1870	45.00	90.00	150	350	—

C# 122   THALER (Krone)
18.5200 g., 0.9000 Silver .5360 oz. ASW   **Ruler:** Ernst II **Subject:** 25th Anniversary of Reign

Date	F	VF	XF	Unc	BU
1869	45.00	85.00	150	250	—

C# 123a   2 THALER (3-1/2 Gulden)
37.1200 g., 0.9000 Silver 1.0743 oz. ASW   **Ruler:** Ernst II

Date	F	VF	XF	Unc	BU
1854	225	425	1,000	2,000	—

REFORM COINAGE

Y# 149 2 MARK
11.1110 g., 0.9000 Silver .3215 oz. ASW **Ruler:** Alfred

Date	F	VF	XF	Unc	BU
1895	250	650	900	1,500	1,800

KM# 152 2 MARK
11.1110 g., 0.9000 Silver .3215 oz. ASW **Ruler:** Karl Eduard

Date	F	VF	XF	Unc	BU
1905-1911	135	285	600	1,100	1,300

Y# 150 5 MARK
27.7770 g., 0.9000 Silver .8038 oz. ASW **Ruler:** Alfred

Date	F	VF	XF	Unc	BU
1895	1,000	2,000	2,600	4,500	5,500

KM# 153 5 MARK
27.7770 g., 0.9000 Silver .8038 oz. ASW **Ruler:** Karl Eduard

Date	F	VF	XF	Unc	BU
1907	300	600	1,000	1,600	2,000

KM# 154 10 MARK
3.9820 g., 0.9000 Gold .1152 oz. AGW **Ruler:** Karl Eduard

Date	F	VF	XF	Unc	BU
1905	650	1,100	1,800	2,250	2,750

Y# 148 20 MARK
1.9650 g., 0.9000 Gold .2304 oz. AGW **Ruler:** Ernst II **Rev:** Type I

Date	F	VF	XF	Unc	BU
1872E	15,000	25,000	35,000	50,000	70,000

Y# 148a 20 MARK
1.9650 g., 0.9000 Gold .2304 oz. AGW **Ruler:** Ernst II

Date	F	VF	XF	Unc	BU
1886	1,000	2,000	3,000	5,000	6,000

Y# 151 20 MARK
1.9650 g., 0.9000 Gold .2304 oz. AGW **Ruler:** Alfred

Date	F	VF	XF	Unc	BU
1895	1,200	2,000	2,500	3,500	4,000

KM# 155 20 MARK
7.9650 g., 0.9000 Gold .2304 oz. AGW **Ruler:** Karl Eduard **Rev:** Type I

Date	F	VF	XF	Unc	BU
1905	700	1,200	1,900	2,500	2,800

SAXE-MEININGEN

(Sachsen-Meiningen)

The duchy of Saxe-Meiningen was located in Thuringia (Thüringen), sandwiched between Saxe-Weimar-Eisenach on the west and north and the enclave of Schmalkalden belonging to Hesse-Cassel on the east. It was founded upon the division of the Ernestine line in Saxe-Gotha in 1680. In 1735, due to an exchange of some territory, the duchy became known as Saxe-Coburg-Meiningen. In 1826, Saxe-Coburg-Gotha assigned Saalfeld to Saxe-Meiningen. The duchy came under the strong influence of Prussia from 1866, when Bernhard II was forced to abdicate because of his support of Austria. The last duke was forced to give up his sovereign power at the end of World War I in 1918.

DUCHY
REGULAR COINAGE

KM# 170 PFENNIG
Copper **Ruler:** Bernhard II

Date	F	VF	XF	Unc	BU
1860-1866	2.00	4.00	8.00	50.00	—

KM# 173 PFENNIG
Copper **Ruler:** Georg II

Date	F	VF	XF	Unc	BU
1867-1868	2.00	4.00	8.00	50.00	—

KM# 171 2 PFENNIG
Copper **Ruler:** Bernhard II

Date	F	VF	XF	Unc	BU
1860-1866	2.00	4.00	8.00	50.00	—

KM# 174 2 PFENNIG
Copper **Ruler:** Georg II

Date	F	VF	XF	Unc	BU
1867-1870	2.00	4.00	8.00	50.00	—

KM# 161 1/4 KREUZER
Copper **Ruler:** Bernhard II **Rev:** Value

Date	F	VF	XF	Unc	BU
1854	2.00	4.00	8.00	40.00	—

KM# 162 1/2 KREUZER
Copper **Ruler:** Bernhard II

Date	F	VF	XF	Unc	BU
1854	2.00	4.00	8.00	40.00	—

KM# 163 KREUZER
Copper **Ruler:** Bernhard II **Obv:** Six-point star below crowned arms

Date	F	VF	XF	Unc	BU
1854	2.50	5.00	10.00	40.00	—

KM# 172 KREUZER
0.8400 g., 0.1650 Silver .0044 oz. ASW **Ruler:** Bernhard II

Date	F	VF	XF	Unc	BU
1864-1866	2.50	5.00	10.00	45.00	—

KM# 164 1/2 GULDEN
5.3000 g., 0.9000 Silver .1533 oz. ASW **Ruler:** Bernhard II

Date	F	VF	XF	Unc	BU
1854	22.00	55.00	120	265	—

KM# 165 GULDEN
10.6000 g., 0.9000 Silver .3067 oz. ASW **Ruler:** Bernhard II

Date	F	VF	XF	Unc	BU
1854	50.00	100	185	300	—

KM# 166 2 GULDEN
21.2100 g., 0.9000 Silver .6138 oz. ASW **Ruler:** Bernhard II

Date	F	VF	XF	Unc	BU
1854	65.00	145	285	485	—

KM# 167 THALER
18.5200 g., 0.9000 Silver .5360 oz. ASW **Ruler:** Bernhard II **Obv:** HELFRICHT on truncation

Date	F	VF	XF	Unc	BU
1859-1866	45.00	85.00	175	350	—

KM# 196 2 MARK
11.1110 g., 0.9000 Silver .3215 oz. ASW **Ruler:** Georg II
Subject: Duke's 75th Birthday

Date	F	VF	XF	Unc	BU
1901	100	250	400	750	900

KM# 198 2 MARK
11.1110 g., 0.9000 Silver .3215 oz. ASW **Ruler:** Georg II **Obv:** Long beard

Date	F	VF	XF	Unc	BU
1902	250	800	1,450	2,200	2,750

KM# 199 2 MARK
11.1110 g., 0.9000 Silver .3215 oz. ASW **Ruler:** Georg II **Obv:** Short beard

Date	F	VF	XF	Unc	BU
1902-1913	100	200	350	750	850

KM# 175 THALER
18.5200 g., 0.9000 Silver .5360 oz. ASW **Ruler:** Georg II **Obv:** HELFRICHT on truncation

Date	F	VF	XF	Unc	BU
1867	90.00	175	400	750	—

KM# 206 2 MARK
11.1110 g., 0.9000 Silver .3215 oz. ASW **Ruler:** Bernhard III
Subject: Death of Georg II

Date	F	VF	XF	Unc	BU
1915	35.00	75.00	150	220	250

KM# 160 2 THALER (3-1/2 Gulden)
37.1200 g., 0.9000 Silver 1.0743 oz. ASW **Ruler:** Bernhard II
Obv: HELFRICHT below bust **Rev:** Similar to KM#156

Date	F	VF	XF	Unc	BU
1853-1854	200	350	750	1,600	—

KM# 203 3 MARK
16.6670 g., 0.9000 Silver .4823 oz. ASW **Ruler:** Georg II

Date	F	VF	XF	Unc	BU
1908-1913	35.00	110	165	250	350

German States • Saxe-Meiningen

KM# 207   3 MARK
16.6670 g., 0.9000 Silver .4823 oz. ASW **Ruler:** Bernhard III
Subject: Death of Georg II

Date	F	VF	XF	Unc	BU
1915	30.00	70.00	150	220	260

KM# 197   5 MARK
27.7770 g., 0.9000 Silver .8038 oz. ASW **Ruler:** Georg II
Subject: Duke's 75th Birthday

Date	F	VF	XF	Unc	BU
1901	85.00	250	450	1,000	1,400

KM# 200   5 MARK
27.7770 g., 0.9000 Silver .8038 oz. ASW **Ruler:** Georg II **Obv:**
Long beard

Date	F	VF	XF	Unc	BU
1902	60.00	185	350	1,000	1,250

KM# 201   5 MARK
27.7770 g., 0.9000 Silver .8038 oz. ASW **Ruler:** Georg II **Obv:**
Short beard

Date	F	VF	XF	Unc	BU
1902-1908	50.00	160	275	850	900

KM# 190   10 MARK
3.9820 g., 0.9000 Gold .1152 oz. AGW **Ruler:** Georg II

Date	F	VF	XF	Unc	BU
1890-1898	1,500	3,000	3,500	5,000	6,000

KM# 202   10 MARK
3.9820 g., 0.9000 Gold .1152 oz. AGW **Ruler:** Georg II

Date	F	VF	XF	Unc	BU
1902-1914	900	2,000	2,750	4,000	5,000

KM# 180   20 MARK
7.9650 g., 0.9000 Gold .2304 oz. AGW **Ruler:** Georg II **Rev:** Type I

Date	F	VF	XF	Unc	BU
1872	3,500	7,000	—	—	—

KM# 185   20 MARK
7.9650 g., 0.9000 Gold .2304 oz. AGW **Ruler:** Georg II **Rev:** Type II

Date	F	VF	XF	Unc	BU
1882	2,500	5,000	6,000	—	—

KM# 186   20 MARK
7.9650 g., 0.9000 Gold .2304 oz. AGW **Ruler:** Georg II

Date	F	VF	XF	Unc	BU
1889	2,000	4,000	6,000	8,000	—

KM# 195   20 MARK
7.9650 g., 0.9000 Gold .2304 oz. AGW **Ruler:** Georg II **Rev:** Type III

Date	F	VF	XF	Unc	BU
1900-1905	3,000	5,000	7,500	—	—

KM# 205 20 MARK
7.9650 g., 0.9000 Gold .2304 oz. AGW **Ruler:** Georg II

Date	F	VF	XF	Unc	BU
1910-1914	1,500	3,000	4,500	6,000	7,500

SAXE-WEIMAR-EISENACH

(Sachsen-Weimar-Eisenach)

When the death of the duke of Saxe-Eisenach in 1741 heralded the extinction of that line, its possessions reverted to Saxe-Weimar, which henceforth was known as Saxe-Weimar-Eisenach. Because of the strong role played by the duke during the Napoleonic Wars, Saxe-Weimar-Eisenach was raised to the rank of a grand duchy in 1814 and granted the territory of Neustadt, taken from Saxony. The last grand duke abdicated at the end of World War I.

GRAND DUCHY
REGULAR COINAGE

C# 81 PFENNIG
Copper

Date	F	VF	XF	Unc	BU
1840-1851	2.00	5.00	10.00	45.00	—

C# 89 PFENNIG
Copper **Note:** Denticled border.

Date	F	VF	XF	Unc	BU
1858-1865	2.00	4.00	8.00	40.00	—

C# 90 2 PFENNIG
Copper **Note:** Denticled border.

Date	F	VF	XF	Unc	BU
1858-1865	2.00	4.00	8.00	28.00	—

C# 91 1/2 GROSCHEN
1.0900 g., 0.2220 Silver .0077 oz. ASW

Date	F	VF	XF	Unc	BU
1858	2.50	50.00	10.00	50.00	—

C# 92 GROSCHEN
2.1900 g., 0.2220 Silver .0156 oz. ASW

Date	F	VF	XF	Unc	BU
1858	2.50	5.00	10.00	50.00	—

C# 93 THALER
22.2700 g., 0.7500 Silver .5370 oz. ASW **Note:** Vereins Thaler.

Date	F	VF	XF	Unc	BU
1858-1870	40.00	75.00	125	250	—

C# 88 2 THALER (3-1/2 Gulden)
37.1200 g., 0.9000 Silver 1.0742 oz. ASW

Date	F	VF	XF	Unc	BU
1840-1848	150	300	600	1,300	—

C# 94 2 THALER (3-1/2 Gulden)
37.1200 g., 0.9000 Silver 1.0742 oz. ASW **Rev:** Similar to C#88

Date	F	VF	XF	Unc	BU
1855	225	400	900	1,750	—

REFORM COINAGE

Y# 168.1   2 MARK
11.1110 g., 0.9000 Silver .3215 oz. ASW   **Subject:** Golden
Wedding of Carl Alexander

Date	F	VF	XF	Unc	BU
1892	100	200	350	575	700

Y# 168.2   2 MARK
11.1110 g., 0.9000 Silver .3215 oz. ASW   **Subject:** 80th Birthday
of the Grand Duke

Date	F	VF	XF	Unc	BU
1898	75.00	150	325	575	700

Y# 170   2 MARK
11.1110 g., 0.9000 Silver .3215 oz. ASW   **Ruler:** Wilhelm Ernst

Date	F	VF	XF	Unc	BU
1901	100	300	450	850	1,200

Y# 172   2 MARK
11.1110 g., 0.9000 Silver .3215 oz. ASW   **Ruler:** Wilhelm Ernst
Subject: Grand Duke's First Marriage

Date	F	VF	XF	Unc	BU
1903	35.00	60.00	100	145	180

Y# 174   2 MARK
11.1110 g., 0.9000 Silver .3215 oz. ASW   **Ruler:** Wilhelm Ernst
Subject: Jena University 350th Anniversary

Date	F	VF	XF	Unc	BU
1908	25.00	55.00	110	135	180

Y# 176   3 MARK
16.6670 g., 0.9000 Silver .4823 oz. ASW   **Ruler:** Wilhelm Ernst
Subject: Grand Duke's Second Marriage

Date	F	VF	XF	Unc	BU
1910	20.00	40.00	85.00	100	140

Y# 177   3 MARK
16.6670 g., 0.9000 Silver .4823 oz. ASW   **Ruler:** Wilhelm Ernst
Subject: Centenary of Grand Duchy

Date	F	VF	XF	Unc	BU
1915	25.00	75.00	125	200	250

Y# 173   5 MARK
27.7770 g., 0.9000 Silver .8038 oz. ASW   **Ruler:** Wilhelm Ernst
Subject: Grand Dule's First Marriage

Date	F	VF	XF	Unc	BU
1903	60.00	125	225	315	350

Y# 175   5 MARK
27.7770 g., 0.9000 Silver .8038 oz. ASW   **Ruler:** Wilhelm Ernst

Subject: Jena University 350th Anniversary

Date	F	VF	XF	Unc	BU
1908	60.00	110	200	280	350

Y# 169   20 MARK
7.9650 g., 0.9000 Gold .2304 oz. AGW **Subject:** Golden Wedding of Carl Alexander

Date	F	VF	XF	Unc	BU
1892-1896	600	1,150	1,600	2,500	3,000

Y# 171   20 MARK
7.9650 g., 0.9000 Gold .2304 oz. AGW   **Ruler:** Wilhelm Ernst
Subject: Golden Wedding of Carl Alexander

Date	F	VF	XF	Unc	BU
1901	1,000	2,000	2,800	4,000	5,000

SAXONY

Saxony, located in southeast Germany was founded in 850. The first coinage was struck c. 990. It was divided into two lines in 1464. The electoral right was obtained by the elder line in 1547. During the time of the Reformation, Saxony was one of the more powerful states in central Europe. It became a kingdom in 1806. At the Congress of Vienna in 1815, they were forced to cede half its territories to Prussia.

KINGDOM

REGULAR COINAGE

KM# 1155   PFENNIG
Copper   **Ruler:** Friedrich August II

Date	F	VF	XF	Unc	BU
1841-1854	1.50	3.00	6.00	30.00	—

KM# 1184   PFENNIG
Copper   **Ruler:** Johann

Date	F	VF	XF	Unc	BU
1855-1859	1.50	3.00	6.00	30.00	—

KM# 1207   PFENNIG
Copper   **Ruler:** Johann

Date	F	VF	XF	Unc	BU
1861	1.50	3.00	6.00	30.00	—

KM# 1216   PFENNIG
Copper   **Ruler:** Johann

Date	F	VF	XF	Unc	BU
1862-1873	1.50	3.00	6.00	30.00	—

KM# 1157   2 PFENNIGE
Copper   **Ruler:** Friedrich August II

Date	F	VF	XF	Unc	BU
1841-1854	1.50	3.00	6.00	40.00	—

KM# 1185   2 PFENNIGE
Copper   **Ruler:** Johann

Date	F	VF	XF	Unc	BU
1855-1859	1.50	3.00	6.00	40.00	—

KM# 1208   2 PFENNIGE
Copper   **Ruler:** Johann

Date	F	VF	XF	Unc	BU
1861	2.00	4.00	8.00	45.00	—

KM# 1217   2 PFENNIGE
Copper   **Ruler:** Johann

Date	F	VF	XF	Unc	BU
1862-1873	1.25	2.50	5.00	30.00	—

KM# 1218 5 PFENNIGE
Copper **Ruler:** Johann

Date	F	VF	XF	Unc	BU
1862-1869	1.50	3.00	6.00	40.00	—

KM# 1158 1/2 NEU-GROSCHEN (5 Pfennig)
1.0600 g., 0.2290 Silver .0078 oz. ASW **Ruler:** Friedrich August II

Date	F	VF	XF	Unc	BU
1841-1856	1.50	3.00	5.00	25.00	—

KM# 1159 NEU-GROSCHEN (10 Pfennig)
2.1200 g., 0.2290 Silver .0156 oz. ASW **Ruler:** Friedrich August II

Date	F	VF	XF	Unc	BU
1841-1856	1.50	3.00	6.00	35.00	—

KM# 1209 NEU-GROSCHEN (10 Pfennig)
2.1200 g., 0.2300 Silver .0156 oz. ASW **Ruler:** Johann **Rev:** B below value

Date	F	VF	XF	Unc	BU
1861	2.50	5.00	7.50	45.00	—

KM# 1219 NEU-GROSCHEN (10 Pfennig)
2.1200 g., 0.2300 Silver .0156 oz. ASW **Ruler:** Johann

Date	F	VF	XF	Unc	BU
1863-1867	1.50	3.00	5.00	30.00	—

KM# 1221 NEU-GROSCHEN (10 Pfennig)
2.1200 g., 0.2300 Silver .0156 oz. ASW **Ruler:** Johann

Date	F	VF	XF	Unc	BU
1867-1873	2.00	4.00	8.00	40.00	—

KM# 1160 2 NEU-GROSCHEN (20 Pfennig)
3.1100 g., 0.3120 Silver .0311 oz. ASW **Ruler:** Friedrich August II

Date	F	VF	XF	Unc	BU
1841-1856	1.50	3.00	6.00	40.00	—

KM# 1220 2 NEU-GROSCHEN (20 Pfennig)
3.2200 g., 0.3000 Silver .0310 oz. ASW **Ruler:** Johann

Date	F	VF	XF	Unc	BU
1863-1866	2.50	5.00	10.00	50.00	—

KM# 1222 2 NEU-GROSCHEN (20 Pfennig)
3.2200 g., 0.3000 Silver .0310 oz. ASW **Ruler:** Johann

Date	F	VF	XF	Unc	BU
1868-1873	4.00	8.00	15.00	55.00	—

KM# 1161 1/6 THALER (1/4 Gulden - 15 Kreuzer)
5.3400 g., 0.5210 Silver .0894 oz. ASW **Ruler:** Friedrich August II

Date	F	VF	XF	Unc	BU
1841-1850	6.00	12.00	30.00	90.00	—

KM# 1176 1/6 THALER (1/4 Gulden - 15 Kreuzer)
5.3400 g., 0.5210 Silver .0894 oz. ASW **Ruler:** Friedrich August II

Date	F	VF	XF	Unc	BU
1851-1852	6.00	12.00	30.00	90.00	—

KM# 1178 1/6 THALER (1/4 Gulden - 15 Kreuzer)
5.3400 g., 0.5210 Silver .0894 oz. ASW **Ruler:** Friedrich August II **Subject:** Death of King Kriedrich August II **Rev:** ER SAEETE. . . in sprays

Date	F	VF	XF	Unc	BU
1854	5.00	10.00	25.00	85.00	—

KM# 1186   1/6 THALER (1/4 Gulden - 15 Kreuzer)
5.3400 g., 0.5210 Silver .0894 oz. ASW   **Ruler:** Johann

Date	F	VF	XF	Unc	BU
1855-1856	5.00	10.00	25.00	100	—

KM# 1205   1/6 THALER (1/4 Gulden - 15 Kreuzer)
5.3420 g., 0.5200 Silver .0893 oz. ASW   **Ruler:** Johann

Date	F	VF	XF	Unc	BU
1860-1871	4.00	8.00	15.00	60.00	—

KM# 1177   1/3 THALER (1/2 Gulden - 30 Kreuzer - 8 Groschen)
8.3520 g., 0.6670 Silver .1790 oz. ASW   **Ruler:** Friedrich August II

Date	F	VF	XF	Unc	BU
1852-1854	15.00	30.00	60.00	125	—

KM# 1179   1/3 THALER (1/2 Gulden - 30 Kreuzer - 8 Groschen)
8.3520 g., 0.6670 Silver .1790 oz. ASW   **Ruler:** Friedrich August II
Subject: Death of King Friedrich August II

Date	F	VF	XF	Unc	BU
1854	20.00	40.00	80.00	125	—

KM# 1191   1/3 THALER (1/2 Gulden - 30 Kreuzer - 8 Groschen)
8.3520 g., 0.6670 Silver .1790 oz. ASW   **Ruler:** Johann **Obv:**
Head right **Rev:** Crowned draped rectangular arms

Date	F	VF	XF	Unc	BU
1856	25.00	50.00	100	175	—

KM# 1198   1/3 THALER (1/2 Gulden - 30 Kreuzer - 8 Groschen)
8.3000 g., 0.6670 Silver .1784 oz. ASW   **Ruler:** Johann

Date	F	VF	XF	Unc	BU
1858-1859	20.00	40.00	80.00	150	—

KM# 1206   1/3 THALER (1/2 Gulden - 30 Kreuzer - 8 Groschen)
8.3000 g., 0.6670 Silver .1784 oz. ASW   **Ruler:** Johann

Date	F	VF	XF	Unc	BU
1860	17.50	35.00	70.00	125	—

KM# 1148   THALER
22.2720 g., 0.7500 Silver .5371 oz. ASW   **Ruler:** Friedrich August II

Date	F	VF	XF	Unc	BU
1839-1849	25.00	50.00	100	250	—

KM# 1162   THALER
22.2720 g., 0.7500 Silver .5371 oz. ASW   **Ruler:** Friedrich August II
Obv: G below head **Note:** Mining Thaler.

Date	F	VF	XF	Unc	BU
1841-1854	50.00	100	200	400	—

KM# 1175   THALER
22.2720 g., 0.7500 Silver .5371 oz. ASW   **Ruler:** Friedrich August II

Date	F	VF	XF	Unc	BU
1850-1854	25.00	50.00	125	325	—

KM# 1180.1   THALER
22.2720 g., 0.7500 Silver .5371 oz. ASW   **Ruler:** Friedrich August II
Subject: Death of King Friedrich August II

Date	F	VF	XF	Unc	BU
1854	30.00	60.00	100	200	—

KM# 1180.2 THALER
22.2720 g., 0.7500 Silver .5371 oz. ASW **Ruler:** Friedrich August II
Edge: SEGEN DES BERGBAUS **Note:** Edge inscription with
crossed hammers.

Date	F	VF	XF	Unc	BU
1854	40.00	75.00	125	250	—

KM# 1181 THALER
22.2720 g., 0.7500 Silver .5371 oz. ASW **Ruler:** Friedrich August II
Note: Convention Thaler.

Date	F	VF	XF	Unc	BU
1854	30.00	60.00	150	450	—

KM# 1182 THALER
22.2720 g., 0.7500 Silver .5371 oz. ASW **Ruler:** Friedrich August II
Rev: Similar to C#269 **Note:** Mining Thaler.

Date	F	VF	XF	Unc	BU
1854	90.00	175	425	1,000	—

KM# 1187 THALER
22.2720 g., 0.7500 Silver .5371 oz. ASW **Ruler:** Johann **Subject:**
Visit to Mint by King Johann **Note:** Convention Thaler.

Date	F	VF	XF	Unc	BU
1855	35.00	65.00	125	300	—

KM# 1188 THALER
22.2720 g., 0.7500 Silver .5371 oz. ASW **Ruler:** Johann **Rev:**
Similar to C#265

Date	F	VF	XF	Unc	BU
1855-1856	25.00	40.00	100	250	—

KM# 1189 THALER
22.2720 g., 0.7500 Silver .5371 oz. ASW **Ruler:** Johann **Note:**
Mining Thaler.

Date	F	VF	XF	Unc	BU
1855-1856	65.00	125	350	800	—

KM# 1192 THALER
18.5200 g., 0.9000 Silver .5360 oz. ASW **Ruler:** Johann **Note:**
Vereins Thaler.

Date	F	VF	XF	Unc	BU
1857-1859	20.00	35.00	90.00	225	—

KM# 1193 THALER
18.5200 g., 0.9000 Silver .5360 oz. ASW **Ruler:** Johann **Obv:**
Similar to C#269. **Note:** Mining Thaler.

Date	F	VF	XF	Unc	BU
1857-1858	75.00	150	400	800	—

KM# 1199 THALER
18.5200 g., 0.9000 Silver .5360 oz. ASW **Ruler:** Johann

Date	F	VF	XF	Unc	BU
1858-1861	25.00	50.00	100	250	—

KM# 1210 THALER
18.5200 g., 0.9000 Silver .5360 oz. ASW **Ruler:** Johann **Note:**
Vereins Thaler.

Date	F	VF	XF	Unc	BU
1860-1861	25.00	50.00	90.00	200	—

KM# 1211   THALER
18.5200 g., 0.9000 Silver .5360 oz. ASW   **Ruler:** Johann **Obv:** Small letters in legend

Date	F	VF	XF	Unc	BU
1861	75.00	150	450	1,000	—

KM# 1212   THALER
18.5200 g., 0.9000 Silver .5360 oz. ASW   **Ruler:** Johann

Date	F	VF	XF	Unc	BU
1861-1867	20.00	40.00	70.00	150	—

KM# 1213   THALER
18.5200 g., 0.9000 Silver .5360 oz. ASW   **Ruler:** Johann **Obv:** KM#1210 **Rev:** KM#1214

Date	F	VF	XF	Unc	BU
1861	300	600	800	1,200	—

KM# 1214   THALER
18.5200 g., 0.9000 Silver .5360 oz. ASW   **Ruler:** Johann

Date	F	VF	XF	Unc	BU
1861-1871	20.00	35.00	70.00	150	—

KM# 1223   THALER
18.5200 g., 0.9000 Silver .5360 oz. ASW   **Ruler:** Johann

Date	F	VF	XF	Unc	BU
1868-1871	20.00	40.00	70.00	150	—

KM# 1230   THALER
18.5200 g., 0.9000 Silver .5360 oz. ASW   **Ruler:** Johann **Subject:** Victory Over France

Date	F	VF	XF	Unc	BU
1871	30.00	50.00	80.00	175	—

KM# 1149   2 THALER (3-1/2 Gulden)
37.1200 g., 0.9000 Silver 1.0742 oz. ASW   **Ruler:** Friedrich August II

Date	F	VF	XF	Unc	BU
1839-1854	50.00	85.00	185	400	—

KM# 1183   2 THALER (3-1/2 Gulden)
37.1200 g., 0.9000 Silver 1.0742 oz. ASW   **Ruler:** Friedrich August II
Subject: Death of King Friedrich August II

Date	F	VF	XF	Unc	BU
1854	100	200	300	500	—

KM# 1200   2 THALER (3-1/2 Gulden)
37.0370 g., 0.9000 Silver 1.0718 oz. ASW   **Ruler:** Johann **Obv:** Similar to KM#1190. **Rev:** Value: VEREINSTHAELR

Date	F	VF	XF	Unc	BU
1858	35.00	90.00	175	375	—

KM# 1190   2 THALER (3-1/2 Gulden)
37.1200 g., 0.9000 Silver 1.0742 oz. ASW   **Ruler:** Johann **Note:** Similar to KM#1149.

Date	F	VF	XF	Unc	BU
1855-1856	50.00	90.00	190	350	—

KM# 1194   2 THALER (3-1/2 Gulden)
37.1200 g., 0.9000 Silver 1.0742 oz. ASW   **Ruler:** Johann **Subject:** Mining Academy at Freiberg **Obv:** Similar to KM#1190. **Note:** Prize Thaler.

Date	F	VF	XF	Unc	BU
1857	700	1,400	2,500	4,000	—

KM# 1215   2 THALER (3-1/2 Gulden)
37.0370 g., 0.9000 Silver 1.0718 oz. ASW   **Ruler:** Johann **Obv:** Similar to KM#1190.

Date	F	VF	XF	Unc	BU
1861	65.00	100	200	350	—

KM# 1195   2 THALER (3-1/2 Gulden)
37.0370 g., 0.9000 Silver 1.0718 oz. ASW   **Ruler:** Johann **Obv:** Similar to KM#1190.

Date	F	VF	XF	Unc	BU
1857-1859	50.00	80.00	180	325	—

KM# 1231.1   2 THALER (3-1/2 Gulden)
37.0370 g., 0.9000 Silver 1.0718 oz. ASW   **Ruler:** Johann
Subject: Golden Wedding Anniversary

Date	F	VF	XF	Unc	BU
1872	50.00	75.00	125	200	—

KM# 1231.2   2 THALER (3-1/2 Gulden)
37.0370 g., 0.9000 Silver 1.0718 oz. ASW   **Ruler:** Johann **Edge:** Plain

Date	F	VF	XF	Unc	BU
1872	100	250	350	500	—

KM# 1164   2-1/2 THALER
3.3410 g., 0.9020 Gold .0970 oz. AGW   **Ruler:** Friedrich August II

Date	F	VF	XF	Unc	BU
1842-1854	250	500	1,000	2,000	—

KM# 1165   5 THALER (August D'or)
6.6820 g., 0.9020 Gold .1940 oz. AGW   **Ruler:** Friedrich August II

Date	F	VF	XF	Unc	BU
1842-1854	250	400	1,000	2,000	—

KM# 1150   10 THALER (2 August D'or)
13.3640 g., 0.9020 Gold .3880 oz. AGW   **Ruler:** Friedrich August II

Date	F	VF	XF	Unc	BU
1839-1854	600	1,250	2,500	3,500	—

KM# 1196   1/2 KRONE
5.5560 g., 0.9000 Gold .1608 oz. AGW   **Ruler:** Johann

Date	F	VF	XF	Unc	BU
1857-1870	475	1,000	2,000	3,000	—

KM# 1197   KRONE
11.1110 g., 0.9000 Gold .3215 oz. AGW   **Ruler:** Johann

Date	F	VF	XF	Unc	BU
1857-1871	525	1,350	2,500	3,200	—

REFORM COINAGE

KM# 1238   2 MARK
11.1110 g., 0.9000 Silver .3215 oz. ASW   **Ruler:** Albert

Date	F	VF	XF	Unc	BU
1876-1888	30.00	80.00	500	1,200	1,400

KM# 1245   2 MARK
11.1110 g., 0.9000 Silver .3215 oz. ASW   **Ruler:** Albert **Note:** Similar to KM#185.

Date	F	VF	XF	Unc	BU
1891-1902	10.00	55.00	110	275	350

KM# 1255   2 MARK
11.1110 g., 0.9000 Silver .3215 oz. ASW   **Ruler:** Georg **Subject:** Death of Albert

Date	F	VF	XF	Unc	BU
1902	15.00	40.00	65.00	125	175

KM# 1257   2 MARK
11.1110 g., 0.9000 Silver .3215 oz. ASW   **Ruler:** Georg

Date	F	VF	XF	Unc	BU
1903-1904	17.50	50.00	100	300	350

KM# 1261   2 MARK
11.1110 g., 0.9000 Silver .3215 oz. ASW **Ruler:** Friedrich August III
Subject: Death of Georg

Date	F	VF	XF	Unc	BU
1904	15.00	35.00	70.00	100	130

KM# 1275   3 MARK
16.6670 g., 0.9000 Silver .4823 oz. ASW **Ruler:** Friedrich August III
Subject: Battle of Leipzig Centennial

Date	F	VF	XF	Unc	BU
1913	12.00	18.00	28.00	45.00	60.00

KM# 1263   2 MARK
11.1110 g., 0.9000 Silver .3215 oz. ASW **Ruler:** Friedrich August III

Date	F	VF	XF	Unc	BU
(1905-1914)-1914	20.00	45.00	70.00	125	160

KM# 1276   3 MARK
16.6670 g., 0.9000 Silver .4823 oz. ASW **Ruler:** Friedrich August III
Subject: Jubilee of Reformation

Date	F	VF	XF	Unc	BU
1917 Proof		Value: 70,000			

KM# 1268   2 MARK
11.1110 g., 0.9000 Silver .3215 oz. ASW **Ruler:** Friedrich August III
Subject: 500th Anniversary - Leipzig University

Date	F	VF	XF	Unc	BU
1909	15.00	35.00	65.00	100	120

KM# 1237   5 MARK
27.7770 g., 0.9000 Silver .8038 oz. ASW **Ruler:** Albert

Date	F	VF	XF	Unc	BU
1875-1889	30.00	60.00	650	1,900	2,200

KM# 1267   3 MARK
16.6670 g., 0.9000 Silver .4823 oz. ASW **Ruler:** Friedrich August III

Date	F	VF	XF	Unc	BU
(1908-1913)-1913	10.00	20.00	35.00	80.00	110

KM# 1239   5 MARK
1.9910 g., 0.9000 Gold .0576 oz. AGW **Ruler:** Albert **Rev:** Type I

Date	F	VF	XF	Unc	BU
1877	175	300	500	750	900

KM# 1249 5 MARK
Silver **Ruler:** Albert **Obv:** Bust right **Rev:** Throne scene,
anniversary dates at base

Date	F	VF	XF	Unc	BU
1889	—	—	2,600	3,500	4,000

KM# 1249a 5 MARK
Bronze **Ruler:** Albert

Date	F	VF	XF	Unc	BU
1889	—	—	350	550	650

KM# 1246 5 MARK
27.7770 g., 0.9000 Silver .8038 oz. ASW **Ruler:** Albert **Note:**
Similar to KM#1256.

Date	F	VF	XF	Unc	BU
1891-1902	20.00	45.00	275	650	1,150

KM# 1256 5 MARK
27.7770 g., 0.9000 Silver .8038 oz. ASW **Ruler:** Georg **Subject:**
Death of Albert

Date	F	VF	XF	Unc	BU
1902	30.00	65.00	145	200	275

KM# 1258 5 MARK
27.7770 g., 0.9000 Silver .8038 oz. ASW **Ruler:** Georg

Date	F	VF	XF	Unc	BU
1903-1904	25.00	50.00	200	650	750

KM# 1262 5 MARK
27.7770 g., 0.9000 Silver .8038 oz. ASW **Ruler:** Friedrich August III
Subject: Death of Georg

Date	F	VF	XF	Unc	BU
1904	45.00	150	245	350	400

KM# 1266 5 MARK
27.7770 g., 0.9000 Silver .8038 oz. ASW **Ruler:** Friedrich August III

Date	F	VF	XF	Unc	BU
1907-1914	17.50	35.00	80.00	200	225

KM# 1233 20 MAR
7.9650 g., 0.9000 Gold .2304 oz. AGW **Ruler:** Johann **Rev:** Type I

Date	F	VF	XF	Unc	BU
1872	160	200	300	600	800

KM# 1269 5 MARK
27.7770 g., 0.9000 Silver .8038 oz. ASW **Ruler:** Friedrich August III
Subject: 500th Anniversary - Leipzig University

Date	F	VF	XF	Unc	BU
1909	40.00	95.00	175	245	300

KM# 1232 10 MARK
3.9820 g., 0.9000 Gold .1152 oz. AGW **Ruler:** Johann

Date	F	VF	XF	Unc	BU
1872-1873	95.00	200	350	600	1,200

KM# 1234 20 MARK
7.9650 g., 0.9000 Gold .2304 oz. AGW **Ruler:** Johann **Obv:** Large letters in legend

Date	F	VF	XF	Unc	BU
1873	160	200	300	600	800

KM# 1236 20 MARK
7.9650 g., 0.9000 Gold .2304 oz. AGW **Ruler:** Albert **Rev:** Type II

Date	F	VF	XF	Unc	BU
1874-1878	160	200	250	—	—

KM# 1235 10 MARK
3.9820 g., 0.9000 Gold .1152 oz. AGW **Ruler:** Albert **Rev:** Type II

Date	F	VF	XF	Unc	BU
1874-1888	80.00	120	200	400	600

KM# 1247 10 MARK
3.9820 g., 0.9000 Gold .1152 oz. AGW **Ruler:** Albert **Rev:** Type III

Date	F	VF	XF	Unc	BU
1891-1902	100	160	200	450	550

KM# 1248 20 MARK
7.9650 g., 0.9000 Gold .2304 oz. AGW **Ruler:** Albert **Rev:** Type III

Date	F	VF	XF	Unc	BU
1894-1895	BV	160	225	350	450

KM# 1259 10 MARK
3.9820 g., 0.9000 Gold .1152 oz. AGW **Ruler:** Georg

Date	F	VF	XF	Unc	BU
1903-1904	100	210	350	600	700

KM# 1260 20 MARK
7.9650 g., 0.9000 Gold .2304 oz. AGW **Ruler:** Georg **Rev:** Type III

Date	F	VF	XF	Unc	BU
1903	BV	200	300	450	550

KM# 1264 10 MARK
3.9820 g., 0.9000 Gold .1152 oz. AGW **Ruler:** Friedrich August III

Date	F	VF	XF	Unc	BU
1905-1912	120	250	325	500	650

KM# 1265 20 MARK
7.9650 g., 0.9000 Gold .2304 oz. AGW **Ruler:** Friedrich August III

Date	F	VF	XF	Unc	BU
1905-1914	BV	200	375	450	550

SCHAUMBURG-LIPPE

The tiny countship of Schaumburg-Lippe, with an area of only 131 square miles (218 square kilometers) in northwest Germany, was surrounded by the larger states of Brunswick-Lüneburg-Calenberg, an enclave of Hesse-Cassel, and the bishopric of Minden (part of Brandenburg-Prussia from 1648). In 1806, the count was raised to the rank of prince and Schaumburg-Lippe was incorporated into the Rhine Confederation. It became a part of the German Confederation in 1815 and joined the North German Confederation in 1866. The principality became a member state in the German Empire in 1871. The last sovereign prince resigned as a result of World War I.

PRINCIPALITY
REGULAR COINAGE

C# 37   PFENNIG
Copper   **Ruler:** Georg Wilhelm

Date	F	VF	XF	Unc	BU
1858	4.00	8.00	25.00	70.00	—

C# 38   2 PFENNIG
Copper   **Ruler:** Georg Wilhelm

Date	F	VF	XF	Unc	BU
1858	3.00	7.00	20.00	50.00	—

C# 39   3 PFENNIG
Copper   **Ruler:** Georg Wilhelm

Date	F	VF	XF	Unc	BU
1858	3.50	8.00	25.00	55.00	—

C# 40   4 PFENNIG
Copper   **Ruler:** Georg Wilhelm

Date	F	VF	XF	Unc	BU
1858	6.00	12.50	30.00	75.00	—

C# 45   1/2 SILBER GROSCHEN (1/60 Thaler)
1.0900 g., 0.2200 Silver .0077 oz. ASW   **Ruler:** Georg Wilhelm

Date	F	VF	XF	Unc	BU
1858	8.00	16.00	40.00	85.00	—

C# 46   SILBER GROSCHEN (1/50 Thaler)
2.1900 g., 0.2200 Silver .0154 oz. ASW   **Ruler:** Georg Wilhelm

Date	F	VF	XF	Unc	BU
1858	7.00	15.00	35.00	75.00	—

C# 47   2-1/2 SILBER GROSCHEN (1/12 Thaler)
3.2200 g., 0.3750 Silver .0388 oz. ASW   **Ruler:** Georg Wilhelm

Date	F	VF	XF	Unc	BU
1858	12.50	25.00	60.00	125	—

C# 48   THALER
18.5200 g., 0.9000 Silver .5360 oz. ASW   **Ruler:** Adolph Georg

Date	F	VF	XF	Unc	BU
1860	60.00	100	250	500	—

C# 51   THALER
18.5200 g., 0.9000 Silver .5360 oz. ASW   **Ruler:** Adolph Georg

Date	F	VF	XF	Unc	BU
1865	40.00	75.00	175	325	—

Y# 204   5 MARK
27.7770 g., 0.9000 Silver 0.8038 oz. ASW **Ruler:** Albrecht Georg
Subject: Death of Prince George

Date	F	VF	XF	Unc	BU
1898-1904	350	775	1,250	2,250	2,600

C# 49   2 THALER
37.0370 g., 0.9000 Silver 1.0718 oz. ASW **Ruler:** Georg Wilhelm
Subject: 50th Anniversary of Reign as Prince **Obv:** Similar to 1
Thaler, C#48.

Date	F	VF	XF	Unc	BU
1857	175	275	400	800	—

REFORM COINAGE

Y# 202   20 MARK
7.9650 g., 0.9000 Gold .2304 oz. AGW **Ruler:** Adolph Georg

Date	F	VF	XF	Unc	BU
1874	2,250	4,000	6,000	9,000	—

Y# 203   2 MARK
11.1110 g., 0.9000 Silver 0.3215 oz. ASW **Ruler:** Albrecht Georg
Subject: Death of Prince George

Date	F	VF	XF	Unc	BU
1898-1904	200	400	700	1,250	1,400

Y# 205   20 MARK
7.9650 g., 0.9000 Gold 0.2304 oz. AGW **Ruler:** Albrecht Georg
Subject: Death of Prince George

Date	F	VF	XF	Unc	BU
1898-1904	750	1,400	2,000	3,000	3,750

SCHLESWIG-HOLSTEIN

Schleswig-Holstein is located along the border area between
Denmark and Germany. The Duchy of Schleswig was predom-
inantly Danish while the Duchy of Holstein was mostly German.
Holstein-Gottorp was the ruling line in most of the territory from
1533 and lost Schleswig to Denmark permanently in 1721. Holstein-Gottorp was transferred by the 1773 Treaty of Zarskoje Selo
to Denmark in exchange for Oldenburg. There was a great deal of
trouble in the area during the 19th century and as a result of a war
with Denmark, Prussia annexed the territory in 1864. After World
War I, a plebiscite was held and the area was divided in 1920. North
Slesvig went to Denmark while South Schleswig and Holstein
became a permanent part of Germany.

STATE

GUTSCHRIFTSMARKE COINAGE
KM# Tn1   5/100 GUTSCHRIFTSMARKE
Aluminum, 23 mm. **Obv:** Provincial arms **Rev:** Denomination

Date	F	VF	XF	Unc	BU
1923	3.00	7.00	14.00	22.50	—

Y# 206   3 MARK
16.6670 g., 0.9000 Silver 0.4823 oz. ASW **Ruler:** Albrecht Georg
Subject: Death of Prince George

Date	F	VF	XF	Unc	BU
1911	30.00	65.00	95.00	180	225

KM# Tn2 10/100 GUTSCHRIFTSMARKE
Aluminum, 27 mm. **Obv:** Provincial arms **Rev:** Denomination

Date	F	VF	XF	Unc	BU
1923	4.00	8.00	16.00	25.00	—

PROVISIONAL GOVERNMENT
1848-1851
REGULAR COINAGE

C# 23 DREILING
Copper **Obv:** Arms of Schleswig-Holstein within wreath **Rev:**
Value and date within area name

Date	F	VF	XF	Unc	BU
1850	10.00	17.50	45.00	75.00	—

C# 24 SECHSLING
Copper **Obv:** Arms of Schleswig-Holstein within wreath **Rev:**
Value and date within area name

Date	F	VF	XF	Unc	BU
1850-1851	10.00	17.50	45.00	75.00	—

SCHWARZBURG-RUDOLSTADT

The Countship of Schwarzburg-Rudolstadt came into being as the younger line upon the division of Schwarzburg-Blankenburg in 1552. Its territory of about 360 square miles (600 square kilometers) is located in the center of Thuringia (Thüringen), surrounded by several of the Saxon duchies and Reuss-Obergreiz. Schwarzburg-Rudolstadt joined the German Confederation at the end of hostilities and subsequently became a member of the North German Confederation in 1867, then the German Empire in 1871. The last prince obtained Schwarzburg-Sondershausen upon the latter's extinction in 1909, then was forced to abdicate in 1918.

PRINCIPALITY
REGULAR COINAGE

C# 73 1/8 KREUZER
Copper **Ruler:** Friedrich Gunther **Obv:** Crowned arms within branches **Rev:** Value

Date	F	VF	XF	Unc	BU
1840-1855	4.00	8.00	20.00	50.00	—

C# 74 1/4 KREUZER
Copper **Ruler:** Friedrich Gunther

Date	F	VF	XF	Unc	BU
1840-1856	3.00	6.00	15.00	35.00	—

C# 74a 1/4 KREUZER
Copper **Ruler:** Friedrich Gunther

Date	F	VF	XF	Unc	BU
1857-1866	2.50	5.00	12.00	32.00	—

C# 82 1/4 KREUZER
Copper **Ruler:** Albert

Date	F	VF	XF	Unc	BU
1868	3.00	6.00	15.00	45.00	—

C# 76a KREUZER
Copper **Ruler:** Friedrich Gunther

Date	F	VF	XF	Unc	BU
1864-1866	2.00	4.00	10.00	30.00	—

C# 83 KREUZER
Copper **Ruler:** Albert

Date	F	VF	XF	Unc	BU
1868	4.00	8.00	18.00	50.00	—

C# 77a 3 KREUZER
1.2300 g., 0.3500 Silver .0138 oz. ASW **Ruler:** Friedrich Gunther
Obv: Legend added

Date	F	VF	XF	Unc	BU
1866	10.00	20.00	50.00	175	—

C# 78a 6 KREUZER
2.4600 g., 0.3500 Silver .0276 oz. ASW **Ruler:** Friedrich Gunther
Obv: Legend added

Date	F	VF	XF	Unc	BU
1866	12.00	25.00	55.00	165	—

C# 70 THALER
18.5200 g., 0.9000 Silver .5360 oz. ASW **Ruler:** Friedrich Gunther
Note: Vereins Thaler.

Date	F	VF	XF	Unc	BU
1858-1859	40.00	65.00	130	275	—

C# 70a THALER
18.5200 g., 0.9000 Silver .5360 oz. ASW **Ruler:** Friedrich Gunther

Date	F	VF	XF	Unc	BU
1862-1863	40.00	65.00	130	275	—

C# 71 THALER
18.5200 g., 0.9000 Silver .5360 oz. ASW **Ruler:** Friedrich Gunther
Subject: 50th Anniversary of Reign

Date	F	VF	XF	Unc	BU
1864	65.00	100	200	350	—

C# 70b   THALER
18.5200 g., 0.9000 Silver .5360 oz. ASW   **Ruler:** Friedrich Gunther

Date	F	VF	XF	Unc	BU
1866	40.00	65.00	130	275	—

C# 84   THALER
18.5200 g., 0.9000 Silver .5360 oz. ASW   **Ruler:** Friedrich Gunther

Date	F	VF	XF	Unc	BU
1867	50.00	80.00	175	450	—

REFORM COINAGE

Y# 207   2 MARK
11.1110 g., 0.9000 Silver .3215 oz. ASW   **Ruler:** Gunther Viktor

Date	F	VF	XF	Unc	BU
1898	150	250	450	650	800

Y# 208   10 MARK
3.9820 g., 0.9000 Gold .1152 oz. AGW   **Ruler:** Gunther Viktor

Date	F	VF	XF	Unc	BU
1898	700	1,500	2,000	3,000	4,000

SCHWARZBURG-SONDERSHAUSEN

The Countship of Schwarzburg-Sondershausen contains territory of about 330 square miles (550 square kilometers) and is located just north of Thuringia (Thüringen), surrounded by the Prussian province of Saxony, between the ducal enclaves of Gotha and Weimar. The count was raised to the rank of prince in 1697 and underwent several minor divisions during the 18th century. Schwarzburg-Sondershausen joined the German Confederation in 1815 and became a member of the North German Confederation in 1867, as well as the German Empire in 1871. When Karl Günther died without an heir in 1909, his lands and titles went to Schwarzburg-Rudolstadt.

PRINCIPALITY
REGULAR COINAGE

C# 18   PFENNIG
Copper   **Ruler:** Gunther Friedrich Carl II **Note:** Struck at Arnstadt Mint.

Date	F	VF	XF	Unc	BU
1846-1858	1.50	3.00	9.00	35.00	—

C# 19   3 PFENNIG
Copper   **Ruler:** Gunther Friedrich Carl II **Note:** Struck at Arnstadt Mint.

Date	F	VF	XF	Unc	BU
1846-1870	3.00	6.00	18.00	50.00	—

C# 20   1/2 SILBER GROSCHEN
1.0900 g., 0.2220 Silver .0077 oz. ASW   **Ruler:** Gunther Friedrich Carl II **Note:** Struck at Arnstadt Mint.

Date	F	VF	XF	Unc	BU
1846-1858	3.00	6.00	18.00	50.00	—

C# 21   SILBER GROSCHEN
2.1900 g., 0.2220 Silver .0156 oz. ASW   **Ruler:** Gunther Friedrich Carl II **Note:** Struck at Arnstadt Mint.

Date	F	VF	XF	Unc	BU
1846-1870	3.00	6.00	18.00	55.00	—

C# 22   THALER
18.5200 g., 0.9000 Silver .5360 oz. ASW **Ruler:**
Gunther Friedrich Carl II **Note:** Vereins Thaler. Struck at Arnstadt
Mint.

Date	F	VF	XF	Unc	BU
1859-1870	50.00	80.00	160	400	—

C# 23   2 THALER (3-1/2 Gulden)
37.1200 g., 0.9000 Silver 1.0741 oz. ASW **Ruler:** Gunther
Friedrich Carl II **Note:** Struck at Arnstadt Mint.

Date	F	VF	XF	Unc	BU
1841-1854	100	200	450	1,000	—

REFORM COINAGE

Y# 209   2 MARK
11.1110 g., 0.9000 Silver .3215 oz. ASW **Ruler:** Karl Gunther
Note: Struck at Arnstadt Mint.

Date	F	VF	XF	Unc	BU
1896	125	250	425	675	850

Y# 211   2 MARK
11.1110 g., 0.9000 Silver .3215 oz. ASW **Ruler:** Karl Gunther
Subject: 25th Anniversary of Reign **Note:** Thick rim.

Date	F	VF	XF	Unc	BU
1905	40.00	80.00	145	220	275

Y# 211a   2 MARK
11.1110 g., 0.9000 Silver .3215 oz. ASW **Ruler:** Karl Gunther
Subject: 25th Anniversary of Reign **Note:** Thin rim.

Date	F	VF	XF	Unc	BU
1905	25.00	50.00	95.00	135	160

Y# 212   3 MARK
16.6670 g., 0.9000 Silver .4823 oz. ASW **Ruler:** Karl Gunther
Subject: Death of Karl Gunther

Date	F	VF	XF	Unc	BU
1909	30.00	60.00	100	175	200

Y# 210   20 MARK
7.9650 g., 0.9000 Gold .2304 oz. AGW **Ruler:** Karl Gunther

Date	F	VF	XF	Unc	BU
1896	850	1,750	2,750	3,500	4,500

WALDECK-PYRMONT

The Count of Waldeck-Eisenberg inherited the Countship of
Pyrmont, located between Lippe and Hannover, in 1625, thus creating an entity which encompassed about 672 square miles (1120
square kilometers). Waldeck and Pyrmont were permanently
united in 1668, thus continuing the Eisenberg line as Waldeck-Pyrmont from that date. The unification of the two territories was confirmed in 1812. Waldeck-Pyrmont joined the German Confederation in 1815 and the North German Confederation in 1867. The
prince renounced his sovereignty on 1 October of that year and
Waldeck-Pyrmont was incorporated into Prussia. However, coinage was struck into the early 20th century for Waldeck-Pyrmont as
a member of the German Empire. The hereditary territorial titles
were lost along with the war in 1918. Some coins were struck for
issue in Pyrmont only in the 18th through 20th centuries and those
are listed separately under that name.

PRINCIPALITY
REGULAR COINAGE

C# 85   PFENNIG
Copper **Ruler:** Georg Victor **Note:** Struck at Hannover Mint.

Date	F	VF	XF	Unc	BU
1855	3.00	6.00	12.00	45.00	—

C# 85a   PFENNIG
Copper **Ruler:** Georg Victor **Note:** Struck at Prussia Mint.

Date	F	VF	XF	Unc	BU
1867	2.00	4.00	8.00	35.00	—

C# 86 3 PFENNIG
Copper **Ruler:** Georg Victor **Note:** Struck at Hannover Mint.

Date	F	VF	XF	Unc	BU
1855	4.00	8.00	16.00	60.00	—

C# 86.1 3 PFENNIG
Copper **Ruler:** Georg Victor **Note:** Struck at Prussia Mint.

Date	F	VF	XF	Unc	BU
1867	3.00	6.00	12.00	50.00	—

C# 87 GROSCHEN
2.1900 g., 0.2220 Silver .0156 oz. ASW **Ruler:** Georg Victor **Rev:** A below value and date **Note:** Struck at Hannover Mint.

Date	F	VF	XF	Unc	BU
1855	7.00	15.00	30.00	125	—

C# 87a GROSCHEN
2.1900 g., 0.2220 Silver .0156 oz. ASW **Ruler:** Georg Victor **Note:** Struck at Prussia Mint.

Date	F	VF	XF	Unc	BU
1867	6.00	12.00	20.00	90.00	—

C# 88 THALER
18.5200 g., 0.9000 Silver .5358 oz. ASW **Ruler:** Georg Victor

Date	F	VF	XF	Unc	BU
1859-1867	40.00	85.00	165	325	—

C# 89 2 THALER (3-1/2 Gulden)
37.1200 g., 0.9000 Silver 1.0742 oz. ASW **Ruler:** Georg Victor **Note:** Struck at Hannover Mint.

Date	F	VF	XF	Unc	BU
1856	200	400	800	1,600	—

REFORM COINAGE

Y# 213 5 MARK
27.7770 g., 0.9000 Silver .8038 oz. ASW **Ruler:** Friedrich

Date	F	VF	XF	Unc	BU
1903	—	3,000	4,000	5,000	6,000

Y# 214 20 MARK
7.9650 g., 0.9000 Gold .2304 oz. AGW **Ruler:** Friedrich

Date	F	VF	XF	Unc	BU
1903	2,400	4,000	5,800	8,000	—

WISMAR

A seaport on the Baltic, the city of Wismar is said to have obtained municipal rights from Mecklenburg in 1229. It was an important member of the Hanseatic League in the 13th and 14th centuries. Their coinage began at the end of the 13th century and terminated in 1854. They belonged to Sweden from 1648 to 1803. A special plate money was struck by the Swedes in 1715 when the town was under siege. In 1803, Sweden sold Wismar to Mecklenburg-Schwerin. The transaction was confirmed in 1815.

SWEDISH ADMINISTRATION
REGULAR COINAGE

C# 4 3 PFENNIG
Copper

Date	F	VF	XF	Unc	BU
1854	6.00	12.00	35.00	75.00	—

WÜRTTEMBERG

Located in South Germany, between Baden and Bavaria, Württemberg takes its name from the ancestral castle of the ruling dynasty. At the close of the Napoleonic Wars (1792-1815), Württemberg joined the German Confederation, but sided with Austria in its war with Prussia in 1866. It sided with Prussia against France in 1870 and became a member of the German Empire in 1871. King Wilhelm II was forced to abdicate at the end of World War I in 1918.

KINGDOM

REGULAR COINAGE

KM# 589   1/4 KREUZER
Copper   **Ruler:** Wilhelm I

Date	F	VF	XF	Unc	BU
1842-1856	3.00	6.50	18.00	50.00	—

KM# 602   1/4 KREUZER
Copper   **Ruler:** Wilhelm I

Date	F	VF	XF	Unc	BU
1858-1864	3.50	7.00	20.00	55.00	—

KM# 610   1/4 KREUZER
Copper   **Ruler:** Karl I

Date	F	VF	XF	Unc	BU
1865-1872	3.00	6.00	14.00	45.00	—

KM# 585   1/2 KREUZER (4 Pfennig)
Copper

Date	F	VF	XF	Unc	BU
1840-1856	3.00	6.00	14.00	45.00	—

KM# 603   1/2 KREUZER (4 Pfennig)
Copper

Date	F	VF	XF	Unc	BU
1858-1864	2.50	5.00	12.00	40.00	—

KM# 611   1/2 KREUZER (4 Pfennig)
Copper

Date	F	VF	XF	Unc	BU
1865-1872	2.50	5.00	12.00	40.00	—

KM# 590   KREUZER
0.6200 g., 0.2500 Silver .0049 oz. ASW

Date	F	VF	XF	Unc	BU
1842-1857	2.00	4.00	8.00	30.00	—

KM# 600   KREUZER
0.8300 g., 0.1660 Silver .0044 oz. ASW

Date	F	VF	XF	Unc	BU
1857-1864	2.00	3.00	6.00	25.00	—

KM# 612   KREUZER
0.8300 g., 0.1660 Silver .0044 oz. ASW

Date	F	VF	XF	Unc	BU
1865-1873	2.00	4.00	7.00	25.00	—

KM# 591   3 KREUZER (Groschen)
1.2900 g., 0.3330 Silver .0138 oz. ASW

Date	F	VF	XF	Unc	BU
1842-1856	2.00	4.00	10.00	40.00	—

KM# 592   6 KREUZER
2.5900 g., 0.3330 Silver .0277 oz. ASW

Date	F	VF	XF	Unc	BU
1842-1856	3.00	6.00	15.00	55.00	—

KM# 573   1/2 GULDEN
5.2900 g., 0.9000 Silver .1530 oz. ASW **Obv:** VOIGT below head

Date	F	VF	XF	Unc	BU
1838-1858	12.00	25.00	65.00	140	—

KM# 604   1/2 GULDEN
5.2900 g., 0.9000 Silver .1530 oz. ASW **Obv:** Without VOIGT below head

Date	F	VF	XF	Unc	BU
1858-1864	15.00	37.50	75.00	140	—

KM# 613   1/2 GULDEN
5.2900 g., 0.9000 Silver .1530 oz. ASW **Obv:** Head right with C.S. on truncation

Date	F	VF	XF	Unc	BU
1865-1868	15.00	50.00	100	250	—

KM# 616   1/2 GULDEN
5.2900 g., 0.9000 Silver .1530 oz. ASW **Obv:** Without C.S. on truncation

Date	F	VF	XF	Unc	BU
1868-1871	15.00	50.00	100	200	—

KM# 574   GULDEN
10.6000 g., 0.9000 Silver .3067 oz. ASW **Obv:** VOIGT below head

Date	F	VF	XF	Unc	BU
1838-1856	15.00	40.00	80.00	175	—

KM# 597   GULDEN
10.6000 g., 0.9000 Silver .3067 oz. ASW

Date	F	VF	XF	Unc	BU
1848	25.00	75.00	125	250	—

KM# 595   2 GULDEN
21.2100 g., 900.0000 Silver .6138 oz. ASW

Date	F	VF	XF	Unc	BU
1845-1856	40.00	60.00	150	350	—

KM# 601   THALER
18.5200 g., 0.9000 Silver .5360 oz. ASW **Note:** Vereins Thaler.

Date	F	VF	XF	Unc	BU
1857-1864	20.00	40.00	135	275	—

KM# 614   THALER
18.5200 g., 0.9000 Silver .5360 oz. ASW **Obv:** C. SCHNITZSPAHN F on truncation

Date	F	VF	XF	Unc	BU
1865	125	225	600	1,250	—

KM# 615   THALER
18.5200 g., 0.9000 Silver .5360 oz. ASW **Rev:** Antlers extend into legend

Date	F	VF	XF	Unc	BU
1865-1867	40.00	75.00	200	475	—

KM# 617 THALER
18.5200 g., 0.9000 Silver .5360 oz. ASW

Date	F	VF	XF	Unc	BU
1868-1870	45.00	80.00	200	500	—

KM# 620 THALER
18.5200 g., 0.9000 Silver .5360 oz. ASW **Subject:** Victorious Conclusion of Franco-Prussian War **Rev:** C. SCH. F at 7 o'clock

Date	F	VF	XF	Unc	BU
1871	25.00	45.00	85.00	150	—

KM# 586 2 THALER (3-1/2 Gulden)
37.1200 g., 0.9000 Silver 1.0742 oz. ASW

Date	F	VF	XF	Unc	BU
1840-1855	125	225	450	1,000	—

KM# 618 2 THALER (3-1/2 Gulden)
37.0400 g., 0.9000 Silver 1.0717 oz. ASW **Subject:** Restoration of Ulm Cathedral

Date	F	VF	XF	Unc	BU
1869-1871	100	200	350	550	—

REFORM COINAGE

KM# 626 2 MARK
11.1110 g., 0.9000 Silver .3215 oz. ASW

Date	F	VF	XF	Unc	BU
1876-1888	30.00	60.00	475	1,100	1,400

KM# 631 2 MARK
11.1110 g., 0.9000 Silver .3215 oz. ASW **Ruler:** Wilhelm II

Date	F	VF	XF	Unc	BU
1892-1900	8.00	15.00	35.00	100	140

KM# 635 3 MARK
16.6670 g., 0.9000 Silver .4823 oz. ASW **Ruler:** Wilhelm II

Date	F	VF	XF	Unc	BU
1908-1914	10.00	17.50	25.00	60.00	90.00

KM# 636 3 MARK
16.6670 g., 0.9000 Silver .4823 oz. ASW **Ruler:** Wilhelm II **Subject:** Silver Wedding Anniversary **Obv:** Normal bar in "H" of "CHARLOTTE"

Date	F	VF	XF	Unc	BU
1911	12.00	18.00	35.00	60.00	80.00

KM# 637 3 MARK
16.6670 g., 0.9000 Silver .4823 oz. ASW **Ruler:** Wilhelm II **Subject:** Silver Wedding Anniversary **Obv:** High bar in "H" of "CHARLOTTE"

Date	F	VF	XF	Unc	BU
1911	125	275	475	650	800

KM# 638 3 MARK
16.6670 g., 0.9000 Silver .4823 oz. ASW **Ruler:** Wilhelm II **Subject:** 25th Year of Reign **Note:** 5,650 were melted.

Date	F	VF	XF	Unc	BU
1916 Proof	Value: 8,500				

KM# 623   5 MARK
27.7770 g., 0.9000 Silver .8038 oz. ASW

Date	F	VF	XF	Unc	BU
1874-1888	30.00	60.00	600	1,700	2,200

KM# 627   5 MARK
1.9910 g., 0.9000 Gold .0576 oz. AGW

Date	F	VF	XF	Unc	BU
1877-1878	150	275	300	500	600

KM# 632   5 MARK
27.7770 g., 0.9000 Silver .8038 oz. ASW   **Ruler:** Wilhelm II

Date	F	VF	XF	Unc	BU
(1892-1900)-1913	15.00	30.00	50.00	200	225

KM# 621   10 MARK
3.9820 g., 0.9000 Gold .1152 oz. AGW   **Rev:** Type I

Date	F	VF	XF	Unc	BU
1872-1873	100	150	300	550	700

KM# 624   10 MARK
3.9820 g., 0.9000 Gold .1152 oz. AGW   **Rev:** Type II

Date	F	VF	XF	Unc	BU
1874-1888	75.00	130	160	300	350

KM# 630   10 MARK
3.9820 g., 0.9000 Gold .1152 oz. AGW   **Rev:** Type III

Date	F	VF	XF	Unc	BU
1890-1891	150	225	300	500	600

KM# 633   10 MARK
3.9820 g., 0.9000 Gold .1152 oz. AGW   **Ruler:** Wilhelm II

Date	F	VF	XF	Unc	BU
1893-1913	80.00	120	175	300	350

KM# 622   20 MARK
7.9650 g., 0.9000 Gold .2304 oz. AGW   **Rev:** Type I

Date	F	VF	XF	Unc	BU
1872-1873	BV	200	250	550	650

KM# 625   20 MARK
7.9650 g., 0.9000 Gold .2304 oz. AGW   **Rev:** Type II

Date	F	VF	XF	Unc	BU
1874-1876	BV	160	200	450	550

KM# 634   20 MARK
7.9650 g., 0.9000 Gold .2304 oz. AGW   **Ruler:** Wilhelm II

Date	F	VF	XF	Unc	BU
1894-1914	—	BV	170	250	300

TRADE COINAGE

KM# 587   DUCAT
3.5000 g., 0.9860 Gold .1109 oz. AGW

Date	F	VF	XF	Unc	BU
1840-1848	200	300	425	750	—

Germany - Empire

1871-1918

Germany, a nation of north-central Europe which from 1871 to 1945 was, successively, an empire, a republic and a totalitarian state, attained its territorial peak as an empire when it comprised a 208,780 sq. mi. (540,740 sq. km.) homeland and an overseas colonial empire.

The empire initiated a colonial endeavor and became one of the world's greatest powers. Germany disintegrated as a result of World War I.

RULERS
Wilhelm II, 1888-1918
MONETARY SYSTEM
(Until 1923)
100 Pfennig = 1 Mark

EMPIRE
STANDARD COINAGE

KM# 1   PFENNIG
Copper

Date	F	VF	XF	Unc	BU
1873-1889	0.75	1.50	6.50	17.50	—

KM# 10   PFENNIG
Copper

Date	F	VF	XF	Unc	BU
1890-1916	0.10	0.20	1.25	5.50	10.00

KM# 24   PFENNIG
Aluminum

Date	F	VF	XF	Unc	BU
1916-1918	0.15	0.75	2.00	6.00	8.00

KM# 2   2 PFENNIG
Copper

Date	VG	F	VF	XF	Unc
1873-1877	0.50	1.00	12.50	50.00	—

KM# 16   2 PFENNIG
Copper

Date	F	VF	XF	Unc	BU
1904-1916	0.10	0.50	2.50	12.00	14.00

KM# 3   5 PFENNIG
Copper-Nickel

Date	F	VF	XF	Unc	BU
1874-1889	0.25	1.00	10.00	35.00	—

KM# 11   5 PFENNIG
Copper-Nickel   **Note:** Struck from 1890-1915.

Date	F	VF	XF	Unc	BU
1890-1915	0.10	0.25	1.00	9.00	10.00

KM# 19   5 PFENNIG
Iron

Date	F	VF	XF	Unc	BU
1915-1922	0.10	0.20	0.50	5.00	8.00

KM# 4   10 PFENNIG
Copper-Nickel

Date	F	VF	XF	Unc	BU
1873-1889	0.25	2.00	12.00	35.00	—

KM# 12   10 PFENNIG
Copper-Nickel

Date	F	VF	XF	Unc	BU
1890-1916	0.10	0.25	1.00	8.00	—

KM# 20   10 PFENNIG
Iron

Date	F	VF	XF	Unc	BU
1916-1922	0.20	0.60	1.50	4.00	—

KM# 25   10 PFENNIG
Zinc   **Note:** Eagle and beaded border similar to KM#20.

Date	F	VF	XF	Unc	BU
1917	90.00	180	380	—	—

KM# 26   10 PFENNIG
Zinc   **Note:** Weight varies: 3.10-3.60 grams. Without mint mark. Variations in planchet thickness exist.

Date	F	VF	XF	Unc	BU
1917-1922	0.10	0.20	1.00	4.00	—

KM# 5   20 PFENNIG
1.1110 g., 0.9000 Silver .0321 oz. ASW

Date	F	VF	XF	Unc	BU
1873-1877	5.00	8.00	14.00	45.00	—

KM# 9.1 20 PFENNIG
Copper-Nickel

Date	F	VF	XF	Unc	BU
1887-1888/7	6.50	18.50	27.50	50.00	—

KM# 9.2 20 PFENNIG
Copper-Nickel **Obv:** Star below value

Date	F	VF	XF	Unc	BU
1887	—	—	—	6,000	—

KM# 13 20 PFENNIG
Copper-Nickel

Date	F	VF	XF	Unc	BU
1890-1892	12.50	35.00	55.00	175	—

KM# 18 25 PFENNIG
Nickel

Date	F	VF	XF	Unc	BU
1909-1912	2.00	6.00	10.00	22.00	—

KM# 6 50 PFENNIG
2.7770 g., 0.9000 Silver .0803 oz. ASW

Date	F	VF	XF	Unc	BU
1875-1877	6.00	12.00	25.00	85.00	—

KM# 8 50 PFENNIG
2.7770 g., 0.9000 Silver .0803 oz. ASW

Date	F	VF	XF	Unc	BU
1877-1878	18.00	35.00	90.00	220	—

KM# 15 50 PFENNIG
2.7770 g., 0.9000 Silver .0803 oz. ASW

Date	F	VF	XF	Unc	BU
1896-1903	100	220	280	500	600

KM# 17 1/2 MARK
2.7770 g., 0.9000 Silver .0803 oz. ASW **Note:** Some coins dated from 1918-19 were issued with a black finish to prevent hoarding.

Date	F	VF	XF	Unc	BU
1808/7-1919/1619	0.80	1.25	2.50	10.00	—

KM# 7 MARK
5.5500 g., 0.9000 Silver .1606 oz. ASW

Date	F	VF	XF	Unc	BU
1873-1887	2.50	4.00	22.00	90.00	—

KM# 14 MARK
5.5500 g., 0.9000 Silver .1606 oz. ASW **Note:** Struck from 1890-1916.

Date	F	VF	XF	Unc	BU
1891-1916	1.25	2.25	3.75	15.00	—

MILITARY COINAGE - WWI

Issued under the authority of the German Military Commander of the East for use in Estonia, Latvia, Lithuania, Poland, and Northwest Russia.

KM# 21 KOPEK
Iron

Date	F	VF	XF	Unc	BU
1916	2.00	6.00	15.00	40.00	—

KM# 22 2 KOPEKS
Iron

Date	F	VF	XF	Unc	BU
1916	2.00	6.00	15.00	40.00	—

KM# 23 3 KOPEKS
Iron

Date	F	VF	XF	Unc	BU
1916	2.50	6.00	18.00	45.00	—

Germany, Weimar Republic

1919-1933

The Imperial German government disintegrated in a flurry of royal abdications as World War I ended. Desperate German parliamentarians, fearful of impending anarchy and civil war, hastily declared a German Republic. The new National Assembly, which was convened Feb. 6, 1919 in Weimar had to establish a legal government, draft a constitution, and then conclude a peace treaty with the Allies. Friedrich Ebert was elected as Reichs President.

MONETARY SYSTEM

(During 1923-1924)
100 Rentenpfennig = 1 Rentenmark
(Commencing 1924)
100 Reichspfennig = 1 Reichsmark

WEIMAR REPUBLIC

MARK COINAGE

1922-1923

KM# 27   50 PFENNIG
Aluminum

Date	F	VF	XF	Unc	BU
1919-1922	0.10	0.15	0.50	3.00	5.00

KM# 28   3 MARK
Aluminum   **Edge:** Reeded

Date	F	VF	XF	Unc	BU
1922	0.25	2.50	7.00	14.00	20.00

KM# 29   3 MARK
Aluminum   **Subject:** 3rd Anniversary Weimar Constitution

Date	F	VF	XF	Unc	BU
1922-1923	0.25	1.00	3.00	10.00	12.00

KM# 35   200 MARK
Aluminum

Date	F	VF	XF	Unc	BU
1923	0.15	0.50	0.75	2.00	3.00

KM# 36   500 MARK
Aluminum

Date	F	VF	XF	Unc	BU
1923	0.20	1.00	1.50	5.00	6.00

RENTENMARK COINAGE

1923-1929

KM# 30   RENTENPFENNIG
Bronze

Date	F	VF	XF	Unc	BU
1923-1929	0.25	0.50	3.00	12.00	14.00

KM# 31   2 RENTENPFENNIG
Bronze

Date	F	VF	XF	Unc	BU
1923-1924	0.20	0.50	1.00	8.00	10.00

KM# 32   5 RENTENPFENNIG
Aluminum-Bronze

Date	F	VF	XF	Unc	BU
1923-1925	0.25	1.00	3.00	20.00	24.00

KM# 33   10 RENTENPFENNIG
Aluminum-Bronze

Date	F	VF	XF	Unc	BU
1923-1925	0.25	1.00	3.00	15.00	17.00

KM# 34   50 RENTENPFENNIG
Aluminum-Bronze

Date	F	VF	XF	Unc	BU
1923-1924	5.00	12.00	20.00	60.00	70.00

REICHSMARK COINAGE
1924-1938

KM# 37   REICHSPFENNIG
Bronze

Date	F	VF	XF	Unc	BU
1924-1936	0.20	0.50	1.00	5.00	8.00

KM# 41   50 REICHSPFENNIG
Aluminum-Bronze

Date	F	VF	XF	Unc	BU
1924-1925	600	1,000	1,600	—	—

KM# 38   2 REICHSPFENNIG
Bronze

Date	F	VF	XF	Unc	BU
1923-1936	0.20	0.50	1.00	7.00	8.00

KM# 49   50 REICHSPFENNIG
Nickel

Date	F	VF	XF	Unc	BU
1927-1938	0.80	2.00	4.00	12.00	14.00

KM# 75   4 REICHSPFENNIG
Bronze

Date	F	VF	XF	Unc	BU
1932	—	9.00	15.00	35.00	40.00

KM# 42   MARK
5.0000 g., 0.5000 Silver .0803 oz. ASW

Date	F	VF	XF	Unc	BU
1924-1925	5.00	12.00	24.00	65.00	75.00

KM# 39   5 REICHSPFENNIG
Aluminum-Bronze

Date	F	VF	XF	Unc	BU
1924-1936	0.20	0.30	1.00	10.00	12.00

KM# 43   3 MARK
15.0000 g., 0.5000 Silver .2411 oz. ASW

Date	F	VF	XF	Unc	BU
1924-1925	16.00	40.00	80.00	110	130

KM# 40   10 REICHSPFENNIG
Aluminum-Bronze

Date	F	VF	XF	Unc	BU
1924-1936	0.20	0.30	1.50	15.00	17.00

KM# 44   REICHSMARK
5.0000 g., 0.5000 Silver .0803 oz. ASW

Date	F	VF	XF	Unc	BU
1925-1927	5.00	12.00	24.00	50.00	55.00

KM# 45   2 REICHSMARK
10.0000 g., 0.5000 Silver .1608 oz. ASW

Date	F	VF	XF	Unc	BU
1925-1931	8.00	16.00	24.00	70.00	80.00

KM# 46   3 REICHSMARK
15.0000 g., 0.5000 Silver .2411 oz. ASW **Subject:** 1000th Year of the Rhineland

Date	F	VF	XF	Unc	BU
1925	25.00	45.00	55.00	100	110

KM# 48   3 REICHSMARK
15.0000 g., 0.5000 Silver .2411 oz. ASW **Subject:** 700 Years of Freedom for Lubeck

Date	F	VF	XF	Unc	BU
1926	60.00	110	180	240	260

KM# 50   3 REICHSMARK
15.0000 g., 0.5000 Silver .2411 oz. ASW **Subject:** 100th Anniversary of Bremerhaven

Date	F	VF	XF	Unc	BU
1927	70.00	130	190	270	290

KM# 52   3 REICHSMARK
15.0000 g., 0.5000 Silver .2411 oz. ASW **Subject:** 1000th Anniversary - Founding of Nordhausen

Date	F	VF	XF	Unc	BU
1927	60.00	120	190	260	290

KM# 53   3 REICHSMARK
15.0000 g., 0.5000 Silver .2411 oz. ASW **Subject:** 400th Anniversary - Philipps University in Marburg

Date	F	VF	XF	Unc	BU
1927	60.00	115	160	240	265

KM# 54   3 REICHSMARK
15.0000 g., 0.5000 Silver .2411 oz. ASW **Subject:** 450th Anniversary - Tubingen University

Date	F	VF	XF	Unc	BU
1927	190	380	520	720	760

KM# 57   3 REICHSMARK
15.0000 g., 0.5000 Silver .2411 oz. ASW **Subject:** 900th Anniversary - Founding of Naumburg

Date	F	VF	XF	Unc	BU
1928	70.00	115	170	230	250

KM# 58   3 REICHSMARK
15.0000 g., 0.5000 Silver .2411 oz. ASW **Subject:** 400th
Anniversary - Death of Albrecht Durer

Date	F	VF	XF	Unc	BU
1928	150	330	530	710	750

KM# 63   3 REICHSMARK
15.0000 g., 0.5000 Silver .2411 oz. ASW **Subject:** 10th
Anniversary - Weimar Constitution

Date	F	VF	XF	Unc	BU
1929	20.00	35.00	65.00	80.00	70.00

KM# 59   3 REICHSMARK
15.0000 g., 0.5000 Silver .2411 oz. ASW **Subject:** 1000th
Anniversary - Founding of Dinkelsbuhl

Date	F	VF	XF	Unc	BU
1928	250	500	750	900	1,000

KM# 65   3 REICHSMARK
15.0000 g., 0.5000 Silver .2411 oz. ASW **Subject:** 1000th
Anniversary - Meissen

Date	F	VF	XF	Unc	BU
1929	30.00	50.00	75.00	115	125

KM# 60   3 REICHSMARK
15.0000 g., 0.5000 Silver .2411 oz. ASW **Subject:** 200th
Anniversary - Birth of Gotthold Lessing

Date	F	VF	XF	Unc	BU
1929	25.00	40.00	80.00	130	140

KM# 67   3 REICHSMARK
15.0000 g., 0.5000 Silver .2411 oz. ASW **Subject:** Graf Zeppelin
Flight

Date	F	VF	XF	Unc	BU
1930	35.00	65.00	90.00	140	150

KM# 62   3 REICHSMARK
15.0000 g., 0.5000 Silver .2411 oz. ASW **Subject:** Waldeck-
Prussia Union

Date	F	VF	XF	Unc	BU
1929	55.00	125	175	250	270

KM# 69   3 REICHSMARK
15.0000 g., 0.5000 Silver .2411 oz. ASW **Subject:** 700th
Anniversary - Death of Von Der Vogelweide **Rev:** Same as Austria,
KM#2845.

Date	F	VF	XF	Unc	BU
1930	35.00	55.00	95.00	120	130

KM# 70   3 REICHSMARK
15.0000 g., 0.5000 Silver .2411 oz. ASW **Subject:** Liberation of Rhineland

Date	F	VF	XF	Unc	BU
1930	25.00	48.00	65.00	100	110

KM# 72   3 REICHSMARK
15.0000 g., 0.5000 Silver .2411 oz. ASW **Subject:** 300th Anniversary - Magdeburg Rebuilding

Date	F	VF	XF	Unc	BU
1931	90.00	170	255	340	370

KM# 73   3 REICHSMARK
15.0000 g., 0.5000 Silver .2411 oz. ASW **Subject:** Centenary - Death of von Stein

Date	F	VF	XF	Unc	BU
1931	55.00	120	180	240	260

KM# 74   3 REICHSMARK
15.0000 g., 0.5000 Silver .2411 oz. ASW

Date	F	VF	XF	Unc	BU
1931-1933	130	260	360	660	750

KM# 76   3 REICHSMARK
15.0000 g., 0.5000 Silver .2411 oz. ASW **Subject:** Centenary - Death of Goethe

Date	F	VF	XF	Unc	BU
1932	35.00	80.00	110	160	175

KM# 47   5 REICHSMARK
25.0000 g., 0.5000 Silver .4019 oz. ASW **Subject:** 1000th Year of the Rhineland

Date	F	VF	XF	Unc	BU
1925	50.00	95.00	125	210	225

KM# 51   5 REICHSMARK
25.0000 g., 0.5000 Silver .4019 oz. ASW **Subject:** 100th Anniversary - Bremerhaven

Date	F	VF	XF	Unc	BU
1927	220	420	580	760	850

KM# 55   5 REICHSMARK
25.0000 g., 0.5000 Silver .4019 oz. ASW **Subject:** 450th Anniversary - University of Tubingen

Date	F	VF	XF	Unc	BU
1927	130	290	550	720	850

KM# 56   5 REICHSMARK
25.0000 g., 0.5000 Silver .4019 oz. ASW   **Rev:** Oaktree

Date	F	VF	XF	Unc	BU
1927-1933	35.00	90.00	130	260	280

KM# 61   5 REICHSMARK
25.0000 g., 0.5000 Silver .4019 oz. ASW   **Subject:** 200th Anniversary - Birth of Gotthold Lessing

Date	F	VF	XF	Unc	BU
1929	60.00	100	145	255	275

KM# 64   5 REICHSMARK
25.0000 g., 0.5000 Silver .4019 oz. ASW   **Subject:** 10th Anniversary - Weimar Constitution

Date	F	VF	XF	Unc	BU
1929	55.00	100	160	260	290

KM# 66   5 REICHSMARK
25.0000 g., 0.5000 Silver .4019 oz. ASW   **Subject:** 1000th Anniversary - Meissen

Date	F	VF	XF	Unc	BU
1929	160	250	400	550	600

KM# 68   5 REICHSMARK
25.0000 g., 0.5000 Silver .4019 oz. ASW   **Subject:** Graf Zeppelin Flight

Date	F	VF	XF	Unc	BU
1930	70.00	120	190	300	330

KM# 71   5 REICHSMARK
25.0000 g., 0.5000 Silver .4019 oz. ASW   **Subject:** Liberation of Rhineland

Date	F	VF	XF	Unc	BU
1930	70.00	125	190	310	340

KM# 77   5 REICHSMARK
25.0000 g., 0.5000 Silver .4019 oz. ASW   **Subject:** Centenary - Death of Goethe

Date	F	VF	XF	Unc	BU
1932	950	2,300	2,850	3,450	3,800

Germany, Third Reich

1933-1945

This period represents the rise and fall of the Nazi Regime led by Adolf Hitler. Until the final German defeat May 8, 1945, known as VE Day.

MONETARY SYSTEMS

(During 1923-1924)
100 Rentenpfennig = 1 Rentenmark
(Commencing 1924)
100 Reichspfennig = 1 Reichsmark

THIRD REICH

STANDARD COINAGE

KM# 89   REICHSPFENNIG
Bronze

Date	F	VF	XF	Unc	BU
1936-1940	0.15	0.30	0.50	3.50	6.00

KM# 97   REICHSPFENNIG
Zinc

Date	F	VF	XF	Unc	BU
1940-1945	0.15	0.20	0.50	4.00	6.00

KM# 90   2 REICHSPFENNIG
Bronze

Date	F	VF	XF	Unc	BU
1936-1940	0.20	0.30	0.60	6.00	9.00

KM# 91   5 REICHSPFENNIG
Aluminum-Bronze

Date	F	VF	XF	Unc	BU
1936-1939	0.50	1.00	1.50	7.00	10.00

KM# 100   5 REICHSPFENNIG
Zinc

Date	F	VF	XF	Unc	BU
1940-1944	0.20	0.25	0.75	5.00	7.00

KM# 92   10 REICHSPFENNIG
Aluminum-Bronze

Date	F	VF	XF	Unc	BU
1936-1939	0.50	1.00	2.00	7.00	12.00

KM# 101   10 REICHSPFENNIG
Zinc

Date	F	VF	XF	Unc	BU
1940-1945	0.20	0.30	0.75	7.00	14.00

KM# 87   50 REICHSPFENNIG
Aluminum

Date	F	VF	XF	Unc	BU
1935	1.00	2.25	9.00	35.00	80.00

KM# 95   50 REICHSPFENNIG
Nickel

Date	F	VF	XF	Unc	BU
1938-1939	15.00	30.00	40.00	50.00	60.00

KM# 96   50 REICHSPFENNIG
Aluminum

Date	F	VF	XF	Unc	BU
1939-1944	2.00	4.50	10.00	25.00	40.00

KM# 78 REICHSMARK
Nickel

Date	F	VF	XF	Unc	BU
1933-1939	1.00	1.75	3.00	9.00	13.00

KM# 79 2 REICHSMARK
8.0000 g., 0.6250 Silver .1607 oz. ASW **Subject:** 450th
Anniversary - Birth of Martin Luther

Date	F	VF	XF	Unc	BU
1933	10.00	22.50	30.00	50.00	70.00

KM# 81 2 REICHSMARK
8.0000 g., 0.6250 Silver .1607 oz. ASW **Subject:** 1st Anniversary
- Nazi Rule **Rev:** Potsdam Garrison Church

Date	F	VF	XF	Unc	BU
1934	4.50	10.00	22.00	50.00	90.00

KM# 84 2 REICHSMARK
8.0000 g., 0.6250 Silver .1607 oz. ASW **Subject:** 175th
Anniversary - Birth of Schiller

Date	F	VF	XF	Unc	BU
1934	40.00	70.00	90.00	120	145

KM# 93 2 REICHSMARK
8.0000 g., 0.6250 Silver .1607 oz. ASW **Subject:** Swastika-
Hindenburg Issue

Date	F	VF	XF	Unc	BU
1936-1939	2.25	3.00	4.50	11.00	15.00

KM# 80 5 REICHSMARK
13.8800 g., 0.9000 Silver .4016 oz. ASW **Subject:** 450th
Anniversary - Birth of Martin Luther

Date	F	VF	XF	Unc	BU
1933	60.00	100	150	200	275

KM# 82 5 REICHSMARK
13.8800 g., 0.9000 Silver .4016 oz. ASW **Subject:** 1st
Anniversary - Nazi Rule **Rev:** Potsdam Garrison Church

Date	F	VF	XF	Unc	BU
1934	10.00	12.00	40.00	100	120

KM# 83 5 REICHSMARK
13.8800 g., 0.9000 Silver .4016 oz. ASW **Subject:** 1st Anniversary
- Nazi Rule **Rev:** Potsdam Garrison Church, date 21 MARZ 1933
dropped

Date	F	VF	XF	Unc	BU
1934-1935	4.00	5.00	9.00	30.00	40.00

KM# 85 5 REICHSMARK
13.8800 g., 0.9000 Silver .4016 oz. ASW **Subject:** 175th
Anniversary - Birth of Schiller

Date	F	VF	XF	Unc	BU
1934	150	200	285	425	475

KM# 86 5 REICHSMARK
13.8800 g., 0.9000 Silver .4016 oz. ASW **Subject:** Hindenburg issue

Date	F	VF	XF	Unc	BU
1935-1936	4.00	5.00	9.00	16.00	20.00

KM# 94 5 REICHSMARK
13.8800 g., 0.9000 Silver .4016 oz. ASW **Subject:** Swastika-Hindenburg Issue

Date	F	VF	XF	Unc	BU
1936-1939	4.00	6.00	9.00	20.00	25.00

MILITARY COINAGE
WWII
KM# 98 5 REICHSPFENNIG
Zinc **Note:** Circulated only in occupied territories.

Date	F	VF	XF	Unc	BU
1940-1941	15.00	20.00	30.00	60.00	90.00

KM# 99 10 REICHSPFENNIG
Zinc **Note:** Circulated only in occupied territories.

Date	F	VF	XF	Unc	BU
1940-1941	15.00	20.00	30.00	50.00	80.00

ALLIED OCCUPATION
POST WW II COINAGE
KM# A102 REICHSPFENNIG
Zinc **Obv:** Modified design, swastika and wreath removed **Rev:** Eagle missing tail feathers

Date	F	VF	XF	Unc	BU
1944	—	—	10,000	—	—

KM# A103 REICHSPFENNIG
Zinc

Date	F	VF	XF	Unc	BU
1945-1946	6.00	12.00	20.00	40.00	60.00

KM# A105 5 REICHSPFENNIG
Zinc

Date	F	VF	XF	Unc	BU
1947-1948	3.00	5.00	7.00	20.00	40.00

KM# A104 10 REICHSPFENNIG
Zinc

Date	F	VF	XF	Unc	BU
1945-1948	2.00	4.00	9.00	20.00	28.00

Germany
Federal Republic

1949-

The Federal Republic of Germany, located in north-central Europe, has an area of 137,744 sq. mi. (356,910 sq. km.) and a population of 81.1 million. Capital: Berlin. The economy centers about one of the world's foremost industrial establishments. Machinery, motor vehicles, iron, steel, yarns and fabrics are exported.

MONETARY SYSTEM
100 Pfennig = 1 Deutsche Mark (DM)

FEDERAL REPUBLIC

STANDARD COINAGE

KM# A101   PFENNIG
Bronze-Clad Steel

Date	F	VF	XF	Unc	BU
1948-1949	—	0.50	6.00	22.50	—

KM# 105   PFENNIG
Copper Plated Steel

Date	F	VF	XF	Unc	BU
1950-2001	—	0.10	0.10	0.10	—

KM# 106   2 PFENNIG
Bronze

Date	F	VF	XF	Unc	BU
1950-1969	—	0.10	0.10	3.00	—

KM# 106a   2 PFENNIG
Bronze Clad Steel

Date	F	VF	XF	Unc	BU
1967-2001	0.25	0.10	0.10	0.15	—

KM# 102   5 PFENNIG
Bronze-Clad Steel

Date	F	VF	XF	Unc	BU
1949	0.25	1.00	7.50	35.00	—

KM# 107   5 PFENNIG
Brass Plated Steel

Date	F	VF	XF	Unc	BU
1950-2001	0.50	2.50	0.10	0.10	—

KM# 103   10 PFENNIG
Brass Clad Steel

Date	F	VF	XF	Unc	BU
1949	—	0.50	7.50	30.00	—

KM# 108   10 PFENNIG
Brass Plated Steel   **Edge:** Plain

Date	F	VF	XF	Unc	BU
1950-2001	0.20	0.15	0.10	0.10	—

KM# 104   50 PFENNIG
Copper-Nickel

Date	F	VF	XF	Unc	BU
1949-1950	—	0.50	3.00	35.00	—

KM# 109.1   50 PFENNIG
Copper-Nickel   **Edge:** Reeded

Date	F	VF	XF	Unc	BU
1950-1971	—	0.45	0.55	1.25	—

KM# 109.2   50 PFENNIG
Copper-Nickel   **Edge:** Plain   **Note:** Counterfeits of 1972 dated coins with reeded edges exist.

Date	F	VF	XF	Unc	BU
1972-2001	1.00	1.00	0.45	0.50	—

KM# 110 MARK
Copper-Nickel

Date	F	VF	XF	Unc	BU
1950-2001	1.00	0.75	0.75	0.90	—

KM# 203 MARK
11.8500 g., 0.9990 Gold .3806 oz. AGW, 23.5 mm. **Subject:** Retirement of the Mark Currency **Obv:** Eagle **Rev:** Denomination **Edge:** Lettered

Date	F	VF	XF	Unc	BU
2001 Proof	Value: 335				

KM# 111 2 MARK
Copper-Nickel

Date	F	VF	XF	Unc	BU
1951	—	25.00	30.00	100	—

KM# 116 2 MARK
Copper-Nickel **Rev:** Head of Max Planck facing left

Date	F	VF	XF	Unc	BU
1957-1971	5.00	1.00	1.25	3.00	—

KM# 124 2 MARK
Copper-Nickel Clad Nickel **Rev:** Head of Konrad Adenauer facing left

Date	F	VF	XF	Unc	BU
1969-1987	—	2.00	1.50	1.75	—

KM# A127 2 MARK
Copper-Nickel Clad Nickel **Rev:** Head of Theodor Heuss facing left

Date	F	VF	XF	Unc	BU
1970-1987	—	2.00	1.50	1.75	—

KM# 149 2 MARK
Copper-Nickel Clad Nickel **Rev:** Head of Dr. Kurt Schumacher facing forward

Date	F	VF	XF	Unc	BU
1979-1993	—	2.00	1.50	1.75	—

KM# 170 2 MARK
Copper-Nickel Clad Nickel **Rev:** Head of Ludwig Erhard facing forward

Date	F	VF	XF	Unc	BU
1988-2001	—	—	3.00	1.65	—

KM# 175 2 MARK
Copper-Nickel Clad Nickel **Rev:** Head of Franz Joseph Strauss facing left

Date	F	VF	XF	Unc	BU
1990-2001	—	—	3.00	1.75	—

KM# 183 2 MARK
Copper-Nickel Clad Nickel **Rev:** Head of Willy Brandt facing forward

Date	F	VF	XF	Unc	BU
1994-2001	—	—	—	2.00	—

KM# 112.1   5 MARK
11.2000 g., 0.6250 Silver .2250 oz. ASW

Date	F	VF	XF	Unc	BU
1951-1974	2.00	3.50	4.50	8.50	—

KM# 112.3   5 MARK
11.2000 g., 0.6250 Silver .2250 oz. ASW **Note:** Error. With edge lettering: GRUSS DICH DEUTSCHLAND AUS HERZENSGRUND.

Date	F	VF	XF	Unc	BU
1957	—	1,250	1,650	2,400	—

KM# 112.2   5 MARK
11.2000 g., 0.6250 Silver .2250 oz. ASW **Note:** Uninscribed plain edge errors.

Date	F	VF	XF	Unc	BU
1959-1967	—	65.00	125	200	—

KM# 112.4   5 MARK
11.2000 g., 0.6250 Silver .2250 oz. ASW **Note:** Error. With edge lettering: ALLE MENSCHEN WERDEN BRUDER.

Date	F	VF	XF	Unc	BU
1970	—	1,250	1,650	2,400	—

KM# 140.1   5 MARK
10.0000 g., Copper-Nickel Clad Nickel

Date	F	VF	XF	Unc	BU
1975-2001	—	—	3.50	4.50	—

KM# 140.2   5 MARK
5.4400 g., Copper-Nickel Clad Nickel **Note:** Thin variety.

Date	F	VF	XF	Unc	BU
1975	—	—	90.00	150	—

COMMEMORATIVE COINAGE

KM# 113   5 MARK
11.2000 g., 0.6250 Silver .2250 oz. ASW **Subject:** Centenary - Nurnberg Museum

Date	F	VF	XF	Unc	BU
1952	—	400	600	800	1,200

KM# 114   5 MARK
11.2000 g., 0.6250 Silver .2250 oz. ASW **Subject:** 150th Anniversary - Death of Friedrich von Schiller

Date	F	VF	XF	Unc	BU
1955	—	200	400	600	800

KM# 115   5 MARK
11.2000 g., 0.6250 Silver .2250 oz. ASW **Subject:** 300th Anniversary - Birth of Ludwig von Baden

Date	F	VF	XF	Unc	BU
1955	—	200	350	500	600

KM# 117   5 MARK
11.2000 g., 0.6250 Silver .2250 oz. ASW **Subject:** Centenary - Death of Joseph Freiherr von Eichendorff

Date	F	VF	XF	Unc	BU
1957	—	200	350	500	600

KM# 118.1   5 MARK
11.2000 g., 0.6250 Silver .2250 oz. ASW **Subject:** 150th Anniversary - Death of Johann Gottlieb Fichte

Date	F	VF	XF	Unc	BU
1964	—	50.00	75.00	125	—

KM# 118.2   5 MARK
11.2000 g., 0.6250 Silver .2250 oz. ASW **Note:** Error. Plain edge.

Date	F	VF	XF	Unc	BU
1964	—	250	500	900	—

KM# 119.1   5 MARK
11.2000 g., 0.6250 Silver .2250 oz. ASW **Subject:** 250th Anniversary - Death of Gottfried Wilhelm Leibniz

Date	F	VF	XF	Unc	BU
1966	—	7.00	12.00	15.00	20.00

KM# 119.2   5 MARK
11.2000 g., 0.6250 Silver .2250 oz. ASW **Note:** Error. Plain edge.

Date	F	VF	XF	Unc	BU
1966	—	225	425	700	

KM# 123.1   5 MARK
11.2000 g., 0.6250 Silver .2250 oz. ASW **Subject:** 150th Anniversary - Birth of Max von Pettenkofer

Date	F	VF	XF	Unc	BU
1968	—	3.50	7.00	9.00	11.00

KM# 123.2   5 MARK
11.2000 g., 0.6250 Silver .2250 oz. ASW **Note:** Polished devices.

Date	F	VF	XF	Unc	BU
1968 Proof	Value: 300				

KM# 120.1   5 MARK
11.2000 g., 0.6250 Silver .2250 oz. ASW **Subject:** Wilhelm and Alexander von Humboldt

Date	F	VF	XF	Unc	BU
1967	—	9.00	12.00	15.00	20.00

KM# 120.2   5 MARK
11.2000 g., 0.6250 Silver .2250 oz. ASW **Note:** Error. Plain edge.

Date	F	VF	XF	Unc	BU
1967	—	225	425	700	—

KM# 125.1   5 MARK
11.2000 g., 0.6250 Silver .2250 oz. ASW **Subject:** 150th Anniversary - Birth of Theodor Fontane

Date	F	VF	XF	Unc	BU
1969	—	3.50	7.00	9.00	11.00

KM# 125.2   5 MARK
11.2000 g., 0.6250 Silver .2250 oz. ASW **Note:** Error. Incomplete nose and hair.

Date	F	VF	XF	Unc	BU
1969 Proof	Value: 140				

KM# 121   5 MARK
11.2000 g., 0.6250 Silver .2250 oz. ASW **Subject:** 150th Anniversary - Birth of Friedrich Raiffeisen

Date	F	VF	XF	Unc	BU
1968	—	3.00	4.50	6.00	8.00

KM# 126.1   5 MARK
11.2000 g., 0.6250 Silver .2250 oz. ASW **Subject:** 375th Anniversary - Death of Gerhard Mercator

Date	F	VF	XF	Unc	BU
1969	—	—	—	5.00	6.00

KM# 126.2   5 MARK
11.2000 g., 0.6250 Silver .2250 oz. ASW **Note:** Error. Plain edge.

Date	F	VF	XF	Unc	BU
1969	—	250	450	750	—

KM# 126.3   5 MARK
11.2000 g., 0.6250 Silver .2250 oz. ASW **Note:** Error. With edge lettering: Einigkeit und Recht und Freiheit.

Date	F	VF	XF	Unc	BU
1969	—	600	1,000	1,600	—

KM# 126.4   5 MARK
11.2000 g., 0.6250 Silver .2250 oz. ASW **Note:** Error. With long "R" in "MERCATOR".

Date	F	VF	XF	Unc	BU
1969	—	25.00	55.00	100	—

KM# 122   5 MARK
11.2000 g., 0.6250 Silver .2250 oz. ASW **Subject:** 500th Anniversary - Death of Johannes Gutenberg

Date	F	VF	XF	Unc	BU
1968	—	3.50	7.00	9.00	11.00

KM# 127   5 MARK
11.2000 g., 0.6250 Silver .2250 oz. ASW   **Subject:** 200th Anniversary - Birth of Ludwig van Beethoven

Date	F	VF	XF	Unc	BU
1970	—	—	3.50	6.00	7.00

KM# 137   5 MARK
11.2000 g., 0.6250 Silver .2250 oz. ASW   **Subject:** 125th Anniversary - Frankfurt Parliament

Date	F	VF	XF	Unc	BU
1973	—	—	—	6.00	7.00

KM# 128.1   5 MARK
11.2000 g., 0.6250 Silver .2250 oz. ASW   **Subject:** Foundation of German Reich 1871

Date	F	VF	XF	Unc	BU
1971	—	3.50	5.00	6.00	7.00

KM# 128.2   5 MARK
11.2000 g., 0.6250 Silver .2250 oz. ASW   **Note:** Error. With weak window details.

Date	F	VF	XF	Unc	BU
1971 Proof	Value: 100				

KM# 138   5 MARK
11.2000 g., 0.6250 Silver .2250 oz. ASW   **Subject:** 25th Anniversary - Constitutional Law

Date	F	VF	XF	Unc	BU
1974	—	—	—	6.00	7.00

KM# 129   5 MARK
11.2000 g., 0.6250 Silver .2250 oz. ASW   **Subject:** 500th Anniversary - Birth of Albrecht Durer

Date	F	VF	XF	Unc	BU
1971	—	—	—	4.00	6.00

KM# 139   5 MARK
11.2000 g., 0.6250 Silver .2250 oz. ASW   **Subject:** 250th Anniversary - Birth of Immanuel Kant

Date	F	VF	XF	Unc	BU
1974	—	—	—	6.00	7.00

KM# 136   5 MARK
11.2000 g., 0.6250 Silver .2250 oz. ASW   **Subject:** 500th Anniversary - Birth of Nicholas Copernicus

Date	F	VF	XF	Unc	BU
1973	—	—	—	6.00	7.00

KM# 141   5 MARK
11.2000 g., 0.6250 Silver .2250 oz. ASW   **Subject:** 50th Anniversary - Death of Friedrich Ebert

Date	F	VF	XF	Unc	BU
1975	—	—	—	6.00	7.00

KM# 142.1   5 MARK
11.2000 g., 0.6250 Silver .2250 oz. ASW   **Subject:** European
Monument Proctection Year **Note:** 2.1mm thick.

Date	F	VF	XF	Unc	BU
1975	—	—	—	6.00	7.00

KM# 142.2   5 MARK
5.3000 g., 0.6250 Silver .2250 oz. ASW   **Note:** 1.4mm thick.

Date	F	VF	XF	Unc	BU
1975	—	—	—	6.00	7.00

KM# 146   5 MARK
5.3000 g., 0.6250 Silver .2250 oz. ASW   **Subject:** 200th
Anniversary - Birth of Heinrich von Kleist

Date	F	VF	XF	Unc	BU
1977	—	—	—	6.00	7.00

KM# 143   5 MARK
5.3000 g., 0.6250 Silver .2250 oz. ASW   **Subject:** Centenary -
Birth of Albert Schweitzer

Date	F	VF	XF	Unc	BU
1975	—	—	—	6.00	7.00

KM# 147   5 MARK
5.3000 g., 0.6250 Silver .2250 oz. ASW   **Subject:** 100th
Anniversary - Birth of Gustav Stresemann

Date	F	VF	XF	Unc	BU
1978	—	—	—	6.00	7.00

KM# 144   5 MARK
5.3000 g., 0.6250 Silver .2250 oz. ASW   **Subject:** 300th
Anniversary - Death of von Grimmelshausen

Date	F	VF	XF	Unc	BU
1976	—	—	—	6.00	7.00

KM# 148   5 MARK
5.3000 g., 0.6250 Silver .2250 oz. ASW   **Subject:** 225th
Anniversary - Death of Balthasar Neumann

Date	F	VF	XF	Unc	BU
1978	—	—	—	6.00	7.00

KM# 145   5 MARK
5.3000 g., 0.6250 Silver .2250 oz. ASW   **Subject:** 200th
Anniversary - Birth of Carl Friedrich Gauss

Date	F	VF	XF	Unc	BU
1977	—	—	—	6.00	7.00

KM# 150   5 MARK
5.3000 g., 0.6250 Silver .2250 oz. ASW   **Subject:** 150th
Anniversary - German Archaeological Institute

Date	F	VF	XF	Unc	BU
1979	—	—	—	6.00	7.00

KM# 151   5 MARK
10.0000 g., Copper-Nickel Clad Nickel   **Subject:** 100th
Anniversary - Birth of Otto Hahn

Date	F	VF	XF	Unc	BU
1979	—	—	3.50	5.00	6.00

KM# 151a   5 MARK
11.2000 g., 0.6250 Silver .2250 oz. ASW

Date	F	VF	XF	Unc	BU
1979	—	—	—	22,500	—

KM# 155   5 MARK
Copper-Nickel Clad Nickel   **Subject:** 150th Anniversary - Death
of Carl vom Stein

Date	F	VF	XF	Unc	BU
1981	—	—	—	4.00	5.00

KM# 152   5 MARK
Copper-Nickel Clad Nickel   **Subject:** 750th Anniversary - Death
of von der Vogelweide

Date	F	VF	XF	Unc	BU
1980	—	—	3.50	5.00	6.00

KM# 156   5 MARK
Copper-Nickel Clad Nickel   **Subject:** 150th Anniversary - Death
of Johann Wolfgang von Goethe

Date	F	VF	XF	Unc	BU
1982	—	—	—	4.00	5.00

KM# 153   5 MARK
Copper-Nickel Clad Nickel   **Subject:** 100th Anniversary - Cologne
Cathedral

Date	F	VF	XF	Unc	BU
1980	—	—	4.00	5.00	6.00

KM# 157   5 MARK
Copper-Nickel Clad Nickel   **Subject:** 10th Anniversary - U.N.
Environmental Conference

Date	F	VF	XF	Unc	BU
1982	—	—	—	4.00	5.00

KM# 154   5 MARK
Copper-Nickel Clad Nickel   **Subject:** 200th Anniversary - Death
of Gotthold Ephraim Lessing

Date	F	VF	XF	Unc	BU
1981	—	—	—	4.00	5.00

KM# 158   5 MARK
Copper-Nickel Clad Nickel   **Subject:** 100th Anniversary - Death
of Karl Marx

Date	F	VF	XF	Unc	BU
1983	—	—	—	4.00	5.00

KM# 159   5 MARK
Copper-Nickel Clad Nickel   **Subject:** 500th Anniversary - Birth of
Martin Luther

Date	F	VF	XF	Unc	BU
1983	—	—	—	4.00	5.00

KM# 163   5 MARK
Copper-Nickel Clad Nickel   **Subject:** 150th Anniversary - German
Railroad

Date	F	VF	XF	Unc	BU
1985	—	—	—	4.00	5.00

KM# 160   5 MARK
Copper-Nickel Clad Nickel   **Subject:** 150th Anniversary - German
Customs Union

Date	F	VF	XF	Unc	BU
1984	—	—	—	4.00	5.00

KM# 164   5 MARK
Copper-Nickel Clad Nickel   **Subject:** 600th Anniversary -
Heidelberg University

Date	F	VF	XF	Unc	BU
1986	—	—	—	4.00	5.00

KM# 165   5 MARK
Copper-Nickel Clad Nickel   **Subject:** 200th Anniversary - Death
of Frederick the Great

Date	F	VF	XF	Unc	BU
1986	—	—	—	4.00	5.00

KM# 161   5 MARK
Copper-Nickel Clad Nickel   **Subject:** 175th Anniversary - Birth of
Felix Bartholdy

Date	F	VF	XF	Unc	BU
1984	—	—	—	4.00	5.00

KM# 130   10 MARK
15.5000 g., 0.6250 Silver .3115 oz. ASW   **Series:** Munich
Olympics **Rev:** "In Deutschland" with spiraling symbol

Date	F	VF	XF	Unc	BU
1972	—	—	—	7.50	10.00

KM# 162   5 MARK
Copper-Nickel Clad Nickel   **Subject:** European Year of Music

Date	F	VF	XF	Unc	BU
1985	—	—	—	4.00	5.00

KM# 131   10 MARK
15.5000 g., 0.6250 Silver .3115 oz. ASW **Series:** Munich
Olympics **Rev:** Schleife (knot)

Date	F	VF	XF	Unc	BU
1972	—	—	—	7.50	10.00

KM# 132   10 MARK
15.5000 g., 0.6250 Silver .3115 oz. ASW **Series:** Munich
Olympics **Rev:** Athletes kneeling

Date	F	VF	XF	Unc	BU
1972	—	—	—	7.00	9.00

KM# 133   10 MARK
15.5000 g., 0.6250 Silver .3115 oz. ASW **Series:** Munich
Olympics **Rev:** Stadium - aerial view

Date	F	VF	XF	Unc	BU
1972	—	—	—	7.00	9.00

KM# 134.1   10 MARK
15.5000 g., 0.6250 Silver .3115 oz. ASW **Series:** Munich
Olympics **Rev:** "In Munchen" - with spiral symbol **Edge:** Lettering
separated by periods

Date	F	VF	XF	Unc	BU
1972	—	—	—	7.50	10.00

KM# 134.2   10 MARK
15.5000 g., 0.6250 Silver .3115 oz. ASW **Edge:** Lettering
separated by arabesques **Note:** Error.

Date	F	VF	XF	Unc	BU
1972	—	200	300	550	—

KM# 135   10 MARK
15.5000 g., 0.6250 Silver .3115 oz. ASW **Series:** Munich
Olympics **Rev:** Olympic Flame - Rings and spiral symbol

Date	F	VF	XF	Unc	BU
1972	—	—	—	7.00	9.00

KM# 166   10 MARK
15.5000 g., 0.6250 Silver .3115 oz. ASW **Subject:** 750th
Anniversary - Berlin

Date	F	VF	XF	Unc	BU
1987	—	—	—	9.00	11.00

KM# 167   10 MARK
15.5000 g., 0.6250 Silver .3115 oz. ASW **Subject:** 30 Years of
European Unity

Date	F	VF	XF	Unc	BU
1987	—	—	—	7.00	9.00

KM# 168   10 MARK
15.5000 g., 0.6250 Silver .3115 oz. ASW **Subject:** 200th
Anniversary - Birth of Arthur Schopenhauer

Date	F	VF	XF	Unc	BU
1988	—	—	—	7.00	9.00

KM# 169 10 MARK
15.5000 g., 0.6250 Silver .3115 oz. ASW **Subject:** 100th Anniversary - Death of Carl Zeiss

Date	F	VF	XF	Unc	BU
1988	—	—	—	7.00	9.00

KM# 171 10 MARK
15.5000 g., 0.6250 Silver .3115 oz. ASW **Subject:** 800th Year - Port of Hamburg

Date	F	VF	XF	Unc	BU
1989	—	—	—	7.00	9.00

KM# 172 10 MARK
15.5000 g., 0.6250 Silver .3115 oz. ASW **Subject:** 2000th Anniversary - City of Bonn

Date	F	VF	XF	Unc	BU
1989	—	—	—	7.00	9.00

KM# 173 10 MARK
15.5000 g., 0.6250 Silver .3115 oz. ASW **Subject:** 40th Anniversary - Republic

Date	F	VF	XF	Unc	BU
1989	—	—	—	7.00	9.00

KM# 174 10 MARK
15.5000 g., 0.6250 Silver .3115 oz. ASW **Subject:** 800th Anniversary - Death of Kaiser Friedrich Barbarossa

Date	F	VF	XF	Unc	BU
1990	—	—	—	7.00	9.00

KM# 176 10 MARK
15.5000 g., 0.6250 Silver .3115 oz. ASW **Subject:** 800th Anniversary - The Teutonic Order

Date	F	VF	XF	Unc	BU
1990	—	—	—	7.00	9.00

KM# 177 10 MARK
15.5000 g., 0.6250 Silver .3115 oz. ASW **Subject:** German Unity - Brandenburg Gate in Berlin

Date	F	VF	XF	Unc	BU
1991	—	—	—	7.00	9.00

KM# 178 10 MARK
15.5000 g., 0.6250 Silver .3115 oz. ASW **Subject:** 125th Anniversary - Birth of Kathe Kollwitz - Artist and Sculptor **Rev:** Kathe Kollwitz at easel drawing

Date	F	VF	XF	Unc	BU
1992	—	—	—	7.00	9.00

KM# 179   10 MARK
15.5000 g., 0.6250 Silver .3115 oz. ASW **Subject:** 150th Anniversary - Civil Pour-le-Merite Order **Rev:** Alexander von Humbolt, 1st chancellor of the Order

Date	F	VF	XF	Unc	BU
1992	—	—	—	7.00	9.00

KM# 180   10 MARK
15.5000 g., 0.6250 Silver .3115 oz. ASW **Subject:** 1000th Anniversary - Potsdam **Rev:** Palace of Sanssouci and Nicolai Church

Date	F	VF	XF	Unc	BU
1993	—	—	—	7.00	9.00

KM# 181   10 MARK
15.5000 g., 0.6250 Silver .3115 oz. ASW **Subject:** 150th Birth Anniversary **Rev:** Head of Robert Koch facing forward

Date	F	VF	XF	Unc	BU
1993	—	—	—	7.00	9.00

KM# 182   10 MARK
15.5000 g., 0.6250 Silver .3115 oz. ASW **Subject:** Attempt on Hitler's Life, July 20, 1944

Date	F	VF	XF	Unc	BU
1994	—	—	—	7.00	9.00

KM# 184   10 MARK
15.5000 g., 0.6250 Silver .3115 oz. ASW **Subject:** 250th Birth Anniversary **Rev:** Head of Johann Gottfried Herder facing right

Date	F	VF	XF	Unc	BU
1994	—	—	—	7.00	9.00

KM# 185   10 MARK
15.5000 g., 0.6250 Silver .3115 oz. ASW **Subject:** 50th Anniversary of Peace and Reconciliation **Rev:** Ruins of Frauen Kirche in Dresden **Edge Lettering:** STEINERNE GLOCKE SYMBOL FUER TOLERANZ

Date	F	VF	XF	Unc	BU
1995	—	—	—	7.00	9.00

KM# 186   10 MARK
15.5000 g., 0.6250 Silver .3115 oz. ASW **Subject:** 500th Anniversary of death - Henry the Lion **Edge Lettering:** HEINRICH DER LOEWE AUS KAISERLICHEM STAMM

Date	F	VF	XF	Unc	BU
1995	—	—	—	7.00	9.00

KM# 187   10 MARK
15.5000 g., 0.6250 Silver .3115 oz. ASW **Subject:** 150th Birth Anniversary - Wilhelm Conrad Rontgen; 100th Anniversary of x-ray **Rev:** Hand and X-rayed hand **Edge Lettering:** ERSTER NOBEL PREIS FUER PHYSIK

Date	F	VF	XF	Unc	BU
1995	—	—	—	7.00	9.00

KM# 188   10 MARK
15.5000 g., 0.6250 Silver .3115 oz. ASW **Subject:** 150th
Anniversary of founding - Kolpingwerk **Edge Lettering:** TAETIGE
LIEBE HEILT ALLE WUNDEN

Date	F	VF	XF	Unc	BU
1996	—	—	—	7.00	9.00

KM# 192   10 MARK
15.5000 g., 0.6250 Silver .3115 oz. ASW **Subject:** Diesel Engine
Centennial **Obv:** Stylized eagle **Rev:** First diesel engine

Date	F	VF	XF	Unc	BU
1997	—	—	—	9.00	11.00

KM# 189.1   10 MARK
15.5000 g., 0.6250 Silver .3115 oz. ASW **Subject:** 500th Birth
Anniversary - Philipp Melanchthon **Obv:** Stylized eagle **Rev:**
Portrait, dates

Date	F	VF	XF	Unc	BU
1997	—	—	—	9.00	11.00

KM# 189.2   10 MARK
15.5000 g., 0.6250 Silver .3115 oz. ASW **Subject:** 500th Birth
Anniversary - Philipp Melanchthon **Rev:** Different forelock on portrait

Date	F	VF	XF	Unc	BU
1997	—	—	—	9.00	11.00

KM# 191   10 MARK
15.5000 g., 0.9250 Silver .4610 oz. ASW **Subject:** 300th
Anniversary end of 30 Years War - Peace of Westphalia **Obv:**
Stylized eagle **Rev:** Clasped hands, dove and quill

Date	F	VF	XF	Unc	BU
1998	—	—	—	9.00	11.00

KM# 190   10 MARK
15.5000 g., 0.6250 Silver .3115 oz. ASW **Subject:** 200th Birth
Anniversary - Heinrich Heine **Obv:** Stylized eagle **Rev:** Portrait
with handwritten text in background

Date	F	VF	XF	Unc	BU
1997	—	—	—	9.00	—

KM# 193   10 MARK
0.9250 Silver **Subject:** 900th Anniversary - Birth of Hildegard von
Bingen (1098-1178AD) **Obv:** Stylized eagle **Rev:** Seated
Hildegard, abbess and scholar, writing **Edge Lettering:** WISSE
DIE WEGE DES HERRN

Date	F	VF	XF	Unc	BU
1998	—	—	—	9.00	11.00

KM# 194   10 MARK
15.5000 g., 0.9000 Silver .5345 oz. ASW **Subject:** 300th
Anniversary Franckesche Charitable Endowment

Date	F	VF	XF	Unc	BU
1998	—	—	—	9.00	11.00

KM# 195   10 MARK
15.5000 g., 0.9250 Silver .4610 oz. ASW **Subject:** 50 Years of German Deutsch Mark **Obv:** Denomination above eagle **Rev:** Seven coin designs **Edge Lettering:** EINIGKEIT UND RECHT UND FREIHEIT

Date	F	VF	XF	Unc	BU
1998	—	—	—	9.00	11.00

KM# 196   10 MARK
15.5000 g., 0.9250 Silver .4610 oz. ASW **Subject:** 50th Anniversary - Bundes Republic Constitution **Obv:** Denomination below eagle **Rev:** German constitution **Edge Lettering:** FUR DAS GESAMTE DEUTSCH VOLK

Date	F	VF	XF	Unc	BU
1999	—	—	—	9.00	11.00

KM# 197   10 MARK
15.5000 g., 0.9250 Silver .4610 oz. ASW **Subject:** 250th Anniversary - Birth of J.W. von Goethe **Obv:** Denomination below eagle **Rev:** Portrait of von Goethe facing inscribed field **Edge Lettering:** WIRKE GUT SO WIRKST DU LANGER

Date	F	VF	XF	Unc	BU
1999	—	—	—	9.00	11.00

KM# 198   10 MARK
15.5000 g., 0.9250 Silver .4610 oz. ASW **Subject:** Charity for children without parents all over the world **Obv:** Denomination

below eagle **Rev:** Stylized globe, children playing **Edge Lettering:** SOS - KINDERDORFER - EINE IDEE FUR DIE WELT

Date	F	VF	XF	Unc	BU
1999	—	—	—	9.00	11.00

KM# 199   10 MARK
15.5000 g., 0.9250 Silver .4610 oz. ASW **Subject:** Expo 2000 **Obv:** Stylized eagle **Rev:** Childlike drawing of human balance scale **Edge Lettering:** WELTAUSSTELLUNG EXPO 2000 HANNOVER

Date	F	VF	XF	Unc	BU
2000	—	—	—	9.00	11.00

KM# 200   10 MARK
15.5000 g., 0.9250 Silver .4610 oz. ASW **Subject:** Founding the Church in Aachen 1200 Years Ago by Charlemagne **Obv:** Stylized eagle **Rev:** Charlemagne handing church model to Madonna and child **Edge Lettering:** URBS AQUENSIS - URBS REGALIS

Date	F	VF	XF	Unc	BU
2000	—	—	—	9.00	11.00

KM# 201   10 MARK
15.5000 g., 0.9250 Silver .4610 oz. ASW, 32.5 mm.   **Subject:** 10th Anniversary of Reunification **Obv:** Eagle and denomination **Rev:** Parliament building **Edge Lettering:** "WIR SIND DAS VOLK WIR SIND EIN VOLK"

Date	F	VF	XF	Unc	BU
2000	—	—	—	9.00	11.00

KM# 202   10 MARK
15.5000 g., 0.9250 Silver .4610 oz. ASW, 32.5 mm.   **Obv:** Eagle and denomination **Rev:** Portrait **Edge Lettering:** "JOHANN SEBASTIAN BACH 250 TODESTAG"

Date	F	VF	XF	Unc	BU
2000	—	—	—	9.00	11.00

KM# 204   10 MARK
15.5000 g., 0.9250 Silver .4610 oz. ASW, 32.5 mm.   **Rev:** Naval Museum, Stralsund **Edge Lettering:** "OHNE WASSER KEIN LEBEN"

Date	F	VF	XF	Unc	BU
2001	—	—	—	9.00	11.00

KM# 205   10 MARK

15.5000 g., 0.9250 Silver .4610 oz. ASW, 32.5 mm.   **Subject:**
200th Anniversary - Birth of Albert Gustav Lortzing **Obv:** Stylized
eagle **Rev:** Portrait and music **Edge Lettering:** "WILDSCHUET *
UNDINE" ZAR UND ZIMMERMANN"

Date	F	VF	XF	Unc	BU
2001	—	—	—	9.00	11.00

KM# 206   10 MARK

15.5000 g., 0.9250 Silver .4610 oz. ASW, 32.5 mm.   **Subject:**
Federal Court of Constitution: 50th Anniversary **Obv:** Stylized
eagle **Rev:** Justice holding books and scale **Edge:** Lettered

Date	F	VF	XF	Unc	BU
2001	—	—	—	9.00	11.00

EURO COINAGE

European Economic Community Issues

KM# 207   EURO CENT

2.2700 g., Copper Plated Steel, 16.3 mm.   **Obv:** Oak leaves **Rev:**
Denomination and globe **Edge:** Plain

Date	F	VF	XF	Unc	BU
2002-2005	—	—	—	0.35	—

KM# 208   2 EURO CENTS

3.0000 g., Copper Plated Steel, 18.7 mm.   **Obv:** Oak leaves **Rev:**
Denomination and globe **Edge:** Grooved

Date	F	VF	XF	Unc	BU
2002-2005	—	—	—	0.50	—

KM# 209   5 EURO CENTS

3.8600 g., Copper Plated Steel, 21.2 mm.   **Obv:** Oak leaves **Rev:**
Denomination and globe **Edge:** Plain

Date	F	VF	XF	Unc	BU
2002-2005	—	—	—	0.75	—

KM# 210   10 EURO CENTS

4.0000 g., Brass, 19.7 mm.   **Obv:** Brandenburg Gate **Rev:**
Denomination and map **Edge:** Reeded

Date	F	VF	XF	Unc	BU
2002-2005	—	—	—	0.75	—

KM# 211   20 EURO CENTS

5.7300 g., Brass, 22.2 mm.   **Obv:** Brandenburg Gate **Rev:**
Denomination and map **Edge:** Notched

Date	F	VF	XF	Unc	BU
2002-2005	—	—	—	1.00	—

KM# 212   50 EURO CENTS

7.8100 g., Brass, 24.2 mm.   **Obv:** Brandenburg Gate **Rev:**
Denomination and map **Edge:** Reeded

Date	F	VF	XF	Unc	BU
2002-2005	—	—	—	1.00	—

KM# 213   EURO

7.5000 g., Bi-Metallic Copper-Nickel center in Brass ring, 23.3 mm.
Obv: Stylized eagle **Rev:** Denomination over map **Edge:** Three
normally reeded and three very finely reeded sections

Date	F	VF	XF	Unc	BU
2002-2005	—	—	—	2.50	—

KM# 214   2 EUROS

8.5200 g., Bi-Metallic Brass center in Copper-Nickel ring,
25.6 mm.   **Obv:** Stylized eagle **Rev:** Denomination and map **Edge:**
Reeded and "EINIGKEIT UND RECHT UND FREIHEIT"

Date	F	VF	XF	Unc	BU
2002-2005	—	—	—	4.50	—

KM# 253　2 EUROS
8.5200 g., Bi-Metallic **Subject:** Lubeck Gate

Date	F	VF	XF	Unc	BU
2006	—	—	—	5.00	—

KM# 215　10 EURO
18.0000 g., 0.9250 Silver 0.5353 oz. ASW, 32.5 mm. **Subject:** Introduction of the Euro Currency **Obv:** Stylized round eagle **Rev:** Euro symbol and map **Edge Lettering:** IM ZEICHEN DER EINIGUNG EUROPAS

Date	F	VF	XF	Unc	BU
2002	—	—	—	20.00	—

KM# 216　10 EURO
18.0000 g., 0.9250 Silver 0.5353 oz. ASW, 32.5 mm. **Subject:** Berlin Subway Centennial **Obv:** Stylized squarish eagle **Rev:** Elevated and subterranean train views **Edge Lettering:** HISTORISCH UND

Date	F	VF	XF	Unc	BU
2002	—	—	—	20.00	—

KM# 217　10 EURO
18.0000 g., 0.9250 Silver 0.5353 oz. ASW, 32.5 mm. **Subject:** "Documenta Kassel" Art Exposition **Obv:** Stylized eagle above inscription **Rev:** Exposition logo **Edge Lettering:** ART (in nine languages)

Date	F	VF	XF	Unc	BU
2002	—	—	—	20.00	—

KM# 218　10 EURO
18.0000 g., 0.9250 Silver 0.5353 oz. ASW, 32.5 mm. **Subject:** Museum Island, Berlin **Obv:** Stylized eagle **Rev:** Aerial view of museum complex **Edge:** Lettered

Date	F	VF	XF	Unc	BU
2002	—	—	—	20.00	—

KM# 219　10 EURO
18.0000 g., 0.9250 Silver 0.5353 oz. ASW, 32.5 mm. **Subject:** 50 Years - German Television **Obv:** Stylized eagle silhouette **Rev:** Television screen silhouette **Edge Lettering:** BILDUNG UNTERHALTUNG INFORMATION

Date	F	VF	XF	Unc	BU
2002	—	—	—	20.00	—

KM# 222　10 EURO
18.0000 g., 0.9250 Silver 0.5353 oz. ASW, 32.5 mm. **Subject:** Justus von Liebig **Obv:** Eagle above denomination **Rev:** Liebig's portrait **Edge Lettering:** FORSCHEN . LEHREN . ANWENDEN ..

Date	F	VF	XF	Unc	BU
2003	—	—	—	20.00	—

KM# 223　10 EURO
18.0000 g., 0.9250 Silver 0.5353 oz. ASW, 32.5 mm. **Subject:** World Cup Soccer **Obv:** Stylized round eagle **Rev:** German map on soccer ball **Edge:** Lettered **Edge Lettering:** "DIE WELT ZU GAST BEI FREUNDEN A. D. F. G.J ." **Note:** Mint is determined by which letter "E" in the edge inscription has a short center bar. If the first letter "E" has the short center bar the coin is from the Berlin mint. Second "E"= Munich, third "E"=Stuttgart, fourth "E"=Karlsruhe, fifth "E"=Hamburg

Date	F	VF	XF	Unc	BU
2003	—	—	—	20.00	—

KM# 224   10 EURO
18.0000 g., 0.9250 Silver 0.5353 oz. ASW, 32.5 mm. **Subject:** Ruhr Industrial District **Obv:** Stylized eagle **Rev:** Various city views **Edge:** Lettered **Edge Lettering:** "RUHRPOTT KULTURLANDSCHAFT"

Date	F	VF	XF	Unc	BU
2003	—	—	—	20.00	—

KM# 225   10 EURO
18.0000 g., 0.9250 Silver 0.5353 oz. ASW, 32.5 mm. **Subject:** German Museum Centennial **Obv:** Stylized eagle **Rev:** Abstract design **Edge:** Lettered **Edge Lettering:** "SAMMELN. AUSSTELLEN. FORSCHEN. BILDEN."

Date	F	VF	XF	Unc	BU
2003	—	—	—	20.00	—

KM# 226   10 EURO
18.0000 g., 0.9250 Silver 0.5353 oz. ASW, 32.5 mm. **Subject:** 50th Anniversary of the Ill-fated East German Revolution **Obv:** Stylized eagle **Rev:** Tank tracks over slogans **Edge:** Lettered **Edge Lettering:** "ERINNERUNG AN DEN VOLKSAUFSTAND IN DER DDR"

Date	F	VF	XF	Unc	BU
2003	—	—	—	20.00	—

![KM# 227 coin]

KM# 227   10 EURO
18.0000 g., 0.9250 Silver 0.5353 oz. ASW, 32.5 mm. **Obv:** Stylized eagle **Rev:** Gottfried Semper and floor plan **Edge:**

Lettered **Edge Lettering:** "ARCHITEKT. FORSCHER. KOSMOPOLIT. DEMOKRAT."

Date	F	VF	XF	Unc	BU
2003	—	—	—	18.50	—

KM# 229   10 EURO
18.0000 g., 0.9250 Silver 0.5353 oz. ASW, 32.5 mm. **Obv:** Stylized eagle **Rev:** Soccer ball orbiting the earth **Edge:** Lettered **Edge Lettering:** "DIE WELT ZU GAST BEI FREUNDEN A D F G J" **Note:** Soccer Series:Mint determination same as KM-223

Date	F	VF	XF	Unc	BU
2004	—	—	—	20.00	—

![KM# 230 coin]

KM# 230   10 EURO
18.0000 g., 0.9250 Silver 0.5353 oz. ASW, 32.5 mm. **Obv:** Stylized eagle, stars and value **Rev:** Bauhaus Dessau geometric shapes design **Edge:** Lettered **Edge Lettering:** "KUNST TECHNIK LEHRE"

Date	F	VF	XF	Unc	BU
2004	—	—	—	20.00	—

KM# 231   10 EURO
18.0000 g., 0.9250 Silver 0.5353 oz. ASW, 32.5 mm. **Obv:** Stylized eagle above value **Rev:** European Union country names and dates **Edge:** Lettered **Edge Lettering:** "FREUDE SCHONER GOTTERFUNKEN"

Date	F	VF	XF	Unc	BU
2004	—	—	—	20.00	—

KM# 232 10 EURO
18.0000 g., 0.9250 Silver 0.5353 oz. ASW, 32.5 mm. **Obv:** Stylized eagle and value **Rev:** Geese flying over Wattenmeer National Park **Edge:** Lettered **Edge Lettering:** "MEERESGRUND TRIFFT HORIZONT"

Date	F	VF	XF	Unc	BU
2004	—	—	—	20.00	—

KM# 233 10 EURO
18.0000 g., 0.9250 Silver 0.5353 oz. ASW, 32.5 mm. **Obv:** Stylized eagle **Rev:** Eduard Moerike **Edge:** Lettered **Edge Lettering:** "OHNE DAS SCHONE WAS SOLL DER GEWINN"

Date	F	VF	XF	Unc	BU
2004	—	—	—	20.00	—

KM# 234 10 EURO
18.0000 g., 0.9250 Silver 0.5353 oz. ASW, 32.5 mm. **Obv:** Stylized eagle **Rev:** Space station above the earth **Edge:** Lettered **Edge Lettering:** "RAUMFAHRT VERBINDET DIE WELT"

Date	F	VF	XF	Unc	BU
2004	—	—	—	20.00	—

KM# 238 10 EURO
18.0000 g., 0.9250 Silver 0.5353 oz. ASW, 32.5 mm. **Subject:** Albert Einstein **Obv:** Stylized eagle **Rev:** E=mc2 on a sphere resting on a net **Edge Lettering:** "NICHT AUFHOREN ZU FRAGEN"

Date	F	VF	XF	Unc	BU
2005	—	—	—	15.00	—

KM# 239 10 EURO
18.0000 g., 0.9250 Silver 0.5353 oz. ASW, 32.5 mm. **Subject:** Friedrich von Schiller **Obv:** Stylized eagle **Rev:** Schiller portrait **Edge Lettering:** "ERNST IST DAS LEBEN. HEITER IST DIE KUNST"

Date	F	VF	XF	Unc	BU
2005	—	—	—	15.00	—

KM# 240 10 EURO
18.0000 g., 0.9250 Silver 0.5353 oz. ASW, 32.5 mm. **Subject:** Magdeburg **Obv:** Stylized eagle **Rev:** Church flanked by landmarks and objects **Edge Lettering:** MAGADOBURG 805..MAGDEBURG 2005..

Date	F	VF	XF	Unc	BU
2005	—	—	—	15.00	—

KM# 241 10 EURO
18.0000 g., 0.9250 Silver 0.5353 oz. ASW, 32.5 mm. **Subject:** Bavarian Forest National Park **Obv:** Stylized eagle **Rev:** Various park scenes **Edge:** Lettered

Date	F	VF	XF	Unc	BU
2005	—	—	—	15.00	—

KM# 242 10 EURO
18.0000 g., 0.9250 Silver 0.5353 oz. ASW, 32.5 mm. **Subject:** Bertha von Suttner **Obv:** Stylized eagle above stars **Rev:** Suttner's portrait **Edge:** Lettered **Edge Lettering:** "EIPHNH PAX FRIEDEN" twice

Date	F	VF	XF	Unc	BU
2005	—	—	—	15.00	—

KM# 243 10 EURO
18.0000 g., 0.9250 Silver 0.5353 oz. ASW, 32.5 mm. **Subject:** World Cup Soccer **Obv:** Round stylized eagle **Rev:** Ball and legs seen through a net **Edge Lettering:** DIE WELT ZU GAST BEI FREUNDEN

Date	F	VF	XF	Unc	BU
2005	—	—	—	15.00	—

KM# 245 10 EURO
18.0000 g., 0.9250 Silver 0.5353 oz. ASW, 32.5 mm. **Subject:** Karl Friedrich Schinkel **Obv:** Stylized eagle **Rev:** Kneeling brick layer **Edge Lettering:** DER MENSCH BILDE SICH IN ALLEM SCHON

Date	F	VF	XF	Unc	BU
2006	—	—	—	20.00	—

KM# 246 10 EURO
18.0000 g., 0.9250 Silver 0.5353 oz. ASW, 32.5 mm. **Subject:** Dresden **Obv:** Stylized eagle **Rev:** City view and reflection **Edge Lettering:** 1206 1485 1547 1697 1832 1945 1989 2006

Date	F	VF	XF	Unc	BU
2006	—	—	—	15.00	—

KM# 247 10 EURO
18.0000 g., 0.9250 Silver 0.5353 oz. ASW, 32.5 mm. **Subject:** Hanseatic League **Obv:** Stylized eagle **Rev:** Old sail boat **Edge Lettering:** Wandel durch Handel - von der Hanse nach Europa

Date	F	VF	XF	Unc	BU
2006	—	—	—	15.00	—

KM# 248 10 EURO
18.0000 g., 0.9250 Silver 0.5353 oz. ASW, 32.5 mm. **Subject:** Mozart **Obv:** Stylized eagle and music **Rev:** Mozart **Edge Lettering:** -- MOZART -- DIE WELT HAT EINEN SINN

Date	F	VF	XF	Unc	BU
2006	—	—	—	15.00	—

KM# 249   10 EURO
18.0000 g., 0.9250 Silver 0.5353 oz. ASW, 32.5 mm. **Subject:**
World Cup Soccer **Obv:** Stylized eagle **Rev:** Brandenburg Gate
on ball on globe

Date	F	VF	XF	Unc	BU
2006	—	—	—	15.00	—

KM# 220   100 EURO
15.5500 g., 0.9990 Gold 0.4994 oz. AGW, 28 mm. **Subject:**
Introduction of the Euro Currency **Obv:** Stylized round eagle **Rev:**
Euro symbol and arches **Edge:** Reeded

Date	F	VF	XF	Unc	BU
2002 Proof		Value: 375			

KM# 228   100 EURO
15.5000 g., 0.9999 Gold 0.4983 oz. AGW, 28 mm. **Obv:** Stylized
eagle **Rev:** Quedlinburg Abbey in monogram **Edge:** Reeded

Date	F	VF	XF	Unc	BU
2003-2003J Proof		Value: 365			

KM# 235   100 EURO
15.5500 g., 0.9999 Gold 0.4999 oz. AGW, 28 mm. **Obv:** Stylized
eagle **Rev:** Bamberg city view **Edge:** Reeded

Date	F	VF	XF	Unc	BU
2004 Proof		Value: 350			

KM# 236   100 EURO
15.5500 g., 0.9990 Gold 0.4994 oz. AGW **Subject:** UNESCO -
Weimar **Obv:** Stylized eagle **Rev:** Historical City of Weimar buildings

Date	F	VF	XF	Unc	BU
2005	—	—	—	—	350

KM# 237   100 EURO
15.5500 g., 0.9990 Gold 0.4994 oz. AGW **Subject:** Soccer -
Germany 2006 **Obv:** Round stylized eagle **Rev:** Aerial view of stadium

Date	F	VF	XF	Unc	BU
2005	—	—	—	—	360

KM# 221   200 EURO
31.1000 g., 0.9990 Gold 0.9989 oz. AGW, 32.5 mm. **Subject:**
Introduction of the Euro Currency **Obv:** Stylized round eagle **Rev:**
Euro symbol and arches **Edge Lettering:**
IM...ZEICHEN...DER...EINIGUNG...EUROPAS

Date	F	VF	XF	Unc	BU
2002 Proof		Value: 1,250			

KM# 250   200 EURO
31.1000 g., 0.9990 Gold 0.9989 oz. AGW **Subject:** Quedlinburg
Abbey

Date	F	VF	XF	Unc	BU
2003 Proof		Value: 950			

KM# 251   200 EURO
31.1000 g., 0.9990 Gold 0.9989 oz. AGW **Subject:** City of Bamberg

Date	F	VF	XF	Unc	BU
2004 Proof		Value: 850			

KM# 252   200 EURO
31.1000 g., 0.9990 Gold 0.9989 oz. AGW **Subject:** 2006 World
Cup - Soccer

Date	F	VF	XF	Unc	BU
2005 Proof		Value: 900			

German - Democratic Republic

1949-1990

The German Democratic Republic, formerly East Germany, was located on the great north European plain, had an area of 41,768 sq. mi. (108,330 sq. km.) and a population of 16.6 million. The figures included East Berlin, which had been incorporated into the G.D.R. Capital: East Berlin. The economy was highly industrialized. Machinery, transport equipment chemicals, and lignite were exported.

MONETARY SYSTEM

100 Pfennig = 1 Mark

DEMOCRATIC REPUBLIC

STANDARD COINAGE

KM# 1   PFENNIG
Aluminum

Date	F	VF	XF	Unc	BU
1948-1950	—	1.00	8.00	35.00	45.00

KM# 5   PFENNIG
Aluminum

Date	F	VF	XF	Unc	BU
1952-1953	—	0.50	3.00	7.00	9.00

KM# 8.1   PFENNIG
Aluminum

Date	F	VF	XF	Unc	BU
1960-1975	—	0.25	0.75	2.50	3.00

KM# 8.2   PFENNIG
Aluminum **Obv:** Smaller design features **Rev:** Smaller design features

Date	F	VF	XF	Unc	BU
1977-1990	—	0.10	0.20	1.00	2.00

KM# 2   5 PFENNIG
Aluminum

Date	F	VF	XF	Unc	BU
1948-1950	—	2.50	6.00	40.00	65.00

KM# 6   5 PFENNIG
Aluminum

Date	F	VF	XF	Unc	BU
1952-1953	—	2.00	5.00	10.00	13.00

KM# 9.1   5 PFENNIG
Aluminum

Date	F	VF	XF	Unc	BU
1968-1975	—	0.50	1.00	2.00	3.00

KM# 9.2   5 PFENNIG
Aluminum **Obv:** Smaller design features **Rev:** Smaller design features **Note:** Varieties exist.

Date	F	VF	XF	Unc	BU
1978-1990	—	0.15	0.25	1.00	2.00

KM# 3   10 PFENNIG
Aluminum **Note:** Also exists with medallic die rotation (1950E).

Date	F	VF	XF	Unc	BU
1948-1950	—	2.50	10.00	70.00	90.00

KM# 7   10 PFENNIG
Aluminum

Date	F	VF	XF	Unc	BU
1952-1953	—	2.00	12.00	60.00	80.00

KM# 10   10 PFENNIG
Aluminum

Date	F	VF	XF	Unc	BU
1963-1990	—	0.15	1.00	2.00	3.00

KM# 35.2   MARK
Aluminum   **Rev:** Small 1

Date	F	VF	XF	Unc	BU
1973-1990	—	0.50	1.00	2.00	3.00

KM# 11   20 PFENNIG
Brass   **Note:** Ribbon width varieties exist.

Date	F	VF	XF	Unc	BU
1969-1990	—	0.20	1.00	2.00	3.00

KM# 14   2 MARK
Aluminum   **Obv:** Larger coat of arms

Date	F	VF	XF	Unc	BU
1957	—	2.00	4.00	8.00	10.00

KM# 4   50 PFENNIG
Aluminum-Bronze

Date	F	VF	XF	Unc	BU
1949-1950	—	3.50	10.00	70.00	—

KM# 12.1   50 PFENNIG
Aluminum   **Obv:** Small coat of arms

Date	F	VF	XF	Unc	BU
1958	—	1.00	3.00	8.00	10.00

KM# 48   2 MARK
Aluminum   **Obv:** Smaller coat of arms

Date	F	VF	XF	Unc	BU
1974-1990	—	1.00	2.00	3.00	4.00

KM# 12.2   50 PFENNIG
Aluminum   **Obv:** Larger coat of arms **Note:** Inscription varieties exist.

Date	F	VF	XF	Unc	BU
1968-1990	—	0.35	0.75	2.50	3.00

KM# 19.1   5 MARK
Copper-Nickel   **Subject:** 125th Anniversary of Birth of Robert Koch, doctor

Date	F	VF	XF	Unc	BU
1968	—	—	10.00	20.00	30.00

KM# 19.2   5 MARK
Copper-Nickel   **Note:** Error: plain edge.

Date	F	VF	XF	Unc	BU
1968	—	—	—	400	450

KM# 13   MARK
Aluminum

Date	F	VF	XF	Unc	BU
1956-1963	—	1.00	2.50	8.00	12.00

KM# 35.1   MARK
Aluminum   **Rev:** Large 1

Date	F	VF	XF	Unc	BU
1972	—	1.00	4.00	5.00	8.00

Germany • Democratic Republic

KM# 22.1 5 MARK
Nickel-Bronze **Subject:** 20th Anniversary D.D.R

Date	F	VF	XF	Unc	BU
1969	—	—	3.00	4.50	7.50

KM# 22.1a 5 MARK
Copper-Nickel

Date	F	VF	XF	Unc	BU
1969	—	50.00	60.00	70.00	80.00

KM# 22.2 5 MARK
Nickel-Bronze **Note:** Error: plain edge.

Date	F	VF	XF	Unc	BU
1969	—	—	—	120	150

KM# 23 5 MARK
Copper-Nickel **Subject:** Heinrich Hertz, physicist

Date	F	VF	XF	Unc	BU
1969	—	—	20.00	35.00	50.00

KM# 26 5 MARK
Copper-Nickel **Subject:** Wilhelm Conrad Rontgen, Physicist

Date	F	VF	XF	Unc	BU
1970	—	—	15.00	20.00	25.00

KM# 29 5 MARK
Copper-Nickel **Subject:** Brandenburg Gate

Date	F	VF	XF	Unc	BU
1971-1990	—	—	3.00	10.00	20.00

KM# 30 5 MARK
Copper-Nickel **Subject:** Johannes Kepler, Scientist

Date	F	VF	XF	Unc	BU
1971	—	—	15.00	20.00	25.00

KM# 36.1 5 MARK
Copper-Nickel **Subject:** 75th Anniversary - Death of Johannes Brahms **Rev:** Name, musical score, dates

Date	F	VF	XF	Unc	BU
1972	—	—	15.00	20.00	25.00

KM# 36.2 5 MARK
Copper-Nickel **Note:** Error: Double edge inscription.

Date	F	VF	XF	Unc	BU
1972	—	—	—	475	575

KM# 37 5 MARK
Copper-Nickel **Subject:** City of Meissen

Date	F	VF	XF	Unc	BU
1972-1983	—	—	4.00	10.00	12.00

KM# 43 5 MARK
Copper-Nickel **Subject:** 125th Anniversary - Birth of Otto Lilienthal, Aviation Pioneer **Obv:** Plane divides dates

Date	F	VF	XF	Unc	BU
1973	—	—	40.00	50.00	60.00

KM# 49 5 MARK
Copper-Nickel **Subject:** Centenary - Death of Philipp Reis, Physicist, Telephone Inventor

Date	F	VF	XF	Unc	BU
1974	—	—	—	20.00	30.00

KM# 54 5 MARK
Copper-Nickel **Subject:** 100th Anniversary - Birth of Thomas Mann, Writer **Rev:** Bust left

Date	F	VF	XF	Unc	BU
1975	—	—	15.00	20.00	25.00

KM# 55   5 MARK
Copper-Nickel   **Subject:** International Women's Year **Rev:**
Profiles of three women right

Date	F	VF	XF	Unc	BU
1975	—	—	15.00	20.00	25.00

KM# 68   5 MARK
Copper-Nickel   **Subject:** Anti-Apartheid Year **Rev:** Raised
clenched fist

Date	F	VF	XF	Unc	BU
1978	—	—	20.00	25.00	30.00

KM# 60   5 MARK
Copper-Nickel   **Subject:** 200th Anniversary - Birth of Ferdinand von
Schill, Military Officer **Rev:** Hat divides dates above sword and name

Date	F	VF	XF	Unc	BU
1976	—	—	20.00	28.00	35.00

KM# 72   5 MARK
Copper-Nickel   **Subject:** 100th Anniversary - Birth of Albert
Einstein, Physicist **Rev:** Head of Einstein half right

Date	F	VF	XF	Unc	BU
1979	—	—	55.00	80.00	95.00

KM# 64   5 MARK
Copper-Nickel   **Subject:** 125th Anniversary - Death of Friedrich
Ludwig Jahn, Father of German Gymnastics **Rev:** Bust of Jahn
half right

Date	F	VF	XF	Unc	BU
1977	—	—	30.00	40.00	50.00

KM# 76   5 MARK
Copper-Nickel   **Subject:** 75th Anniversary - Death of Adolph von
Menzel **Rev:** Bust left

Date	F	VF	XF	Unc	BU
1980	—	—	35.00	50.00	60.00

KM# 67   5 MARK
Copper-Nickel   **Subject:** 175th Anniversary - Death of Friedrich
Klopstock, Poet **Rev:** Bust left

Date	F	VF	XF	Unc	BU
1978	—	—	30.00	40.00	50.00

KM# 79   5 MARK
Copper-Nickel   **Subject:** 450th Anniversary - Death of Tilman
Riemenschneider, Sculptor **Rev:** Bust half left

Date	F	VF	XF	Unc	BU
1981	—	—	40.00	60.00	70.00

KM# 84   5 MARK
Copper-Nickel **Subject:** 200th Anniversary - Birth of Friedrich Frobel **Rev:** Three children with building blocks

Date	F	VF	XF	Unc	BU
1982	—	—	40.00	60.00	75.00

KM# 90   5 MARK
Copper-Nickel **Subject:** Martin Luther's Birthplace

Date	F	VF	XF	Unc	BU
1983	—	—	25.00	40.00	50.00

KM# 85   5 MARK
Copper-Nickel-Zinc **Subject:** Goethe's Weimar Cottage

Date	F	VF	XF	Unc	BU
1982	—	—	25.00	35.00	42.00

KM# 91   5 MARK
Copper-Nickel-Zinc **Subject:** 125th Anniversary - Birth of Max Planck **Rev:** Head right

Date	F	VF	XF	Unc	BU
1983	—	—	32.00	45.00	55.00

KM# 86   5 MARK
Copper-Nickel-Zinc **Subject:** Wartburg Castle

Date	F	VF	XF	Unc	BU
1982-1983	—	—	25.00	40.00	45.00

KM# 96   5 MARK
Copper-Nickel **Subject:** Leipzig Old City Hall

Date	F	VF	XF	Unc	BU
1984	—	—	25.00	40.00	50.00

KM# 89   5 MARK
Copper-Nickel **Subject:** Wittenberg Church

Date	F	VF	XF	Unc	BU
1983	—	—	25.00	40.00	50.00

KM# 97   5 MARK
Copper-Nickel **Subject:** Thomas Church of Leipzig

Date	F	VF	XF	Unc	BU
1984	—	—	25.00	40.00	50.00

Germany • Democratic Republic

KM# 98   5 MARK
Copper-Nickel **Subject:** 150th Anniversary - Death of Adolf
Freiherr von Lutzow

Date	F	VF	XF	Unc	BU
1984	—	—	55.00	70.00	80.00

KM# 102   5 MARK
Copper-Nickel **Subject:** Restoration of Dresden Women's Church

Date	F	VF	XF	Unc	BU
1985	—	—	25.00	35.00	40.00

KM# 103   5 MARK
Copper-Nickel **Subject:** Restoration of Dresden Zwinger

Date	F	VF	XF	Unc	BU
1985	—	—	25.00	35.00	45.00

KM# 104   5 MARK
Copper-Nickel **Subject:** 225th Anniversary - Death of Caroline
Neuber **Rev:** Caroline on stage, 1697-1760

Date	F	VF	XF	Unc	BU
1985	—	—	75.00	90.00	100

KM# 110   5 MARK
Copper-Nickel **Subject:** Potsdam - Sanssouci Palace

Date	F	VF	XF	Unc	BU
1986	—	—	9.00	12.00	17.50

KM# 111   5 MARK
Copper-Nickel **Subject:** Potsdam - New Palace

Date	F	VF	XF	Unc	BU
1986	—	—	9.00	12.00	17.50

KM# 112   5 MARK
Copper-Nickel **Subject:** 175th Anniversary - Death of Heinrich
von Kleist **Rev:** Bust of von Kleist left

Date	F	VF	XF	Unc	BU
1986	—	—	130	150	180

KM# 114   5 MARK
Copper-Zinc-Nickel **Subject:** Berlin - Nikolai Quarter

Date	F	VF	XF	Unc	BU
1987	—	—	8.00	12.00	15.00

KM# 115 5 MARK
Copper-Zinc-Nickel **Subject:** Berlin - Red City Hall

Date	F	VF	XF	Unc	BU
1987	—	—	8.00	12.00	15.00

KM# 122 5 MARK
Copper-Nickel **Subject:** 50th Anniversary - Death of Ernst Barlach **Rev:** Full-length figure of Barlach playing horn

Date	F	VF	XF	Unc	BU
1988	—	—	50.00	65.00	80.00

KM# 116 5 MARK
Copper-Zinc-Nickel **Subject:** Berlin - Universal Time Clock

Date	F	VF	XF	Unc	BU
1987	—	—	8.00	12.00	15.00

KM# 129 5 MARK
Copper-Zinc-Nickel **Subject:** Katharinen Kirche in Zwickau

Date	F	VF	XF	Unc	BU
1989	—	—	7.00	9.00	11.50

KM# 120 5 MARK
Copper-Nickel **Subject:** Germany's First Railroad

Date	F	VF	XF	Unc	BU
1988	—	—	8.00	9.00	12.50

KM# 130 5 MARK
Copper-Zinc-Nickel **Subject:** Marien Kirche in Muhlhausen

Date	F	VF	XF	Unc	BU
1989	—	—	7.00	9.00	11.50

KM# 121 5 MARK
Copper-Nickel **Subject:** Port City of Rostock

Date	F	VF	XF	Unc	BU
1988	—	—	8.00	9.00	12.50

KM# 131 5 MARK
Copper-Zinc-Nickel **Subject:** 100th Anniversary - Birth of Carl von Ossietzky **Rev:** Bust of Ossietzky left

Date	F	VF	XF	Unc	BU
1989	—	—	60.00	75.00	90.00

KM# 133 5 MARK
Copper-Zinc-Nickel **Subject:** 100th Anniversary - Birth of Kurt
Tucholsky **Rev:** Head of Tucholsky facing

Date	F	VF	XF	Unc	BU
1990	—	—	40.00	60.00	70.00

KM# 134 5 MARK
Copper-Zinc-Nickel **Subject:** 500 Years of Postal Service

Date	F	VF	XF	Unc	BU
1990	—	—	7.00	9.00	11.00

KM# 135 5 MARK
Copper-Zinc-Nickel **Subject:** Zeughaus Museum

Date	F	VF	XF	Unc	BU
1990	—	—	7.00	8.00	10.00

KM# 15.1 10 MARK
17.0000 g., 0.8000 Silver .4373 oz. ASW **Subject:** 125th
Anniversary - Death of Karl Friedrich Schinkel, Artist, Painter **Edge
Lettering:** 10 MARK DER DEUTSCHEN NOTEN BANK

Date	F	VF	XF	Unc	BU
1966	—	—	325	400	425

KM# 17.1 10 MARK
17.0000 g., 0.8000 Silver .4373 oz. ASW **Subject:** 100th
Anniversary - Birth of Kathe Kollwitz, Artist **Edge Lettering:** 10
MARK DER DEUTSCHEN NOTENBANK

Date	F	VF	XF	Unc	BU
1967	—	—	60.00	70.00	90.00

KM# 17.2 10 MARK
17.0000 g., 0.8000 Silver .4373 oz. ASW **Subject:** 100th
Anniversary - Birth of Kathe Kollwitz **Note:** Error, edge: 10
MARK*10 MARK*10 MARK*

Date	F	VF	XF	Unc	BU
1967	—	—	—	200	250

KM# 20.1 10 MARK
17.0000 g., 0.6250 Silver .3416 oz. ASW **Subject:** 500th
Anniversary - Death of Johann Gutenberg

Date	F	VF	XF	Unc	BU
1968	—	—	55.00	65.00	85.00

KM# 20.2 10 MARK
17.0000 g., 0.6250 Silver .3416 oz. ASW **Subject:** 500th
Anniversary - Death of Johann Gutenberg **Note:** Error: Plain edge.

Date	F	VF	XF	Unc	BU
1968	—	—	—	700	800

KM# 24 10 MARK
17.0000 g., 0.6250 Silver .3416 oz. ASW **Subject:** 250th
Anniversary - Death of Johann Friedrich Bottger

Date	F	VF	XF	Unc	BU
1969	—	—	50.00	60.00	75.00

KM# 27.1 10 MARK
17.0000 g., 0.6250 Silver .3416 oz. ASW **Subject:** Ludwig Van
Beethoven, Composer **Rev:** Head left

Date	F	VF	XF	Unc	BU
1970	—	—	50.00	60.00	70.00

KM# 27.2 10 MARK
17.0000 g., 0.6250 Silver .3416 oz. ASW **Rev:** Head left **Note:**
Error: Plain edge.

Date	F	VF	XF	Unc	BU
1970	—	—	—	—	600

KM# 31   10 MARK
17.0000 g., 0.6250 Silver .3416 oz. ASW **Subject:** Albrecht
Durer, Artist **Rev:** Durer's monogram

Date	F	VF	XF	Unc	BU
1971	—	—	50.00	60.00	75.00

KM# 45   10 MARK
17.0000 g., 0.6250 Silver .3416 oz. ASW **Subject:** 75th
Anniversary - Birth of Bertolt Brecht, Poet

Date	F	VF	XF	Unc	BU
1973	—	—	50.00	60.00	80.00

KM# 38   10 MARK
Copper-Nickel **Subject:** Buchenwald Memorial

Date	F	VF	XF	Unc	BU
1972	—	—	—	8.00	10.00

KM# 50   10 MARK
Copper-Nickel **Subject:** 25th Anniversary (with state motto)

Date	F	VF	XF	Unc	BU
1974	—	—	—	6.00	14.00

KM# 39   10 MARK
17.0000 g., 0.6250 Silver .3416 oz. ASW **Subject:** 175th
Anniversary - Birth of Heinrich Heine, Poet **Rev:** Bust of Heine half
left between dates, name below

Date	F	VF	XF	Unc	BU
1972	—	—	55.00	65.00	80.00

KM# 51   10 MARK
17.0000 g., 0.6250 Silver .3416 oz. ASW **Subject:** 25th
Anniversary D.D.R.

Date	F	VF	XF	Unc	BU
1974	—	—	50.00	60.00	80.00

KM# 44   10 MARK
Copper-Nickel **Subject:** 10th Youth Festival Games

Date	F	VF	XF	Unc	BU
1973	—	—	—	5.00	12.00

KM# 52   10 MARK
17.0000 g., 0.6250 Silver .3416 oz. ASW **Subject:** 200th
Anniversary - Birth of Caspar David Friedrich, Painter **Rev:** Bust
of Friedrich right within inner circle

Date	F	VF	XF	Unc	BU
1974	—	—	50.00	60.00	75.00

KM# 56   10 MARK
17.0000 g., 0.6250 Silver .3416 oz. ASW **Subject:** Centenary - Birth of Albert Schweitzer, Doctor and Philosopher **Rev:** Head of Schweitzer left

Date	F	VF	XF	Unc	BU
1975	—	—	50.00	60.00	80.00

KM# 57   10 MARK
17.0000 g., 0.5000 Silver .2733 oz. ASW **Subject:** Mule **Obv:** KM#58 **Rev:** KM#56 **Edge:** Plain

Date	F	VF	XF	Unc	BU
1975	—	—	—	—	180

KM# 58   10 MARK
Copper-Nickel **Subject:** 20th Anniversary - Warsaw Pact

Date	F	VF	XF	Unc	BU
1974-1975	—	—	7.00	10.00	15.00

KM# 61   10 MARK
Copper-Nickel **Subject:** 20th Anniversary - National People's Army **Rev:** Bust of soldier half left

Date	F	VF	XF	Unc	BU
1976	—	—	10.00	15.00	20.00

KM# 62   10 MARK
17.0000 g., 0.5000 Silver .2733 oz. ASW **Subject:** 150th Anniversary - Death of Carl Maria von Weber, Composer **Rev:** Bust of Weber right

Date	F	VF	XF	Unc	BU
1976	—	—	70.00	80.00	95.00

KM# 65   10 MARK
17.0000 g., 0.5000 Silver .2733 oz. ASW **Subject:** 375th Anniversary - Birth of Otto von Guericke

Date	F	VF	XF	Unc	BU
1977	—	—	100	115	125

KM# 69   10 MARK
17.0000 g., 0.5000 Silver .2733 oz. ASW **Subject:** 175th Anniversary - Birth of Justus von Liebig, Chemist **Rev:** Bust of Liebig right

Date	F	VF	XF	Unc	BU
1978	—	—	80.00	115	130

KM# 70   10 MARK
Copper-Nickel **Subject:** Joint USSR-DDR Orbital Flight

Date	F	VF	XF	Unc	BU
1978	—	—	20.00	30.00	40.00

KM# 73   10 MARK
17.0000 g., 0.5000 Silver .2733 oz. ASW **Subject:** 175th
Anniversary - Birth of Ludwig Feuerbach, Philosopher

Date	F	VF	XF	Unc	BU
1979	—	—	150	175	190

KM# 77   10 MARK
17.0000 g., 0.5000 Silver .2733 oz. ASW **Subject:** 225th
Anniversary - Birth of Gerhard von Scharnhorst **Rev:** Bust left

Date	F	VF	XF	Unc	BU
1980	—	—	40.00	50.00	60.00

KM# 80   10 MARK
Copper-Nickel **Subject:** 25th Anniversary - National People's
Army **Rev:** Plane above, ship at center, tank below, dates at sides

Date	F	VF	XF	Unc	BU
1981	—	—	12.00	22.00	25.00

KM# 81   10 MARK
17.0000 g., 0.5000 Silver .2733 oz. ASW **Subject:** 150th
Anniversary - Death of Georg Hegel, Philosopher **Rev:** Head of
Hegel right

Date	F	VF	XF	Unc	BU
1981	—	—	45.00	55.00	65.00

KM# 82   10 MARK
Copper-Nickel **Subject:** 700th Anniversary - Berlin Mint

Date	F	VF	XF	Unc	BU
1981	—	—	40.00	45.00	55.00

KM# 87   10 MARK
17.0000 g., 0.5000 Silver .2733 oz. ASW **Subject:** Leipzig
Gewandhaus

Date	F	VF	XF	Unc	BU
1982	—	—	50.00	60.00	70.00

KM# 92   10 MARK
17.1100 g., 0.5000 Silver .2751 oz. ASW **Subject:** 100th
Anniversary - Death of Richard Wagner

Date	F	VF	XF	Unc	BU
1983	—	—	50.00	60.00	70.00

KM# 93   10 MARK
Copper-Nickel-Zinc **Subject:** 30th Anniversary - Worker's Militia
Rev: Worker and soldier facing left

Date	F	VF	XF	Unc	BU
1983	—	—	12.00	20.00	30.00

KM# 99   10 MARK
17.0000 g., 0.5000 Silver .2733 oz. ASW **Subject:** 100th Anniversary - Death of Alfred Brehm **Rev:** Marabou stork left

Date	F	VF	XF	Unc	BU
1984	—	—	65.00	85.00	100

KM# 109   10 MARK
Copper-Nickel **Subject:** 100th Anniversary - Birth of Ernst Thalmann

Date	F	VF	XF	Unc	BU
1986	—	—	10.00	17.50	25.00

KM# 101   10 MARK
17.0000 g., 0.5000 Silver .2733 oz. ASW **Subject:** Restoration of Semper Opera in Dresden

Date	F	VF	XF	Unc	BU
1985	—	—	60.00	70.00	85.00

KM# 113   10 MARK
17.0000 g., 0.5000 Silver .2733 oz. ASW **Subject:** Charite - Berlin

Date	F	VF	XF	Unc	BU
1986	—	—	70.00	80.00	90.00

KM# 106   10 MARK
Copper-Nickel-Zinc **Subject:** 40th Anniversary - Liberation from Fascism

Date	F	VF	XF	Unc	BU
1985	—	—	10.00	20.00	25.00

KM# 118   10 MARK
17.0000 g., 0.5000 Silver .2733 oz. ASW **Subject:** Berlin - Theater

Date	F	VF	XF	Unc	BU
1987	—	—	60.00	70.00	85.00

KM# 107   10 MARK
17.0000 g., 0.5000 Silver 0.2733 oz. ASW **Subject:** 175th Anniversary - Humboldt University

Date	F	VF	XF	Unc	BU
1985	—	—	75.00	90.00	100

KM# 123   10 MARK
17.0000 g., 0.5000 Silver .2733 oz. ASW **Subject:** 500th Anniversary - Birth of Ulrich von Hutten

Date	F	VF	XF	Unc	BU
1988	—	—	70.00	90.00	110

KM# 125 10 MARK
Copper-Nickel **Subject:** East German Sports **Rev:** Three women running left

Date	F	VF	XF	Unc	BU
1988	—	—	10.00	20.00	28.00

KM# 126 10 MARK
Copper-Nickel **Subject:** Council of Mutual Economic Aid

Date	F	VF	XF	Unc	BU
1989	—	—	30.00	50.00	60.00

KM# 128 10 MARK
17.0000 g., 0.5000 Silver .2733 oz. ASW **Subject:** 225th Anniversary - Birth of Johann Gottfried Schadow

Date	F	VF	XF	Unc	BU
1989	—	—	95.00	120	150

KM# 132 10 MARK
Copper-Nickel-Zinc **Subject:** 40th Anniversary - East German Government **Edge Lettering:** 10 MARK (repeated)

Date	F	VF	XF	Unc	BU
1989	—	—	12.00	15.00	20.00

KM# 136 10 MARK
Copper-Nickel-Zinc **Subject:** International Labor Day **Edge Lettering:** 10 MARK (repeated)

Date	F	VF	XF	Unc	BU
1990	—	—	4.00	7.00	10.00

KM# 137 10 MARK
17.0000 g., 0.5000 Silver .2733 oz. ASW **Rev:** Johann Gottlieb Fichte at lectern facing left

Date	F	VF	XF	Unc	BU
1990	—	—	70.00	90.00	110

KM# 16.1 20 MARK
20.9000 g., 0.8000 Silver .5376 oz. ASW **Subject:** 250th Anniversary - Death of Gottfried Wilhelm Leibniz **Edge Lettering:** 20 MARK DER DEUTSCHEN NOTEN BANK

Date	F	VF	XF	Unc	BU
1966	—	—	175	225	275

KM# 18.1 20 MARK
20.9000 g., 0.8000 Silver .5376 oz. ASW **Subject:** 200th Anniversary - Birth of Wilhelm von Humboldt **Edge Lettering:** 20 MARK DER DEUTSCHEN NOTENBANK

Date	F	VF	XF	Unc	BU
1967	—	—	160	180	210

KM# 18.2 20 MARK

20.9000 g., 0.8000 Silver .5376 oz. ASW **Edge:** Error: In inscription
Edge Lettering: 20 MARK*20 MARK*20 MARK*20 MARK

Date	F	VF	XF	Unc	BU
1967	—	—	—	—	275

KM# 32 20 MARK

20.9000 g., 0.6250 Silver .4200 oz. ASW **Subject:** Karl
Kiebknecht - Rosa Luxemburg **Rev:** Conjoined busts left **Edge
Lettering:** 20 MARK (repeated)

Date	F	VF	XF	Unc	BU
1971	—	—	75.00	90.00	100

KM# 21 20 MARK

20.9000 g., 0.8000 Silver .5376 oz. ASW **Subject:** 150th
Anniversary - Birth of Karl Marx **Rev:** Head of Marx left

Date	F	VF	XF	Unc	BU
1968	—	—	80.00	100	120

KM# 33 20 MARK

Copper-Nickel **Subject:** 100th Anniversary - Birth of Heinrich Mann,
Writer **Rev:** Head of Mann left **Edge Lettering:** 20 MARK (repeated)

Date	F	VF	XF	Unc	BU
1971	—	—	4.00	6.50	28.00

KM# 25 20 MARK

20.9000 g., 0.6250 Silver .4200 oz. ASW **Subject:** 240th Birth
Anniversary - Johann Wolfgang von Goethe, poet **Rev:** Head of
Goethe left

Date	F	VF	XF	Unc	BU
1969	—	—	140	160	180

KM# 34 20 MARK

Copper-Nickel **Subject:** 85th Birthday of Ernst Thalmann **Rev:**
Head of Thalmann left **Edge Lettering:** 20 MARK (repeated) **Note:**
Edge varieties exist.

Date	F	VF	XF	Unc	BU
1971	—	—	4.00	5.50	20.00

KM# 28 20 MARK

20.9000 g., 0.6250 Silver .4200 oz. ASW **Subject:** 150th
Anniversary - Birth of Friedrich Engels **Rev:** Head of Engels left

Date	F	VF	XF	Unc	BU
1970	—	—	85.00	100	120

KM# 40 20 MARK

Copper-Nickel **Subject:** Freiedrich von Schiller, Poet **Rev:** Head
of Schiller right

Date	F	VF	XF	Unc	BU
1972	—	—	4.00	15.00	18.00

KM# 41 20 MARK
20.9000 g., 0.6250 Silver .4200 oz. ASW **Subject:** 500th Anniversary - Birth of Lucas Cranach, Painter **Edge Lettering:** 20 MARK (repeated)

Date	F	VF	XF	Unc	BU
1972	—	—	60.00	90.00	110

KM# 53 20 MARK
20.9000 g., 0.6250 Silver .4200 oz. ASW **Subject:** 250th Anniversary - Death of Immanuel Kant, Philosopher **Rev:** Bust of Kant half left

Date	F	VF	XF	Unc	BU
1974	—	—	60.00	85.00	150

KM# 42 20 MARK
Copper-Nickel **Rev:** Head of Wilhelm Pieck left

Date	F	VF	XF	Unc	BU
1972	—	—	4.00	15.00	20.00

KM# 59 20 MARK
20.9000 g., 0.6250 Silver .4200 oz. ASW **Subject:** 225th Anniversary - Death of Johann Sebastian Bach, Composer **Rev:** Musical score

Date	F	VF	XF	Unc	BU
1975	—	—	100	125	145

KM# 46 20 MARK
20.9000 g., 0.6250 Silver .4200 oz. ASW **Subject:** 60th Anniversary - Death of August Bebel **Rev:** Bust of Bebel half facing

Date	F	VF	XF	Unc	BU
1973	—	—	60.00	70.00	90.00

KM# 63 20 MARK
20.9000 g., 0.6250 Silver .4200 oz. ASW **Subject:** 150th Anniversary - Birth of Wilhelm Liebknecht **Rev:** Bust of Liebknecht half left

Date	F	VF	XF	Unc	BU
1976	—	—	60.00	70.00	90.00

KM# 47 20 MARK
Copper-Nickel **Rev:** Head of Otto Grotewohl left **Edge Lettering:** 20 MARK (repeated)

Date	F	VF	XF	Unc	BU
1973	—	—	5.00	10.00	15.00

KM# 66 20 MARK
20.9000 g., 0.5000 Silver .3360 oz. ASW **Subject:** 200th Anniversary - Birth of Carl Friedrich Gauss, Scientist

Date	F	VF	XF	Unc	BU
1977	—	—	90.00	110	125

KM# 71 20 MARK
20.9000 g., 0.5000 Silver .3360 oz. ASW **Subject:** 175th Anniversary - Death of Johann von Herder, Philosopher **Rev:** Head of Herder half left

Date	F	VF	XF	Unc	BU
1978	—	—	90.00	100	120

KM# 74 20 MARK
20.9000 g., 0.5000 Silver .3360 oz. ASW **Subject:** 250th Anniversary - Birth of Gotthold Ephraim Lessing, Poet

Date	F	VF	XF	Unc	BU
1979	—	—	100	130	150

KM# 75 20 MARK
Copper-Nickel **Subject:** 30th Anniversary - East German Regime

Date	F	VF	XF	Unc	BU
1979	—	—	—	15.00	25.00

KM# 78 20 MARK
20.9200 g., 0.5000 Silver .3360 oz. ASW **Subject:** 75th Anniversary - Death of Ernst Abbe, Physicist

Date	F	VF	XF	Unc	BU
1980	—	—	70.00	90.00	110

KM# 83 20 MARK
20.9200 g., 0.5000 Silver .3360 oz. ASW **Subject:** 150th Anniversary - Death of vom Stein **Rev:** Small bust half left below name

Date	F	VF	XF	Unc	BU
1981	—	—	60.00	70.00	90.00

KM# 88 20 MARK
20.9200 g., 0.5000 Silver .3360 oz. ASW **Subject:** 125th Anniversary - Birth of Clara Zetkin **Rev:** Bust of Zetkin half left

Date	F	VF	XF	Unc	BU
1982	—	—	65.00	80.00	100

KM# 94 20 MARK
20.9200 g., 0.5000 Silver .3360 oz. ASW **Subject:** 500th Anniversary - Birth of Martin Luther **Rev:** Bust of Luther holding bible half left

Date	F	VF	XF	Unc	BU
1983	—	—	600	700	750

KM# 95 20 MARK
Copper-Nickel **Subject:** 100th Anniversary - Death of Karl Marx

Date	F	VF	XF	Unc	BU
1983	—	—	12.00	20.00	30.00

KM# 100   20 MARK
20.9200 g., 0.5000 Silver .3360 oz. ASW **Subject:** 225th Anniversary - Death of Georg Friedrich Handel **Rev:** Bust of Handel half right

Date	F	VF	XF	Unc	BU
1984	—	—	160	190	220

KM# 105   20 MARK
20.9200 g., 0.5000 Silver .3360 oz. ASW **Subject:** 125th Anniversary - Death of Ernst Moritz Arndt **Rev:** Bust of Arndt half right

Date	F	VF	XF	Unc	BU
1985	—	—	130	150	175

KM# 108   20 MARK
20.9000 g., 0.6250 Silver .4200 oz. ASW **Subject:** 200th Anniversary - Birth of Jacob and Wilhelm Grimm **Rev:** "Puss 'n Boots"

Date	F	VF	XF	Unc	BU
1986	—	—	245	300	350

KM# 119.1   20 MARK
20.9000 g., 0.6250 Silver .4200 oz. ASW **Subject:** Berlin - City Seal

Date	F	VF	XF	Unc	BU
1987	—	—	425	500	575

KM# 119.2   20 MARK
20.9000 g., 0.6250 Silver .4200 oz. ASW **Rev:** Fields in seal polished

Date	F	VF	XF	Unc	BU
1987 Proof		Value: 1,500			

KM# 124   20 MARK
20.9000 g., 0.6250 Silver .4200 oz. ASW **Subject:** 100th Anniversary - Death of Carl Zeiss **Rev:** Microscope

Date	F	VF	XF	Unc	BU
1988	—	—	225	250	300

KM# 127   20 MARK
20.9000 g., 0.6250 Silver .4200 oz. ASW **Subject:** 500th Anniversary - Birth of Thomas Muntzer **Rev:** Head of Muntzer left

Date	F	VF	XF	Unc	BU
1989	—	—	80.00	95.00	110

KM# 138   20 MARK
20.9000 g., 0.6250 Silver .4200 oz. ASW **Subject:** Andreas Schluter

Date	F	VF	XF	Unc	BU
1990	—	—	90.00	130	160

KM# 139   20 MARK
Copper-Nickel **Subject:** Opening of Brandenburg Gate **Obv:** State emblem, value and legend

Date	F	VF	XF	Unc	BU
1990	—	—	7.00	10.00	15.00

KM# 139a   20 MARK
18.2000 g., 0.9990 Silver .5852 oz. ASW **Subject:** Opening of Brandenburg Gate **Obv:** State emblem, value and legend

Date	F	VF	XF	Unc	BU
1990	—	—	16.00	20.00	25.00

Great Britain

The United Kingdom of Great Britain and Northern Ireland, located off the northwest coast of the European continent, has an area of 94,227sq. mi. (244,820 sq. km.) and a population of 54 million. Capital: London. The economy is based on industrial activity and trading. Machinery, motor vehicles, chemicals, and textile yarns and fabrics are exported.

RULERS
Victoria, 1837-1901
Edward VII, 1901-1910
George V, 1910-1936
Edward VIII, 1936
George VI, 1936-1952
Elizabeth II, 1952--

MONETARY SYSTEM
Colloquial Denomination Terms
Ha'penny = 1/2 Penny
Tanner = 6 Pence
Bob = 1 Shilling
Half a Crown (Half a Dollar) = 2 Shillings 6 Pence
Dollar = 5 Shillings
Half a quid = 10 Shillings
Quid = 1 Pound
Tenner = 10 Pounds
Pony = 20 Pounds

(Until 1970)

4 Farthings = 1 Penny
12 Pence = 1 Shilling
2 Shillings = 1 Florin
5 Shillings = 1 Crown
20 Shillings = 1 Pound (Sovereign)
21 Shillings = 1 Guinea

NOTE: Pound Coinage - Strictly red, original mint luster coins in the copper series command premiums.

KINGDOM
Resumed

POUND COINAGE

KM# 737   1/4 FARTHING
Copper   **Ruler:** Victoria

Date	F	VF	XF	Unc	BU
1839-1853	15.00	30.00	75.00	150	—

KM# 737a   1/4 FARTHING
Bronzed Copper   **Ruler:** Victoria

Date	F	VF	XF	Unc	BU
1852 Proof		Value: 600			

KM# 743   1/3 FARTHING
Copper   **Ruler:** Victoria

Date	F	VF	XF	Unc	BU
1844	25.00	45.00	120	250	—

KM# 750   1/3 FARTHING
Bronze   **Ruler:** Victoria

Date	F	VF	XF	Unc	BU
1866-1885	2.50	7.00	18.00	40.00	—

KM# 791   1/3 FARTHING
0.9500 g., Bronze   **Ruler:** Edward VII **Obv:** Bust right **Rev:** Value crowned within oak wreath **Note:** Homeland style struck for Malta.

Date	F	VF	XF	Unc	BU
1902	2.50	5.00	10.00	35.00	—

KM# 823   1/3 FARTHING
0.9500 g., Bronze **Ruler:** George V **Obv:** Head left **Rev:** Crowned value within oak wreath **Note:** Homeland style struck for Malta.

Date	F	VF	XF	Unc	BU
1913	2.50	5.00	10.00	35.00	—

KM# 738   1/2 FARTHING
Copper   **Ruler:** Victoria **Note:** Although the design of the 1/2 Farthing is of the homeland type, the issues were originally struck for Ceylon; the issue was made legal tender in the United Kingdom by proclamation in 1842.

Date	F	VF	XF	Unc	BU
1839-1856	2.50	5.00	22.00	65.00	—

KM# 725   FARTHING
Copper   **Ruler:** Victoria **Obv:** Bust of Victoria left **Rev:** Britannia

Date	F	VF	XF	Unc	BU
1838-1864	5.00	9.00	30.00	85.00	—

KM# 725a   FARTHING
Bronzed Copper   **Ruler:** Victoria

Date	F	VF	XF	Unc	BU
1839-1853 Proof, rare	—	—	—	—	—

KM# 747.1   FARTHING
Bronze   **Ruler:** Victoria **Note:** Beaded border.

Date	F	VF	XF	Unc	BU
1860	2.00	6.00	30.00	90.00	—

KM# 747.2   FARTHING
Bronze   **Ruler:** Victoria **Obv:** Draped bust of Victoria left **Rev:** Britannia **Note:** Toothed border.

Date	F	VF	XF	Unc	BU
1860-1873	1.00	2.75	22.00	75.00	—

KM# 753   FARTHING
Bronze   **Ruler:** Victoria **Obv:** Mature bust

Date	F	VF	XF	Unc	BU
1874-1895	0.75	1.50	12.00	40.00	—

KM# 788.1 FARTHING
Bronze **Ruler:** Victoria

Date	F	VF	XF	Unc	BU
1895-1897	0.50	2.00	5.00	22.00	—

KM# 788.2 FARTHING
2.8000 g., Bronze **Ruler:** Victoria **Obv:** Veiled bust left **Rev:** Britannia seated right **Note:** Blackened finish.

Date	F	VF	XF	Unc	BU
1897-1901	0.30	0.50	2.00	17.00	—

KM# 792 FARTHING
Bronze **Ruler:** Edward VII **Obv:** Head right **Rev:** Britannia seated right

Date	F	VF	XF	Unc	BU
1902-1910	0.50	1.25	5.00	25.00	—

KM# 808.1 FARTHING
Bronze **Ruler:** George V **Obv:** Head left **Rev:** Britannia seated right

Date	F	VF	XF	Unc	BU
1911-1918	0.15	0.35	1.50	10.00	—

KM# 808.2 FARTHING
Bronze **Ruler:** George V **Obv:** Head left **Rev:** Britannia seated right **Note:** Bright finish.

Date	F	VF	XF	Unc	BU
1918-1925	0.20	0.40	1.00	7.50	—

KM# 825 FARTHING
Bronze **Ruler:** George V **Obv:** Head left, modified effigy **Rev:** Britannia seated right

Date	F	VF	XF	Unc	BU
1926-1936	0.15	0.35	1.00	5.00	—

KM# 843 FARTHING
Bronze **Ruler:** George VI **Obv:** Head left **Rev:** Wren

Date	F	VF	XF	Unc	BU
1937-1948	0.10	0.15	0.50	4.50	—

KM# 867 FARTHING
Bronze **Ruler:** George VI **Obv:** Head left **Rev:** Wren

Date	F	VF	XF	Unc	BU
1949-1952	0.10	0.20	0.50	6.00	—

KM# 881 FARTHING
Bronze **Ruler:** Elizabeth II **Rev:** Wren

Date	F	VF	XF	Unc	BU
1953	0.15	0.25	0.50	3.00	—

KM# 895 FARTHING
Bronze **Ruler:** Elizabeth II **Obv:** Bust right **Rev:** Wren

Date	F	VF	XF	Unc	BU
1954-1956	0.10	0.15	0.50	5.00	—

KM# 726 1/2 PENNY
Copper **Ruler:** Victoria

Date	F	VF	XF	Unc	BU
1838-1860	2.00	9.00	23.00	90.00	—

KM# 726a 1/2 PENNY
Bronzed Copper **Ruler:** Victoria

Date	F	VF	XF	Unc	BU
1839 Proof	Value: 350				

KM# 748.1   1/2 PENNY
Bronze   **Ruler:** Victoria **Note:** Beaded border.

Date	F	VF	XF	Unc	BU
1860	1.50	6.00	30.00	125	—

KM# 748.2   1/2 PENNY
Bronze   **Ruler:** Victoria **Note:** Toothed border.

Date	F	VF	XF	Unc	BU
1860-1874	1.25	5.00	28.00	100	—

KM# 754   1/2 PENNY
Bronze   **Ruler:** Victoria **Obv:** Mature bust

Date	F	VF	XF	Unc	BU
1874-1894	1.25	5.00	26.00	100	—

KM# 789   1/2 PENNY
5.7000 g., Bronze   **Ruler:** Victoria **Obv:** Veiled bust left **Rev:** Britannia seated right

Date	F	VF	XF	Unc	BU
1895-1901	0.75	2.00	6.00	30.00	—

KM# 793.1   1/2 PENNY
Bronze   **Ruler:** Edward VII **Obv:** Head right **Rev:** Britannia seated right, low horizon line

Date	F	VF	XF	Unc	BU
1902	10.00	30.00	75.00	180	—

KM# 793.2   1/2 PENNY
Bronze   **Ruler:** Edward VII **Obv:** Head right **Rev:** Britannia seated right, high horizon line

Date	F	VF	XF	Unc	BU
1902-1910	0.50	1.25	5.00	25.00	—

KM# 809   1/2 PENNY
Bronze   **Ruler:** George V **Obv:** Head left **Rev:** Britannia seated right

Date	F	VF	XF	Unc	BU
1911-1925	0.50	1.25	5.00	25.00	—

KM# 824   1/2 PENNY
Bronze   **Ruler:** George V **Obv:** Head left, modified effigy **Rev:** Britannia seated right

Date	F	VF	XF	Unc	BU
1925-1927	0.75	1.50	5.00	35.00	—

KM# 837   1/2 PENNY
Bronze   **Ruler:** George V **Obv:** Smaller head left **Rev:** Britannia seated right

Date	F	VF	XF	Unc	BU
1928-1936	0.25	0.50	2.50	19.00	—

KM# 844   1/2 PENNY
Bronze   **Ruler:** George VI **Obv:** Head left **Rev:** The Golden Hind

Date	F	VF	XF	Unc	BU
1937-1948	0.10	0.20	0.50	7.00	—

KM# 868   1/2 PENNY
Bronze   **Ruler:** George VI **Obv:** Legend without IND IMP **Rev:** The Golden Hind

Date	F	VF	XF	Unc	BU
1949-1952	0.10	0.25	1.00	10.00	—

KM# 882   1/2 PENNY
Bronze **Ruler:** Elizabeth II **Obv:** Bust right **Rev:** The Golden Hind

Date	F	VF	XF	Unc	BU
1953	0.20	0.40	1.00	5.00	—

KM# 896   1/2 PENNY
Bronze **Ruler:** Elizabeth II **Obv:** Legend without BRITT OMN
Rev: The Golden Hind

Date	F	VF	XF	Unc	BU
1954-1970	0.10	0.10	0.10	0.55	—

KM# 727   PENNY
0.4713 g., 0.9250 Silver .0140 oz. ASW **Ruler:** Victoria

Date	F	VF	XF	Unc	BU
1838-1887	—	—	—	35.00	60.00

KM# 739   PENNY
Copper **Ruler:** Victoria

Date	F	VF	XF	Unc	BU
1841-1860/59	2.00	10.00	70.00	125	—

KM# 739a   PENNY
Bronzed Copper **Ruler:** Victoria

Date	F	VF	XF	Unc	BU
1839-1841 Proof	Value: 900				

KM# 749.1   PENNY
Bronze **Ruler:** Victoria **Note:** Beaded border.

Date	F	VF	XF	Unc	BU
1860	10.00	27.00	75.00	375	—

KM# 749.2   PENNY
Bronze **Ruler:** Victoria **Note:** Toothed border, wtihout die number.

Date	F	VF	XF	Unc	BU
1860-1874	2.00	12.00	50.00	250	—

KM# 749.3   PENNY
Bronze **Ruler:** Victoria **Note:** Toothed border, wtih die number.

Date	F	VF	XF	Unc	BU
1863	100	180	450	1,200	—

KM# 755   PENNY
Bronze **Ruler:** Victoria **Obv:** Mature bust, without die number

Date	F	VF	XF	Unc	BU
1874-1894	2.50	8.50	30.00	125	—

KM# 770   PENNY
0.4713 g., 0.9250 Silver .0140 oz. ASW **Ruler:** Victoria

Date	F	VF	XF	Unc	BU
1888-1892	—	—	—	25.00	45.00

KM# 775   PENNY
0.4713 g., 0.9250 Silver .0140 oz. ASW **Ruler:** Victoria **Obv:**
Veiled bust left **Rev:** Crowned value within oak wreath

Date	F	VF	XF	Unc	BU
1893-1901	—	—	—	20.00	35.00

KM# 790 PENNY
9.4500 g., Bronze **Ruler:** Victoria **Obv:** Veiled bust left **Rev:** Britannia seated right

Date	F	VF	XF	Unc	BU
1895-1901	0.30	1.00	10.00	25.00	—

KM# 794.1 PENNY
9.4500 g., Bronze **Ruler:** Edward VII **Obv:** Head right **Rev:** Britannia seated right, low horizon line

Date	F	VF	XF	Unc	BU
1902	5.00	20.00	75.00	180	—

KM# 794.2 PENNY
Bronze **Ruler:** Edward VII **Obv:** Head right **Rev:** Britannia seated right, high horizon line

Date	F	VF	XF	Unc	BU
1902-1910	0.35	1.50	5.00	30.00	—

KM# 795 PENNY
0.4713 g., 0.9250 Silver .0140 oz. ASW **Ruler:** Edward VII **Obv:** Head right **Rev:** Crowned value within oak wreath

Date	F	VF	XF	Unc	BU
1902-1910	—	—	—	25.00	40.00

KM# 810 PENNY
9.4500 g., Bronze **Ruler:** George V **Obv:** Head left **Rev:** Britannia seated right **Note:** Fully struck and orginal mint lustre coins command a premium.

Date	F	VF	XF	Unc	BU
1911-1926	0.30	1.00	8.00	35.00	—

KM# 811 PENNY
0.4713 g., 0.9250 Silver .0140 oz. ASW **Ruler:** George V **Obv:** Head left **Rev:** Crowned value within oak wreath

Date	F	VF	XF	Unc	BU
1911-1920	—	—	—	35.00	45.00

KM# 811a PENNY
0.4713 g., 0.5000 Silver .0076 oz. ASW **Ruler:** George V **Obv:** Head left **Rev:** Crowned value within oak wreath

Date	F	VF	XF	Unc	BU
1921-1927	—	—	—	35.00	45.00

KM# 826 PENNY
Bronze **Ruler:** George V **Obv:** Modified head left **Rev:** Britannia seated right

Date	F	VF	XF	Unc	BU
1926-1927	0.35	0.75	8.00	30.00	—

KM# 838 PENNY
Bronze **Ruler:** George V **Obv:** Smaller head left **Rev:** Britannia seated right

Date	F	VF	XF	Unc	BU
1928-1936	0.25	0.40	5.00	25.00	—

KM# 839 PENNY
0.4713 g., 0.5000 Silver .0076 oz. ASW **Ruler:** George V **Obv:** Modified head left **Rev:** Crowned value within oak wreath

Date	F	VF	XF	Unc	BU
1928-1936	—	—	—	45.00	50.00

KM# 845 PENNY
9.4500 g., Bronze **Ruler:** George VI **Obv:** Head left **Rev:** Britannia seated right

Date	F	VF	XF	Unc	BU
1937-1948	0.15	0.25	0.75	7.50	—

KM# 846 PENNY
0.4713 g., 0.5000 Silver .0076 oz. ASW **Ruler:** George VI **Obv:**
Head left **Rev:** Crowned value within oak wreath

Date	F	VF	XF	Unc	BU
1937-1946	—	—	—	35.00	40.00

KM# 846a PENNY
0.4713 g., 0.9250 Silver .0140 oz. ASW **Ruler:** George VI **Obv:**
Head left **Rev:** Crowned value within oak wreath

Date	F	VF	XF	Unc	BU
1947-1948	—	—	—	40.00	45.00

KM# 869 PENNY
Bronze **Ruler:** George VI **Obv:** Head left **Rev:** Britannia seated right

Date	F	VF	XF	Unc	BU
1949-1951	0.20	0.35	0.75	7.50	—

KM# 870 PENNY
0.4713 g., 0.9250 Silver .0140 oz. ASW **Ruler:** George VI **Obv:**
Head left **Rev:** Crowned value within oak wreath

Date	F	VF	XF	Unc	BU
1949-1952	—	—	—	40.00	45.00

KM# 883 PENNY
Bronze **Ruler:** Elizabeth II **Obv:** Mary Gillick **Rev:** Britannia
seated right

Date	F	VF	XF	Unc	BU
1953	0.75	1.25	5.00	18.00	—

KM# 884 PENNY
0.4713 g., 0.9250 Silver .0140 oz. ASW **Ruler:** Elizabeth II **Obv:**
Bust right **Rev:** Britannia seated right

Date	F	VF	XF	Unc	BU
1953	—	—	—	170	185

KM# 898 PENNY
0.4713 g., 0.9250 Silver .0140 oz. ASW **Ruler:** Elizabeth II **Obv:**
Bust right **Rev:** Crowned value within oak wreath

Date	F	VF	XF	Unc	BU
1954-2006	—	—	—	35.00	40.00

KM# 897 PENNY
Bronze **Ruler:** Elizabeth II **Obv:** Bust right **Rev:** Britannia seated
right

Date	F	VF	XF	Unc	BU
1954-1970	—	0.10	0.10	0.30	—

KM# 728 1-1/2 PENCE
0.7069 g., 0.9250 Silver .0210 oz. ASW **Ruler:** Victoria

Date	F	VF	XF	Unc	BU
1838-1870	3.50	7.00	25.00	50.00	—

KM# 729 2 PENCE
0.9426 g., 0.9250 Silver .0280 oz. ASW **Ruler:** Victoria

Date	F	VF	XF	Unc	BU
1838-1887	2.00	4.00	10.00	20.00	60.00

KM# 771 2 PENCE
0.9426 g., 0.9250 Silver .0280 oz. ASW **Ruler:** Victoria

Date	F	VF	XF	Unc	BU
1888-1892	—	—	—	25.00	45.00

KM# 776 2 PENCE
0.9426 g., 0.9250 Silver .0280 oz. ASW **Ruler:** Victoria **Obv:**
Veiled bust left **Rev:** Crowned value within oak wreath

Date	F	VF	XF	Unc	BU
1893-1901	—	—	—	20.00	35.00

KM# 796 2 PENCE
0.9426 g., 0.9250 Silver .0280 oz. ASW **Ruler:** Edward VII **Obv:**
Head right **Rev:** Crowned value within oak wreath

Date	F	VF	XF	Unc	BU
1902-1910	—	—	—	25.00	40.00

KM# 812 2 PENCE
0.9426 g., 0.9250 Silver .0280 oz. ASW **Ruler:** George V **Obv:**
Head left **Rev:** Crowned value within oak wreath

Date	F	VF	XF	Unc	BU
1911-1920	—	—	—	45.00	50.00

KM# 812a 2 PENCE
0.9426 g., 0.5000 Silver .0152 oz. ASW **Ruler:** George V **Obv:**
Head left **Rev:** Crowned value within oak wreath

Date	F	VF	XF	Unc	BU
1921-1927	—	—	—	45.00	50.00

KM# 840   2 PENCE
0.9426 g., 0.5000 Silver .0152 oz. ASW **Ruler:** George V **Obv:**
Modified head left **Rev:** Crowned value within oak wreath

Date	F	VF	XF	Unc	BU
1928-1936	—	—	—	50.00	60.00

KM# 847   2 PENCE
0.9426 g., 0.5000 Silver .0152 oz. ASW **Ruler:** George VI **Obv:**
Head left **Rev:** Crowned value within oak wreath

Date	F	VF	XF	Unc	BU
1937-1946	—	—	—	35.00	40.00

KM# 847a   2 PENCE
0.9426 g., 0.9250 Silver .0280 oz. ASW **Ruler:** George VI **Obv:**
Head left **Rev:** Crowned value within oak wreath

Date	F	VF	XF	Unc	BU
1947-1948	—	—	—	40.00	45.00

KM# 871   2 PENCE
0.9426 g., 0.9250 Silver .0280 oz. ASW **Ruler:** George VI **Obv:**
Head left **Rev:** Crowned value within oak wreath

Date	F	VF	XF	Unc	BU
1949-1952	—	—	—	40.00	45.00

KM# 885   2 PENCE
0.9426 g., 0.9250 Silver .0280 oz. ASW **Ruler:** Elizabeth II **Obv:**
Bust right **Rev:** Crowned value within oak wreath

Date	F	VF	XF	Unc	BU
1953	—	—	—	170	185

KM# 899   2 PENCE
0.9426 g., 0.9250 Silver .0280 oz. ASW **Ruler:** Elizabeth II **Obv:**
Legend without BRITT OMN

Date	F	VF	XF	Unc	BU
1954-2006	—	—	—	35.00	40.00

KM# 730   3 PENCE
1.4138 g., 0.9250 Silver .0420 oz. ASW **Ruler:** Victoria

Date	F	VF	XF	Unc	BU
1838-1887	2.25	6.00	35.00	75.00	145

KM# 758   3 PENCE
1.4138 g., 0.9250 Silver .0420 oz. ASW **Ruler:** Victoria

Date	F	VF	XF	Unc	BU
1887-1893	1.25	2.25	6.50	15.00	—

KM# 777   3 PENCE
1.4138 g., 0.9250 Silver .0420 oz. ASW **Ruler:** Victoria **Obv:**
Veiled bust left **Rev:** Crowned value within oak wreath

Date	F	VF	XF	Unc	BU
1893-1901	1.00	2.00	5.00	20.00	—

KM# 797.1   3 PENCE
1.4138 g., 0.9250 Silver .0420 oz. ASW **Ruler:** Edward VII **Obv:**
Head right **Rev:** Crowned value within oak wreath **Note:** The
prooflike coins come with a mirror or satin finish.

Date	F	VF	XF	Unc	BU
1902-1904	0.75	4.00	8.00	18.00	—

KM# 797.2   3 PENCE
1.4138 g., 0.9250 Silver .0420 oz. ASW **Ruler:** Edward VII **Obv:**
Head right **Rev:** Crowned value within oak wreath

Date	F	VF	XF	Unc	BU
1904-1910	0.75	1.50	10.00	30.00	—

KM# 813   3 PENCE
1.4138 g., 0.9250 Silver .0420 oz. ASW **Ruler:** George V **Obv:**
Head left **Rev:** Crowned value within oak wreath

Date	F	VF	XF	Unc	BU
1911-1920	0.50	1.00	3.00	15.00	—

KM# 813a   3 PENCE
1.4138 g., 0.5000 Silver .0227 oz. ASW **Ruler:** George V **Obv:**
Head left **Rev:** Crowned value within oak wreath

Date	F	VF	XF	Unc	BU
1920-1927	0.65	1.00	3.00	18.00	60.00

KM# 827   3 PENCE
1.4138 g., 0.5000 Silver .0227 oz. ASW **Ruler:** George V **Obv:**
Modified head left **Rev:** Crowned value within oak wreath

Date	F	VF	XF	Unc	BU
1926-1936	0.75	1.75	8.00	45.00	50.00

KM# 831   3 PENCE
1.4138 g., 0.5000 Silver .0227 oz. ASW **Ruler:** George V **Obv:**
Head left **Rev:** Three oak leaves and acorns

Date	F	VF	XF	Unc	BU
1927-1936	BV	0.50	1.25	12.00	—

KM# 848 3 PENCE
1.4138 g., 0.5000 Silver .0227 oz. ASW **Ruler:** George VI **Obv:** Head left **Rev:** St. George shield on Tudor rose

Date	F	VF	XF	Unc	BU
1937-1945	BV	0.50	1.25	10.00	—

KM# 849 3 PENCE
Nickel-Brass **Ruler:** George VI **Obv:** Head left **Rev:** Thrift plant (allium porrum) **Shape:** 12-sided

Date	F	VF	XF	Unc	BU
1937-1948	0.25	0.40	2.00	12.00	—

KM# 850 3 PENCE
1.4138 g., 0.5000 Silver .0227 oz. ASW **Ruler:** George VI **Obv:** Head left **Rev:** Crowned value within oak wreath

Date	F	VF	XF	Unc	BU
1937-1946	—	—	—	45.00	50.00

KM# 850a 3 PENCE
1.4138 g., 0.9250 Silver .0420 oz. ASW **Ruler:** George VI **Obv:** Head left **Rev:** Crowned value within oak wreath

Date	F	VF	XF	Unc	BU
1947-1948	—	—	—	50.00	55.00

KM# 872 3 PENCE
1.4138 g., 0.9250 Silver .0420 oz. ASW **Ruler:** George VI **Obv:** Head left **Rev:** Crowned value within oak wreath

Date	F	VF	XF	Unc	BU
1949-1952	—	—	—	50.00	55.00

KM# 873 3 PENCE
Nickel-Brass **Ruler:** George VI **Obv:** Head left **Rev:** Thrift plant (allium porrum)

Date	F	VF	XF	Unc	BU
1949-1952	0.25	0.50	5.00	19.00	—

KM# 886 3 PENCE
Nickel-Brass **Ruler:** Elizabeth II **Obv:** Bust right **Rev:** Crowned portcullis

Date	F	VF	XF	Unc	BU
1953	0.25	0.50	0.75	6.00	—

KM# 887 3 PENCE
1.4138 g., 0.9250 Silver .0420 oz. ASW **Ruler:** Elizabeth II **Obv:** Bust right **Rev:** Crowned portcullis

Date	F	VF	XF	Unc	BU
1953	—	—	—	180	200

KM# 900 3 PENCE
Nickel-Brass **Ruler:** Elizabeth II **Obv:** Bust right **Rev:** Crowned portcullis **Shape:** 12-sided

Date	F	VF	XF	Unc	BU
1954-1970	—	0.15	0.25	0.50	—

KM# 901 3 PENCE
1.4138 g., 0.9250 Silver .0420 oz. ASW **Ruler:** Elizabeth II **Obv:** Bust right **Rev:** Crowned value within oak wreath

Date	F	VF	XF	Unc	BU
1954-2006	—	—	—	45.00	50.00

KM# 731.1 4 PENCE (Groat)
1.8851 g., 0.9250 Silver .0561 oz. ASW **Ruler:** Victoria **Note:** This issue was produced for circulation in both Great Britain and British Guiana.

Date	F	VF	XF	Unc	BU
1838-1862	2.25	8.00	30.00	80.00	—

KM# 731.2 4 PENCE (Groat)
1.8851 g., 0.9250 Silver .0561 oz. ASW **Ruler:** Victoria **Edge:** Plain

Date	F	VF	XF	Unc	BU
1838-1839 Proof	Value: 200				

KM# 732 4 PENCE (Groat)
1.8851 g., 0.9250 Silver .0561 oz. ASW **Ruler:** Victoria

Date	F	VF	XF	Unc	BU
1838-1887	—	—	—	60.00	100

KM# 772 4 PENCE (Groat)
1.8851 g., 0.9250 Silver .0561 oz. ASW **Ruler:** Victoria **Note:** This piece was exclusively for use in British Guiana and the West Indies.

Date	F	VF	XF	Unc	BU
1888	9.00	25.00	50.00	100	—

KM# 773   4 PENCE (Groat)
1.8851 g., 0.9250 Silver .0561 oz. ASW **Ruler:** Victoria

Date	F	VF	XF	Unc	BU
1888-1892	—	—	—	35.00	60.00

KM# 778   4 PENCE (Groat)
1.8851 g., 0.9250 Silver .0561 oz. ASW **Ruler:** Victoria **Obv:**
Veiled bust left **Rev:** Crowned value within oak wreath

Date	F	VF	XF	Unc	BU
1893-1901	—	—	—	30.00	50.00

KM# 798   4 PENCE (Groat)
1.8851 g., 0.9250 Silver .0561 oz. ASW **Ruler:** Edward VII **Obv:**
Head left **Rev:** Crowned value within oak wreath

Date	F	VF	XF	Unc	BU
1902-1910	—	—	—	30.00	45.00

KM# 814   4 PENCE (Groat)
1.8851 g., 0.9250 Silver .0561 oz. ASW **Ruler:** George V **Obv:**
Head left **Rev:** Crowned value within oak wreath

Date	F	VF	XF	Unc	BU
1911-1920	—	—	—	45.00	50.00

KM# 814a   4 PENCE (Groat)
1.8851 g., 0.5000 Silver .0303 oz. ASW **Ruler:** George V **Obv:**
Head left **Rev:** Crowned value within oak wreath

Date	F	VF	XF	Unc	BU
1921-1927	—	—	—	45.00	50.00

KM# 841   4 PENCE (Groat)
1.8851 g., 0.5000 Silver .0303 oz. ASW **Ruler:** George V **Obv:**
Modified head left **Rev:** Crowned value within oak wreath

Date	F	VF	XF	Unc	BU
1928-1936	—	—	—	45.00	50.00

KM# 851   4 PENCE (Groat)
1.8851 g., 0.5000 Silver .0303 oz. ASW **Ruler:** George VI **Obv:**
Head left **Rev:** Crowned value within oak wreath

Date	F	VF	XF	Unc	BU
1937-1946	—	—	—	45.00	50.00

KM# 851a   4 PENCE (Groat)
1.8851 g., 0.9250 Silver .0561 oz. ASW **Ruler:** George VI **Obv:**
Head left **Rev:** Crowned value within oak wreath

Date	F	VF	XF	Unc	BU
1947-1948	—	—	—	50.00	55.00

KM# 874   4 PENCE (Groat)
1.8851 g., 0.9250 Silver .0561 oz. ASW **Ruler:** George VI **Obv:**
Head left **Rev:** Crowned value within oak wreath

Date	F	VF	XF	Unc	BU
1949-1952	—	—	—	50.00	55.00

KM# 888   4 PENCE (Groat)
1.8851 g., 0.9250 Silver .0561 oz. ASW **Ruler:** Elizabeth II **Obv:**
Bust right **Rev:** Crowned value within oak wreath

Date	F	VF	XF	Unc	BU
1953	—	—	—	180	200

KM# 902   4 PENCE (Groat)
1.8851 g., 0.9250 Silver .0561 oz. ASW **Ruler:** Elizabeth II **Obv:**
Bust right **Obv. Inscription:** without BRITT OMN **Rev:** Crowned
value within oak wreath

Date	F	VF	XF	Unc	BU
1954-2006	—	—	—	45.00	50.00

KM# 733.1   6 PENCE
3.0100 g., 0.9250 Silver .0895 oz. ASW **Ruler:** Victoria **Rev:**
Without die number

Date	F	VF	XF	Unc	BU
1838-1866	5.50	15.00	85.00	135	—

KM# 733.2   6 PENCE
3.0100 g., 0.9250 Silver .0895 oz. ASW **Ruler:** Victoria **Rev:** With
die number

Date	F	VF	XF	Unc	BU
1864-1866	8.00	19.00	70.00	175	—

KM# 751.1   6 PENCE
3.0100 g., 0.9250 Silver .0895 oz. ASW **Ruler:** Victoria **Obv:**
New portrait **Rev:** With die number

Date	F	VF	XF	Unc	BU
1867-1878/7	6.00	15.00	75.00	150	—

KM# 751.2   6 PENCE
3.0100 g., 0.9250 Silver .0895 oz. ASW **Ruler:** Victoria **Rev:**
Without die number

Date	F	VF	XF	Unc	BU
1871-1880	9.00	20.00	60.00	150	—

KM# 757 6 PENCE
3.0100 g., 0.9250 Silver .0895 oz. ASW **Ruler:** Victoria **Obv:**
New portrait, longer hair waves

Date	F	VF	XF	Unc	BU
1880-1887	5.00	12.00	35.00	85.00	—

KM# 759 6 PENCE
3.0100 g., 0.9250 Silver .0895 oz. ASW **Ruler:** Victoria

Date	F	VF	XF	Unc	BU
1887	2.50	6.00	12.00	28.00	—

KM# 760 6 PENCE
3.0100 g., 0.9250 Silver .0895 oz. ASW **Ruler:** Victoria

Date	F	VF	XF	Unc	BU
1887-1893	2.00	6.00	12.00	25.00	—

KM# 779 6 PENCE
3.0100 g., 0.9250 Silver .0895 oz. ASW **Ruler:** Victoria **Obv:**
Veiled bust left **Rev:** Crowned value within oak wreath

Date	F	VF	XF	Unc	BU
1893-1901	4.00	7.00	19.00	45.00	—

KM# 799 6 PENCE
3.0100 g., 0.9250 Silver .0895 oz. ASW **Ruler:** Edward VII **Obv:**
Head right **Rev:** Crowned value within oak wreath

Date	F	VF	XF	Unc	BU
1902-1910	3.00	5.00	25.00	50.00	—

KM# 815 6 PENCE
3.0100 g., 0.9250 Silver .0895 oz. ASW **Ruler:** George V **Obv:**
Head left **Rev:** Lion atop crown

Date	F	VF	XF	Unc	BU
1911-1920	2.00	8.00	15.00	30.00	—

KM# 815a.1 6 PENCE
2.8276 g., 0.5000 Silver .0455 oz. ASW **Ruler:** George V **Obv:**
Head left **Rev:** Lion atop crown **Note:** Narrow rim.

Date	F	VF	XF	Unc	BU
1920-1925	2.00	4.00	12.00	30.00	—

KM# 815a.2 6 PENCE
2.8276 g., 0.5000 Silver .0455 oz. ASW **Ruler:** George V **Obv:**
Head left **Rev:** Lion atop crown **Note:** Wide rim.

Date	F	VF	XF	Unc	BU
1925-1926	2.00	4.00	12.00	35.00	—

KM# 828 6 PENCE
2.8276 g., 0.5000 Silver .0455 oz. ASW **Ruler:** George V **Obv:**
Modified head left **Rev:** Lion atop crown

Date	F	VF	XF	Unc	BU
1926-1927	BV	3.00	10.00	22.50	—

KM# 832 6 PENCE
2.8276 g., 0.5000 Silver .0455 oz. ASW **Ruler:** George V **Obv:**
Head left **Rev:** Six oak leaves and acorns **Note:** Varieties in edge
milling exist.

Date	F	VF	XF	Unc	BU
1927-1936	BV	2.00	4.50	15.00	—

KM# 852 6 PENCE
2.8276 g., 0.5000 Silver .0455 oz. ASW **Ruler:** George VI **Obv:**
Head left **Rev:** Crowned monogram

Date	F	VF	XF	Unc	BU
1937-1946	—	BV	1.00	10.00	—

KM# 862 6 PENCE
Copper-Nickel **Ruler:** George VI **Obv:** Head left **Rev:** Crowned
monogram

Date	F	VF	XF	Unc	BU
1947-1948	—	0.20	0.50	5.00	—

KM# 875 6 PENCE
Copper-Nickel **Ruler:** George VI **Obv:** Head left **Rev:** Crowned
monogram

Date	F	VF	XF	Unc	BU
1949-1952	1.25	0.20	1.00	10.00	—

KM# 889   6 PENCE
Copper-Nickel   **Ruler:** Elizabeth II **Obv:** Bust right **Rev:** Flora - leek, rose, thistle and shamrock

Date	F	VF	XF	Unc	BU
1953	—	0.15	0.50	2.50	—

KM# 903   6 PENCE
Copper-Nickel   **Ruler:** Elizabeth II **Obv:** Bust right **Rev:** Flora - leek, rose, thistle and shamrock

Date	F	VF	XF	Unc	BU
1954-1970	—	0.10	0.20	1.00	—

KM# 734.1   SHILLING
5.6552 g., 0.9250 Silver .1682 oz. ASW   **Ruler:** Victoria **Obv:** High relief **Note:** Without die number.

Date	F	VF	XF	Unc	BU
1838-1863	12.00	26.00	80.00	200	—

KM# 734.3   SHILLING
5.6552 g., 0.9250 Silver .1682 oz. ASW   **Ruler:** Victoria **Note:** With die number.

Date	F	VF	XF	Unc	BU
1864-1867	11.00	25.00	85.00	225	—

KM# 734.2   SHILLING
5.6552 g., 0.9250 Silver .1682 oz. ASW   **Ruler:** Victoria **Obv:** Low relief **Note:** With die number.

Date	F	VF	XF	Unc	BU
1867-1879	12.00	26.00	80.00	175	—

KM# 734.4   SHILLING
5.6552 g., 0.9250 Silver .1682 oz. ASW   **Ruler:** Victoria **Note:** Without die number.

Date	F	VF	XF	Unc	BU
1879-1887	11.00	22.00	75.00	150	—

KM# 761   SHILLING
5.6552 g., 0.9250 Silver .1682 oz. ASW   **Ruler:** Victoria **Obv:** Small bust

Date	F	VF	XF	Unc	BU
1887-1889	3.50	6.00	12.00	35.00	—

KM# 774   SHILLING
5.6552 g., 0.9250 Silver .1682 oz. ASW   **Ruler:** Victoria **Obv:** Large bust

Date	F	VF	XF	Unc	BU
1889-1892	6.00	10.00	50.00	90.00	—

KM# 780   SHILLING
5.6552 g., 0.9250 Silver .1682 oz. ASW   **Ruler:** Victoria **Obv:** Veiled bust left **Rev:** Crowned shields of England, Scotland and Ireland

Date	F	VF	XF	Unc	BU
1893-1901	4.00	7.50	35.00	60.00	—

KM# 800   SHILLING
5.6552 g., 0.9250 Silver .1682 oz. ASW   **Ruler:** Edward VII **Obv:** Head right **Rev:** Lion atop crown

Date	F	VF	XF	Unc	BU
1902-1910	3.00	10.00	45.00	80.00	—

KM# 816 SHILLING
5.6552 g., 0.9250 Silver .1682 oz. ASW **Ruler:** George V **Obv:**
Head left **Rev:** Lion atop crown **Note:** Fully struck 1914-1918
pieces command a premium.

Date	F	VF	XF	Unc	BU
1911-1919	2.00	3.50	20.00	40.00	—

KM# 816a SHILLING
5.6552 g., 0.5000 Silver .0909 oz. ASW **Ruler:** George V **Obv:**
Head left **Rev:** Lion atop crown

Date	F	VF	XF	Unc	BU
1920-1926	2.00	3.50	21.00	50.00	—

KM# 829 SHILLING
5.6552 g., 0.5000 Silver .0909 oz. ASW **Ruler:** George V **Obv:**
Modified head left **Rev:** Lion atop crown

Date	F	VF	XF	Unc	BU
1926-1927	1.50	3.50	18.00	50.00	—

KM# 833 SHILLING
5.6552 g., 0.5000 Silver .0909 oz. ASW **Ruler:** George V **Obv:**
Head left **Rev:** English crest, Lion atop crown

Date	F	VF	XF	Unc	BU
1927-1936	BV	2.00	8.00	25.00	—

KM# 853 SHILLING
5.6552 g., 0.5000 Silver .0909 oz. ASW **Ruler:** George VI **Obv:**
Head left **Rev:** English crest, lion atop crown

Date	F	VF	XF	Unc	BU
1937-1946	—	BV	1.25	8.00	—

KM# 854 SHILLING
5.6552 g., 0.5000 Silver .0909 oz. ASW **Ruler:** George VI **Obv:**

Head left **Rev:** Scottish crest, lion seated atop crown, holding
sowrd and sceptre

Date	F	VF	XF	Unc	BU
1937-1946	—	BV	1.50	8.00	—

KM# 863 SHILLING
Copper-Nickel **Ruler:** George VI **Rev:** English crest

Date	F	VF	XF	Unc	BU
1947-1948	0.10	0.20	1.00	6.00	—

KM# 864 SHILLING
Copper-Nickel **Ruler:** George VI **Rev:** Scottish crest, lion seated
atop crown, holding sword and sceptre

Date	F	VF	XF	Unc	BU
1947-1948	0.10	0.20	1.00	6.00	—

KM# 876 SHILLING
Copper-Nickel **Ruler:** George VI **Obv:** Legend without IND IMP
Rev: English crest, lion atop crown

Date	F	VF	XF	Unc	BU
1949-1952	0.10	0.25	1.50	15.00	—

KM# 877 SHILLING
Copper-Nickel **Ruler:** George VI **Rev:** Scottish crest, lion seated
atop crown, holding sword and shield

Date	F	VF	XF	Unc	BU
1949-1951	0.10	0.25	1.50	19.00	—

KM# 890 SHILLING
Copper-Nickel **Ruler:** Elizabeth II **Rev:** Crowned English shield

Date	F	VF	XF	Unc	BU
1953	—	0.15	0.50	4.50	—

KM# 891 SHILLING

Copper-Nickel **Ruler:** Elizabeth II **Obv:** Bust right **Rev:** Crowned
Scottish shield

Date	F	VF	XF	Unc	BU
1953	—	0.15	0.50	5.00	—

KM# 904 SHILLING

Copper-Nickel **Ruler:** Elizabeth II **Obv:** Bust right **Rev:** Crowned
English shield

Date	F	VF	XF	Unc	BU
1954-1970	0.25	0.15	0.25	1.25	—

KM# 905 SHILLING

Copper-Nickel **Ruler:** Elizabeth II **Obv:** Bust right **Rev:** Crowned
Scottish shield

Date	F	VF	XF	Unc	BU
1954-1970	0.50	0.15	0.25	1.25	—

KM# 745 FLORIN (Two Shillings)

11.3104 g., 0.9250 Silver .3364 oz. ASW **Ruler:** Victoria

Date	F	VF	XF	Unc	BU
1848-1849	23.00	45.00	125	325	—

KM# 746.1 FLORIN (Two Shillings)

11.3104 g., 0.9250 Silver .3364 oz. ASW **Ruler:** Victoria **Obv:**
Without die number **Note:** Gothic type.

Date	F	VF	XF	Unc	BU
1851-1863	21.00	50.00	150	275	—

KM# 746.3 FLORIN (Two Shillings)

11.3104 g., 0.9250 Silver .3364 oz. ASW **Ruler:** Victoria **Obv:**
With die number

Date	F	VF	XF	Unc	BU
1864-1867	23.00	40.00	150	350	—

KM# 746.2 FLORIN (Two Shillings)

11.3104 g., 0.9250 Silver .3364 oz. ASW **Ruler:** Victoria **Obv:**
With die number

Date	F	VF	XF	Unc	BU
1868-1878	22.00	50.00	150	250	—

KM# 746.4 FLORIN (Two Shillings)

11.3104 g., 0.9250 Silver .3364 oz. ASW **Ruler:** Victoria **Obv:**
Without die number **Note:** Varieties exist.

Date	F	VF	XF	Unc	BU
1877-1887	19.00	32.00	175	275	—

KM# 762 FLORIN (Two Shillings)

11.3104 g., 0.9250 Silver .3364 oz. ASW **Ruler:** Victoria

Date	F	VF	XF	Unc	BU
1887-1892	6.00	10.00	30.00	75.00	—

KM# 781 FLORIN (Two Shillings)
11.3104 g., 0.9250 Silver .3364 oz. ASW **Ruler:** Victoria **Obv:**
Veiled bust left **Rev:** Crown above shields of England, Scotland
and Ireland

Date	F	VF	XF	Unc	BU
1893-1901	6.00	12.00	60.00	100	—

KM# 801 FLORIN (Two Shillings)
11.3104 g., 0.9250 Silver .3364 oz. ASW **Ruler:** Edward VII **Obv:**
Head right **Rev:** Britannia standing

Date	F	VF	XF	Unc	BU
1902-1910	8.00	20.00	60.00	120	—

KM# 817 FLORIN (Two Shillings)
11.3104 g., 0.9250 Silver .3364 oz. ASW **Ruler:** George V **Obv:**
Head left **Rev:** Cross of crowned shield, sceptres in angles

Date	F	VF	XF	Unc	BU
1911-1919	BV	6.00	25.00	60.00	—

KM# 817a FLORIN (Two Shillings)
11.3104 g., 0.5000 Silver .1818 oz. ASW **Ruler:** George V **Obv:**
Head left **Rev:** Cross of crowned shields, sceptres in angles

Date	F	VF	XF	Unc	BU
1920-1926	2.00	3.50	23.00	45.00	—

KM# 834 FLORIN (Two Shillings)
11.3104 g., 0.5000 Silver .1818 oz. ASW **Ruler:** George V **Obv:**
Head left **Rev:** Cross of crowned sceptres, shields in angles

Date	F	VF	XF	Unc	BU
1927-1936	BV	2.25	11.50	25.00	—

KM# 855 FLORIN (Two Shillings)
11.3104 g., 0.5000 Silver .1818 oz. ASW **Ruler:** George VI **Obv:**
Head left **Rev:** Crowned rose, thistle and shamrock flanking

Date	F	VF	XF	Unc	BU
1937-1946	—	BV	3.00	10.00	—

KM# 865 FLORIN (Two Shillings)
Copper-Nickel **Ruler:** George VI **Obv:** Head left **Rev:** Crowned
rose, thistle and shamrock flanking

Date	F	VF	XF	Unc	BU
1947-1948	0.20	0.35	1.00	10.00	—

KM# 878 FLORIN (Two Shillings)
Copper-Nickel **Ruler:** George VI **Obv:** Head left **Rev:** Crowned
rose, thistle and shamrock flanking

Date	F	VF	XF	Unc	BU
1949-1951	0.20	0.35	1.00	18.00	—

KM# 892 FLORIN (Two Shillings)
Copper-Nickel **Ruler:** Elizabeth II **Obv:** Bust right **Rev:** Tudor
rose at center, thistle, leek and shamrock wreath around

Date	F	VF	XF	Unc	BU
1953	0.25	0.50	1.00	8.00	—

KM# 906 FLORIN (Two Shillings)
Copper-Nickel **Ruler:** Elizabeth II **Obv:** Bust right **Rev:** Tudor rose at center, thistle, leek and shamrock wreath around

Date	F	VF	XF	Unc	BU
1954-1970	0.20	0.20	0.30	2.00	—

KM# 740 1/2 CROWN
14.1380 g., 0.9250 Silver .4205 oz. ASW **Ruler:** Victoria

Date	F	VF	XF	Unc	BU
1839-1864	25.00	60.00	375	650	—

KM# 756 1/2 CROWN
14.1380 g., 0.9250 Silver .4205 oz. ASW **Ruler:** Victoria **Obv:** Second young head

Date	F	VF	XF	Unc	BU
1874-1887	17.00	40.00	125	375	—

KM# 764 1/2 CROWN
14.1380 g., 0.9250 Silver .4205 oz. ASW **Ruler:** Victoria

Date	F	VF	XF	Unc	BU
1887-1892	9.00	15.00	26.00	80.00	—

KM# 782 1/2 CROWN
14.1380 g., 0.9250 Silver .4205 oz. ASW **Ruler:** Victoria **Obv:** Veiled bust left **Rev:** Crowned spade shield

Date	F	VF	XF	Unc	BU
1893-1901	16.00	26.00	40.00	150	—

KM# 802 1/2 CROWN
14.1380 g., 0.9250 Silver .4205 oz. ASW **Ruler:** Edward VII **Obv:** Head right **Rev:** Crowned shield within Garter band **Note:** Particular attention should be given to quality of detail in hair and beard on obverse.

Date	F	VF	XF	Unc	BU
1902-1910	15.00	35.00	60.00	150	—

KM# 818.1 1/2 CROWN
14.1380 g., 0.9250 Silver .4205 oz. ASW **Ruler:** George V **Obv:** Head left **Rev:** Crowned shield within Garter band **Note:** Fully struck World War I (1914-1918) specimens command a premium.

Date	F	VF	XF	Unc	BU
1911-1919	BV	10.00	28.00	65.00	—

KM# 818.1a 1/2 CROWN
14.1380 g., 0.5000 Silver .2273 oz. ASW **Ruler:** George V **Obv:** Head left **Rev:** Crowned shield within Garter rose, crown touches shield **Note:** Fully struck coins command a premium.

Date	F	VF	XF	Unc	BU
1920-1922	5.00	8.00	25.00	75.00	—

KM# 818.2 1/2 CROWN
14.1380 g., 0.5000 Silver .2273 oz. ASW **Ruler:** George V **Obv:** Head left **Rev:** Crowned shield within Garter band, groove between crown and shield **Note:** Fully struck coins command a premium.

Date	F	VF	XF	Unc	BU
1922-1926	3.50	5.00	15.00	50.00	—

KM# 830 1/2 CROWN
14.1380 g., 0.5000 Silver .2273 oz. ASW **Ruler:** George V **Obv:** Modified head left, larger beads **Rev:** Crowned shield within Garter band

Date	F	VF	XF	Unc	BU
1926-1927	4.50	7.00	28.00	70.00	—

KM# 835 1/2 CROWN
14.1380 g., 0.5000 Silver .2273 oz. ASW **Ruler:** George V **Obv:**
Head left **Rev:** Shield

Date	F	VF	XF	Unc	BU
1927-1936	BV	3.00	9.00	25.00	—

KM# 893 1/2 CROWN
Copper-Nickel **Ruler:** Elizabeth II **Obv:** Bust left **Rev:** Crowned
shield

Date	F	VF	XF	Unc	BU
1953	0.50	0.75	1.75	10.50	—

KM# 856 1/2 CROWN
14.1380 g., 0.5000 Silver .2273 oz. ASW **Ruler:** George VI **Obv:**
Head left **Rev:** Crowned shield

Date	F	VF	XF	Unc	BU
1937-1946	—	BV	3.00	10.00	—

KM# 907 1/2 CROWN
Copper-Nickel **Ruler:** Elizabeth II **Obv:** Bust right **Rev:** Crowned
shield

Date	F	VF	XF	Unc	BU
1954-1970	0.20	0.30	0.50	1.50	—

KM# 866 1/2 CROWN
Copper-Nickel **Ruler:** George VI **Obv:** Head left **Rev:** Crowned
shield

Date	F	VF	XF	Unc	BU
1947-1948	0.25	0.50	1.00	10.00	—

KM# 763 DOUBLE FLORIN
22.6207 g., 0.9250 Silver 0.6727 oz. ASW **Ruler:** Victoria

Date	F	VF	XF	Unc	BU
1887-1890	16.00	20.00	50.00	85.00	—

KM# 879 1/2 CROWN
Copper-Nickel **Ruler:** George VI **Obv:** Head left **Rev:** Crowned
shield

Date	F	VF	XF	Unc	BU
1949-1952	0.25	0.50	1.25	10.00	—

KM# 741 CROWN
28.2759 g., 0.9250 Silver .8409 oz. ASW **Ruler:** Victoria

Date	F	VF	XF	Unc	BU
1839-1847	35.00	125	850	2,250	—

KM# 744 CROWN
28.2759 g., 0.9250 Silver .8409 oz. ASW **Ruler:** Victoria

Date	F	VF	XF	Unc	BU
1847-1853	500	850	1,400	—	—

KM# 803 CROWN
28.2759 g., 0.9250 Silver .8409 oz. ASW **Ruler:** Edward VII **Obv:** Head right **Rev:** St. George slaying the dragon

Date	F	VF	XF	Unc	BU
1902	50.00	75.00	125	250	—

KM# 765 CROWN
28.2759 g., 0.9250 Silver .8409 oz. ASW **Ruler:** Victoria

Date	F	VF	XF	Unc	BU
1887-1892	16.50	27.50	75.00	125	—

KM# 836 CROWN
28.2759 g., 0.5000 Silver .4546 oz. ASW **Ruler:** George V **Obv:** Head left **Rev:** Crown within wreath

Date	F	VF	XF	Unc	BU
1927-1936	50.00	100	200	350	—

KM# 842 CROWN
28.2759 g., 0.5000 Silver .4546 oz. ASW **Ruler:** George V **Subject:** Silver Jubilee **Obv:** Bust left **Rev:** St. George slaying the dragon

Date	F	VF	XF	Unc	BU
1935	10.00	15.00	20.00	50.00	—

KM# 842a CROWN
0.9250 Silver **Ruler:** George V **Subject:** Silver Jubilee **Obv:** Head left **Rev:** St. George slaying the dragon

Date	F	VF	XF	Unc	BU
1935 Proof	Value: 400				

KM# 842b CROWN
47.8300 g., 0.9170 Gold 1.4096 oz. AGW **Ruler:** George V **Subject:** Silver Jubilee **Obv:** Head left **Rev:** St. George slaying the dragon

Date	F	VF	XF	Unc	BU
1935 Proof	Value: 14,500				

KM# 783 CROWN
28.2759 g., 0.9250 Silver .8409 oz. ASW **Ruler:** Victoria **Obv:** Crowned and veiled bust left **Rev:** St. George slaying dragon **Edge Lettering:** DECVS ET TVTAMEN ANNO REGNI

Date	F	VF	XF	Unc	BU
1893-LVI-1900-LXIV	15.00	32.00	150	275	—

KM# 857 CROWN
0.5000 Silver **Ruler:** George VI **Obv:** Head left **Rev:** Crowned shield with supporters

Date	F	VF	XF	Unc	BU
1937	8.00	12.00	25.00	50.00	—

KM# 880 CROWN
Copper-Nickel **Ruler:** George VI **Subject:** Festival of Britain **Obv:** Head left **Rev:** St. George slaying the dragon

Date	F	VF	XF	Unc	BU
1951	—	—	—	20.00	—

KM# 894 CROWN
Copper-Nickel **Ruler:** Elizabeth II **Subject:** Coronation of Queen Elizabeth II **Obv:** Queen on horseback left **Rev:** Crown at center of cross formed by Rose, shamrock, leek and thistle, shields in angles **Edge Lettering:** FAITH AND TRUTH I WILL BEAR UNTO YOU

Date	F	VF	XF	Unc	BU
1953	—	—	7.50	15.00	—

KM# 909 CROWN
Copper-Nickel **Ruler:** Elizabeth II **Subject:** British Exhibition in New York **Obv:** Bust right **Rev:** Crown at center of cross formed by Rose, shamrock, leek and thistle, shields in angles

Date	F	VF	XF	Unc	BU
1960	—	—	6.00	12.00	—

KM# 910 CROWN
Copper-Nickel **Ruler:** Elizabeth II **Obv:** Bust right **Rev:** Head of Winston Churchill right

Date	F	VF	XF	Unc	BU
1965	—	—	0.65	2.00	—

SOVEREIGN COINAGE

KM# 735.1 1/2 SOVEREIGN
3.9940 g., 0.9170 Gold .1177 oz. AGW **Ruler:** Victoria **Rev:** Without die number

Date	F	VF	XF	Unc	BU
1838-1885/3	80.00	100	225	425	—

KM# 735.2 1/2 SOVEREIGN
3.9940 g., 0.9170 Gold .1177 oz. AGW **Ruler:** Victoria **Rev:** With die number

Date	F	VF	XF	Unc	BU
1863-1880	85.00	100	175	400	—

KM# 766   1/2 SOVEREIGN
3.9940 g., 0.9170 Gold .1177 oz. AGW   **Ruler:** Victoria **Rev:** Without die number

Date	F	VF	XF	Unc	BU
1887-1893	BV	85.00	120	160	—

KM# 784   1/2 SOVEREIGN
3.9940 g., 0.9170 Gold .1177 oz. AGW   **Ruler:** Victoria **Obv:** Veiled bust left **Rev:** St. George slaying the dragon

Date	F	VF	XF	Unc	BU
1893-1901	—	BV	90.00	130	—

KM# 804   1/2 SOVEREIGN
3.9940 g., 0.9170 Gold .1177 oz. AGW   **Ruler:** Edward VII **Obv:** Head right **Rev:** St. George slaying the dragon

Date	F	VF	XF	Unc	BU
1902-1910	—	BV	75.00	120	—

KM# 819   1/2 SOVEREIGN
3.9940 g., 0.9170 Gold .1177 oz. AGW   **Ruler:** George V **Obv:** Head left **Rev:** St. George slaying the dragon

Date	F	VF	XF	Unc	BU
1911-1915	—	BV	75.00	120	—

KM# 858   1/2 SOVEREIGN
3.9940 g., 0.9170 Gold .1177 oz. AGW   **Ruler:** George VI **Obv:** Head left **Rev:** St. George slaying the dragon

Date	F	VF	XF	Unc	BU
1937 Proof		Value: 400			

KM# 922   1/2 SOVEREIGN
3.9900 g., 0.9170 Gold .1176 oz. AGW   **Ruler:** Elizabeth II **Obv:** Bust right **Rev:** St. George slaying the dragon

Date	F	VF	XF	Unc	BU
1980-1984	—	—	—	80.00	—

KM# 942   1/2 SOVEREIGN
3.9900 g., 0.9170 Gold .1176 oz. AGW   **Ruler:** Elizabeth II **Obv:** Head right **Rev:** St. George slaying the dragon

Date	F	VF	XF	Unc	BU
1985-1997 Proof		Value: 100			

KM# 955   1/2 SOVEREIGN
3.9900 g., 0.9170 Gold .1176 oz. AGW   **Ruler:** Elizabeth II **Subject:** 500th Anniversary of the Gold Sovereign **Obv:** Elizabeth II seated on the Coronation throne **Rev:** Crowned shield on rose

Date	F	VF	XF	Unc	BU
ND(1989) Proof		Value: 200			

KM# 1001   1/2 SOVEREIGN
3.9900 g., 0.9170 Gold .1176 oz. AGW   **Ruler:** Elizabeth II **Obv:** Head right **Rev:** St. George slaying the dragon

Date	F	VF	XF	Unc	BU
1998-2006	—	—	—	90.00	—

KM# 1025   1/2 SOVEREIGN
3.9900 g., 0.9167 Gold 0.1176 oz. AGW, 19.3 mm.   **Ruler:** Elizabeth II **Subject:** Queen Elizabeth II's Golden Jubilee **Obv:** Queen's head right **Rev:** Crowned arms **Edge:** Reeded

Date	F	VF	XF	Unc	BU
2002 Proof		Value: 145			

KM# 1064   1/2 SOVEREIGN
3.9940 g., 0.9167 Gold 0.1177 oz. AGW, 19.3 mm.   **Ruler:** Elizabeth II **Obv:** Elizabeth II **Rev:** Knight fighting dragon with sword **Edge:** Reeded

Date	F	VF	XF	Unc	BU
2005 Proof		Value: 175			

KM# 736.1   SOVEREIGN
7.9881 g., 0.9170 Gold .2354 oz. AGW   **Ruler:** Victoria **Rev:** Without die number

Date	F	VF	XF	Unc	BU
1838-1872	BV	155	175	350	—

Great Britain

KM# 736.2   SOVEREIGN
7.9881 g., 0.9170 Gold .2354 oz. AGW   **Ruler:** Victoria **Rev:** Die number below wreath

Date	F	VF	XF	Unc	BU
1863-1874	BV	155	165	325	—

KM# 736.3   SOVEREIGN
7.9881 g., 0.9170 Gold .2354 oz. AGW   **Ruler:** Victoria **Obv:** Additional line on lower edge of ribbon **Rev:** Without die number **Note:** Ansell variety.

Date	F	VF	XF	Unc	BU
1859	650	950	3,000	—	—

KM# 752   SOVEREIGN
7.9881 g., 0.9170 Gold .2354 oz. AGW   **Ruler:** Victoria

Date	F	VF	XF	Unc	BU
1871-1885	BV	155	175	350	—

KM# 767   SOVEREIGN
7.9881 g., 0.9170 Gold .2354 oz. AGW   **Ruler:** Victoria

Date	F	VF	XF	Unc	BU
1887-1892	—	BV	155	175	—

KM# 785   SOVEREIGN
7.9881 g., 0.9170 Gold .2354 oz. AGW   **Ruler:** Victoria **Obv:** Veiled bust left **Rev:** St. George slaying the dragon

Date	F	VF	XF	Unc	BU
1893-1901	—	—	BV	160	—

KM# 805   SOVEREIGN
7.9881 g., 0.9170 Gold .2354 oz. AGW   **Ruler:** Edward VII **Obv:** Head right **Rev:** St. George slaying the dragon

Date	F	VF	XF	Unc	BU
1902-1910	—	—	BV	130	—

KM# 820   SOVEREIGN
7.9881 g., 0.9170 Gold .2354 oz. AGW   **Ruler:** George V **Obv:** Head left **Rev:** St. George slaying the dragon

Date	F	VF	XF	Unc	BU
1911-1925	—	—	BV	150	—

KM# 859   SOVEREIGN
7.9881 g., 0.9170 Gold .2354 oz. AGW   **Ruler:** George VI **Obv:** Head left **Rev:** St. George slaying the dragon

Date	F	VF	XF	Unc	BU
1937 Proof	Value: 2,000				

KM# 908   SOVEREIGN
7.9881 g., 0.9170 Gold .2354 oz. AGW   **Ruler:** Elizabeth II **Obv:** Bust right **Rev:** St. George slaying the dragon

Date	F	VF	XF	Unc	BU
1957-1968	—	—	BV	145	—

KM# 919   SOVEREIGN
7.9881 g., 0.9170 Gold .2354 oz. AGW   **Ruler:** Elizabeth II **Obv:** Bust right **Rev:** St. George slaying the dragon

Date	F	VF	XF	Unc	BU
1974-1984	—	—	BV	145	—

KM# 943 SOVEREIGN

7.9881 g., 0.9170 Gold .2354 oz. AGW **Ruler:** Elizabeth II **Obv:** Head right **Rev:** St. George slaying the dragon

Date	F	VF	XF	Unc	BU
1985-1997 Proof			Value: 225		

KM# 956 SOVEREIGN

7.9881 g., 0.9170 Gold .2354 oz. AGW **Ruler:** Elizabeth II **Subject:** 500th Anniversary of the Gold Sovereign **Obv:** Elizabeth II seated on coronation throne **Rev:** Crowned shield on rose

Date	F	VF	XF	Unc	BU
ND(1989) Proof			Value: 400		

KM# 768 2 POUNDS

15.9761 g., 0.9170 Gold .4708 oz. AGW **Ruler:** Victoria

Date	F	VF	XF	Unc	BU
1887	320	350	400	700	—

KM# 1002 SOVEREIGN

7.9881 g., 0.9170 Gold .2354 oz. AGW **Ruler:** Elizabeth II **Obv:** Head right **Rev:** St. George slaying the dragon

Date	F	VF	XF	Unc	BU
1998-2006	—	—	—	165	—

KM# 786 2 POUNDS

15.9761 g., 0.9170 Gold .4708 oz. AGW **Ruler:** Victoria

Date	F	VF	XF	Unc	BU
1893	320	400	675	900	—

KM# 1026 SOVEREIGN

7.9800 g., 0.9167 Gold 0.2352 oz. AGW, 22 mm. **Ruler:** Elizabeth II **Subject:** Queen Elizabeth II's Golden Jubilee **Obv:** Queen's head right **Rev:** Crowned arms **Edge:** Reeded

Date	F	VF	XF	Unc	BU
2002	—	—	—	165	—

KM# 806 2 POUNDS

15.9761 g., 0.9170 Gold .4708 oz. AGW **Ruler:** Edward VII **Obv:** Head right **Rev:** St. George slaying the dragon

Date	F	VF	XF	Unc	BU
1902	BV	325	400	700	—

KM# 1065 SOVEREIGN

7.9880 g., 0.9176 Gold 0.2357 oz. AGW, 22.05 mm. **Ruler:** Elizabeth II **Obv:** Elizabeth II **Rev:** Knight fighting dragon with sword **Edge:** Reeded

Date	F	VF	XF	Unc	BU
2005	—	—	—	—	175

KM# 821 2 POUNDS

15.9761 g., 0.9170 Gold .4708 oz. AGW **Ruler:** George V **Obv:** Head left **Rev:** St. George slaying the dragon

Date	F	VF	XF	Unc	BU
1911 Proof			Value: 1,100		

KM# 860 2 POUNDS
15.9761 g., 0.9170 Gold .4708 oz. AGW **Ruler:** George VI **Obv:**
Head left **Rev:** St. George slaying the dragon

Date	F	VF	XF	Unc	BU
1937 Proof		Value: 1,100			

KM# 923 2 POUNDS
15.9200 g., 0.9170 Gold .4694 oz. AGW **Ruler:** Elizabeth II **Obv:**
Bust right

Date	F	VF	XF	Unc	BU
1980-1983 Proof		Value: 300			

KM# 944 2 POUNDS
15.9200 g., 0.9170 Gold .4694 oz. AGW **Ruler:** Elizabeth II **Obv:**
Head right **Rev:** St. George slaying the dragon

Date	F	VF	XF	Unc	BU
1985-1999 Proof		Value: 350			

KM# 957 2 POUNDS
15.9800 g., 0.9170 Gold .4708 oz. AGW **Ruler:** Elizabeth II
Subject: 500th Anniversary of the Gold Sovereign **Obv:** Elizabeth
II seated on Coronation throne **Rev:** Crowned shield on rose

Date	F	VF	XF	Unc	BU
ND(1989) Proof		Value: 350			

KM# 1027 2 POUNDS
15.9700 g., 0.9167 Gold 0.4707 oz. AGW, 28.4 mm. **Ruler:**
Elizabeth II **Subject:** Queen Elizabeth II's Golden Jubilee **Obv:**
Queen's head right **Rev:** Crowned arms **Edge:** Reeded **Note:** In
proof sets only.

Date	F	VF	XF	Unc	BU
2002 Proof		Value: 435			

KM# 742 5 POUNDS
39.9403 g., 0.9170 Gold 1.1773 oz. AGW **Ruler:** Victoria

Date	F	VF	XF	Unc	BU
1839 Proof		Value: 35,000			

KM# 769 5 POUNDS
39.9403 g., 0.9170 Gold 1.1773 oz. AGW **Ruler:** Victoria

Date	F	VF	XF	Unc	BU
1887	775	850	1,000	1,500	—

KM# 787 5 POUNDS
39.9403 g., 0.9170 Gold 1.1773 oz. AGW **Ruler:** Victoria

Date	F	VF	XF	Unc	BU
1893	775	850	1,200	2,000	—

KM# 807 5 POUNDS
39.9403 g., 0.9170 Gold 1.1773 oz. AGW **Ruler:** Edward VII
Obv: Head right **Rev:** St. George slaying the dragon

Date	F	VF	XF	Unc	BU
1902	—	BV	775	1,500	—

KM# 822 5 POUNDS
39.9403 g., 0.9170 Gold 1.1773 oz. AGW **Ruler:** George V **Obv:**
Head left **Rev:** St. George slaying the dragon

Date	F	VF	XF	Unc	BU
1911 Proof	Value: 2,750				

KM# 861 5 POUNDS
39.9403 g., 0.9170 Gold 1.1773 oz. AGW **Ruler:** George V **Obv:**
Head left **Rev:** St. George slaying the dragon

Date	F	VF	XF	Unc	BU
1937 Proof	Value: 1,500				

KM# 924 5 POUNDS
39.9400 g., 0.9170 Gold 1.1775 oz. AGW **Ruler:** Elizabeth II
Obv: Bust right **Rev:** St. George slaying the dragon

Date	F	VF	XF	Unc	BU
1980-1984	—	—	—	725	—

KM# 945 5 POUNDS
39.9400 g., 0.9170 Gold 1.1775 oz. AGW **Ruler:** Elizabeth II
Obv: Head right **Rev:** St. George slaying the dragon

Date	F	VF	XF	Unc	BU
1985-1997	—	—	—	725	—

KM# 949 5 POUNDS
39.9400 g., 0.9170 Gold 1.1775 oz. AGW **Ruler:** Elizabeth II
Obv: Draped bust right **Rev:** St. George slaying the dragon

Date	F	VF	XF	Unc	BU
1987-1988	—	—	—	725	—

KM# 958 5 POUNDS
39.9400 g., 0.9170 Gold 1.1775 oz. AGW **Ruler:** Elizabeth II
Subject: 500th Anniversary of the Gold Sovereign **Obv:** Elizabeth
II seated on Coronation throne **Rev:** Crowned shield on rose

Date	F	VF	XF	Unc	BU
1989	—	—	—	725	—

KM# 1003 5 POUNDS
39.9400 g., 0.9170 Gold 1.1775 oz. AGW, 36 mm. **Ruler:**
Elizabeth II **Obv:** Portrait of Queen Elizabeth II **Rev:** St. George
slaying dragon **Edge:** Reeded

Date	F	VF	XF	Unc	BU
1999-2006	—	—	—	775	—

KM# 1028 5 POUNDS
39.9400 g., 0.9167 Gold 1.1771 oz. AGW, 36 mm. **Ruler:**
Elizabeth II **Subject:** Queen Elizabeth II's Golden Jubilee **Obv:**
Queen's head right **Rev:** Crowned arms **Edge:** Reeded

Date	F	VF	XF	Unc	BU
2002 Proof		Value: 875			

KM# 1067 5 POUNDS
39.9400 g., 0.9167 Gold 1.1771 oz. AGW, 36 mm. **Ruler:**
Elizabeth II **Obv:** Elizabeth II **Rev:** Knight fighting dragon with
sword **Edge:** Reeded

Date	F	VF	XF	Unc	BU
2005 Proof		Value: 950			

DECIMAL COINAGE
1971-1981, 100 New Pence = 1 Pound; 1982,
100 Pence = 1 Pound

KM# 914 1/2 NEW PENNY
Bronze **Ruler:** Elizabeth II **Obv:** Bust right **Rev:** Crown, value below

Date	F	VF	XF	Unc	BU
1971-1981	—	—	0.10	0.20	—

KM# 926 1/2 PENNY
Bronze **Ruler:** Elizabeth II **Obv:** Bust right **Rev:** "HALF PENNY"
above crown and fraction **Note:** Denomination now demonetized.

Date	F	VF	XF	Unc	BU
1982-1984	—	—	0.15	0.20	—

KM# 915 NEW PENNY
Bronze **Ruler:** Elizabeth II **Obv:** Bust right **Rev:** Crowned portocullis

Date	F	VF	XF	Unc	BU
1971-1981	—	—	0.15	0.20	—

KM# 927 PENNY
Bronze **Ruler:** Elizabeth II **Obv:** Bust right **Rev:** Crowned portocullis

Date	F	VF	XF	Unc	BU
1982-1984	—	—	0.15	0.20	—

KM# 935 PENNY
Bronze **Ruler:** Elizabeth II **Obv:** Head right **Rev:** Crowned
portcullis **Note:** Queen's head reduced size.

Date	F	VF	XF	Unc	BU
1985-1992	—	—	0.15	0.25	—

KM# 935a PENNY
Copper Plated Steel **Ruler:** Elizabeth II **Obv:** Head right **Rev:**
Crowned portcullis

Date	F	VF	XF	Unc	BU
1992-1997	—	—	0.15	0.25	—

KM# 935b PENNY
0.9250 Silver **Ruler:** Elizabeth II **Obv:** Head right **Rev:** Crowned
portcullis

Date	F	VF	XF	Unc	BU
1996 Proof		Value: 16.50			

KM# 986 PENNY
Copper Plated Steel **Ruler:** Elizabeth II **Obv:** Head right **Rev:**
Crowned portcullis

Date	F	VF	XF	Unc	BU
1998-2006	—	—	—	0.20	—

KM# 986a PENNY
Bronze, 20.3 mm. **Ruler:** Elizabeth II **Obv:** Head right **Rev:**
Crowned portcullis **Edge:** Plain **Note:** Issued in sets only

Date	F	VF	XF	Unc	BU
1999-2004	—	—	—	0.20	—

KM# 986b   PENNY
3.5600 g., 0.9250 Silver 0.1059 oz. ASW, 20.3 mm. **Ruler:**
Elizabeth II **Obv:** Head left **Rev:** Crowned portcullis **Edge:** Plain

Date	F	VF	XF	Unc	BU
2000 Proof		Value: 16.50			

KM# 916   2 NEW PENCE
Bronze **Ruler:** Elizabeth II **Obv:** Bust right **Rev:** Welsh plumes
and crown

Date	F	VF	XF	Unc	BU
1971-1981	—	—	0.10	0.20	—

KM# 928   2 PENCE
Bronze **Ruler:** Elizabeth II **Obv:** Bust right **Rev:** Welsh plumes
and crown

Date	F	VF	XF	Unc	BU
1982-1984	—	—	—	1.00	—

KM# 936   2 PENCE
Bronze **Ruler:** Elizabeth II **Obv:** Head right **Rev:** Welsh plumes
and crown

Date	F	VF	XF	Unc	BU
1985-1992	—	—	0.15	0.25	—

KM# 936a   2 PENCE
Copper Plated Steel **Ruler:** Elizabeth II **Obv:** Head right **Rev:**
Welsh plumes and crown

Date	F	VF	XF	Unc	BU
1992-1997	—	—	0.10	0.25	—

KM# 936b   2 PENCE
0.9250 Silver **Ruler:** Elizabeth II **Obv:** Head right **Rev:** Welsh
plumes and crown

Date	F	VF	XF	Unc	BU
1996 Proof		Value: 17.50			

KM# 987   2 PENCE
Copper Plated Steel **Ruler:** Elizabeth II **Obv:** Head right **Rev:**
Welsh plumes and crown

Date	F	VF	XF	Unc	BU
1998-2006	—	—	—	0.25	—

KM# 987a   2 PENCE
Bronze **Ruler:** Elizabeth II **Obv:** Head right **Rev:** Welsh plumes
and crown

Date	F	VF	XF	Unc	BU
1998-2004	—	—	—	0.25	—

KM# 987b   2 PENCE
7.1200 g., 0.9250 Silver 0.2117 oz. ASW, 25.9 mm. **Ruler:**
Elizabeth II **Obv:** Head right **Rev:** Welsh plumes and crown **Edge:**
Plain

Date	F	VF	XF	Unc	BU
2000 Proof		Value: 17.50			

KM# 911   5 NEW PENCE
Copper-Nickel **Ruler:** Elizabeth II **Obv:** Bust right **Rev:** Crowned
thistle

Date	F	VF	XF	Unc	BU
1968-1981	—	—	0.15	0.30	—

KM# 929   5 PENCE
Copper-Nickel **Ruler:** Elizabeth II **Obv:** Head right **Rev:** Crowned
thistle

Date	F	VF	XF	Unc	BU
1982-1984	—	—	—	1.75	—

KM# 937   5 PENCE
Copper-Nickel **Ruler:** Elizabeth II **Obv:** Head right **Rev:** Crowned
thistle

Date	F	VF	XF	Unc	BU
1985-1990	—	—	0.15	0.30	—

KM# 937a   5 PENCE
5.6000 g., 0.9250 Silver .1683 oz. ASW **Ruler:** Elizabeth II **Obv:**
Head right **Rev:** Crowned thistle

Date	F	VF	XF	Unc	BU
1990 Proof		Value: 22.00			

KM# 937b   5 PENCE
Copper-Nickel **Ruler:** Elizabeth II **Obv:** Head right **Rev:** Crowned
thistle **Note:** Reduced size. Varieties in thickness and edge milling
exist.

Date	F	VF	XF	Unc	BU
1990-1997	—	—	—	0.35	—

KM# 937c   5 PENCE
3.2500 g., 0.9250 Silver .0967 oz. ASW **Ruler:** Elizabeth II **Obv:**
Bust right **Rev:** Crowned thistle

Date	F	VF	XF	Unc	BU
1990-1996 Proof		Value: 20.00			

KM# 937d   5 PENCE
6.5000 g., 0.9250 Silver .1933 oz. ASW **Ruler:** Elizabeth II **Obv:**
Head right **Rev:** Crowned thistle **Note:** Piefort.

Date	F	VF	XF	Unc	BU
1990 Proof		Value: 25.00			

KM# 988   5 PENCE
Copper-Nickel **Ruler:** Elizabeth II **Obv:** Head right **Rev:** Crowned
thistle

Date	F	VF	XF	Unc	BU
1998-2006	—	—	—	0.30	—

KM# 988a   5 PENCE
3.2500 g., 0.9250 Silver 0.0967 oz. ASW, 18 mm. **Ruler:**
Elizabeth II **Obv:** Head right **Rev:** Crowned thistle **Edge:** Reeded

Date	F	VF	XF	Unc	BU
2000 Proof		Value: 20.00			

KM# 912   10 NEW PENCE
Copper-Nickel **Ruler:** Elizabeth II **Obv:** Bust right **Rev:** Crowned
lion prancing left

Date	F	VF	XF	Unc	BU
1968-1981	—	0.25	0.25	0.50	—

KM# 930   10 PENCE
Copper-Nickel **Ruler:** Elizabeth II **Obv:** Bust right **Rev:** Crowned
lion prancing left

Date	F	VF	XF	Unc	BU
1982-1984	—	—	—	2.00	—

KM# 938   10 PENCE
Copper-Nickel **Ruler:** Elizabeth II **Obv:** Head left **Rev:** Crowned
lion prancing left

Date	F	VF	XF	Unc	BU
1985-1992	—	—	—	1.75	—

KM# 938a   10 PENCE
11.3100 g., 0.9250 Silver .3363 oz. ASW **Ruler:** Elizabeth II **Obv:**
Head right **Rev:** Crowned lion prancing left **Note:** Date varieties exist.

Date	F	VF	XF	Unc	BU
1992 Proof		Value: 25.00			

KM# 938b   10 PENCE
Copper-Nickel **Ruler:** Elizabeth II **Obv:** Head right **Rev:** Crowned
lion prancing left **Note:** Reduced size. Varieties in thickness and
edge milling exist.

Date	F	VF	XF	Unc	BU
1992-1997	—	—	0.25	0.50	—

KM# 938c   10 PENCE
6.5000 g., 0.9250 Silver .1933 oz. ASW **Ruler:** Elizabeth II **Obv:**
Head right **Rev:** Crowned lion prancing left

Date	F	VF	XF	Unc	BU
1992-1996 Proof		Value: 17.50			

KM# 989   10 PENCE
Copper-Nickel **Ruler:** Elizabeth II **Obv:** Head right **Rev:** Crowned lion prancing left

Date	F	VF	XF	Unc	BU
1998-2006	—	—	—	0.40	—

KM# 989a   10 PENCE
6.5000 g., 0.9250 Silver 0.1933 oz. ASW, 24.5 mm. **Ruler:** Elizabeth II **Obv:** Head right **Rev:** Crowned lion prancing left **Edge:** Reeded

Date	F	VF	XF	Unc	BU
2000 Proof		Value: 17.50			

KM# 931   20 PENCE
Copper-Nickel **Ruler:** Elizabeth II **Obv:** Bust right **Rev:** Crowned rose **Shape:** 7-sided

Date	F	VF	XF	Unc	BU
1982-1984	—	—	0.45	0.65	—

KM# 939   20 PENCE
Copper-Nickel **Ruler:** Elizabeth II **Obv:** Head right **Rev:** Crowned rose **Shape:** 7-sided

Date	F	VF	XF	Unc	BU
1985-1997	—	—	0.45	0.75	—

KM# 939a   20 PENCE
0.9250 Silver **Ruler:** Elizabeth II **Obv:** Head right **Rev:** Crowned rose **Shape:** 7-sided

Date	F	VF	XF	Unc	BU
1996 Proof		Value: 18.50			

KM# 990   20 PENCE
Copper-Nickel **Ruler:** Elizabeth II **Obv:** Effigy of Queen Elizabeth II **Rev:** Crowned rose **Shape:** 7-sided

Date	F	VF	XF	Unc	BU
1998-2006	—	—	—	0.60	—

KM# 990a   20 PENCE
5.0000 g., 0.9250 Silver 0.1487 oz. ASW, 21.4 mm. **Ruler:** Elizabeth II **Obv:** Head right **Rev:** Crowned rose **Edge:** Plain **Shape:** 7-sided

Date	F	VF	XF	Unc	BU
2000 Proof		Value: 18.50			

KM# 917   25 NEW PENCE
Copper-Nickel **Ruler:** Elizabeth II **Subject:** Royal Silver Wedding Anniversary **Obv:** Bust right **Rev:** Crowned EP monogram

Date	F	VF	XF	Unc	BU
ND(1972)	—	—	0.65	2.50	—

KM# 917a   25 NEW PENCE
28.2759 g., 0.9250 Silver .8409 oz. ASW **Ruler:** Elizabeth II **Obv:** Bust right **Rev:** Crowned EP monogram

Date	F	VF	XF	Unc	BU
ND(1972) Proof		Value: 25.00			

KM# 920   25 NEW PENCE
Copper-Nickel **Ruler:** Elizabeth II **Subject:** Silver Jubilee of Reign **Obv:** Queen on horseback left **Rev:** Eagle and spoon, crown above

Date	F	VF	XF	Unc	BU
1977	—	—	0.65	1.50	—

KM# 920a 25 NEW PENCE
28.2759 g., 0.9250 Silver .8409 oz. ASW **Ruler:** Elizabeth II **Obv:**
Queen on horseback left **Rev:** Eagle and spoon, crown above

Date	F	VF	XF	Unc	BU
1977 Proof		Value: 20.00			

KM# 921 25 NEW PENCE
Copper-Nickel **Ruler:** Elizabeth II **Subject:** 80th Birthday of
Queen Mother **Obv:** Bust right **Rev:** Queen Mother's profile left,
circle of rampant lions and banners

Date	F	VF	XF	Unc	BU
ND(1980)	—	—	0.65	2.50	—

KM# 921a 25 NEW PENCE
28.2759 g., 0.9250 Silver .8409 oz. ASW **Ruler:** Elizabeth II **Obv:**
Bust right **Rev:** Queen Mother's profile left in circle of rampant
lions and banners

Date	F	VF	XF	Unc	BU
ND(1980) Proof		Value: 55.00			

KM# 925 25 NEW PENCE
Copper-Nickel **Ruler:** Elizabeth II **Subject:** Wedding of Prince
Charles and Lady Diana **Obv:** Bust right **Rev:** Conjoined heads
of Diana and Prince Charles left

Date	F	VF	XF	Unc	BU
1981	—	—	0.65	2.50	—

KM# 925a 25 NEW PENCE
28.2759 g., 0.9250 Silver .8409 oz. ASW **Ruler:** Elizabeth II **Obv:**
Bust right **Rev:** Conjoined heads of Diana and Prince Charles
facing left

Date	F	VF	XF	Unc	BU
1981 Proof		Value: 27.50			

KM# 913 50 NEW PENCE
Copper-Nickel **Ruler:** Elizabeth II **Obv:** Bust right **Rev:** Britannia
seated **Shape:** 7-sided

Date	F	VF	XF	Unc	BU
1969-1981	—	—	1.25	2.25	—

KM# 918 50 PENCE
Copper-Nickel **Ruler:** Elizabeth II **Subject:** Britain's entry into
E.E.C **Obv:** Bust right **Rev:** Nine clasped hands **Shape:** 7-sided

Date	F	VF	XF	Unc	BU
1973	—	—	1.25	2.00	—

KM# 932 50 PENCE
Copper-Nickel **Ruler:** Elizabeth II **Obv:** Bust right **Rev:** Britannia
seated **Shape:** 7-sided

Date	F	VF	XF	Unc	BU
1982-1984	—	—	1.25	1.75	—

KM# 940.1 50 PENCE
Copper-Nickel **Ruler:** Elizabeth II **Obv:** Head right **Rev:** Britannia
seated **Shape:** 7-sided

Date	F	VF	XF	Unc	BU
1985-1997	—	—	1.25	2.75	—

KM# 963   50 PENCE
Copper-Nickel **Ruler:** Elizabeth II **Subject:** British Presidency of European Council of Ministers **Obv:** Head right **Rev:** Stars on conference table **Shape:** 7-sided

Date	F	VF	XF	Unc	BU
ND(1992)	—	—	—	5.75	—

KM# 963a   50 PENCE
13.5000 g., 0.9250 Silver .4014 oz. ASW **Ruler:** Elizabeth II **Obv:** Head right **Rev:** Stars on conference table

Date	F	VF	XF	Unc	BU
ND(1992) Proof			Value: 30.00		

KM# 963b   50 PENCE
26.3200 g., 0.9170 Gold .7757 oz. AGW **Ruler:** Elizabeth II **Subject:** British Presidency of European Council of Ministers **Obv:** Head right **Rev:** Stars on conference table

Date	F	VF	XF	Unc	BU
ND(1992) Proof			Value: 475		

KM# 966   50 PENCE
Copper-Nickel **Ruler:** Elizabeth II **Subject:** 50th Anniversary of Normandy Invasion **Obv:** Head right **Rev:** Boats and planes **Shape:** 7-sided

Date	F	VF	XF	Unc	BU
1994	—	—	—	2.50	—

KM# 966a   50 PENCE
13.5000 g., 0.9250 Silver .4014 oz. ASW **Ruler:** Elizabeth II **Obv:** Head right **Rev:** Boats and planes

Date	F	VF	XF	Unc	BU
1994 Proof			Value: 45.00		

KM# 966b   50 PENCE
26.3200 g., 0.9170 Gold .7757 oz. AGW **Ruler:** Elizabeth II **Obv:** Bust right **Rev:** Boats and planes

Date	F	VF	XF	Unc	BU
1994 Proof			Value: 500		

KM# 940.1a   50 PENCE
Silver **Ruler:** Elizabeth II **Obv:** Head right **Rev:** Britannia seated

Date	F	VF	XF	Unc	BU
1996 Proof			Value: 30.00		

KM# 940.2   50 PENCE
Copper-Nickel **Ruler:** Elizabeth II **Obv:** Head right **Rev:** Britannia seated **Shape:** 7-sided **Note:** Reduced size.

Date	F	VF	XF	Unc	BU
1997	—	—	—	2.50	—

KM# 991   50 PENCE
Copper-Nickel **Ruler:** Elizabeth II **Obv:** Portrait of Queen Elizabeth II **Rev:** Britannia seated **Shape:** 7-sided

Date	F	VF	XF	Unc	BU
1998-2006	—	—	—	1.75	—

KM# 992   50 PENCE
Copper-Nickel **Ruler:** Elizabeth II **Subject:** 25th Anniversary - Britain in the Common Market **Obv:** Head right **Rev:** Bouquet of stars **Shape:** 7-sided

Date	F	VF	XF	Unc	BU
1998	—	—	—	2.75	—

KM# 992a   50 PENCE
8.0000 g., 0.9250 Silver .2379 oz. ASW **Ruler:** Elizabeth II **Obv:** Head right **Rev:** Bouquet of stars

Date	F	VF	XF	Unc	BU
1998 Proof			Value: 45.00		

KM# 996   50 PENCE
Copper-Nickel **Ruler:** Elizabeth II **Subject:** National Health Service **Obv:** Head right **Rev:** Radiant hands **Shape:** 7-sided

Date	F	VF	XF	Unc	BU
1998	—	—	—	2.75	—

KM# 996a   50 PENCE
8.0000 g., 0.9250 Silver .2379 oz. ASW **Ruler:** Elizabeth II **Obv:** Head right **Rev:** Radiant hands

Date	F	VF	XF	Unc	BU
1998 Proof			Value: 45.00		

KM# 996b   50 PENCE
15.5000 g., 0.9167 Gold .4568 oz. AGW **Ruler:** Elizabeth II **Subject:** National Health Service **Obv:** Head right **Rev:** Radiant hands

Date	F	VF	XF	Unc	BU
1998 Proof			Value: 475		

KM# 1004   50 PENCE
Copper-Nickel **Ruler:** Elizabeth II **Subject:** Public Library **Obv:**
Bust Queen right **Rev:** Open book above building, CDs in pediment
Edge: Plain edge **Shape:** 7-sided

Date	F	VF	XF	Unc	BU
2000	—	—	—	2.75	—

KM# 991a   50 PENCE
8.0000 g., 0.9250 Silver 0.2379 oz. ASW, 27.3 mm. **Ruler:**
Elizabeth II **Obv:** Queen Elizabeth II **Rev:** Britannia seated **Edge:**
Plain **Shape:** 7-sided

Date	F	VF	XF	Unc	BU
2000 Proof		Value: 25.00			

KM# 1017   50 PENCE
8.1100 g., 0.9584 Silver .2499 oz. ASW, 22 mm. **Ruler:**
Elizabeth II **Subject:** Britannia Bullion **Obv:** Queen's portrait **Rev:**
Stylized "Britannia and the Lion" **Edge:** Reeded

Date	F	VF	XF	Unc	BU
2001 Proof		Value: 25.00			

KM# 1036   50 PENCE
8.0000 g., Copper-Nickel, 27.3 mm. **Ruler:** Elizabeth II **Subject:**
Woman's Suffrage **Obv:** Queen's portrait **Rev:** Standing woman
with banner **Edge:** Plain **Shape:** 7-sided

Date	F	VF	XF	Unc	BU
2003	—	—	—	2.50	—

KM# 1036a   50 PENCE
8.0000 g., 0.9250 Silver 0.2379 oz. ASW, 27.3 mm. **Ruler:**
Elizabeth II **Edge:** Plain **Shape:** 7-sided

Date	F	VF	XF	Unc	BU
2003 Proof		Value: 45.00			

KM# 1036b   50 PENCE
15.5000 g., 0.9166 Gold 0.4568 oz. AGW, 27.3 mm. **Ruler:**
Elizabeth II **Edge:** Plain **Shape:** 7-sided

Date	F	VF	XF	Unc	BU
2003 Proof		Value: 475			

KM# 1047   50 PENCE
8.0000 g., Copper-Nickel, 27.3 mm. **Ruler:** Elizabeth II **Subject:**
The First Four Minute Mile **Obv:** Queen Elizabeth II **Rev:** Running
legs, stop watch and value **Edge:** Plain

Date	F	VF	XF	Unc	BU
2004	—	—	—	5.00	6.00

KM# 1050   50 PENCE
8.0000 g., Copper-Nickel, 27.3 mm. **Ruler:** Elizabeth II **Obv:**
Queen Elizabeth II **Rev:** Text from the first English dictionary by
Samuel Johnson **Edge:** Plain

Date	F	VF	XF	Unc	BU
2005	—	—	—	2.50	3.50

KM# 1050a   50 PENCE
8.0000 g., 0.9250 Silver 0.461 oz. ASW, 27.3 mm. **Ruler:**
Elizabeth II **Subject:** First English Dictionary **Obv:** Elizabeth II
Rev: Sample page from Johnson's 1755 dictionary **Edge:** Plain
Shape: 7-sided

Date	F	VF	XF	Unc	BU
2005 Proof		Value: 45.00			

KM# 1050b   50 PENCE
15.5000 g., 0.9167 Gold 0.4568 oz. AGW, 27.3 mm. **Ruler:**
Elizabeth II **Subject:** First English Dictionary **Rev:** Sample page
from Johnson's 1755 dictionary **Edge:** Plain **Shape:** 7-sided

Date	F	VF	XF	Unc	BU
2005 Proof		Value: 550			

KM# 1057   50 PENCE
8.0000 g., Copper-Nickel, 27.3 mm. **Ruler:** Elizabeth II **Obv:**
Queen Elizabeth II **Rev:** Victoria Cross obverse and reverse views
Edge: Plain **Shape:** 7-sided

Date	F	VF	XF	Unc	BU
2006	—	—	—	5.00	6.00

KM# 1058   50 PENCE
8.0000 g., Copper-Nickel, 27.3 mm. **Ruler:** Elizabeth II **Obv:**
Queen Elizabeth II **Rev:** Heroic Act scene with cross shape in
background **Edge:** Plain **Shape:** 7-sided

Date	F	VF	XF	Unc	BU
2006	—	—	—	5.00	6.00

KM# 933 POUND
Nickel-Brass **Ruler:** Elizabeth II **Obv:** Bust right **Rev:** Shield of
Great Britain within the Garter, all crowned and supported **Edge
Lettering:** DECUS ET TUTAMEN

Date	F	VF	XF	Unc	BU
1983	—	—	2.25	4.00	5.50

KM# 933a POUND
9.5000 g., 0.9250 Silver .2825 oz. ASW **Ruler:** Elizabeth II **Obv:**
Bust right **Rev:** Arms of Great Britain within the Garter, all crowned
and supported

Date	F	VF	XF	Unc	BU
1983 Proof	Value: 27.50				

KM# 934 POUND
Nickel-Brass **Ruler:** Elizabeth II **Obv:** Bust right **Rev:** Scottish
thistle **Edge Lettering:** NEMO ME IMPUNE LACESSIT

Date	F	VF	XF	Unc	BU
1984	—	—	2.25	4.00	5.50

KM# 934a POUND
9.5000 g., 0.9250 Silver .2825 oz. ASW **Ruler:** Elizabeth II **Obv:**
Bust right **Rev:** Scottish thistle

Date	F	VF	XF	Unc	BU
1984 Proof	Value: 27.50				

KM# 941 POUND
Nickel-Brass **Ruler:** Elizabeth II **Obv:** Bust right **Rev:** Welsh leek
Edge Lettering: PLEIDIOL WYF I'M GWLAD

Date	F	VF	XF	Unc	BU
1985-1990	—	—	2.00	3.50	5.00

KM# 941a POUND
9.5000 g., 0.9250 Silver .2825 oz. ASW **Ruler:** Elizabeth II **Obv:**
Bust right **Rev:** Welsh leek

Date	F	VF	XF	Unc	BU
1985-1990 Proof	Value: 27.50				

KM# 946 POUND
Nickel-Brass **Ruler:** Elizabeth II **Obv:** Bust right **Rev:** Northern
Ireland - Blooming flax **Edge Lettering:** DECUS ET TUTAMEN

Date	F	VF	XF	Unc	BU
1986-1991	—	—	2.00	4.00	5.50

KM# 946a POUND
9.5000 g., 0.9250 Silver .2825 oz. ASW **Ruler:** Elizabeth II **Obv:**
Bust right **Rev:** Northern Ireland - Blooming flax

Date	F	VF	XF	Unc	BU
1986-1991 Proof	Value: 27.50				

KM# 948 POUND
Nickel-Brass **Ruler:** Elizabeth II **Obv:** Bust right **Rev:** Oak tree
Edge Lettering: DECUS ET TUTAMEN

Date	F	VF	XF	Unc	BU
1987-1992	—	—	—	3.50	5.00

KM# 948a POUND
9.5000 g., 0.9250 Silver .2825 oz. ASW **Ruler:** Elizabeth II **Obv:**
Bust right **Rev:** Oak tree

Date	F	VF	XF	Unc	BU
1987-1992 Proof	Value: 27.50				

KM# 954 POUND
Nickel-Brass **Ruler:** Elizabeth II **Obv:** Head right **Rev:** Crowned
shield of the United Kingdom **Edge Lettering:** DECUS ET
TUTAMEN

Date	F	VF	XF	Unc	BU
1988	—	—	—	4.00	5.50

KM# 954a POUND
9.5000 g., 0.9250 Silver .2825 oz. ASW **Ruler:** Elizabeth II **Obv:**
Head right **Rev:** Crowned shield of the United Kingdom

Date	F	VF	XF	Unc	BU
1988 Proof	Value: 40.00				

KM# 959 POUND
Nickel-Brass **Ruler:** Elizabeth II **Obv:** Head right **Rev:** Scottish
thistle **Edge Lettering:** NEMO ME IMPUNE LACESSIT

Date	F	VF	XF	Unc	BU
1989	—	—	—	4.00	5.50

KM# 959a POUND
9.5000 g., 0.9250 Silver .2825 oz. ASW **Ruler:** Elizabeth II **Obv:**
Head right **Rev:** Scottish thistle

Date	F	VF	XF	Unc	BU
1989 Proof	Value: 32.50				

KM# 964 POUND
Nickel-Brass **Ruler:** Elizabeth II **Obv:** Head right **Rev:** Shield of
Great Britain with Garter, all crowned and supported **Edge
Lettering:** DECUS ET TUTAMEN

Date	F	VF	XF	Unc	BU
1993	—	—	—	4.00	5.50

KM# 964a POUND
9.5000 g., 0.9250 Silver .2825 oz. ASW **Ruler:** Elizabeth II **Obv:** Head right **Rev:** Shield of Great Britain within Garter, all crowned and supported

Date	F	VF	XF	Unc	BU
1993 Proof		Value: 40.00			

KM# 967 POUND
Nickel-Brass **Ruler:** Elizabeth II **Obv:** Head right **Rev:** Scottish arms **Edge Lettering:** NEMO ME IMPUNE LACESSIT

Date	F	VF	XF	Unc	BU
1994	—	—	2.00	3.50	5.50

KM# 967a POUND
9.5000 g., 0.9250 Silver .2825 oz. ASW **Ruler:** Elizabeth II **Obv:** Head right **Rev:** Scottish arms

Date	F	VF	XF	Unc	BU
1994 Proof		Value: 60.00			

KM# 969 POUND
Nickel-Brass **Ruler:** Elizabeth II **Obv:** Head right **Rev:** Welsh Dragon **Edge Lettering:** PLEIDIOL WYF I'M GWLAD

Date	F	VF	XF	Unc	BU
1995	—	—	2.50	5.50	7.00

KM# 969a POUND
9.5000 g., 0.9250 Silver .2825 oz. ASW **Ruler:** Elizabeth II **Obv:** Head right **Rev:** Welsh dragon

Date	F	VF	XF	Unc	BU
1995 Proof		Value: 37.50			

KM# 972 POUND
Nickel-Brass **Ruler:** Elizabeth II **Obv:** Head right **Rev:** Celtic Cross **Edge Lettering:** DECUS ET TUTAMEN

Date	F	VF	XF	Unc	BU
1996	—	—	—	3.50	5.00

KM# 972a POUND
9.5000 g., 0.9250 Silver .2825 oz. ASW **Ruler:** Elizabeth II **Obv:** Head right **Rev:** Celtic cross

Date	F	VF	XF	Unc	BU
1996 Proof		Value: 37.50			

KM# 975 POUND
9.5000 g., Nickel-Brass **Ruler:** Elizabeth II **Obv:** Head right **Rev:** Plantagenet lions **Edge Lettering:** DECUS ET TUTAMEN

Date	F	VF	XF	Unc	BU
1997	—	—	—	3.50	5.50

KM# 975a POUND
9.5000 g., 0.9250 Silver .2825 oz. ASW **Ruler:** Elizabeth II **Obv:** Head right **Rev:** Plantagenet lions **Edge Lettering:** DECUS ET TUTAMEN

Date	F	VF	XF	Unc	BU
1997 Proof		Value: 40.00			

KM# 993 POUND
Nickel-Brass **Ruler:** Elizabeth II **Obv:** Head right **Rev:** Shield of Great Britian within Garter, all crowned and supported **Edge Lettering:** DECUS ET TUTAMEN

Date	F	VF	XF	Unc	BU
1998-2003	—	—	—	4.50	6.00

KM# 993a POUND
9.5000 g., 0.9250 Silver .2825 oz. ASW **Ruler:** Elizabeth II **Obv:** Head right **Rev:** Shield of Great Britiain within Garter, all crowned and supported

Date	F	VF	XF	Unc	BU
1998	—	—	—	40.00	—

KM# 998 POUND
Nickel-Brass **Ruler:** Elizabeth II **Obv:** Head right **Rev:** Scottish lion **Edge Lettering:** NEMO ME IMPUNE LACESSTT

Date	F	VF	XF	Unc	BU
1999	—	—	2.00	3.50	5.50

KM# 998a POUND
9.5000 g., 0.9250 Silver .2825 oz. ASW **Ruler:** Elizabeth II **Obv:** Head right **Rev:** Scottish lion

Date	F	VF	XF	Unc	BU
1999 Proof		Value: 40.00			

KM# 1005 POUND
Nickel-Brass **Ruler:** Elizabeth II **Obv:** Head right **Rev:** Welsh dragon **Edge:** Reeded and lettered **Edge Lettering:** PLEIDIOL WYF I'M GWLAD

Date	F	VF	XF	Unc	BU
2000	—	—	—	3.50	5.00

KM# 1005a POUND
9.5000 g., 0.9250 Silver 0.2825 oz. ASW, 22.5 mm. **Ruler:** Elizabeth II **Subject:** Wales **Obv:** Head right **Rev:** Welsh dragon **Edge:** Reeded **Edge Lettering:** PLEIDIOL WYF I'M GWLAD

Date	F	VF	XF	Unc	BU
2000 Proof		Value: 40.00			

KM# 1013 POUND
9.5000 g., Nickel-Brass, 22.5 mm. **Ruler:** Elizabeth II **Subject:** Northern Ireland **Obv:** Queen's new portrait **Rev:** Celtic style cross **Edge:** Reeding **Edge Lettering:** DEBUS ET TUTAMEN

Date	F	VF	XF	Unc	BU
2001	—	—	—	3.50	5.00

KM# 1013a POUND
9.5000 g., 0.9250 Silver 0.2825 oz. ASW, 22.5 mm. **Ruler:** Elizabeth II **Subject:** Northern Ireland **Obv:** Queen's new portrait **Rev:** Celtic cross design **Edge:** Reeded **Edge Lettering:** DECUS ET TUTAMEN

Date	F	VF	XF	Unc	BU
2001 Proof		Value: 40.00			

KM# 1030 POUND
9.5000 g., Nickel-Brass, 22.5 mm. **Ruler:** Elizabeth II **Obv:** Queen's new portrait **Rev:** Three lions **Edge:** Reeded **Edge Lettering:** DECUS ET TUTAMEN

Date	F	VF	XF	Unc	BU
2002	—	—	—	3.50	5.00

KM# 1030a POUND
9.5000 g., 0.9250 Silver 0.2825 oz. ASW **Ruler:** Elizabeth II **Obv:** Queen's new portrait **Rev:** Three lions **Edge:** Reeded **Edge Lettering:** DECUS ET TUTAMEN

Date	F	VF	XF	Unc	BU
2002 Proof		Value: 40.00			

KM# 1048 POUND
9.5000 g., Nickel-Brass, 22.5 mm. **Ruler:** Elizabeth II **Obv:** Queen Elizabeth II **Rev:** "Forth Rail Bridge" in Scotland **Edge:** Reeded and lettered **Edge Lettering:** "NEMO ME IMPUNE LACESSIT"

Date	F	VF	XF	Unc	BU
2004	—	—	—	6.00	7.50

KM# 1051 POUND
9.5000 g., Nickel-Brass, 22.5 mm. **Ruler:** Elizabeth II **Obv:** Queen Elizabeth II **Rev:** Menai Bridge in Wales **Edge:** Reeded and lettered **Edge Lettering:** "PLEIDOL WYF I'M GWLAD"

Date	F	VF	XF	Unc	BU
2005	—	—	—	3.00	4.00

KM# 1051a POUND
9.5000 g., 0.9250 Silver 0.2825 oz. ASW, 22.5 mm. **Ruler:** Elizabeth II **Obv:** Elizabeth II **Rev:** Menai Bridge **Edge Lettering:** 'PLEIDOL WYF I'M GWLAD"

Date	F	VF	XF	Unc	BU
2005 Proof		Value: 45.00			

KM# 1051b POUND
19.6190 g., 0.9167 Gold 0.5782 oz. AGW, 22.5 mm. **Ruler:** Elizabeth II **Obv:** Elizabeth II **Rev:** Menai Bridge **Edge Lettering:** 'PLEIDOL WYF I'M GWLAD"

Date	F	VF	XF	Unc	BU
2005 Proof		Value: 725			

KM# 1059 POUND
9.5000 g., Nickel-Brass, 22.5 mm. **Ruler:** Elizabeth II **Obv:** Queen Elizabeth II **Rev:** Egyptian Arch Bridge at Newry, Northern Ireland **Edge:** Reeded and lettered

Date	F	VF	XF	Unc	BU
2006	—	—	—	8.00	9.00

KM# 1059a POUND
9.5000 g., 0.9250 Silver 0.2825 oz. ASW, 22.5 mm. **Ruler:** Elizabeth II **Obv:** Elizabeth II **Rev:** Egyptian Arch Bridge **Edge Lettering:** "DECUS ET TUTAMEN"

Date	F	VF	XF	Unc	BU
2006 Proof		Value: 50.00			

KM# 1059b POUND
19.6190 g., 0.9167 Gold 0.5782 oz. AGW, 22.5 mm. **Ruler:** Elizabeth II **Obv:** Elizabeth II **Rev:** Egyptian Arch Bridge **Edge Lettering:** "DECUS ET TUTAMEN"

Date	F	VF	XF	Unc	BU
2006 Proof		Value: 725			

KM# 947 2 POUNDS
Nickel-Brass **Ruler:** Elizabeth II **Subject:** Commonwealth Games **Obv:** Head right **Rev:** Thistle on St. Andrew's Cross **Edge Lettering:** XIII COMMONWEALTH GAMES SCOTLAND 1986

Date	F	VF	XF	Unc	BU
1986	—	—	4.50	6.50	10.00

KM# 947a 2 POUNDS
15.9800 g., 0.5000 Silver .2569 oz. ASW **Ruler:** Elizabeth II **Subject:** Commonwealth Games **Obv:** Head right **Rev:** Thistle on St. Andrew's cross

Date	F	VF	XF	Unc	BU
1986	—	—	—	15.00	20.00

KM# 947b 2 POUNDS
15.9800 g., 0.9250 Silver .4752 oz. ASW **Ruler:** Elizabeth II **Subject:** Commonwealth Games **Obv:** Head right **Rev:** Thistle on St. Andrew's Cross

Date	F	VF	XF	Unc	BU
1986 Proof		Value: 25.00			

KM# 947c 2 POUNDS
15.9800 g., 0.9170 Gold .4710 oz. AGW **Ruler:** Elizabeth II **Subject:** Commonwealth Games **Obv:** Head right **Rev:** Thistle on St. Andrew's Cross

Date	F	VF	XF	Unc	BU
1986 Proof		Value: 290			

KM# 960 2 POUNDS
Nickel-Brass **Ruler:** Elizabeth II **Subject:** Tercentenary - Bill of Rights **Obv:** Head right **Rev:** St. Edward's crown above sceptre and WM monogram

Date	F	VF	XF	Unc	BU
ND(1989)	—	—	—	6.50	10.00

KM# 960a   2 POUNDS
15.9800 g., 0.9250 Silver .4752 oz. ASW   **Ruler:** Elizabeth II
Subject: Tercentenary - Bill of Rights **Obv:** Head right **Rev:** St.
Edward's crowned above sceptre and WM monogram

Date	F	VF	XF	Unc	BU
ND(1989) Proof		Value: 25.00			

KM# 961   2 POUNDS
Nickel-Brass   **Ruler:** Elizabeth II **Subject:** Tercentenary - Claim
of Right **Obv:** Head left **Rev:** Crown of Scotland above sceptre
and WM monogram

Date	F	VF	XF	Unc	BU
ND(1989)	—	—	—	9.00	15.00

KM# 961a   2 POUNDS
15.9800 g., 0.9250 Silver .4752 oz. ASW   **Ruler:** Elizabeth II
Subject: Tercentenary - Claim of Right **Obv:** Head right **Rev:**
Crown of Scotland above sceptre and WM monogram

Date	F	VF	XF	Unc	BU
ND(1989) Proof		Value: 25.00			

KM# 1012   2 POUNDS
15.9800 g., 0.9170 Gold .4710 oz. AGW   **Ruler:** Elizabeth II **Obv:**
2 Pounds, KM#944, Sovereign Obverse **Rev:** 2 Pounds, KM#968c,
Bank of England Commemorative **Note:** Muled die error.

Date	F	VF	XF	Unc	BU
ND(1994)	—	—	—	625	—

KM# 968   2 POUNDS
Nickel-Brass   **Ruler:** Elizabeth II **Subject:** 300th Anniversary -
Bank of England **Obv:** Head right **Rev:** Britiannia seated within
oval, Crowned WM monogram above **Edge Lettering:** SIC VOS
NON VOBIS

Date	F	VF	XF	Unc	BU
ND(1994)	—	—	—	5.50	9.00

KM# 968a   2 POUNDS
15.9800 g., 0.9250 Silver .4752 oz. ASW   **Ruler:** Elizabeth II
Subject: 300th Anniversary - Bank of England **Obv:** Head right
Rev: Britiannia seated within oval, Crowned WM monogram above

Date	F	VF	XF	Unc	BU
ND(1994) Proof		Value: 40.00			

KM# 968c   2 POUNDS
15.9800 g., 0.9170 Gold .4710 oz. AGW   **Ruler:** Elizabeth II
Subject: 300th Anniversary - Bank of England **Obv:** Head right
Rev: Britiannia seated within oval, Crowned WM monogram above

Date	F	VF	XF	Unc	BU
ND(1994) Proof		Value: 470			

KM# 970   2 POUNDS
Nickel-Brass   **Ruler:** Elizabeth II **Subject:** 50th Anniversary, end
of World War II **Obv:** Head right **Rev:** Dove with laurel branch
Edge Lettering: 1945 IN PEACE GOODWILL 1995

Date	F	VF	XF	Unc	BU
ND(1995)	—	—	—	6.00	10.00

KM# 970a   2 POUNDS
15.9800 g., 0.9250 Silver .4752 oz. ASW   **Ruler:** Elizabeth II **Obv:**
Head right **Rev:** Dove with laurel branch

Date	F	VF	XF	Unc	BU
ND(1995) Proof		Value: 40.00			

KM# 970c   2 POUNDS
15.9800 g., 0.9170 Gold .4710 oz. AGW   **Ruler:** Elizabeth II
Subject: 50th Anniversary, end of World War II **Obv:** Head right
Rev: Dove with laurel branch

Date	F	VF	XF	Unc	BU
ND(1995) Proof		Value: 475			

KM# 971   2 POUNDS
Nickel-Brass   **Ruler:** Elizabeth II **Subject:** 50th Anniversary -
United Nations **Obv:** Head right **Rev:** Flags and UN Logo **Note:**
Mintage included with KM#970.

Date	F	VF	XF	Unc	BU
ND(1995)	—	—	—	6.00	9.00

KM# 971a   2 POUNDS
15.9760 g., 0.9250 Silver .4751 oz. ASW   **Ruler:** Elizabeth II
Subject: 50th Anniversary - United Nations **Obv:** Head right **Rev:**
Flags and UN Logo

Date	F	VF	XF	Unc	BU
ND(1995) Proof		Value: 40.00			

KM# 971c   2 POUNDS
15.9760 g., 0.9170 Gold .4708 oz. AGW   **Ruler:** Elizabeth II
Subject: 50th Anniversary - United Nations **Obv:** Head right **Rev:**
Flags and UN Logo

Date	F	VF	XF	Unc	BU
ND(1995) Proof		Value: 475			

KM# 973   2 POUNDS
Nickel-Brass   **Ruler:** Elizabeth II **Obv:** Head right **Rev:** Soccer
ball **Edge Lettering:** TENTH EUROPEAN CHAMPIONSHIP

Date	F	VF	XF	Unc	BU
1996	—	—	—	6.50	10.00

KM# 973a 2 POUNDS
15.9760 g., 0.9250 Silver .4751 oz. ASW **Ruler:** Elizabeth II **Obv:** Head right **Rev:** Soccer ball

Date	F	VF	XF	Unc	BU
1996 Proof			Value: 40.00		

KM# 976 2 POUNDS
Bi-Metallic Copper-Nickel center in Nickel-Brass ring **Ruler:** Elizabeth II **Obv:** Head right **Rev:** Celtic designs **Edge Lettering:** STANDING ON THE SHOULDERS OF GIANTS

Date	F	VF	XF	Unc	BU
1997	—	—	—	7.50	12.50

KM# 976a 2 POUNDS
12.0000 g., 0.9250 Silver .3568 oz. ASW **Ruler:** Elizabeth II **Obv:** Head right **Rev:** Celtic designs **Note:** Gold plated silver ring, silver center.

Date	F	VF	XF	Unc	BU
1997 Proof			Value: 45.00		

KM# 976b 2 POUNDS
15.9800 g., 0.9170 Gold .4710 oz. AGW **Ruler:** Elizabeth II **Obv:** Head right **Rev:** Celtic design **Note:** Red gold ring, yellow gold center.

Date	F	VF	XF	Unc	BU
1997 Proof			Value: 650		

KM# 994 2 POUNDS
Bi-Metallic Copper-Nickel center in Nickel-Brass ring, 28.35 mm. **Ruler:** Elizabeth II **Obv:** Head right **Rev:** Celtic design **Edge Lettering:** STANDING ON THE SHOULDERS OF GIANTS

Date	F	VF	XF	Unc	BU
1998-2006	—	—	—	6.00	8.50

KM# 994a 2 POUNDS
12.0000 g., 0.9250 Silver .3568 oz. ASW **Ruler:** Elizabeth II **Obv:** Head right **Rev:** Celtic design **Note:** Gold plated silver ring, silver center.

Date	F	VF	XF	Unc	BU
1998 Proof			Value: 50.00		

KM# 994b 2 POUNDS
12.0000 g., 0.9250 Silver .3568 oz. ASW **Ruler:** Elizabeth II **Obv:** Head right **Rev:** Celtic design **Note:** Without gold plating.

Date	F	VF	XF	Unc	BU
1998 Proof			Value: 40.00		

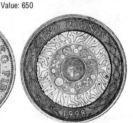

KM# 999 2 POUNDS
Bi-Metallic Copper-Nickel center in Nickel-Brass ring **Ruler:** Elizabeth II **Subject:** Rugby World Cup **Obv:** Head right **Rev:** 2-tone rugby design **Note:** Varieties exist.

Date	F	VF	XF	Unc	BU
1999	—	—	—	7.00	9.00

KM# 999a 2 POUNDS
12.0000 g., 0.9250 Silver .3569 oz. ASW **Ruler:** Elizabeth II **Obv:** Head right **Rev:** Rugby design **Edge:** Reeded, lettered edge **Note:** Gold plated ring.

Date	F	VF	XF	Unc	BU
1999 Proof			Value: 47.50		

KM# 999b 2 POUNDS
15.9800 g., 0.9170 Gold .4710 oz. AGW **Ruler:** Elizabeth II **Obv:** Head right **Rev:** Rugby design

Date	F	VF	XF	Unc	BU
1999 Proof			Value: 525		

KM# 999c 2 POUNDS
24.0000 g., 0.9250 Silver .7137 oz. ASW **Ruler:** Elizabeth II **Obv:** Head right within gold-plated ring **Rev:** Multicolor hologram center within gold-plated ring **Edge:** Reeded, lettered edge

Date	F	VF	XF	Unc	BU
1999 Proof			Value: 80.00		

KM# 1014 2 POUNDS
11.9700 g., Bi-Metallic Copper-Nickel center in Nickel-Brass ring, 28.4 mm. **Ruler:** Elizabeth II **Subject:** First Transatlantic Radio Transmission **Obv:** Head right **Rev:** Symbolic design **Edge:** Reeded and inscribed

Date	F	VF	XF	Unc	BU
2001	—	—	—	5.00	6.50

KM# 1014a 2 POUNDS
24.0000 g., 0.9250 Silver Gold plated ring .7137 oz. ASW, 28.4 mm. **Ruler:** Elizabeth II **Edge:** Reeded and inscribed **Edge Lettering:** "WIRELESS BRIDGES THE ATLANTIC...MARCONI 1901..."

Date	F	VF	XF	Unc	BU
2001 Proof			Value: 33.50		

KM# 1014b 2 POUNDS
15.9700 g., 0.9166 Gold Yellow gold plated Red Gold center in Red Gold ring .4706 oz. AGW, 28.4 mm. **Ruler:** Elizabeth II

Date	F	VF	XF	Unc	BU
2001 Proof			Value: 445		

KM# 1019 2 POUNDS
32.4500 g., 0.9584 Silver .9999 oz. ASW, 40 mm. **Ruler:** Elizabeth II **Subject:** Britannia Bullion **Obv:** Queen's portrait **Rev:** Stylized "Britannia and the Lion" **Edge:** Reeded

Date	F	VF	XF	Unc	BU
2001	—	—	—	25.00	30.00

KM# 1031 2 POUNDS

12.0000 g., Bi-Metallic Copper-Nickel center in Nickel-Brass ring, 28.4 mm. **Ruler:** Elizabeth II **Subject:** Commonwealth Games - England **Obv:** Head of Queen Elizabeth II right **Rev:** Runner breaking ribbon at finish line **Edge:** Reeded and lettered

Date	F	VF	XF	Unc	BU
2002	—	—	—	5.00	6.00

KM# 1031a 2 POUNDS

12.0000 g., Silver Gold plated ring, 28.4 mm. **Ruler:** Elizabeth II **Subject:** Commonwealth Games - England **Obv:** Head of Queen Elizabeth II right **Rev:** Runner breaking ribbon at finish line **Edge:** Reeded and lettered

Date	F	VF	XF	Unc	BU
2002	—	—	—	30.00	35.00

KM# 1031b 2 POUNDS

15.9800 g., 0.9160 Gold Yellow gold center in Red Gold ring, 28.4 mm. **Ruler:** Elizabeth II **Subject:** Commonwealth Games - England **Obv:** Head of Queen Elizabeth II right **Rev:** Runner breaking ribbon at finish line **Edge:** Reeded and lettered

Date	F	VF	XF	Unc	BU
2002 Proof		Value: 500			

KM# 1032 2 POUNDS

12.0000 g., Bi-Metallic Copper-Nickel center in Nickel-Brass ring, 28.4 mm. **Ruler:** Elizabeth II **Subject:** Commonwealth Games - Scotland **Obv:** Head of Queen Elizabeth II right **Rev:** Runner breaking ribbon at finish line **Edge:** Reeded and lettered

Date	F	VF	XF	Unc	BU
2002	—	—	—	5.00	6.00

KM# 1032a 2 POUNDS

Bi-Metallic Silver center with Gold plated ring, 28.4 mm. **Ruler:** Elizabeth II **Subject:** Commonwealth Games - Scotland **Obv:** Head of Queen Elizabeth II right **Rev:** Runner breaking ribbon at finish line **Edge:** Reeded and lettered

Date	F	VF	XF	Unc	BU
2002 Proof		Value: 30.00			

KM# 1032b 2 POUNDS

15.9800 g., 0.9160 Gold Yellow gold center in Red Gold ring, 28.4 mm. **Ruler:** Elizabeth II **Subject:** Commonwealth Games - Scotland **Obv:** Head of Queen Elizabeth II right **Rev:** Runner breaking ribbon at finish line **Edge:** Reeded and lettered

Date	F	VF	XF	Unc	BU
2002 Proof		Value: 500			

KM# 1033 2 POUNDS

12.0000 g., Bi-Metallic Copper-Nickel center in Nickel-Brass ring, 28.4 mm. **Ruler:** Elizabeth II **Subject:** Commonwealth Games - Wales **Obv:** Head of Queen Elizabeth II right **Rev:** Runner breaking ribbon at finish line **Edge:** Reeded and lettered

Date	F	VF	XF	Unc	BU
2002	—	—	—	5.00	6.00

KM# 1033a 2 POUNDS

12.0000 g., Silver Silver center in Gold plated ring, 28.4 mm. **Ruler:** Elizabeth II **Subject:** Commonwealth Games - Wales **Obv:** Head of Queen Elizabeth II right **Rev:** Runner breaking ribbon at finish line **Edge:** Reeded and lettered

Date	F	VF	XF	Unc	BU
2002 Proof		Value: 30.00			

KM# 1033b 2 POUNDS

15.9800 g., 0.9160 Gold Yellow Gold center in Red Gold ring, 28.4 mm. **Ruler:** Elizabeth II **Subject:** Commonwealth Games - Wales **Obv:** Head of Queen Elizabeth II right **Rev:** Runner breaking ribbon at finish line **Edge:** Reeded and lettered

Date	F	VF	XF	Unc	BU
2002 Proof		Value: 500			

KM# 1034 2 POUNDS

12.0000 g., Bi-Metallic Copper-Nickel center in Nickel-Brass ring, 28.4 mm. **Ruler:** Elizabeth II **Subject:** Commonwealth Games - Northern Ireland **Obv:** Head of Queen Elizabeth II right **Rev:** Runner breaking ribbon at finish line **Edge:** Reeded and lettered

Date	F	VF	XF	Unc	BU
2002	—	—	—	5.00	6.00

KM# 1034a 2 POUNDS

12.0000 g., Silver Silver center in Gold plated ring, 28.4 mm. **Ruler:** Elizabeth II **Subject:** Commonwealth Games - Northern Ireland **Obv:** Head of Queen Elizabeth II right **Rev:** Runner breaking ribbon at finish line **Edge:** Reeded and lettered

Date	F	VF	XF	Unc	BU
2002 Proof		Value: 30.00			

KM# 1034b 2 POUNDS

15.9800 g., 0.9160 Gold Yellow Gold center in Red Gold ring, 28.4 mm. **Ruler:** Elizabeth II **Subject:** Commonwealth Games - Northern Ireland **Obv:** Head of Queen Elizabeth II right **Rev:** Runner breaking ribbon at finish line **Edge:** Reeded and lettered

Date	F	VF	XF	Unc	BU
2002 Proof		Value: 500			

KM# 1037   2 POUNDS
12.0000 g., Bi-Metallic Copper-Nickel center in Nickel-Brass ring,
28.4 mm. **Ruler:** Elizabeth II **Subject:** D N A **Obv:** Queen's
portrait **Rev:** DNA Double Helix **Edge:** Reeded and inscribed

Date	F	VF	XF	Unc	BU
ND(2003)	—	—	—	5.00	6.50

KM# 1037a   2 POUNDS
12.0000 g., 0.9250 Silver Silver center in Gold plated silver ring
0.3569 oz. ASW, 28.4 mm. **Ruler:** Elizabeth II **Obv:** Queen
Elizabeth II **Rev:** DNA Double Helix **Edge:** Reeded and lettered

Date	F	VF	XF	Unc	BU
ND(2003) Proof		Value: 30.00			

KM# 1037b   2 POUNDS
15.9800 g., 0.9167 Gold Yellow gold center in Red gold ring
0.471 oz. AGW, 28.4 mm. **Ruler:** Elizabeth II **Obv:** Queen
Elizabeth II **Rev:** DNA Double Helix **Edge:** Reeded and lettered

Date	F	VF	XF	Unc	BU
ND(2003) Proof		Value: 550			

KM# 1049   2 POUNDS
12.0000 g., Bi-Metallic Nickel-Brass center in Copper-Nickel ring,
28.4 mm. **Ruler:** Elizabeth II **Obv:** Queen Elizabeth II **Rev:** First
steam locomotive **Edge:** Reeded and lettered

Date	F	VF	XF	Unc	BU
2004	—	—	—	7.50	8.50

KM# 1049a   2 POUNDS
12.0000 g., 0.9250 Bi-Metallic .925 Silver center in Gold Plated .925
Silver ring 0.3569 oz., 28.4 mm. **Ruler:** Elizabeth II **Obv:** Queen
Elizabeth II **Rev:** First steam locomotive **Edge:** Reeded and lettered

Date	F	VF	XF	Unc	BU
2004 Proof		Value: 30.00			

KM# 1049b   2 POUNDS
15.9800 g., 0.9166 Bi-Metallic .9166 Yellow Gold center in .9166
Red Gold ring 0.4709 oz., 28.4 mm. **Ruler:** Elizabeth II **Obv:**
Queen Elizabeth II **Rev:** First steam locomotive **Edge:** Reeded
and lettered

Date	F	VF	XF	Unc	BU
2004 Proof		Value: 450			

KM# 1052   2 POUNDS
12.0000 g., Bi-Metallic Nickel-Brass center in Copper-Nickel ring,
28.4 mm. **Ruler:** Elizabeth II **Subject:** 400th Anniversary - The
Gunpowder Plot **Obv:** Queen Elizabeth II **Rev:** Circular design of
Royal scepters, swords and crosiers **Edge:** Reeded and lettered

Date	F	VF	XF	Unc	BU
ND(2005)	—	—	—	6.00	7.00

KM# 1056   2 POUNDS
12.0000 g., 0.9250 Silver Gold plated outer ring 0.3569 oz. ASW,
28.4 mm. **Ruler:** Elizabeth II **Subject:** End of WW II **Obv:**
Elizabeth II **Rev:** St. Paul's Cathedral amid search light beams
Edge: Reeded and lettered **Edge Lettering:** "IN VICTORY
MAGNANIMITY IN PEACE GOODWILL"

Date	F	VF	XF	Unc	BU
ND (2005) Proof		Value: 30.00			

KM# 1061   2 POUNDS
12.0000 g., Bi-Metallic Copper-Nickel center in Nickel-Brass ring,
28.4 mm. **Ruler:** Elizabeth II **Obv:** Queen Elizabeth II **Rev:**
Paddington Station structural supports **Edge:** Lettered

Date	F	VF	XF	Unc	BU
2006	—	—	—	16.00	17.50

KM# 962   5 POUNDS
Copper-Nickel **Ruler:** Elizabeth II **Subject:** 90th Birthday of
Queen Mother **Obv:** Head right **Rev:** Crowned E monogram with
rose and thistle flanking

Date	F	VF	XF	Unc	BU
ND(1990)	—	—	—	15.00	—

KM# 962a   5 POUNDS
28.2800 g., 0.9250 Silver .8411 oz. ASW **Ruler:** Elizabeth II **Obv:**
Head right **Rev:** Crowned E monogram with rose and thistle flanking

Date	F	VF	XF	Unc	BU
ND(1990) Proof		Value: 40.00			

KM# 962b   5 POUNDS
39.9400 g., 0.9170 Gold 1.1775 oz. AGW **Ruler:** Elizabeth II
Subject: 90th Birthday of Queen Mother **Obv:** Head right **Rev:**
Crowned E monogram with rose and thistle flanking

Date	F	VF	XF	Unc	BU
ND(1990) Proof		Value: 725			

KM# 965   5 POUNDS
Copper-Nickel   **Ruler:** Elizabeth II **Subject:** 40th Anniversary of Reign **Obv:** Head right with circle of bugling horsemen **Rev:** Crown within rays

Date	F	VF	XF	Unc	BU
ND(1993)	—	—	—	13.50	—

KM# 965a   5 POUNDS
28.2800 g., 0.9250 Silver .8411 oz. ASW   **Ruler:** Elizabeth II **Obv:** Head right with circle of bugling horsemen **Rev:** Crown within rays

Date	F	VF	XF	Unc	BU
ND(1993) Proof		Value: 45.00			

KM# 965b   5 POUNDS
39.9400 g., 0.9170 Gold 1.1775 oz. AGW   **Ruler:** Elizabeth II **Subject:** 40th Anniversary of Reign **Obv:** Head right with circle of bugling horsemen **Rev:** Crown within rays

Date	F	VF	XF	Unc	BU
ND(1993) Proof		Value: 950			

KM# 974   5 POUNDS
Copper-Nickel   **Ruler:** Elizabeth II **Subject:** 70th Birthday of Queen Elizabeth II **Obv:** Head right **Rev:** Five banners above Windsor Castle **Edge Lettering:** VIVAT REGINA ELIZABETHA

Date	F	VF	XF	Unc	BU
ND(1996)	—	—	—	14.00	—

KM# 974a   5 POUNDS
28.2800 g., 0.9250 Silver .8411 oz. ASW   **Ruler:** Elizabeth II **Obv:** Head right **Rev:** Five banners above Windsor Castle

Date	F	VF	XF	Unc	BU
ND(1996) Proof		Value: 45.00			

KM# 974b   5 POUNDS
39.9400 g., 0.9170 Gold 1.1775 oz. AGW   **Ruler:** Elizabeth II **Subject:** 70th Birthday of Queen Elizabeth II **Obv:** Head right **Rev:** Five banners above Windsor Castle

Date	F	VF	XF	Unc	BU
ND(1996) Proof		Value: 1,000			

KM# 977   5 POUNDS
Copper-Nickel   **Ruler:** Elizabeth II **Subject:** Queen Elizabeth II's Golden Wedding Anniversary **Obv:** Conjoined busts right of Elizabeth II and Prince Philip **Rev:** Two shields, crown above, anchor below

Date	F	VF	XF	Unc	BU
ND(1997)	—	—	—	15.00	—

KM# 977a   5 POUNDS
28.2800 g., 0.9250 Silver .8411 oz. ASW   **Ruler:** Elizabeth II **Obv:** Conjoined busts right of Elizabeth II and Prince Philip **Rev:** Two shields, crown above, anchor below

Date	F	VF	XF	Unc	BU
ND(1997) Proof		Value: 50.00			

KM# 977b   5 POUNDS
39.9400 g., 0.9170 Gold 1.1775 oz. AGW   **Ruler:** Elizabeth II **Obv:** Conjoined busts right of Elizabeth II and Prince Philip **Rev:** Two shields, crown above, anchor below

Date	F	VF	XF	Unc	BU
ND(1997) Proof		Value: 995			

KM# 995   5 POUNDS
Copper-Nickel   **Ruler:** Elizabeth II **Subject:** 50th Birthday - Prince Charles **Obv:** Head right **Rev:** Portrait of Prince Charles

Date	F	VF	XF	Unc	BU
1998	—	—	—	15.00	—

KM# 995a   5 POUNDS
28.2800 g., 0.9250 Silver .8411 oz. ASW   **Ruler:** Elizabeth II **Subject:** 50th Birthday - Prince Charles **Obv:** Head right **Rev:** Portrait of Prince Charles

Date	F	VF	XF	Unc	BU
1998 Proof		Value: 50.00			

KM# 995b   5 POUNDS
39.9400 g., 0.9167 Gold 1.1771 oz. AGW   **Ruler:** Elizabeth II **Subject:** 50th Birthday - Prince Charles **Obv:** Head right **Rev:** Portrait of Prince Charles

Date	F	VF	XF	Unc	BU
1998 Proof		Value: 900			

KM# 1006   5 POUNDS
Copper-Nickel   **Ruler:** Elizabeth II **Obv:** Head right **Rev:** Map with Greenwich Meridian **Edge Lettering:** WHAT'S PAST IS PROLOGUE

Date	F	VF	XF	Unc	BU
1999-2000	—	—	—	14.00	—

KM# 1006.1 5 POUNDS
Copper-Nickel **Ruler:** Elizabeth II **Rev:** Map with Greenwich Meridian, world globe at 3 o'clock in inner circle

Date	F	VF	XF	Unc	BU
2000	—	—	—	20.00	—

KM# 1006a 5 POUNDS
28.2800 g., 0.9250 Silver .8410 oz. ASW **Ruler:** Elizabeth II **Obv:** Head right **Rev:** Map with Greenwich Meridian

Date	F	VF	XF	Unc	BU
1999-2000 Proof		Value: 55.00			

KM# 1006b 5 POUNDS
39.9400 g., 0.9170 Gold 1.1771 oz. AGW **Ruler:** Elizabeth II **Obv:** Head right **Rev:** Map with Greenwich Meridian

Date	F	VF	XF	Unc	BU
1999-2000 Proof		Value: 995			

KM# 1006c 5 POUNDS
28.2800 g., 0.9990 Silver 0.9083 oz. ASW **Ruler:** Elizabeth II **Obv:** Head right **Rev:** Map with Greenwich Meridian **Note:** With gold-plated British map.

Date	F	VF	XF	Unc	BU
2000 Proof		Value: 65.00			

KM# 997 5 POUNDS
28.2800 g., 0.9250 Silver .8411 oz. ASW **Ruler:** Elizabeth II **Obv:** Head right **Rev:** Profile right of Princess Diana, dates

Date	F	VF	XF	Unc	BU
1999	—	—	—	16.00	—

KM# 997a 5 POUNDS
28.2800 g., 0.9250 Silver .8410 oz. ASW **Ruler:** Elizabeth II **Obv:** Head right **Rev:** Profile right of Princess Diana, dates

Date	F	VF	XF	Unc	BU
1999 Proof		Value: 50.00			

KM# 997b 5 POUNDS
39.9400 g., 0.9170 Gold 1.1775 oz. AGW **Ruler:** Elizabeth II **Obv:** Head right **Rev:** Profile right of Princess Diana, dates

Date	F	VF	XF	Unc	BU
1999 Proof		Value: 925			

KM# 1007 5 POUNDS
Copper-Nickel **Ruler:** Elizabeth II **Subject:** 100th Birthday - Queen Elizabeth, The Queen Mother **Obv:** Head right **Rev:** Queen Mother's profile left with signature below **Edge:** Reeded

Date	F	VF	XF	Unc	BU
2000	—	—	—	15.00	—

KM# 1007a 5 POUNDS
28.2800 g., 0.9250 Silver .8410 oz. ASW **Ruler:** Elizabeth II **Subject:** Queen Mother's Centennial **Obv:** Head right **Rev:** Queen Mother's profile left with signature below **Edge:** Reeded

Date	F	VF	XF	Unc	BU
2000 Proof		Value: 55.00			

KM# 1007b 5 POUNDS
39.9400 g., 0.9167 Gold 1.0003 oz. AGW **Ruler:** Elizabeth II **Obv:** Head right **Rev:** Queen Mother's profile left with signature below

Date	F	VF	XF	Unc	BU
2000 Proof		Value: 950			

KM# 1015 5 POUNDS
28.2800 g., Copper-Nickel, 38.6 mm. **Ruler:** Elizabeth II **Subject:** Centennial of Queen Victoria **Obv:** Queen Elizabeth's portrait **Rev:** Queen Victoria's portrait **Edge:** Reeded

Date	F	VF	XF	Unc	BU
2001	—	—	—	14.00	16.00

KM# 1015a 5 POUNDS
28.2800 g., 0.9250 Silver 0.841 oz. ASW, 38.6 mm. **Ruler:** Elizabeth II **Subject:** Centennial of Queen Victoria **Obv:** Queen Elizabeth's portrait **Rev:** Queen Victoria's portrait

Date	F	VF	XF	Unc	BU
2001 Proof		Value: 65.00			

KM# 1015b 5 POUNDS
39.9400 g., 0.9167 Gold 1.1771 oz. AGW **Ruler:** Elizabeth II

Date	F	VF	XF	Unc	BU
2001 Proof		Value: 1,000			

KM# 1024   5 POUNDS
28.2800 g., Copper-Nickel, 38.6 mm. **Ruler:** Elizabeth II
Subject: Queen's Golden Jubilee of Reign **Obv:** Queen's portrait
Rev: Queen on horse **Edge:** Reeded

Date	F	VF	XF	Unc	BU
2002	—	—	—	12.50	14.50

KM# 1024a   5 POUNDS
28.2800 g., 0.9250 Silver .8410 oz. ASW, 38.6 mm. **Ruler:**
Elizabeth II **Edge:** Reeded

Date	F	VF	XF	Unc	BU
2002 Proof		Value: 50.00			

KM# 1024b   5 POUNDS
39.9400 g., 0.9167 Gold 1.0003 oz. AGW, 38.6 mm. **Ruler:**
Elizabeth II **Edge:** Reeded

Date	F	VF	XF	Unc	BU
2002 Proof		Value: 950			

KM# 1035   5 POUNDS
28.2800 g., Copper Nickel, 38.6 mm. **Ruler:** Elizabeth II **Subject:**
Queen Mother **Obv:** Bust of Queen Elizabeth II right **Rev:** Queen
Mother's portrait in wreath **Edge:** Reeded

Date	F	VF	XF	Unc	BU
ND(2002) Proof		Value: 20.00			

KM# 1035a   5 POUNDS
28.2800 g., Silver, 38.6 mm. **Ruler:** Elizabeth II **Subject:** Queen
Mother **Obv:** Bust of Queen Elizabeth II right **Rev:** Queen Mother's
portrait in wreath **Edge:** Reeded

Date	F	VF	XF	Unc	BU
ND(2002) Proof		Value: 50.00			

KM# 1035b   5 POUNDS
39.9400 g., 0.9167 Gold 1.1771 oz. AGW, 38.6 mm. **Ruler:**
Elizabeth II **Subject:** Queen Mother **Obv:** Bust of Queen Elizabeth
II right **Rev:** Queen Mother's portrait in wreath **Edge:** Reeded

Date	F	VF	XF	Unc	BU
ND(2002) Proof		Value: 950			

KM# 1038   5 POUNDS
28.2800 g., Copper Nickel, 38.6 mm. **Ruler:** Elizabeth II **Subject:**
Queen's Golden Jubilee **Obv:** Queen's stylized portrait **Rev:**
Childlike lettering **Edge:** Reeded

Date	F	VF	XF	Unc	BU
2003	—	—	—	12.50	14.50

KM# 1038a   5 POUNDS
28.2800 g., 0.9250 Silver 0.841 oz. ASW, 38.6 mm. **Ruler:**
Elizabeth II **Edge:** Reeded

Date	F	VF	XF	Unc	BU
2003 Proof		Value: 50.00			

KM# 1038b   5 POUNDS
39.9400 g., 0.9166 Gold 1.177 oz. AGW, 38.6 mm. **Ruler:**
Elizabeth II **Edge:** Reeded

Date	F	VF	XF	Unc	BU
2003 Proof		Value: 950			

KM# 1055   5 POUNDS
28.2800 g., Copper-Nickel, 38.6 mm. **Ruler:** Elizabeth II
Subject: Entente Cordiale **Obv:** Elizabeth II **Rev:** Britannia and
Marianne **Edge:** Reeded

Date	F	VF	XF	Unc	BU
2004	—	—	—	15.00	17.50

KM# 1055a   5 POUNDS
28.2800 g., 0.9250 Silver 0.841 oz. ASW, 38.6 mm. **Ruler:**
Elizabeth II **Subject:** Entente Cordiale **Obv:** Elizabeth II **Rev:**
Britannia and Marianne **Edge:** Reeded

Date	F	VF	XF	Unc	BU
2004 Proof		Value: 50.00			

KM# 1055b   5 POUNDS
39.9400 g., 0.9167 Gold 1.1771 oz. AGW, 38.6 mm. **Ruler:**
Elizabeth II **Subject:** Entente Cordiale **Obv:** Elizabeth II **Rev:**
Britannia and Marianne **Edge:** Reeded

Date	F	VF	XF	Unc	BU
2004 Proof		Value: 1,000			

KM# 1055c   5 POUNDS
94.2000 g., 0.9995 Platinum 3.0271 oz. APW, 38.6 mm. **Ruler:**
Elizabeth II **Subject:** Entente Cordiale **Obv:** Elizabeth II **Rev:**
Britannia and Marianne **Edge:** Reeded

Date	F	VF	XF	Unc	BU
2004 Proof		Value: 4,000			

KM# 1053   5 POUNDS
28.2800 g., Copper-Nickel, 38.6 mm. **Ruler:** Elizabeth II
Subject: Battle of Trafalgar **Obv:** Queen Elizabeth II **Rev:** HMS
Victory and HMS Temeraire at Trafalgar **Edge:** Reeded

Date	F	VF	XF	Unc	BU
2005	—	—	—	15.00	16.50

KM# 1053a 5 POUNDS
28.2800 g., 0.9250 Silver 0.841 oz. ASW, 38.6 mm. **Ruler:**
Elizabeth II **Subject:** Battle of Trafalgar **Obv:** Queen Elizabeth II **Rev:**
Ships HMS Victory and Temeraire at Trafalgar **Edge:** Reeded

Date	F	VF	XF	Unc	BU
2005 Proof			Value: 60.00		

KM# 1053b 5 POUNDS
39.9400 g., 0.9167 Gold 1.1771 oz. AGW, 38.6 mm. **Ruler:**
Elizabeth II **Subject:** Battle of Trafalgar **Obv:** Queen Elizabeth II **Rev:**
Ships HMS Victory and Temeraire at Trafalgar **Edge:** Reeded

Date	F	VF	XF	Unc	BU
2005 Proof			Value: 1,100		

KM# 1054 5 POUNDS
28.2800 g., Copper-Nickel, 38.6 mm. **Ruler:** Elizabeth II **Obv:**
Queen Elizabeth II **Rev:** Admiral Horatio Nelson in uniform **Edge:**
Reeded

Date	F	VF	XF	Unc	BU
2005	—	—	—	15.00	16.50

KM# 1062 5 POUNDS
28.2800 g., Copper-Nickel, 38.6 mm. **Ruler:** Elizabeth II **Obv:**
Queen Elizabeth II **Rev:** Three bannered trumpets **Edge:** Reeded

Date	F	VF	XF	Unc	BU
2006	—	—	—	20.00	22.00

KM# 1060 25 POUNDS (1/4 Ounce - Britannia)
12.0000 g., Bi-Metallic Copper-Nickel center in Nickel-Brass ring,
28.4 mm. **Ruler:** Elizabeth II **Obv:** Queen Elizabeth II **Rev:**
Isambard Brunel **Edge:** Lettered

Date	F	VF	XF	Unc	BU
2006	—	—	—	16.00	18.00

BULLION COINAGE

Until 1990, .917 Gold was commonly alloyed with copper
by the British Royal Mint.

All proof issues have designers name as P. Nathan. The
uncirculated issues use only Nathan.

KM# 978 20 PENCE
3.2400 g., 0.9580 Silver .0098 oz. ASW **Ruler:** Elizabeth II **Obv:**
Head right **Rev:** Britannia in chariot **Note:** Similar to 2 Pounds,
KM#981.

Date	F	VF	XF	Unc	BU
1997 Proof			Value: 25.00		

KM# 1016 20 PENCE
3.2400 g., 0.9580 Silver .0098 oz. ASW, 16.5 mm. **Ruler:**
Elizabeth II **Subject:** Britannia Bullion **Obv:** Queen's portrait **Rev:**
Stylized "Britannia and the Lion" **Edge:** Reeded

Date	F	VF	XF	Unc	BU
2001 Proof			Value: 25.00		

KM# 1044 20 PENCE
3.2400 g., 0.9584 Silver 0.0098 oz. ASW, 16.5 mm. **Ruler:**
Elizabeth II **Obv:** Queen Elizabeth II **Rev:** Britannia portrait behind
wavy lines **Edge:** Reeded

Date	F	VF	XF	Unc	BU
2003 Proof			Value: 35.00		

KM# 979 50 PENCE
8.1100 g., 0.9580 Silver .2498 oz. ASW **Ruler:** Elizabeth II **Obv:**
Queen's portrait **Rev:** Britannia in chariot **Note:** Similar to 2
Pounds, KM#981.

Date	F	VF	XF	Unc	BU
1997 Proof			Value: 25.00		

KM# 1045 50 PENCE
8.1100 g., 0.9584 Silver 0.2499 oz. ASW, 22 mm. **Ruler:**
Elizabeth II **Obv:** Queen Elizabeth II **Rev:** Britannia portrait behind
wavy lines **Edge:** Reeded

Date	F	VF	XF	Unc	BU
2003 Proof			Value: 35.00		

KM# 980 POUND
16.2200 g., 0.9580 Silver .4996 oz. ASW **Ruler:** Elizabeth II **Obv:**
Head right **Rev:** Britannia in chariot **Note:** Similar to 2 Pounds,
KM#981.

Date	F	VF	XF	Unc	BU
1997 Proof			Value: 40.00		

KM# 1018 POUND
16.2200 g., 0.9584 Silver .4998 oz. ASW, 27 mm. **Ruler:**
Elizabeth II **Subject:** Britannia Bullion **Obv:** Queen's portrait **Rev:**
Stylized "Britannia and the Lion" **Edge:** Reeded

Date	F	VF	XF	Unc	BU
2001 Proof			Value: 40.00		

KM# 1046 POUND
16.2200 g., 0.9584 Silver 0.4998 oz. ASW, 27 mm. **Ruler:**
Elizabeth II **Obv:** Queen Elizabeth II **Rev:** Britannia portrait behind
wavy lines **Edge:** Reeded

Date	F	VF	XF	Unc	BU
2003 Proof			Value: 50.00		

KM# 981 2 POUNDS
32.5400 g., 0.9580 Silver .9995 oz. ASW **Ruler:** Elizabeth II **Obv:**
Head right **Rev:** Britannia in chariot

Date	F	VF	XF	Unc	BU
1997 Proof			Value: 50.00		

KM# 1029   2 POUNDS
32.5400 g., 0.9580 Silver .9995 oz. ASW, 40 mm. **Ruler:** Elizabeth II
Obv: Head right **Rev:** Standing Britannia **Edge:** Reeded

Date	F	VF	XF	Unc	BU
1998-2006	—	—	—	20.00	22.00

KM# 1000   2 POUNDS
32.5400 g., 0.9580 Silver .9995 oz. ASW **Ruler:** Elizabeth II **Obv:**
Head right **Rev:** Britannia in chariot

Date	F	VF	XF	Unc	BU
1999 Proof		Value: 45.00			

KM# 1039   2 POUNDS
32.4500 g., 0.9580 Silver 0.9995 oz. ASW, 40 mm. **Ruler:**
Elizabeth II **Subject:** Britannia Bullion **Obv:** Queen's portrait **Rev:**
Britannia portrait behind wavy puzzle-like lines **Edge:** Reeded

Date	F	VF	XF	Unc	BU
2003	—	—	—	—	20.00

KM# 1063   2 POUNDS
32.4500 g., 0.9580 Silver 0.9995 oz. ASW, 40 mm. **Ruler:**
Elizabeth II **Obv:** Elizabeth II **Rev:** Seated Britannia **Edge:** Reeded

Date	F	VF	XF	Unc	BU
2005	—	—	—	—	25.00

KM# 1066   2 POUNDS
15.9760 g., 0.9167 Gold 0.4709 oz. AGW, 28.4 mm. **Ruler:**
Elizabeth II **Obv:** Elizabeth II **Rev:** Knight fighting dragon with
sword **Edge:** Reeded

Date	F	VF	XF	Unc	BU
2005 Proof		Value: 450			

KM# 1000a   2 POUNDS
32.4500 g., 0.9580 Silver 0.9995 oz. ASW, 40 mm. **Ruler:**
Elizabeth II **Subject:** Golden Silhouette Britannias **Obv:** Queen
Elizabeth II **Rev:** Gold plated Britannia in chariot **Edge:** Reeded

Date	F	VF	XF	Unc	BU
2006 Proof		Value: 100			

KM# 1012a   2 POUNDS
32.4500 g., 0.9580 Silver 0.9995 oz. ASW, 40 mm. **Ruler:**
Elizabeth II **Subject:** Golden Silhouette Britannias **Obv:** Queen
Elizabeth II **Rev:** Gold plated Britannia standing with shield **Edge:**
Reeded

Date	F	VF	XF	Unc	BU
2006 Proof		Value: 100			

KM# 1018a   2 POUNDS
32.4500 g., 0.9580 Silver 0.9995 oz. ASW, 40 mm. **Ruler:**
Elizabeth II **Subject:** Golden Silhouette Britannias **Obv:** Queen
Elizabeth II **Rev:** Gold plated Britannia and Lion **Edge:** Reeded

Date	F	VF	XF	Unc	BU
2006 Proof		Value: 100			

KM# 1039a 2 POUNDS
32.4500 g., 0.9580 Silver 0.9995 oz. ASW, 40 mm. **Ruler:**
Elizabeth II **Subject:** Golden Silhouette Britannias **Obv:** Queen
Elizabeth II **Rev:** Gold plated Britannia head **Edge:** Reeded

Date	F	VF	XF	Unc	BU
2006 Proof			Value: 100		

KM# 1063a 2 POUNDS
32.4500 g., 0.9580 Gold 0.9995 oz. AGW, 40 mm. **Ruler:**
Elizabeth II **Subject:** Golden Silhouette Britannias **Obv:** Queen
Elizabeth II **Rev:** Gold plated Britannia seated **Edge:** Reeded

Date	F	VF	XF	Unc	BU
2006 Proof			Value: 100		

KM# 1072 2 POUNDS
15.9700 g., 0.9167 Gold 0.4707 oz. AGW, 28.4 mm. **Ruler:**
Elizabeth II **Obv:** Elizabeth II by Ian Rank-Broadley **Rev:** St.
George slaying the Dragon **Edge:** Reeded

Date	F	VF	XF	Unc	BU
2006 Proof			Value: 450		

KM# 950 10 POUNDS (1/10 Ounce - Britannia)
3.4120 g., 0.9170 Gold .1000 oz. AGW **Ruler:** Elizabeth II **Obv:**
Head right **Rev:** Britannia standing **Note:** Copper alloy.

Date	F	VF	XF	Unc	BU
1987-1989	—	—	—BV+16%	—	

KM# 950a 10 POUNDS (1/10 Ounce - Britannia)
3.4120 g., 0.9170 Gold .1000 oz. AGW **Ruler:** Elizabeth II **Obv:**
Head right **Rev:** Britannia standing **Note:** Silver alloy.

Date	F	VF	XF	Unc	BU
1990-1999 Proof			Value: 80.00		

KM# 982 10 POUNDS (1/10 Ounce - Britannia)
3.41 g., 0.9167 Gold .1005 oz. AGW **Ruler:** Elizabeth II **Obv:** Head
right **Rev:** Britannia in chariot **Note:** Similar to 2 Pounds, KM#981.

Date	F	VF	XF	Unc	BU
1997 Proof			Value: 120		

KM# 1008 10 POUNDS (1/10 Ounce - Britannia)
3.4100 g., 0.9167 Gold .1005 oz. AGW **Ruler:** Elizabeth II **Obv:**
Head right **Rev:** Britannia standing **Edge:** Reeded

Date	F	VF	XF	Unc	BU
1999-2004 Proof			Value: 100		

KM# 1008 10 POUNDS (1/10 Ounce - Britannia)
3.4100 g., 0.9167 Gold .1005 oz. AGW **Ruler:** Elizabeth II **Obv:**
Head right **Rev:** Britannia standing **Edge:** Reeded

Date	F	VF	XF	Unc	BU
1999-2004 Proof			Value: 100		

KM# 1020 10 POUNDS (1/10 Ounce - Britannia)
3.4100 g., 0.9167 Gold .1005 oz. AGW, 16.5 mm. **Ruler:**
Elizabeth II **Subject:** Britannia Bullion **Obv:** Queen's portrait **Rev:**
Stylized "Britannia and the Lion" **Edge:** Reeded

Date	F	VF	XF	Unc	BU
2001	—	—	—BV+16%	—	

KM# 1040 10 POUNDS (1/10 Ounce - Britannia)
3.4100 g., 0.9167 Gold 0.1005 oz. AGW, 16.5 mm. **Ruler:**
Elizabeth II **Obv:** Queen Elizabeth II **Rev:** Britannia portrait behind
wavy lines **Edge:** Reeded

Date	F	VF	XF	Unc	BU
2003	—	—	—BV+16%	—	

KM# 1068 10 POUNDS (1/10 Ounce - Britannia)
3.4100 g., 0.9167 Gold 0.1005 oz. AGW, 16.5 mm. **Ruler:**
Elizabeth II **Obv:** Elizabeth II **Rev:** Seated Britannia **Edge:** Reeded

Date	F	VF	XF	Unc	BU
2005 Proof			Value: 150		

KM# 951 25 POUNDS (1/4 Ounce - Britannia)
8.5130 g., 0.9170 Gold .2500 oz. AGW **Ruler:** Elizabeth II **Obv:**
Head right **Rev:** Britannia standing **Note:** Copper alloy.

Date	F	VF	XF	Unc	BU
1987-1989	—	—	— BV+8%	—	

KM# 951a 25 POUNDS (1/4 Ounce - Britannia)
8.5130 g., 0.9170 Gold .2500 oz. AGW **Ruler:** Elizabeth II **Obv:**
Head right **Rev:** Britannia standing **Note:** Silver alloy.

Date	F	VF	XF	Unc	BU
1990-1999 Proof			Value: 165		

KM# 983 25 POUNDS (1/4 Ounce - Britannia)
8.51 g., 0.9167 Gold .2508 oz. AGW **Ruler:** Elizabeth II **Obv:** Head
right **Rev:** Britannia in chariot **Note:** Similar to 2 Pounds, KM#981.

Date	F	VF	XF	Unc	BU
1997 Proof			Value: 215		

KM# 1009 25 POUNDS (1/4 Ounce - Britannia)
8.5100 g., 0.9167 Gold .2508 oz. AGW **Ruler:** Elizabeth II **Obv:**
Head right **Rev:** Britannia standing **Edge:** Reeded

Date	F	VF	XF	Unc	BU
1999-2004 Proof			Value: 200		

KM# 1021 25 POUNDS (1/4 Ounce - Britannia)
8.5100 g., 0.9167 Gold .2508 oz. AGW, 22 mm. **Ruler:**
Elizabeth II **Subject:** Britannia Bullion **Obv:** Queen's portrait **Rev:**
Stylized "Britannia and the Lion" **Edge:** Reeded

Date	F	VF	XF	Unc	BU
2001	—	—	—BV+35%	—	

KM# 1041 25 POUNDS (1/4 Ounce - Britannia)
8.5100 g., 0.9167 Gold 0.2508 oz. AGW, 22 mm. **Ruler:**
Elizabeth II **Obv:** Queen Elizabeth II **Rev:** Britannia portrait behind
wavy lines **Edge:** Reeded

Date	F	VF	XF	Unc	BU
2003	—	—	—BV+35%	—	

KM# 1069 25 POUNDS (1/4 Ounce - Britannia)
8.5100 g., 0.9167 Gold 0.2508 oz. AGW, 22 mm. **Ruler:** Elizabeth II
Obv: Elizabeth II **Rev:** Seated Britannia **Edge:** Reeded

Date	F	VF	XF	Unc	BU
2005 Proof			Value: 300		

KM# 952 50 POUNDS (1/2 Ounce - Britannia)
17.0250 g., 0.9170 Gold .5000 oz. AGW **Ruler:** Elizabeth II **Obv:**
Head right **Rev:** Britannia standing **Note:** Copper alloy.

Date	F	VF	XF	Unc	BU
1987-1989	—	—	— BV+6%	—	

KM# 952a   50 POUNDS (1/2 Ounce - Britannia)
17.0250 g., 0.9170 Gold .5000 oz. AGW **Obv:** Elizabeth II **Obv:** Head right **Rev:** Britannia standing **Note:** Silver alloy.

Date	F	VF	XF	Unc	BU
1990-1999 Proof				Value: 325	

KM# 984   50 POUNDS (1/2 Ounce - Britannia)
17.03 g., 0.9167 Gold .5019 oz. AGW **Ruler:** Elizabeth II **Obv:** Head right **Rev:** Britannia in chariot **Note:** Similar to 2 Pounds, KM#281.

Date	F	VF	XF	Unc	BU
1997 Proof				Value: 400	

KM# 1010   50 POUNDS (1/2 Ounce - Britannia)
17.0300 g., 0.9167 Gold .5019 oz. AGW **Ruler:** Elizabeth II **Obv:** Head right **Rev:** Britannia standing **Edge:** Reeded

Date	F	VF	XF	Unc	BU
1999-2004 Proof				Value: 425	

KM# 1022   50 POUNDS (1/2 Ounce - Britannia)
17.0200 g., 0.9167 Gold .5016 oz. AGW, 27 mm. **Ruler:** Elizabeth II **Subject:** Britannia Bullion **Obv:** Queen's portrait **Rev:** Stylized "Britannia and the Lion" **Edge:** Reeded

Date	F	VF	XF	Unc	BU
2001	—	—	—BV+35%		—

KM# 1042   50 POUNDS (1/2 Ounce - Britannia)
17.0200 g., 0.9167 Gold 0.5016 oz. AGW, 27 mm. **Ruler:** Elizabeth II **Obv:** Queen Elizabeth II **Rev:** Britannia portrait behind wavy lines **Edge:** Reeded

Date	F	VF	XF	Unc	BU
2003	—	—	—BV+25%		—

KM# 1070   50 POUNDS (1/2 Ounce - Britannia)
17.03 g., 0.9167 Gold 0.5019 oz. AGW, 27 mm. **Ruler:** Elizabeth II **Obv:** Elizabeth II **Rev:** Seated Britannia **Edge:** Reeded

Date	F	VF	XF	Unc	BU
2005 Proof				Value: 450	

KM# 953   100 POUNDS (1 Ounce - Britannia)
34.0500 g., 0.9170 Gold 1.0000 oz. AGW **Ruler:** Elizabeth II **Obv:** Head right **Rev:** Britannia standing **Note:** Copper alloy.

Date	F	VF	XF	Unc	BU
1987-1989	—	—		BV+4%	—

KM# 953a   100 POUNDS (1 Ounce - Britannia)
34.0500 g., 0.9170 Gold 1.0000 oz. AGW **Ruler:** Elizabeth II **Obv:** Head right **Rev:** Britannia standing **Note:** Silver alloy.

Date	F	VF	XF	Unc	BU
1990-1999 Proof				Value: 625	

KM# 985   100 POUNDS (1 Ounce - Britannia)
34.0500 g., 0.9167 Gold 1.0035 oz. AGW **Ruler:** Elizabeth II **Obv:** Head right **Rev:** Britannia in chariot

Date	F	VF	XF	Unc	BU
1997	—	—	—BV+15%		—

KM# 1011   100 POUNDS (1 Ounce - Britannia)
34.0500 g., 0.9167 Gold 1.0035 oz. AGW **Ruler:** Elizabeth II **Obv:** Head right **Rev:** Britannia standing **Edge:** Reeded

Date	F	VF	XF	Unc	BU
1999-2004 Proof				Value: 850	

KM# 1023   100 POUNDS (1 Ounce - Britannia)
34.0500 g., 0.9167 Gold 1.0035 oz. AGW, 32.7 mm. **Ruler:** Elizabeth II **Subject:** Britannia Bullion **Obv:** Queen's portrait **Rev:** Stylized "Britannia and the Lion" **Edge:** Reeded

Date	F	VF	XF	Unc	BU
2001	—	—	—BV+15%		—

KM# 1043   100 POUNDS (1 Ounce - Britannia)
34.0500 g., 0.9167 Gold 1.0035 oz. AGW, 32.7 mm. **Ruler:** Elizabeth II **Obv:** Queen Elizabeth II **Rev:** Britannia portrait behind wavy lines **Edge:** Reeded

Date	F	VF	XF	Unc	BU
2003	—	—	—BV+15%		—

KM# 1071   100 POUNDS (1 Ounce - Britannia)
34.0500 g., 0.9167 Gold 1.0035 oz. AGW, 32.7 mm. **Ruler:** Elizabeth II **Obv:** Elizabeth II **Rev:** Seated Britannia **Edge:** Reeded

Date	F	VF	XF	Unc	BU
2005 Proof				Value: 875	

TRADE COINAGE
Britannia Issues

Issued to facilitate British trade in the Orient, the reverse design incorporated the denomination in Chinese characters and Malay script.

This issue was struck at the Bombay (B) and Calcutta (C) Mints in India, except for 1925 and 1930 issues which were struck at London. Through error the mint marks did not appear on some early (1895-1900) issues as indicated.

KM# T5   DOLLAR
26.9568 g., 0.9000 Silver .7800 oz. ASW **Obv:** Britannia standing **Rev:** Oriental design

Date	F	VF	XF	Unc	BU
1895-1935	12.00	20.00	25.00	60.00	—

KM# T5a   DOLLAR
Gold **Obv:** Britannia standing **Rev:** Oriental design

Date	F	VF	XF	Unc	BU
1895-1902 Proof				Value: 7,500	

Greenland

Greenland, an integral part of the Danish realm is situated between the North Atlantic Ocean and the Polar Sea, almost entirely within the Arctic Circle. An island nation, it has an area of 840,000 sq. mi. (2,175,600 sq. km.) and a population of 57,000. Capital: Nuuk (formerly Godthaab). Greenland is the world's only source of natural cryolite, a fluoride of sodium and aluminum important in making aluminum. Fish products and minerals are exported.

MONETARY SYSTEM
100 Øre = 1 Krone

DANISH COLONY
MILLED COINAGE

KM# 5   25 ORE
Copper-Nickel **Obv:** Crowned arms of Denmark **Rev:** Value over polar bear walking left, date below

Date	F	VF	XF	Unc	BU
1926	4.00	7.00	12.50	37.50	50.00

KM# 7   50 ORE
Aluminum-Bronze **Obv:** Crowned arms of Denmark **Rev:** Value over polar bear walking left, date below

Date	F	VF	XF	Unc	BU
1926	6.00	9.50	15.00	37.50	55.00

KM# 8   KRONE
Aluminum-Bronze **Obv:** Crowned arms of Denmark **Rev:** Value over polar bear walking left, date below

Date	F	VF	XF	Unc	BU
1926	4.50	10.00	18.00	55.00	70.00

KM# 9   5 KRONER
Brass **Obv:** Crowned arms of Denmark **Rev:** Value over polar bear walking left, date below **Note:** Mainly struck for use by American forces in Greenland during WWII, when 5 Kroner was equal to one US dollar.

Date	F	VF	XF	Unc	BU
1944	40.00	60.00	80.00	125	—

GREENLAND MINING LTD.
Josvas (Innatsiaq)

A place in southwest Greenland, where the Gronlandsk Minedrifts Aktieselskab run a copper mine from 1907-1914, yielding little more than 60 tons of copper, as a minor bonus, over 50 kg of silver and half a kg of gold.

KM# Tn1   10 ORE
Nickel Plated Zinc **Rev:** Crossed hammers over "10" **Note:** Struck at L. Chr. Lauer, Nürnberg, Germany.

Date	VG	F	VF	XF	Unc
1911	3.00	8.00	12.00	32.00	—

KM# Tn2   25 ORE
Nickel Plated Zinc **Rev:** Crossed hammers over "25" **Note:** Struck at L. Chr. Lauer, Nürnberg, Germany.

Date	VG	F	VF	XF	Unc
1911	3.00	8.00	12.00	32.00	—

KM# Tn3   100 ORE
Nickel Plated Zinc **Rev:** Crossed hammers over "100" **Note:** Struck at L. Chr. Lauer, Nürnberg, Germany.

Date	VG	F	VF	XF	Unc
1911	3.00	8.00	12.00	35.00	—

A. GIBBS & SONS

British trading and mining company located in eastern Greenland.

KM# Tn11   SKILLING
Brass

Date	VG	F	VF	XF	Unc
1863	450	850	1,400	—	—

KM# Tn12   6 SKILLING
Brass

Date	VG	F	VF	XF	Unc
1863	175	300	500	—	—

KM# Tn13   24 SKILLING
Brass

Date	VG	F	VF	XF	Unc
1863	225	400	650	—	—

KM# Tn14   DALER
Brass

Date	VG	F	VF	XF	Unc
1863	275	500	850	—	—

ORESUND
1859-1865

Danish company for mining cryolite located in Ivigtut, southwest Greenland.

KM# Tn51 SKILLING
Zinc **Obv. Legend:** ØRESUND above "1" **Note:** Uniface.

Date	VG	F	VF	XF	Unc
ND	100	200	350	500	—

KM# Tn52 4 SKILLING
Zinc **Obv. Legend:** ØRESUND above "4"

Date	VG	F	VF	XF	Unc
ND	135	275	450	650	—

KM# Tn53 16 SKILLING
Zinc **Obv. Legend:** ORESUND above "16" **Note:** Uniface.

Date	VG	F	VF	XF	Unc
ND	165	325	550	750	—

KM# Tn54 48 SKILLING
Zinc **Obv. Legend:** ØRESUND above "48" **Note:** Uniface.

Date	VG	F	VF	XF	Unc
ND	200	425	700	950	—

KM# Tn55 RIGSDALER
Zinc **Obv. Legend:** ØRESUND above "1 Rd" **Note:** Uniface.

Date	VG	F	VF	XF	Unc
ND	275	500	900	1,200	—

IVIGTUT CRYOLITE MINING & TRADING CO.
Series I, 1875-1882

KM# Tn26 ORE
Zinc, 26 mm. **Obv. Legend:** IVIGTUT above "1" **Note:** Uniface. Currently unknown.

Date	VG	F	VF	XF	Unc
ND	—	—	—	—	—

KM# Tn27 5 ORE
Zinc, 26.5 mm. **Note:** Uniface.

Date	VG	F	VF	XF	Unc
ND	—	—	450	—	—

KM# Tn28 10 ORE
Zinc, 26 mm. **Obv. Legend:** IVIGTUT above "10" **Note:** Uniface.

Date	VG	F	VF	XF	Unc
ND	—	—	—	—	—

KM# Tn29 70 ORE
Zinc, 26 mm. **Obv. Legend:** IVIGTUT above "70" **Note:** Uniface.

Date	VG	F	VF	XF	Unc
ND	—	—	—	—	—

KM# Tn30 85 ORE
Zinc, 30 mm. **Obv. Legend:** IVIGTUT above "85" **Note:** Uniface.

Date	VG	F	VF	XF	Unc
ND	—	—	—	—	—

KM# Tn31 100 ORE
Zinc, 43.5 mm. **Note:** Uniface.

Date	VG	F	VF	XF	Unc
ND	—	—	600	900	—

IVIGTUT CRYOLITE MINING & TRADING CO.
Series II, Pre-1882

KM# Tn32 ORE
Zinc, 27.1 mm. **Obv. Legend:** IVIGTUT above "1" **Note:** 1.0mm thick, uniface.

Date	VG	F	VF	XF	Unc
ND	—	—	—	—	—

KM# Tn33.1 5 ORE
Zinc, 27.3 mm. **Obv. Legend:** IVIGTUT above "5" **Note:** 1.0mm thick, uniface.

Date	VG	F	VF	XF	Unc
ND	—	—	—	—	—

KM# Tn33.2 5 ORE
Zinc **Note:** 26.6-27.0mm, 1.4-1.5mm thick, uniface

Date	VG	F	VF	XF	Unc
ND(1875-82)	—	—	125	200	—

KM# Tn34 10 ORE
Zinc, 27.2 mm. **Obv. Legend:** IVIGTUT above "10" **Note:** 1.0mm thick, uniface.

Date	VG	F	VF	XF	Unc
ND	—	—	—	—	—

KM# Tn35 50 ORE
Zinc, 30.8 mm. **Obv. Legend:** IVIGTUT above "50" **Note:** 1.0mm thick, uniface.

Date	VG	F	VF	XF	Unc
ND	—	—	—	—	—

KM# Tn36 85 ORE
Zinc, 30.6 mm. **Note:** 1.0mm thick, uniface

Date	VG	F	VF	XF	Unc
ND	—	—	3,500	—	—

KM# Tn37 100 ORE
Zinc **Note:** 38.3-39.8mm, 1.4-1.5mm thick, uniface

Date	VG	F	VF	XF	Unc
ND	185	350	550	850	—

IVIGTUT CRYOLITE MINING & TRADING CO.
Series III, 1892-

The Cryolite Mining and Trading Company at Ivigtut at the southwest coast of Greenland issued its own tokens since 1873. The uncommon mineral Cryolite (Na_3AlF_6, Sodium Aluminum Fluoride) was used in the aluminum industry. In large quantities it was only found on the west coast of Greenland.

NOTE: The 1922 tokens were struck at the Royal Mint, Copenhagen.

KM# Tn38 ORE
Zinc, 27 mm. **Note:** .75mm thick, uniface

Date	VG	F	VF	XF	Unc
ND	—	225	375	575	—

KM# Tn39 5 ORE
Zinc, 26.6-27 mm. **Note:** .75mm thick, uniface

Date	VG	F	VF	XF	Unc
ND	—	65.00	110	175	—

KM# Tn40 10 ORE
Zinc, 30.5 mm. **Note:** .75mm thick, uniface

Date	VG	F	VF	XF	Unc
ND	—	60.00	100	160	—

KM# Tn46   10 ORE
Copper-Nickel   **Obv:** Seated polar bear on frame

Date	VG	F	VF	XF	Unc
1922	5.00	10.00	15.00	32.50	50.00

KM# Tn48   2 KRONER
Copper-Nickel   **Obv:** Seated polar bear on frame

Date	VG	F	VF	XF	Unc
1922	15.00	35.00	70.00	100	165

KM# Tn49   10 KRONER
Copper-Nickel   **Obv:** Seated polar bear on frame   **Edge:** Reeded

Date	VG	F	VF	XF	Unc
1922	20.00	55.00	85.00	135	200

KM# Tn49a   10 KRONER
Aluminum-Bronze   **Edge:** Plain

Date	VG	F	VF	XF	Unc
1922	—	—	800	1,100	1,500

ROYAL GREENLAND TRADE (COMPANY)
(Den Kongelige Grønlandske Handel)

Located on Angmagssalik Island off the east coast of Greenland just below the Arctic Circle.

KM# Tn15   ORE
Zinc, 26.8 mm.   **Obv:** Crowned "1"

Date	VG	F	VF	XF	Unc
ND	—	—	—	—	—

KM# Tn16   5 ORE
Zinc, 30 mm.   **Obv:** Crowned "5"   **Note:** Uniface

Date	VG	F	VF	XF	Unc
ND	—	—	—	—	—

KM# Tn17   10 ORE
Zinc   **Obv:** Crowned "10"   **Note:** Uniface

Date	VG	F	VF	XF	Unc
ND	—	—	—	—	—

KM# Tn41   50 ORE
Zinc, 38 mm.   **Note:** .75mm thick, uniface

Date	VG	F	VF	XF	Unc
ND	—	200	350	525	—

KM# Tn18   25 ORE
Zinc   **Obv:** Crowned "25"   **Note:** Uniface

Date	VG	F	VF	XF	Unc
ND	—	—	—	—	—

KM# Tn47   50 ORE
Copper-Nickel   **Obv:** Seated polar bear on frame

Date	VG	F	VF	XF	Unc
1922	16.00	35.00	60.00	100	150

KM# Tn42.1   100 ORE
Zinc, 44 mm.   **Note:** .75mm thick, uniface

Date	VG	F	VF	XF	Unc
ND	—	250	400	575	—

KM# Tn42.2   100 ORE
Zinc   **Obv. Legend:** IVIGTUT/IVIGTUT   **Note:** Uniface.

Date	VG	F	VF	XF	Unc
ND	—	250	400	575	—

KM# Tn43   500 ORE
Zinc   **Note:** Uniface. Not seen since 1917.

Date	VG	F	VF	XF	Unc
ND	—	—	—	—	—

KM# Tn44   1000 ORE
Zinc   **Obv. Legend:** IVIGTUT above "1000"   **Note:** Uniface. 0.9mm thick.

Date	VG	F	VF	XF	Unc
ND	—	—	—	—	—

KM# Tn45   20 KRONER
Zinc   **Obv. Legend:** iVIGTUT above "20 Kr"   **Rev. Inscription:** 28 JULI 95

Date	VG	F	VF	XF	Unc
ND	—	—	—	—	—

KM# Tn19.1   50 ORE
Zinc   **Obv:** Crowned "50"   **Note:** Uniface, holed.

Date	VG	F	VF	XF	Unc
ND	60.00	120	200	300	—

Greenland

KM# Tn19.2   50 ORE
Zinc   **Note:** Without hole

Date	VG	F	VF	XF	Unc
ND	150	220	300	500	—

KM# Tn21.1   100 ORE
Zinc   **Obv:** Crowned "100"

Date	VG	F	VF	XF	Unc
ND	30.00	60.00	100	185	—

KM# Tn23.2   500 ORE
Zinc   **Rev:** Am.

Date	VG	F	VF	XF	Unc
ND	75.00	150	250	400	—

KM# Tn25   500 ORE
Aluminum   **Note:** Uniface

Date	VG	F	VF	XF	Unc
ND (1905)	40.00	80.00	150	260	—

DANISH STATE
1953-1979
MILLED COINAGE

KM# 10   KRONE
Aluminum-Bronze   **Issuer:** Royal Greenland Trade Company **Obv:** Crowned arms of Denmark and Greenland **Rev:** Value in flowers

Date	F	VF	XF	Unc	BU
1957	8.00	12.50	22.50	55.00	—

KM# 10a   KRONE
Copper-Nickel   **Issuer:** Royal Greenland Trade Company

Date	F	VF	XF	Unc	BU
1960-1964	3.75	7.50	12.50	22.50	—

THULE-KAP YORK

The Thule (gaanaaq)-Cape York Arctic trading station located in northwestern Greenland on the coast of the Hayes Peninsula north of Cap York was established in 1910 by polar explorer Knud Rasmussen. U.S. military bases are currently there.

TOKEN COINAGE

KM# Tn5.1   5 ORE
Aluminum   **Rev:** "5" above date, with hole in center

Date	F	VF	XF	Unc	BU
1910	2.00	4.50	8.00	17.50	—

KM# Tn5.2   5 ORE
Aluminum   **Note:** Error, struck without center hole

Date	F	VF	XF	Unc	BU
1910	—	—	—	—	—

KM# Tn6   25 ORE
Aluminum   **Rev:** "25" above date, with hole in center

Date	F	VF	XF	Unc	BU
1910	2.00	5.00	8.00	17.50	—

KM# Tn7   100 ORE
Aluminum   **Rev:** "100" above date, with hole in center

Date	F	VF	XF	Unc	BU
1910	4.00	10.00	18.00	38.00	—

KM# Tn8   500 ORE
Aluminum   **Rev:** "500" above date, with hole in center

Date	F	VF	XF	Unc	BU
1910	6.00	18.00	25.00	55.00	—

KM# Tn9   5 KRONER
Aluminum   **Rev:** "5 KRONER" above date, with hole in center

Date	F	VF	XF	Unc	BU
1932	15.00	30.00	60.00	110	—

KM# Tn10   10 KRONER
Aluminum   **Rev:** "10 KRONER" above date, with hole in center

Date	F	VF	XF	Unc	BU
1932	40.00	100	160	260	—

Guernsey

The Bailiwick of Guernsey, a British crown dependency located in the English Channel 30 miles (48 km.) west of Normandy, France, has an area of 30 sq. mi. (194 sq. km.)(including the isles of Alderney, Jethou, Herm, Brechou, and Sark), and a population of 54,000. Capital: St. Peter Port. Agriculture and cattle breeding are the main occupations.

MONETARY SYSTEM
8 Doubles = 1 Penny
12 Pence = 1 Shilling
5 Shillings = 1 Crown
20 Shillings = 1 Pound

NOTICE:
Non-circulating commemorative coins issued after 1971 are not presented in this volume. Please see the *Standard Catalog of World Coins*, either the 20th or 21st century edition, by Krause Publications, an imprint of F+W Publications

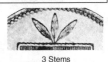

1 Stem	3 Stems

BRITISH DEPENDENCY
STANDARD COINAGE

KM# 1   DOUBLE
Copper

Date	F	VF	XF	Unc	BU
1830	2.00	6.00	23.00	70.00	—

KM# 1a   DOUBLE
Bronzed Copper

Date	F	VF	XF	Unc	BU
1830 Proof		Value: 250			

KM# 10   DOUBLE
Bronze

Date	F	VF	XF	Unc	BU
1868-1911	0.25	0.50	2.25	5.00	—

KM# 10a   DOUBLE
Bronzed Copper

Date	F	VF	XF	Unc	BU
1885 Proof		Value: 275			

KM# 11   DOUBLE
Bronze

Date	F	VF	XF	Unc	BU
1911-1938	0.30	0.85	2.50	5.50	—

KM# 4   2 DOUBLES
Copper   **Rev:** Leaves with 1 stem

Date	F	VF	XF	Unc	BU
1858	11.00	35.00	100	300	—

Greenland (side margin)

KM# 9 2 DOUBLES
Bronze **Obv:** Leaves with 3 stems above shield

Date	F	VF	XF	Unc	BU
1868-1911	0.85	2.75	6.00	15.00	—

KM# 9a 2 DOUBLES
Bronzed Copper

Date	F	VF	XF	Unc	BU
1885 Proof	Value: 275				

KM# 12 2 DOUBLES
Bronzed Copper

Date	F	VF	XF	Unc	BU
1914-1929	0.35	1.25	6.00	10.00	—

KM# 2 4 DOUBLES
Copper **Note:** A rare mule restrike of the St. Helena obverse 1/2 Penny 1821 and reverse of Guernsey 4 Doubles dated 1830 exists. Market valuation $600.00 (VF).

Date	F	VF	XF	Unc	BU
1830-1858	2.25	7.50	30.00	175	—

KM# 2a 4 DOUBLES
Bronzed Copper

Date	F	VF	XF	Unc	BU
1830 Proof	Value: 325				

KM# 5 4 DOUBLES
Bronze **Obv:** Leaves with 3 stems above shield **Note:** Varieties exist.

Date	F	VF	XF	Unc	BU
1864/54-1911	0.75	1.25	5.00	22.00	—

KM# 6 4 DOUBLES
Bronze **Obv:** Leaves with one stem **Note:** Mintage included with KM#5.

Date	F	VF	XF	Unc	BU
1864	2.00	5.00	45.00	95.00	—

KM# 5a 4 DOUBLES
Bronzed Copper **Obv:** Leaves with three stems

Date	F	VF	XF	Unc	BU
1885 Proof	Value: 275				

KM# 13 4 DOUBLES
Bronze

Date	F	VF	XF	Unc	BU
1914-1949	0.45	1.25	4.50	10.00	—

KM# 15 4 DOUBLES
Bronze **Note:** Guernsey Lily

Date	F	VF	XF	Unc	BU
1956-1966	0.25	0.45	0.75	2.00	3.50

KM# 3 8 DOUBLES
Copper

Date	F	VF	XF	Unc	BU
1834-1858	5.00	12.50	65.00	300	—

KM# 3a 8 DOUBLES
Bronzed Copper

Date	F	VF	XF	Unc	BU
1834 Proof	Value: 600				

KM# 7 8 DOUBLES
Bronze

Date	F	VF	XF	Unc	BU
1864-1911	1.00	4.00	11.00	27.00	—

KM# 7a 8 DOUBLES
Bronzed Copper

Date	F	VF	XF	Unc	BU
1885 Proof	Value: 325				

KM# 14 8 DOUBLES
Bronze

Date	F	VF	XF	Unc	BU
1914-1949	0.30	0.60	2.00	5.00	—

KM# 16 8 DOUBLES
Bronze **Obv:** Three-flowered lily

Date	F	VF	XF	Unc	BU
1956-1966	0.10	0.20	0.50	1.25	2.50

KM# 17 3 PENCE
Copper Nickel **Rev:** Guernsey cow (bos primigenius taurus)
Shape: Scalloped **Note:** Thin flan.

Date	F	VF	XF	Unc	BU
1956	0.10	0.20	0.50	1.50	2.00

KM# 18 3 PENCE
Copper Nickel **Rev:** Guernsey cow (bos primigenius taurus)
Shape: Scalloped **Note:** Thick flan.

Date	F	VF	XF	Unc	BU
1959-1966	0.10	0.20	0.50	1.50	2.00

KM# 19 10 SHILLING
Copper Nickel **Subject:** 900th Anniversary - Norman Conquest
Rev: William I portrait left **Shape:** 4-sided

Date	F	VF	XF	Unc	BU
1966	—	1.00	1.25	1.75	—

DECIMAL COINAGE
100 Pence = 1 Pound

KM# 20 1/2 NEW PENNY
Bronze

Date	F	VF	XF	Unc	BU
1971	—	—	0.15	0.30	0.50

KM# 21 NEW PENNY
Bronze **Rev:** Gannet

Date	F	VF	XF	Unc	BU
1971	—	—	0.15	0.45	0.75

KM# 22 2 NEW PENCE
Bronze **Rev:** Windmill from Sark

Date	F	VF	XF	Unc	BU
1971	—	—	0.15	0.35	0.50

KM# 23 5 NEW PENCE
Copper-Nickel **Rev:** Guernsey lily

Date	F	VF	XF	Unc	BU
1968-1971	—	0.15	0.25	0.45	0.65

KM# 24 10 NEW PENCE
Copper-Nickel **Rev:** Guernsey cow

Date	F	VF	XF	Unc	BU
1968-1971	—	0.20	0.40	1.50	1.75

KM# 25 50 NEW PENCE
Copper-Nickel **Rev:** Ducal cap of the Duke of Normandy **Shape:**
7-sided

Date	F	VF	XF	Unc	BU
1969-1971	—	1.00	1.50	2.50	3.50

Iceland

The Republic of Iceland, an island of recent volcanic origin in the North Atlantic east of Greenland and immediately south of the Arctic Circle, has an area of 39,768sq. mi. (103,000 sq. km.) and a population of 275,264. Capital: Reykjavik. Fishing is the chief industry and accounts for more than 70 percent of the exports.

MONETARY SYSTEM
100 Aurar = 1 Krona

KINGDOM

DECIMAL COINAGE

KM# 5.1   EYRIR
Bronze   **Ruler:** Christian X **Obv:** Crowned monogram **Rev:** Large value

Date	F	VF	XF	Unc	BU
1926-1939	1.00	2.00	3.50	12.50	—

KM# 5.2   EYRIR
Bronze   **Obv:** Crowned monogram **Rev:** Large value

Date	F	VF	XF	Unc	BU
1940-1942	0.25	0.40	0.75	2.00	—

KM# 6.1   2 AURAR
Bronze   **Obv:** Crowned monogram **Rev:** Large value **Note:** Varieties exist in the appearance of the numeral 8 in 1938 dated coins. As the die slowly deteriorated, "globs" were added to the upper loop and later to the lower loop.

Date	F	VF	XF	Unc	BU
1926-1940	1.00	2.50	7.00	29.00	—

KM# 6.2   2 AURAR
Bronze   **Obv:** Crowned monogram **Rev:** Large value

Date	F	VF	XF	Unc	BU
1940-1942	0.20	0.50	1.00	2.00	—

KM# 7.1   5 AURAR
Bronze   **Obv:** Crowned monogram **Rev:** Large value

Date	F	VF	XF	Unc	BU
1926-1931	5.00	10.00	25.00	85.00	—

KM# 7.2   5 AURAR
Bronze   **Obv:** Crowned monogram **Rev:** Large value

Date	F	VF	XF	Unc	BU
1940-1942	0.35	0.85	1.50	3.00	—

KM# 1.1   10 AURAR
Copper-Nickel   **Obv:** Large value **Rev:** Crowned shield, monogram flanking

Date	F	VF	XF	Unc	BU
1922-1939/6	2.00	3.50	7.00	32.50	—

KM# 1.2   10 AURAR
Copper-Nickel   **Obv:** Large value **Rev:** Crowned shield flanked by monogram

Date	F	VF	XF	Unc	BU
1940	0.35	0.75	1.50	4.50	—

KM# 1a   10 AURAR
Zinc **Obv:** Large value **Rev:** Crowned shield flanked by monogram

Date	F	VF	XF	Unc	BU
1942	1.50	3.00	6.00	—	—

KM# 2.1   25 AURAR
Copper-Nickel   **Obv:** Large value **Rev:** Crowned shield flanked by monogram

Date	F	VF	XF	Unc	BU
1922-1937	1.00	2.50	4.00	35.00	—

KM# 2.2   25 AURAR
Copper-Nickel   **Obv:** Large value **Rev:** Crowned shield flanked by monogram

Date	F	VF	XF	Unc	BU
1940	0.25	0.50	1.00	2.50	—

KM# 2a   25 AURAR
Zinc **Obv:** Large value **Rev:** Crowned shield flanked by monogram

Date	F	VF	XF	Unc	BU
1942	1.00	2.50	5.00	—	—

KM# 3.1   KRONA
Aluminum-Bronze **Obv:** Large value **Rev:** Crowned shield flanked by monogram

Date	F	VF	XF	Unc	BU
1925-1940	1.50	2.50	5.00	15.00	—

KM# 3.2 KRONA

Aluminum-Bronze **Obv:** Large value **Rev:** Crowned shield flanked by monogram

Date	F	VF	XF	Unc	BU
1940	1.00	2.00	4.00	10.00	—

KM# 4.1 2 KRONUR

Aluminum-Bronze **Obv:** Large value **Rev:** Crowned shield flanked by monogram

Date	F	VF	XF	Unc	BU
1925-1929	7.50	12.50	40.00	235	—

KM# 4.2 2 KRONUR

Aluminum-Bronze **Obv:** Large value **Rev:** Crowned shield flanked by monogram

Date	F	VF	XF	Unc	BU
1940	0.75	1.50	3.50	10.00	—

TOKEN COINAGE

Olafur Arnason
Stokkseyri

KM# Tn1 10 AURAR
2.2000 g., Bronze **Issuer:** Olafur Arnason, Stokkseyri **Obv:** Merchant's name and shop location in legend, denomination **Rev:** GEGN VORUM (against goods) in wreath

Date	VG	F	VF	XF	Unc
ND(1900)	10.00	25.00	50.00	130	—

KM# Tn2 25 AURAR
2.2000 g., Bronze **Issuer:** Olafur Arnason, Stokkseyri **Note:** Similar to KM#Tn1.

Date	VG	F	VF	XF	Unc
ND(1900)	7.00	20.00	40.00	100	—

J.R.B. Lefolii
Eyrarbakka

KM# Tn5 10 AURAR
1.6000 g., Bronze **Issuer:** J.R.B. Lefolii, Eyrarbakka **Obv:** Merchant's name and shop location in legend, denomination **Rev:** GEGN VORUM (against goods) in wreath

Date	VG	F	VF	XF	Unc
ND(1900)	12.00	25.00	60.00	135	—

KM# Tn6 25 AURAR
2.3000 g., Bronze **Issuer:** J.R.B. Lefolii, Eyrarbakka **Obv:** Merchant's name and shop location in legend, denomination **Rev:** GEGN VORUM (against goods) in wreath

Date	VG	F	VF	XF	Unc
ND(1900)	12.00	25.00	60.00	135	—

KM# Tn7 100 AURAR
3.3000 g., Bronze **Issuer:** J.R.B. Lefolii, Eyrarbakka **Obv:** Merchant's name and shop location in legend, denomination **Rev:** GEGN VORUM (against goods) in wreath

Date	VG	F	VF	XF	Unc
ND(1900)	15.00	30.00	75.00	150	—

C.F. Siemsen
Reykjavik

KM# Tn8 4 SKILDINGAR
1.5000 g., Bronze **Issuer:** C.F. Siemsen, Reykjavik **Obv:** Merchant's initials **Rev:** Denomination **Note:** Also valid at C. F. Siemsen's store on the Faeroe Islands

Date	VG	F	VF	XF	Unc
ND(1846)	40.00	80.00	180	325	—

KM# Tn9 16 SKILDINGAR
2.5000 g., Bronze **Issuer:** C.F. Siemsen, Reykjavik **Obv:** Merchant's initials **Rev:** Denomination **Note:** Also valid at C. F. Siemsen's store on the Faeroe Islands

Date	VG	F	VF	XF	Unc
ND(1846)	30.00	60.00	125	200	—

P.J. Thorsteinsson
Bildudal

KM# Tn12 10 AURAR
1.7000 g., Brass **Issuer:** P.J. Thorsteinsson, Bildudal **Note:** Similar to 100 Aurar, KM#Tn21. Struck by L. Chr. Lauer of Nurnberg.

Date	VG	F	VF	XF	Unc
ND(1901)	12.00	25.00	50.00	130	—

KM# Tn13 25 AURAR
3.7000 g., Bronze **Issuer:** P.J. Thorsteinsson, Bildudal **Obv:** PT monogram **Rev:** Denomination

Date	VG	F	VF	XF	Unc
ND(1880)	20.00	40.00	80.00	165	—

KM# Tn14 25 AURAR
3.7000 g., Bronze **Issuer:** P.J. Thorsteinsson, Bildudal **Obv:** PT monogram above 97 **Rev:** Denomination

Date	VG	F	VF	XF	Unc
xx97	15.00	30.00	60.00	135	—

KM# Tn15 25 AURAR
1.7000 g., Brass **Issuer:** P.J. Thorsteinsson, Bildudal **Note:** Similar to 100 Aurar, KM#Tn21. Struck by L. Chr. Lauer of Nurnberg.

Date	VG	F	VF	XF	Unc
ND(1901)	6.00	12.00	25.00	60.00	—

KM# Tn16 50 AURAR
Bronze **Issuer:** P.J. Thorsteinsson, Bildudal **Obv:** PT monogram **Rev:** Denomination

Date	VG	F	VF	XF	Unc
ND(1880)	20.00	40.00	80.00	165	—

KM# Tn17 50 AURAR
Bronze **Issuer:** P.J. Thorsteinsson, Bildudal **Obv:** PT monogram above 97 **Rev:** Denomination

Date	VG	F	VF	XF	Unc
xx97	15.00	30.00	60.00	145	—

KM# Tn18 50 AURAR
2.2000 g., Brass **Issuer:** P.J. Thorsteinsson, Bildudal **Note:** Similar to 100 Aurar, KM#Tn21. Struck by L. Chr. Lauer of Nurnberg.

Date	VG	F	VF	XF	Unc
ND(1901)	6.00	12.00	25.00	60.00	—

KM# Tn22 500 AURAR
1.1000 g., Aluminum **Issuer:** P.J. Thorsteinsson, Bildudal **Note:** Similar to 100 Aurar, KM#Tn21. Struck by L. Chr. Lauer of Nurnberg.

Date	VG	F	VF	XF	Unc
ND(1901)	7.00	15.00	30.00	75.00	—

REPUBLIC

DECIMAL COINAGE

KM# 8 EYRIR
Bronze **Obv:** Large value **Rev:** Shield within wreath **Note:** Values for the 1953-59 proof issues are for impaired proofs. Brilliant proofs may bring 3 to 4 times these figures.

Date	F	VF	XF	Unc	BU
1946-1966	0.10	0.15	0.40	0.75	—

KM# 9　5 AURAR
Bronze **Obv:** Large value **Rev:** Shield within wreath **Note:** Values for the 1958-63 proof issues are for impaired proofs. Brilliant proofs may bring 3 to 4 times these figures.

Date	F	VF	XF	Unc	BU
1946-1966	0.10	0.20	0.50	1.00	—

KM# 10　10 AURAR
Copper-Nickel **Obv:** Large value **Rev:** Shield within wreath **Note:** Values for the 1953-63 proof issues are for impaired proofs. Brilliant proofs may bring 3 to 4 times these figures.

Date	F	VF	XF	Unc	BU
1946-1969	0.10	0.10	0.10	0.20	—

KM# 10a　10 AURAR
Aluminum **Obv:** Large value **Rev:** Shield within wreath

Date	F	VF	XF	Unc	BU
1970-1974	—	—	0.10	0.20	—

KM# 11　25 AURAR
Copper-Nickel **Obv:** Large value **Rev:** Shield within wreath **Note:** Values for the 1951-63 proof issues are for impaired proofs. Brilliant proofs may bring 3 to 4 times these figures.

Date	F	VF	XF	Unc	BU
1946-1967	0.10	0.15	0.10	0.25	—

KM# 17　50 AURAR
Nickel-Brass **Obv:** Large value **Rev:** Shield within wreath

Date	F	VF	XF	Unc	BU
1969-1974	—	—	0.10	0.30	—

KM# 12　KRONA
Aluminum-Bronze **Obv:** Large value **Rev:** Shield with supporters

Date	F	VF	XF	Unc	BU
1946	—	0.10	0.40	1.50	—

KM# 12a　KRONA
Nickel-Brass **Obv:** Large value **Rev:** Shield with supporters **Note:** Values for the 1957-63 proof issues are for impaired proofs. Brilliant proofs may bring 3 to 4 times these figures.

Date	F	VF	XF	Unc	BU
1957-1975	0.10	0.10	0.10	0.25	—

KM# 23　KRONA
Aluminum **Obv:** Large value **Rev:** Shield with supporters

Date	F	VF	XF	Unc	BU
1976-1980	—	—	0.10	0.20	—

KM# 13　2 KRONUR
Aluminum-Bronze **Obv:** Large value **Rev:** Shield with supporters **Note:** Republic

Date	F	VF	XF	Unc	BU
1946	0.20	0.40	0.80	3.50	—

KM# 13a.1　2 KRONUR
Nickel-Brass **Obv:** Large value **Rev:** Shield with supporters **Note:** Values for the 1958-63 proof issues are for impaired proofs. Brilliant proofs may bring 3 to 4 times these figures.

Date	F	VF	XF	Unc	BU
1958-1966	0.10	0.20	0.40	1.50	—

KM# 13a.2　2 KRONUR
11.5000 g., Nickel-Brass **Obv:** Large value **Rev:** Shield with supporters **Note:** Thick planchet.

Date	F	VF	XF	Unc	BU
1966	—	—	360	475	—

KM# 18　5 KRONUR
Copper-Nickel

Date	F	VF	XF	Unc	BU
1969-1980	0.10	0.10	0.15	0.25	—

KM# 15 10 KRONUR
Copper-Nickel **Obv:** Large value **Rev:** Shield with supporters

Date	F	VF	XF	Unc	BU
1967-1980	0.15	0.10	0.25	0.60	—

KM# 16 50 KRONUR
Nickel **Subject:** 50th Anniversary of Sovereignty **Obv:** Large value **Rev:** Parliament Building in Reyjavik

Date	F	VF	XF	Unc	BU
1968	1.50	2.50	4.00	7.00	—

KM# 19 50 KRONUR
Copper-Nickel **Obv:** Large value **Rev:** Parliament Building in Reykjavic

Date	F	VF	XF	Unc	BU
1970-1980	0.20	0.35	0.50	1.00	—

KM# 14 500 KRONUR
8.9604 g., 0.9000 Gold .2593 oz. AGW **Subject:** Jon Sigurdsson Sesquicentennial **Obv:** Shield with supporters **Rev:** Head right

Date	F	VF	XF	Unc	BU
ND(1961)	—	—	—	200	—

KM# 20 500 KRONUR
20.0000 g., 0.9250 Silver .5968 oz. ASW **Subject:** 1100th Anniversary - 1st Settlement **Obv:** Quartered design of eagle, dragon, bull, giant **Rev:** Female and cow

Date	F	VF	XF	Unc	BU
ND(1974)	—	—	—	10.00	13.00

KM# 21 1000 KRONUR
30.0000 g., 0.9250 Silver .8923 oz. ASW **Subject:** 1100th Anniversary - 1st Settlement **Obv:** Quartered design of eagle, dragon, bull, giant **Rev:** Two Vikings and fire

Date	F	VF	XF	Unc	BU
ND(1974)	—	—	—	13.50	16.00

KM# 22 10000 KRONUR
15.5000 g., 0.9000 Gold .4485 oz. AGW **Subject:** 1100th Anniversary - 1st Settlement **Obv:** Quartered design of eagle, dragon, bull, giant **Rev:** Ingulfur Arnason getting ready to throw his home posts on the beach

Date	F	VF	XF	Unc	BU
ND(1974)	—	—	—	300	—

Iceland

REFORM COINAGE
100 Old Kronur = 1 New Krona

KM# 24   5 AURAR
Bronze   **Obv:** Eagle with upraised wing **Rev:** Skate

Date	F	VF	XF	Unc	BU
1981	—	—	—	0.35	0.75

KM# 25   10 AURAR
Bronze   **Obv:** bull's head facing **Rev:** Flying squid

Date	F	VF	XF	Unc	BU
1981	—	—	—	0.45	1.00

KM# 26   50 AURAR
Bronze   **Obv:** Dragon **Rev:** Northern shrimp

Date	F	VF	XF	Unc	BU
1981	—	—	0.10	0.50	1.00

KM# 26a   50 AURAR
Bronze Coated Steel   **Obv:** Dragon **Rev:** Northern shrimp

Date	F	VF	XF	Unc	BU
1986	—	—	—	0.50	1.00

KM# 27   KRONA
4.5000 g., Copper-Nickel, 21.5 mm.   **Obv:** Giant **Rev:** Cod **Edge:** Reeded

Date	F	VF	XF	Unc	BU
1981-1987	—	—	0.15	0.75	1.25

KM# 27a   KRONA
4.0000 g., Nickel Coated Steel, 21.5 mm.   **Obv:** Giant **Rev:** Cod **Edge:** Reeded

Date	F	VF	XF	Unc	BU
1989-2006	—	—	—	0.75	1.25

KM# 28   5 KRONUR
6.5000 g., Copper-Nickel, 24.5 mm.   **Obv:** Eagle, dragon, bull, giant **Rev:** Two dolphins, denomination **Edge:** Reeded

Date	F	VF	XF	Unc	BU
1981-1992	—	—	0.25	1.50	2.00

KM# 28a   5 KRONUR
5.6000 g., Nickel Clad Steel, 24.5 mm.   **Obv:** Eagle, dragon, bull, giant **Rev:** Two dolphins, denomination **Edge:** Reeded

Date	F	VF	XF	Unc	BU
1996-2005	—	—	—	1.50	2.00

KM# 29.1   10 KRONUR
Copper-Nickel   **Obv:** Eagle, dragon, bull, giant **Rev:** Four capelins, denomination **Edge:** Reeded

Date	F	VF	XF	Unc	BU
1984-1994	—	—	0.35	1.75	2.50

KM# 29.2   10 KRONUR
8.0000 g., Nickel Clad Steel, 24.5 mm.   **Obv:** Eagle, dragon, bull, giant **Edge:** Reeded **Note:** Struck on flan of Indian Rupee in error.

Date	F	VF	XF	Unc	BU
1984	—	—	100	150	—

KM# 29.1a   10 KRONUR
8.0000 g., Nickel Clad Steel, 27.5 mm.   **Obv:** Eagle, dragon, bull, giant **Rev:** Four capelins, denomination **Edge:** Reeded

Date	F	VF	XF	Unc	BU
1996-2005	—	—	—	1.75	2.50

KM# 31   50 KRONUR
8.2500 g., Nickel-Brass, 23 mm. **Rev:** Northern shrimp **Edge:** Reeded

Date	F	VF	XF	Unc	BU
1987-2005	—	—	—	4.00	5.00

KM# 35   100 KRONUR
8.5000 g., Nickel-Brass, 25.5 mm. **Obv:** Eagle, dragon, bull, giant **Rev:** Lumpfish **Edge:** Reeded

Date	F	VF	XF	Unc	BU
1995-2004	—	—	—	6.00	7.00

KM# 30   500 KRONUR
20.0000 g., 0.5000 Silver .3215 oz. ASW **Subject:** 100th Anniversary of Icelandic Banknotes **Obv:** Fishing vessel **Rev:** Female seated with sword and shield

Date	F	VF	XF	Unc	BU
ND(1986)	—	—	—	55.00	60.00

KM# 30a   500 KRONUR
20.0000 g., 0.9250 Silver .5968 oz. ASW **Subject:** 100th Anniversary of Icelandic Banknotes **Obv:** Fishing vessel **Rev:** Female seated with sword and shield

Date	F	VF	XF	Unc	BU
ND(1986) Proof	Value: 67.50				

KM# 32   1000 KRONUR
30.0000 g., 0.9250 Silver .8922 oz. ASW **Subject:** 50th Anniversary of Icelandic Republic **Obv:** Arms **Rev:** Head of Sveinn Bjornsson left **Note:** In sets only.

Date	F	VF	XF	Unc	BU
ND(1994)	—	—	—	55.00	62.50

KM# 33   1000 KRONUR
30.0000 g., 0.9250 Silver .8922 oz. ASW **Obv:** Arms **Rev:** Head of Asgeir Asgeirsson left **Note:** In sets only.

Date	F	VF	XF	Unc	BU
ND(1994)	—	—	—	55.00	62.50

KM# 34   1000 KRONUR
30.0000 g., 0.9250 Silver .8922 oz. ASW **Obv:** Arms **Rev:** Head of Kristjan Eldjarn left **Note:** In sets only.

Date	F	VF	XF	Unc	BU
ND(1994)	—	—	—	55.00	62.50

KM# 37   1000 KRONUR
27.7300 g., 0.9000 Silver .7720 oz. ASW **Subject:** Leif Ericson Millennium

Date	F	VF	XF	Unc	BU
2000 Proof	Value: 60.00				

KM# 36   10000 KRONUR
8.6500 g., 0.9000 Gold .2503 oz. AGW **Subject:** 1000 Years of Christianity **Obv:** National arms **Rev:** Old crosier top

Date	F	VF	XF	Unc	BU
ND(2000) Proof	Value: 285				

Ireland

Ireland, the island located in the Atlantic Ocean west of Great Britain, was settled by a race of tall, red-haired Celts from Gaul about 400 BC. English control did not become reasonably absolute until 1800 when England and Ireland became the "United Kingdom of Great Britain and Ireland". Religious freedom was restored to the Irish in 1829, but agitation for political autonomy continued until the Irish Free State was established as a Dominion on Dec. 6, 1921 while Northern Ireland remained under the British rule.

MONETARY SYSTEM
4 Farthings = 1 Penny
12 Pence = 1 Shilling
5 Shillings = 1 Crown
20 Shillings = 1 Pound

BRITISH INFLUENCE - COLONIAL
STANDARD COINAGE

KM# 150   1/2 PENNY
Copper

Date	F	VF	XF	Unc	BU
1822-1823	8.00	25.00	75.00	250	—

KM# 151   PENNY
Copper

Date	F	VF	XF	Unc	BU
1822-1823	20.00	75.00	225	600	—

Ireland Republic

The Republic of Ireland, which occupies five-sixths of the island of Ireland located in the Atlantic Ocean west of Great Britain, has an area of 27,136 sq. mi. (70,280 sq. km.) and a population of 4.3 million. Capital: Dublin. Agriculture and dairy farming are the principal industries. Meat, livestock, dairy products and textiles are exported.

Ireland proclaimed itself a republic on April 18, 1949. The government, however, does not use the term 'Republic of Ireland', which tacitly acknowledges the partitioning of the island into Ireland and Northern Ireland, but refers to the country simply as 'Ireland'.

MONETARY SYSTEM

(1928-1971)

4 Farthings = 1 Penny
12 Pence = 1 Shilling
2 Shillings = 1 Florin
20 Shillings = 1 Pound

REPUBLIC
STERLING COINAGE

KM# 1   FARTHING
2.8300 g., Bronze, 20.3 mm. **Rev:** Woodcock (Scolopax rusticola) **Edge:** Plain

Date	F	VF	XF	Unc	BU
1928-1937	0.50	1.50	3.00	10.00	—

KM# 9   FARTHING
2.8300 g., Bronze, 20.3 mm. **Rev:** Woodcock (Scolopax rusticola) **Edge:** Plain

Date	F	VF	XF	Unc	BU
1939-1966	0.25	0.50	1.25	3.00	—

KM# 2   1/2 PENNY
5.6700 g., Bronze, 25.5 mm. **Rev:** Sow with piglets (Sus scrofa domestica) **Edge:** Plain

Date	F	VF	XF	Unc	BU
1928-1937	0.75	2.00	5.00	14.00	—

KM# 10   1/2 PENNY
5.6700 g., Bronze, 25.5 mm. **Rev:** Sow with piglets (Sus scrofa domestica) **Edge:** Plain

Date	F	VF	XF	Unc	BU
1939-1967	0.10	0.15	0.25	1.50	—

KM# 3   PENNY
9.4500 g., Bronze, 30.9 mm. **Rev:** Hen with chicks (Gallus gallus domesticus)

Date	F	VF	XF	Unc	BU
1928-1937	0.50	1.00	4.00	20.00	—

KM# 11   PENNY
9.4500 g., Bronze, 30.9 mm. **Rev:** Hen with chicks (Gallus gallus domesticus) **Edge:** Plain **Note:** Varieties exist.

Date	F	VF	XF	Unc	BU
1940-1968	0.20	0.40	0.75	1.50	—

KM# 4   3 PENCE
3.2400 g., Nickel, 17.6 mm. **Rev:** Hare (Lepus timidus hibernicus) **Edge:** Plain

Date	F	VF	XF	Unc	BU
1928-1935	0.50	1.00	3.50	10.00	—

KM# 12   3 PENCE
3.2400 g., Nickel, 17.6 mm. **Rev:** Hare (Lepus timidus hibernicus)

Date	F	VF	XF	Unc	BU
1939-1940	1.50	3.00	12.50	50.00	—

KM# 12a   3 PENCE
3.2400 g., Copper-Nickel **Rev:** Hare (lepus timidus)

Date	F	VF	XF	Unc	BU
1942-1968	0.10	0.15	0.25	1.50	—

KM# 5   6 PENCE
4.5400 g., Nickel, 20.8 mm. **Rev:** Irish Wolfhound (Canis familiaris leineri) **Edge:** Plain

Date	F	VF	XF	Unc	BU
1928-1935	0.50	1.00	5.00	17.50	—

KM# 13   6 PENCE
4.5400 g., Nickel, 20.8 mm. **Rev:** Irish Wolfhound (canis familiaris leineri)

Date	F	VF	XF	Unc	BU
1939-1940	0.75	2.00	6.00	45.00	—

KM# 13a   6 PENCE
4.5400 g., Copper-Nickel, 20.8 mm. **Rev:** Irish Wolfhound (canis familiaris leineri)

Date	F	VF	XF	Unc	BU
1942-1969	0.15	0.25	0.50	3.00	—

KM# 6   SHILLING
5.6552 g., 0.7500 Silver .1364 oz. ASW, 23.6 mm. **Rev:** Bull **Edge:** Reeded

Date	F	VF	XF	Unc	BU
1928-1937	1.75	5.00	10.00	30.00	—

KM# 14 SHILLING
5.6552 g., 0.7500 Silver .1364 oz. ASW, 23.6 mm. **Rev:** Bull

Date	F	VF	XF	Unc	BU
1939-1942	2.50	4.50	12.50	40.00	—

KM# 14a SHILLING
5.6600 g., Copper-Nickel, 23.6 mm. **Rev:** Bull

Date	F	VF	XF	Unc	BU
1951-1968	0.25	0.50	1.00	2.50	—

KM# 7 FLORIN
11.3104 g., 0.7500 Silver .2727 oz. ASW, 28.5 mm. **Rev:** Salmon (salmo salar) **Edge:** Reeded

Date	F	VF	XF	Unc	BU
1928-1937	3.50	7.00	15.00	40.00	—

KM# 15 FLORIN
11.3104 g., 0.7500 Silver .2727 oz. ASW, 28.5 mm. **Rev:** Salmon (salmo salar)

Date	F	VF	XF	Unc	BU
1939-1943	3.25	6.00	18.00	45.00	—

KM# 15a FLORIN
11.3100 g., Copper-Nickel, 28.5 mm. **Rev:** Salmon (salmo salar)

Date	F	VF	XF	Unc	BU
1951-1968	0.25	0.35	0.75	2.00	—

KM# 8 1/2 CROWN
14.1380 g., 0.7500 Silver .3409 oz. ASW, 32.3 mm. **Rev:** Horse - Irish Hunter **Edge:** Reeded **Note:** Close O and I in COROIN. 8 tufts in horse's tail, with 156 beads.

Date	F	VF	XF	Unc	BU
1928-1937	4.50	10.00	20.00	50.00	—

KM# 16 1/2 CROWN
14.1380 g., 0.7500 Silver .3409 oz. ASW, 32.3 mm. **Rev:** Irish Hunter **Note:** Normal spacing between O and I in COROIN, 7 tufts in horse's tail, with 151 beads in border.

Date	F	VF	XF	Unc	BU
1939-1943	4.00	9.00	15.00	50.00	—

KM# 16a 1/2 CROWN
14.1400 g., Copper-Nickel, 32.3 mm. **Rev:** Irish hunter **Note:** Normal spacing between O and I on "COROIN", 7 tufts in horse's tail, with 151 beads in border.

Date	F	VF	XF	Unc	BU
1951-1967	0.50	1.00	2.00	7.50	—

KM# 17 1/2 CROWN
Copper-Nickel **Obv:** KM#16a **Rev:** KM#8 **Note:** Mule.

Date	VG	F	VF	XF	Unc
1961	9,876	8.00	25.00	200	

KM# 18 10 SHILLING
18.1400 g., 0.8333 Silver .4858 oz. ASW, 30.5 mm. **Subject:** 50th Anniversary - Irish Uprising of Easter, 1916 **Obv:** Padraig Henry Pearse bust 3/4 right **Edge Lettering:** EIRI AMAC NA CASCA 1916

Date	F	VF	XF	Unc	BU
1966	—	—	6.00	15.00	—

DECIMAL COINAGE

100 Pence = 1 Pound (Punt)

KM# 19   1/2 PENNY

1.7800 g., Bronze, 17.1 mm. **Rev:** Stylized bird adapted from an illumination in a celtic manuscript from Cologne Cathedral **Edge:** Plain

Date	F	VF	XF	Unc	BU
1971-1986	—	—	0.10	0.25	0.45

KM# 20   PENNY

3.5600 g., Bronze, 20.3 mm. **Rev:** Stylized bird adapted from an ornamental detail in the Book of Kells **Edge:** Plain

Date	F	VF	XF	Unc	BU
1971-1988	—	—	0.10	0.30	0.50

KM# 20a   PENNY

3.5600 g., Copper-Plated-Steel, 20.3 mm.

Date	F	VF	XF	Unc	BU
1988-2000	—	—	0.10	0.15	0.50

KM# 21   2 PENCE

7.1200 g., Bronze, 25.9 mm. **Rev:** Stylized bird detail from the Second Bible of Charles the Bald **Edge:** Plain

Date	F	VF	XF	Unc	BU
1971-1988	—	—	0.10	0.50	0.75

KM# 21a   2 PENCE

7.1200 g., Copper-Plated-Steel, 25.9 mm.

Date	F	VF	XF	Unc	BU
1990-2000	—	—	0.10	0.25	0.50

KM# 22   5 PENCE

5.6600 g., Copper-Nickel, 23.6 mm. **Rev:** Bull right **Edge:** Reeded

Date	F	VF	XF	Unc	BU
1969-1990	—	0.10	0.10	0.75	1.20

KM# 28   5 PENCE

3.2500 g., Copper-Nickel, 18.5 mm. **Rev:** Bull left **Edge:** Reeded **Note:** Reduced size: 18.5mm. Varieties exist.

Date	F	VF	XF	Unc	BU
1992-2000	—	—	0.10	0.50	0.75

KM# 23   10 PENCE

11.3200 g., Copper-Nickel, 28.5 mm. **Rev:** Salmon right (salmo salar) **Edge:** Reeded

Date	F	VF	XF	Unc	BU
1969-1986	—	2.00	0.25	1.00	1.75

KM# 29   10 PENCE

5.4500 g., Copper-Nickel, 22 mm. **Rev:** Salmon left (salmo salar) **Edge:** Reeded **Note:** Reduced size.

Date	F	VF	XF	Unc	BU
1993-2000	—	—	—	0.75	1.25

KM# 25   20 PENCE

8.4700 g., Nickel-Bronze, 27.1 mm. **Rev:** Horse - Irish Hunter **Edge:** Alternating plain and reeded

Date	F	VF	XF	Unc	BU
1986-2000	—	—	0.50	1.75	3.00

KM# 24   50 PENCE

13.3000 g., Copper-Nickel **Obv:** Harp **Rev:** Woodcock (Scolopax rusticola) **Edge:** Plain **Shape:** 7-sided

Date	F	VF	XF	Unc	BU
1970-2000	—	1.00	1.00	2.00	3.50

KM# 26 50 PENCE

13.5000 g., Copper-Nickel **Subject:** Dublin Millennium

Date	F	VF	XF	Unc	BU
1988	—	—	—	2.50	3.50

KM# 27 PUNT (Pound)

10.0000 g., Copper-Nickel, 31.1 mm. **Obv:** Harp **Rev:** Irish Red Deer left (Cervus elephus) **Note:** The normal KM27 was struck with an milled and engrailed edge. Examples with plain edge, or partial engrailing command a premium of approximately four times the values listed here.

Date	F	VF	XF	Unc	BU
1990-2000	—	—	—	7.00	8.00

KM# 30 PUNT (Pound)

28.2800 g., 0.9250 Silver .8328 oz. ASW, 38.6 mm. **Subject:** 50th Anniversary - United Nations **Obv:** Harp **Rev:** Dove and UN logo **Rev. Inscription:** United for Peace

Date	F	VF	XF	Unc	BU
ND(1995) Proof	Value: 100				

KM# 31 PUNT (Pound)

10.0000 g., Copper-Nickel **Subject:** Millennium **Obv:** Harp **Rev:** Stylized ancient ship **Edge:** Milled and engrailed **Note:** Struck at Sandyford.

Date	F	VF	XF	Unc	BU
2000	—	—	—	7.50	8.50

EURO COINAGE
European Economic Community Issues

KM# 32 EURO CENT

2.2700 g., Copper Plated Steel, 16.25 mm. **Obv:** Harp **Rev:** Denomination and globe **Edge:** Plain

Date	VG	F	VF	XF	Unc
2002-2006	9,876	—	—	—	0.35

KM# 33 2 EURO CENT

3.0000 g., Copper Plated Steel, 18.75 mm. **Obv:** Harp **Rev:** Denomination and globe **Edge:** Plain

Date	VG	F	VF	XF	Unc
2002-2006	9,876	—	—	—	0.50

KM# 34 5 EURO CENT

3.8600 g., Copper-Plated-Steel, 21.25 mm. **Obv:** Harp **Rev:** Denomination and globe **Edge:** Plain

Date	VG	F	VF	XF	Unc
2002-2006	9,876	—	—	—	0.75

KM# 35 10 EURO CENT

4.0700 g., Aluminum-Bronze, 19.75 mm. **Obv:** Harp **Rev:** Denomination and map **Edge:** Reeded

Date	VG	F	VF	XF	Unc
2002-2006	9,876	—	—	—	1.00

KM# 36 20 EURO CENT

5.7300 g., Aluminum-Bronze, 22.25 mm. **Obv:** Harp **Rev:** Denomination and map **Edge:** Notched

Date	VG	F	VF	XF	Unc
2002-2006	9,876	—	—	—	1.25

KM# 37 50 EURO CENT

7.8100 g., Aluminum-Bronze, 24.25 mm. **Obv:** Harp **Edge:** Reeded

Date	VG	F	VF	XF	Unc
2002-2006	9,876	—	—	—	1.50

KM# 38 EURO

7.5000 g., Bi-Metallic Copper-Nickel center in Brass ring,
23.25 mm. **Obv:** Harp **Rev:** Denomination and map **Edge:**
Reeded and plain sections

Date	VG	F	VF	XF	Unc
2002-2006	9,876	—	—	—	2.75

KM# 39 2 EUROS

8.5200 g., Bi-Metallic Brass center in Copper-Nickel ring,
25.7 mm. **Obv:** Harp **Rev:** Denomination and map **Edge:** Reeded
with 2's and stars

Date	VG	F	VF	XF	Unc
2002-2006	9,876	—	—	—	4.00

KM# 42 10 EURO

28.3400 g., 0.9250 Silver 0.8428 oz. ASW, 38.6 mm. **Obv:** Harp
Rev: Stylized Celtic swan **Edge:** Reeded

Date	F	VF	XF	Unc	BU
2004 Proof		Value: 50.00			

KM# 40 5 EURO

14.1900 g., Copper-Nickel, 28.4 mm. **Subject:** Special Olympics
Obv: Harp **Rev:** Multicolor games logo **Edge:** Reeded

Date	F	VF	XF	Unc	BU
2003	—	—	—	15.00	18.00

KM# 44 10 EURO

28.2800 g., 0.9250 Silver 0.841 oz. ASW, 38.6 mm. **Subject:** Sir
William R. Hamilton **Obv:** Harp **Rev:** Triangle in circle of Greek
letters used as math symbols **Edge:** Reeded

Date	F	VF	XF	Unc	BU
2005 Proof		Value: 50.00			

KM# 45 10 EURO

28.5000 g., 0.9250 Silver 0.8476 oz. ASW, 38.6 mm. **Subject:**
Samuel Beckett 1906-1989 **Obv:** Harp **Rev:** Face, value and play
scene **Edge:** Reeded

Date	F	VF	XF	Unc	BU
2006 Proof		Value: 45.00			

KM# 46 20 EURO

1.2400 g., 0.9990 Gold 0.0398 oz. AGW, 14 mm. **Subject:**
Samuel Beckett 1906-1989 **Obv:** Harp scene **Rev:** Face, value
and play **Edge:** Reeded

Date	F	VF	XF	Unc	BU
2006 Proof		Value: 65.00			

KM# 41 10 EURO

28.3000 g., 0.9250 Silver 0.8416 oz. ASW, 38.6 mm. **Subject:**
Special Olympics **Obv:** Gold highlighted harp **Rev:** Gold
highlighted games logo **Edge:** Reeded

Date	F	VF	XF	Unc	BU
2003 Proof		Value: 40.00			

Isle of Man

The Isle of Man, a dependency of the British Crown located in the Irish Sea equidistant from Ireland, Scotland and England, has an area of 227 sq. mi. (588 sq. km.) and a population of 68,000. Capital: Douglas. Agriculture, dairy farming, fishing and tourism are the chief industries.

NOTICE:

Non-circulating commemorative coins issued after 1971 are not presented in this volume. Please see the *Standard Catalog of World Coins*, either the 20th or 21st century edition, by Krause Publications, an imprint of F+W Publications

BRITISH DEPENDENCY
STANDARD COINAGE

KM# 12 FARTHING
Copper

Date	F	VF	XF	Unc	BU
1839-1860	10.00	27.00	55.00	150	—

KM# 12a FARTHING
Copper-Gilt

Date	F	VF	XF	Unc	BU
1839-1860 Proof, rare	—	—	—	—	—

KM# 13 1/2 PENNY
Copper

Date	F	VF	XF	Unc	BU
1839-1860	12.00	30.00	60.00	175	—

KM# 14 PENNY
Copper

Date	F	VF	XF	Unc	BU
1839-1859	20.00	35.00	85.00	275	—

DECIMAL COINAGE
5 New Pence = 1 Shilling; 25 New Pence = 1 Crown; 100 New Pence = 1 Pound

KM# 19 1/2 NEW PENNY
Bronze **Obv:** Bust of Queen Elizabeth II right **Rev:** St. James' Weed; Cushaq; Ragwort (senecio jacobaea)

Date	F	VF	XF	Unc	BU
1971-1975	—	—	0.10	0.15	—

KM# 20 NEW PENNY
Bronze **Obv:** Bust of Queen Elizabeth II right **Rev:** Celtic cross

Date	F	VF	XF	Unc	BU
1971-1975	—	—	0.10	0.20	—

KM# 21 2 NEW PENCE
Bronze **Obv:** Bust of Queen Elizabeth II right **Rev:** Cast of falcons (falco rusticolus)

Date	F	VF	XF	Unc	BU
1971-1975	—	—	0.25	1.00	—

KM# 23 10 NEW PENCE
Copper-Nickel **Obv:** Bust of Queen Elizabeth II right **Rev:** Triskelion

Date	F	VF	XF	Unc	BU
1971-1975	—	—	0.20	0.40	—

KM# 24 50 NEW PENCE
Copper-Nickel **Obv:** Bust of Queen Elizabeth II right **Rev:** Viking ship sailing right **Shape:** 7-sided

Date	F	VF	XF	Unc	BU
1971-1975	—	—	1.00	5.00	7.50

KM# 15   1/2 SOVEREIGN (1/2 Pound)
3.9940 g., 0.9170 Gold .1177 oz. AGW **Subject:** 200th
Anniversary of Acquisition **Obv:** Bust of Queen Elizabeth II right

Date	F	VF	XF	Unc	BU
1965	—	—	—	80.00	—

KM# 15a   1/2 SOVEREIGN (1/2 Pound)
4.0000 g., 0.9800 Gold .1260 oz. AGW **Subject:** 200th
Anniversary of Acquisition **Obv:** Bust of Queen Elizabeth II right

Date	F	VF	XF	Unc	BU
1965 Proof		Value: 85.00			

KM# 16   SOVEREIGN (Pound)
7.9881 g., 0.9170 Gold .2355 oz. AGW **Subject:** 200th
Anniversary of Acquisition **Obv:** Bust of Queen Elizabeth II right
Rev: Triskeles symbol in inner circle

Date	F	VF	XF	Unc	BU
1965	—	—	—	165	—

KM# 16a   SOVEREIGN (Pound)
8.0000 g., 0.9800 Gold .2520 oz. AGW **Subject:** 200th
Anniversary of Acquisition **Obv:** Bust of Queen Elizabeth II right
Rev: Triskeles symbol in inner circle

Date	F	VF	XF	Unc	BU
1965 Proof		Value: 175			

KM# 17   5 POUNDS
39.9403 g., 0.9170 Gold 1.1776 oz. AGW **Subject:** 200th
Anniversary of Acquisition **Obv:** Bust of Queen Elizabeth II right

Date	F	VF	XF	Unc	BU
1965	—	—	—	775	—

KM# 17a   5 POUNDS
39.9500 g., 0.9800 Gold 1.2588 oz. AGW **Subject:** 200th
Anniversary of Acquisition **Obv:** Bust of Queen Elizabeth II right

Date	F	VF	XF	Unc	BU
1965 Proof		Value: 825			

KM# 18   CROWN
Copper-Nickel **Obv:** Bust of Queen Elizabeth II right **Rev:** Manx cat

Date	F	VF	XF	Unc	BU
1970	—	—	—	10.00	12.00

KM# 18a   CROWN
28.2800 g., 0.9250 Silver .8411 oz. ASW **Obv:** Bust of Queen
Elizabeth II right **Rev:** Manx cat

Date	F	VF	XF	Unc	BU
1970 Proof		Value: 17.50			

WW II P.O.W TOKEN COINAGE

KM# Tn23   1/2 PENNY
Brass

Date	F	VF	XF	Unc	BU
ND	17.50	35.00	75.00	165	—

KM# Tn24   PENNY
Brass

Date	F	VF	XF	Unc	BU
ND	6.00	15.00	35.00	80.00	—

KM# Tn25   6 PENCE
Brass

Date	F	VF	XF	Unc	BU
ND	12.00	28.00	60.00	135	—

Isle of Man

Jersey

The Bailiwick of Jersey, a British Crown dependency located in the English Channel 12 miles (19 km.) west of Normandy, France, has an area of 45 sq. mi. (117 sq. km.) and a population of 74,000. Capital: St. Helier. The economy is based on agriculture and cattle breeding – the importation of cattle is prohibited to protect the purity of the island's world-famous strain of milch cows.

Jersey was occupied by Neanderthal man by 100,000 B.C., and by Iberians of 2000 B.C. who left their chamber tombs in the island's granite cliffs. Roman legions almost certainly visited the island although they left no evidence of settlement. The country folk of Jersey still speak an archaic form of Norman-French, lingering evidence of the Norman annexation of the island in 933 A.D. Jersey was annexed to England in 1206, 140 years after the Norman Conquest. The dependency is administered by its own laws and customs; laws enacted by the British Parliament do not apply to Jersey unless it is specifically mentioned. During World War II, German troops occupied the island from July 1, 1940 until May 9, 1945.

Coins of pre-Roman Gaul and of Rome have been found in abundance on Jersey.

MONETARY SYSTEM
Commencing 1877
12 Pence = 1 Shilling
5 Shillings = 1 Crown
20 Shillings = 1 Pound
100 New Pence = 1 Pound

BRITISH DEPENDENCY
STANDARD COINAGE

KM# 1 1/52 SHILLING
Copper

Date	F	VF	XF	Unc	BU
1841-1861	20.00	50.00	175	350	—

KM# 1a 1/52 SHILLING
Bronze

Date	F	VF	XF	Unc	BU
1861 Proof	—	—	—	—	—

KM# 6 1/48 SHILLING
Bronze

Date	F	VF	XF	Unc	BU
1877	15.00	30.00	95.00	175	—

KM# 2 1/26 SHILLING
Copper

Date	F	VF	XF	Unc	BU
1841-1861	3.00	12.00	40.00	100	—

KM# 4 1/26 SHILLING
Bronze

Date	F	VF	XF	Unc	BU
1866-1871	1.00	6.00	30.00	95.00	—

KM# 7 1/24 SHILLING
Bronze

Date	F	VF	XF	Unc	BU
1877-1894	1.25	4.00	12.00	32.00	—

KM# 9 1/24 SHILLING
Bronze **Obv:** Bust of King Edward VII right **Rev:** Arms

Date	F	VF	XF	Unc	BU
1909	1.00	2.50	11.50	40.00	—

KM# 11 1/24 SHILLING
Bronze **Obv:** Bust of King George V left **Rev:** Arms

Date	F	VF	XF	Unc	BU
1911-1923	1.00	2.50	11.50	28.00	—

KM# 13 1/24 SHILLING
Bronze **Obv:** Bust of King George V leftsey

Date	F	VF	XF	Unc	BU
1923-1926	0.75	2.50	4.50	20.00	—

KM# 15   1/24 SHILLING
Bronze   **Obv:** Bust of King George V left **Rev:** Arms

Date	F	VF	XF	Unc	BU
1931-1935	0.50	1.00	3.00	15.00	—

KM# 10   1/12 SHILLING
Bronze   **Obv:** Bust of King Edward VII right **Rev:** Arms

Date	F	VF	XF	Unc	BU
1909	0.75	3.50	12.50	60.00	—

KM# 17   1/24 SHILLING
Bronze   **Obv:** Bust of King George VI left **Rev:** Arms

Date	F	VF	XF	Unc	BU
1937-1947	0.50	1.00	3.00	15.00	—

KM# 3   1/13 SHILLING
Copper

Date	F	VF	XF	Unc	BU
1841-1865	2.00	20.00	80.00	175	—

KM# 12   1/12 SHILLING
Bronze   **Obv:** Bust of King George V left **Rev:** Arms

Date	F	VF	XF	Unc	BU
1911-1923	0.50	1.50	5.00	35.00	—

KM# 5   1/13 SHILLING
Bronze

Date	F	VF	XF	Unc	BU
1866-1871	1.00	6.50	35.00	100	—

KM# 14   1/12 SHILLING
Bronze   **Obv:** Bust of King George V left **Rev:** Arms

Date	F	VF	XF	Unc	BU
1923-1926	0.75	2.50	8.00	30.00	—

KM# 8   1/12 SHILLING
Bronze

Date	F	VF	XF	Unc	BU
1877-1894	0.50	2.00	15.00	50.00	—

KM# 16   1/12 SHILLING
Bronze   **Obv:** Bust of King George V left **Rev:** Arms

Date	F	VF	XF	Unc	BU
1931-1935	0.50	1.25	3.00	19.00	—

Jersey

KM# 18   1/12 SHILLING
Bronze   **Obv:** Bust of King George VI left **Rev:** Arms

Date	F	VF	XF	Unc	BU
1937-1947	0.25	0.50	1.50	7.50	—

KM# 19   1/12 SHILLING
Bronze   **Subject:** Liberation Commemorative **Obv:** Bust of King George VI left **Rev:** Arms

Date	F	VF	XF	Unc	BU
1945	0.25	0.50	1.00	5.00	—

KM# 20   1/12 SHILLING
Bronze   **Obv:** Head of Queen Elizabeth II right **Rev:** Arms

Date	F	VF	XF	Unc	BU
ND (1954)	0.25	0.50	1.00	3.50	—

KM# 21   1/12 SHILLING
Bronze   **Obv:** Head of Queen Elizabeth II right

Date	F	VF	XF	Unc	BU
1957-1964	0.25	0.45	0.75	1.50	—

KM# 23   1/12 SHILLING
Bronze   **Subject:** 300th Anniversary - Accession of King Charles II **Obv:** Head of Queen Elizabeth II right

Date	F	VF	XF	Unc	BU
ND (1960)	0.25	0.45	0.75	1.50	—

KM# 24   1/12 SHILLING
Bronze   **Obv:** Head of Queen Elizabeth II right **Rev:** KM#23

Date	F	VF	XF	Unc	BU
ND(1960) Proof	Value: 65.00				

KM# 26   1/12 SHILLING
Bronze   **Subject:** Norman Conquest **Obv:** Head of Queen Elizabeth II right

Date	F	VF	XF	Unc	BU
ND (1966)	0.25	0.45	0.75	1.50	—

KM# 22   1/4 SHILLING (3 Pence)
Nickel-Brass   **Obv:** Head of Queen Elizabeth II right

Date	F	VF	XF	Unc	BU
1957-1960	0.10	0.15	0.50	3.00	—

KM# 25   1/4 SHILLING (3 Pence)
Nickel-Brass   **Obv:** Head of Queen Elizabeth II right **Edge:** 12-sided

Date	F	VF	XF	Unc	BU
1964	0.10	0.15	0.20	0.75	—

KM# 27   1/4 SHILLING (3 Pence)
Nickel-Brass   **Subject:** Norman Conquest **Obv:** Head of Queen
Elizabeth II right **Shape:** 12-sided

Date	F	VF	XF	Unc	BU
ND (1966)	0.10	0.15	0.35	1.25	—

KM# 28   5 SHILLING
Copper-Nickel   **Subject:** Norman Conquest **Obv:** Head of Queen
Elizabeth II right

Date	F	VF	XF	Unc	BU
ND (1966)	—	1.00	2.00	3.50	—

DECIMAL COINAGE
100 New Pence = 1 Pound

Many of the following coins are also struck in silver, gold,
and platinum for collectors

KM# 29   1/2 NEW PENNY
Bronze   **Obv:** Bust of Queen Elizabeth II right

Date	F	VF	XF	Unc	BU
1971-1980	—	—	0.10	0.20	—

KM# 30   NEW PENNY
Bronze   **Obv:** Bust of Queen Elizabeth II right

Date	F	VF	XF	Unc	BU
1971-1980	—	—	0.10	0.20	—

KM# 31   2 NEW PENCE
Bronze   **Obv:** Bust of Queen Elizabeth II right

Date	F	VF	XF	Unc	BU
1971-1980	—	—	0.15	0.30	—

KM# 32   5 NEW PENCE
Copper-Nickel   **Obv:** Bust of Queen Elizabeth II right

Date	F	VF	XF	Unc	BU
1968-1980	—	0.15	0.25	1.00	—

KM# 33   10 NEW PENCE
Copper-Nickel   **Obv:** Bust of Queen Elizabeth II right

Date	F	VF	XF	Unc	BU
1968-1980	—	0.20	0.30	0.75	—

KM# 34   50 PENCE
Copper-Nickel   **Obv:** Bust of Queen Elizabeth II right **Shape:** 7-sided

Date	F	VF	XF	Unc	BU
1969-1980	—	—	0.90	1.50	—

NOTICE:
Non-circulating commemorative coins issued after
1971 are not presented in this volume. Please see
the *Standard Catalog of World Coins*, either the
20th or 21st century edition, by Krause Publications,
an imprint of F+W Publications

Jersey

Latvia

The Republic of Latvia, the central Baltic state in east Europe, has an area of 24,749 sq. mi. (43,601 sq. km.) and a population of *2.6 million. Capital: Riga. Livestock raising and manufacturing are the chief industries. Butter, bacon, fertilizers and telephone equipment are exported.

The coinage issued during the early 20th Century Republic is now obsolete.

Latvia declared their independence from the U.S.S.R. on August 22, 1991.

MONETARY SYSTEM
100 Santimu = 1 Lats

FIRST REPUBLIC
1918-1939

STANDARD COINAGE
100 Santimu = 1 Lats

KM# 1   SANTIMS
1.6500 g., Bronze, 17 mm. **Edge:** Plain **Note:** Struck at Huguenin Freres, Le Locle, Switzerland.

Date	F	VF	XF	Unc	BU
1922-1935	1.00	2.00	3.50	8.00	—

KM# 10   SANTIMS
1.8000 g., Bronze, 17 mm. **Edge:** Plain

Date	F	VF	XF	Unc	BU
1937-1939	0.50	1.00	2.00	3.00	—

KM# 2   2 SANTIMI
2.0000 g., Bronze, 19.5 mm. **Edge:** Plain

Date	F	VF	XF	Unc	BU
1922-1932	1.00	2.00	5.00	9.00	—

KM# 11.1   2 SANTIMI
2.0000 g., Bronze, 19 mm. **Edge:** Plain

Date	F	VF	XF	Unc	BU
1937	10.00	20.00	30.00	60.00	—

KM# 11.2   2 SANTIMI
2.0000 g., Bronze, 19.5 mm. **Edge:** Plain

Date	F	VF	XF	Unc	BU
1939	2.00	3.00	4.00	9.00	—

KM# 3   5 SANTIMI
3.0000 g., Bronze, 22 mm.

Date	F	VF	XF	Unc	BU
1922-1923	1.00	2.00	3.00	8.00	—

KM# 4   10 SANTIMU
3.0000 g., Nickel, 19 mm. **Edge:** Plain **Note:** Struck at Huguenin.

Date	F	VF	XF	Unc	BU
1922	1.00	2.00	4.00	6.00	—

KM# 5   20 SANTIMU
6.0000 g., Nickel, 21 mm. **Edge:** Plain **Note:** Struck at Huguenin.

Date	F	VF	XF	Unc	BU
1922	1.00	2.00	5.00	9.00	—

KM# 6   50 SANTIMU
6.5000 g., Nickel, 25 mm. **Edge:** Plain **Note:** Struck at Huguenin.

Date	F	VF	XF	Unc	BU
1922	2.00	4.00	6.00	10.00	—

KM# 7   LATS
5.0000 g., 0.8350 Silver .1342 oz. ASW, 23 mm. **Edge:** Milled

Date	F	VF	XF	Unc	BU
1923-1924	3.50	6.00	9.00	—	—

KM# 8   2 LATI
10.0000 g., 0.8350 Silver .2684 oz. ASW, 27 mm.   **Edge:** Milled

Date	F	VF	XF	Unc	BU
1925-1926	3.75	6.00	10.00	30.00	—

KM# 9   5 LATI
25.0000 g., 0.8350 Silver .6712 oz. ASW, 37 mm.   **Edge:** Plain with   DIEVS *** SVETI *** LATVOJU ***

Date	F	VF	XF	Unc	BU
1929-1932	10.00	15.00	18.00	40.00	—

MODERN REPUBLIC
1991-present

STANDARD COINAGE
100 Santimu = 1 Lats

KM# 15   SANTIMS
Copper Plated Iron

Date	F	VF	XF	Unc	BU
1992-2005	—	—	—	0.25	0.35

KM# 21   2 SANTIMI
Bronze Plated Steel

Date	F	VF	XF	Unc	BU
1992-2000	—	—	—	0.50	0.65

KM# 16   5 SANTIMI
Brass

Date	F	VF	XF	Unc	BU
1992	—	—	—	0.75	1.00

KM# 17   10 SANTIMU
Brass

Date	F	VF	XF	Unc	BU
1992	—	—	—	1.25	1.50

KM# 22   20 SANTIMU
Brass

Date	F	VF	XF	Unc	BU
1992	—	—	—	1.50	1.75

KM# 13   50 SANTIMU
Copper-Nickel

Date	F	VF	XF	Unc	BU
1992	—	—	—	3.00	3.50

KM# 12   LATS
Copper-Nickel

Date	F	VF	XF	Unc	BU
1992	—	—	—	4.00	4.50

Latvia

KM# 45 LATS
31.4700 g., 0.9250 Silver .9359 oz. ASW, 38.6 mm. **Subject:**
European mink **Obv:** National arms **Rev:** Mink on rock **Edge:**
Lettered

Date	F	VF	XF	Unc	BU
1999 Proof			Value: 60.00		

KM# 23 LATS
28.2800 g., 0.9250 Silver .8411 oz. ASW **Series:** UN 50th
Anniversary **Rev:** Many people holding hands

Date	F	VF	XF	Unc	BU
1995 Proof			Value: 42.50		

KM# 39 LATS
15.2000 g., 0.9250 Silver .4520 oz. ASW **Subject:** Millennium
Note: Button design.

Date	F	VF	XF	Unc	BU
1999-2000 Proof			Value: 55.00		

KM# 46 LATS
31.4700 g., 0.9250 Silver .9359 oz. ASW, 38.6 mm. **Subject:**
Hanseatic City of Ventspils **Obv:** City arms above denomination
Rev: Building and ship **Edge Lettering:** "LATVIJAS REPUBLIKA
LATVIJAS BANKA"

Date	F	VF	XF	Unc	BU
2000 Proof			Value: 50.00		

KM# 44 LATS
20.0000 g., 0.9250 Silver .5948 oz. ASW, 34 mm. **Series:**
Olympics **Obv:** National arms **Rev:** Two cyclists **Edge:** Lettered

Date	F	VF	XF	Unc	BU
1999 Proof			Value: 35.00		

KM# 47 LATS
31.4700 g., 0.9250 Silver .9359 oz. ASW, 38.6 mm. **Subject:**
Earth - Roots **Obv:** Stylized "Roots" pattern **Rev:** Landscape and
denomination **Edge:** Plain

Date	F	VF	XF	Unc	BU
2000 Proof			Value: 50.00		

KM# 48 LATS
31.4700 g., 0.9250 Silver .9359 oz. ASW, 38.6 mm. **Subject:**
UNICEF **Obv:** National arms **Rev:** Child art and logo **Edge**
Lettering: "LATVIJAS BANKA" twice

Date	F	VF	XF	Unc	BU
2000 Proof		Value: 50.00			

KM# 51 LATS
31.4700 g., 0.9250 Silver 0.9359 oz. ASW, 38.6 mm. **Series:**
Roots - Heaven **Obv:** Stylized Roots pattern **Rev:** Woman holding
the sun **Edge:** Plain

Date	F	VF	XF	Unc	BU
2001 Proof		Value: 50.00			

KM# 54 LATS
4.7500 g., Copper-Nickel, 21.7 mm. **Obv:** National arms **Rev:** Stork
above denomination **Edge Lettering:** "LATVIJAS BANKA" twice

Date	F	VF	XF	Unc	BU
2001	—	—	—	5.50	6.00

KM# 49 LATS
31.4700 g., 0.9250 Silver .9359 oz. ASW, 38.6 mm. **Subject:**
Hanseatic City of Cesis **Obv:** City arms **Rev:** Castle and ship **Edge**
Lettering: "LATVIJAS REPUBLIKA.LATVIJAS BANKA"

Date	F	VF	XF	Unc	BU
2001 Proof		Value: 50.00			

KM# 50 LATS
31.4700 g., 0.9250 Silver .9359 oz. ASW **Series:** Ice Hockey
Obv: National arms **Rev:** Hockey player

Date	F	VF	XF	Unc	BU
2001 Proof		Value: 50.00			

KM# 52 LATS
31.4700 g., 0.9250 Silver 0.9359 oz. ASW, 38.6 mm. **Series:**
Roots - Destiny **Obv:** Stylized Roots pattern **Rev:** Apple tree and
landscape **Edge:** Plain

Date	F	VF	XF	Unc	BU
2002 Proof		Value: 50.00			

KM# 53 LATS
31.4700 g., 0.9250 Silver 0.9359 oz. ASW, 38.6 mm. **Subject:** Hanseatic City of Kuldiga **Obv:** City arms **Rev:** City view and ships **Edge:** Lettered

Date	F	VF	XF	Unc	BU
2002 Proof		Value: 50.00			

KM# 57 LATS
31.4700 g., 0.9250 Silver 0.9359 oz. ASW, 38.6 mm. **Subject:** Olympics 2004 **Obv:** National arms **Rev:** Ancient wrestlers **Edge:** Lettered **Edge Lettering:** LATVIJAS BANKA repeated twice

Date	F	VF	XF	Unc	BU
2002 Proof		Value: 50.00			

KM# 58 LATS
4.8000 g., Copper Nickel, 21.8 mm. **Obv:** National arms **Rev:** Ant above value **Edge:** Lettered **Edge Lettering:** LATVIJAS BANKA

Date	F	VF	XF	Unc	BU
2003	—	—	—	5.00	6.00

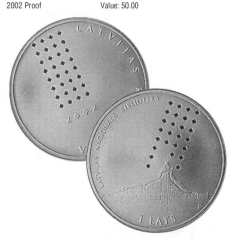

KM# 55 LATS
31.4700 g., 0.9250 Silver 0.9359 oz. ASW, 38.6 mm. **Subject:** National Library **Obv:** Country name and diamonds pattern **Rev:** Library building sketch and diamonds design **Edge Lettering:** "GAISMU SAUCA-GAISMA AUSA"

Date	F	VF	XF	Unc	BU
2002 Proof		Value: 50.00			

KM# 56 LATS
15.0000 g., 0.9250 Silver 0.4461 oz. ASW, 28 mm. **Subject:** "Fortune" **Obv:** Totally gold plated. Sun above country name **Rev:** Waning moon, date and value **Edge:** Plain

Date	F	VF	XF	Unc	BU
2002 Proof		Value: 35.00			

KM# 60 LATS
31.4700 g., 0.9250 Silver 0.9359 oz. ASW, 38.6 mm. **Obv:** Crowned arms of Courland above a partially built ship **Rev:** Hemp weighing scene with Iron foundry and brick wall in background **Edge:** Lettered **Edge Lettering:** "REPUBLIKA LATVIJAS BANKA LATVIJA" **Note:** Western Latvia formerly Courland

Date	F	VF	XF	Unc	BU
2003 Proof		Value: 50.00			

KM# 61 LATS
4.8000 g., Copper-Nickel, 21.7 mm. **Obv:** National arms **Rev:** Child with shovel above value **Edge:** Lettered **Edge Lettering:** "LATVIJAS BANKA" twice

Date	F	VF	XF	Unc	BU
2004	—	—	—	5.50	6.00

KM# 62 LATS
17.1500 g., Bi-Metallic Dark Blue Niobium 7.15g center in .900 Silver 10g ring, 34 mm. **Obv:** Heraldic Rose **Rev:** Astronomical Clock **Edge:** Plain

Date	F	VF	XF	Unc	BU
2004	—	—	—	50.00	55.00

KM# 63 LATS
31.4700 g., 0.9250 Silver 0.9359 oz. ASW, 38.6 mm. **Obv:** National arms **Rev:** World Cup Soccer player **Edge:** "LATVIJA" three times

Date	F	VF	XF	Unc	BU
2004 Proof		Value: 50.00			

KM# 64 LATS
31.4700 g., 0.9250 Silver 0.9359 oz. ASW, 38.6 mm. **Subject:** Latvian European Union Membership **Obv:** National arms askew **Rev:** "P.S. LATVIJA-ES 2004" above value **Edge:** Lettered **Edge Lettering:** "LATVIJAS BANKA" twice

Date	F	VF	XF	Unc	BU
2004 Proof		Value: 50.00			

KM# 65 LATS
14.8400 g., Copper-Nickel, 21.7 mm. **Obv:** National arms **Rev:** Chicken above value **Edge:** Lettered **Edge Lettering:** :LATVIJAS BANKA" twice

Date	F	VF	XF	Unc	BU
2005	—	—	—	5.50	6.00

KM# 66 LATS
4.8500 g., Copper-Nickel, 21.7 mm. **Obv:** National arms **Rev:** Pretzel **Edge Lettering:** "LATVIJAS BANKA"

Date	F	VF	XF	Unc	BU
2005	—	—	—	4.00	5.00

KM# 14 2 LATI
Copper-Nickel

Date	F	VF	XF	Unc	BU
1992	—	—	—	7.00	8.00

KM# 18 2 LATI
Copper-Nickel **Subject:** 75th Anniversary - Declaration of Independence

Date	F	VF	XF	Unc	BU
ND(1993)	—	—	—	9.00	10.00

KM# 38 2 LATI
Ring Composition: Copper-Nickel **Center Composition:** Brass **Rev:** Cow above denomination

Date	F	VF	XF	Unc	BU
1999	—	—	—	10.00	11.50

KM# 59 5 LATI
1.2442 g., 0.9999 Gold 0.04 oz. AGW, 13.92 mm. **Obv:** Latvian maiden **Rev:** National arms above value **Edge:** Reeded **Note:** Remake of the popular KM-9 design

Date	F	VF	XF	Unc	BU
2003 Proof			Value: 60.00		

KM# 19 10 LATU
25.1750 g., 0.9250 Silver .7484 oz. ASW **Subject:** 75th Anniversary - Declaration of Independence

Date	F	VF	XF	Unc	BU
ND(1993) Proof			Value: 35.00		

KM# 24 10 LATU
31.4700 g., 0.9250 Silver .9359 oz. ASW **Series:** Olympics **Rev:** Canoeing event - Man paddling canoe right

Date	F	VF	XF	Unc	BU
1994 Proof			Value: 35.00		

KM# 25 10 LATU
31.4700 g., 0.9250 Silver .9359 oz. ASW **Subject:** Julia Maria **Rev:** 3-masted schooner

Date	F	VF	XF	Unc	BU
1995 Proof			Value: 50.00		

KM# 26 10 LATU
31.4700 g., 0.9250 Silver .9359 oz. ASW **Subject:** Riga 800 **Rev:** First city seal

Date	F	VF	XF	Unc	BU
1995 (1996) Proof			Value: 50.00		

KM# 27 10 LATU
31.4700 g., 0.9250 Silver .9359 oz. ASW **Subject:** 800th Anniversary - Riga **Obv:** Coat of arms from 1368 **Rev:** The Great Gould's coat of arms from 1354

Date	F	VF	XF	Unc	BU
1995 (1996) Proof			Value: 50.00		

KM# 33 10 LATU
31.4700 g., 0.9250 Silver .9359 oz. ASW **Series:** Endangered Wildlife **Obv:** National arms **Rev:** Grieze (corn-crake) bird **Edge:** Lettered **Edge Lettering:** LATVIJAS BANKA \ (2x)

Date	F	VF	XF	Unc	BU
1996 Proof			Value: 50.00		

KM# 34 10 LATU
31.4700 g., 0.9250 Silver .9359 oz. ASW **Subject:** Riga - XVI Century **Obv:** Old coin design above denomination **Rev:** Old city view

Date	F	VF	XF	Unc	BU
1996 Proof			Value: 50.00		

KM# 36   10 LATU
31.3500 g., 0.9990 Silver 1.0069 oz. ASW **Subject:** 800th Anniversary of Riga **Obv:** Old coin design with St. Christopher **Rev:** Old coin design with city arms **Edge:** Lettered **Edge Lettering:** LATVIJAS REPUBLIKA LATVIJAS BANKA

Date	F	VF	XF	Unc	BU
1996 Proof		Value: 50.00			

KM# 28   10 LATU
31.3200 g., 0.9250 Silver .9314 oz. ASW **Obv:** National arms **Rev:** 12th-century ship above its sunken remains **Edge:** Lettered **Edge Lettering:** LATIJAS BANKAS

Date	F	VF	XF	Unc	BU
1997 Proof		Value: 50.00			

KM# 35   10 LATU
31.4700 g., 0.9250 Silver .9359 oz. ASW **Subject:** Riga - XVII Century **Obv:** Old coin design **Rev:** Aerial view of walled city

Date	F	VF	XF	Unc	BU
1997 Proof		Value: 50.00			

KM# 42   10 LATU
1.2442 g., 0.9990 Gold .0400 oz. AGW, 13.92 mm. **Obv:** National arms **Rev:** Sailing ship "Julia Maria" **Edge:** Reeded

Date	F	VF	XF	Unc	BU
1997 Proof		Value: 55.00			

KM# 29   10 LATU
1.2441 g., 0.9999 Gold .0400 oz. AGW **Subject:** 800th Anniversary - Riga **Obv:** City arms on old coin design **Rev:** City arms and ship on old coin design

Date	F	VF	XF	Unc	BU
1998 Proof		Value: 55.00			

KM# 30   10 LATU
31.4700 g., 0.9250 Silver .9359 oz. ASW **Subject:** 800th Anniversary - Riga **Obv:** National song festival procession **Rev:** Riga city arms

Date	F	VF	XF	Unc	BU
1998 Proof		Value: 50.00			

KM# 31   10 LATU
31.4700 g., 0.9250 Silver .9359 oz. ASW **Subject:** 800th Anniversary - Riga **Obv:** Liberty Monument in Riga **Rev:** Lions supporting city arms of Riga

Date	F	VF	XF	Unc	BU
1998 Proof		Value: 55.00			

KM# 32   10 LATU
31.4700 g., 0.9250 Silver .9359 oz. ASW **Obv:** National arms **Rev:** 1925 Icebreaker "Krisjanis Valdemars"

Date	F	VF	XF	Unc	BU
1998 Proof		Value: 50.00			

KM# 43 10 LATU
3.1100 g., 0.5830 Gold .0583 oz. AGW, 18.5 mm. **Series:**
Olympics **Obv:** National arms **Rev:** Javelin thrower **Edge:** Reeded

Date	F	VF	XF	Unc	BU
1999 Proof			Value: 60.00		

KM# 37 20 LATU
31.4100 g., 0.9210 Silver .9341 oz. ASW **Obv:** City arms **Rev:**
Melngalvgu **Edge:** Lettered **Edge Lettering:** LATVIJAS
REPUBLIKA LATVIJAS BANKA

Date	F	VF	XF	Unc	BU
1997 Proof			Value: 50.00		

KM# 41 20 LATU
7.7760 g., 0.5830 Gold .1458 oz. AGW, 25 mm. **Obv:** National
arms **Rev:** Sailing ship "Gekronte Ehlendt" **Edge:** Reeded **Note:**
Struck at Valcambi.

Date	F	VF	XF	Unc	BU
1997 Proof			Value: 110		

KM# 20 100 LATU
13.3380 g., 0.8330 Gold .2501 oz. AGW **Subject:** 75th
Anniversary - Declaration of Independence

Date	F	VF	XF	Unc	BU
ND(1993) Proof			Value: 250		

KM# 40 100 LATU
16.2000 g., 0.9990 Gold .5203 oz. AGW, 24 mm. **Subject:**
Development **Obv:** National arms **Rev:** Partial circle and
denomination **Edge:** Reeded and plain sections

Date	F	VF	XF	Unc	BU
1998 Proof			Value: 500		

Lithuania

The Republic of Lithuania, southernmost of the Baltic states
in east Europe, has an area of 25,174 sq. mi.(65,201 sq. km.) and
a population of *3.6 million. Capital: Vilnius. The economy is based
on livestock raising and manufacturing. Hogs, cattle, hides and
electric motors are exported.

REPUBLIC
1918-1940

STANDARD COINAGE
100 Centas = 1 Litas

KM# 71 CENTAS
1.6000 g., Aluminum-Bronze, 16 mm. **Edge:** Plain **Note:** Struck
at King's Norton.

Date	F	VF	XF	Unc	BU
1925	4.00	8.00	15.00	35.00	—

KM# 79 CENTAS
Bronze, 16.6 mm. **Edge:** Plain

Date	F	VF	XF	Unc	BU
1936	2.00	3.00	5.00	28.00	—

KM# 80 2 CENTAI
2.3000 g., Bronze, 18.5 mm. **Edge:** Plain

Date	F	VF	XF	Unc	BU
1936	3.00	5.00	10.00	40.00	—

KM# 72 5 CENTAI
Aluminum-Bronze

Date	F	VF	XF	Unc	BU
1925	2.00	4.00	8.00	30.00	—

KM# 81 5 CENTAI
2.5000 g., Bronze, 20 mm. **Edge:** Plain

Date	F	VF	XF	Unc	BU
1936	2.00	4.00	8.00	35.00	—

KM# 73   10 CENTU
3.0000 g., Aluminum-Bronze, 21 mm.   **Edge:** Plain

Date	F	VF	XF	Unc	BU
1925	3.00	5.00	8.00	30.00	—

KM# 74   20 CENTU
4.0000 g., Aluminum-Bronze, 23 mm.   **Edge:** Plain

Date	F	VF	XF	Unc	BU
1925	2.00	5.00	10.00	30.00	—

KM# 75   50 CENTU
5.0000 g., Aluminum-Bronze, 25 mm.   **Edge:** Plain

Date	F	VF	XF	Unc	BU
1925	4.00	8.00	15.00	35.00	—

KM# 76   LITAS
2.7000 g., 0.5000 Silver .0434 oz. ASW, 19 mm.   **Edge:** Milled
Note: Struck at Royal Mint, London.

Date	F	VF	XF	Unc	BU
1925	2.00	3.00	8.00	30.00	—

KM# 77   2 LITU
5.4000 g., 0.5000 Silver .0868 oz. ASW, 22.9 mm.   **Edge:** Milled

Date	F	VF	XF	Unc	BU
1925	4.00	6.00	12.00	35.00	—

KM# 78   5 LITAI
13.5000 g., 0.5000 Silver .217 oz. ASW, 29.5 mm.   **Edge:** Milled

Date	F	VF	XF	Unc	BU
1925	6.00	10.00	18.00	65.00	—

KM# 82   5 LITAI
9.0000 g., 0.7500 Silver .217 oz. ASW, 27 mm.   **Rev:** Dr. Jonas Basanavicius bust facing left **Edge Lettering:** TAUTOS GEROVE TAVO GEROVE **Note:** Designers initials below bust

Date	F	VF	XF	Unc	BU
1936	4.00	6.00	9.00	20.00	—

KM# 83   10 LITU
18.0000 g., 0.7500 Silver .434 oz. ASW, 32 mm.   **Rev:** Grand Duke Vytautas Didysis (Vytautas the Great) bust facing left **Edge Lettering:** VIENYBEJE TAUTOS JEGA

Date	F	VF	XF	Unc	BU
1936	9.00	12.00	18.00	30.00	55.00

KM# 84   10 LITU
18.0000 g., 0.7500 Silver .434 oz. ASW   **Subject:** 20th Anniversary of Republic **Rev:** President Smetona head facing left **Edge Lettering:** VIENYBEJE TAUTOS JEGA

Date	F	VF	XF	Unc	BU
ND(1938)	15.00	25.00	35.00	60.00	90.00

MODERN REPUBLIC
1991-present

REFORM COINAGE
100 Centas = 1 Litas

KM# 85   CENTAS
Aluminum

Date	F	VF	XF	Unc	BU
1991	—	—	—	0.20	—

KM# 86　2 CENTAI
Aluminum

Date	F	VF	XF	Unc	BU
1991	—	—	—	0.25	—

KM# 87　5 CENTAI
Aluminum

Date	F	VF	XF	Unc	BU
1991	—	—	—	0.30	—

KM# 88　10 CENTU
Bronze

Date	F	VF	XF	Unc	BU
1991	—	—	—	0.50	—

KM# 106　10 CENTU
2.6000 g., Brass, 16 mm.　**Obv:** Lithuanian knight **Rev:** Denomination **Edge:** Milled

Date	F	VF	XF	Unc	BU
1997-2003	—	—	—	0.40	—

KM# 89　20 CENTU
Bronze

Date	F	VF	XF	Unc	BU
1991	0.30	0.40	0.50	1.50	—

KM# 107　20 CENTU
4.8000 g., Brass, 20 mm.　**Obv:** Lithuanian knight **Rev:** Denomination **Edge:** Milled

Date	F	VF	XF	Unc	BU
1997-2003	—	—	—	0.75	—

KM# 90　50 CENTU
Bronze

Date	F	VF	XF	Unc	BU
1991	0.50	0.75	1.00	5.00	—

KM# 108　50 CENTU
6.0000 g., Brass

Date	F	VF	XF	Unc	BU
1997-2003	—	—	—	1.00	—

KM# 91　LITAS
Copper-Nickel　**Obv:** Knight with raised sword on horse left, date below **Rev:** Value with lines above

Date	F	VF	XF	Unc	BU
1991	0.50	1.00	1.50	4.00	—

KM# 109　LITAS
Copper-Nickel　**Subject:** 75th Anniversary - Bank of Lithuania **Obv:** Knight and denomination **Rev:** Vladas Jurgutis

Date	F	VF	XF	Unc	BU
1997	—	—	—	6.00	—

KM# 109a　LITAS
7.7759 g., 0.9990 Gold .25 oz. AGW, 22.3 mm.　**Subject:** 75th Anniversary - Bank of Lithuania **Obv:** Knight and denomination **Rev:** Vladas Jurgutis

Date	F	VF	XF	Unc	BU
1997 Proof	Value: 600				

KM# 111　LITAS
Copper-Nickel　**Obv:** Lithuanian knight **Rev:** Denomination **Edge:** Reeded

Date	F	VF	XF	Unc	BU
1998-2003	—	—	—	1.25	—

KM# 117　LITAS
Copper-Nickel　**Subject:** The Baltic Highway **Rev:** Six clasped hands **Edge:** Reeded and plain sections

Date	F	VF	XF	Unc	BU
1999	—	—	—	3.00	—

KM# 137   LITAS
6.1500 g., Copper-Nickel, 22.2 mm. **Subject:** 425th Anniversary - University of Vilnius **Obv:** Lithuanian knight above value **Rev:** Old university buildings **Edge:** Segmented reeding

Date	F	VF	XF	Unc	BU
2004	—	—	—	5.00	—

KM# 142   LITAS
6.4100 g., Copper-Nickel, 22.35 mm. **Obv:** Lithuanian Knight **Rev:** Vilnius Ducal Palace **Edge:** Segmented reeding

Date	F	VF	XF	Unc	BU
2005	—	—	—	3.50	—

KM# 92   2 LITAI
Copper-Nickel

Date	F	VF	XF	Unc	BU
1991	1.00	1.50	2.00	4.00	—

KM# 112   2 LITAI
Bi-Metallic Copper-Nickel ring in Brass center **Obv:** Lithuanian knight **Rev:** Denomination **Edge:** Segmented reeding

Date	F	VF	XF	Unc	BU
1998-2003	—	—	—	2.75	—

KM# 93   5 LITAI
Copper-Nickel

Date	F	VF	XF	Unc	BU
1991	2.50	3.50	6.00	12.00	—

KM# 113   5 LITAI
Bi-Metallic Copper-Nickel ring in Brass center **Obv:** Lithuanian knight **Rev:** Denomination **Edge Lettering:** PENKI LITAI

Date	F	VF	XF	Unc	BU
1998-2003	—	—	—	5.00	—

KM# 127   5 LITAI
Outer **Weight:** 28.2800 g. Outer **Composition:** 0.9250 Silver .841 oz. ASW AGW , 38.61 mm. **Series:** UNICEF **Subject:** For the Children of the World **Obv:** Hill of Geoiminas Castle **Rev:** Child with pinwheel **Edge Lettering:** LIETUVOS BANKAS

Date	F	VF	XF	Unc	BU
1998 Proof		Value: 45.00			

KM# 132   5 LITAI
28.2800 g., 0.9250 Silver 0.841 oz. ASW, 38.6 mm. **Series:** Endangered Wildlife **Obv:** Knight on horse **Rev:** Barn owl in flight **Edge Lettering:** LIETUVOS BANKAS

Date	F	VF	XF	Unc	BU
2002 Proof		Value: 45.00			

KM# 94   10 LITU
Copper-Nickel, 28.70 mm.   **Subject:** 60th Anniversary - Darius and Girenas flight across the Atlantic **Edge Lettering:** SLOVE ATLANTO NUGALETOJAMS

Date	F	VF	XF	Unc	BU
ND(1993)	—	—	—	45.00	—

KM# 115   10 LITU
Copper-Nickel, 28.70 mm.   **Obv:** National arms above denomination **Rev:** Vilnus building tops as seen from ground level **Edge Lettering:** VILNIUS-LIETUVOS SOSTINE

Date	F	VF	XF	Unc	BU
1998 Proof		Value: 15.00			

KM# 95   10 LITU
Copper-Nickel, 28.70 mm.   **Subject:** Papal visit **Edge Lettering:** TIKEJIMAS MEILE VILTIS

Date	F	VF	XF	Unc	BU
1993	—	—	—	65.00	—

KM# 116   10 LITU
Copper-Nickel, 28.70 mm.   **Obv:** Lithuanian knight **Rev:** Kaunas city arms and buildings **Edge Lettering:** LAISUAS BUDAMAS, LAISVES NEISSIZADESI

Date	F	VF	XF	Unc	BU
1999 Proof		Value: 12.00			

KM# 96   10 LITU
Copper-Nickel, 28.70 mm.   **Subject:** International Song Fest **Edge Lettering:** SKRISKIT SKAISCIOS DAINOS

Date	F	VF	XF	Unc	BU
1994 Proof		Value: 12.00			

KM# 120   10 LITU
1.2440 g., 0.9999 Gold .04 oz. AGW, 28.70 mm.   **Subject:** Lithuanian gold coinage **Rev:** Medieval minter

Date	F	VF	XF	Unc	BU
1999 Proof		Value: 65.00			

KM# 131   10 LITU
13.1500 g., Copper-Nickel, 28.7 mm.   **Obv:** National arms above an aerial harbor view **Rev:** Klaipeda (Memel) city arms and city view **Edge Lettering:** KLAIPEDAI - 75 (twice)

Date	F	VF	XF	Unc	BU
2002 Proof		Value: 15.00			

KM# 97   10 LITU
Copper-Nickel, 28.70 mm.   **Subject:** 5th World Sport Games **Edge Lettering:** LIETUVIAIS ESAME MES GIME

Date	F	VF	XF	Unc	BU
1995 Proof		Value: 12.00			

KM# 98   50 LITU
23.3000 g., 0.9250 Silver .6929 oz. ASW, 34 mm.   **Subject:** 5th Anniversary - Independence **Edge Lettering:** TEGUL MEILE LIETUVOS DEGA MUSU SIRDYSE

Date	F	VF	XF	Unc	BU
ND(1995) Proof		Value: 80.00			

KM# 102   50 LITU
23.3000 g., 0.9250 Silver .6929 oz. ASW, 34 mm.   **Rev:** King Mindaugas **Edge Lettering:** IS PRAEITIES TAVO SUNUS TE STIPRYBE SEMIA

Date	F	VF	XF	Unc	BU
1996 Proof		Value: 40.00			

KM# 99   50 LITU
23.3000 g., 0.9250 Silver .6929 oz. ASW, 34 mm.   **Subject:** 120th Birth Anniversary Mikalojaus K. Ciurlionis **Edge Lettering:** PASAULIS KAIP DIDELE SIMFONIJA

Date	F	VF	XF	Unc	BU
1995 Proof		Value: 40.00			

KM# 103   50 LITU
23.3000 g., 0.9250 Silver .6929 oz. ASW, 34 mm.   **Rev:** Grand Duke Gediminas **Edge Lettering:** IS PRAEITIES TAVO SUNUS TE STIPRYBE SEMIA

Date	F	VF	XF	Unc	BU
1996 Proof		Value: 45.00			

KM# 100   50 LITU
23.3000 g., 0.9250 Silver .6929 oz. ASW, 34 mm.   **Subject:** 5th Anniversary - 13 January 1991 Assault **Edge Lettering:** IR KRAUJU KRIKSTYTI TAMPA VEL GYUYBE

Date	F	VF	XF	Unc	BU
ND(1996) Proof		Value: 40.00			

KM# 104   50 LITU
23.3000 g., 0.9250 Silver .6929 oz. ASW, 34 mm.   **Subject:** 450th Anniversary - First Lithuanian Book **Obv:** Mounted Lithuanian knight with sword **Rev:** Page from book **Edge Lettering:** MARTYNAS MAZVYDAS IMKIT MANE IR SKAITYKIT

Date	F	VF	XF	Unc	BU
1997 Proof		Value: 47.50			

KM# 105   50 LITU
23.3000 g., 0.9250 Silver .6929 oz. ASW, 34 mm.   **Subject:** 600th Anniversary - Karaims and Tartars settlement in Lithuania **Obv:** Mounted Lithuanian knight with sword **Rev:** Karaim castle guard and Tartar warrior **Edge Lettering:** LIETUVA TEVYNE MUSU

Date	F	VF	XF	Unc	BU
1997 Proof		Value: 47.50			

KM# 110   50 LITU
23.3000 g., 0.9250 Silver .6929 oz. ASW   **Obv:** Mounted Grand Duke Algirdas with sword left **Rev:** Half bust of knight facing and holding scepter

Date	F	VF	XF	Unc	BU
1998 Proof		Value: 42.50			

KM# 114   50 LITU
23.3000 g., 0.9250 Silver .6929 oz. ASW   **Subject:** 200th Anniversary - Birth of Adam Mickiewicz **Obv:** Feather, denomination **Rev:** Laureated profile of Adomas Mickievicius, building

Date	F	VF	XF	Unc	BU
1998 Proof		Value: 42.50			

KM# 101   50 LITU
23.3000 g., 0.9250 Silver .6929 oz. ASW, 34 mm.   **Series:** Altanta Olympics **Rev:** Basketball players **Edge Lettering:** CITIUS. ALTIUS. FORTIUS.

Date	F	VF	XF	Unc	BU
1996 Proof		Value: 30.00			

KM# 118 50 LITU

23.3000 g., 0.9250 Silver .6929 oz. ASW, 34 mm. **Subject:**
Grand Duke Kestutis **Rev:** Half bust Grand Duke Kestutis facing
Edge Lettering: IS PRAEITIES TAVO SUNVS TE STIPRYBE
SEMIA **Note:** Lithuanian Mint.

Date	F	VF	XF	Unc	BU
1999 Proof		Value: 47.50			

KM# 119 50 LITU

28.2800 g., 0.9250 Silver .841 oz. ASW, 38.6 mm. **Subject:**
100th Anniversary - Death of Vincas Kudirka **Obv:** National arms
on stylized bell **Rev:** Head of Kudirka **Edge Lettering:** VARDAN
TOS LIETUVOS VIENYBE TEZYDI **Note:** Lithuanian Mint.

Date	F	VF	XF	Unc	BU
1999 Proof		Value: 50.00			

KM# 123 50 LITU

28.2800 g., 0.9250 Silver .841 oz. ASW, 38.1 mm. **Subject:** 10th
Anniversary - Baltic Way Highway **Rev:** Three pairs of clasped hands
Edge Lettering: VILNIUS RYGA TALINAS **Note:** Lithuanian Mint.

Date	F	VF	XF	Unc	BU
1999 Proof		Value: 37.50			

KM# 121 50 LITU

28.2800 g., 0.9250 Silver .841 oz. ASW, 38.61 mm. **Subject:**
350th Anniversary - The Great Art of Artillery Book **Obv:** National
arms on frame **Rev:** Old rocket designs **Edge Lettering:** ARS
MAGNA ARTILLERIAE * MDCL

Date	F	VF	XF	Unc	BU
2000 Proof		Value: 42.50			

KM# 122 50 LITU

28.2800 g., 0.9250 Silver .841 oz. ASW, 38.6 mm. **Subject:** 10th
Anniversary of Independence **Obv:** Republic of Lithuania coat of arms
Rev: Statue of independence **Edge Lettering:** LAISVE - AMZINOJI
TAUTOS VERTYBE **Note:** Struck at Lietuvos Monetu Kalykla.

Date	F	VF	XF	Unc	BU
ND(2000) Proof		Value: 40.00			

KM# 124 50 LITU

28.2800 g., 0.9250 Silver .841 oz. ASW, 38.61 mm. **Series:** XXVII
Summer Olympic Games **Obv:** Republic of Lithuania coat of arms
Rev: Man throwing discus, Olympic emblem, year, and SIDNEJUS
(Sydney) **Edge Lettering:** NUGALI STIPRUS DVASIA IR KUNU

Date	F	VF	XF	Unc	BU
2000 Proof		Value: 37.50			

KM# 125   50 LITU

23.3000 g., 0.9250 Silver .6929 oz. ASW, 34 mm.   **Subject:**
Grand Duke Vytautas **Obv:** National arms above four shields **Rev:**
Crowned portrait holding sword **Edge Lettering:** IS PRAEITIES
TAVO SUNUS TESTIPRYBE SEMIA

Date	F	VF	XF	Unc	BU
2000 Proof		Value: 40.00			

KM# 128   50 LITU

28.2800 g., 0.9250 Silver .841 oz. ASW, 38.61 mm.   **Subject:**
Millennium **Obv:** National arms, denomination **Rev:** Radiant cross,
arch **Edge Lettering:** SALVE NOVUM MILLENNIUM

Date	F	VF	XF	Unc	BU
2000 Proof		Value: 38.00			

KM# 129   50 LITU

28.2800 g., 0.9250 Silver .8410 oz. ASW, 38.61 mm.   **Subject:**
Motiejus Valancius' 200th Birthday **Obv:** National arms and church
landscape **Rev:** Bishop's portrait **Edge Lettering:** LIETUVISKAS
ZODIS RASTAS IR TIKEJMAS TAUTOS GYVASTIS

Date	F	VF	XF	Unc	BU
2001 Proof		Value: 42.50			

KM# 130   50 LITU

28.2800 g., 0.9250 Silver 0.841 oz. ASW, 38.61 mm.   **Subject:**
Jonas Basanavicius (1851-1927) **Obv:** Mounted knight left **Rev:**
Jonas Basanavlcius **Edge Lettering:** KAD AUSRAI AUSTANT
PRAVISTU IR LIETUVOS DVASIA

Date	F	VF	XF	Unc	BU
2001 Proof		Value: 45.00			

KM# 133   50 LITU

28.2800 g., 0.9250 Silver 0.8410 oz. ASW   **Obv:** Republic of
Lithuania coat of arms **Rev:** Trakai Island Castle **Edge Lettering:**
ISTORIJOS IR ARCHITEKTUROS PAMINKLAI

Date	F	VF	XF	Unc	BU
2002 Proof		Value: 45.00			

KM# 134   50 LITU

28.2800 g., 0.9250 Silver 0.841 oz. ASW, 38.6 mm.   **Obv:**
Lithuanian knight above value **Rev:** Vilnius Cathedral **Edge
Lettering:** ISTORIJOS IR ARCHITEKTUROS PAMINKLAI

Date	F	VF	XF	Unc	BU
2003 Proof		Value: 45.00			

KM# 135 50 LITU
28.2800 g., 0.9250 Silver 0.841 oz. ASW, 38.6 mm. **Subject:**
Olympics **Obv:** Lithuanian knight above value **Rev:** Stylized
cyclists **Edge Lettering:** XXVIII OLIMPIADOS ZAIDYNEMS

Date	F	VF	XF	Unc	BU
2003 Proof		Value: 42.50			

KM# 138 50 LITU
28.2800 g., 0.9250 Silver 0.841 oz. ASW, 38.6 mm. **Subject:**
425th Anniversary - University of Vilnius **Obv:** Lithuanian Knight
Rev: Old university buildings **Edge:** Lettered

Date	F	VF	XF	Unc	BU
2004 Proof		Value: 35.00			

KM# 139 50 LITU
28.2800 g., 0.9250 Silver 0.841 oz. ASW, 38.6 mm. **Obv:**
Lithuanian knight **Rev:** Pazaislis Monastery **Edge:** Lettered **Edge
Lettering:** ISTORIJOS IR ARCHITEKTUROS PAMINKLAI

Date	F	VF	XF	Unc	BU
2004 Proof		Value: 42.50			

KM# 140 50 LITU
28.2800 g., 0.9250 Silver 0.841 oz. ASW, 38.6 mm. **Subject:**
First Lithuanian Statute of 1529 **Obv:** Lithuanian Knight **Rev:** King

Sigismond the Old and Chancellor Gostaustas **Edge:** Lettered
Edge Lettering: "BUKIME TEISES VERGAI, KAD GALETUME
NAUDOTIS LAISVEMIS"

Date	F	VF	XF	Unc	BU
2004 Proof		Value: 47.50			

KM# 141 50 LITU
28.2800 g., 0.9250 Silver 0.841 oz. ASW, 38.6 mm. **Subject:**
Curonian Spit **Obv:** Lithuanian Knight **Rev:** Shifting sand dunes
design **Edge:** Ornamented pattern from Neringa emblem

Date	F	VF	XF	Unc	BU
2004 Proof		Value: 40.00			

KM# 143 50 LITU
28.2800 g., 0.9250 Silver 0.841 oz. ASW, 38.6 mm. **Obv:** Denar
coin with Lithuanian knight **Rev:** Kernavé hill fort **Edge Lettering:**
ISTORIJOS IR ARCHITEKTUROS PAMINKLAI

Date	F	VF	XF	Unc	BU
2005 Proof		Value: 40.00			

KM# 144 50 LITU
28.2800 g., 0.9250 Silver 0.841 oz. ASW, 38.6 mm. **Subject:** 150th
Anniversary - National Museum **Obv:** Trio of ancient Lithuanian coins
Rev: Man blowing horn **Edge Lettering:** PRO PUBLICO BONO

Date	F	VF	XF	Unc	BU
2005 Proof		Value: 40.00			

KM# 145 50 LITU
28.2800 g., 0.9250 Silver 0.841 oz. ASW, 38.6 mm. **Subject:**
Lithuanian knight, cross **Rev:** Cardinal Vincentas Sladkevicius **Edge
Lettering:** LET OUR LIFE BE BUILT ON GOODNESS AND HOPE

Date	F	VF	XF	Unc	BU
2005 Proof		Value: 40.00			

KM# 147 50 LITU
28.2800 g., 0.9250 Silver 0.841 oz. ASW, 38.6 mm. **Subject:**
1905 Lithuanian Congress **Obv:** Lithuanian Knight **Rev:** Legend
and inscription **Edge:** Ornamented

Date	F	VF	XF	Unc	BU
2005 Proof		Value: 50.00			

KM# 148 50 LITU
28.2800 g., 0.9250 Silver 0.841 oz. ASW, 38.6 mm. **Obv:** National
arms on forest background **Rev:** Lynx prowling **Edge:** Stylized lynx
paw prints

Date	F	VF	XF	Unc	BU
2006 Proof		Value: 35.00			

KM# 149 50 LITU
28.2800 g., 0.9250 Silver 0.841 oz. ASW, 38.6 mm. **Obv:** National
arms against castle wall background **Rev:** Medininkai Castle **Edge
Lettering:** "ISTORIJOS IR ARCHITEKTUROS PAMINKLAI"

Date	F	VF	XF	Unc	BU
2006 Proof		Value: 35.00			

KM# 126 100 LITU
7.7800 g., 0.9999 Gold .2501 oz. AGW, 22.3 mm. **Subject:**
Grand Duke Vytautas **Obv:** Knight on horse **Rev:** Crowned portrait
and sword hilt **Edge Lettering:** IS PRAEITIES TAVO SUNUS TE
STIPRYBE SEMIA

Date	F	VF	XF	Unc	BU
2000 Proof		Value: 600			

KM# 136 200 LITU
15.0000 g., Bi-Metallic .900 Gold 7.9g. center in a .925 Silver 7.1g.
ring, 27 mm. **Subject:** 750th Anniversary - King Mindaugas **Obv:**
Lithuanian Knight **Rev:** Seated King Mindaugas **Edge Lettering:**
LIETUVOS KARALYSTE 1253

Date	F	VF	XF	Unc	BU
2003 Proof		Value: 450			

KM# 146 500 LITU
31.1000 g., 0.9999 Gold 0.9998 oz. AGW, 32.5 mm. **Obv:**
Lithuanian Knight **Rev:** Vilnius Ducal Palace **Edge:** Plain

Date	F	VF	XF	Unc	BU
2005 Proof		Value: 950			

Luxembourg

The Grand Duchy of Luxembourg is located in western Europe between Belgium, Germany and France, has an area of 1,103 sq. mi. (2,586 sq. km.) and a population of 377,100. Capital: Luxembourg. The economy is based on steel.

MONETARY SYSTEM
100 Centimes = 1 Franc

GRAND DUCHY
STANDARD COINAGE RESUMED
100 Centimes = 1 Franc

KM# 21   2-1/2 CENTIMES
Bronze

Date	F	VF	XF	Unc	BU
1854-1908	0.50	1.50	7.50	40.00	—

KM# 22.1   5 CENTIMES
Bronze

Date	F	VF	XF	Unc	BU
1854-1870	5.00	15.00	60.00	120	—

KM# 22.2   5 CENTIMES
Bronze

Date	F	VF	XF	Unc	BU
1855-1860	7.00	22.00	85.00	175	—

KM# 24   5 CENTIMES
Copper-Nickel

Date	F	VF	XF	Unc	BU
1901	0.25	0.75	4.50	16.00	—

KM# 26   5 CENTIMES
Copper-Nickel

Date	F	VF	XF	Unc	BU
1908	0.35	1.00	6.50	20.00	—

KM# 27   5 CENTIMES
Zinc

Date	F	VF	XF	Unc	BU
1915	1.00	6.00	15.00	30.00	—

KM# 30   5 CENTIMES
Iron

Date	F	VF	XF	Unc	BU
1918-1922	1.00	4.00	8.00	30.00	—

KM# 33   5 CENTIMES
Copper-Nickel

Date	F	VF	XF	Unc	BU
1924	0.20	0.40	3.00	10.00	—

KM# 40   5 CENTIMES
Bronze

Date	F	VF	XF	Unc	BU
1930	0.10	0.25	2.00	4.00	—

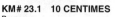

KM# 23.1   10 CENTIMES
Bronze

Date	F	VF	XF	Unc	BU
1854-1870	3.00	6.00	40.00	120	—

KM# 23.2   10 CENTIMES
Bronze

Date	F	VF	XF	Unc	BU
1855-1865	3.00	6.00	40.00	120	—

KM# 25   10 CENTIMES
Copper-Nickel

Date	F	VF	XF	Unc	BU
1901	0.25	0.75	6.00	12.00	—

KM# 28   10 CENTIMES
Zinc

Date	F	VF	XF	Unc	BU
1915	1.25	4.00	8.00	20.00	—

KM# 31   10 CENTIMES
Iron

Date	F	VF	XF	Unc	BU
1918-1923	1.50	3.50	10.00	25.00	—

KM# 34   10 CENTIMES
Copper-Nickel

Date	F	VF	XF	Unc	BU
1924	0.25	0.50	2.00	8.00	—

KM# 41   10 CENTIMES
Bronze

Date	F	VF	XF	Unc	BU
1930	0.10	0.25	2.00	4.00	—

KM# 29   25 CENTIMES
Zinc

Date	F	VF	XF	Unc	BU
1916-1920	1.50	6.00	12.00	25.00	—

KM# 32   25 CENTIMES
Iron

Date	F	VF	XF	Unc	BU
1919-1922	2.75	6.50	12.50	35.00	—

KM# 37   25 CENTIMES
Copper-Nickel

Date	F	VF	XF	Unc	BU
1927	0.35	0.65	5.00	25.00	—

KM# 42   25 CENTIMES
Bronze

Date	F	VF	XF	Unc	BU
1930	0.35	1.00	8.00	30.00	—

KM# 42a.1   25 CENTIMES
Copper-Nickel   **Note:** Coin alignment.

Date	F	VF	XF	Unc	BU
1938	0.35	1.00	3.00	10.00	—

KM# 42a.2   25 CENTIMES
Copper-Nickel   **Note:** Medal alignment.

Date	F	VF	XF	Unc	BU
1938	50.00	75.00	100	200	—

KM# 45   25 CENTIMES
Bronze

Date	F	VF	XF	Unc	BU
1946-1947	—	0.15	0.25	0.75	—

KM# 45a.1   25 CENTIMES
Aluminum   **Note:** Coin alignment.

Date	F	VF	XF	Unc	BU
1954-1972	0.10	0.25	0.50	0.10	—

KM# 45a.2   25 CENTIMES
Aluminum   **Note:** Medal alignment.

Date	F	VF	XF	Unc	BU
1954-1967	5.00	10.00	15.00	20.00	—

KM# 45b   25 CENTIMES
2.9600 g., 0.9250 Silver .088 oz. ASW

Date	F	VF	XF	Unc	BU
1980 Proof	Value: 12.00				

KM# 43   50 CENTIMES
Nickel

Date	F	VF	XF	Unc	BU
1930	0.25	1.00	10.00	20.00	—

KM# 35   FRANC
Nickel

Date	F	VF	XF	Unc	BU
1924-1935	0.20	1.50	10.00	20.00	—

KM# 44   FRANC
Copper-Nickel

Date	F	VF	XF	Unc	BU
1939	0.25	0.75	1.50	5.00	—

KM# 46.1   FRANC
Copper-Nickel

Date	F	VF	XF	Unc	BU
1946-1947	0.15	0.35	0.50	1.50	—

KM# 46.2   FRANC
Copper-Nickel

Date	F	VF	XF	Unc	BU
1962-1964	0.10	0.10	0.25	1.00	—

KM# 46.2a   FRANC
4.4500 g., 0.9250 Silver .1323 oz. ASW

Date	F	VF	XF	Unc	BU
1980 Proof	Value: 20.00				

KM# 55   FRANC
Copper-Nickel

Date	F	VF	XF	Unc	BU
1965-1984	—	—	0.10	0.20	—

KM# 55a   FRANC
4.4700 g., 0.9250 Silver .1329 oz. ASW

Date	F	VF	XF	Unc	BU
1980 Proof	Value: 20.00				

KM# 59   FRANC
Copper-Nickel   **Rev:** IML added

Date	F	VF	XF	Unc	BU
1986-1987	—	—	0.10	0.20	—

KM# 63 FRANC
Nickel-Steel

Date	F	VF	XF	Unc	BU
1988-1995	—	—	—	0.40	—

KM# 36 2 FRANCS
Nickel

Date	F	VF	XF	Unc	BU
1924	1.00	4.00	20.00	40.00	—

KM# 38 5 FRANCS
8.0000 g., 0.6250 Silver .1608 oz. ASW

Date	F	VF	XF	Unc	BU
1929	BV	3.50	12.50	25.00	—

KM# 50 5 FRANCS
Copper-Nickel

Date	F	VF	XF	Unc	BU
1949	0.30	0.60	1.00	3.50	—

KM# 51 5 FRANCS
Copper-Nickel

Date	F	VF	XF	Unc	BU
1962	0.10	0.25	0.40	1.00	—

KM# 51a 5 FRANCS
6.7400 g., 0.9250 Silver .2004 oz. ASW

Date	F	VF	XF	Unc	BU
1980 Proof		Value: 25.00			

KM# 56 5 FRANCS
Copper-Nickel

Date	F	VF	XF	Unc	BU
1971-1981	—	—	0.15	0.50	—

KM# 56a 5 FRANCS
6.7800 g., 0.9250 Silver .2016 oz. ASW

Date	F	VF	XF	Unc	BU
1980 Proof		Value: 25.00			

KM# 60.1 5 FRANCS
Brass **Rev:** IML added

Date	F	VF	XF	Unc	BU
1986-1988	—	—	0.15	0.40	—

KM# 60.2 5 FRANCS
Brass **Rev:** Larger crown with cross touching rim

Date	F	VF	XF	Unc	BU
1986-1987	—	—	0.15	0.40	—

KM# 65 5 FRANCS
Brass

Date	F	VF	XF	Unc	BU
1989-1995	—	—	—	0.60	—

KM# 39 10 FRANCS
13.5000 g., 0.7500 Silver .3255 oz. ASW

Date	F	VF	XF	Unc	BU
1929	BV	6.00	12.00	32.50	—

KM# 57 10 FRANCS
Nickel

Date	F	VF	XF	Unc	BU
1971-1980	—	—	0.30	0.60	—

KM# 57a 10 FRANCS
8.7900 g., 0.9250 Silver .2614 oz. ASW

Date	F	VF	XF	Unc	BU
1980 Proof		Value: 30.00			

KM# 47 20 FRANCS
8.5000 g., 0.8350 Silver .2282 oz. ASW **Subject:** 600th Anniversary - John the Blind

Date	F	VF	XF	Unc	BU
ND(1946)	BV	5.00	12.00	18.00	—

KM# 62 50 FRANCS
Nickel

Date	F	VF	XF	Unc	BU
1987-1989	—	—	1.50	3.50	—

KM# 66 50 FRANCS
Nickel **Note:** Similar to 5 Francs, KM#65.

Date	F	VF	XF	Unc	BU
1989-1995	—	—	—	3.50	—

KM# 58 20 FRANCS
Bronze **Edge:** Dashes all around

Date	F	VF	XF	Unc	BU
1980-1983	—	—	0.60	1.00	—

KM# 58a 20 FRANCS
10.2100 g., 0.9250 Silver .3036 oz. ASW

Date	F	VF	XF	Unc	BU
1980 Proof	Value: 30.00				

KM# 49 100 FRANCS
25.0000 g., 0.8350 Silver .6711 oz. ASW **Subject:** 600th Anniversary - John the Blind

Date	F	VF	XF	Unc	BU
ND(1946)	—	20.00	40.00	50.00	—

KM# 64 20 FRANCS
6.2200 g., 0.9990 Gold .2 oz. AGW **Subject:** 150th Anniversary of the Grand Duchy

Date	F	VF	XF	Unc	BU
ND(1989) Proof	Value: 120				

KM# 52 100 FRANCS
18.0000 g., 0.8350 Silver .4832 oz. ASW

Date	F	VF	XF	Unc	BU
1963	—	—	10.00	15.00	—

KM# 67 20 FRANCS
Bronze

Date	F	VF	XF	Unc	BU
1990-1995	—	—	—	2.00	—

KM# 48 50 FRANCS
12.5000 g., 0.8350 Silver .3356 oz. ASW **Subject:** 600th Anniversary - John the Blind

Date	F	VF	XF	Unc	BU
ND(1946)	—	10.00	15.00	35.00	—

KM# 54 100 FRANCS
18.0000 g., 0.8350 Silver .4832 oz. ASW

Date	F	VF	XF	Unc	BU
1964	—	—	8.00	13.50	—

Luxembourg

KM# 70   100 FRANCS
16.1000 g., 0.9250 Silver .4788 oz. ASW **Subject:** 50th
Anniversary - United Nations

Date	F	VF	XF	Unc	BU
ND(1995) Proof		Value: 28.50			

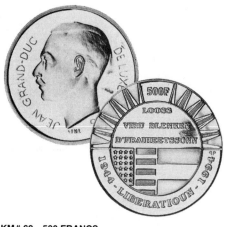

KM# 69   500 FRANCS
22.8500 g., 0.9250 Silver .6795 oz. ASW **Subject:** 50th
Anniversary of Liberation

Date	F	VF	XF	Unc	BU
ND(1994)	—	—	—	35.00	—

KM# 53.1   250 FRANCS
25.0000 g., 0.9000 Silver .7234 oz. ASW **Subject:** Millennium of
Luxembourg City

Date	F	VF	XF	Unc	BU
ND(1963)	—	—	25.00	45.00	—

KM# 53.2   250 FRANCS
25.0000 g., 0.9000 Silver .7234 oz. ASW **Subject:** Millennium of
Luxembourg City **Note:** Darkly toned by the mint.

Date	F	VF	XF	Unc	BU
ND(1963)	—	—	40.00	60.00	—

KM# 71   500 FRANCS
22.8500 g., 0.9250 Silver .6795 oz. ASW **Subject:** Luxembourg
- European Cultural City **Obv:** Segmented head of Jean Grand-
Duc

Date	F	VF	XF	Unc	BU
(19)95 Proof		Value: 45.00			

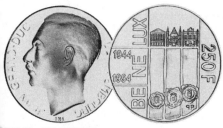

KM# 68   250 FRANCS
18.7500 g., 0.9250 Silver .5577 oz. ASW **Subject:** BE-NE-LUX
Treaty

Date	F	VF	XF	Unc	BU
ND(1994) Proof		Value: 30.00			

KM# 72   500 FRANCS
22.8500 g., 0.9250 Silver .6795 oz. ASW **Subject:** Presidency
of the European Community **Obv:** Segmented portrait **Rev:**
Symbolic design, dates

Date	F	VF	XF	Unc	BU
(19)97 Proof		Value: 40.00			

Luxembourg

KM# 73 500 FRANCS
22.8500 g., 0.9250 Silver .6795 oz. ASW **Subject:** 1,300 years of Echternach **Obv:** Duke's segmented portrait **Rev:** City seal and anniversary dates

Date	F	VF	XF	Unc	BU
ND(1998) Proof		Value: 40.00			

KM# 74 500 FRANCS
22.8500 g., 0.9250 Silver .6795 oz. ASW, 37 mm. **Subject:** Coronation of Henry III **Obv:** Portrait **Rev:** Crowned "H"

Date	F	VF	XF	Unc	BU
2000 Proof		Value: 50.00			

EURO COINAGE
European Economic Community Issues

KM# 75 EURO CENT
2.2700 g., Copper Plated Steel, 16.2 mm. **Ruler:** Henri **Obv:** Prince's portrait **Rev:** Denominaton and globe **Edge:** Plain

Date	F	VF	XF	Unc	BU
2002-2006	—	—	—	0.35	—

KM# 76 2 EURO CENTS
3.0300 g., Copper Plated Steel, 18.7 mm. **Ruler:** Henri **Obv:** Prince's portrait **Rev:** Denomination and globe **Edge:** Grooved

Date	F	VF	XF	Unc	BU
2002-2006	—	—	—	0.50	—

KM# 77 5 EURO CENTS
3.8600 g., Copper Plated Steel, 21.2 mm. **Ruler:** Henri **Obv:** Prince's portrait **Rev:** Denomination and globe **Edge:** Plain

Date	F	VF	XF	Unc	BU
2002-2006	—	—	—	0.75	—

KM# 78 10 EURO CENTS
4.0700 g., Brass, 19.7 mm. **Ruler:** Henri **Obv:** Prince's portrait **Rev:** Denomination and map **Edge:** Reeded

Date	F	VF	XF	Unc	BU
2002-2006	—	—	—	0.75	—

KM# 79 20 EURO CENTS
5.7300 g., Brass, 22.1 mm. **Ruler:** Henri **Obv:** Prince's portrait **Rev:** Denomination and map **Edge:** Notched

Date	F	VF	XF	Unc	BU
2002-2006	—	—	—	1.00	—

KM# 80 50 EURO CENTS
7.8100 g., Brass, 24.1 mm. **Ruler:** Henri **Obv:** Prince's portrait **Rev:** Denomination and map **Edge:** Reeded

Date	F	VF	XF	Unc	BU
2002-2006	—	—	—	1.25	—

KM# 81 EURO
7.5000 g., Bi-Metallic Copper-Nickel center in Brass ring, 23.2 mm. **Ruler:** Henri **Obv:** Prince's portrait **Rev:** Denomination and map **Edge:** Reeded and plain sections

Date	F	VF	XF	Unc	BU
2002-2006	—	—	—	2.50	—

KM# 82 2 EUROS
8.5200 g., Bi-Metallic Brass center in Copper-Nickel ring, 25.7 mm. **Ruler:** Henri **Obv:** Prince's portrait **Rev:** Denomination and map **Edge:** Reeded with 2's and stars

Date	F	VF	XF	Unc	BU
2002-2006	—	—	—	3.75	—

KM# 85　2 EUROS
8.5200 g., Bi-Metallic Brass center in Copper-Nickel ring, 25.7 mm.
Ruler: Henri **Obv:** Grand Duke and crowned monogram **Rev:** Value and map

Date	F	VF	XF	Unc	BU
2004	—	—	—	5.50	—

KM# 87　2 EUROS
8.5200 g., Bi-Metallic Brass center in Copper-Nickel ring, 25.7 mm. **Obv:** Grand Dukes Henri and Adolph **Rev:** Value and map **Edge:** Reeding over stars and 2's

Date	F	VF	XF	Unc	BU
2005	—	—	—	5.00	—

KM# 88　2 EUROS
8.5000 g., Bi-Metallic, 25.7 mm. **Ruler:** Henri **Obv:** Grand Duke and son **Rev:** Value **Edge:** Reeding over 2's and stars

Date	F	VF	XF	Unc	BU
2006	—	—	—	5.00	—

KM# 84　5 EURO
6.2200 g., 0.9990 Gold 0.1998 oz. AGW, 20 mm. **Ruler:** Henri **Subject:** European Central Bank **Obv:** Grand Duke Henri **Rev:** Building

Date	F	VF	XF	Unc	BU
2003 Proof	Value: 225				

KM# 83　25 EURO
22.8500 g., 0.9250 Silver 0.6795 oz. ASW, 37 mm. **Ruler:** Henri **Subject:** European Court System **Obv:** Grand Duke Henri **Rev:** Sword-scale on law book

Date	F	VF	XF	Unc	BU
2002 Proof	Value: 100				

KM# 86　25 EURO
22.8500 g., 0.9250 Silver 0.6795 oz. ASW, 37 mm. **Ruler:** Henri **Subject:** European Parliament **Obv:** Grand Duke Henri

Date	F	VF	XF	Unc	BU
2004 Proof	Value: 100				

Netherlands

The Kingdom of the Netherlands, a country of western Europe fronting on the North Sea and bordered by Belgium and Germany, has an area of 15,770 sq. mi. (41,500 sq. km.) and a population of 16.1 million. Capital: Amsterdam, but the seat of government is at The Hague. The economy is based on dairy farming and a variety of industrial activities. Chemicals, yarns and fabrics, and meat products are exported.

WORLD WAR II COINAGE
U.S. mints in the name of the government in exile and its remaining Curacao and Suriname Colonies during the years 1941-45 minted coinage of the Netherlands Homeland Types -KM #152, 153, 163, 164, 161.1 and 161.2 -. The Curacao and Suriname strikes, distinguished by the presence of a palm tree in combination with a mint mark (P-Philadelphia; D-Denver; S-San Francisco) flanking the date, are incorporated under those titles in this volume. Pieces of this period struck in the name of the homeland bear an acorn and mint mark and are incorporated in the following tabulation.

NOTE: Excepting the World War II issues struck at U.S. mints, all of the modern coins were struck at the Utrecht Mint and bear the caduceus mint mark of that facility. They also bear the mintmasters' marks.

KINGDOM OF THE NETHERLANDS
STANDARD COINAGE

KM# 90　1/2 CENT
Copper

Date	F	VF	XF	Unc	BU
1850-1877	5.00	15.00	30.00	65.00	100

KM# 91　5 CENTS
0.6850 g., 0.6400 Silver .0141 oz. ASW, 12.5 mm. **Obv:** Head right **Rev:** Value and date within wreath

Date	F	VF	XF	Unc	BU
1850.-1887	2.00	5.00	12.00	25.00	35.00

KM# 80　10 CENTS
1.4000 g., 0.6400 Silver .0288 oz. ASW, 15 mm. **Obv:** Head right **Rev:** Value and date within legend **Edge:** Reeded

Date	F	VF	XF	Unc	BU
1849-1890	5.00	20.00	50.00	90.00	130

KM# 81　25 CENTS
3.5750 g., 0.6400 Silver .0736 oz. ASW, 19 mm. **Obv:** Head right **Rev:** Value and date within wreath **Edge:** Reeded

Date	F	VF	XF	Unc	BU
1849-1890.	60.00	150	250	400	600

KM# 92   1/2 GULDEN
5.0000 g., 0.9450 Silver .1519 oz. ASW, 22 mm. **Obv:** Head right
Edge: Reeded

Date	F	VF	XF	Unc	BU
1850-1868	8.00	25.00	50.00	120	170

KM# 93   GULDEN
10.0000 g., 0.9450 Silver .3038 oz. ASW, 28 mm. **Obv:** Head
right **Rev:** Weapon, 1-G flanking **Edge:** GOD ZY MET ONS

Date	F	VF	XF	Unc	BU
1850-1867	10.00	20.00	40.00	120	170

KM# 82   2-1/2 GULDEN
25.0000 g., 0.9450 Silver .7596 oz. ASW, 38 mm. **Obv:** Head
right **Rev:** Crowned weapon, 2 1/2-G flanking **Edge Lettering:**
GOD ZY MET ONS

Date	F	VF	XF	Unc	BU
1849-1874	8.00	15.00	40.00	100	150

KM# 94   5 GULDEN
3.3645 g., 0.9000 Gold .0973 oz. AGW, 18.5 mm. **Obv:** Head
left **Rev:** Crowned arms within branches **Edge:** Reeded

Date	F	VF	XF	Unc	BU
1850-1851	400	1,200	2,000	2,600	3,000

KM# 95   10 GULDEN
6.7290 g., 0.9000 Gold .1947 oz. AGW, 22.5 mm. **Obv:** Bust left
Rev: Crowned weapon in wreath **Edge Lettering:** GOD ZY MET
ONS

Date	F	VF	XF	Unc	BU
1850-1851	500	1,000	1,750	2,500	3,000

KM# 96   20 GULDEN
13.4580 g., 0.9000 Gold .3894 oz. AGW **Obv:** Head left **Rev:**
Crowned arms within branches **Edge Lettering:** GOD ZY MET ONS

Date	F	VF	XF	Unc	BU
1850-1853	600	2,000	3,000	4,000	5,000

DECIMAL COINAGE

KM# 109   1/2 CENT
1.2500 g., Bronze, 14 mm. **Obv:** 17 small shields in field **Rev:**
Value within wreath **Edge:** Reeded

Date	F	VF	XF	Unc	BU
1878-1901	1.50	3.00	6.00	20.00	30.00

KM# 133   1/2 CENT
1.2500 g., Bronze, 14 mm. **Obv:** 17 small shields in field **Rev:**
Value within wreath **Edge:** Reeded

Date	F	VF	XF	Unc	BU
1903-1906	1.00	2.00	3.00	10.00	15.00

KM# 138   1/2 CENT
1.2500 g., Bronze, 14 mm. **Obv:** 15 large shields in field around
larger lion, smaller date and legend **Rev:** CENT in larger letters
Edge: Reeded

Date	F	VF	XF	Unc	BU
1909-1940	0.75	1.50	2.00	3.00	5.00

KM# 100 CENT
Copper

Date	F	VF	XF	Unc	BU
1860-1877	2.50	5.50	12.50	25.00	30.00

KM# 107 CENT
2.5000 g., Bronze, 19 mm. **Obv:** 17 small shields in field **Rev:** Value within wreath **Edge:** Reeded

Date	F	VF	XF	Unc	BU
1877-1900	0.50	2.00	6.00	15.00	20.00

KM# 130 CENT
2.5000 g., Bronze, 19 mm. **Obv:** 15 large shields in field **Rev:** Value within wreath **Edge:** Reeded

Date	F	VF	XF	Unc	BU
1901	1.00	2.50	5.00	20.00	45.00

KM# 131 CENT
2.5000 g., Bronze, 19 mm. **Obv:** 10 large shields in field **Rev:** Value within wreath **Edge:** Reeded

Date	F	VF	XF	Unc	BU
1901	1.00	2.50	5.00	20.00	45.00

KM# 132.1 CENT
2.5000 g., Bronze, 19 mm. **Obv:** 15 medium shields in field **Rev:** Value within wreath **Edge:** Reeded

Date	F	VF	XF	Unc	BU
1902-1907	1.00	2.00	3.00	15.00	25.00

KM# 132.2 CENT
2.5000 g., Bronze, 19 mm. **Obv:** 15 medium shields in field **Rev:** Value within wreath **Edge:** Plain

Date	F	VF	XF	Unc	BU
1906 Proof	Value: 875				

KM# 152 CENT
Bronze

Date	F	VF	XF	Unc	BU
1913-1941	0.25	0.60	1.00	2.50	4.00

KM# 170 CENT
2.0000 g., Zinc, 17 mm. **Rev:** Value and four waves **Edge:** Reeded

Date	F	VF	XF	Unc	BU
1941-1944	0.25	0.50	1.00	3.00	8.00

KM# 175 CENT
2.0000 g., Bronze, 14 mm. **Obv:** Head left **Edge:** Plain

Date	F	VF	XF	Unc	BU
1948	0.10	0.25	0.50	3.50	9.00

KM# 180 CENT
2.0000 g., Bronze, 14 mm. **Obv:** Head right

Date	F	VF	XF	Unc	BU
1950-1980	0.10	0.20	0.10	0.20	0.50

KM# 108 2-1/2 CENT
4.0000 g., Bronze, 23.5 mm. **Obv:** 17 small shields in field **Edge:** Reeded

Date	F	VF	XF	Unc	BU
1877-1898	2.50	5.00	15.00	45.00	55.00

KM# 134 2-1/2 CENT
4.0000 g., Bronze, 23.5 mm. **Obv:** 15 large shields in field **Rev:** Value within wreath **Edge:** Reeded

Date	F	VF	XF	Unc	BU
1903-1906	2.00	3.50	6.50	20.00	35.00

KM# 150   2-1/2 CENT

Bronze **Obv:** 15 large shields in field

Date	F	VF	XF	Unc	BU
1912-1941	1.25	2.00	3.00	6.00	9.00

KM# 171   2-1/2 CENT

2.0000 g., Zinc, 20 mm. **Obv:** Two swans on roof **Rev:** Value with four waves

Date	F	VF	XF	Unc	BU
1941-1942	1.00	3.00	5.00	15.00	—

KM# 137   5 CENTS

4.5000 g., Copper-Nickel, 12 mm. **Obv:** Crown between leaves **Rev:** Value within wreath

Date	F	VF	XF	Unc	BU
1907-1909	3.00	6.00	10.00	20.00	35.00

KM# 153   5 CENTS

4.5000 g., Copper-Nickel, 21.3 mm. **Obv:** Orange branch **Rev:** Value within shells **Shape:** 4-sided

Date	F	VF	XF	Unc	BU
1913-1940	1.50	3.00	4.00	9.00	15.00

KM# 172   5 CENTS

2.6000 g., Zinc, 18 mm. **Obv:** Two horse heads **Rev:** Value and nine waves **Shape:** 4-sided

Date	F	VF	XF	Unc	BU
1941-1943	1.00	2.50	6.00	18.00	35.00

KM# 176   5 CENTS

2.5000 g., Bronze, 21 mm. **Obv:** Head left **Rev:** Value with orange branch

Date	F	VF	XF	Unc	BU
1948	—	0.50	0.75	7.00	16.50

KM# 181   5 CENTS

3.5000 g., Bronze, 21 mm. **Obv:** Head right **Rev:** Value with orange branch

Date	F	VF	XF	Unc	BU
1950-1980	—	0.10	0.10	0.10	0.35

KM# 202   5 CENTS

3.5000 g., Bronze, 21 mm. **Obv:** Head left **Rev:** Value and vertical lines

Date	F	VF	XF	Unc	BU
1982-2001	—	—	—	—	0.40

KM# 116   10 CENTS

1.4000 g., 0.6400 Silver .0288 oz. ASW, 15 mm. **Obv:** Queen head left with long hair **Edge:** Reeded

Date	F	VF	XF	Unc	BU
1892-1897	5.00	15.00	30.00	65.00	90.00

KM# 119   10 CENTS

1.4000 g., 0.6400 Silver .0288 oz. ASW, 15 mm. **Obv:** Small head, divided legend **Rev:** Value within wreath **Edge:** Reeded

Date	F	VF	XF	Unc	BU
1898-1901	10.00	25.00	60.00	135	200

KM# 135   10 CENTS

1.4000 g., 0.6400 Silver .0288 oz. ASW, 15 mm. **Obv:** Large head **Rev:** Value in wreath

Date	F	VF	XF	Unc	BU
1903	4.00	12.00	30.00	50.00	65.00

KM# 136 10 CENTS
1.4000 g., 0.6400 Silver .0288 oz. ASW, 15 mm. **Obv:** Small head, continous legend **Rev:** Value in wreath

Date	F	VF	XF	Unc	BU
1904-1906	4.00	14.50	25.00	55.00	100

KM# 145 10 CENTS
1.4000 g., 0.6400 Silver .0288 oz. ASW, 15 mm. **Obv:** Small head, continuous legend **Rev:** Value within wreath **Edge:** Reeded

Date	F	VF	XF	Unc	BU
1910-1925	1.00	2.50	5.00	13.50	30.00

KM# 163 10 CENTS
1.4000 g., 0.6400 Silver .0288 oz. ASW, 15 mm. **Obv:** Small head, continuous legend **Rev:** Value within wreath **Edge:** Reeded

Date	F	VF	XF	Unc	BU
1926-1945	0.35	0.50	1.25	2.00	3.00

KM# 173 10 CENTS
3.3000 g., Zinc, 22 mm. **Obv:** Value and two twigs **Edge:** Reeded

Date	F	VF	XF	Unc	BU
1941-1943	0.25	0.50	2.00	5.00	10.00

KM# 177 10 CENTS
1.5000 g., Nickel, 15 mm. **Obv:** Head left **Rev:** Crowned value **Edge:** Reeded

Date	F	VF	XF	Unc	BU
1948	—	0.25	0.50	3.00	8.50

KM# 182 10 CENTS
1.5000 g., Nickel, 15 mm. **Obv:** Head right **Rev:** Crowned value **Edge:** Reeded

Date	F	VF	XF	Unc	BU
1950-1980	—	0.10	0.10	0.10	0.50

KM# 203 10 CENTS
1.5000 g., Nickel, 15 mm. **Obv:** Head left **Rev:** Value and vertical lines **Edge:** Reeded

Date	F	VF	XF	Unc	BU
1982-2001	—	—	—	—	0.50

KM# 115 25 CENTS
3.5750 g., 0.6400 Silver .0736 oz. ASW

Date	F	VF	XF	Unc	BU
1892-1897	6.00	25.00	60.00	120	160

KM# 120.1 25 CENTS
3.5750 g., 0.6400 Silver .0736 oz. ASW, 19 mm. **Obv:** Bust with wide truncation **Rev:** Value within wreath **Edge:** Reeded

Date	F	VF	XF	Unc	BU
1898-1901	40.00	85.00	175	450	750

KM# 120.2 25 CENTS
3.5750 g., 0.6400 Silver .0736 oz. ASW, 19 mm. **Obv:** Bust with narrow truncation **Rev:** Value within wreath **Edge:** Reeded

Date	F	VF	XF	Unc	BU
1901-1906	6.00	18.00	35.00	85.00	125

KM# 146 25 CENTS
3.5750 g., 0.6400 Silver .0736 oz. ASW, 19 mm. **Obv:** Small head, continuous legend **Rev:** Value within wreath **Edge:** Reeded

Date	F	VF	XF	Unc	BU
1910-1925	2.00	6.00	12.00	32.00	50.00

KM# 164 25 CENTS
3.5750 g., 0.6400 Silver .0736 oz. ASW, 19 mm. **Obv:** Small head left **Rev:** Value within wreath **Edge:** Reeded

Date	F	VF	XF	Unc	BU
1926-1945	BV	0.85	1.50	2.50	4.50

KM# 174   25 CENTS
5.0000 g., Zinc, 26 mm.   **Obv:** Sailing boat **Rev:** Value between two twigs

Date	F	VF	XF	Unc	BU
1941-1943	0.75	1.50	3.50	12.00	25.00

KM# 178   25 CENTS
3.0000 g., Nickel, 19 mm.   **Obv:** Head left **Rev:** Crowned value
Edge: Reeded

Date	F	VF	XF	Unc	BU
1948	—	0.25	0.50	4.00	10.00

KM# 183   25 CENTS
3.0000 g., Nickel, 19 mm.   **Obv:** Head right **Rev:** Crowned value
Edge: Reeded

Date	F	VF	XF	Unc	BU
1950-1980	—	0.20	0.20	0.20	0.50

KM# 183a   25 CENTS
Aluminum **Note:** Thought by many sources to be a pattern.

Date	F	VF	XF	Unc	BU
1980	—	—	—	—	500

KM# 204   25 CENTS
3.0000 g., Nickel, 19 mm.   **Obv:** Half head silhouette of Queen Beatrix left, 3-line inscription vertically at right **Obv. Inscription:** Beatrix/Konincin Der/Nederlanden **Rev:** Vertical and horizontal lines **Edge:** Reeded

Date	F	VF	XF	Unc	BU
1982-2001	—	—	—	0.20	0.60

KM# 121.1   1/2 GULDEN
5.0000 g., 0.9450 Silver .1519 oz. ASW, 22 mm.   **Obv:** Queen's head left **Rev:** Weapon, 1/2-G flanking, 50 C below **Edge:** Reeded

Date	F	VF	XF	Unc	BU
1898	25.00	60.00	110	180	250

KM# 121.2   1/2 GULDEN
5.0000 g., 0.9450 Silver .1519 oz. ASW, 22 mm.   **Obv:** Head left **Rev:** Crowned shield without 50 C. below shield **Edge:** Reeded

Date	F	VF	XF	Unc	BU
1904-1909	7.00	15.00	35.00	90.00	135

KM# 147   1/2 GULDEN
5.0000 g., 0.9450 Silver .1519 oz. ASW, 22 mm.   **Obv:** Head left **Rev:** Crowned shield **Edge:** Reeded

Date	F	VF	XF	Unc	BU
1910-1919	6.00	10.00	30.00	65.00	90.00

KM# 160   1/2 GULDEN
5.0000 g., 0.7200 Silver .1157 oz. ASW, 22 mm.   **Obv:** Head left **Rev:** Crowned shield **Edge:** Reeded

Date	F	VF	XF	Unc	BU
1921-1930	BV	1.50	2.50	9.00	15.00

KM# 117   GULDEN
10.0000 g., 0.9450 Silver .3038 oz. ASW, 28 mm.   **Obv:** Queen's head left with long hair **Rev:** Weapon, 1-G flanking **Edge Lettering:** GOD ZY MET ONS

Date	F	VF	XF	Unc	BU
1892-1897	6.00	20.00	60.00	150	200

Netherlands

KM# 122.1 GULDEN
10.0000 g., 0.9450 Silver .3038 oz. ASW, 28 mm. **Obv:** Young head left **Rev:** Crowned shield with 100 C below **Edge Lettering:** GOD * ZIJ * MET * ONS *

Date	F	VF	XF	Unc	BU
1898-1901	22.00	45.00	90.00	225	325

KM# 122.2 GULDEN
10.0000 g., 0.9450 Silver .3038 oz. ASW **Rev:** Without 100 C. below shield

Date	F	VF	XF	Unc	BU
1904-1909	8.00	20.00	35.00	90.00	120

KM# 148 GULDEN
10.0000 g., 0.9450 Silver .3038 oz. ASW, 28 mm. **Obv:** Small head left **Edge Lettering:** GOD * ZIJ * MET * ONS *

Date	F	VF	XF	Unc	BU
1910-1917	5.00	15.00	32.50	65.00	100

KM# 161.1 GULDEN
10.0000 g., 0.7200 Silver .2315 oz. ASW, 28 mm. **Obv:** Older head left **Rev:** Crowned shield **Edge Lettering:** GOD * ZIJ * MET * ONS *

Date	F	VF	XF	Unc	BU
1922-1944	—	BV	3.00	7.00	12.00

KM# 161.2 GULDEN
10.0000 g., 0.7200 Silver .2315 oz. ASW, 28 mm. **Obv:** Older head left **Edge Lettering:** GOD * ZIJ * MET * ONS * **Note:** For similar coins dated 1943D with palm tree privy mark, see Netherlands East Indies

Date	F	VF	XF	Unc	BU
1944-1945	7.50	20.00	35.00	55.00	80.00

KM# 184 GULDEN
6.5000 g., 0.7200 Silver .1504 oz. ASW, 25 mm. **Obv:** Head right **Rev:** Crowned shield **Edge Lettering:** GOD * ZIJ * MET * ONS *

Date	F	VF	XF	Unc	BU
1954-1967	—	—	BV	2.00	4.00

KM# 184a GULDEN
6.0000 g., Nickel

Date	F	VF	XF	Unc	BU
1967-1980	—	—	0.75	0.65	1.00

KM# 200 GULDEN
6.0000 g., Nickel, 25 mm. **Subject:** Investiture of New Queen **Obv:** Conjoined busts of Queens Juliana and Beatrix left **Rev:** Crowned shield **Edge Lettering:** GOD * ZIJ * MET * ONS *

Date	F	VF	XF	Unc	BU
1980	—	—	—	0.65	1.00

KM# 200a GULDEN
6.5000 g., Silver, 25 mm. **Subject:** Investiture of New Queen **Obv:** Conjoined busts of Queens Juliana and Beatrix left **Edge Lettering:** GOD * ZIJ * MET * ONS * **Note:** Z added (for silver).

Date	F	VF	XF	Unc	BU
1980	—	—	—	—	700

KM# 200b GULDEN
Gold, 25 mm. **Subject:** Investiture of New Queen **Obv:** Conjoined busts of Queens Juliana and Beatrix left **Note:** G added (for gold).

Date	F	VF	XF	Unc	BU
1980 Rare	—	—	—	—	—

KM# 205 GULDEN
6.0000 g., Nickel, 25 mm. **Obv:** Head left **Rev:** Vertical and horizontal lines **Edge Lettering:** GOD * ZIJ * MET * ONS *

Date	F	VF	XF	Unc	BU
1982-2001	—	—	—	—	1.25

KM# 205a GULDEN
7.1000 g., 0.9250 Silver 0.2111 oz. ASW **Edge Lettering:** GOD*ZIJ*MET*OMS*

Date	F	VF	XF	Unc	BU
2001	—	—	—	17.50	

KM# 205b GULDEN
13.2000 g., 0.9990 Gold .4243 oz. AGW **Edge Lettering:**
GOD*ZIJ*MET*ONS* **Note:** Prev. KM#205a.

Date	F	VF	XF	Unc	BU
2001	—	—	—	—	325

KM# 205c GULDEN
13.2000 g., 0.9990 Gold 0.424 oz. AGW **Edge:** Plain

Date	F	VF	XF	Unc	BU
2001	—	—	—	—	550

KM# 230 GULDEN
11.0000 g., 0.7500 Gold .2652 oz. AGW **Rev:** Small tulip, "750"
added **Edge Lettering:** GOD ZIJ MET ONS **Note:** Similar to
KM#205.

Date	F	VF	XF	Unc	BU
1999 Proof	Value: 700				

KM# 233 GULDEN
6.0400 g., Nickel, 25 mm. **Obv:** Queen's portrait **Rev:** Child art
design **Edge Lettering:** GOD ZIJ MET ONS

Date	F	VF	XF	Unc	BU
2001	—	—	—	—	4.00

KM# 233a GULDEN
7.1000 g., 0.9250 Silver .3926 oz. ASW, 25 mm. **Obv:** Queen's
portrait **Rev:** Child art design **Edge Lettering:** GOD * ZIJ * MET
* ONS *

Date	F	VF	XF	Unc	BU
2001	—	—	—	—	800

KM# 233b GULDEN
13.2000 g., 0.9990 Gold .4240 oz. AGW, 25 mm. **Obv:** Queen's
portrait **Rev:** Child art design **Note:** 98 of 100 pieces melted down,
with 2 known in museum collections.

Date	F	VF	XF	Unc	BU
2001	—	—	—	—	2,750

KM# 123 2-1/2 GULDEN
25.0000 g., 0.9450 Silver .7596 oz. ASW, 38 mm. **Obv:** Young
head left **Rev:** Crowned shield, 2 1/2-G flanking **Edge Lettering:**
GOD * ZJ * MET * ONS *

Date	F	VF	XF	Unc	BU
1898	150	275	500	1,000	1,250

KM# 165 2-1/2 GULDEN
25.0000 g., 0.7200 Silver .5787 oz. ASW, 38 mm. **Obv:** Head
left **Rev:** Crowned shield, value flanking **Edge Lettering:** GOD *
ZIJ * MET * ONS *

Date	F	VF	XF	Unc	BU
1929-1940	BV	7.50	10.00	20.00	30.00

KM# 185 2-1/2 GULDEN
15.0000 g., 0.7200 Silver .3472 oz. ASW, 38 mm. **Obv:** Head
right **Rev:** Crowned shield, value flanking **Edge Lettering:** GOD
* ZIJ * MET * ONS *

Date	F	VF	XF	Unc	BU
1959-1966	—	—	BV	4.75	9.00

KM# 191 2-1/2 GULDEN
10.0000 g., Nickel, 29 mm. **Obv:** Head right **Rev:** Crowned shield,
value flanking **Edge Lettering:** GOD * ZIJ * MET * ONS *

Date	F	VF	XF	Unc	BU
1969-1980	—	—	1.00	1.50	4.00

KM# 197 2-1/2 GULDEN
10.0000 g., Nickel, 29 mm. **Subject:** 400th Anniversary - The
Union of Utrecht **Obv:** Head right **Rev:** Text, value, date **Edge
Lettering:** GOD * ZIJ * MET * ONS *

Date	F	VF	XF	Unc	BU
1979	—	—	—	1.50	2.00

KM# 201 2-1/2 GULDEN
10.0000 g., Nickel **Subject:** Investiture of New Queen **Obv:**
Conjoined busts of Queens Juliana and Beatrix left **Rev:** Crowned
shield with value **Edge Lettering:** GOD * ZIJ * MET * ONS *

Date	F	VF	XF	Unc	BU
1980	—	—	—	1.50	2.00

KM# 201a 2-1/2 GULDEN
Silver **Subject:** Investiture of New Queen **Obv:** Conjoined busts
of Queens Juliana and Beatrix left **Edge Lettering:** GOD * ZIJ *
MET * ONS * **Note:** Z added (for silver).

Date	F	VF	XF	Unc	BU
1980	—	—	—	—	500

KM# 201b 2-1/2 GULDEN
Gold **Subject:** Investiture of New Queen **Obv:** Conjoined busts of
Queens Juliana and Beatrix left **Edge Lettering:** GOD * ZIJ * MET
* ONS * **Note:** G added (for gold).

Date	F	VF	XF	Unc	BU
1980 Rare	—	—	—	—	—

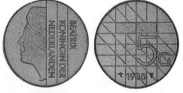

KM# 206 2-1/2 GULDEN
10.0000 g., Nickel, 29 mm. **Obv:** Head left **Rev:** Value with
horizontal, vertical and diagonal lines **Edge Lettering:** GOD * ZIJ
* MET * ONS *

Date	F	VF	XF	Unc	BU
1982-2001	—	—	—	—	2.00

KM# 151 5 GULDEN
3.3600 g., 0.9000 Gold .0973 oz. AGW, 18 mm. **Obv:** Bust right
Rev: Crowned shield, 5G flanking **Edge:** Reeded

Date	F	VF	XF	Unc	BU
1912	70.00	80.00	100	160	185

KM# 210 5 GULDEN
9.2500 g., Bronze Clad Nickel, 23.5 mm. **Obv:** Head left **Rev:**
Value with horizontal, vertical and diagonal lines **Edge:** GOD * ZIJ
* MET * ONS *

Date	F	VF	XF	Unc	BU
1988-2001	—	—	—	—	3.50

KM# 231 5 GULDEN
9.2500 g., Brass Plated Nickel **Subject:** Soccer **Obv:** Head left
Rev: Soccerball and value **Edge:** Reeded **Edge Lettering:** GOD
* ZIJ * MET * ONS * **Note:** A joint issue proof set exists containing
the Netherlands KM#231, Belgium KM#213-214 plus a medal.

Date	F	VF	XF	Unc	BU
2000	—	—	—	4.00	8.50

KM# 105 10 GULDEN
6.7290 g., 0.9000 Gold .1947 oz. AGW, 22.5 mm. **Obv:** Head
right **Rev:** Crowned weapon, 10-G flanking, date above crown
Edge: Reeded

Date	F	VF	XF	Unc	BU
1875	—	—	BV	125	145

KM# 106 10 GULDEN
6.7290 g., 0.9000 Gold .1947 oz. AGW, 22.5 mm. **Obv:** Crowned
weapon, 10-G flanking, date under weapon **Edge:** Reeded

Date	F	VF	XF	Unc	BU
1876-1889	—	—	BV	130	

KM# 118 10 GULDEN
6.7290 g., 0.9000 Gold .1947 oz. AGW, 22.5 mm. **Obv:** Bust left
with long hair **Rev:** Crowned weapon, 10-G flanking **Edge:** Reeded

Date	F	VF	XF	Unc	BU
1892-1897	—	—	BV	135	160

KM# 124 10 GULDEN
6.7290 g., 0.9000 Gold .1947 oz. AGW, 22.5 mm. **Obv:** Head with
tiara right **Rev:** Crowned weapon, 10-G flanking **Edge:** Reeded

Date	F	VF	XF	Unc	BU
1898	BV	150	200	350	450

KM# 149   10 GULDEN
6.7290 g., 0.9000 Gold .1947 oz. AGW, 22.5 mm.   **Obv:** Head right **Rev:** Crowned shield, 10G flanking **Edge:** Reeded

Date	F	VF	XF	Unc	BU
1911-1917	—	—	—	BV	130

KM# 162   10 GULDEN
6.7290 g., 0.9000 Gold .1947 oz. AGW, 22.5 mm.   **Obv:** Head right **Rev:** Crowned shield, 10G flanking **Edge:** Reeded

Date	F	VF	XF	Unc	BU
1925-1933	—	—	—	BV	130

KM# 195   10 GULDEN
25.0000 g., 0.7200 Silver .5787 oz. ASW, 38 mm.   **Subject:** 25th Anniversary of Liberation **Obv:** Queen Juliana right **Rev:** Queen Wilhelmina left **Edge Lettering:** GOD * ZIJ * MET * ONS *

Date	F	VF	XF	Unc	BU
ND(1970)	—	—	—	—	10.00

KM# 196   10 GULDEN
25.0000 g., 0.7200 Silver .5787 oz. ASW, 38 mm.   **Subject:** 25th Anniversary of Reign **Obv:** Head right **Rev:** Crowned shield **Edge Lettering:** GOD * ZIJ * MET * ONS *

Date	F	VF	XF	Unc	BU
1973	—	—	—	8.50	10.00

KM# 216   10 GULDEN
15.0000 g., 0.7200 Silver .3473 oz. ASW, 33 mm.   **Subject:** BE-NE-LUX Treaty **Obv:** Head left. **Rev:** Three Parliament buildings **Edge Lettering:** GOD * ZIJ * MET * ONS *

Date	F	VF	XF	Unc	BU
1994	—	—	—	—	12.50

KM# 220   10 GULDEN
15.0000 g., 0.8000 Silver, 33 mm.   **Subject:** 300th Anniversary - Death of Hugo de Groot **Obv:** Head left **Rev:** Escape of Hugo in book chest **Edge Lettering:** GOD * ZIJ * MET * ONS *

Date	F	VF	XF	Unc	BU
1995	—	—	—	—	12.50

KM# 223   10 GULDEN
15.0000 g., 0.8000 Silver, 33 mm.   **Subject:** Artist Jan Steen -

Lute Player **Obv:** Head left **Rev:** Jan Steen as a lute player **Edge Lettering:** GOD * ZIJ * MET * ONS *

Date	F	VF	XF	Unc	BU
1996	—	—	—	—	12.50

KM# 224   10 GULDEN
15.0000 g., 0.8000 Silver .3858 oz. ASW, 33 mm. **Subject:** Marshall Plan **Obv:** Head of Queen Beatrix left **Rev:** George C. Marshall **Edge Lettering:** GOD * ZIJ * MET * ONS *

Date	F	VF	XF	Unc	BU
1997	—	—	—	—	20.00

KM# 228   10 GULDEN
15.0000 g., 0.8000 Silver .3858 oz. ASW, 33 mm. **Subject:** Millennium **Obv:** Head of Queen above 12 concentric rings, 1999 **Rev:** Head of Queen above 12 concentric rings, 2000 **Edge:** GOD ZIJ MET ONS

Date	F	VF	XF	Unc	BU
1999	—	—	—	—	20.00

KM# 207   50 GULDEN
25.0000 g., 0.9250 Silver .7435 oz. ASW, 38 mm. **Subject:** Dutch-American Friendship **Obv:** Head left **Rev:** Dutch lion and American eagle **Edge Lettering:** GOD * ZIJ * MET * ONS *

Date	F	VF	XF	Unc	BU
ND(1982)	—	—	—	25.00	35.00

KM# 208   50 GULDEN
25.0000 g., 0.9250 Silver .7435 oz. ASW, 38 mm. **Subject:** 400th Anniversary - Death of William of Orange **Obv:** Head left **Rev:** Signature of William **Edge Lettering:** GOD * ZIJ * MET * ONS *

Date	F	VF	XF	Unc	BU
1984	—	—	—	—	20.00

KM# 209   50 GULDEN
25.0000 g., 0.9250 Silver .7435 oz. ASW **Subject:** Golden Wedding Anniversary - Queen Mother and Prince Bernhard **Edge Lettering:** GOD * ZIJ * MET * ONS *

Date	F	VF	XF	Unc	BU
1987	—	—	—	—	20.00

KM# 212   50 GULDEN
25.0000 g., 0.9250 Silver .7435 oz. ASW, 38 mm. **Subject:** 300th Anniversary of William and Mary **Obv:** Beatrix's head left **Rev:** Conjoined busts of William and Mary right **Edge Lettering:** GOD * ZIJ * MET * ONS *

Date	F	VF	XF	Unc	BU
1988	—	—	—	—	20.00

KM# 214   50 GULDEN
25.0000 g., 0.9250 Silver .7435 oz. ASW, 38 mm. **Subject:** 100 Years of Queens **Obv:** Heads of Queens Emma, Wilhelmina, Juliana, and Beatrix like rocks **Edge Lettering:** GOD * ZIJ * MET * ONS *

Date	F	VF	XF	Unc	BU
1990	—	—	—	—	20.00

KM# 219   50 GULDEN
25.0000 g., 0.9250 Silver .7435 oz. ASW, 38 mm. **Subject:** 50th Anniversary of Liberation **Obv:** Head left **Rev:** Value and text of Liberation **Edge Lettering:** GOD * ZIJ * MET * ONS *

Date	F	VF	XF	Unc	BU
ND(1995)	—	—	—	—	35.00

KM# 215   50 GULDEN
25.0000 g., 0.9250 Silver .7435 oz. ASW, 38 mm. **Subject:** Silver Wedding Anniversary **Obv:** Face of Beatrix left **Rev:** Prince Claus face left **Edge Lettering:** GOD * ZIJ * MET * ONS *

Date	F	VF	XF	Unc	BU
1991	—	—	—	—	20.00

KM# 227   50 GULDEN
25.0000 g., 0.9250 Silver .7435 oz. ASW, 38 mm. **Subject:** 350th Anniversary - Treaty of Munster **Obv:** Head left **Rev:** Mirror image of obverse **Edge Lettering:** GOD*'ZIJ*MET*ONS*

Date	F	VF	XF	Unc	BU
1998	—	—	—	—	40.00

EURO COINAGE
European Economic Community Issues

KM# 217   50 GULDEN
25.0000 g., 0.9250 Silver .7435 oz. ASW, 38 mm. **Subject:** Maastricht Treaty **Obv:** Head left **Rev:** Value and Maastricht Treaty **Edge Lettering:** GOD * ZIJ * MET * ONS *

Date	F	VF	XF	Unc	BU
1994	—	—	—	—	35.00

KM# 234   EURO CENT
2.3000 g., Copper Plated Steel, 16.2 mm. **Obv:** Head of Queen Beatrix left **Rev:** Denomination and globe **Edge:** Plain

Date	F	VF	XF	Unc	BU
1999-2006	—	—	—	0.35	—

KM# 235 2 EURO CENTS
3.0000 g., Copper Plated Steel, 18.7 mm. **Obv:** Head of Queen
Beatrix left **Rev:** Denomination and globe **Edge:** Grooved

Date	F	VF	XF	Unc	BU
1999-2006	—	—	—	0.50	—

KM# 236 5 EURO CENTS
3.9000 g., Copper Plated Steel, 21.2 mm. **Obv:** Head of Queen
Beatrix left **Rev:** Denomination and globe **Edge:** Plain

Date	F	VF	XF	Unc	BU
1999-2006	—	—	—	0.50	—

KM# 237 10 EURO CENTS
4.1000 g., Brass, 19.7 mm. **Obv:** Head of Queen Beatrix left **Rev:**
Denomination and map

Date	F	VF	XF	Unc	BU
1999-2006	—	—	—	0.75	—

KM# 238 20 EURO CENTS
5.7000 g., Brass, 22.2 mm. **Obv:** Head of Queen Beatrix left **Rev:**
Denomination and map **Edge:** Notched

Date	F	VF	XF	Unc	BU
1999-2006	—	—	—	1.00	—

KM# 239 50 EURO CENTS
7.8000 g., Brass, 24.2 mm. **Obv:** Head of Queen Beatrix left **Rev:**
Denomination and map **Edge:** Notched

Date	F	VF	XF	Unc	BU
1999-2006	—	—	—	1.25	—

KM# 240 EURO
7.5000 g., Bi-Metallic Copper-Nickel center in Brass ring,
23.2 mm. **Obv:** Queen's profile left **Rev:** Denomination and map
Edge: Plain and reeded sections

Date	F	VF	XF	Unc	BU
1999-2006	—	—	—	2.50	—

KM# 241 2 EURO
8.5000 g., Bi-Metallic Brass center in Copper-Nickel ring,
25.7 mm. **Obv:** Queen's profile left **Rev:** Denomination and map
Edge: Reeded **Edge Lettering:** "GOD*ZIJ*MET*ONS*"

Date	F	VF	XF	Unc	BU
1999-2006	—	—	—	4.00	—

KM# 245 5 EURO
11.9900 g., 0.9250 Silver 0.3566 oz. ASW, 29 mm. **Subject:**
Vincent Van Gogh **Obv:** Queen's portrait **Rev:** Van Gogh's portrait
Edge: Lettered **Edge Lettering:** GOD ZIJ MET ONS

Date	F	VF	XF	Unc	BU
(2003)-ND(2003)	—	—	—	—	8.00
ND(2003)-ND(2003)	—	—	—	—	20.00

KM# 252 5 EURO
11.9000 g., 0.9250 Silver 0.3539 oz. ASW **Ruler:** Beatrix **Obv:**
Queen Beatrix head left **Rev:** Names of old and new member
countries

Date	F	VF	XF	Unc	BU
2004	—	—	—	—	10.00

KM# 253 5 EURO
11.9000 g., 0.9250 Silver 0.3539 oz. ASW **Ruler:** Beatrix
Subject: 50th Anniversary - End of colonization of Netherlands
Antilles **Obv:** Queen Beatrix head left **Rev:** Fruit **Edge Lettering:**
GOD*ZIJ*MET*ONS*

Date	F	VF	XF	Unc	BU
2004	—	—	—	—	10.00

KM# 254   5 EURO
11.9100 g., 0.9250 Silver 0.3542 oz. ASW, 29 mm. **Subject:** 60th
Anniversary of Liberation **Obv:** Queen's image **Rev:** Value and
dots **Edge:** Lettered

Date	F	VF	XF	Unc	BU
2005	—	—	—	12.00	15.00

KM# 255   5 EURO
11.9100 g., 0.9250 Silver 0.3542 oz. ASW, 29 mm. **Ruler:** Beatrix
Obv: Queen's silhouette centered on a world globe **Rev:** Value above
Australia on a world globe **Edge Lettering:** "GOD ZIJ MET ONS"

Date	F	VF	XF	Unc	BU
2006	—	—	—	15.00	18.00

KM# 243   10 EURO
17.8000 g., 0.9250 Silver 0.5294 oz. ASW, 33 mm. **Subject:**
Crown Prince's Wedding **Obv:** Head of Queen Beatrix left **Rev:**
Two facing silhouettes **Edge:** Plain

Date	F	VF	XF	Unc	BU
2002	—	—	—	—	30.00

KM# 244   10 EURO
6.7200 g., 0.9000 Gold 0.1944 oz. AGW, 22.5 mm. **Subject:** Crown
Prince's Wedding **Obv:** Head of Queen Beatrix right **Rev:** Two facing
silhouettes of Willem Alexander and Maxima **Edge:** Reeded

Date	F	VF	XF	Unc	BU
2002	—	—	—	—	160

KM# 246   10 EURO
6.7200 g., 0.9000 Gold 0.1944 oz. AGW, 22.5 mm. **Subject:**
Vincent Van Gogh **Obv:** Queen's portrait **Rev:** Van Gogh's portrait
Edge: Reeded

Date	F	VF	XF	Unc	BU
ND(2003)	—	—	—	—	160

KM# 247   10 EURO
6.7200 g., 0.9000 Gold 0.1944 oz. AGW, 22.5 mm. **Ruler:** Beatrix
Subject: New EEC members **Obv:** Head of Queen Beatrix half
left **Rev:** Value, legend around **Edge:** Reeded

Date	F	VF	XF	Unc	BU
2004 Proof		Value: 165			

KM# 248   10 EURO
0.9250 Silver **Ruler:** Beatrix **Obv:** Queen Beatrix head left **Rev:**
Multi-views of Prince Willem-Alexander, Princess Catherina-
Amalia and Princess Maxima

Date	F	VF	XF	Unc	BU
2004	—	—	—	—	18.00

KM# 251   10 EURO
Gold **Ruler:** Beatrix **Subject:** 50 Years of Domestic Autonomy,
1954-2004 (for Netherlands Antilles) **Obv:** Small head facing left
Edge: Reeded

Date	F	VF	XF	Unc	BU
2004 Proof		Value: 185			

KM# 261   10 EURO
17.8000 g., 0.9250 Silver 0.5294 oz. ASW, 33 mm. **Ruler:** Beatrix
Subject: Silver Jubilee of Reign **Obv:** Queen's photo **Rev:** Queen
taking oath photo

Date	F	VF	XF	Unc	BU
2005	—	—	—	—	20.00

KM# 264   10 EURO
6.7200 g., 0.9000 Gold 0.1944 oz. AGW, 22.5 mm. **Ruler:** Beatrix
Subject: 60th Anniversary of Liberation **Obv:** Queen and dots
Rev: Value and dots

Date	F	VF	XF	Unc	BU
2005 Proof		Value: 200			

KM# 249   20 EURO
8.5000 g., 0.9000 Gold 0.2460 oz. AGW, 25 mm. **Ruler:** Beatrix
Subject: Birth of Crown-Princess - Catharina-Amalia - July 12,
2003 **Obv:** Bust of Queen Beatrix left **Rev:** Holographic images:
left, Princess Maxima; front, Princess Catharina-Amalia; right,
Prince Willem-Alexander **Edge:** Reeded

Date	F	VF	XF	Unc	BU
2004 Proof		Value: 300			

KM# 262   20 EURO
8.5000 g., 0.9000 Gold 0.246 oz. AGW, 25 mm. **Ruler:** Beatrix
Subject: Silver Jubilee of Reign **Obv:** Queen's photo **Rev:** Queen
taking oath photo

Date	F	VF	XF	Unc	BU
2005 Proof		Value: 345			

KM# 250   50 EURO
13.4400 g., 0.9000 Gold 0.3889 oz. AGW, 27 mm. **Ruler:** Beatrix
Subject: Birth of Crown-Princess - Catharina-Amalia - July 12,
2003 **Obv:** Bust of Queen Beatrix left **Rev:** Holographic images:
left, Princess Maxima; front, Princess Catharina-Amalia; right,
Prince Willem-Alexander **Edge:** Reeded

Date	F	VF	XF	Unc	BU
2004 Proof		Value: 500			

KM# 263   50 EURO
13.4400 g., 0.9000 Gold 0.3889 oz. AGW, 27 mm. **Ruler:** Beatrix
Subject: Silver Jubilee of Reign **Obv:** Queen's photo **Rev:** Queen
taking oath photo

Date	F	VF	XF	Unc	BU
2005 Proof		Value: 575			

TRADE COINAGE

KM# 83.1   DUCAT
3.4940 g., 0.9830 Gold .1106 oz. AGW, 21 mm. **Obv:** Standing
knight with sword **Rev:** Inscription within decorated square **Edge:**
Slant-reeded

Date	F	VF	XF	Unc	BU
1849-1937	—	—	—	BV	60.00

Netherlands (side text)

KM# 190.1 DUCAT
3.4940 g., 0.9830 Gold .1106 oz. AGW, 21 mm. **Obv:** Knight with right leg bent, larger letters in legend **Rev:** Inscription within decorated square

Date	F	VF	XF	Unc	BU
1960-1985	BV	100	75.00	—	75.00

KM# 190.2 DUCAT
3.4940 g., 0.9830 Gold .1106 oz. AGW **Obv:** Knight with left leg bent, larger letters in legend **Rev:** Inscription within decorated square

Date	F	VF	XF	Unc	BU
1986-2006	—	—	—	—	75.00

KM# 97 2 DUCAT
6.9880 g., 0.9830 Gold .2209 oz. AGW, 27 mm. **Obv:** Standing knight with sword and arrows **Rev:** Inscription within decorated square

Date	F	VF	XF	Unc	BU
1854-1867 Proof	Value: 9,000				

KM# 211 2 DUCAT
6.9880 g., 0.9830 Gold .2209 oz. AGW, 26 mm. **Obv:** Knight standing **Rev:** Inscription within decorated square

Date	F	VF	XF	Unc	BU
1988-2006	—	—	—	—	145

SILVER BULLION COINAGE

KM# 213 SILVER DUCAT
28.2500 g., 0.8730 Silver .7948 oz. ASW, 40 mm. **Obv:** Crowned arms of the Netherlands **Rev:** Knight standing with the arms of Utrecht

Date	F	VF	XF	Unc	BU
1989-1993 Proof	Value: 20.00				

KM# 218 SILVER DUCAT
28.2500 g., 0.8730 Silver .7948 oz. ASW, 40 mm. **Subject:** Seven Provinces - Groningen **Obv:** Crowned arms of the Netherlands **Rev:** Knight standing with arms of Groningen

Date	F	VF	XF	Unc	BU
1994 Proof	Value: 75.00				

KM# 221 SILVER DUCAT
28.2500 g., 0.8730 Silver .7948 oz. ASW, 40 mm. **Subject:** Seven Provinces - Zeeland **Obv:** Crowned arms of the Netherlands **Rev:** Knight standing with arms of Zeeland

Date	F	VF	XF	Unc	BU
1995 Proof	Value: 40.00				

KM# 222 SILVER DUCAT
28.2500 g., 0.8730 Silver .7948 oz. ASW, 40 mm. **Subject:** Seven Provinces - Holland **Obv:** Crowned arms of the Netherlands **Rev:** Knight standing with arms of Holland

Date	F	VF	XF	Unc	BU
1996 Proof	Value: 40.00				

KM# 225 SILVER DUCAT
28.2500 g., 0.8730 Silver .7948 oz. ASW, 40 mm. **Subject:** Seven Provinces - Gelderland **Obv:** Crowned arms of the Netherlands **Rev:** Knight standing with arms of Gelderland

Date	F	VF	XF	Unc	BU
1997 Proof	Value: 40.00				

KM# 226 SILVER DUCAT
28.2500 g., 0.8730 Silver .7948 oz. ASW, 40 mm. **Subject:** Seven Provinces - Friesland **Obv:** Crowned arms of the Netherlands **Rev:** Knight standing with shield of Friesland

Date	F	VF	XF	Unc	BU
1998 Proof	Value: 40.00				

KM# 229 SILVER DUCAT
28.2500 g., 0.8730 Silver .7948 oz. ASW, 40 mm. **Subject:**
Seven Provinces - Utrecht **Obv:** Crowned arms of the Netherlands
Rev: Knight standing with arms of Utrecht

Date	F	VF	XF	Unc	BU
1999 Proof		Value: 40.00			

KM# 232 SILVER DUCAT
28.2500 g., 0.8730 Silver .7948 oz. ASW, 40 mm. **Obv:** Crowned
arms of the Netherlands **Rev:** Standing knight with the arms of
Overijssel **Edge:** Reeded

Date	F	VF	XF	Unc	BU
2000-2002 Proof		Value: 40.00			

KM# 242 SILVER DUCAT
28.2500 g., 0.8730 Silver 0.7929 oz. ASW, 40 mm. **Obv:**
Crowned arms of Netherlands **Rev:** Standing knight with sword
and arms of Utrecht **Edge:** Reeded **Note:** Utrecht coin design circa
1659 based on KM#48.

Date	F	VF	XF	Unc	BU
2001 Proof		Value: 40.00			

KM# 256 SILVER DUCAT
28.2500 g., 0.8730 Silver 0.7929 oz. ASW, 40 mm. **Ruler:** Beatrix
Obv: Crowned arms of Netherlands **Rev:** Standing knight with
Gelderland arms **Edge:** Reeded

Date	F	VF	XF	Unc	BU
2002 Proof		Value: 45.00			

KM# 257 SILVER DUCAT
28.2500 g., 0.8730 Silver 0.7929 oz. ASW, 40 mm. **Ruler:** Beatrix
Obv: Crowned arms of Netherlands **Rev:** Standing knight with
sword holding arms of Holland **Edge:** Reeded

Date	F	VF	XF	Unc	BU
2003 Proof		Value: 45.00			

KM# 258 SILVER DUCAT
28.2500 g., 0.8730 Silver 0.7929 oz. ASW, 40 mm. **Ruler:** Beatrix
Obv: Crowned arms of Netherlands **Rev:** Standing knight holding
sword with Zeeland arms **Edge:** Reeded

Date	F	VF	XF	Unc	BU
2004 Proof		Value: 45.00			

KM# 259 SILVER DUCAT
28.2500 g., 0.8730 Silver 0.7929 oz. ASW, 40 mm. **Ruler:** Beatrix
Obv: Crowned arms of Netherlands **Rev:** Standing knight holding
sword with Friesland arms **Edge:** Reeded

Date	F	VF	XF	Unc	BU
2005 Proof		Value: 45.00			

KM# 260 SILVER DUCAT
28.2500 g., 0.8730 Silver 0.7929 oz. ASW, 40 mm. **Obv:**
Crowned arms of Netherlands **Rev:** Standing knight holding sword
with Groningen arms **Edge:** Reeded

Date	F	VF	XF	Unc	BU
2006 Proof		Value: 45.00			

Norway

The Kingdom of Norway (*Norge, Noreg*), a constitutional monarchy located in northwestern Europe, has an area of 150,000 sq. mi. (324,220 sq. km.), including the island territories of Spitzbergen (Svalbard) and Jan Mayen, and a population of *4.2 million. Capital: Oslo (Christiania). The diversified economic base of Norway includes shipping, fishing, forestry, agriculture, and manufacturing. Nonferrous metals, paper and paperboard, paper pulp, iron, steel and oil are exported.

MONETARY SYSTEM
100 Ore = 1 Krone (30 Skilling)

KINGDOM

STANDARD COINAGE

KM# 324   1/2 SKILLING
Copper

Date	VG	F	VF	XF	Unc
1863	4.50	9.50	28.00	70.00	175

KM# 329   1/2 SKILLING
Copper

Date	VG	F	VF	XF	Unc
1867	1.50	3.00	6.50	15.00	40.00

KM# 335   SKILLING
Copper

Date	VG	F	VF	XF	Unc
1870	3.50	7.00	17.00	50.00	125

KM# 336.1   2 SKILLING
1.5000 g., 0.2500 Silver .0120 oz. ASW   **Rev:** Rosettes

Date	VG	F	VF	XF	Unc
1870-1871	2.50	6.00	12.00	25.00	55.00

KM# 336.2   2 SKILLING
1.5000 g., 0.2500 Silver .0120 oz. ASW   **Rev:** Stars

Date	VG	F	VF	XF	Unc
1871	2.50	6.00	12.00	25.00	55.00

KM# 330.1   3 SKILLING
2.2500 g., 0.2500 Silver .0181 oz. ASW   **Rev:** Rosettes

Date	VG	F	VF	XF	Unc
1868-1869	5.00	10.00	21.00	40.00	60.00

KM# 330.2   3 SKILLING
2.2500 g., 0.2500 Silver .0181 oz. ASW   **Rev:** Stars

Date	VG	F	VF	XF	Unc
1869	5.00	10.00	21.00	40.00	60.00

KM# 338.1   3 SKILLING
2.2500 g., 0.2500 Silver .0181 oz. ASW   **Rev:** Rosettes

Date	VG	F	VF	XF	Unc
1872	5.00	10.00	21.00	40.00	60.00

KM# 338.2   3 SKILLING
2.2500 g., 0.2500 Silver .0181 oz. ASW   **Rev:** Stars

Date	VG	F	VF	XF	Unc
1872-1873	5.00	10.00	20.00	40.00	60.00

KM# 337   4 SKILLING
3.0000 g., 0.2500 Silver .0241 oz. ASW

Date	VG	F	VF	XF	Unc
1871	7.00	17.00	29.00	50.00	80.00

KM# 314.1   12 SKILLING
2.8900 g., 0.8750 Silver .0813 oz. ASW   **Note:** Plain border.

Date	VG	F	VF	XF	Unc
1845-1848	9.00	20.00	35.00	85.00	—

KM# 314.2   12 SKILLING
2.8900 g., 0.8750 Silver .0813 oz. ASW   **Note:** Beaded border.

Date	VG	F	VF	XF	Unc
1850-1856/5	8.00	17.00	30.00	75.00	—

KM# 320   12 SKILLING
2.8900 g., 0.8750 Silver .813 oz. ASW   **Obv:** Small head

Date	VG	F	VF	XF	Unc
1861-1862	250	500	1,300	2,000	3,000

KM# 326   12 SKILLING
2.8900 g., 0.8750 Silver .0813 oz. ASW **Obv:** Large head

Date	VG	F	VF	XF	Unc
1865	35.00	75.00	150	300	475

KM# 339   12 SKILLING
2.8900 g., 0.8750 Silver .0813 oz. ASW

Date	VG	F	VF	XF	Unc
1873	20.00	45.00	80.00	150	245

KM# 315.1   24 SKILLING
5.7800 g., 0.8750 Silver .1626 oz. ASW **Note:** Plain border.

Date	VG	F	VF	XF	Unc
1845-1848	22.00	50.00	80.00	125	—

KM# 315.2   24 SKILLING
5.7800 g., 0.8750 Silver .1626 oz. ASW **Note:** Beaded border.

Date	VG	F	VF	XF	Unc
1850-1855	25.00	50.00	95.00	175	—

KM# 321   24 SKILLING
5.7800 g., 0.8750 Silver .1626 oz. ASW **Obv:** Small head

Date	VG	F	VF	XF	Unc
1862	300	600	1,100	2,100	3,600

KM# 327   24 SKILLING
5.7800 g., 0.8750 Silver .1626 oz. ASW **Obv:** Large head

Date	VG	F	VF	XF	Unc
1865	40.00	100	225	350	700

KM# 316   1/2 SPECIE DALER
14.4500 g., 0.8750 Silver .4065 oz. ASW **Obv:** Head right **Rev:** Crowned arms divide value within spray, date below

Date	VG	F	VF	XF	Unc
1846-1855	60.00	100	175	350	—

KM# 322   1/2 SPECIE DALER
14.4500 g., 0.8750 Silver .4065 oz. ASW **Obv:** Head right **Rev:** Crowned arms divide value within spray, date below

Date	VG	F	VF	XF	Unc
1862	150	250	400	700	—

KM# 328   1/2 SPECIE DALER
14.4500 g., 0.8750 Silver .4065 oz. ASW **Obv:** Larger head

Date	VG	F	VF	XF	Unc
1865 Rare	—	—	—	—	—

KM# 340   1/2 SPECIE DALER
14.4500 g., 0.8750 Silver .4065 oz. ASW **Obv:** Head of Carl XV right **Rev:** Crowned arms divide value within spray, date below

Date	VG	F	VF	XF	Unc
1873	3,000	4,500	6,000	8,800	—

KM# 317   SPECIE DALER
28.8900 g., 0.8750 Silver .8127 oz. ASW **Obv:** Head of Oscar right **Rev:** Crowned arms divide value within spray, date below

Date	VG	F	VF	XF	Unc
1846-1857	100	225	400	600	—

KM# 323   SPECIE DALER
28.8900 g., 0.8750 Silver .8127 oz. ASW **Obv:** Head of Carl XV
right **Rev:** Crowned arms divide value within spray, date below

Date	VG	F	VF	XF	Unc
1861-1862	125	350	700	1,350	2,000

KM# 325   SPECIE DALER
28.8900 g., 0.8750 Silver .8127 oz. ASW **Obv:** Head of Carl XV
right **Rev:** Crowned arms divide value within spray, date below

Date	VG	F	VF	XF	Unc
1864-1869	150	300	550	750	1,200

DECIMAL COINAGE

KM# 352   ORE
2.0000 g., Bronze **Note:** Varieties exist.

Date	VG	F	VF	XF	BU
1876-1902	9,876	2.00	5.00	15.00	45.00

KM# 361   ORE
2.0000 g., Bronze

Date	VG	F	VF	XF	BU
1906-1907	9,876	2.00	3.00	10.00	25.00

KM# 367   ORE
2.0000 g., Bronze

Date	VG	F	VF	XF	BU
1908-1952	9,876	0.10	0.25	0.90	4.00

KM# 367a   ORE
1.7400 g., Iron

Date	VG	F	VF	XF	BU
1918-1921	9,876	1.50	3.50	12.00	30.00

KM# 387   ORE
1.7400 g., Iron **Subject:** World War II German Occupation

Date	VG	F	VF	XF	BU
1941-1945	9,876	0.15	0.50	1.75	6.00

KM# 398   ORE
2.0000 g., Bronze

Date	VG	F	VF	XF	BU
1952-1957	9,876	—	0.10	0.50	3.25

KM# 403   ORE
2.0000 g., Bronze **Rev:** Squirrel (sciurus vulgaris) **Note:** Varieties
exist.

Date	VG	F	VF	XF	BU
1958-1972	9,876	0.10	0.10	0.10	0.45

KM# 353   2 ORE
4.0000 g., Bronze

Date	VG	F	VF	XF	BU
1876-1902	9,876	1.50	4.00	12.00	60.00

KM# 362   2 ORE
4.0000 g., Bronze

Date	VG	F	VF	XF	BU
1906-1907	9,876	3.00	5.00	25.00	120

KM# 371   2 ORE
4.0000 g., Bronze

Date	VG	F	VF	XF	BU
1909-1952	9,876	0.10	0.25	1.00	5.00

KM# 371a   2 ORE
3.4800 g., Iron

Date	VG	F	VF	XF	BU
1917-1920	9,876	10.00	15.00	55.00	235

KM# 394   2 ORE
3.4700 g., Iron **Note:** World War II German occupation issue.

Date	VG	F	VF	XF	BU
1943-1945	9,876	0.50	0.75	1.75	9.00

KM# 399   2 ORE
4.0000 g., Bronze

Date	VG	F	VF	XF	BU
1952-1957	9,876	—	0.10	0.85	7.00

KM# 404   2 ORE
4.0000 g., Bronze **Rev:** Moor hen (lyrurus tetrix), small lettering

Date	VG	F	VF	XF	BU
1958	9,876	0.20	0.50	1.75	10.00

KM# 410   2 ORE
4.0000 g., Bronze **Rev:** Moor hen, large lettering

Date	VG	F	VF	XF	BU
1959-1972	9,876	0.10	0.10	0.10	1.00

KM# 349   5 ORE
8.0000 g., Bronze

Date	VG	F	VF	XF	BU
1875-1902	9,876	2.50	6.00	40.00	185

KM# 364   5 ORE
8.0000 g., Bronze

Date	VG	F	VF	XF	BU
1907	9,876	3.50	12.50	70.00	285

KM# 368   5 ORE
Bronze

Date	VG	F	VF	XF	BU
1908-1952	9,876	0.25	0.50	2.25	20.00

KM# 368a   5 ORE
6.6900 g., Iron

Date	VG	F	VF	XF	BU
1917-1920	9,876	12.00	30.00	70.00	125

KM# 388   5 ORE
6.9400 g., Iron **Note:** World War II German occupation issue.

Date	VG	F	VF	XF	BU
1941-1945	9,876	0.50	1.50	5.00	20.00

KM# 400   5 ORE
8.0000 g., Bronze

Date	VG	F	VF	XF	BU
1952-1957	9,876	0.10	0.35	2.25	12.50

KM# 405   5 ORE
8.0000 g., Bronze **Rev:** Moose

Date	VG	F	VF	XF	BU
1958-1973	9,876	0.10	0.10	0.15	1.00

KM# 415   5 ORE
3.0000 g., Bronze **Note:** Varieties exist.

Date	VG	F	VF	XF	BU
1973-1982	9,876	—	—	0.10	0.25

KM# 345   10 ORE
1.5000 g., 0.4000 Silver 0.0193 oz. ASW

Date	VG	F	VF	XF	BU
1874-1875	9,876	19.00	40.00	90.00	200

KM# 350   10 ORE
1.5000 g., 0.4000 Silver .0192 oz. ASW

Date	VG	F	VF	XF	BU
1875-1903	9,876	10.00	22.00	30.00	50.00

KM# 372   10 ORE
1.4500 g., 0.4000 Silver

Date	VG	F	VF	XF	BU
1909-1919/7	9,876	1.50	3.00	5.00	15.00

KM# 378   10 ORE
1.5000 g., Copper-Nickel

Date	VG	F	VF	XF	BU
1920-1923	9,876	5.00	15.00	20.00	50.00

KM# 383   10 ORE
1.5000 g., Copper-Nickel

Date	VG	F	VF	XF	BU
1924-1951	5.00	0.10	0.25	1.75	6.50

KM# 389   10 ORE
1.2500 g., Zinc **Note:** World War II German occupation issue.

Date	VG	F	VF	XF	BU
1941-1945	9,876	0.35	1.00	3.50	12.50

KM# 391   10 ORE
1.1500 g., Nickel-Brass **Note:** World War II government in exile issue.

Date	VG	F	VF	XF	BU
1942	9,876	—	—	120	200

KM# 396   10 ORE
1.5000 g., Copper-Nickel

Date	VG	F	VF	XF	BU
1951-1957	9,876	0.10	0.20	1.50	12.00

KM# 406   10 ORE
1.5000 g., Copper-Nickel **Rev:** Honey bee (apis melifica) small lettering

Date	VG	F	VF	XF	BU
1958	9,876	0.50	1.50	3.00	30.00

KM# 411   10 ORE
1.5000 g., Copper-Nickel **Rev:** Honey bee, large lettering

Date	VG	F	VF	XF	BU
1959-1973	9,876	0.50	0.10	0.25	1.00

KM# 416   10 ORE
1.2500 g., Copper-Nickel   **Note:** Varieties exist in monogram.

Date	VG	F	VF	XF	BU
1974-1991	9,876	—	—	0.10	0.35

KM# 354   25 ORE
2.4000 g., 0.6000 Silver .0463 oz. ASW

Date	VG	F	VF	XF	BU
1876	9,876	21.00	40.00	100	165

KM# 360   25 ORE
2.4200 g., 0.6000 Silver .0463 oz. ASW

Date	VG	F	VF	XF	BU
1896-1904	9.00	20.00	35.00	60.00	120

KM# 373   25 ORE
2.4200 g., 0.6000 Silver .0463 oz. ASW

Date	VG	F	VF	XF	BU
1909-1919	3.50	6.00	12.00	25.00	65.00

KM# 381   25 ORE
4.4000 g., Copper-Nickel

Date	VG	F	VF	XF	BU
1921-1923	4.00	10.00	15.00	20.00	40.00

KM# 382   25 ORE
2.4000 g., Copper-Nickel

Date	VG	F	VF	XF	BU
1921-1923	1.50	1.50	3.00	25.00	190

KM# 384   25 ORE
2.4000 g., Copper-Nickel

Date	VG	F	VF	XF	BU
1924-1950	9,876	0.20	0.50	1.75	12.00

KM# 392   25 ORE
2.4000 g., Nickel-Brass   **Note:** World War II government in exile issue.

Date	VG	F	VF	XF	BU
1942	9,876	—	—	120	225

KM# 395   25 ORE
2.0000 g., Zinc   **Note:** World War II German occupation.

Date	VG	F	VF	XF	BU
1943-1945	2.00	1.00	1.50	4.00	25.00

KM# 401   25 ORE
2.4000 g., Copper-Nickel   **Note:** Mint marks exist with mint mark on square or without square.

Date	VG	F	VF	XF	BU
1952-1957	9,876	0.10	0.25	1.20	20.00

KM# 407   25 ORE
2.4000 g., Copper-Nickel   **Rev:** Siberian tit (parus cinctus)

Date	VG	F	VF	XF	BU
1958-1973	9,876	0.50	0.10	0.10	1.25

KM# 417   25 ORE
2.0000 g., Copper-Nickel

Date	VG	F	VF	XF	BU
1974-1982	9,876	—	—	0.10	0.50

KM# 346   50 ORE
5.0000 g., 0.6000 Silver .0964 oz. ASW

Date	VG	F	VF	XF	BU
1874-1875	9,876	125	225	450	650

KM# 356   50 ORE
5.0000 g., 0.6000 Silver .0964 oz. ASW   **Rev:** Without 15 SK

Date	VG	F	VF	XF	BU
1877-1904	7.00	13.00	24.00	65.00	185

KM# 374 50 ORE
5.0000 g., 0.6000 Silver .0964 oz. ASW

Date	VG	F	VF	XF	BU
1909-1919	2.50	5.00	8.00	12.00	50.00

KM# 379 50 ORE
4.8000 g., Copper-Nickel

Date	VG	F	VF	XF	BU
1920-1923	4.00	8.00	12.00	25.00	50.00

KM# 380 50 ORE
4.8000 g., Copper-Nickel **Note:** Respective mintages are included with KM#379.

Date	VG	F	VF	XF	BU
1920-1923	9,876	2.50	6.00	60.00	350

KM# 386 50 ORE
4.8000 g., Copper-Nickel

Date	VG	F	VF	XF	BU
1926-1949	9,876	0.20	0.40	1.75	12.50

KM# 390 50 ORE
Zinc **Note:** World War II German occupation issue.

Date	VG	F	VF	XF	BU
1941-1945	5.00	1.00	2.50	7.00	45.00

KM# 393 50 ORE
4.8000 g., Nickel-Brass **Note:** World War II government in exile issue.

Date	VG	F	VF	XF	BU
1942	9,876	—	—	125	250

KM# 402 50 ORE
4.8000 g., Copper-Nickel

Date	VG	F	VF	XF	BU
1953-1957	1.25	0.10	0.40	1.75	32.50

KM# 408 50 ORE
4.8000 g., Copper-Nickel **Rev:** Hound (canis familiaris intermedius)

Date	VG	F	VF	XF	BU
1958-1973	9,876	0.25	0.10	0.25	3.00

KM# 418 50 ORE
4.8000 g., Copper-Nickel **Note:** Varieties in shield exist.

Date	VG	F	VF	XF	BU
1974-1996	9,876	—	0.10	0.15	0.35

KM# 460 50 ORE
3.6000 g., Bronze **Obv:** Crown **Rev:** Stylized animal, denomination

Date	VG	F	VF	XF	BU
1996-2006	9,876	—	—	—	0.40

KM# 351 KRONE
7.5000 g., 0.8000 Silver .1929 oz. ASW

Date	VG	F	VF	XF	BU
1875	9,876	150	300	550	1,400

KM# 357   KRONE
7.5000 g., 0.8000 Silver .1929 oz. ASW   **Note:** Without 30 SK

Date	VG	F	VF	XF	BU
1877-1904	17.00	30.00	45.00	90.00	250

KM# 409   KRONE
7.0000 g., Copper-Nickel   **Rev:** Fjord horse

Date	VG	F	VF	XF	BU
1958-1973	9,876	3.00	0.20	0.40	4.75

KM# 369   KRONE
7.5000 g., 0.8000 Silver .1929 oz. ASW

Date	VG	F	VF	XF	BU
1908-1917	11.00	19.00	30.00	50.00	95.00

KM# 419   KRONE
7.0000 g., Copper-Nickel   **Note:** Varieties with and without star mint mark exist.

Date	VG	F	VF	XF	BU
1974-1991	9,876	—	0.20	0.35	0.65

KM# 385   KRONE
7.0000 g., Copper-Nickel

Date	VG	F	VF	XF	BU
1925-1951	9,876	0.20	0.50	3.00	15.00

KM# 436   KRONE
7.0000 g., Copper-Nickel

Date	VG	F	VF	XF	BU
1992-1996	9,876	—	0.20	0.35	0.65

KM# 397   KRONE
7.0000 g., Copper-Nickel

Date	VG	F	VF	XF	BU
1951-1957	9,876	0.20	0.50	2.50	32.50

KM# 462   KRONE
4.3000 g., Copper-Nickel   **Obv:** Monogram cross **Rev:** Bird on vine above date and denomination

Date	VG	F	VF	XF	BU
1997-2006	9,876	—	—	—	0.65

KM# 359   2 KRONER
15.0000 g., 0.8000 Silver .3858 oz. ASW   **Note:** Restrikes are made by the Royal Mint, Norway, in gold, silver and bronze.

Date	VG	F	VF	XF	BU
1878-1904	35.00	65.00	125	225	500

KM# 363   2 KRONER
15.0000 g., 0.8000 Silver .3858 oz. ASW **Subject:** Norway
Independence **Obv:** Large shield

Date	VG	F	VF	XF	BU
1906	23.00	35.00	60.00	100	175

KM# 365   2 KRONER
15.0000 g., 0.8000 Silver .3858 oz. ASW **Obv:** Smaller shield

Date	VG	F	VF	XF	BU
1907	30.00	55.00	100	175	250

KM# 366   2 KRONER
15.0000 g., 0.8000 Silver .3858 oz. ASW **Subject:** Border watch

Date	VG	F	VF	XF	BU
1907	100	200	350	550	850

KM# 370   2 KRONER
15.0000 g., 0.8000 Silver .3858 oz. ASW

Date	VG	F	VF	XF	BU
1908-1917	9,876	30.00	40.00	60.00	150

KM# 377   2 KRONER
15.0000 g., 0.8000 Silver .3858 oz. ASW **Subject:** Constitution
centennial

Date	VG	F	VF	XF	BU
1914	10.00	17.00	30.00	60.00	110

KM# 412   5 KRONER
11.5000 g., Copper-Nickel

Date	VG	F	VF	XF	BU
1963-1973	9,876	1.00	1.00	1.25	3.50

KM# 420   5 KRONER
11.5000 g., Copper-Nickel **Note:** Varieties exist with large and
small shields.

Date	VG	F	VF	XF	BU
1974-1988	9,876	—	—	1.00	1.50

KM# 421   5 KRONER
11.5000 g., Copper-Nickel **Subject:** 100th Anniversary of Krone
System

Date	VG	F	VF	XF	BU
ND(1975)	9,876	—	1.00	1.50	3.50

KM# 422   5 KRONER
11.5000 g., Copper-Nickel   **Subject:** 150th Anniversary - Immigration to America **Rev:** The "Restaurasjonen"(Restoration)

Date	VG	F	VF	XF	BU
ND(1975)	9,876	—	1.00	1.50	3.50

KM# 437   5 KRONER
11.5000 g., Copper-Nickel   **Obv:** Harald V

Date	VG	F	VF	XF	BU
1992-1994	9,876	—	—	—	2.00

KM# 423   5 KRONER
11.5000 g., Copper-Nickel   **Subject:** 350th Anniversary of Norwegian Army

Date	VG	F	VF	XF	BU
ND(1978)	9,876	—	1.00	1.50	3.00

KM# 456   5 KRONER
11.5000 g., Copper-Nickel   **Obv:** 1,000 years of Norwegian coinage

Date	VG	F	VF	XF	BU
1995	9,876	—	—	—	3.50

KM# 428   5 KRONER
11.5000 g., Copper-Nickel   **Subject:** 300th Anniversary of the Mint

Date	VG	F	VF	XF	BU
1986	9,876	—	1.00	1.50	—

KM# 458   5 KRONER
11.5000 g., Copper-Nickel   **Subject:** 50th Anniversary - United Nations

Date	VG	F	VF	XF	BU
ND(1995)	9,876	—	—	—	3.50

KM# 430   5 KRONER
11.5000 g., Copper-Nickel   **Subject:** 175th Anniversary of the National Bank

Date	VG	F	VF	XF	BU
1991	9,876	—	—	—	7.00

KM# 459   5 KRONER
11.5000 g., Copper-Nickel   **Subject:** Centennial - Nasen's Return From the Arctic

Date	VG	F	VF	XF	BU
1996	9,876	—	—	—	3.00

KM# 461 5 KRONER
11.5000 g., Copper-Nickel **Subject:** 350th Anniversary - Norwegian Postal Service

Date	VG	F	VF	XF	BU
ND(1997)	9,876	—	—	—	3.00

KM# 463 5 KRONER
7.8500 g., Copper-Nickel **Subject:** Order of St. Olaf **Rev:** Denomination and date

Date	VG	F	VF	XF	BU
1998-2006	9,876	—	—	—	1.50

KM# 347 10 KRONER
4.4803 g., 0.9000 Gold .1296 oz. AGW

Date	VG	F	VF	XF	Unc
1874	9,876	200	450	700	1,000

KM# 358 10 KRONER
4.4803 g., 0.9000 Gold .1296 oz. AGW

Date	VG	F	VF	XF	Unc
1877-1902	9,876	100	200	375	600

KM# 375 10 KRONER
4.4803 g., 0.9000 Gold .1296 oz. AGW

Date	F	VF	XF	Unc	BU
1910	BV	165	275	450	—

KM# 413 10 KRONER
20.0000 g., 0.9000 Silver .5707 oz. ASW **Subject:** Constitution sesquicentennial **Rev:** Eidsval Mansion **Edge Lettering:** ENIGE OG TRO TIL DOVRE FALLER **Note:** Edge lettering varieties exist.

Date	VG	F	VF	XF	BU
ND(1964)	9,876	—	—	6.00	10.00

KM# 427 10 KRONER
9.0000 g., Copper-Zinc-Nickel

Date	VG	F	VF	XF	BU
1983-1991	9,876	—	—	1.75	2.75

KM# 457 10 KRONER
6.8000 g., Copper-Zinc-Nickel **Rev:** Church rooftop

Date	VG	F	VF	XF	BU
1995-2006	9,876	—	—	—	3.50

KM# 348 20 KRONER
8.9606 g., 0.9000 Gold .2593 oz. AGW

Date	VG	F	VF	XF	Unc
1874-1875	9,876	100	150	300	450

KM# 355 20 KRONER
8.9600 g., 0.9000 Gold .2593 oz. AGW

Date	VG	F	VF	XF	Unc
1876-1902	9,876	—	BV	200	350

KM# 376 20 KRONER
8.9600 g., 0.9000 Gold .2593 oz. AGW

Date	F	VF	XF	Unc	BU
1910	BV	165	275	450	—

KM# 453 20 KRONER
Copper-Zinc-Nickel

Date	VG	F	VF	XF	BU
1994-2005	9,876	—	—	—	6.50

KM# 464 20 KRONER
9.9000 g., Copper-Zinc-Nickel **Subject:** 700th Anniversary - Akershus Fortress **Obv:** Seal of King Hakon V **Rev:** Fortress

Date	F	VF	XF	Unc	BU
1999	—	—	—	7.50	—

KM# 465 20 KRONER
9.9000 g., Nickel-Bronze **Subject:** Vinland **Obv:** King's portrait **Rev:** Viking ship hull

Date	F	VF	XF	Unc	BU
1999	—	—	—	7.50	—

KM# 468 20 KRONER
9.9000 g., Nickel-Brass **Subject:** Millennium **Obv:** King's head right **Rev:** Unknown road into the future

Date	F	VF	XF	Unc	BU
2000	—	—	—	12.50	—

KM# 471 20 KRONER
9.7300 g., Nickel-Brass, 27.4 mm. **Ruler:** Harald V **Subject:** Niels Henrik Abel **Obv:** King's portrait **Rev:** Mathematical graphs **Edge:** Plain

Date	F	VF	XF	Unc	BU
2002	—	—	—	10.00	12.50

KM# 478 20 KRONER (5 Speciedaler)
9.9000 g., Copper-Zinc-Nickel, 27.5 mm. **Ruler:** Harald V **Subject:** First Norwegian Railroad **Obv:** King Harald V **Rev:** Switch track and value **Edge:** Plain

Date	F	VF	XF	Unc	BU
2005	—	—	—	17.50	20.00

KM# 414 25 KRONER
29.0000 g., 0.8750 Silver .8159 oz. ASW **Subject:** 25th Anniversary of Liberation

Date	VG	F	VF	XF	BU
1970	9,876	—	—	—	12.00

KM# 424 50 KRONER
27.0000 g., 0.9250 Silver .8030 oz. ASW **Subject:** 75th Birthday of King Olav V

Date	VG	F	VF	XF	BU
ND(1978)	9,876	—	—	—	15.00

Norway

KM# 431   50 KRONER
16.8100 g., 0.9250 Silver .5000 oz. ASW **Subject:** 1994 Olympics
Rev: Skiers

Date		VG	F	VF	XF	BU
1991		9,876	—	—	—	37.50

KM# 447   50 KRONER
16.8100 g., 0.9250 Silver .5000 oz. ASW **Subject:** 1994 Olympics
Rev: Cross-country skiers

Date		VG	F	VF	XF	BU
1993		9,876	—	—	—	37.50

KM# 432   50 KRONER
16.8100 g., 0.9250 Silver .5000 oz. ASW **Subject:** 1994 Olympics
Rev: Child skiing

Date		VG	F	VF	XF	BU
1991		9,876	—	—	—	37.50

KM# 448   50 KRONER
16.8100 g., 0.9250 Silver .5000 oz. ASW **Subject:** 1994 Olympics
Rev: Children ice skating

Date		VG	F	VF	XF	BU
1993		9,876	—	—	—	37.50

KM# 438   50 KRONER
16.8100 g., 0.9250 Silver .5000 oz. ASW **Subject:** 1994 Olympics
Rev: Grandfather and child

Date		VG	F	VF	XF	BU
1992		9,876	—	—	—	37.50

KM# 454   50 KRONER
16.8100 g., 0.9250 Silver .5000 oz. ASW **Subject:** 50th
Anniversary - United Nations

Date	VG	F	VF	XF	BU
ND(1995) Proof	Value: 42.50				

KM# 439   50 KRONER
16.8100 g., 0.9250 Silver .5000 oz. ASW **Subject:** 1994 Olympics
Rev: 2 children on sled

Date		VG	F	VF	XF	BU
1992		9,876	—	—	—	37.50

KM# 455   50 KRONER
16.8100 g., 0.9250 Silver .5000 oz. ASW **Subject:** 50th
Anniversary - End of World War II

Date	VG	F	VF	XF	BU
ND(1995) Proof	Value: 45.00				

KM# 426   100 KRONER
24.7300 g., 0.9250 Silver .7355 oz. ASW **Subject:** 25th
Anniversary of King Olav's Reign

Date	VG	F	VF	XF	BU
1982	9,876	—	—	—	25.00

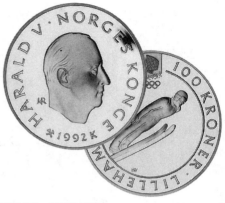

KM# 440   100 KRONER
33.6200 g., 0.9250 Silver 1 oz. ASW **Subject:** 1994 Olympics
Rev: Ski jumper

Date	VG	F	VF	XF	BU
1992	9,876	—	—	—	60.00

KM# 433   100 KRONER
33.6200 g., 0.9250 Silver 1 oz. ASW **Subject:** 1994 Olympics
Obv: Similar to 50 Kroner, KM#431 **Rev:** Cross-country skier

Date	VG	F	VF	XF	BU
1991	9,876	—	—	—	60.00

KM# 441   100 KRONER
33.6200 g., 0.9250 Silver 1 oz. ASW **Subject:** 1994 Olympics
Rev: Hockey players

Date	VG	F	VF	XF	BU
1992	9,876	—	—	—	60.00

KM# 434   100 KRONER
33.6200 g., 0.9250 Silver 1 oz. ASW **Subject:** 1994 Olympics
Rev: 2 speed skaters

Date	VG	F	VF	XF	BU
1991	9,876	—	—	—	60.00

KM# 443   100 KRONER
33.6200 g., 0.9250 Silver 1 oz. ASW **Subject:** World Cycling
Championships **Rev:** Cyclist

Date	VG	F	VF	XF	BU
1993	9,876	—	—	—	70.00

KM# 444 100 KRONER
33.6200 g., 0.9250 Silver 1 oz. ASW **Subject:** World Cycling
Championships **Rev:** 7 cyclists

Date	VG	F	VF	XF	BU
1993	9,876	—	—	—	70.00

KM# 466 100 KRONER
33.8000 g., 0.9250 Silver 1.0052 oz. ASW **Subject:** Year 2000
Obv: National arms **Rev:** Cut tree trunk exposing rings

Date	F	VF	XF	Unc	BU
1999 Proof		Value: 70.00			

KM# 449 100 KRONER
33.6200 g., 0.9250 Silver 1 oz. ASW **Subject:** 1984 Olympics
Rev: Female figure skater

Date	VG	F	VF	XF	BU
1993	9,876	—	—	—	60.00

KM# 469 100 KRONER
33.6000 g., 0.9250 Silver .9992 oz. ASW, 39 mm. **Subject:** Nobel
Peace Prize Centennial **Obv:** National arms **Rev:** Nobel's portrait
Edge: Plain

Date	F	VF	XF	Unc	BU
2001 Proof		Value: 60.00			

KM# 472 100 KRONER
33.8000 g., 0.9250 Silver 1.0052 oz. ASW, 39 mm. **Ruler:**
Harald V **Subject:** 1905 Liberation **Obv:** Three kings **Rev:** Farm
field **Edge:** Plain

Date	F	VF	XF	Unc	BU
2003 Proof		Value: 70.00			

KM# 474 100 KRONER
33.8000 g., 0.9250 Silver 1.0052 oz. ASW, 39 mm. **Ruler:**
Harald V **Subject:** 1905 Liberation **Obv:** Three kings **Rev:** Off
shore ocean oil well **Edge:** Plain

Date	F	VF	XF	Unc	BU
2004 Proof		Value: 70.00			

KM# 450 100 KRONER
33.6200 g., 0.9250 Silver 1 oz. ASW **Subject:** 1984 Olympics
Rev: Alpine skier

Date	VG	F	VF	XF	BU
1993	9,876	—	—	—	60.00

KM# 476 100 KRONER
33.8000 g., 0.9250 Silver 1.0052 oz. ASW, 39 mm. **Ruler:**
Harald V **Obv:** Three kings **Rev:** Circuit board **Edge:** Plain

Date	F	VF	XF	Unc	BU
2005 Proof		Value: 70.00			

KM# 442   1500 KRONER
17.0000 g., 0.9170 Gold .5 oz. AGW   **Subject:** 1994 Olympics
Rev: Birkebeiners

Date	VG	F	VF	XF	BU
1992 Proof		Value: 375			

KM# 429   175 KRONER
26.5000 g., 0.9250 Silver .7882 oz. ASW   **Subject:** 175th
Anniversary of Constitution

Date	VG	F	VF	XF	BU
ND(1989)	9,876	—	—	—	75.00

KM# 445   1500 KRONER
17.0000 g., 0.9170 Gold .5 oz. AGW   **Subject:** World Cycling
Championships **Rev:** 2 19th century cyclists

Date	VG	F	VF	XF	BU
1993 Proof		Value: 500			

KM# 446   1500 KRONER
17.0000 g., 0.9170 Gold .5 oz. AGW   **Subject:** Edvard Grieg

Date	VG	F	VF	XF	BU
1993 Proof		Value: 550			

KM# 425   200 KRONER
26.8000 g., 0.6250 Silver .5385 oz. ASW   **Subject:** 35th
Anniversary of Liberation **Rev:** Akershus Castle

Date	VG	F	VF	XF	BU
1980	9,876	—	—	—	45.00

KM# 451   1500 KRONER
17.0000 g., 0.9170 Gold .5 oz. AGW   **Subject:** 1994 Olympics
Rev: Telemark skier

Date	VG	F	VF	XF	BU
1993 Proof		Value: 385			

KM# 435   1500 KRONER
17.0000 g., 0.9170 Gold .5 oz. AGW   **Subject:** 1994 Olympics
Obv: Head of King Olav V left **Rev:** Ancient Norwegian skier

Date	VG	F	VF	XF	BU
1991 Proof		Value: 375			

Norway

KM# 452   1500 KRONER
7.0000 g., 0.9170 Gold .5 oz. AGW   **Subject:** Roald Amundsen

Date	VG	F	VF	XF	BU
1993 Proof		Value: 450			

KM# 467   1500 KRONER
6.9600 g., 0.9170 Gold .4994 oz. AGW   **Subject:** Year 2000
Obv: King Harald V right   **Rev:** Tree and roots

Date	VG	F	VF	XF	BU
2000 Proof		Value: 425			

KM# 470   1500 KRONER
6.9600 g., 0.9170 Gold .5000 oz. AGW, 27 mm.   **Ruler:** Harald V
Subject: Nobel Peace Prize Centennial **Obv:** King's portrait **Rev:**
Reverse design of the prize medal **Edge:** Plain

Date	VG	F	VF	XF	BU
ND(2001) Proof		Value: 385			

KM# 473   1500 KRONER
6.9600 g., 0.9170 Gold 0.5 oz. AGW, 27 mm.   **Ruler:** Harald V
Subject: 1905 Liberation **Obv:** Three kings **Rev:** Various leaf
types **Edge:** Plain

Date	F	VF	XF	Unc	BU
2003 Proof		Value: 500			

KM# 475   1500 KRONER
6.9600 g., 0.9170 Gold 0.5 oz. AGW, 27 mm.   **Ruler:** Harald V
Subject: 1905 Liberation **Obv:** Three kings **Rev:** Liquid drops on
hard surface **Edge:** Plain

Date	F	VF	XF	Unc	BU
2004 Proof		Value: 500			

KM# 477   1500 KRONER
6.9600 g., 0.9170 Gold 0.5 oz. AGW, 27 mm.   **Obv:** Three kings
Rev: Binary language **Edge:** Plain

Date	F	VF	XF	Unc	BU
2005 Proof		Value: 500			

Poland

The Republic of Poland, located in central Europe, has an area of 120,725 sq. mi. (312,680 sq. km.) and a population of *38.2 million. Capital: Warszawa (Warsaw). The economy is essentially agricultural, but industrial activity provides the products for foreign trade. Machinery, coal, coke, iron, steel and transport equipment are exported.

CONGRESS - KINGDOM OF POLAND

STANDARD COINAGE

C# 105   GROSZ
Copper

Date	VG	F	VF	XF	Unc
1828-1835	2.00	3.00	6.00	12.00	—

C# 106   GROSZ
Copper   **Note:** Varieties exist.

Date	VG	F	VF	XF	Unc
1835-1840	2.00	4.00	7.50	14.00	—

C# 106a   GROSZ
Copper   **Rev:** Without wreath, pearl rim

Date	VG	F	VF	XF	Unc
1840	12.00	18.00	35.00	65.00	—

C# 107   GROSZ
Copper **Rev:** JEDEN or IEDEN above value

Date	VG	F	VF	XF	Unc
1840MW Rare	—	—	—	—	—

C# 109   3 GROSZE
Copper

Date	VG	F	VF	XF	Unc
1827-1835	3.00	5.00	8.00	25.00	—

C# 110.1   3 GROSZE
Copper   **Rev:** Wreath surrounds value **Note:** Varieties exist.

Date	VG	F	VF	XF	Unc
1835-1839	3.00	5.00	8.00	25.00	—

C# 110.2   3 GROSZE
Copper   **Obv:** Eagle's head larger, shield smaller

Date	VG	F	VF	XF	Unc
1839-1841	3.00	6.00	8.00	22.00	—

C# 111   5 GROSZY
1.4500 g., 0.1920 Silver .0090 oz. ASW

Date	VG	F	VF	XF	Unc
1826-1832	3.00	5.00	12.00	25.00	—

C# 111a 5 GROSZY
1.4500 g., 0.1920 Silver .0090 oz. ASW

Date	VG	F	VF	XF	Unc
1836-1840	3.00	5.00	15.00	28.00	—

C# 112 5 GROSZY
1.4500 g., 0.1920 Silver .0090 oz. ASW **Obv:** Similar to 25 Zlotych, C#118

Date	VG	F	VF	XF	Unc
1841 Proof, rare	—	—	—	—	—

C# 113 10 GROSZY
2.9000 g., 0.1920 Silver .0180 oz. ASW

Date	VG	F	VF	XF	Unc
1826-1831	4.00	7.50	12.50	25.00	—

C# 113a 10 GROSZY
2.9000 g., 0.1920 Silver .0180 oz. ASW

Date	VG	F	VF	XF	Unc
1835-1840WW	2.50	6.00	10.00	15.00	—

C# 130 40 GROSZY-20 KOPEKS
4.1000 g., 0.8680 Silver .1144 oz. ASW

Date	VG	F	VF	XF	Unc
1842-1850	10.00	17.50	25.00	50.00	—

C# 131 50 GROSZY-25 KOPEKS
5.1800 g., 0.8680 Silver .1445 oz. ASW

Date	VG	F	VF	XF	Unc
1842-1850	10.00	17.50	30.00	50.00	—

C# 114.1 ZLOTY
4.5500 g., 0.5930 Silver .0872 oz. ASW **Obv:** Large head **Note:** Varieties exist.

Date	VG	F	VF	XF	Unc
1827-1832	6.00	10.00	20.00	38.00	—

C# 114.2 ZLOTY
4.5500 g., 0.5930 Silver .0872 oz. ASW **Obv:** Small head

Date	VG	F	VF	XF	Unc
1832-1834	6.00	10.00	20.00	38.00	—

C# 129 ZLOTY - 15 KOPEKS
3.0700 g., 0.8680 Silver .0857 oz. ASW **Note:** Varieties exist.

Date	VG	F	VF	XF	Unc
1832-1841	5.00	7.50	10.00	25.00	—

C# 115 2 ZLOTE
9.0900 g., 0.5930 Silver .1733 oz. ASW **Obv:** Laureated head

Date	VG	F	VF	XF	Unc
1826-1830	12.00	20.00	35.00	75.00	—

C# 132 2 ZLOTE - 30 KOPEKS
6.2100 g., 0.8680 Silver .1733 oz. ASW

Date	VG	F	VF	XF	Unc
1834-1841	10.00	16.00	25.00	45.00	—

C# 116 5 ZLOTYCH
15.5900 g., 0.8680 Silver .4351 oz. ASW **Note:** Large and small bust varieties exist.

Date	VG	F	VF	XF	Unc
1829-1834	32.50	50.00	80.00	200	—

C# 116a 5 ZLOTYCH
15.5900 g., 0.8680 Silver .4351 oz. ASW **Obv:** Legend with retrograde "S"

Date	VG	F	VF	XF	Unc
1833	22.50	32.50	60.00	120	—

C# 133 5 ZLOTYCH - 3/4 RUBLE
15.5400 g., 0.8680 Silver .4337 oz. ASW

Date	VG	F	VF	XF	Unc
1833-1841	15.00	30.00	50.00	85.00	—

C# 134 10 ZLOTYCH - 1-1/2 RUBLES
31.1000 g., 0.8680 Silver .8679 oz. ASW

Date	VG	F	VF	XF	Unc
1833-1841	35.00	50.00	100	200	—

C# 136.1　20 ZLOTYCH - 3 RUBLES
3.8900 g., 0.9170 Gold .1147 oz. AGW

Date	F	VF	XF	Unc	BU
1834-1840	850	2,450	4,250	7,500	—

C# 136.2　20 ZLOTYCH - 3 RUBLES
3.8900 g., 0.9170 Gold .1147 oz. AGW　**Note:** Mint mark: St. Petersburg "USB".

Date	F	VF	XF	Unc	BU
1834-1839	200	300	600	1,000	—

C# 136.3　20 ZLOTYCH - 3 RUBLES
3.8900 g., 0.9170 Gold .1147 oz. AGW

Date	F	VF	XF	Unc	BU
1840	275	475	600	1,250	—

C# 118　25 ZLOTYCH
4.8900 g., 0.9170 Gold .1442 oz. AGW　**Note:** Struck in collar.

Date	F	VF	XF	Unc	BU
1828-1833	900	1,650	4,000	6,000	—

REVOLUTIONARY COINAGE
1830-1831

C# 120　3 GROSZE
Copper　**Note:** Varieties in eagle exist.

Date	VG	F	VF	XF	Unc
1831	12.00	18.00	30.00	65.00	—

C# 121　10 GROSZY
2.8000 g., 0.1920 Silver .0173 oz. ASW　**Note:** Varieties in eagle exist.

Date	VG	F	VF	XF	Unc
1831	10.00	15.00	25.00	60.00	—

C# 123　2 ZLOTE
8.9800 g., 0.5930 Silver .1712 oz. ASW　**Note:** Varieties exist.

Date	VG	F	VF	XF	Unc
1831	30.00	45.00	60.00	120	—

C# 124　5 ZLOTYCH
15.4900 g., 0.8680 Silver .4323 oz. ASW　**Note:** Varieties in fraction numerator fineness exist.

Date	VG	F	VF	XF	Unc
1831	50.00	75.00	120	200	—

TRADE COINAGE

C# 125　DUKAT
3.5000 g., 0.9860 Gold .1109 oz. AGW　**Obv:** Eagle in legend at one o'clock

Date	F	VF	XF	Unc	BU
1831	200	300	400	750	—

GERMAN OCCUPATION

REGENCY COINAGE
100 Fenigow = 1 Marka

Y# 4　FENIG
Iron

Date	F	VF	XF	Unc	BU
1918	0.50	1.00	3.00	10.00	30.00

Y# 5　5 FENIGOW
Iron

Date	F	VF	XF	Unc	BU
1917-1918	0.25	0.75	1.50	3.50	—

Y# 6   10 FENIGOW
Iron

Date	F	VF	XF	Unc	BU
1917-1918	0.25	0.75	1.25	3.50	—

Y# 6a   10 FENIGOW
Zinc **Note:** Error planchet.

Date	F	VF	XF	Unc	BU
1917	25.00	45.00	85.00	150	—

Y# 7   20 FENIGOW
Iron

Date	F	VF	XF	Unc	BU
1917-1918	0.75	1.25	2.50	5.50	—

Y# 7a   20 FENIGOW
Zinc **Note:** Error planchet.

Date	F	VF	XF	Unc	BU
1917	35.00	60.00	100	200	—

REPUBLIC

STANDARD COINAGE
100 Groszy = 1 Zloty

Y# 8   GROSZ
Brass **Note:** Some authorities consider this strike a pattern.

Date	F	VF	XF	Unc	BU
1923	—	—	—	200	—

Y# 8a   GROSZ
Bronze

Date	F	VF	XF	Unc	BU
1923-1939	0.25	0.50	0.75	2.50	—

Y# 9   2 GROSZE
Brass

Date	F	VF	XF	Unc	BU
1923	3.50	12.50	22.50	45.00	60.00

Y# 9a   2 GROSZE
Bronze

Date	F	VF	XF	Unc	BU
1925-1939	0.20	0.40	0.60	2.50	—

Y# 10   5 GROSZY
Brass

Date	F	VF	XF	Unc	BU
1923	0.50	2.00	5.00	10.00	—

Y# 10a   5 GROSZY
Bronze

Date	F	VF	XF	Unc	BU
1923-1939	0.20	0.40	0.60	2.50	—

Y# 11   10 GROSZY
Nickel

Date	F	VF	XF	Unc	BU
1923	0.20	0.45	0.80	1.25	—

Y# 12   20 GROSZY
Nickel

Date	F	VF	XF	Unc	BU
1923	0.35	0.75	1.25	2.00	—

Y# 13   50 GROSZY
Nickel

Date	F	VF	XF	Unc	BU
1923	0.40	0.80	1.50	3.50	—

Y# 15   ZLOTY
5.0000 g., 0.7500 Silver .1206 oz. ASW

Date	F	VF	XF	Unc	BU
1924-1925	2.50	5.00	12.00	30.00	—

Y# 30   2 ZLOTE
4.4000 g., 0.7500 Silver .1061 oz. ASW **Subject:** 15th Anniversary of Gdynia Seaport **Rev:** Sail training ship "Dar Pomorza"

Date	F	VF	XF	Unc	BU
1936	3.00	6.00	12.00	30.00	—

Y# 14   ZLOTY
Nickel

Date	F	VF	XF	Unc	BU
1929	0.75	1.50	2.50	7.00	—

Y# 16   2 ZLOTE
10.0000 g., 0.7500 Silver .2400 oz. ASW

Date	F	VF	XF	Unc	BU
1924-1925	4.00	8.00	17.50	47.50	—

Y# 20   2 ZLOTE
4.4000 g., 0.7500 Silver .1061 oz. ASW

Date	F	VF	XF	Unc	BU
1932-1934	2.00	4.00	7.00	13.50	16.50

Y# 27   2 ZLOTE
4.4000 g., 0.7500 Silver .1061 oz. ASW

Date	F	VF	XF	Unc	BU
1934-1936	3.00	6.00	10.00	25.00	—

Y# 17.1   5 ZLOTYCH
25.0000 g., 0.9000 Silver .7234 oz. ASW **Subject:** Adoption of the Constitution **Rev:** 100 pearls in circle

Date	F	VF	XF	Unc	BU
1925	150	300	700	1,500	—

Y# 17.1a   5 ZLOTYCH
Gold

Date	F	VF	XF	Unc	BU
1925(w) Rare	—	—	—	—	—

Y# 17.2   5 ZLOTYCH
25.0000 g., 0.9000 Silver .7234 oz. ASW **Obv:** Without monogram by date

Date	F	VF	XF	Unc	BU
1925	—	—	450	950	—

Y# 17.2a   5 ZLOTYCH
Bronze

Date	F	VF	XF	Unc	BU
1925	—	—	200	300	—

Y# 17.3   5 ZLOTYCH
25.0000 g., 0.9000 Silver .7234 oz. ASW **Obv:** Monogram by date **Rev:** 81 pearls in circle

Date	F	VF	XF	Unc	BU
1925	—	—	450	950	—

Y# 17.3a   5 ZLOTYCH
43.3300 g., 0.9000 Gold 1.3407 oz. AGW **Obv:** Mink mark right of date **Edge Lettering:** SALUS REIPUBLICAE SUPREMA LEX

Date	F	VF	XF	Unc	BU
1925(w) Rare	—	—	—	—	—

Y# 17.4   5 ZLOTYCH
43.3300 g., 0.9000 Gold 1.3407 oz. AGW **Obv:** Without monogram by date, with mint mark

Date	F	VF	XF	Unc	BU
1925	—	—	925	1,150	—

Y# 17.4a   5 ZLOTYCH
Tombac

Date	F	VF	XF	Unc	BU
1925	—	—	200	300	—

Y# 18   5 ZLOTYCH
18.0000 g., 0.7500 Silver .4340 oz. ASW   **Rev:** Nike right

Date	F	VF	XF	Unc	BU
1928-1932	12.50	22.50	55.00	120	—

Y# 28   5 ZLOTYCH
11.0000 g., 0.7500 Silver .2652 oz. ASW   **Rev:** Bust of Jozef Pilsudski left

Date	F	VF	XF	Unc	BU
1934-1938	BV	4.00	9.00	20.00	25.00

Y# 19.1   5 ZLOTYCH
18.0000 g., 0.7500 Silver .4340 oz. ASW   **Subject:** Centennial of 1830 Revolution **Edge Lettering:** SALUS REIPUBLICAE SUPREMA LEX

Date	F	VF	XF	Unc	BU
1930	7.00	16.50	35.00	90.00	—

Y# 19.2   5 ZLOTYCH
18.0000 g., 0.7500 Silver .4340 oz. ASW   **Note:** High relief.

Date	F	VF	XF	Unc	BU
1930	70.00	175	375	750	—

Y# 31   5 ZLOTYCH
11.0000 g., 0.7500 Silver .2652 oz. ASW   **Subject:** 15th Anniversary of Gdynia Seaport

Date	F	VF	XF	Unc	BU
1936	7.00	12.00	25.00	50.00	—

Y# 21   5 ZLOTYCH
11.0000 g., 0.7500 Silver .2652 oz. ASW

Date	F	VF	XF	Unc	BU
1932-1934	—	BV	5.00	12.50	—

Y# 32   10 ZLOTYCH
3.2258 g., 0.9000 Gold .0933 oz. AGW   **Rev:** Boleslaw I **Note:** Never released into circulation; similar design to Y#33.

Date	F	VF	XF	Unc	BU
ND(1925)	—	BV	80.00	150	200

Y# 25   5 ZLOTYCH
11.0000 g., 0.7500 Silver .2652 oz. ASW   **Obv:** Rifle Corps symbol below eagle **Rev:** Jozef Pilsudski

Date	F	VF	XF	Unc	BU
1934	5.00	8.00	16.50	40.00	—

Y# 22   10 ZLOTYCH
22.0000 g., 0.7500 Silver .5305 oz. ASW

Date	F	VF	XF	Unc	BU
1932-1933	6.00	8.50	12.50	30.00	38.00

Y# 23   10 ZLOTYCH
22.0000 g., 0.7500 Silver .5305 oz. ASW **Subject:** Jan III
Sobieski's Victory Over the Turks **Obv:** Similar to Y#22 **Rev:** Bust
of Sobieski right

Date	F	VF	XF	Unc	BU
ND(1933)	8.00	16.00	25.00	55.00	—

Y# 24   10 ZLOTYCH
22.0000 g., 0.7500 Silver .5305 oz. ASW **Subject:** 70th
Anniversary of 1863 Insurrection **Obv:** Similar to Y#23 **Rev:** Bust
of Romuald Traugutt 1/4 right

Date	F	VF	XF	Unc	BU
ND(1933)	10.00	20.00	40.00	65.00	—

Y# 26   10 ZLOTYCH
22.0000 g., 0.7500 Silver .5305 oz. ASW **Obv:** Rifle Corps symbol
below eagle **Rev:** Jozef Pilsudski

Date	F	VF	XF	Unc	BU
1934	9.00	17.50	25.00	50.00	—

Y# 29   10 ZLOTYCH
22.0000 g., 0.7500 Silver .5305 oz. ASW **Obv:** No symbol below
eagle

Date	F	VF	XF	Unc	BU
1934-1939	BV	7.00	14.00	30.00	—

Y# 33   20 ZLOTYCH
6.4516 g., 0.9000 Gold .1867 oz. AGW **Rev:** Boleslaw I **Note:**
Never released into circulation.

Date	F	VF	XF	Unc	BU
ND(1925)	—	BV	135	210	325

WWII GERMAN OCCUPATION

OCCUPATION COINAGE

Y# 34   GROSZ
Zinc

Date	F	VF	XF	Unc	BU
1939	0.50	1.00	1.75	3.50	—

Y# 35   5 GROSZY
Zinc

Date	F	VF	XF	Unc	BU
1939	0.50	1.50	2.00	5.00	—

Y# 36   10 GROSZY
Zinc

Date	F	VF	XF	Unc	BU
1923	0.10	0.20	0.40	2.00	—

Y# 37   20 GROSZY
Zinc

Date	F	VF	XF	Unc	BU
1923	0.15	0.25	0.50	2.00	—

Y# 38   50 GROSZY
Nickel Plated Iron

Date	F	VF	XF	Unc	BU
1938	1.00	2.00	4.00	8.50	—

Y# 38a 50 GROSZY
Iron

Date	F	VF	XF	Unc	BU
1938	1.25	2.50	5.00	10.00	—

TOKEN COINAGE
Lodz Ghetto, 1942-1944

A major industrial city in western Poland before World War II and site of the first wartime ghetto under German occupation (May 1940). It was also the last ghetto to close during the war (August 1944). Token coinage was struck in 1942 and 1943, in the name of the Jewish Elders of Litzmannstadt. This series has seen very little circulation, but is commonly found in conditions from slightly to badly corroded. The badly corroded specimens have the appearance of zinc.

KM# Tn1 10 PFENNIG
Aluminum-Magnesium

Date	VG	F	VF	XF	Unc
1942	60.00	125	200	—	—

KM# Tn5 10 PFENNIG
Aluminum-Magnesium

Date	VG	F	VF	XF	Unc
1942	35.00	50.00	65.00	125	—

KM# Tn2 5 MARK
Aluminum

Date	VG	F	VF	XF	Unc
1943	5.00	10.00	25.00	45.00	—

KM# Tn2a 5 MARK
Aluminum-Magnesium

Date	VG	F	VF	XF	Unc
1943	20.00	40.00	75.00	—	—

KM# Tn3 10 MARK
Aluminum Note: Thick and thin planchets exist.

Date	VG	F	VF	XF	Unc
1943	5.00	10.00	25.00	45.00	—

KM# Tn3a 10 MARK
Aluminum-Magnesium

Date	VG	F	VF	XF	Unc
1943	25.00	45.00	85.00	—	—

KM# Tn4 20 MARK
Aluminum Note: Beware of numerous counterfeits.

Date	VG	F	VF	XF	Unc
1943	75.00	110	150	250	—

REPUBLIC
Post War

STANDARD COINAGE

Y# 39 GROSZ
Aluminum Note: 116,000 were struck at Warsaw, the remainder at Budapest.

Date	F	VF	XF	Unc	BU
1949	0.10	0.20	0.30	0.75	—

Y# 40 2 GROSZE
Aluminum Note: 106,000 were struck at Warsaw, the remainder at Budapest.

Date	F	VF	XF	Unc	BU
1949	0.10	0.25	0.50	1.00	—

Y# 41 5 GROSZY
Bronze Note: Struck at Basel.

Date	F	VF	XF	Unc	BU
1949	0.10	0.25	0.50	1.00	—

Y# 41a 5 GROSZY
Aluminum Note: Struck at Kremnica.

Date	F	VF	XF	Unc	BU
1949	0.10	0.25	0.75	1.50	—

Y# 42   10 GROSZY
Copper-Nickel   **Note:** Struck at Kremnica.

Date	F	VF	XF	Unc	BU
1949	0.20	0.40	0.60	1.50	—

Y# 42a   10 GROSZY
Aluminum   **Note:** Struck at Warsaw.

Date	F	VF	XF	Unc	BU
1949	0.10	0.25	0.75	2.50	—

Y# 43   20 GROSZY
Copper-Nickel   **Note:** Struck at Kremnica.

Date	F	VF	XF	Unc	BU
1949	0.25	0.45	0.75	2.00	—

Y# 43a   20 GROSZY
Aluminum

Date	F	VF	XF	Unc	BU
1949	0.10	0.25	0.75	2.50	—

Y# 44   50 GROSZY
Copper-Nickel   **Note:** Struck at Kremnica.

Date	F	VF	XF	Unc	BU
1949	0.35	0.65	1.00	2.50	—

Y# 44a   50 GROSZY
Aluminum   **Note:** Struck at Warsaw.

Date	F	VF	XF	Unc	BU
1949	0.10	0.25	1.50	5.00	—

Y# 45   ZLOTY
Copper-Nickel   **Note:** Struck at Kremnica.

Date	F	VF	XF	Unc	BU
1949	1.00	1.50	2.25	4.00	—

Y# 45a   ZLOTY
Aluminum   **Note:** Struck at Warsaw.

Date	F	VF	XF	Unc	BU
1949	0.10	0.25	2.50	6.00	—

PEOPLES REPUBLIC
STANDARD COINAGE

Y# A46   5 GROSZY
Aluminum

Date	F	VF	XF	Unc	BU
1958-1972	—	0.50	0.10	0.15	—

Y# AA47   10 GROSZY
Aluminum   **Note:** Varieties in date size exist.

Date	F	VF	XF	Unc	BU
1961-1985	—	0.25	0.10	0.10	—

Y# A47   20 GROSZY
Aluminum   **Note:** Date varieties exist.

Date	F	VF	XF	Unc	BU
1957-1985	—	1.75	0.10	0.20	—

Y# 48.1   50 GROSZY
Aluminum

Date	F	VF	XF	Unc	BU
1957-1985	—	0.10	0.20	0.40	—

Y# 48.2   50 GROSZY
Aluminum   **Obv:** Redesigned eagle

Date	F	VF	XF	Unc	BU
1986-1987	—	0.10	0.20	0.40	—

Poland

Y# 49.1 ZLOTY
Aluminum

Date	F	VF	XF	Unc	BU
1957-1985	—	0.10	0.15	0.25	—

Y# 80.2 2 ZLOTE
Brass **Obv:** Redesigned eagle

Date	F	VF	XF	Unc	BU
1986-1988	—	0.15	0.25	0.50	—

Y# 49.2 ZLOTY
Aluminum **Obv:** Redesigned eagle

Date	F	VF	XF	Unc	BU
1986-1988	—	0.10	0.15	0.25	—

Y# 80.3 2 ZLOTE
Aluminum, 17.9 mm.

Date	F	VF	XF	Unc	BU
1989-1990	—	0.10	0.20	0.40	—

Y# 49.3 ZLOTY
Aluminum

Date	F	VF	XF	Unc	BU
1989-1990	—	0.10	0.15	0.25	—

Y# 47 5 ZLOTYCH
Aluminum **Rev:** Fisherman with net

Date	F	VF	XF	Unc	BU
1958-1974	—	0.20	0.50	2.50	—

Y# 46 2 ZLOTE
Aluminum

Date	F	VF	XF	Unc	BU
1958-1974	—	0.15	0.30	1.00	—

Y# 81.1 5 ZLOTYCH
Brass **Note:** Variety of size of letters exist.

Date	F	VF	XF	Unc	BU
1975-1985	—	0.20	0.40	0.85	—

Y# 80.1 2 ZLOTE
Brass

Date	F	VF	XF	Unc	BU
1975-1985	—	0.15	0.25	0.50	—

Y# 81.2 5 ZLOTYCH
Brass, 24 mm. **Obv:** Redesigned eagle

Date	F	VF	XF	Unc	BU
1986-1988	—	0.20	0.40	0.85	—

Poland

Y# 81.3   5 ZLOTYCH
Aluminum, 20 mm.

Date	F	VF	XF	Unc	BU
1989-1990	—	0.15	0.30	0.65	—

Y# 50   10 ZLOTYCH
Copper-Nickel, 31 mm.   **Rev:** Tadeusz Kosciuszko left

Date	F	VF	XF	Unc	BU
1959-1966	—	0.60	2.00	6.50	—

Y# 50a   10 ZLOTYCH
Copper-Nickel, 28 mm.   **Rev:** Tadeusz Kosciuszko facing **Note:** Reduced size.

Date	F	VF	XF	Unc	BU
1969-1973	—	0.50	1.00	2.00	—

Y# 51   10 ZLOTYCH
Copper-Nickel   **Rev:** Mikolaj Kopernik

Date	F	VF	XF	Unc	BU
1959-1965	—	0.75	1.25	2.50	—

Y# 51a   10 ZLOTYCH
Copper-Nickel   **Rev:** Mikolaj Kopernik **Note:** Reduced size.

Date	F	VF	XF	Unc	BU
1967-1969	—	0.75	1.25	2.50	—

Y# 52   10 ZLOTYCH
Copper-Nickel   **Subject:** 600th Anniversary of Jagiello University
Rev: Kasimir the Great crowned head left **Note:** Legends raised.

Date	F	VF	XF	Unc	BU
ND(1964)	—	0.50	1.50	3.50	—

Y# 52a   10 ZLOTYCH
Copper-Nickel   **Subject:** 600th Anniversary of Jagiello University
Rev: Kasimir the Great crowned head left **Note:** Legends incuse.

Date	F	VF	XF	Unc	BU
ND(1964)	—	0.50	1.50	3.50	—

Y# 54   10 ZLOTYCH
Copper-Nickel   **Subject:** 700th Anniversary of Warsaw **Rev:** Nike
of Warsaw

Date	F	VF	XF	Unc	BU
1965	—	0.75	2.00	3.50	5.00

Y# 55   10 ZLOTYCH
Copper-Nickel   **Subject:** 700th Anniversary of Warsaw **Rev:**
Sigismund Pillar

Date	F	VF	XF	Unc	BU
1965	—	0.75	2.00	3.50	5.00

Y# 56   10 ZLOTYCH
Copper-Nickel **Subject:** 200th Anniversary of Warsaw Mint **Rev:** Sigismund Pillar **Edge Lettering:** W DWNSETNA ROCZNICE MENNICY WARSZAWSKIEJ

Date	F	VF	XF	Unc	BU
1966	—	2.50	6.50	22.50	40.00

Y# 61   10 ZLOTYCH
Copper-Nickel **Subject:** 25th Anniversary - Peoples Republic

Date	F	VF	XF	Unc	BU
1969	—	0.50	1.00	2.25	—

Y# 62   10 ZLOTYCH
Copper-Nickel **Subject:** 25th Anniversary - Provincial Annexations

Date	F	VF	XF	Unc	BU
1970	—	0.50	1.00	2.25	—

Y# 58   10 ZLOTYCH
Copper-Nickel **Subject:** 20th Anniversary - Death of General Swierczewski

Date	F	VF	XF	Unc	BU
1967	—	0.50	1.00	2.25	—

Y# 63   10 ZLOTYCH
Copper-Nickel **Series:** F.A.O. **Rev:** Atlantic turbot and ear of barley

Date	F	VF	XF	Unc	BU
1971	—	0.75	1.50	3.50	5.0

Y# 59   10 ZLOTYCH
Copper-Nickel **Subject:** Centennial - Birth of Marie Sklodowska Curie

Date	F	VF	XF	Unc	BU
1967	—	0.50	1.00	2.25	—

Y# 64   10 ZLOTYCH
Copper-Nickel **Subject:** 50th Anniversary - Battle of Upper Silesia

Date	F	VF	XF	Unc	BU
1971	—	0.50	1.00	2.25	B

Y# 60   10 ZLOTYCH
Copper-Nickel **Subject:** 25th Anniversary - Peoples Army

Date	F	VF	XF	Unc	BU
1968	—	0.50	1.00	2.25	—

Y# 65   10 ZLOTYCH
Copper-Nickel **Subject:** 50th Anniversary - Gdynia Seaport

Date	F	VF	XF	Unc
1972	—	0.50	1.00	2.25

Y# 73　10 ZLOTYCH
Copper-Nickel　**Rev:** Boleslaw Prus, Writer, head left

Date	F	VF	XF	Unc	BU
1975-1984	—	0.25	0.65	1.25	—

Y# 74　10 ZLOTYCH
Copper-Nickel　**Rev:** Adam Mickiewicz, Poet

Date	F	VF	XF	Unc	BU
1975-1976	—	0.25	0.65	1.25	—

Y# 152.1　10 ZLOTYCH
Copper-Nickel, 25 mm.

Date	F	VF	XF	Unc	BU
1984-1988	—	0.20	0.50	1.00	—

Y# 152.2　10 ZLOTYCH
Brass, 21.8 mm.

Date	F	VF	XF	Unc	BU
1989-1990	—	0.20	0.40	0.80	—

Y# 67　20 ZLOTYCH
Copper-Nickel

Date	F	VF	XF	Unc	BU
1973-1976	—	0.25	0.75	1.50	—

Y# 69　20 ZLOTYCH
Copper-Nickel　**Rev:** Marceli Nowotko

Date	F	VF	XF	Unc	BU
1974-1983	—	0.25	0.75	1.50	—

Y# 70　20 ZLOTYCH
Copper-Nickel　**Subject:** 25th Anniversary of the Comcon　**Rev:** Half sunflower, half cog wheel

Date	F	VF	XF	Unc	BU
1974	—	0.75	1.25	2.50	—

Y# 75　20 ZLOTYCH
Copper-Nickel　**Subject:** International Women's Year

Date	F	VF	XF	Unc	BU
1975	—	0.75	1.25	2.50	—

Y# 95　20 ZLOTYCH
Copper-Nickel　**Rev:** Maria Konopnicka

Date	F	VF	XF	Unc	BU
1978	—	0.75	1.25	2.75	—

Y# 97　20 ZLOTYCH
Copper-Nickel　**Subject:** First Polish Cosmonaut

Date	F	VF	XF	Unc	BU
1978	—	0.75	1.25	2.75	—

Y# 99   20 ZLOTYCH
Copper-Nickel   **Series:** International Year of the Child

Date	F	VF	XF	Unc	BU
1979	—	1.00	1.50	3.00	—

Y# 108   20 ZLOTYCH
Copper-Nickel   **Series:** 1980 Olympics **Rev:** Runner

Date	F	VF	XF	Unc	BU
1980	—	1.00	1.75	5.00	—

Y# 112   20 ZLOTYCH
Copper-Nickel   **Subject:** 50th Anniversary - Training Ship Daru Pomorza

Date	F	VF	XF	Unc	BU
1980	—	1.00	1.75	3.50	—

Y# 153.1   20 ZLOTYCH
Copper-Nickel   **Note:** Circulation coinage.

Date	F	VF	XF	Unc	BU
1984-1988	—	0.25	0.60	1.25	1.50

Y# 153.2   20 ZLOTYCH
Copper-Nickel, 23.9 mm.   **Note:** Reduced size.

Date	F	VF	XF	Unc	BU
1989-1990	—	0.25	0.35	0.75	1.00

Y# 66   50 ZLOTYCH
12.6400 g., 0.7500 Silver .3048 oz. ASW   **Rev:** Fryderyk Chopin, pianist

Date	F	VF	XF	Unc	BU
1972-1974 Proof		Value: 11.50			

Y# 100   50 ZLOTYCH
Copper-Nickel   **Rev:** Duke Mieszko I

Date	F	VF	XF	Unc	BU
1979	—	1.00	2.00	5.00	—

Y# 114   50 ZLOTYCH
Copper-Nickel   **Rev:** King Boleslaw I Chrobry

Date	F	VF	XF	Unc	BU
1980	—	1.00	2.00	5.00	—

Y# 117   50 ZLOTYCH
Copper-Nickel   **Rev:** Duke Kazimierz I Odnowiciel

Date	F	VF	XF	Unc	BU
1980	—	1.00	2.00	5.00	—

Y# 122   50 ZLOTYCH
Copper-Nickel   **Rev:** General Broni Wladyslaw Sikorski

Date	F	VF	XF	Unc	B
1981	—	1.00	2.00	5.00	

Y# 124   50 ZLOTYCH
Copper-Nickel   **Rev:** King Boleslaw II Smialy

Date	F	VF	XF	Unc	B
1981	—	1.00	2.00	4.50	

Y# 127   50 ZLOTYCH
Copper-Nickel   **Series:** F.A.O. - World Food Day

Date	F	VF	XF	Unc	BU
1981	—	1.00	2.00	4.50	—

Y# 146   50 ZLOTYCH
Copper-Nickel   **Rev:** Ignacy Lukasiewicz

Date	F	VF	XF	Unc	BU
1983	—	1.00	4.00	8.00	—

Y# 128   50 ZLOTYCH
Copper-Nickel   **Rev:** King Wladyslaw I Herman

Date	F	VF	XF	Unc	BU
1981	—	1.00	2.00	4.50	—

Y# 133   50 ZLOTYCH
Copper-Nickel   **Rev:** King Boleslaw III Krzywousty

Date	F	VF	XF	Unc	BU
1982	—	1.00	2.00	4.50	—

Y# 57   100 ZLOTYCH
20.0000 g., 0.9000 Silver .5787 oz. ASW   **Subject:** Polish Millennium   **Rev:** Miezka I and Dabrowka standing behind shield

Date	F	VF	XF	Unc	BU
1966	—	—	7.50	12.50	—

Y# 68   100 ZLOTYCH
16.5000 g., 0.6250 Silver .3316 oz. ASW   **Subject:** 500th Anniversary - Birth of Mikolaj Kopernik, scientist

Date	F	VF	XF	Unc	BU
1973-1974 Proof		Value: 9.00			

Y# 142   50 ZLOTYCH
Copper-Nickel   **Subject:** 150th Anniversary of Great Theater

Date	F	VF	XF	Unc	BU
1983	—	1.00	4.00	8.00	—

145   50 ZLOTYCH
Copper-Nickel   **Rev:** King Jan III Sobieski

Date	F	VF	XF	Unc	BU
1983	—	1.00	2.00	4.50	—

Y# 71   100 ZLOTYCH
16.5000 g., 0.6250 Silver .3316 oz. ASW   **Subject:** 40th Anniversary - Death of Maria Sklodowska Curie   **Rev:** Profile left of Curie with radiation lines running from the symbol of the element at right

Date	F	VF	XF	Unc	BU
1974 Proof		Value: 7.50			

Y# 76   100 ZLOTYCH
16.5000 g., 0.6250 Silver .3316 oz. ASW   **Rev:** Royal castle in Warsaw

Date	F	VF	XF	Unc	BU
1975 Proof		Value: 7.50			

Y# 77   100 ZLOTYCH
16.5000 g., 0.6250 Silver .3316 oz. ASW   **Rev:** Ignacy Jan Paderewski, Composer, left

Date	F	VF	XF	Unc	BU
1975 Proof		Value: 6.50			

Y# 78   100 ZLOTYCH
16.5000 g., 0.6250 Silver .3316 oz. ASW   **Rev:** Helena Modrzejewska, Actress, right

Date	F	VF	XF	Unc	BU
1975 Proof		Value: 6.50			

Y# 82   100 ZLOTYCH
16.5000 g., 0.6250 Silver .3316 oz. ASW   **Rev:** Tadeusz Kosciuszko right

Date	F	VF	XF	Unc	BU
1976 Proof		Value: 6.50			

Y# 84   100 ZLOTYCH
16.50 g., 0.6250 Silver .3316 oz. ASW   **Rev:** Kazimierz Pulaski left

Date	F	VF	XF	Unc	BU
1976 Proof		Value: 7.00			

Y# 87   100 ZLOTYCH
16.5000 g., 0.6250 Silver .3316 oz. ASW   **Series:** Environment Protection **Rev:** Aurochs

Date	F	VF	XF	Unc	BU
1977 Proof		Value: 30.00			

Y# 88   100 ZLOTYCH
16.5000 g., 0.6250 Silver .3316 oz. ASW   **Rev:** Henryk Sienkiewicz, Writer, left

Date	F	VF	XF	Unc	BU
1977 Proof		Value: 8.50			

Y# 89   100 ZLOTYCH
16.5000 g., 0.6250 Silver .3316 oz. ASW   **Rev:** Wladyslaw Reymont, Story Teller, half right

Date	F	VF	XF	Unc	BU
1977 Proof		Value: 8.50			

Y# 91   100 ZLOTYCH
16.5000 g., 0.6250 Silver .3316 oz. ASW   **Rev:** Wawel Castle in Krakow

Date	F	VF	XF	Unc	B
1977 Proof		Value: 11.50			

Y# 92   100 ZLOTYCH
16.5000 g., 0.6250 Silver .3316 oz. ASW   **Rev:** Adam Mickiewicz Poet, facing

Date	F	VF	XF	Unc	B
1978 Proof		Value: 11.50			

Y# 93   100 ZLOTYCH
16.5000 g., 0.6250 Silver .3316 oz. ASW **Series:** Environment
Protection **Rev:** Moose heading left

Date	F	VF	XF	Unc	BU
1978 Proof		Value: 27.50			

Y# 94   100 ZLOTYCH
16.5000 g., 0.6250 Silver .3316 oz. ASW **Subject:** 100th
Anniversary - Birth of Janusz Korczak **Rev:** Bust facing

Date	F	VF	XF	Unc	BU
1978 Proof		Value: 9.00			

Y# 105   100 ZLOTYCH
16.5000 g., 0.6250 Silver .3316 oz. ASW **Series:** Environment
Protection **Rev:** Chamois

Date	F	VF	XF	Unc	BU
1979 Proof		Value: 27.50			

Y# 96   100 ZLOTYCH
16.5000 g., 0.6250 Silver .3316 oz. ASW **Series:** Environment
Protection **Rev:** Beaver

Date	F	VF	XF	Unc	BU
1978 Proof		Value: 27.50			

Y# 103   100 ZLOTYCH
16.5000 g., 0.6250 Silver .3316 oz. ASW **Rev:** Ludwik Zamenhof left

Date	F	VF	XF	Unc	BU
1979 Proof		Value: 9.00			

Y# 98   100 ZLOTYCH
16.5000 g., 0.6250 Silver .3316 oz. ASW **Rev:** Henryk
Wieniawski, Composer, left

Date	F	VF	XF	Unc	BU
1979 Proof		Value: 15.00			

Y# 104   100 ZLOTYCH
16.5000 g., 0.6250 Silver .3316 oz. ASW **Series:** Environment
Protection **Rev:** Lynx

Date	F	VF	XF	Unc	BU
1979 Proof		Value: 27.50			

Y# 109   100 ZLOTYCH
16.5000 g., 0.6250 Silver .3316 oz. ASW **Series:** 1980 Olympics
Rev: Olympic rings and runner

Date	F	VF	XF	Unc	BU
1980 Proof		Value: 32.50			

Y# 120   100 ZLOTYCH
16.5000 g., 0.6250 Silver .3316 oz. ASW **Subject:** 450th
Anniversary - Birth of Jan Kochanowski, Poet

Date	F	VF	XF	Unc	BU
1980 Proof		Value: 17.50			

Poland

Y# 121   100 ZLOTYCH
16.5000 g., 0.6250 Silver .3316 oz. ASW   **Series:** Environment
Protection **Rev:** Cappercaillie

Date	F	VF	XF	Unc	BU
1980 Proof		Value: 27.50			

Y# 123   100 ZLOTYCH
16.5000 g., 0.6250 Silver .3316 oz. ASW   **Rev:** General Broni
Wladyslaw Sikorski left

Date	F	VF	XF	Unc	BU
1981 Proof		Value: 16.00			

Y# 126   100 ZLOTYCH
16.5000 g., 0.6250 Silver .3316 oz. ASW   **Series:** Environment
Protection **Rev:** Horse right

Date	F	VF	XF	Unc	BU
1981 Proof		Value: 27.50			

Y# 136   100 ZLOTYCH
14.1500 g., 0.7500 Silver .3412 oz. ASW   **Subject:** Visit of Pope
John Paul II **Rev:** Bust left

Date	F	VF	XF	Unc	BU
1982-1986	—	—	—	45.00	—

Y# 141   100 ZLOTYCH
16.5000 g., 0.6250 Silver .3316 oz. ASW   **Series:** Environment
Protection **Rev:** Stork walking right

Date	F	VF	XF	Unc	BU
1982 Proof		Value: 27.50			

Y# 147   100 ZLOTYCH
16.5000 g., 0.6250 Silver .3316 oz. ASW   **Series:** Environment
Protection **Rev:** Bear walking right

Date	F	VF	XF	Unc	BU
1983 Proof		Value: 40.00			

Y# 148   100 ZLOTYCH
Copper-Nickel   **Rev:** Wincenty Witos

Date	F	VF	XF	Unc	BU
1984	—	—	—	3.00	4.50

Y# 151   100 ZLOTYCH
Copper-Nickel   **Subject:** 40th Anniversary of Peoples Republic

Date	F	VF	XF	Unc	BU
1984	—	—	—	3.00	4.5

Y# 155   100 ZLOTYCH
Copper-Nickel   **Rev:** King Przemyslaw II

Date	F	VF	XF	Unc	B
1985	—	—	—	3.00	4.5

Y# 157   100 ZLOTYCH
Nickel Plated Steel **Subject:** Polish Women's Memorial Hospital
Center **Rev:** Woman breast-feeding Child

Date	F	VF	XF	Unc	BU
1985	—	—	—	3.00	4.50

Y# 160   100 ZLOTYCH
Copper-Nickel **Rev:** King Wladyslaw I Lokietek half right

Date	F	VF	XF	Unc	BU
1986	—	—	—	3.00	4.50

Y# 167   100 ZLOTYCH
Copper-Nickel **Rev:** King Kazimierz III half left

Date	F	VF	XF	Unc	BU
1987	—	—	—	3.50	5.00

Y# 182   100 ZLOTYCH
Copper-Nickel **Subject:** 70th Anniversary - Wielkopolskiego
Insurrection

Date	F	VF	XF	Unc	BU
1988	—	—	—	3.00	4.50

Y# 183   100 ZLOTYCH
Copper-Nickel **Rev:** Queen Jadwiga 1384-1399

Date	F	VF	XF	Unc	BU
1988	—	—	—	3.00	4.50

Y# 72   200 ZLOTYCH
14.4700 g., 0.6250 Silver .2907 oz. ASW **Subject:** 30th
Anniversary - Polish Peoples Republic

Date	F	VF	XF	Unc	BU
1974	—	—	—	4.50	6.00

Y# 79   200 ZLOTYCH
14.4700 g., 0.7500 Silver .3490 oz. ASW **Subject:** 30th
Anniversary - Victory Over Fascism

Date	F	VF	XF	Unc	BU
1975	—	—	—	5.00	6.50

Y# 86   200 ZLOTYCH
14.4700 g., 0.6250 Silver .2907 oz. ASW **Series:** XXI Olympics
Rev: Rings and torch

Date	F	VF	XF	Unc	BU
1976	—	—	—	8.50	10.00

Y# 101   200 ZLOTYCH
17.6000 g., 0.7500 Silver .4244 oz. ASW **Rev:** Duke Mieszko I
half left

Date	F	VF	XF	Unc	BU
1979 Proof		Value: 35.00			

Y# 110   200 ZLOTYCH
17.6000 g., 0.7500 Silver .4244 oz. ASW **Series:** Winter
Olympics **Rev:** Torch below ski jumper

Date	F	VF	XF	Unc	BU
1980 Proof		Value: 16.50			

Y# 110a   200 ZLOTYCH
17.6000 g., 0.7500 Silver .4244 oz. ASW   **Rev:** Without torch below ski jumper

Date	F	VF	XF	Unc	BU
1980 Proof		Value: 11.50			

Y# 130   200 ZLOTYCH
17.6000 g., 0.7500 Silver .4244 oz. ASW   **Subject:** World Soccer Championship Games in Spain

Date	F	VF	XF	Unc	BU
1982 Proof		Value: 16.50			

Y# 132   200 ZLOTYCH
17.6000 g., 0.7500 Silver .4244 oz. ASW   **Rev:** King Boleslaw III Krzywousty

Date	F	VF	XF	Unc	BU
1982 Proof		Value: 20.00			

Y# 115   200 ZLOTYCH
17.6000 g., 0.7500 Silver .4244 oz. ASW   **Rev:** King Boleslaw I Chrobry

Date	F	VF	XF	Unc	BU
1980 Proof		Value: 35.00			

Y# 118   200 ZLOTYCH
17.6000 g., 0.7500 Silver .4244 oz. ASW   **Rev:** Duke Kazimierz I facing

Date	F	VF	XF	Unc	BU
1980 Proof		Value: 15.00			

Y# 125   200 ZLOTYCH
17.6000 g., 0.7500 Silver .4244 oz. ASW   **Rev:** King Bolaslaw II Smialy

Date	F	VF	XF	Unc	BU
1981 Proof		Value: 18.50			

Y# 129   200 ZLOTYCH
17.6000 g., 0.7500 Silver .4244 oz. ASW   **Rev:** King Wladyslaw I Herman

Date	F	VF	XF	Unc	BU
1981 Proof		Value: 20.00			

Y# 137   200 ZLOTYCH
28.3000 g., 0.7500 Silver .6825 oz. ASW   **Subject:** Visit of Pope John Paul II **Obv:** Similar to Y#132 **Rev:** Bust of Pope left

Date	F	VF	XF	Unc	BU
1982-1986	—	—	—	125	

Y# 143   200 ZLOTYCH
17.6000 g., 0.7500 Silver .4244 oz. ASW   **Rev:** King Jan III Sobieski

Date	F	VF	XF	Unc	B
1983 Proof		Value: 25.00			

Y# 149   200 ZLOTYCH
17.6000 g., 0.7500 Silver .4244 oz. ASW   **Series:** Winter
Olympics **Rev:** Ice skater

Date	F	VF	XF	Unc	BU
1984 Proof		Value: 22.50			

Y# 150   200 ZLOTYCH
17.6000 g., 0.7500 Silver .4244 oz. ASW   **Series:** Summer
Olympics **Rev:** Hurdler

Date	F	VF	XF	Unc	BU
1984 Proof		Value: 20.00			

Y# 83   500 ZLOTYCH
0.0000 g., 0.9000 Gold .8681 oz. AGW   **Rev:** Tadeusz
Kosciuszko right

Date	F	VF	XF	Unc	BU
1976	—	—	—	850	—

Y# 85   500 ZLOTYCH
0.0000 g., 0.9000 Gold .8681 oz. AGW   **Rev:** Kazimierz Pulaski
left

Date	F	VF	XF	Unc	BU
1976	—	—	—	850	—

Y# 154   500 ZLOTYCH
16.5000 g., 0.6250 Silver .3283 oz. ASW   **Series:** Environment
Protection **Rev:** Mute Swan and two cygnets

Date	F	VF	XF	Unc	BU
1984 Proof		Value: 35.00			

Y# 156   500 ZLOTYCH
16.5000 g., 0.7500 Silver .3979 oz. ASW   **Rev:** King Przemyslaw II

Date	F	VF	XF	Unc	BU
1985 Proof		Value: 25.00			

Y# 158   500 ZLOTYCH
16.5000 g., 0.7500 Silver .3979 oz. ASW   **Subject:** 40th
Anniversary of United Nations

Date	F	VF	XF	Unc	BU
1985 Proof		Value: 22.50			

Y# 159   500 ZLOTYCH
16.5000 g., 0.7500 Silver .3979 oz. ASW   **Series:** Environmental
Protection **Rev:** Red squirrel

Date	F	VF	XF	Unc	BU
1985 Proof		Value: 35.00			

Y# 161 500 ZLOTYCH
16.5000 g., 0.7500 Silver .3979 oz. ASW **Rev:** King Wladyslaw
I Lokietek half right

Date	F	VF	XF	Unc	BU
1986 Proof		Value: 22.00			

Y# 172 500 ZLOTYCH
16.5000 g., 0.7500 Silver .3979 oz. ASW **Series:** Winter
Olympics **Rev:** Ice hockey goalie

Date	F	VF	XF	Unc	BU
1987 Proof		Value: 18.50			

Y# 162 500 ZLOTYCH
16.5000 g., 0.7500 Silver .3979 oz. ASW **Series:** Environment
Protection **Rev:** Eagle Owl

Date	F	VF	XF	Unc	BU
1986 Proof		Value: 40.00			

Y# 173 500 ZLOTYCH
16.5000 g., 0.7500 Silver .3979 oz. ASW **Rev:** King Kazimierz III

Date	F	VF	XF	Unc	BU
1987 Proof		Value: 25.00			

Y# 181 500 ZLOTYCH
16.5000 g., 0.7500 Silver .3979 oz. ASW **Rev:** Queen Jadwiga
1384-1399

Date	F	VF	XF	Unc	BU
1988 Proof		Value: 22.50			

Y# 225 500 ZLOTYCH
16.5000 g., 0.7500 Silver .3979 oz. ASW **Rev:** Soccer ball in net

Date	F	VF	XF	Unc	BU
1986 Proof		Value: 30.00			

Y# 184 500 ZLOTYCH
16.5000 g., 0.7500 Silver .3979 oz. ASW **Rev:** Colosseum in
Rome - Soccer 1990

Date	F	VF	XF	Unc	BU
1988 Proof		Value: 22.50			

Y# 165 500 ZLOTYCH
16.5000 g., 0.7500 Silver .3979 oz. ASW **Series:** Olympics **Rev:**
Equestrian

Date	F	VF	XF	Unc	BU
1987 Proof		Value: 25.00			

Y# 166 500 ZLOTYCH
16.5000 g., 0.7500 Silver .3979 oz. ASW **Subject:** European
Championship Soccer Games

Date	F	VF	XF	Unc	BU
1987 Proof		Value: 30.00			

Y# 185 500 ZLOTYCH
Copper-Nickel **Subject:** 50th Anniversary - Beginning of WWII
Rev: Infantry soldiers advancing

Date	F	VF	XF	Unc	BU
1989	—	—	—	2.50	—

Y# 194 500 ZLOTYCH
Copper-Nickel **Rev:** King Wladyslaw II 1386-1434

Date	F	VF	XF	Unc	BU
1989	—	—	—	3.00	—

Y# 138 1000 ZLOTYCH
3.4000 g., 0.9000 Gold .0984 oz. AGW **Subject:** Visit of Pope John Paul II

Date	F	VF	XF	Unc	BU
1982-1986	—	—	—	350	—

Y# 144 1000 ZLOTYCH
14.5000 g., 0.7500 Silver .3497 oz. ASW **Subject:** Visit of Pope John Paul II **Rev:** Bust left

Date	F	VF	XF	Unc	BU
1982-1983	—	—	—	9.00	—

Y# 168 1000 ZLOTYCH
3.1100 g., 0.9990 Gold .1000 oz. AGW **Subject:** Papal Visit in America **Note:** Similar to KM#163.

Date	F	VF	XF	Unc	BU
1987 Proof		Value: 345			

Y# 174 1000 ZLOTYCH
3.1100 g., 0.9990 Gold .1000 oz. AGW **Subject:** 10th Anniversary of Pope John Paul II **Note:** Similar to KM#177.

Date	F	VF	XF	Unc	BU
1988 Proof		Value: 175			

Y# 186 1000 ZLOTYCH
3.1100 g., 0.9990 Gold .1000 oz. AGW **Subject:** Pope John Paul II **Obv:** Similar to Y#174 **Rev:** Similar to 200,000 Zlotych, Y#190

Date	F	VF	XF	Unc	BU
1989	—	—	—	175	—

Y# 90 2000 ZLOTYCH
8.0000 g., 0.9000 Gold .2315 oz. AGW **Rev:** Fryderyk Chopin, Pianist

Date	F	VF	XF	Unc	BU
1977 Proof		Value: 175			

Y# 102 2000 ZLOTYCH
8.0000 g., 0.9000 Gold .2315 oz. AGW **Rev:** Duke Mieszko I

Date	F	VF	XF	Unc	BU
1979 Proof		Value: 175			

Y# 106 2000 ZLOTYCH
8.0000 g., 0.9000 Gold .2315 oz. AGW **Rev:** Mikolaj Kopernik, Scientist

Date	F	VF	XF	Unc	BU
1979 Proof		Value: 175			

Y# 107 2000 ZLOTYCH
8.0000 g., 0.9000 Gold .2315 oz. AGW **Rev:** Maria Sklodowska Curie, Scientist

Date	F	VF	XF	Unc	BU
1979 Proof		Value: 175			

Y# 111 2000 ZLOTYCH
8.0000 g., 0.9000 Gold .2315 oz. AGW **Series:** Winter Olympics **Obv:** Similar to Y#107 **Rev:** Ski jumper

Date	F	VF	XF	Unc	BU
1980 Proof		Value: 175			

Y# 116 2000 ZLOTYCH
8.0000 g., 0.9000 Gold .2315 oz. AGW **Rev:** King Boleslaw I Chrobry

Date	F	VF	XF	Unc	BU
1980 Proof		Value: 175			

Y# 119 2000 ZLOTYCH
8.0000 g., 0.9000 Gold .2315 oz. AGW **Rev:** Kazimierz I

Date	F	VF	XF	Unc	BU
1980 Proof		Value: 180			

Y# 131 2000 ZLOTYCH
8.0000 g., 0.9000 Gold .2315 oz. AGW **Rev:** Wladyslaw I Herman **Note:** Similar to 200 Zlotych, Y#129.

Date	F	VF	XF	Unc	BU
1981 Proof		Value: 180			

Y# 135 2000 ZLOTYCH
8.0000 g., 0.9000 Gold .2315 oz. AGW **Rev:** Boleslaw II

Date	F	VF	XF	Unc	BU
1981 Proof		Value: 180			

Y# 139 2000 ZLOTYCH
6.8000 g., 0.9000 Gold .1968 oz. AGW **Subject:** Visit of Pope John Paul II

Date	F	VF	XF	Unc	BU
1982-1986	—	—	—	750	—

Y# 169   2000 ZLOTYCH
7.7700 g., 0.9990 Gold .2500 oz. AGW   **Subject:** Papal Visit in America **Note:** Similar to KM#163.

Date	F	VF	XF	Unc	BU
1987 Proof		Value: 400			

Y# 175   2000 ZLOTYCH
7.7700 g., 0.9990 Gold .2500 oz. AGW   **Subject:** 10th Anniversary of Pope John Paul II **Note:** Similar to KM#177.

Date	F	VF	XF	Unc	BU
1988 Proof		Value: 220			

Y# 187   2000 ZLOTYCH
7.7700 g., 0.9990 Gold .2500 oz. AGW   **Obv:** Similar to Y#175 **Rev:** Similar to 200,000 Zlotych, Y#190 **Note:** Pope John Paul II.

Date	F	VF	XF	Unc	BU
1989	—	—	—	220	—

Y# 170   5000 ZLOTYCH
15.5500 g., 0.9990 Gold .5000 oz. AGW   **Subject:** Papal Visit in America **Note:** Similar to KM#163.

Date	F	VF	XF	Unc	BU
1987 Proof		Value: 650			

Y# 176   5000 ZLOTYCH
15.5500 g., 0.9990 Gold .5000 oz. AGW   **Subject:** 10th Anniversary of Pope John Paul II **Note:** Similar to KM#177.

Date	F	VF	XF	Unc	BU
1988 Proof		Value: 350			

Y# 188   5000 ZLOTYCH
15.5500 g., 0.9990 Gold .5000 oz. AGW   **Obv:** Similar to Y#176 **Rev:** Similar to 200,000 Zlotych, Y#190 **Note:** Pope John Paul II.

Date	F	VF	XF	Unc	BU
1989	—	—	—	345	—

Y# 191   5000 ZLOTYCH
16.5000 g., 0.7500 Silver .3978 oz. ASW   **Rev:** Torun - Kopernik

Date	F	VF	XF	Unc	BU
1989 Proof		Value: 30.00			

Y# 192   5000 ZLOTYCH
16.5000 g., 0.7500 Silver .3978 oz. ASW   **Rev:** Torunia Town Hall

Date	F	VF	XF	Unc	BU
1989 Proof		Value: 30.00			

Y# 193   5000 ZLOTYCH
16.5000 g., 0.7500 Silver .3978 oz. ASW   **Rev:** Henryk Sucharski

Date	F	VF	XF	Unc	BU
1989 Proof		Value: 27.50			

Y# 197   5000 ZLOTYCH
16.5000 g., 0.7500 Silver .3978 oz. ASW   **Rev:** Bust of King Wladyslaw II

Date	F	VF	XF	Unc	BU
1989 Proof		Value: 65.00			

Y# 198   5000 ZLOTYCH
16.5000 g., 0.7500 Silver .3978 oz. ASW   **Rev:** Half-length portrait of King Wladyslaw II

Date	F	VF	XF	Unc	BU
1989 Proof		Value: 300			

Y# 140   10000 ZLOTYCH
34.5000 g., 0.9000 Gold .9984 oz. AGW   **Subject:** Visit of Pope John Paul II

Date	F	VF	XF	Unc	BU
1982	—	—	—	1,750	—

Y# 399   10000 ZLOTYCH
28.3100 g., 0.9000 Silver .8192 oz. ASW, 40.2 mm.   **Subject:** Pope John Paul II **Obv:** Eagle **Rev:** Bust of Pope John Paul II left **Edge:** Plain

Date	F	VF	XF	Unc	BL
1986 Proof		Value: 1,900			

Y# 164   10000 ZLOTYCH
19.0600 g., 0.7500 Silver .4582 oz. ASW **Subject:** Papal Visit

Date	F	VF	XF	Unc	BU
1987	—	—	—	25.00	—

Y# 171   10000 ZLOTYCH
31.1030 g., 0.9990 Gold 1.0000 oz. AGW **Subject:** Papal Visit in America **Note:** Similar to KM#163.

Date	F	VF	XF	Unc	BU
1987 Proof	Value: 1,150				

Y# 177   10000 ZLOTYCH
31.1030 g., 0.9990 Gold 1.0000 oz. AGW **Subject:** 10th Anniversary of Pope John Paul II

Date	F	VF	XF	Unc	BU
1988	—	—	—	675	—

Y# 177a   10000 ZLOTYCH
31.1030 g., 0.9990 Silver 1.0000 oz. ASW **Subject:** 10th Anniversary of Pope John Paul II

Date	F	VF	XF	Unc	BU
1988	—	—	—	45.00	—

Y# 237   10000 ZLOTYCH
31.1000 g., 0.9990 Silver 1.0000 oz. ASW **Rev:** Pope John Paul II

Date	F	VF	XF	Unc	BU
1989 Proof	Value: 40.00				

Y# 179   10000 ZLOTYCH
31.1030 g., 0.9990 Silver 1.0000 oz. ASW **Subject:** Pope John Paul - Christmas

Date	F	VF	XF	Unc	BU
1988 Proof	Value: 55.00				

Y# 223   20000 ZLOTYCH
19.0000 g., 0.7500 Silver .4558 oz. ASW **Rev:** Soccer ball, map, and globe

Date	F	VF	XF	Unc	BU
1989 Proof	Value: 35.00				

Y# 224   20000 ZLOTYCH
19.0000 g., 0.7500 Silver .4558 oz. ASW **Rev:** Soccer player behind vertical lines

Date	F	VF	XF	Unc	BU
1989 Proof	Value: 35.00				

Y# 189   10000 ZLOTYCH
31.1030 g., 0.9990 Gold 1.0000 oz. AGW **Rev:** Pope John Paul II

Date	F	VF	XF	Unc	BU
1989 Proof	Value: 675				

Y# 189a   10000 ZLOTYCH
31.1000 g., 0.9990 Silver 1.0000 oz. ASW **Rev:** Pope John Paul II

Date	F	VF	XF	Unc	BU
1989	—	—	—	40.00	—

Y# 180   50000 ZLOTYCH
19.3000 g., 0.7500 Silver .4654 oz. ASW **Subject:** 70 Years of Polish Independence

Date	F	VF	XF	Unc	BU
1988	—	—	—	10.00	—

Y# 163   200000 ZLOTYCH
373.2420 g., 0.9990 Gold 12.0000 oz. AGW, 70 mm. **Subject:**
Papal Visit in America **Note:** Illustration reduced.

Date	F	VF	XF	Unc	BU
1987 Proof		Value: 8,500			

Y# 178   200000 ZLOTYCH
373.2420 g., 0.9990 Gold 12.0000 oz. AGW, 70 mm. **Subject:**
10th Anniversary of Pope John Paul II **Note:** Illustration reduced.

Date	F	VF	XF	Unc	BU
1988 Proof		Value: 8,250			

Y# 190   200000 ZLOTYCH
373.2420 g., 0.9990 Gold 12.0000 oz. AGW **Rev:** Pope John
Paul II **Note:** Similar to KM#189.

Date	F	VF	XF	Unc	BU
1989 Proof		Value: 8,250			

REPUBLIC
Democratic

STANDARD COINAGE

Y# 216   50 ZLOTYCH

Date	F	VF	XF	Unc	BU
1990	—	—	—	1.25	2.00

Y# 214   100 ZLOTYCH

Date	F	VF	XF	Unc	BU
1990	—	—	—	2.00	3.00

Y# 195   10000 ZLOTYCH
Copper-Nickel **Subject:** 10th Anniversary of Solidarity

Date	F	VF	XF	Unc	BU
1990	—	—	—	4.50	6.00

Y# 217   10000 ZLOTYCH
Nickel Plated Steel **Subject:** 200th Anniversary of Polish Constitution

Date	F	VF	XF	Unc	BU
1991	—	—	—	6.00	—

Y# 246   10000 ZLOTYCH
Copper-Nickel **Rev:** Wladyslaw III

Date	F	VF	XF	Unc	BU
1992	—	—	—	3.50	—

Y# 219   20000 ZLOTYCH
3.1100 g., 0.9990 Gold .1 oz. AGW **Subject:** 10th Anniversary
of Solidarity **Note:** Similar to 10000 Zlotych, Y#195.

Date	F	VF	XF	Unc	BU
1990 Proof		Value: 125			

Y# 215   20000 ZLOTYCH
Copper-Nickel center in Brass ring **Subject:** 225th Anniversary of
Warsaw Mint **Rev:** Crowned monogram of Stanislow August
Poniatowski, mint founder

Date	F	VF	XF	Unc	BU
1991	—	—	—	18.00	—

Y# 243   20000 ZLOTYCH
Copper-Nickel   **Rev:** Barn swallows

Date	F	VF	XF	Unc	BU
1993	—	—	—	7.50	—

Y# 265   20000 ZLOTYCH
Copper-Nickel   **Subject:** 75th Anniversary - Disabled Association

Date	F	VF	XF	Unc	BU
1994	—	—	—	4.50	—

Y# 244   20000 ZLOTYCH
Copper-Nickel   **Rev:** Lancut Castle

Date	F	VF	XF	Unc	BU
1993	—	—	—	4.50	—

Y# 270   20000 ZLOTYCH
Copper-Nickel   **Rev:** New mint building

Date	F	VF	XF	Unc	BU
1994	—	—	—	4.50	—

Y# 256   20000 ZLOTYCH
Copper-Nickel   **Rev:** Kazimierz IV

Date	F	VF	XF	Unc	BU
1993	—	—	—	4.50	—

Y# 271   20000 ZLOTYCH
Copper-Nickel   **Subject:** 200th Anniversary - Kosciuszko Insurrection

Date	F	VF	XF	Unc	BU
1994	—	—	—	5.00	—

Y# 261   20000 ZLOTYCH
Copper-Nickel   **Series:** Olympics **Rev:** Slalom skier

Date	F	VF	XF	Unc	BU
1993	—	—	—	7.50	—

Y# 272   20000 ZLOTYCH
Copper-Nickel   **Rev:** Zygmunt I, 1506-1548

Date	F	VF	XF	Unc	BU
1994	—	—	—	4.50	—

Y# 220   50000 ZLOTYCH
13.1000 g., 0.9990 Gold .4212 oz. AGW   **Subject:** 10th
Anniversary of Solidarity **Note:** Similar to 10000 Zlotych, Y#195.

Date	F	VF	XF	Unc	BU
1990 Proof		Value: 300			

Y# 229 50000 ZLOTYCH
Copper-Nickel **Subject:** 200th Anniversary of Order Virtuti Militari
Shape: Octagonal

Date	F	VF	XF	Unc	BU
1992 Proof		Value: 12.50			

Y# 196.1 100000 ZLOTYCH
31.1000 g., 0.9990 Silver 1.0000 oz. ASW **Subject:** 10th
Anniversary of Solidarity

Date	F	VF	XF	Unc	BU
1990	—	—	—	18.00	22.00

Y# 196.2 100000 ZLOTYCH
31.1000 g., 0.9990 Silver 1.0000 oz. ASW, 31.9 mm. **Subject:**
10th Anniversary of Solidarity **Note:** Reduced size.

Date	F	VF	XF	Unc	BU
1990 Proof		Value: 60.00			

Y# 199 100000 ZLOTYCH
31.1000 g., 0.9990 Silver 1.0000 oz. ASW **Rev:** Fryderyk Chopin

Date	F	VF	XF	Unc	BU
1990 Proof		Value: 35.00			

Y# 200 100000 ZLOTYCH
31.1000 g., 0.9990 Silver 1.0000 oz. ASW **Rev:** Tadeusz Kosciuszko

Date	F	VF	XF	Unc	BU
1990 Proof		Value: 35.00			

Y# 201 100000 ZLOTYCH
31.1000 g., 0.9990 Silver 1.0000 oz. ASW **Rev:** Marszalek Pilsudski

Date	F	VF	XF	Unc	BU
1990 Proof		Value: 35.00			

Y# 221 100000 ZLOTYCH
15.5500 g., 0.9990 Gold .5000 oz. AGW **Subject:** 10th
Anniversary of Solidarity **Note:** Similar to 10000 Zlotych, Y#195

Date	F	VF	XF	Unc	BU
1990 Proof		Value: 350			

Poland

Y# 235 100000 ZLOTYCH
16.5000 g., 0.7500 Silver .3979 oz. ASW **Series:** WWII **Rev:**
Major Henrik Dobrzanski - Hubal - Cavalry

Date	F	VF	XF	Unc	BU
1991 Proof			Value: 27.50		

Y# 236 100000 ZLOTYCH
16.5000 g., 0.7500 Silver .3979 oz. ASW **Series:** WWII **Subject:**
Defense of Narvik **Rev:** Polish troops

Date	F	VF	XF	Unc	BU
1991 Proof			Value: 27.50		

Y# 238 100000 ZLOTYCH
16.5000 g., 0.7500 Silver .3979 oz. ASW **Series:** WWII **Rev:**
Polish troops at Battle of Tobruk

Date	F	VF	XF	Unc	BU
1991 Proof			Value: 27.50		

Y# 239 100000 ZLOTYCH
16.5000 g., 0.7500 Silver .3979 oz. ASW **Series:** WWII **Rev:**
Polish pilots in Battle of Britain

Date	F	VF	XF	Unc	BU
1991 Proof			Value: 27.50		

Y# 227 100000 ZLOTYCH
16.5000 g., 0.7500 Silver .3979 oz. ASW **Subject:** Unification of
Upper Silesia and Poland

Date	F	VF	XF	Unc	BU
1992 Proof			Value: 27.50		

Y# 268 100000 ZLOTYCH
16.5000 g., 0.9000 Silver .4775 oz. ASW **Subject:** Warsaw Uprising

Date	F	VF	XF	Unc	BU
1994 Proof			Value: 32.50		

Y# 202 200000 ZLOTYCH
155.5000 g., 0.9990 Silver 5.0000 oz. ASW **Rev:** Fryderyk
Chopin **Note:** Similar to 100,000 Zlotych, Y#199.

Date	F	VF	XF	Unc	BU
1990 Proof			Value: 175		

Y# 203 200000 ZLOTYCH
155.5000 g., 0.9990 Silver 5.0000 oz. ASW **Rev:** Tadeusz
Kosciuszko **Note:** Similar to 100,000 Zlotych, Y#200.

Date	F	VF	XF	Unc	BU
1990 Proof			Value: 175		

Y# 204 200000 ZLOTYCH
155.5000 g., 0.9990 Silver 5.0000 oz. ASW **Rev:** Marszalck
Pilsudski **Note:** Similar to 100,000 Zlotych, Y#201.

Date	F	VF	XF	Unc	BU
1990 Proof			Value: 175		

Y# 205 200000 ZLOTYCH
31.1000 g., 0.9990 Gold 1.0000 oz. AGW **Rev:** Fryderyk Chopin

Date	F	VF	XF	Unc	BU
1990 Proof			Value: 675		

Y# 206 200000 ZLOTYCH
31.1000 g., 0.9990 Gold 1.0000 oz. AGW **Rev:** Tadeusz Kosciuszko

Date	F	VF	XF	Unc	BU
1990 Proof			Value: 675		

Y# 207 200000 ZLOTYCH
31.1000 g., 0.9990 Gold 1.0000 oz. AGW **Rev:** Marszalck Pilsudski

Date	F	VF	XF	Unc	BU
1990 Proof			Value: 675		

Y# 222 200000 ZLOTYCH
31.1000 g., 0.9990 Gold 1.0000 oz. AGW **Subject:** Solidarity
Rev: Solidarity monument with city view background

Date	F	VF	XF	Unc	BU
1990 Proof			Value: 750		

Y# 240   200000 ZLOTYCH
19.0600 g., 0.9990 Silver .6122 oz. ASW **Rev:** General Dyw.
Stefan Rowecki "Grot"

Date	F	VF	XF	Unc	BU
1990-1991 Proof		Value: 45.00			

Y# 250   200000 ZLOTYCH
19.2650 g., 0.9990 Silver .6188 oz. ASW **Rev:** General Komorowski

Date	F	VF	XF	Unc	BU
1990 Proof		Value: 27.50			

Y# 228   200000 ZLOTYCH
31.1000 g., 0.9250 Silver .9250 oz. ASW **Series:** Barcelona
Olympics **Rev:** Weight lifter

Date	F	VF	XF	Unc	BU
1991 Proof		Value: 28.50			

Y# 218   200000 ZLOTYCH
38.9000 g., 0.9990 Silver 1.2496 oz. ASW **Subject:** 200th
Anniversary of Polish Constitution

Date	F	VF	XF	Unc	BU
1991	—	—	—	22.50	—

Y# 241   200000 ZLOTYCH
31.1600 g., 0.9250 Silver .9267 oz. ASW **Series:** Barcelona
Olympics **Rev:** Two sailboats

Date	F	VF	XF	Unc	BU
1991 Proof		Value: 37.50			

Y# 242   200000 ZLOTYCH
19.3300 g., 0.7500 Silver .4661 oz. ASW **Subject:** 70th
Anniversary of Poznan Fair

Date	F	VF	XF	Unc	BU
1991 Proof		Value: 27.50			

Y# 226   200000 ZLOTYCH
31.1000 g., 0.9250 Silver .9250 oz. ASW **Series:** Albertville
Olympics **Rev:** Slalom skier

Date	F	VF	XF	Unc	BU
1991 Proof		Value: 28.50			

Poland

Y# 251   200000 ZLOTYCH
19.3300 g., 0.7500 Silver .4661 oz. ASW   **Rev:** General Okulicki

Date	F	VF	XF	Unc	BU
1991 Proof		Value: 27.50			

Y# 252   200000 ZLOTYCH
19.3300 g., 0.7500 Silver .4661 oz. ASW   **Rev:** General
Tokarzewski - Karaszewicz

Date	F	VF	XF	Unc	BU
1991 Proof		Value: 27.50			

Y# 230   200000 ZLOTYCH
31.1000 g., 0.9990 Silver 1.0000 oz. ASW   **Subject:** Discovery
of America **Rev:** Portrait and ship

Date	F	VF	XF	Unc	BU
1992 Proof		Value: 40.00			

Y# 231   200000 ZLOTYCH
31.1000 g., 0.9990 Silver 1.0000 oz. ASW   **Subject:** Seville Expo '92

Date	F	VF	XF	Unc	BU
1992 Proof		Value: 28.00			

Y# 232   200000 ZLOTYCH
16.5000 g., 0.7500 Silver .3979 oz. ASW   **Series:** WWII **Rev:**
Polish protection of WWII sea convoys

Date	F	VF	XF	Unc	BU
1992 Proof		Value: 27.50			

Y# 233   200000 ZLOTYCH
16.5000 g., 0.7500 Silver .3979 oz. ASW   **Rev:** Stanislaw Staszic

Date	F	VF	XF	Unc	BU
1992 Proof		Value: 27.50			

Y# 253   200000 ZLOTYCH
16.5000 g., 0.7500 Silver .3979 oz. ASW   **Rev:** Full bust Wladyslaw III

Date	F	VF	XF	Unc	BU
1992 Proof		Value: 27.50			

Y# 254   200000 ZLOTYCH
16.5000 g., 0.7500 Silver .3979 oz. ASW   **Rev:** Half bust
Wladyslaw III

Date	F	VF	XF	Unc	BU
1992 Proof		Value: 30.00			

Y# 255   200000 ZLOTYCH
16.5000 g., 0.7500 Silver .3979 oz. ASW **Subject:** 750th
Anniversary - City of Stettin

Date	F	VF	XF	Unc	BU
1993 Proof		Value: 25.00			

Y# 262   200000 ZLOTYCH
16.5000 g., 0.7500 Silver .3979 oz. ASW **Series:** WWII **Rev:**
Battle of Monte Cassino

Date	F	VF	XF	Unc	BU
1994 Proof		Value: 37.50			

Y# 257   200000 ZLOTYCH
16.5000 g., 0.7500 Silver .3979 oz. ASW **Rev:** Kazimierz IV

Date	F	VF	XF	Unc	BU
1993 Proof		Value: 25.00			

Y# 266   200000 ZLOTYCH
16.5000 g., 0.7500 Silver .3979 oz. ASW **Subject:** 75th
Anniversary - Disabled Association

Date	F	VF	XF	Unc	BU
1994 Proof		Value: 27.50			

Y# 258   200000 ZLOTYCH
16.5000 g., 0.7500 Silver .3979 oz. ASW **Rev:** Enthroned
Kazimierz IV

Date	F	VF	XF	Unc	BU
1993 Proof		Value: 55.00			

Y# 273   200000 ZLOTYCH
16.5000 g., 0.7500 Silver .3979 oz. ASW **Rev:** Sigismund I, 1506-48

Date	F	VF	XF	Unc	BU
1994 Proof		Value: 27.50			

Y# 259   200000 ZLOTYCH
16.5000 g., 0.7500 Silver .3979 oz. ASW **Series:** WWII **Rev:**
Polish partisans sabotaging railways

Date	F	VF	XF	Unc	BU
1993 Proof		Value: 27.50			

Y# 274   200000 ZLOTYCH
16.5000 g., 0.7500 Silver .3979 oz. ASW **Rev:** Half-length portrait
of Sigismund I

Date	F	VF	XF	Unc	BU
1994 Proof		Value: 55.00			

Y# 275   200000 ZLOTYCH
16.5000 g., 0.7500 Silver .3979 oz. ASW   **Subject:** 200th
Anniversary - Kosciuszko Insurrection

Date	F	VF	XF	Unc	BU
1994 Proof		Value: 32.50			

Y# 245   300000 ZLOTYCH
31.1600 g., 0.9250 Silver .9267 oz. ASW   **Subject:** 50th
Anniversary of Warsaw Ghetto Uprising

Date	F	VF	XF	Unc	BU
1993 Proof		Value: 37.50			

Y# 247   300000 ZLOTYCH
31.1600 g., 0.9250 Silver .9267 oz. ASW   **Series:** 1994 Olympics
Rev: Lillehammer

Date	F	VF	XF	Unc	BU
1993 Proof		Value: 27.50			

Y# 248   300000 ZLOTYCH
31.1450 g., 0.9990 Silver 1.0004 oz. ASW   **Rev:** Barn swallow
feeding young

Date	F	VF	XF	Unc	BU
1993 Proof		Value: 45.00			

Y# 249   300000 ZLOTYCH
31.1450 g., 0.9990 Silver 1.0004 oz. ASW   **Rev:** Lancut Castle

Date	F	VF	XF	Unc	BU
1993 Proof		Value: 37.50			

Y# 260   300000 ZLOTYCH
31.1000 g., 0.9990 Silver .9990 oz. ASW   **Rev:** Aerial view of Zamosc

Date	F	VF	XF	Unc	BU
1993 Proof		Value: 32.50			

Y# 263   300000 ZLOTYCH
31.1600 g., 0.9250 Silver .9267 oz. ASW **Rev:** St. Maksymilian Kolbe

Date	F	VF	XF	Unc	BU
1994 Proof		Value: 37.50			

Y# 264   300000 ZLOTYCH
31.1000 g., 0.9250 Silver .9250 oz. ASW **Subject:** 70th
Anniversary - Polish National Bank **Shape:** 7-sided

Date	F	VF	XF	Unc	BU
1994 Proof		Value: 45.00			

Y# 269   300000 ZLOTYCH
31.1035 g., 0.9990 Silver 1.0000 oz. ASW **Subject:** Warsaw
Uprising

Date	F	VF	XF	Unc	BU
1994 Proof		Value: 35.00			

Y# 208   500000 ZLOTYCH
62.2000 g., 0.9990 Gold 2.0000 oz. AGW **Rev:** Fryderyk Chopin
Note: Similar to 100,000 Zlotych, Y#199.

Date	F	VF	XF	Unc	BU
1990 Proof		Value: 1,400			

Y# 209   500000 ZLOTYCH
62.2000 g., 0.9990 Gold 2.0000 oz. AGW **Rev:** Tadeusz
Kosciuszko **Note:** Similar to 100,000 Zlotych, Y#200.

Date	F	VF	XF	Unc	BU
1990 Proof		Value: 1,400			

Y# 210   500000 ZLOTYCH
62.2000 g., 0.9990 Gold 2.0000 oz. AGW **Rev:** Marszalek
Pilsudski **Note:** Similar to 100,000 Zlotych, Y#201.

Date	F	VF	XF	Unc	BU
1990 Proof		Value: 1,400			

Y# 211   1000000 ZLOTYCH
373.2000 g., 0.9990 Gold 12.0000 oz. AGW **Rev:** Fryderyk
Chopin **Note:** Similar to 100,000 Zlotych, Y#199.

Date	F	VF	XF	Unc	BU
1990 Proof		Value: 8,250			

Y# 212   1000000 ZLOTYCH
373.2000 g., 0.9990 Gold 12.0000 oz. AGW **Rev:** Tadeusz
Kosciuszko **Note:** Similar to 100,000 Zlotych, Y#200.

Date	F	VF	XF	Unc	BU
1990 Proof		Value: 8,250			

Y# 213   1000000 ZLOTYCH
373.2000 g., 0.9990 Gold 12.0000 oz. AGW **Rev:** Marszalek
Pilsudski **Note:** Similar to 100,000 Zlotych, Y#201.

Date	F	VF	XF	Unc	BU
1990 Proof		Value: 8,250			

REFORM COINAGE

100 Old Zlotych = 1 Grosz; 10,000 Old Zlotych = 1 Zloty

As far back as 1990, production was initiated for the new
1 Grosz - 1 Zlotych coins for a forthcoming monetary reform. It
wasn't announced until the Act of July 7, 1994 and was
enacted on January 1, 1995.

Y# 276   GROSZ
Brass

Date	F	VF	XF	Unc	BU
1990-2005	—	—	—	0.10	0.20

Y# 277   2 GROSZE
Brass

Date	F	VF	XF	Unc	BU
1990-2005	—	—	—	0.15	0.25

Y# 278   5 GROSZY
Brass

Date	F	VF	XF	Unc	BU
1990-2005	—	—	—	0.25	0.45

Y# 279   10 GROSZY
Copper-Nickel

Date	F	VF	XF	Unc	BU
1990-2005	—	—	—	0.40	0.60

Y# 280   20 GROSZY
Copper-Nickel

Date	F	VF	XF	Unc	BU
1990-2005	—	—	—	0.65	0.85

Y# 281   50 GROSZY
Copper-Nickel

Date	F	VF	XF	Unc	BU
1990-1995	—	—	—	1.00	1.25

Y# 282   ZLOTY
Copper-Nickel

Date	F	VF	XF	Unc	BU
1990-1995	—	—	—	1.75	2.00

Y# 283   2 ZLOTE
Bi-Metallic Copper-Nickel center in Brass ring

Date	F	VF	XF	Unc	BU
1994-2005	—	—	—	4.00	4.50

Y# 285   2 ZLOTE
Copper-Nickel **Subject:** 55th Anniversary - Katyn Forest Massacre

Date	F	VF	XF	Unc	BU
1995	—	—	—	3.50	

Y# 289   2 ZLOTE
Copper-Nickel **Rev:** European catfish

Date	F	VF	XF	Unc	BU
1995	—	—	—	12.00	—

Y# 297   2 ZLOTE
Copper-Nickel **Subject:** 75th Anniversary - Battle of Warsaw

Date	F	VF	XF	Unc	BU
1995	—	—	—	3.50	—

Y# 300   2 ZLOTE
Copper-Nickel **Series:** 1996 Olympic Games **Rev:** Centennial

Date	F	VF	XF	Unc	BU
1995	—	—	—	3.50	—

Y# 313   2 ZLOTE
Copper-Aluminum-Zinc-Tin **Rev:** Ligzbark Warminski Castle, with Bishop's arms

Date	F	VF	XF	Unc	BU
1996	—	—	—	3.00	—

Y# 303   2 ZLOTE
Copper-Nickel **Series:** 1996 Olympics - Atlanta **Rev:** Wrestling

Date	F	VF	XF	Unc	BU
1995	—	—	—	3.50	—

Y# 315   2 ZLOTE
Copper-Aluminum-Zinc-Tin   **Rev:** Henryk Sienkiewicz

Date	F	VF	XF	Unc	BU
1996	—	—	—	3.00	—

Y# 310   2 ZLOTE
Copper-Nickel **Series:** 1996 Olympics - Atlanta **Rev:** Lazienki Royal Palace

Date	F	VF	XF	Unc	BU
1995	—	—	—	3.75	—

Y# 325   2 ZLOTE
Brass **Obv:** Polish eagle **Rev:** Stefan Batory

Date	F	VF	XF	Unc	BU
1997	—	—	—	3.50	—

Y# 306   2 ZLOTE
Brass **Rev:** Bust of Zygmunt II

Date	F	VF	XF	Unc	BU
1996	—	—	—	10.00	—

Y# 329   2 ZLOTE
Brass **Obv:** Polish eagle **Rev:** Stag beetle **Note:** Jelenek Rogacz - Lucanus cervus.

Date	F	VF	XF	Unc	BU
1997	—	—	—	10.00	—

Y# 311   2 ZLOTE
Copper-Zinc-Tin   **Rev:** Hedgehog with young

Date	F	VF	XF	Unc	BU
1996	—	—	—	15.00	—

Y# 331   2 ZLOTE
Brass **Obv:** Polish eagle **Rev:** Zamek W Pieskowej Skale

Date	F	VF	XF	Unc	BU
1997	—	—	—	3.00	—

Y# 333   2 ZLOTE
Copper-Aluminum-Zinc-Tin   **Obv:** Polish eagle **Rev:** Pawel
Edmund Strzelecki

Date	F	VF	XF	Unc	BU
1997	—	—	—	5.00	—

Y# 344   2 ZLOTE
Brass   **Subject:** Discovery of Radium and Polomium **Obv:** Polish
eagle

Date	F	VF	XF	Unc	BU
1998	—	—	—	3.00	—

Y# 335   2 ZLOTE
Brass   **Series:** Nagano Olympics **Obv:** Polish eagle **Rev:** Snow
boarder

Date	F	VF	XF	Unc	BU
1998	—	—	—	3.00	—

Y# 347   2 ZLOTE
Brass   **Obv:** Polish eagle **Rev:** Zamek W. Korniku - Palace

Date	F	VF	XF	Unc	BU
1998	—	—	—	3.50	—

Y# 336   2 ZLOTE
Brass   **Obv:** Polish eagle **Rev:** Sigismund III (1587-1632)

Date	F	VF	XF	Unc	BU
1998	—	—	—	3.00	—

Y# 349   2 ZLOTE
Brass   **Subject:** 80th Anniversary - Polish Independence **Obv:**
Polish eagle **Rev:** 1918 on flaming map

Date	F	VF	XF	Unc	BU
1998	—	—	—	3.00	—

Y# 340   2 ZLOTE
Brass   **Obv:** Polish eagle **Rev:** Popucha Paskowka - Toad (bufo
calamita)

Date	F	VF	XF	Unc	BU
1998	—	—	—	12.00	—

Y# 352   2 ZLOTE
Brass   **Subject:** 200th Birthday - Adam Mickiewicz **Obv:** Polish
eagle **Rev:** Portrait, dates

Date	F	VF	XF	Unc	BU
1998	—	—	—	3.00	—

Poland

Y# 355 2 ZLOTE
Brass **Obv:** Polish eagle **Rev:** Gray wolves and cubs **Edge Lettering:** POLSKI NARODOWY BANK

Date	F	VF	XF	Unc	BU
1999	—	—	—	14.00	—

Y# 363 2 ZLOTE
Brass **Obv:** Polish eagle **Rev:** Portraits of Laski and Erasmus **Edge Lettering:** NARODOWY BANK POLSKI

Date	F	VF	XF	Unc	BU
1999	—	—	—	3.00	—

Y# 356 2 ZLOTE
Brass **Obv:** Polish eagle **Rev:** Portrait Juliusz Slowacki, dates

Date	F	VF	XF	Unc	BU
1999	—	—	—	3.00	—

Y# 365 2 ZLOTE
Brass **Obv:** Polish eagle **Rev:** Fryderyk Chopin with stylized piano and music score

Date	F	VF	XF	Unc	BU
1999	—	—	—	3.00	—

Y# 357 2 ZLOTE
Brass **Subject:** Poland's Accession to NATO **Obv:** Polish eagle **Rev:** NATO globe, soldiers rapelling from helicopter **Edge Lettering:** NARODOWY BANK POLSKI

Date	F	VF	XF	Unc	BU
1999	—	—	—	3.00	—

Y# 368 2 ZLOTE
Brass **Obv:** Polish eagle **Rev:** Portrait of Wladyslaw IV **Edge Lettering:** NARODOWY BANK POLSKI

Date	F	VF	XF	Unc	BU
1999	—	—	—	3.00	—

Y# 358 2 ZLOTE
Brass **Obv:** Polish eagle **Rev:** Portrait of Ernest Malinowsky above slanted text

Date	F	VF	XF	Unc	BU
1999	—	—	—	3.00	—

Y# 372 2 ZLOTE
Brass **Obv:** Polish eagle **Rev:** Palace behind Potlocki family arms

Date	F	VF	XF	Unc	BU
1999	—	—	—	3.50	—

Y# 374   2 ZLOTE

8.3100 g., Bi-Metallic Copper-Nickel center in Brass ring **Subject:** Millennium **Obv:** Crowned eagle in center **Rev:** Latent image dates in center **Edge Lettering:** NARODOWY BANK POLSKI

Date	F	VF	XF	Unc	BU
2000	—	—	—	3.00	—

Y# 376   2 ZLOTE

8.1500 g., Brass **Subject:** Holy Year **Obv:** Polish eagle **Rev:** Cross with holy symbolic animals

Date	F	VF	XF	Unc	BU
2000	—	—	—	5.00	—

Y# 377   2 ZLOTE

8.1500 g., Brass **Subject:** 1000th Anniversary - Gniezno Convention **Rev:** Denar coin design of Boleslaw Chrobry

Date	F	VF	XF	Unc	BU
2000	—	—	—	5.00	—

Y# 388   2 ZLOTE

8.1400 g., Brass, 26.8 mm. **Subject:** "Dudek-Upupa epops" **Obv:** Polish eagle **Rev:** Long-billed Hoopoe **Edge Lettering:** NARODOWY BANK POLSKI

Date	F	VF	XF	Unc	BU
2000	—	—	—	4.00	6.00

Y# 389   2 ZLOTE

8.1400 g., Brass **Subject:** 1000th Anniversary - Wroclawia (Breslau) **Obv:** Polish eagle **Rev:** Jesus with city view in background

Date	F	VF	XF	Unc	BU
2000	—	—	—	3.00	—

Y# 390   2 ZLOTE

8.1400 g., Brass   **Rev:** Wilanowie Palace

Date	F	VF	XF	Unc	BU
2000	—	—	—	3.00	—

Y# 394   2 ZLOTE

8.2200 g., Brass **Subject:** Solidarity **Rev:** Solidarity logo, map, children **Edge Lettering:** NARODOWY BANK POLSKI

Date	F	VF	XF	Unc	BU
2000	—	—	—	3.00	—

Y# 398   2 ZLOTE

8.2200 g., Brass **Obv:** Crowned eagle **Rev:** Bust Jan II Kazimierz facing **Edge Lettering:** POLSKA NARODOWY BANK **Note:** Jan II Kazimierz - 1648-68.

Date	F	VF	XF	Unc	BU
2000	—	—	—	3.00	—

Y# 404   2 ZLOTE

8.1500 g., Brass, 26.7 mm. **Subject:** Workers revolt in December 1970 **Obv:** Crowned eagle **Rev:** Fist **Edge:** "NBP" repeatedly

Date	F	VF	XF	Unc	BU
2000	—	—	—	3.00	—

Poland

Y# 408   2 ZLOTE

8.1500 g., Brass   **Subject:** Wieliczka Salt Mine **Obv:** Crowned eagle **Rev:** Ancient salt miners

Date	F	VF	XF	Unc	BU
2001	—	—	—	3.00	—

Y# 418   2 ZLOTE

8.1500 g., Brass, 27 mm.   **Subject:** Cardinal Stefan Wyszynski **Obv:** Polish eagle **Rev:** Cardinal wearing mitre **Edge:** "NBP" eight times

Date	F	VF	XF	Unc	BU
2001	—	—	—	3.00	—

Y# 410   2 ZLOTE

8.1500 g., Brass   **Subject:** Amber Route **Obv:** Crowned eagle **Rev:** Ancient Roman coin and map with route marked in stars

Date	F	VF	XF	Unc	BU
2001	—	—	—	3.00	—

Y# 421   2 ZLOTE

8.1000 g., Brass, 26.8 mm.   **Subject:** Michal Siedlecki **Obv:** Eagle **Rev:** Portrait and art work **Edge:** "NBP" eight times

Date	F	VF	XF	Unc	BU
2001	—	—	—	3.00	—

Y# 412   2 ZLOTE

8.1500 g., Brass, 27 mm.   **Subject:** 15 Years of the Constitutional Court **Obv:** Crowned eagle **Rev:** Crowned eagle head and scale **Edge:** "*NBP*" eight times

Date	F	VF	XF	Unc	BU
2001	—	—	—	3.00	—

Y# 422   2 ZLOTE

Brass   **Subject:** Koledicy **Obv:** Eagle **Rev:** Christmas celebration scene

Date	F	VF	XF	Unc	BU
2001	—	—	—	3.00	—

Y# 423   2 ZLOTE

8.1500 g., Brass, 26.8 mm.   **Subject:** Jan III Sobieski **Obv:** Polish eagle **Rev:** Half bust of Sobieski facing **Edge Lettering:** *NBP* repeated

Date	F	VF	XF	Unc	BU
2001	—	—	—	3.00	—

Y# 414   2 ZLOTE

8.1500 g., Brass, 27 mm.   **Obv:** Crowned eagle **Rev:** Flying Swallowtail butterfly **Edge:** "*NBP*" eight times

Date	F	VF	XF	Unc	BU
2001	—	—	—	6.00	—

Y# 426   2 ZLOTE

8.1500 g., Brass, 26.8 mm.   **Subject:** Henryk Wieniawski **Obv:** Polish eagle **Rev:** Bust of Wieniawski facing right **Edge Lettering:** *NBP* repeated

Date	F	VF	XF	Unc	BU
2001	—	—	—	3.00	—

Y# 427 2 ZLOTE
8.1000 g., Brass, 26.7 mm. **Obv:** Crowned eagle **Rev:** Two pond
turtles **Edge:** Lettered **Edge Lettering:** "NBP" repeatedly

Date	F	VF	XF	Unc	BU
2002	—	—	—	6.00	7.50

Y# 431 2 ZLOTE
8.1500 g., Brass, 27 mm. **Subject:** Bronislaw Malinowski **Obv:**
Crowned eagle **Rev:** Portrait and Trobriand Islanders **Edge
Lettering:** "NBP" eight times

Date	F	VF	XF	Unc	BU
2002	—	—	—	3.50	—

Y# 433 2 ZLOTE
8.1500 g., Brass, 27 mm. **Subject:** World Cup Soccer **Obv:**
Crowned eagle **Rev:** Two soccer players **Edge Lettering:** "NBP"
eight times

Date	F	VF	XF	Unc	BU
2002	—	—	—	3.50	—

Y# 439 2 ZLOTE
8.1000 g., Brass, 26.8 mm. **Subject:** August II (1697-1706, 1709-
1733) **Obv:** Crowned eagle **Rev:** Portrait **Edge:** "NBP*" repeatedly

Date	F	VF	XF	Unc	BU
2002	—	—	—	3.00	—

Y# 440 2 ZLOTE
8.1300 g., Brass, 26.7 mm. **Subject:** Gen. Wladyslaw Anders
Obv: Crowned eagle **Rev:** Military portrait and cross **Edge:** "NBP"
repeated eight times

Date	F	VF	XF	Unc	BU
2002	—	—	—	3.00	—

Y# 443 2 ZLOTE
8.1500 g., Brass, 26.8 mm. **Subject:** Zamek W. Malborku **Obv:**
Crowned eagle **Rev:** Castle **Edge:** ""NBP* "repeatedly

Date	F	VF	XF	Unc	BU
2002	—	—	—	3.00	—

Y# 444 2 ZLOTE
8.1300 g., Brass, 26.8 mm. **Subject:** Jan Matejko **Obv:**
Denomination, crowned eagle and artist's palette **Rev:** Jester
behind portrait **Edge:** "NBP" repeatedly

Date	F	VF	XF	Unc	BU
2002	—	—	—	3.00	—

Y# 445 2 ZLOTE
8.1300 g., Brass, 26.8 mm. **Subject:** Eels **Obv:** Crowned eagle
Rev: Two eels **Edge:** "NBP" repeatedly

Date	F	VF	XF	Unc	BU
2003	—	—	—	5.00	—

Y# 446 2 ZLOTE
7.7500 g., Brass, 26.7 mm. **Subject:** Children **Obv:** Children and
square design above crowned eagle, date and denomination **Rev:**
Children on square design **Edge:** "NBP" repeatedly **Note:** minted
with center hole

Date	F	VF	XF	Unc	BU
2003	—	—	—	4.50	—

Y# 447 2 ZLOTE
8.1500 g., Brass, 26.8 mm. **Subject:** City of Poznan (Posen)
Obv: Crowned eagle **Rev:** Clock face and tower between two goat
heads **Edge:** NBP repeated eight times

Date	F	VF	XF	Unc	BU
2003	—	—	—	4.50	—

Y# 451 2 ZLOTE
8.2100 g., Brass, 26.8 mm. **Subject:** Easter Monday Festival
Obv: Crowned eagle **Rev:** Festival scene **Edge:** Lettered **Edge
Lettering:** NBP eight times

Date	F	VF	XF	Unc	BU
2003	—	—	—	3.00	—

Y# 455 2 ZLOTE
8.1400 g., Brass, 26.7 mm. **Subject:** Petroleum and Gas Industry
150th Anniversary **Obv:** Crowned eagle **Rev:** Portrait and refinery
Edge: "NBP" repeated eight times

Date	F	VF	XF	Unc	BU
2003	—	—	—	3.50	—

Y# 456 2 ZLOTE
8.1400 g., Brass, 26.7 mm. **Subject:** General B. S. Maczek **Obv:**
Crowned eagle **Rev:** Military uniformed portrait **Edge:** "NBP"
repeated eight times

Date	F	VF	XF	Unc	BU
2003	—	—	—	3.00	—

Y# 465 2 ZLOTE
8.1700 g., Aluminum-Bronze, 26.7 mm. **Obv:** Small Polish eagle
with large cross background **Rev:** Pope in prayer with cross
background **Edge:** Lettered **Edge Lettering:** "NBP" repeated

Date	F	VF	XF	Unc	BU
2003	—	—	—	3.00	—

Y# 473   2 ZLOTE
8.1500 g., Brass, 27 mm. **Obv:** Crowned eagle **Rev:** Stanislaus Leszcywski **Edge:** Lettered **Edge Lettering:** "NBP" repeated eight times

Date	F	VF	XF	Unc	BU
2003	—	—	—	3.50	—

Y# 477   2 ZLOTE
8.1500 g., Brass, 27 mm. **Obv:** Crowned eagle and artists palette **Rev:** Self portrait of Jacek Malczewski **Edge:** Lettered **Edge Lettering:** "NPB" repeated eight times

Date	F	VF	XF	Unc	BU
2003	—	—	—	3.50	—

Y# 464   2 ZLOTE
8.1300 g., Brass, 26.8 mm. **Obv:** Crowned eagle **Rev:** Two dolphins **Edge:** Lettered **Edge Lettering:** "NBP" repeated

Date	F	VF	XF	Unc	BU
2004	—	—	—	4.00	—

Y# 479   2 ZLOTE
8.1500 g., Brass, 27 mm. **Subject:** 80th Anniversary of the Modern Zloty Currency **Obv:** Crowned eagle above value **Rev:** Reverse design of the 1 Zloty Y-15 **Edge:** Lettered **Edge Lettering:** "NBP" eight times

Date	F	VF	XF	Unc	BU
2004	—	—	—	3.00	—

Y# 481   2 ZLOTE
8.1500 g., Brass, 27 mm. **Subject:** Poland Joining the European Union **Obv:** Crowned eagle above value **Rev:** Polish map and stars **Edge:** Lettered **Edge Lettering:** "NBP" eight times

Date	F	VF	XF	Unc	BU
2004	—	—	—	3.00	—

Y# 484   2 ZLOTE
8.1500 g., Brass, 27 mm. **Subject:** Dolnoslaskie (Lower Silesian) District **Obv:** Crowned eagle on map **Rev:** Silesian eagle on shield **Edge:** Lettered **Edge Lettering:** "NBP" eight times

Date	F	VF	XF	Unc	BU
2004	—	—	—	3.00	—

Y# 485   2 ZLOTE
8.1500 g., Brass, 27 mm. **Subject:** Kujawsko-Pomorskie District **Obv:** Crowned eagle on map **Rev:** Shield with crowned half eagle and griffin **Edge:** Lettered **Edge Lettering:** "NBP" eight times

Date	F	VF	XF	Unc	BU
2004	—	—	—	3.00	—

Y# 486   2 ZLOTE
8.1500 g., Brass, 27 mm. **Subject:** Lubuskie District **Obv:** Crowned eagle on map **Rev:** Shield with half eagle and two stars **Edge:** Lettered **Edge Lettering:** "NBP" eight times

Date	F	VF	XF	Unc	BU
2004	—	—	—	3.00	—

Y# 487   2 ZLOTE
8.1500 g., Brass, 27 mm. **Subject:** Lodzkie District **Obv:** Crowned eagle on map **Rev:** Shield with two creatures above an eagle **Edge:** Lettered **Edge Lettering:** "NBP" eight times

Date	F	VF	XF	Unc	BU
2004	—	—	—	3.00	—

Y# 488   2 ZLOTE
8.1500 g., Brass, 27 mm. **Subject:** Malopolskie District **Obv:** Crowned eagle on map **Rev:** Shield with crowned eagle **Edge:** Lettered **Edge Lettering:** "NBP" eight times

Date	F	VF	XF	Unc	BU
2004	—	—	—	3.00	—

Y# 489   2 ZLOTE
8.1500 g., Brass, 27 mm. **Subject:** Mazowieckie District **Obv:** Crowned eagle on map **Rev:** Uncrowned eagle on shield **Edge:** Lettered **Edge Lettering:** "NBP" eight times

Date	F	VF	XF	Unc	BU
2004	—	—	—	3.00	—

Y# 490   2 ZLOTE
8.1500 g., Brass, 27 mm. **Subject:** Podkarpackie District **Obv:** Crowned eagle on map **Rev:** Shield with iron cross above griffin and lion **Edge:** Lettered **Edge Lettering:** "NBP" eight times

Date	F	VF	XF	Unc	BU
2004	—	—	—	3.00	—

Y# 491   2 ZLOTE
8.1500 g., Brass, 27 mm. **Subject:** Podlaskie District **Obv:** Crowned eagle on map **Rev:** Shield with Polish eagle above Lithuanian knight **Edge:** Lettered **Edge Lettering:** "NBP" eight times

Date	F	VF	XF	Unc	BU
2004	—	—	—	3.00	—

Y# 492   2 ZLOTE
8.1500 g., Brass, 27 mm. **Subject:** Pomorskie District **Obv:** Crowned eagle on map **Rev:** Griffin on shield **Edge:** Lettered **Edge Lettering:** "NBP" eight times

Date	F	VF	XF	Unc	BU
2004	—	—	—	3.00	—

Y# 493   2 ZLOTE
8.1500 g., Brass, 27 mm. **Subject:** Slaskie (Silesia) District **Obv:** Crowned eagle on map **Rev:** Eagle on shield **Edge:** Lettered **Edge Lettering:** "NBP" eight times

Date	F	VF	XF	Unc	BU
2004	—	—	—	3.00	—

Y# 496   2 ZLOTE
8.1500 g., Brass, 27 mm. **Subject:** Warsaw Uprising 60th Anniversary **Obv:** Crowned eagle **Rev:** Resistance symbol on brick wall **Edge:** Lettered **Edge Lettering:** "NBP" eight times

Date	F	VF	XF	Unc	BU
2004	—	—	—	3.00	—

Y# 499   2 ZLOTE
8.1500 g., Brass, 27 mm. **Obv:** Crowned eagle **Rev:** Gen. Stanislaw F. Sosabowski **Edge:** Lettered **Edge Lettering:** "NBP" eight times

Date	F	VF	XF	Unc	BU
2004	—	—	—	3.00	—

Y# 501   2 ZLOTE
8.1500 g., Brass, 27 mm. **Subject:** Polish Police 85th Anniversary **Obv:** Crowned eagle **Rev:** Police badge **Edge:** Lettered **Edge Lettering:** "NBP" eight times

Date	F	VF	XF	Unc	BU
2004	—	—	—	3.00	—

Y# 503   2 ZLOTE
8.1500 g., Brass, 27 mm. **Subject:** Polish Senate **Obv:** Crowned eagle **Rev:** Senate eagle and speaker's staff **Edge:** Lettered **Edge Lettering:** "NBP" eight times

Date	F	VF	XF	Unc	BU
2004	—	—	—	3.00	—

Y# 505   2 ZLOTE
8.1500 g., Brass, 27 mm. **Obv:** Crowned eagle **Rev:** Aleksander Czekanowski (1833-1876) **Edge:** Lettered **Edge Lettering:** "NBP" eight times

Date	F	VF	XF	Unc	BU
2004	—	—	—	3.00	—

Y# 507   2 ZLOTE
8.1500 g., Brass, 27 mm. **Obv:** Crowned eagle **Rev:** Harvest fest couple in folk costume **Edge:** Lettered **Edge Lettering:** "NBP" eight times

Date	F	VF	XF	Unc	BU
2004	—	—	—	3.00	—

Y# 509   2 ZLOTE
8.1500 g., Brass, 27 mm. **Subject:** Warsaw Fine Arts Academy Centennial **Obv:** Crowned eagle **Rev:** Painter's hands **Edge:** Lettered **Edge Lettering:** "NBP" eight times

Date	F	VF	XF	Unc	BU
2004	—	—	—	3.00	—

Y# 512   2 ZLOTE
8.1500 g., Brass, 27 mm. **Obv:** Crowned eagle and artists palette **Rev:** Stanislaw Wyspianski (1869-1907) **Edge:** Lettered **Edge Lettering:** "NBP" eight times

Date	F	VF	XF	Unc	BU
2004	—	—	—	3.00	—

Y# 516   2 ZLOTE
8.1500 g., Brass, 27 mm. **Subject:** Olympics **Obv:** Crowned eagle **Rev:** Ancient runners **Edge:** Lettered **Edge Lettering:** "NBP" eight times

Date	F	VF	XF	Unc	BU
2004	—	—	—	3.00	—

Y# 520   2 ZLOTE
8.1500 g., Brass, 26.8 mm.   **Obv:** Crowned eagle **Rev:** Eagle Owl
on nest with chicks **Edge:** Lettered **Edge Lettering:** "NBP"
repeated eight times

Date	F	VF	XF	Unc	BU
2005	—	—	—	3.50	—

Y# 521   2 ZLOTE
8.1500 g., Brass, 26.8 mm.   **Obv:** Crowned Polish eagle **Rev:** 2
Zlote ship coin design of 1936 **Edge:** Lettered **Edge Lettering:**
"NBP" repeatedly

Date	F	VF	XF	Unc	BU
2005	—	—	—	3.50	—

Y# 522   2 ZLOTE
8.1500 g., Brass, 26.8 mm.   **Subject:** Japan's Aichi Expo **Obv:**
Crowned Polish eagle **Rev:** Two cranes flying over Mt. Fuji with rising
sun background **Edge:** Lettered **Edge Lettering:** "NBP" repeatedly

Date	F	VF	XF	Unc	BU
2005	—	—	—	3.50	—

Y# 524   2 ZLOTE
8.1300 g., Brass, 26.7 mm.   **Subject:** Obrony Jasnej Cory **Obv:**
Polish eagle above value **Rev:** Monk **Edge:** Lettered **Edge
Lettering:** "NBP" repeatedly

Date	F	VF	XF	Unc	BU
2005	—	—	—	4.00	—

Y# 525   2 ZLOTE
8.1300 g., Brass, 26.7 mm.   **Obv:** Polish eagle above value **Rev:**
Pope John Paul II **Edge:** Lettered **Edge Lettering:** "NBP" repeatedly

Date	F	VF	XF	Unc	BU
2005	—	—	—	4.00	—

Y# 527   2 ZLOTE
8.2000 g., Brass, 26.7 mm.   **Obv:** Eagle above value **Rev:**
Konstanty Ildefons Galczynski **Edge Lettering:** "NBP" repeatedly

Date	F	VF	XF	Unc	BU
2005	—	—	—	3.00	—

Y# 528   2 ZLOTE
8.2000 g., Brass, 26.7 mm.   **Obv:** Eagle and value above wall
Rev: Kolobrzeg light house **Edge Lettering:** "NBP" repeatedly

Date	F	VF	XF	Unc	BU
2005	—	—	—	3.00	—

Y# 529   2 ZLOTE
8.2000 g., Brass, 26.7 mm.   **Obv:** Eagle and value above wall
Rev: Wloclawek Cathedral **Edge Lettering:** "NBP" repeatedly

Date	F	VF	XF	Unc	BU
2005	—	—	—	3.00	—

Y# 530   2 ZLOTE
8.2000 g., Brass, 26.7 mm.   **Obv:** Eagle above value **Rev:**
Stanislaw August Poniatowski **Edge Lettering:** "NBP" repeatedly

Date	F	VF	XF	Unc	BU
2005	—	—	—	3.00	—

Y# 284   5 ZLOTYCH
Bi-Metallic Brass center in Copper-Nickel ring

Date	F	VF	XF	Unc	BU
1994-1996	—	—	—	7.00	8.00

Y# 287   10 ZLOTYCH
16.5500 g., 0.7500 Silver .3979 oz. ASW **Rev:** Capture of Berlin

Date	F	VF	XF	Unc	BU
1995 Proof	Value: 22.50				

Y# 301   10 ZLOTYCH
16.4400 g., 0.9250 Silver .4889 oz. ASW **Series:** 1996 Olympics
Rev: Centennial - Atlanta

Date	F	VF	XF	Unc	BU
1995 Proof	Value: 20.00				

Y# 305   10 ZLOTYCH
16.5000 g., 0.9250 Silver .4907 oz. ASW **Subject:** Centennial of
Organized Peasant Movement **Rev:** Wincenty Witos

Date	F	VF	XF	Unc	BU
1995 Proof	Value: 25.00				

Y# 307   10 ZLOTYCH
16.5000 g., 0.9250 Silver .4907 oz. ASW **Rev:** Bust of Zygmunt
II August left

Date	F	VF	XF	Unc	BU
1996 Proof	Value: 25.00				

Y# 308   10 ZLOTYCH
16.5000 g., 0.9250 Silver .4907 oz. ASW **Rev:** Half-length figure
of Zygmunt II August

Date	F	VF	XF	Unc	BU
1996 Proof	Value: 60.00				

Y# 317   10 ZLOTYCH
16.5000 g., 0.9250 Silver .4907 oz. ASW **Rev:** Stanislaw Mikolajczyk

Date	F	VF	XF	Unc	BU
1996 Proof	Value: 25.00				

Y# 318   10 ZLOTYCH
16.5000 g., 0.9250 Silver .4907 oz. ASW **Rev:** Mazurka of Dabrowski

Date	F	VF	XF	Unc	BU
1996 Proof	Value: 35.00				

Poland

Y# 324 10 ZLOTYCH
16.5000 g., 0.9250 Silver .4907 oz. ASW **Subject:** 40th
Anniversary - Poznan Workers Protest **Obv:** Polish eagle

Date	F	VF	XF	Unc	BU
1996 Proof		Value: 25.00			

Y# 334 10 ZLOTYCH
14.1400 g., 0.9250 Silver .4205 oz. ASW **Obv:** Polish eagle **Rev:**
Pawel Edmund Strzelecki **Edge Lettering:** 200 LECIE URODZIN

Date	F	VF	XF	Unc	BU
1997 Proof		Value: 25.00			

Y# 321 10 ZLOTYCH
14.1400 g., 0.9250 Silver .4205 oz. ASW **Subject:** St. Adalbert's
Martyrdom **Obv:** Polish eagle **Rev:** Birth and funeral scenes

Date	F	VF	XF	Unc	BU
1997 Proof		Value: 25.00			

Y# 322 10 ZLOTYCH
14.1400 g., 0.9250 Silver .4205 oz. ASW **Subject:** 46th
Eucharistic Congress **Obv:** Polish eagle in design **Rev:** Pope

Date	F	VF	XF	Unc	BU
1997 Proof		Value: 28.00			

Y# 337 10 ZLOTYCH
14.1400 g., 0.9250 Silver .4205 oz. ASW **Obv:** Polish eagle **Rev:**
Sigismund III (1587-1632)

Date	F	VF	XF	Unc	BU
1998 Proof		Value: 25.00			

Y# 326 10 ZLOTYCH
14.1400 g., 0.9250 Silver .4205 oz. ASW **Obv:** Polish eagle **Rev:**
Stefan Batory

Date	F	VF	XF	Unc	BU
1997 Proof		Value: 60.00			

Y# 327 10 ZLOTYCH
14.1400 g., 0.9250 Silver .4205 oz. ASW **Obv:** Polish eagle **Rev:**
Stefan Batory

Date	F	VF	XF	Unc	BU
1997 Proof		Value: 22.50			

Y# 338 10 ZLOTYCH
14.1400 g., 0.9250 Silver .4205 oz. ASW **Subject:** Sigismund III
(1587-1632) **Obv:** Polish eagle **Rev:** King seated

Date	F	VF	XF	Unc	BU
1998 Proof		Value: 27.50			

Y# 341 10 ZLOTYCH
14.1400 g., 0.9250 Silver .4205 oz. ASW **Series:** 1998 Winter
Olympics **Obv:** Polish eagle **Rev:** Snow boarder

Date	F	VF	XF	Unc	BU
1998 Proof		Value: 18.50			

Y# 342 10 ZLOTYCH
14.1400 g., 0.9250 Silver .4205 oz. ASW **Obv:** Polish eagle **Rev:** Brigadier General August Emil Fieldorf

Date	F	VF	XF	Unc	BU
1998 Proof		Value: 32.50			

Y# 345 10 ZLOTYCH
14.1400 g., 0.9250 Silver .4205 oz. ASW **Obv:** Denomination and eagles in cross design **Rev:** Pope John Paul II

Date	F	VF	XF	Unc	BU
1998 Proof		Value: 35.00			

Y# 350 10 ZLOTYCH
14.1400 g., 0.9250 Silver .4205 oz. ASW **Subject:** 80th Anniversary - Polish Independence **Obv:** Polish eagle on stylized flames **Rev:** Anniversary dates

Date	F	VF	XF	Unc	BU
1998 Proof		Value: 27.50			

Y# 351 10 ZLOTYCH
14.1400 g., 0.9250 Silver .4205 oz. ASW **Subject:** Universal Declaration of Human Rights **Obv:** Polish eagle **Rev:** Human figure between two hands **Edge Lettering:** 50 ROCZNICA UCHWALENIA (three times)

Date	F	VF	XF	Unc	BU
1998 Proof		Value: 27.50			

Y# 359 10 ZLOTYCH
14.1400 g., 0.9250 Silver .4205 oz. ASW **Subject:** Poland's Accession to NATO **Obv:** Polish eagle **Rev:** NATO globe, soldiers rapelling from helicopter

Date	F	VF	XF	Unc	BU
1999 Proof		Value: 20.00			

Y# 360 10 ZLOTYCH
14.1400 g., 0.9250 Silver .4205 oz. ASW **Obv:** Crucifix designs and Polish eagle **Rev:** Portrait of Pope John Paul II and dove

Date	F	VF	XF	Unc	BU
1999 Proof		Value: 30.00			

Y# 362 10 ZLOTYCH
14.1400 g., 0.9250 Silver .4205 oz. ASW **Obv:** Polish eagle **Rev:** Queen Jadwiga and coat of arms **Edge Lettering:** 1400-2000. (five times) **Note:** Cracow University.

Date	F	VF	XF	Unc	BU
1999 Proof		Value: 21.50			

Y# 364 10 ZLOTYCH
14.1400 g., 0.9250 Silver .4205 oz. ASW **Obv:** Polish eagle above windowed brick wall **Rev:** Portrait of Laski with Erasmus in background **Note:** Jan Laski 1490-1560.

Date	F	VF	XF	Unc	BU
1999 Proof		Value: 21.50			

Y# 366   10 ZLOTYCH
14.1400 g., 0.9250 Silver .4205 oz. ASW   **Obv:** Polish eagle over twisted chords **Rev:** Portrait of Fryderyk Chopin with stylized design

Date	F	VF	XF	Unc	BU
1999 Proof		Value: 21.50			

Y# 369   10 ZLOTYCH
14.1400 g., 0.9250 Silver .4205 oz. ASW   **Obv:** Polish eagle **Rev:** Portrait of Wladyslaw IV, dates

Date	F	VF	XF	Unc	BU
1999 Proof		Value: 21.50			

Y# 370   10 ZLOTYCH
14.1400 g., 0.9250 Silver .4205 oz. ASW   **Obv:** Polish eagle **Rev:** Framed half-length portrait of Wladyslaw IV

Date	F	VF	XF	Unc	BU
1999 Proof		Value: 25.00			

Y# 378   10 ZLOTYCH
14.1400 g., 0.9250 Silver .4205 oz. ASW   **Obv:** World globe and Polish eagle **Rev:** Bust Ernest Malinowski facing, train in background **Edge Lettering:** 100-LECIE SMIERCI twice

Date	F	VF	XF	Unc	BU
1999 Proof		Value: 32.50			

Y# 379   10 ZLOTYCH
14.1400 g., 0.9250 Silver .4205 oz. ASW   **Obv:** Inscription and Polish eagle **Rev:** Bust Juliusz Slowacki half right **Edge:** Plain

Date	F	VF	XF	Unc	BU
1999 Proof		Value: 27.50			

Y# 380   10 ZLOTYCH
14.1400 g., 0.9250 Silver .4205 oz. ASW   **Subject:** Holy Year **Obv:** Polish eagle in frame **Rev:** Cross with symbols of the evangelists **Edge Lettering:** WIELKI JUBILEUSZ ROKU 2000

Date	F	VF	XF	Unc	BU
2000 Proof		Value: 32.50			

Y# 381   10 ZLOTYCH
14.1400 g., 0.9250 Silver .4205 oz. ASW   **Subject:** 1000th Anniversary - Gniezno Convention **Obv:** Old coin designs in oxidized center **Rev:** Seated figures of Boleslaw Chrobry and Otto III in oxidized center **Edge:** Plain

Date	F	VF	XF	Unc	BU
2000 Proof		Value: 32.50			

Y# 392   10 ZLOTYCH
14.2000 g., 0.9250 Silver .4223 oz. ASW   **Subject:** 1000 Years Wroclaw (Breslau) **Obv:** Polish eagle in front of city view **Rev:** City arms in arch **Edge:** Plain

Date	F	VF	XF	Unc	BU
2000 Proof		Value: 25.00			

Y# 395   10 ZLOTYCH
14.2200 g., 0.9250 Silver .4229 oz. ASW, 32 mm.   **Subject:** Solidarity **Obv:** Polish eagle **Rev:** Solidarity logo and two children **Edge:** Plain

Date	F	VF	XF	Unc	BU
2000 Proof		Value: 27.50			

Poland

Y# 400   10 ZLOTYCH
14.1400 g., 0.9250 Silver .4205 oz. ASW, 32 mm. **Subject:** Jan Kazimierz II (1648-68) **Obv:** Crowned eagle **Rev:** Half-length portrait with crown **Edge:** Plain

Date	F	VF	XF	Unc	BU
2000	—	—	—	27.50	—

Y# 401   10 ZLOTYCH
14.1400 g., 0.9250 Silver .4205 oz. ASW **Subject:** Jan Kazimierz II (1648-68) **Obv:** Crowned eagle **Rev:** Portrait

Date	F	VF	XF	Unc	BU
2000	—	—	—	27.50	—

Y# 406   10 ZLOTYCH
14.1400 g., 0.9250 Silver .4205 oz. ASW **Subject:** Year 2001 **Obv:** Crowned eagle **Rev:** Printed circuit board

Date	F	VF	XF	Unc	BU
2001 Proof			Value: 27.50		

Y# 403   10 ZLOTYCH
14.1400 g., 0.9250 Silver .4205 oz. ASW **Subject:** Rapperswil Polish Museum **Obv:** Crowned eagle and denomination between two buildings **Rev:** Eagle-topped column **Edge:** GDANSK GDYNIA SZCZECIN ELBLAG SLUPSK

Date	F	VF	XF	Unc	BU
2000	—	—	—	27.50	—

Y# 413   10 ZLOTYCH
14.1400 g., 0.9250 Silver .4205 oz. ASW, 32 mm. **Subject:** 15 Years of the Constitutional Court **Obv:** Crowned eagle suspended from a judge's neck chain **Rev:** Crowned eagle head and balance scale **Edge Lettering:** "TRYBUNAL KONSTYTUCYJNY W SLUZBIE PANSTWA PRAWA"

Date	F	VF	XF	Unc	BU
2001 Proof			Value: 22.50		

Y# 405   10 ZLOTYCH
14.1400 g., 0.9250 Silver .4205 oz. ASW **Subject:** Grudnia 1970 **Obv:** Two crowned eagles **Rev:** Shadow figures on pavement

Date	F	VF	XF	Unc	BU
2000	—	—	—	27.50	—

Y# 419   10 ZLOTYCH
14.1400 g., 0.9250 Silver .4205 oz. ASW, 32 mm. **Subject:** Cardinal Stefan Wyszynski **Obv:** Polish eagle above ribbon **Rev:** Portrait with raised hands **Edge Lettering:** "100.ROCZNIA URODZIN"

Date	F	VF	XF	Unc	BU
2001 Proof			Value: 27.50		

Y# 425   10 ZLOTYCH
14.2100 g., 0.9250 Silver 0.4226 oz. ASW, 32 mm. **Subject:** Jan III Sobieski **Obv:** Polish eagle above denomination **Rev:** 3/4 bust Jan III Sobieski lower left, army in background **Edge:** Plain

Date	F	VF	XF	Unc	BU
2001 Proof			Value: 30.00		

Y# 458 10 ZLOTYCH
14.1400 g., 0.9250 Silver 0.4205 oz. ASW, 32 mm. **Obv:** Polish
eagle **Rev:** Jan Sobieski, type II **Edge:** Plain

Date	F	VF	XF	Unc	BU
2001 Proof	Value: 35.00				

Y# 459 10 ZLOTYCH
14.1400 g., 0.9250 Silver 0.4205 oz. ASW, 32 mm. **Obv:** Three
violins **Rev:** Henryk Wieniawski **Edge:** Plain

Date	F	VF	XF	Unc	BU
2001 Proof	Value: 35.00				

Y# 460 10 ZLOTYCH
14.1400 g., 0.9250 Silver 0.4205 oz. ASW, 32 mm. **Obv:** Polish
eagle above fish **Rev:** Michal Siedlecki **Edge:** Plain

Date	F	VF	XF	Unc	BU
2001 Proof	Value: 35.00				

Y# 432 10 ZLOTYCH
14.1400 g., 0.9250 Silver 0.4205 oz. ASW, 32 mm. **Subject:**
Bronislaw Malinowski **Obv:** Portrait and crowned eagle **Rev:**
Trobriand Islands village scene **Edge Lettering:** "etnolog,
antropolog kultury"

Date	F	VF	XF	Unc	BU
2002 Proof	Value: 20.00				

Y# 434 10 ZLOTYCH
14.1400 g., 0.9250 Silver 0.4205 oz. ASW, 32 mm. **Subject:**
World Cup Soccer **Obv:** Crowned eagle **Rev:** Soccer player **Edge
Lettering:** "etnolog, antropolog kultury"

Date	F	VF	XF	Unc	BU
2002 Proof	Value: 20.00				

Y# 435 10 ZLOTYCH
14.1400 g., 0.9250 Silver 0.4205 oz. ASW, 32 mm. **Subject:**
World Cup Soccer **Obv:** Amber soccer ball inset entering goal net
Rev: Two soccer players with amber soccer ball inset **Edge
Lettering:** "etnolog, antropolog kultury"

Date	F	VF	XF	Unc	BU
2002 Proof	Value: 25.00				

Y# 437 10 ZLOTYCH
14.1400 g., 0.9250 Silver 0.4205 oz. ASW, 32 mm. **Subject:**
Pope John Paul II **Obv:** Polish eagle and two views of praying
Pope **Rev:** Pope facing radiant Holy Door **Edge:** Plain

Date	F	VF	XF	Unc	BU
2002 Proof	Value: 27.50				

Y# 441 10 ZLOTYCH
14.2000 g., 0.9250 Silver 0.4223 oz. ASW, 32 mm. **Subject:** Gen.
Wladyslaw Anders **Obv:** Crowned eagle, cross and multicolor
flowers **Rev:** Military portrait **Edge:** Plain

Date	F	VF	XF	Unc	BU
2002 Proof	Value: 35.00				

Y# 450 10 ZLOTYCH
14.1400 g., 0.9250 Silver 0.4205 oz. ASW, 32 mm. **Subject:**
August II (1697-1706, 1709-1735) **Obv:** Crowned eagle above
value **Rev:** Portrait and Order of the White Eagle **Edge:** Plain

Date	F	VF	XF	Unc	BU
2002 Proof	Value: 25.00				

Y# 461 10 ZLOTYCH
14.1400 g., 0.9250 Silver 0.4205 oz. ASW, 32 mm. **Obv:** Polish
eagle above value **Rev:** August II **Edge:** Plain

Date	F	VF	XF	Unc	BU
2002 Proof	Value: 27.50				

Y# 448 10 ZLOTYCH
14.1400 g., 0.9250 Silver 0.4205 oz. ASW, 32 mm. **Subject:** City
of Poznan (Posen) **Obv:** Old coin design and door **Rev:** Old coin
design and city view **Edge:** Plain

Date	F	VF	XF	Unc	BU
2003 Proof	Value: 25.00				

Y# 453   10 ZLOTYCH
14.1400 g., 0.9250 Silver 0.4205 oz. ASW, 32 mm. **Subject:**
Great Orchestra of Christmas Charity **Obv:** Large inscribed heart
Rev: Boy playing flute **Edge:** Plain

Date	F	VF	XF	Unc	BU
2003	—	—	—	—	25.00

Y# 468   10 ZLOTYCH
14.1400 g., 0.9250 Silver 0.4205 oz. ASW, 32 mm. **Obv:** Tanks
on battlefield **Rev:** General Maczek (1892-1994) **Edge:** Plain

Date	F	VF	XF	Unc	BU
2003 Proof		Value: 25.00			

Y# 469   10 ZLOTYCH
14.1400 g., 0.9250 Silver 0.4205 oz. ASW, 32 mm. **Subject:** Gas
and Oil Industry **Obv:** Crowned eagle and highway leading to city
view **Rev:** Portrait and refinery **Edge:** Plain

Date	F	VF	XF	Unc	BU
2003 Proof		Value: 25.00			

Y# 474   10 ZLOTYCH
14.1400 g., 0.9250 Silver 0.4205 oz. ASW, 32 mm. **Obv:**
Crowned eagle **Rev:** Stanislaus I and wife's portrait **Edge:** Plain

Date	F	VF	XF	Unc	BU
2003 Proof		Value: 25.00			

Y# 475   10 ZLOTYCH
14.1400 g., 0.9250 Silver 0.4205 oz. ASW, 32 mm. **Obv:**
Crowned eagle **Rev:** Half-length figure of Stanislaus I with his wife
in background **Edge:** Plain

Date	F	VF	XF	Unc	BU
2003 Proof		Value: 25.00			

Y# 480   10 ZLOTYCH
14.1400 g., 0.9250 Silver 0.4205 oz. ASW, 32 mm. **Subject:** 80th
Anniversary of the Modern Zloty Currency **Obv:** Man wearing
glasses behind obverse design of 1 zloty Y-15 **Rev:** Reverse
design of 1 Zloty Y-15 **Edge:** Plain

Date	F	VF	XF	Unc	BU
2004 Proof		Value: 25.00			

Y# 482   10 ZLOTYCH
14.1400 g., 0.9250 Silver 0.4205 oz. ASW, 32 mm. **Subject:**
Poland Joining the European Union **Obv:** Crowned eagle in blue
circle with yellow stars **Rev:** Multicolor European Union and Polish
flags **Edge:** Plain

Date	F	VF	XF	Unc	BU
2004 Proof		Value: 25.00			

Y# 497   10 ZLOTYCH
14.1400 g., 0.9250 Silver 0.4205 oz. ASW, 32 mm. **Subject:**
Warsaw Uprising 60th Anniversary **Obv:** Crowned eagle and value
on resistance symbol **Rev:** Polish soldier wearing captured
German helmet **Edge:** Plain

Date	F	VF	XF	Unc	BU
2004 Proof		Value: 25.00			

Y# 500   10 ZLOTYCH
14.1400 g., 0.9250 Silver 0.4205 oz. ASW, 32 mm. **Obv:** Polish
paratrooper badge **Rev:** Gen. Sosabowski and descending
paratrooper **Edge:** Plain

Date	F	VF	XF	Unc	BU
2004 Proof		Value: 25.00			

Y# 502   10 ZLOTYCH
14.1400 g., 0.9250 Silver 0.4205 oz. ASW, 32 mm. **Subject:**
Polish Police 85th Anniversary **Obv:** Crowned eagle **Rev:** Seal
partially overlapping police badge **Edge:** Plain

Date	F	VF	XF	Unc	BU
2004 Proof		Value: 25.00			

Y# 506   10 ZLOTYCH
14.1400 g., 0.9250 Silver 0.4205 oz. ASW, 32 mm. **Obv:** Siberian
landscape above crowned eagle and value **Rev:** Aleksander
Czekanowski (1833-1876) **Edge:** Plain

Date	F	VF	XF	Unc	BU
2004 Proof		Value: 25.00			

Y# 510   10 ZLOTYCH
14.1400 g., 0.9250 Silver 0.4205 oz. ASW, 32 mm. **Subject:**
Warsaw Fine Arts Academy Centennial **Obv:** Crowned eagle in
city square **Rev:** Art studio **Edge:** Plain

Date	F	VF	XF	Unc	BU
2004	—	—	—	—	25.00

Y# 517   10 ZLOTYCH
14.1400 g., 0.9250 Silver 0.4205 oz. ASW, 32 mm. **Subject:**
Olympics **Obv:** Woman and crowned eagle **Rev:** Fencers in front
of Parthenon **Edge:** Plain

Date	F	VF	XF	Unc	BU
2004 Proof		Value: 25.00			

Y# 518   10 ZLOTYCH
14.1400 g., 0.9250 Silver 0.4205 oz. ASW, 32 mm. **Subject:**
Olympics **Obv:** Crowned eagle in gold plated center **Rev:** Ancient
athlete within gold plated circle **Edge:** Plain

Date	F	VF	XF	Unc	BU
2004 Proof		Value: 35.00			

Y# 523   10 ZLOTYCH
14.2300 g., 0.9250 Silver 0.4232 oz. ASW, 43.2 x 29.2 mm.
Subject: Japan's Aichi Expo **Obv:** Frederic Chopin Monument
Rev: Two cranes **Edge:** Plain **Shape:** Fan

Date	F	VF	XF	Unc	BU
2005 Proof		Value: 30.00			

Y# 526   10 ZLOTYCH
14.1400 g., 0.9250 Silver Gold plated reverse 0.4205 oz. ASW,
32.1 mm. **Obv:** Polish eagle above hands **Rev:** Pope John Paul
II and church **Edge:** Plain

Date	F	VF	XF	Unc	BU
2005 Proof		Value: 30.00			

Poland

Y# 286 20 ZLOTYCH
31.1100 g., 0.9990 Silver .9990 oz. ASW **Subject:** Katyn Forest
Massacre

Date	F	VF	XF	Unc	BU
1995 Proof		Value: 32.50			

Y# 291 20 ZLOTYCH
31.1100 g., 0.9990 Silver .9990 oz. ASW **Subject:** 50th
Anniversary - United Nations

Date	F	VF	XF	Unc	BU
1995 Proof		Value: 32.50			

Y# 288 20 ZLOTYCH
31.1100 g., 0.9990 Silver .9990 oz. ASW **Subject:** 500th
Anniversary - Plock Province

Date	F	VF	XF	Unc	BU
1995 Proof		Value: 35.00			

Y# 296 20 ZLOTYCH
31.1700 g., 0.9990 Silver 1.0011 oz. ASW **Rev:** Lazienki Royal
Palace

Date	F	VF	XF	Unc	BU
1995 Proof		Value: 35.00			

Y# 290 20 ZLOTYCH
31.1100 g., 0.9990 Silver .9990 oz. ASW **Rev:** European catfish

Date	F	VF	XF	Unc	BU
1995 Proof		Value: 38.00			

Y# 298 20 ZLOTYCH
30.9200 g., 0.9250 Silver .9195 oz. ASW **Subject:** 75th
Anniversary - Battle of Warsaw

Date	F	VF	XF	Unc	BU
1995 Proof		Value: 32.50			

Y# 302　20 ZLOTYCH
31.0500 g., 0.9250 Silver .9234 oz. ASW　**Rev:** Copernicus and Ecu

Date	F	VF	XF	Unc	BU
1995 Proof		Value: 37.50			

Y# 319　20 ZLOTYCH
31.1000 g., 0.9250 Silver .9240 oz. ASW　**Subject:** Millennium of Gdansk (Danzig) **Edge Lettering:** MONUMENTUM MILLENNII CIVITATIS GEDANENSIS

Date	F	VF	XF	Unc	BU
1996 Proof		Value: 37.50			

Y# 304　20 ZLOTYCH
31.1000 g., 0.9250 Silver .9240 oz. ASW　**Series:** 1996 Olympics - Atlanta **Rev:** Wrestlers

Date	F	VF	XF	Unc	BU
1995 Proof		Value: 55.00			

Y# 330　20 ZLOTYCH
28.5200 g., 0.9250 Silver .8482 oz. ASW　**Obv:** Polish eagle **Rev:** Stag beetle

Date	F	VF	XF	Unc	BU
1997 Proof		Value: 60.00			

Y# 309　20 ZLOTYCH
31.1000 g., 0.9250 Silver .9240 oz. ASW　**Subject:** 400th Anniversary - Warsaw as Capital City

Date	F	VF	XF	Unc	BU
1996 Proof		Value: 27.50			

Y# 312　20 ZLOTYCH
31.1000 g., 0.9250 Silver .9240 oz. ASW　**Rev:** Hedgehog with young

Date	F	VF	XF	Unc	BU
1996 Proof		Value: 60.00			

Y# 314　20 ZLOTYCH
31.1000 g., 0.9250 Silver .9240 oz. ASW　**Rev:** Bishop's arms and Lidzibark Warminski castle

Date	F	VF	XF	Unc	BU
1996 Proof		Value: 40.00			

Y# 332　20 ZLOTYCH
28.5200 g., 0.9250 Silver .8482 oz. ASW　**Obv:** Polish eagle **Rev:** Zemek W Pieskowej Skale

Date	F	VF	XF	Unc	BU
1997 Proof		Value: 40.00			

Poland

Y# 343   20 ZLOTYCH
28.4700 g., 0.9250 Silver .8467 oz. ASW **Obv:** Polish eagle **Rev:**
Ropucha Paskowka - Natterjack Toad

Date	F	VF	XF	Unc	BU
1998 Proof		Value: 50.00			

Y# 348   20 ZLOTYCH
28.2800 g., 0.9250 Silver .8410 oz. ASW **Obv:** Polish eagle **Rev:**
Zamek W. Koniku - Palace

Date	F	VF	XF	Unc	BU
1998 Proof		Value: 37.50			

Y# 382   20 ZLOTYCH
28.3000 g., 0.9250 Silver .8416 oz. ASW   **Rev:** Wolf family

Date	F	VF	XF	Unc	BU
1999 Proof		Value: 60.00			

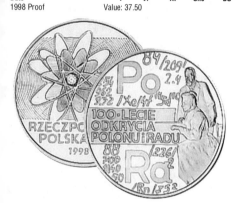

Y# 354   20 ZLOTYCH
28.1500 g., 0.9250 Silver .8372 oz. ASW **Subject:** Discovery of
Radium and Polonium **Obv:** Atom **Rev:** Madame and Monsieur
Curie and formulas

Date	F	VF	XF	Unc	BU
1998 Proof		Value: 32.50			

Y# 387   20 ZLOTYCH
28.3700 g., 0.9250 Silver .8437 oz. ASW   **Rev:** Dudek - Upupa
epops - Eurasian Hoopoe

Date	F	VF	XF	Unc	BU
2000 Proof		Value: 35.00			

Y# 373   20 ZLOTYCH
28.2800 g., 0.9250 Silver .8410 oz. ASW **Obv:** Polish eagle within
inner circle **Rev:** Palace behind Potlocki family arms

Date	F	VF	XF	Unc	BU
1999 Proof		Value: 32.50			

Y# 391   20 ZLOTYCH
28.2400 g., 0.9250 Silver .8398 oz. ASW, 38.5 mm.   **Obv:** Polish
eagle **Rev:** View of Wilanowie Palace through front gate **Edge:** Plain

Date	F	VF	XF	Unc	BU
2000 Proof		Value: 35.00			

Poland

Y# 409   20 ZLOTYCH
28.2800 g., 0.9250 Silver .8410 oz. ASW, 38.6 mm. **Subject:**
Wieliezce Salt Mine **Obv:** Crowned eagle and rock **Rev:** Ancient
salt miners **Edge:** Plain

Date	F	VF	XF	Unc	BU
2001 Proof		Value: 57.50			

Y# 411   20 ZLOTYCH
28.2800 g., 0.9250 Silver .8410 oz. ASW, 38.6 mm. **Subject:**
Amber Route **Obv:** Crowned eagle and two ancient Roman silver
cups **Rev:** Piece of amber mounted above an ancient Roman coin
design and map with the route marked with stars **Edge:** Plain

Date	F	VF	XF	Unc	BU
2001	—	—	—	80.00	—

Y# 415   20 ZLOTYCH
28.2800 g., 0.9250 Silver .8410 oz. ASW, 38.6 mm. **Obv:**
Crowned eagle between two flags **Rev:** Flying Swallowtail butterfly
Edge: Plain

Date	F	VF	XF	Unc	BU
2001 Proof		Value: 50.00			

Y# 424   20 ZLOTYCH
28.7700 g., 0.9250 Silver 0.8556 oz. ASW, 38.6 mm. **Subject:**
Christmas **Obv:** Ornate city view **Rev:** Celebration scene including
an attached zirconia star **Edge:** Plain **Note:** Antiqued finish.

Date	F	VF	XF	Unc	BU
2001	—	—	—	35.00	—

Y# 428   20 ZLOTYCH
28.2800 g., 0.9250 Silver 0.841 oz. ASW, 38.6 mm. **Obv:**
Crowned eagle **Rev:** Two pond turtles **Edge:** Plain

Date	F	VF	XF	Unc	BU
2002 Proof		Value: 45.00			

Y# 442   20 ZLOTYCH
28.0500 g., 0.9250 Silver 0.8342 oz. ASW **Subject:** Jan Matejko
Obv: Seated figure with crowned eagle at lower right **Rev:** Portrait
with multicolor artist's palette **Edge:** Plain **Shape:** Rectangular
Note: Actual size 40 x 37.9mm.

Date	F	VF	XF	Unc	BU
2002 Proof		Value: 40.00			

Y# 457   20 ZLOTYCH
28.2800 g., 0.9250 Silver 0.841 oz. ASW, 38.6 mm. **Obv:**
Crowned eagle and castle **Rev:** Malborku castle and ceramic
applique **Edge:** Plain **Note:** Antiqued finish

Date	F	VF	XF	Unc	BU
2002	—	—	—	35.00	—

Y# 449   20 ZLOTYCH
28.4700 g., 0.9250 Silver 0.8467 oz. ASW, 38.6 mm. **Obv:**
Crowned eagle **Rev:** Eels and world globe **Edge:** Plain

Date	F	VF	XF	Unc	BU
2003 Proof		Value: 40.00			

Y# 452   20 ZLOTYCH
28.2800 g., 0.9250 Silver 0.841 oz. ASW, 38.6 mm. **Subject:** Easter
Monday Festival **Obv:** Crowned eagle on lace curtain above lamb
and multicolor Easter eggs **Rev:** Festival scene **Edge:** Plain

Date	F	VF	XF	Unc	BU
2003 Proof		Value: 36.00			

Y# 471   20 ZLOTYCH
28.2800 g., 0.9250 Silver 0.841 oz. ASW, 40 x 40 mm. **Obv:**
Standing Pope John Paul II **Rev:** Pope"s portrait **Edge:** Plain
Shape: Square

Date	F	VF	XF	Unc	BU
2003 Proof		Value: 35.00			

Y# 478   20 ZLOTYCH
28.2800 g., 0.9250 Silver 0.841 oz. ASW, 28 mm. **Obv:** "Death"
allegory closing an old man's eyes **Rev:** Self portrait of Jacek
Malczewski **Edge:** Plain **Shape:** Rectangular

Date	F	VF	XF	Unc	BU
2003 Proof		Value: 35.00			

Y# 498   20 ZLOTYCH
28.2800 g., 0.9250 Silver 0.841 oz. ASW, 38.6 mm. **Subject:**
Lodz Ghetto (1940-1944) **Obv:** Silhouette on wall **Rev:** Child with
a pot **Edge:** Plain

Date	F	VF	XF	Unc	BU
2004	—	—	—	—	35.00

Y# 504   20 ZLOTYCH
28.2800 g., 0.9250 Silver 0.841 oz. ASW, 38.6 mm. **Subject:**
Polish Senate **Obv:** Crowned eagle above Senate chamber **Rev:**
Senate eagle and speaker's staff **Edge:** Plain

Date	F	VF	XF	Unc	BU
2004 Proof		Value: 35.00			

Y# 508   20 ZLOTYCH
28.2800 g., 0.9250 Silver 0.841 oz. ASW, 38.6 mm. **Obv:** Crowned
eagle in harvest wreath **Rev:** Harvest fest parade **Edge:** Plain

Date	F	VF	XF	Unc	BU
2004 Proof		Value: 35.00			

Y# 513 20 ZLOTYCH
28.2800 g., 0.9250 Silver 0.841 oz. ASW, 40x28 mm. **Obv:** Mother and children **Rev:** Stanislaw Wyspianski (1869-1907) **Edge:** Plain

Date	F	VF	XF	Unc	BU
2004 Proof			Value: 35.00		

Y# 515 20 ZLOTYCH
28.2800 g., 0.9250 Silver 0.841 oz. ASW, 38.6 mm. **Obv:** Crowned eagle **Rev:** Two porpoises **Edge:** Plain

Date	F	VF	XF	Unc	BU
2004 Proof			Value: 35.00		

Y# 292 50 ZLOTYCH
3.1000 g., 0.9999 Gold .1000 oz. AGW **Rev:** Golden eagle

Date	F	VF	XF	Unc	BU
1995	—	—	—	140	—

Y# 293 100 ZLOTYCH
7.7800 g., 0.9999 Gold .2500 oz. AGW **Rev:** Golden eagle

Date	F	VF	XF	Unc	BU
1995	—	—	—	245	—

Y# 328 100 ZLOTYCH
8.0000 g., 0.9000 Gold .2315 oz. AGW **Obv:** Polish eagle **Rev:** Stefan Batory

Date	F	VF	XF	Unc	BU
1997 Proof			Value: 220		

Y# 339 100 ZLOTYCH
8.0000 g., 0.9000 Gold .2315 oz. AGW **Obv:** Polish eagle **Rev:** Sigismund III

Date	F	VF	XF	Unc	BU
1998 Proof			Value: 220		

Y# 361 100 ZLOTYCH
8.0000 g., 0.9000 Gold .2315 oz. AGW **Obv:** Polish eagle in inner circle **Rev:** Pope John Paul II and crucifix

Date	F	VF	XF	Unc	BU
1999 Proof			Value: 190		

Y# 371 100 ZLOTYCH
8.0000 g., 0.9000 Gold .2315 oz. AGW **Obv:** Polish eagle **Rev:** Framed portrait of Wladyslaw IV

Date	F	VF	XF	Unc	BU
1999 Proof			Value: 220		

Y# 383 100 ZLOTYCH
8.0000 g., 0.9000 Gold .2315 oz. AGW **Obv:** Polish eagle **Rev:** Bust King Zygmunt II left

Date	F	VF	XF	Unc	BU
1999 Proof			Value: 175		

Y# 384 100 ZLOTYCH
8.0000 g., 0.9000 Gold .2315 oz. AGW **Subject:** 100th Anniversary - Gniezno Convention **Obv:** Old coin designs **Rev:** Seated figures of Boleslaw Chrobry and Otto III

Date	F	VF	XF	Unc	BU
2000 Proof			Value: 175		

Y# 396 100 ZLOTYCH
8.0000 g., 0.9000 Gold .2315 oz. AGW **Obv:** Polish eagle **Rev:** Half-length bust of Queen Jadwiga facing **Edge:** Plain

Date	F	VF	XF	Unc	BU
2000 Proof			Value: 220		

Y# 402 100 ZLOTYCH
8.0000 g., 0.9000 Gold .2315 oz. AGW, 21 mm. **Subject:** Jan Kazimierz II (1648-68) **Obv:** Crowned eagle **Rev:** Portrait with name and dates **Edge:** Plain

Date	F	VF	XF	Unc	BU
2000 Proof			Value: 225		

Y# 416   100 ZLOTYCH

8.0000 g., 0.9000 Gold .2315 oz. AGW, 21 mm. **Subject:** Wladyslaw I (1320-33) **Obv:** Crowned eagle **Rev:** Crowned portrait **Edge:** Plain

Date	F	VF	XF	Unc	BU
2001 Proof		Value: 225			

Y# 417   100 ZLOTYCH

8.0000 g., 0.9000 Gold .2315 oz. AGW, 21 mm. **Subject:** Boleslaw III (1102-1138) **Obv:** Polish eagle **Rev:** Portrait **Edge:** Plain

Date	F	VF	XF	Unc	BU
2001 Proof		Value: 220			

Y# 462   100 ZLOTYCH

8.0000 g., 0.9000 Gold 0.2315 oz. AGW, 21 mm. **Obv:** Polish eagle **Rev:** Jan Sobieski III **Edge:** Plain

Date	F	VF	XF	Unc	BU
2001 Proof		Value: 225			

Y# 429   100 ZLOTYCH

8.0000 g., 0.9000 Gold 0.2315 oz. AGW, 21 mm. **Obv:** Crowned eagle **Rev:** Bust of crowned King Kazimierz III (1333-1370) **Edge:** Plain

Date	F	VF	XF	Unc	BU
2002 Proof		Value: 225			

Y# 430   100 ZLOTYCH

8.0000 g., 0.9000 Gold 0.2315 oz. AGW, 21 mm. **Obv:** Crowned eagle **Rev:** Bust of crowned King Wladyslaw II Jagiello (1386-1434) half left **Edge:** Plain

Date	F	VF	XF	Unc	BU
2002 Proof		Value: 225			

Y# 436   100 ZLOTYCH

8.0000 g., 0.9000 Gold 0.2315 oz. AGW, 21 mm. **Subject:** World Cup Soccer **Obv:** Crowned eagle with world background **Rev:** Soccer player **Edge:** Plain

Date	F	VF	XF	Unc	BU
2002 Proof		Value: 225			

Y# 454   100 ZLOTYCH

8.0000 g., 0.9000 Gold 0.2315 oz. AGW, 21 mm. **Obv:** Crowned eagle **Rev:** King Wladyslaw III (1434-1444) **Edge:** Plain

Date	F	VF	XF	Unc	BU
2003 Proof		Value: 225			

Y# 466   100 ZLOTYCH

8.0000 g., 0.9000 Gold 0.2315 oz. AGW, 21 mm. **Subject:** 750th Anniversary - City Charter **Obv:** Door knocker and church **Rev:** Clock face and tower **Edge:** Plain

Date	F	VF	XF	Unc	BU
2003 Proof		Value: 225			

Y# 467   100 ZLOTYCH

8.0000 g., 0.9000 Gold 0.2315 oz. AGW, 21 mm. **Obv:** Crowned eagle **Rev:** Kazimierz IV (1447-1492) **Edge:** Plain

Date	F	VF	XF	Unc	BU
2003 Proof		Value: 225			

Y# 476   100 ZLOTYCH

8.0000 g., 0.9000 Gold 0.2315 oz. AGW, 21 mm. **Obv:** Crowned eagle **Rev:** Stanislaus I and eagle **Edge:** Plain

Date	F	VF	XF	Unc	BU
2003 Proof		Value: 225			

Y# 494   100 ZLOTYCH

8.0000 g., 0.9000 Gold 0.2315 oz. AGW, 21 mm. **Obv:** Crowned eagle **Rev:** King Przemysi II (1295-1296) **Edge:** Plain

Date	F	VF	XF	Unc	BU
2004 Proof		Value: 225			

Y# 495   100 ZLOTYCH

8.0000 g., 0.9000 Gold 0.2315 oz. AGW, 21 mm. **Obv:** Crowned eagle **Rev:** King Zygmunt I (1506-1548) **Edge:** Plain

Date	F	VF	XF	Unc	BU
2004 Proof		Value: 225			

Y# 294   200 ZLOTYCH

15.5000 g., 0.9000 Gold .4485 oz. AGW **Rev:** Golden eagle

Date	F	VF	XF	Unc	BU
1995	—	—	—	485	—

Y# 299   200 ZLOTYCH

15.5000 g., 0.9000 Gold .4485 oz. AGW **Subject:** XII Chopin Piano Competition **Edge:** Lettered

Date	F	VF	XF	Unc	BU
1995 Proof		Value: 925			

Y# 316   200 ZLOTYCH
15.5000 g., 0.9000 Gold .4485 oz. AGW **Rev:** Henryk Sienkiewicz

Date	F	VF	XF	Unc	BU
1996 Proof		Value: 400			

Y# 353   200 ZLOTYCH
15.5000 g., 0.9000 Gold .4485 oz. AGW **Subject:** 200th Birthday - Adam Mickiewicz **Obv:** Small Polish eagle, quote **Rev:** Portrait with silhouette

Date	F	VF	XF	Unc	BU
1998 Proof		Value: 350			

Y# 320   200 ZLOTYCH
15.5000 g., 0.9000 Gold .4485 oz. AGW **Subject:** Millennium of Gdansk (Danzig) **Rev:** City arms in old coin style

Date	F	VF	XF	Unc	BU
1996	—	—	—	—	360

Y# 367   200 ZLOTYCH
15.5000 g., 0.9000 Gold .4485 oz. AGW **Obv:** Polish eagle on sash, music **Rev:** Portrait of Fryderyk Chopin with music background

Date	F	VF	XF	Unc	BU
1999 Proof		Value: 350			

Y# 323   200 ZLOTYCH
15.5000 g., 0.9000 Gold .4485 oz. AGW **Subject:** St. Adalbert's Martyrdom **Obv:** Polish eagle

Date	F	VF	XF	Unc	BU
1997 Proof		Value: 360			

Y# 385   200 ZLOTYCH
15.5000 g., 0.9000 Gold .4485 oz. AGW **Obv:** Polish eagle **Rev:** Head Juliusz Slowacki left

Date	F	VF	XF	Unc	BU
1999 Proof		Value: 350			

Y# 346   200 ZLOTYCH
15.5000 g., 0.9000 Gold .4485 oz. AGW **Obv:** Polish eagle **Rev:** Pope John Paul II

Date	F	VF	XF	Unc	BU
1998 Proof		Value: 360			

Y# 375   200 ZLOTYCH
13.6000 g., Gold And Silver **Subject:** Millennium **Obv:** Crowned eagle and world globe **Rev:** Various computer, DNA and atomic symbols **Note:** .900 Gold center in .925 Silver inner ring in a .900 Gold outer ring.

Date	F	VF	XF	Unc	BU
2000 Proof		Value: 200			

Poland

Y# 386   200 ZLOTYCH
15.5000 g., 0.9000 Gold .4485 oz. AGW **Subject:** 1000th
Anniversary - Gniezno Convention **Obv:** Old coin designs **Rev:**
Seated figures of Boleslaw Chrobry and Otto III

Date	F	VF	XF	Unc	BU
2000 Proof		Value: 350			

Y# 420   200 ZLOTYCH
15.5000 g., 0.9000 Gold .4485 oz. AGW, 27 mm. **Subject:** Cardinal
Stefan Wyszynski **Obv:** Pillar divides arms and eagle **Rev:** Cardinal's
portrait **Edge Lettering:** "100 ROCZNIA URODZIN"

Date	F	VF	XF	Unc	BU
2001 Proof		Value: 350			

Y# 463   200 ZLOTYCH
15.5000 g., 0.9000 Gold 0.4485 oz. AGW, 27 mm. **Obv:** Standing
violinist **Rev:** Henry Wieniawski **Edge:** Lettered **Edge Lettering:**
"XII MIEDZYNARODOWY KONKURS SKRZYPCOWY IM
HENRYKA WIENIAWSKIEGO"

Date	F	VF	XF	Unc	BU
2001 Proof		Value: 365			

Y# 393   200 ZLOTYCH
15.5000 g., 0.9000 Gold .4485 oz. AGW, 27 mm. **Subject:** 1000
Years - Wroclzaw (Breslau) **Obv:** Polish eagle **Rev:** Bust of Jesus
holding city arms **Edge:** Plain

Date	F	VF	XF	Unc	BU
2000 Proof		Value: 350			

Y# 438   200 ZLOTYCH
15.5000 g., 0.9000 Gold 0.4485 oz. AGW, 27 mm. **Subject:** Pope
John Paul II **Obv:** Bust of Pope at right facing left, small eagle in
background **Rev:** Pope facing radiant Holy Door **Edge:** Plain

Date	F	VF	XF	Unc	BU
2002 Proof		Value: 350			

Y# 470   200 ZLOTYCH
15.5000 g., 0.9000 Gold 0.4485 oz. AGW, 27 mm. **Subject:** Gas
and Oil Industry **Obv:** Crowned eagle, oil wells and refinery **Rev:**
Scientist at work **Edge:** Plain

Date	F	VF	XF	Unc	BU
2003 Proof		Value: 375			

Y# 472   200 ZLOTYCH
15.5000 g., 0.9000 Gold 0.4485 oz. AGW, 27 mm. **Obv:** Standing
Pope John Paul II **Rev:** Seated Pope **Edge:** Plain

Date	F	VF	XF	Unc	BU
2003 Proof		Value: 375			

Y# 397   200 ZLOTYCH
23.3200 g., 0.9000 Gold .6748 oz. AGW **Subject:** Solidarity **Obv:**
Polish eagle **Rev:** Multicolor Soldiarity logo, map and two children
Edge: Plain

Date	F	VF	XF	Unc	BU
2000 Proof		Value: 500			

Y# 483   200 ZLOTYCH
15.5000 g., 0.9000 Gold 0.4485 oz. AGW, 27 mm. **Subject:**
Poland Joining the European Union **Obv:** Polish euro coin design
elements **Rev:** Polish euro coin design elements **Edge:** Plain

Date	F	VF	XF	Unc	BU
2004 Proof		Value: 350			

Y# 407   200 ZLOTYCH
Tri-Metallic Gold with Palladium center, Gold with Silver ring, Gold
with Copper outer limit, 27 mm. **Subject:** Year 2001 **Obv:** Crowned
eagle in a swirl **Rev:** Couple looking into the future **Edge:** Plain

Date	F	VF	XF	Unc	BU
2001 Proof		Value: 225			

Y# 511   200 ZLOTYCH
15.5000 g., 0.9000 Gold 0.4485 oz. AGW, 27 mm. **Subject:**
Warsaw Fine Arts Academy Centennial **Obv:** Campus view **Rev:**
Statue and building **Edge:** Plain

Date	F	VF	XF	Unc	BU
2004 Proof			Value: 350		

Y# 519   200 ZLOTYCH
15.5000 g., 0.9000 Gold 0.4485 oz. AGW, 27 mm. **Subject:**
Olympics **Obv:** Woman and crowned eagle **Rev:** Ancient runners
painted on pottery **Edge:** Plain

Date	F	VF	XF	Unc	BU
2004 Proof			Value: 350		

Y# 295   500 ZLOTYCH
31.1035 g., 0.9999 Gold 1.0000 oz. AGW

Date	F	VF	XF	Unc	BU
1995	—	—	—	775	—

 # 267   1000 ZLOTYCH
.9500 g., 0.9250 Silver .8313 oz. ASW **Subject:** World Cup
occer **Rev:** Soccer stadium

ate	F	VF	XF	Unc	BU
94 Proof			Value: 45.00		

Russia

Russia, formerly the central power of the Union of Soviet
Socialist Republics and now of the Commonwealth of Independent
States occupies the northern part of Asia and the eastern part of
Europe, has an area of 17,075,400 sq. km. Capital: Moscow.

EMPIRE

MONETARY SYSTEM
1/4 Kopek = Polushka ПОЛУШКА
1/2 Kopek = Denga, Denezhka ДЕНГА, ДЕНЕЖКА
Kopek = КОП_ИКА
(2, 3 & 4) Kopeks КОП_ИКИ
(5 and up) Kopeks КОП_ЕКЪ
(1924 – 5 and up) Kopeks КОПЕЕКРУБЛЪ
50 Kopeks = Poltina, Poltinnik ПОЛТИНА, ПОЛТИННИК
100 Kopeks = Rouble, Ruble РУБЛЪ
10 Roubles = Imperial ИМПЕРІАЛЪРУБЛЪ
10 Roubles = Chervonetz ЧЕРВОНЕЦ

STANDARD COINAGE

Y# 1.1   POLUSHKA (1/4 Kopek)
3.0000 g., Copper **Ruler:** Alexander II **Note:** Plain border.

Date	F	VF	XF	Unc	BU
1855-1859	7.00	15.00	30.00	60.00	—

Y# 1.2   POLUSHKA (1/4 Kopek)
3.0000 g., Copper **Ruler:** Alexander II

Date	F	VF	XF	Unc	BU
1855-1860	15.00	30.00	60.00	120	—

Y# 1.3   POLUSHKA (1/4 Kopek)
3.0000 g., Copper **Ruler:** Alexander II **Note:** Toothed border.

Date	F	VF	XF	Unc	BU
1859-1867	3.00	7.00	15.00	30.00	—

Y# 1.4   POLUSHKA (1/4 Kopek)
3.0000 g., Copper **Ruler:** Alexander II

Date	F	VF	XF	Unc	BU
1861	5.00	10.00	25.00	50.00	—

Y# 7.1   POLUSHKA (1/4 Kopek)
3.0000 g., Copper **Ruler:** Alexander II

Date	F	VF	XF	Unc	BU
1867-1875	3.00	7.00	15.00	30.00	—

Y# 7.2   POLUSHKA (1/4 Kopek)
3.0000 g., Copper **Ruler:** Alexander II

Date	F	VF	XF	Unc	BU
1867-1881	2.00	5.00	12.00	25.00	—

Y# 29   POLUSHKA (1/4 Kopek)
3.0000 g., Copper **Ruler:** Alexander III

Date	F	VF	XF	Unc	BU
1881-1893	1.50	3.50	7.00	15.00	—

Y# 47.1   POLUSHKA (1/4 Kopek)
3.0000 g., Copper

Date	F	VF	XF	Unc	BU
1894-1910	1.00	2.00	4.00	10.00	—

Y# 47.2 POLUSHKA (1/4 Kopek)
3.0000 g., Copper

Date	F	VF	XF	Unc	BU
1915-1916	2.00	5.00	10.00	20.00	—

Y# 48.1 1/2 KOPEK
4.0000 g., Copper **Ruler:** Nicholas II

Date	F	VF	XF	Unc	BU
1894-1914	0.75	1.50	3.00	6.00	—

Y# 48.1 1/2 KOPEK
4.0000 g., Copper **Ruler:** Nicholas II

Date	F	VF	XF	Unc	BU
1894-1914	0.75	1.50	3.00	6.00	—

Y# 48.2 1/2 KOPEK
4.0000 g., Copper **Note:** Struck at Petrograd without mint mark.

Date	F	VF	XF	Unc	BU
1915-1916	1.50	3.00	7.00	15.00	20.00

Y# 2.1 DENGA (1/2 Kopek)
4.0000 g., Copper **Ruler:** Alexander II **Note:** Plain border.

Date	F	VF	XF	Unc	BU
1855-1859	5.00	10.00	20.00	40.00	—

Y# 2.2 DENGA (1/2 Kopek)
4.0000 g., Copper **Ruler:** Alexander II

Date	F	VF	XF	Unc	BU
1855-1860	7.00	15.00	30.00	60.00	—

Y# 2.3 DENGA (1/2 Kopek)
4.0000 g., Copper **Ruler:** Alexander II **Note:** Toothed border.

Date	F	VF	XF	Unc	BU
1859-1867	15.00	30.00	60.00	100	—

Y# 2.4 DENGA (1/2 Kopek)
4.0000 g., Copper **Ruler:** Alexander II

Date	F	VF	XF	Unc	BU
1861-1863	10.00	20.00	45.00	85.00	—

Y# 8.1 DENGA (1/2 Kopek)
4.0000 g., Copper **Ruler:** Alexander II

Date	F	VF	XF	Unc	BU
1867-1876	5.00	10.00	25.00	50.00	—

Y# 8.2 DENGA (1/2 Kopek)
4.0000 g., Copper **Ruler:** Alexander II

Date	F	VF	XF	Unc	BU
1867-1881	5.00	10.00	25.00	50.00	—

Y# 30 DENGA (1/2 Kopek)
4.0000 g., Copper **Ruler:** Alexander III

Date	F	VF	XF	Unc	BU
1881-1894	4.00	8.00	16.00	30.00	—

Y# 3.1 KOPEK
4.0000 g., Copper **Ruler:** Alexander II **Obv:** Crowned small A
Edge: Plain

Date	F	VF	XF	Unc	BU
1854-1859	5.00	10.00	20.00	40.00	—

Y# 3.2 KOPEK
4.0000 g., Copper **Ruler:** Alexander II **Obv:** Crowned tall A **Rev:** Large date

Date	F	VF	XF	Unc	BU
1855-1860	15.00	30.00	60.00	120	—

Y# 3.3 KOPEK
4.0000 g., Copper **Ruler:** Alexander II **Obv:** Crowned small A
Note: Toothed border.

Date	F	VF	XF	Unc	BU
1859-1867	4.00	10.00	20.00	30.00	—

Y# 3.4 KOPEK
4.0000 g., Copper **Ruler:** Alexander II **Obv:** Crowned tall A

Date	F	VF	XF	Unc
1861-1864	20.00	40.00	70.00	150

Y# 9.1 KOPEK
4.0000 g., Copper **Ruler:** Alexander II

Date	F	VF	XF	Unc
1867-1876	2.00	4.00	7.50	15.00

Y# 9.2 KOPEK
4.0600 g., Copper

Date	F	VF	XF	Unc	BU
1867-1914	0.50	1.00	2.00	8.00	—

Y# 9.3 KOPEK
4.0000 g., Copper **Note:** Struck at Petrograd without mint mark.

Date	F	VF	XF	Unc	BU
1915-1916	0.50	1.00	2.00	8.00	—

C# 150.1 2 KOPEKS
Copper **Ruler:** Alexander II

Date	VG	F	VF	XF	Unc
1850-1859	3.00	7.00	15.00	30.00	—

C# 150.3 2 KOPEKS
Copper **Ruler:** Alexander II

Date	VG	F	VF	XF	Unc
1850-1860	5.00	10.00	20.00	40.00	—

4a.1 2 KOPEKS
Copper **Ruler:** Alexander II **Obv:** Ribbons added to crown

Date	F	VF	XF	Unc	BU
1859-1867	3.00	7.00	15.00	30.00	—

4a.2 2 KOPEKS
Copper **Ruler:** Alexander II

Date	F	VF	XF	Unc	BU
1860-1863	10.00	20.00	35.00	70.00	—

10.1 2 KOPEKS
Copper **Ruler:** Alexander II

Date	F	VF	XF	Unc	BU
1867-1876	3.00	7.00	15.00	30.00	—

Y# 10.2 2 KOPEKS
Copper

Date	F	VF	XF	Unc	BU
1867-1914	1.50	2.50	5.00	10.00	—

Y# 10.3 2 KOPEKS
Copper **Note:** Struck at Petrograd without mint mark.

Date	F	VF	XF	Unc	BU
1915-1916	1.00	2.00	3.00	5.00	—

C# 151.1 3 KOPEKS
Copper **Obv:** First variety - 6 coats of arms, no ribbons at crown

Date	VG	F	VF	XF	Unc
1850-1859	3.00	7.00	15.00	35.00	—

C# 151.3 3 KOPEKS
Copper

Date	VG	F	VF	XF	Unc
1850-1859	12.00	25.00	50.00	100	—

Y# 5a.1 3 KOPEKS
Copper **Ruler:** Alexander II **Obv:** Second variety - 8 coats of arms, ribbons from crown

Date	F	VF	XF	Unc	BU
1859-1867	10.00	20.00	40.00	25.00	—

Y# 5a.2 3 KOPEKS
Copper **Ruler:** Alexander II

Date	F	VF	XF	Unc	BU
1860-1863	25.00	50.00	100	200	—

Y# 11.1 3 KOPEKS
Copper **Ruler:** Alexander II **Note:** Similar to 2 Kopeks, Y#10.2

Date	F	VF	XF	Unc	BU
1867-1876	4.00	8.00	16.00	35.00	—

Y# 11.2   3 KOPEKS
Copper   **Obv:** Double-headed eagle

Date	F	VF	XF	Unc	BU
1867-1914	1.50	3.00	6.00	15.00	—

Y# 11.3   3 KOPEKS
Copper   **Note:** Struck at Petrograd without mint mark.

Date	F	VF	XF	Unc	BU
1915-1916	1.00	2.00	6.00	20.00	—

C# 163   5 KOPEKS
1.0366 g., 0.8680 Silver .0289 oz. ASW   **Ruler:** Nicholas I

Date	VG	F	VF	XF	Unc
1832-1858	2.50	4.00	8.00	20.00	—

C# 152.1   5 KOPEKS
Copper   **Obv:** 6 coats of arms, no ribbons at crown

Date	F	VF	XF	Unc	BU
1850-1859	4.00	40.00	120	225	—

C# 152.4   5 KOPEKS
Copper

Date	F	VF	XF	Unc	BU
1850-1856	40.00	80.00	175	350	—

Y# 19.1   5 KOPEKS
1.0366 g., 0.7500 Silver .0250 oz. ASW   **Ruler:** Alexander II **Obv:** Ribbons added to crown

Date	F	VF	XF	Unc	BU
1859-1860	7.00	15.00	30.00	100	—

Y# 6a   5 KOPEKS
Copper   **Ruler:** Alexander II **Obv:** 8 coats of arms, ribbons at crown

Date	F	VF	XF	Unc	BU
1859-1867	7.00	15.00	30.00	65.00	—

Y# 19.2   5 KOPEKS
1.0366 g., 0.7500 Silver .0250 oz. ASW   **Ruler:** Alexander II **Obv:** Redesigned eagle, engrailed edge

Date	F	VF	XF	Unc	BU
1860-1866	5.00	12.00	25.00	60.00	—

Y# 12.1   5 KOPEKS
Copper   **Ruler:** Alexander II

Date	F	VF	XF	Unc	BU
1867-1876	3.00	7.00	15.00	30.00	—

Y# 12.2   5 KOPEKS
Copper, 32.6 mm.

Date	F	VF	XF	Unc	BU
1867-1912	3.00	7.00	15.00	30.00	—

Y# 19a.1   5 KOPEKS
0.8998 g., 0.5000 Silver .0144 oz. ASW   **Obv:** Eagle **Edge:** Reeded

Date	F	VF	XF	Unc	BU
1867-1914	1.50	3.00	7.00	15.00	30.0

Y# 19a.2   5 KOPEKS
0.8998 g., 0.5000 Silver .0144 oz. ASW   **Note:** Struck at Petrograd without mint mark.

Date	F	VF	XF	Unc	BU
1915	1.50	3.00	7.00	15.00	30.0

Y# 12.3   5 KOPEKS
Copper   **Note:** Struck at Petrograd without mint mark.

Date	F	VF	XF	Unc	BU
1916	40.00	80.00	150	250	B

C# 164.1   10 KOPEKS (Grivennik)
2.0700 g., 0.8680 Silver .0577 oz. ASW

Date	VG	F	VF	XF	U
1832-1858	3.00	7.00	15.00	30.00	

Y# 20.1 10 KOPEKS (Grivennik)
2.0732 g., 0.7500 Silver .0499 oz. ASW **Ruler:** Alexander II **Note:** Type 1, reticulated edge.

Date	F	VF	XF	Unc	BU
1859-1860	6.00	12.00	25.00	50.00	—

Y# 20.2 10 KOPEKS (Grivennik)
2.0732 g., 0.7500 Silver .0499 oz. ASW **Ruler:** Alexander II **Note:** Type 2, eagle redesigned.

Date	F	VF	XF	Unc	BU
1860-1866	4.00	8.00	16.00	35.00	—

Y# 20a.2 10 KOPEKS
1.7996 g., 0.5000 Silver .0289 oz. ASW **Edge:** Reeded

Date	F	VF	XF	Unc	BU
1867-1914	1.00	2.00	3.50	15.00	—

Y# 20a.3 10 KOPEKS
1.7996 g., 0.5000 Silver .0289 oz. ASW **Note:** Struck at Petrograd without mintmaster initials.

Date	F	VF	XF	Unc	BU
1915-1917	1.00	2.00	3.00	6.00	—

Y# 20a.1 10 KOPEKS
1.7996 g., 0.5000 Silver .0289 oz. ASW **Note:** Struck at Osaka, Japan without mintmaster initials.

Date	F	VF	XF	Unc	BU
1916	BV	1.00	2.00	10.00	—

Y# 21 15 KOPEKS
1.1097 g., 0.7500 Silver .0750 oz. ASW **Ruler:** Alexander II **Edge:** Reticulated

Date	F	VF	XF	Unc	BU
1860-1866	4.00	8.00	16.00	35.00	—

Y# 21a.2 15 KOPEKS
0.6994 g., 0.5000 Silver .0434 oz. ASW **Edge:** Reeded

Date	F	VF	XF	Unc	BU
1867-1914	1.50	3.00	7.00	15.00	—

Y# 21a.3 15 KOPEKS
0.6994 g., 0.5000 Silver .0434 oz. ASW **Note:** Struck at Petrograd without mintmaster initials.

Date	F	VF	XF	Unc	BU
1915-1917	1.00	2.00	3.00	10.00	—

Y# 21a.1 15 KOPEKS
0.6994 g., 0.5000 Silver .0434 oz. ASW **Edge:** Reeded **Note:** Struck at Osaka, Japan without mintmaster initials.

Date	F	VF	XF	Unc	BU
1916	BV	1.50	3.00	10.00	—

C# 165 20 KOPEKS
4.1463 g., 0.8680 Silver .1157 oz. ASW **Ruler:** Nicholas I **Obv:** Variety I eagle

Date	VG	F	VF	XF	Unc
1832-1858	5.00	10.00	20.00	40.00	—

Y# 22.1 20 KOPEKS
4.1463 g., 0.7500 Silver .0999 oz. ASW **Ruler:** Alexander II **Edge:** Reticulated

Date	F	VF	XF	Unc	BU
1859-1860	3.00	7.00	15.00	—	—

Y# 22.2 20 KOPEKS
4.1463 g., 0.7500 Silver .0999 oz. ASW **Ruler:** Alexander II **Obv:** Eagle redesigned **Note:** Varieties of eagle exist for 1860 dated coins.

Date	F	VF	XF	Unc	BU
1860-1866	3.00	7.00	15.00	30.00	—

Y# 22a.1 20 KOPEKS
3.5992 g., 0.5000 Silver .0579 oz. ASW

Date	F	VF	XF	Unc	BU
1867-1914	BV	2.00	5.00	10.00	—

Y# 22a.2 20 KOPEKS
3.5992 g., 0.5000 Silver .0579 oz. ASW **Note:** Struck at Petrograd without mint mark.

Date	F	VF	XF	Unc	BU
1915-1917	BV	2.00	4.00	10.00	15.00

C# 166.1 25 KOPEKS
5.1830 g., 0.8680 Silver .1446 oz. ASW **Ruler:** Nicholas I **Obv:** Variety I eagle **Note:** Varieties of eagle and crown exist.

Date	VG	F	VF	XF	Unc
1832-1858	5.00	10.00	20.00	40.00	—

C# 166.2 25 KOPEKS
5.1830 g., 0.8680 Silver .1446 oz. ASW

Date	VG	F	VF	XF	Unc
1854-1857	20.00	40.00	85.00	175	—

Y# 23   25 KOPEKS
5.1830 g., 0.8680 Silver .1446 oz. ASW **Ruler:** Alexander II **Obv:**
Eagle redesigned

Date	F	VF	XF	Unc	BU
1859-1885	10.00	20.00	40.00	80.00	—

Y# 44   25 KOPEKS
4.9990 g., 0.9000 Silver .1446 oz. ASW **Ruler:** Alexander III
Note: Without mint mark.

Date	F	VF	XF	Unc	BU
1886-1894/3	20.00	40.00	80.00	150	—

Y# 57   25 KOPEKS
4.9990 g., 0.9000 Silver .1446 oz. ASW **Note:** Struck at St.
Petersburg without mint mark.

Date	F	VF	XF	Unc	BU
1895-1901	5.00	10.00	25.00	75.00	—

Y# 45   50 KOPEKS
9.9980 g., 0.9000 Silver .2893 oz. ASW **Ruler:** Alexander III
Note: Without mint mark.

Date	F	VF	XF	Unc	BU
1886-1894	30.00	65.00	14.00	325	—

Y# 58.2   50 KOPEKS
9.9980 g., 0.9000 Silver .2893 oz. ASW **Note:** Without mint mark.

Date	F	VF	XF	Unc	BU
1895-1914	5.00	8.00	15.00	45.00	—

Y# 58.1   50 KOPEKS
9.9980 g., 0.9000 Silver .2893 oz. ASW **Ruler:** Nicholas II **Note:**
Mint mark: Star on rim.

Date	F	VF	XF	Unc	BU
1896-1899	10.00	20.00	35.00	80.00	—

C# 167.1   POLTINA (1/2 Rouble)
10.3600 g., 0.8680 Silver .2892 oz. ASW **Ruler:** Nicholas I **Note:**
Variety I eagle. Varieties of eagle and wreath exist.

Date	VG	F	VF	XF	Unc
1832-1858	7.00	15.00	30.00	50.00	—

Y# 24   POLTINA (1/2 Rouble)
10.3600 g., 0.8680 Silver .2892 oz. ASW **Ruler:** Alexander II
Note: Variety II eagle. Edge varieties exist.

Date	F	VF	XF	Unc	BU
1859-1885	15.00	30.00	65.00	175	—

C# 168.1   ROUBLE
20.7300 g., 0.8680 Silver .5785 oz. ASW **Note:** Superior
Goodman sale 2-91 P/L Unc realized $10,450.

Date	F	VF	XF	Unc	B
1832-1858	20.00	40.00	120	300	—

Y# 25   ROUBLE
20.7300 g., 0.8680 Silver .5785 oz. ASW **Ruler:** Alexander II

Date	F	VF	XF	Unc	
1859-1885	30.00	65.00	125	300	4

Y# 28   ROUBLE
20.7300 g., 0.8680 Silver .5785 oz. ASW   **Ruler:** Alexander II
Subject: Nicholas I Memorial **Note:** Without mint mark.

Date	F	VF	XF	Unc	BU
1859	175	325	600	1,250	—

Y# 43   ROUBLE
20.7300 g., 0.8680 Silver .5785 oz. ASW   **Ruler:** Alexander III
Subject: Alexander III Coronation **Note:** Without mint mark.

Date	F	VF	XF	Unc	BU
1883	40.00	90.00	175	450	—

46   ROUBLE
9.9960 g., 0.9000 Silver .5786 oz. ASW   **Ruler:** Alexander III
Note: Mintmasters initials and stars found on edge

ate	F	VF	XF	Unc	BU
886-1894	45.00	95.00	250	1,150	3,750

59.3   ROUBLE
.9960 g., 0.9000 Silver .5786 oz. ASW   **Note:** Struck at St.
etersburg without mint mark.

te	F	VF	XF	Unc	BU
95-1915	12.00	25.00	45.00	250	375

Y# 59.2   ROUBLE
19.9960 g., 0.9000 Silver .5786 oz. ASW   **Ruler:** Nicholas II **Note:**
Mint mark: Star on rim.

Date	F	VF	XF	Unc	BU
1896-1898	15.00	30.00	60.00	325	750

Y# 60   ROUBLE
19.9960 g., 0.9000 Silver .5786 oz. ASW   **Ruler:** Nicholas II
Subject: Nicholas II Coronation

Date	F	VF	XF	Unc	BU
1896	25.00	45.00	100	350	800

Y# 59.1   ROUBLE
19.9960 g., 0.9000 Silver .5786 oz. ASW   **Ruler:** Nicholas II **Note:**
Mint mark 2 stars on rim.

Date	F	VF	XF	Unc	BU
1897-1899	20.00	50.00	100	300	700

Y# 61   ROUBLE
19.9960 g., 0.9000 Silver .5786 oz. ASW   **Ruler:** Nicholas II
Subject: Alexander II Memorial

Date	F	VF	XF	Unc	BU
1898	300	650	1,250	3,000	—

Y# 68   ROUBLE
19.9960 g., 0.9000 Silver .5786 oz. ASW   **Subject:** Centennial -
Napolean's Defeat

Date	F	VF	XF	Unc	BU
1912	175	350	650	950	2,750

Y# 69   ROUBLE
19.9960 g., 0.9000 Silver .5786 oz. ASW **Subject:** Alexander III Memorial

Date	F	VF	XF	Unc	BU
1912	750	1,600	2,750	5,000	9,500

Y# 70   ROUBLE
19.9960 g., 0.9000 Silver .5786 oz. ASW **Subject:** 300th Anniversary - Romanov Dynasty **Obv:** Michael Feodorovich and Nicholas II **Note:** Struck at St. Petersburg without mint mark.

Date	F	VF	XF	Unc	BU
1913	15.00	25.00	65.00	125	185

Y# 71   ROUBLE
19.9960 g., 0.9000 Silver .5786 oz. ASW **Subject:** 200th Anniversary - Battle of Gangut

Date	F	VF	XF	Unc	BU
1914	1,250	3,500	6,000	8,000	9,500

Y# 26   3 ROUBLES
3.9260 g., 0.9170 Gold .1157 oz. AGW

Date	F	VF	XF	Unc	BU
1869-1885	175	225	350	1,500	2,000

Y# A26   5 ROUBLES
6.5440 g., 0.9170 Gold .1929 oz. AGW **Ruler:** Alexander II

Date	F	VF	XF	Unc	BU
1855-1858	150	200	300	525	900

Y# B26   5 ROUBLES
6.5440 g., 0.9170 Gold .1929 oz. AGW

Date	F	VF	XF	Unc	BU
1859-1885	145	185	275	475	850

Y# 42   5 ROUBLES
6.4516 g., 0.9000 Gold .1867 oz. AGW **Ruler:** Alexander III **Note:** Without mint mark. Edge varieties exist.

Date	F	VF	XF	Unc	BU
1886-1894	150	200	300	475	850

Y# A61   5 ROUBLES
6.4516 g., 0.9000 Gold .1867 oz. AGW **Ruler:** Nicholas II **Note:** Without mint mark.

Date	F	VF	XF	Unc	BU
1895-1896	—	9,000	—	—	—

Y# 62   5 ROUBLES
4.3013 g., 0.9000 Gold .1244 oz. AGW **Note:** Struck at St. Petersburg without mint mark.

Date	F	VF	XF	Unc	BU
1897-1911	—	—	BV	95.00	2(

Y# 63 7 ROUBLES 50 KOPEKS
6.4516 g., 0.9000 Gold .1867 oz. AGW **Ruler:** Nicholas II **Note:**
Without mint mark.

Date	F	VF	XF	Unc	BU
1897	140	170	250	450	—

Y# A42 10 ROUBLES
12.9039 g., 0.9000 Gold .3734 oz. AGW **Ruler:** Alexander III
Note: Without mint mark.

Date	F	VF	XF	Unc	BU
1886-1894	400	650	1,250	2,850	—

Y# A63 10 ROUBLES
12.9039 g., 0.9000 Gold .3734 oz. AGW **Ruler:** Nicholas II

Date	F	VF	XF	Unc	BU
1895-1897	—	15,000	25,000	35,000	—

Y# 64 10 ROUBLES
8.6026 g., 0.9000 Gold .2489 oz. AGW **Note:** Without mint mark.

Date	F	VF	XF	Unc	BU
1898-1911	—	—	BV	175	360

Y# 65.1 15 ROUBLES
12.9039 g., 0.9000 Gold .3734 oz. AGW **Ruler:** Nicholas II **Note:**
Without mint mark. Wide rim, legend ends at back of neck.

Date	F	VF	XF	Unc	BU
1897	BV	275	375	575	—

Y# 65.2 15 ROUBLES
12.9039 g., 0.9000 Gold .3734 oz. AGW **Ruler:** Nicholas II **Note:**
Narrow rim, 4 letters of legend under neck.

Date	F	VF	XF	Unc	BU
1897	BV	275	375	500	—

Y# 27 25 ROUBLES
32.7200 g., 0.9170 Gold .9640 oz. AGW **Ruler:** Alexander II

Date	F	VF	XF	Unc	BU
1876 Proof		Value: 100,000			

Y# A65 25 ROUBLES
32.2500 g., 0.9000 Gold .9332 oz. AGW **Ruler:** Nicholas II **Note:**
Struck at St. Petersburg without mint mark.

Date	F	VF	XF	Unc	BU
1896-1908	—	50,000		65,000	—

Y# B65 37 ROUBLES 50 KOPEKS
32.2500 g., 0.9000 Gold .9335 oz. AGW **Note:** Without mint mark.

Date	F	VF	XF	Unc	BU
1902	—	—	—	75,000	—

Y# B65a 37 ROUBLES 50 KOPEKS
Copper-Nickel **Rev:** Letter "P" after "1902 G" **Edge:** Plain **Note:**
Gold plated specimens were done outside the mint.

Date	F	VF	XF	Unc	BU
1902 (1991)	—	—	—	15.00	—

РСФСР (R.S.F.S.R.)
(Russian Soviet Federated Socialist Republic)
STANDARD COINAGE

Y# 80   10 KOPEKS
1.8000 g., 0.5000 Silver .0289 oz. ASW

Date	F	VF	XF	Unc	BU
1921-1923	1.00	2.00	4.00	10.00	—

Y# 81   15 KOPEKS
2.7000 g., 0.5000 Silver .0434 oz. ASW

Date	F	VF	XF	Unc	BU
1921-1923	1.50	2.50	4.50	12.00	—

Y# 82   20 KOPEKS
3.6000 g., 0.5000 Silver .0578 oz. ASW   **Note:** Varieties exist.

Date	F	VF	XF	Unc	BU
1921-1923	2.00	3.50	7.00	15.00	—

Y# 83   50 KOPEKS
9.9980 g., 0.9000 Silver .2893 oz. ASW   **Edge Lettering:** Mintmaster's initials

Date	F	VF	XF	Unc	BU
1921-1922	5.50	7.50	12.00	28.00	—

Y# 84   ROUBLE
19.9960 g., 0.9000 Silver .5786 oz. ASW   **Edge Lettering:** Mintmaster's initials **Note:** Varieties exist.

Date	F	VF	XF	Unc	BU
1921-1922	8.50	13.50	25.00	70.00	95.00

TRADE COINAGE

Y# 85   CHERVONETZ (10 Roubles)
8.6026 g., 0.9000 Gold .2489 oz. AGW   **Obv:** РСФСР below arms
Edge Lettering: Mintmaster's initials

Date	F	VF	XF	Unc	BU
1923-1982	—	—	—BV+10%	—	—

CCCP (U.S.S.R.)
(Union of Soviet Socialist Republics)
STANDARD COINAGE

Y# 75   1/2 KOPEK
Copper

Date	F	VF	XF	Unc	BU
1925-1928	4.00	8.00	16.00	30.00	—

Y# 76   KOPEK
Bronze

Date	F	VF	XF	Unc	BU
1924-1925	5.00	10.00	20.00	45.00	—

Y# 91   KOPEK
Aluminum-Bronze   **Note:** Varieties exist.

Date	F	VF	XF	Unc	BU
1926-1935	0.50	1.00	2.00	5.00	—

Y# 98   KOPEK
Aluminum-Bronze

Date	F	VF	XF	Unc	BU
1935-1936	1.00	2.00	4.00	8.00	—

Y# 105   KOPEK
Aluminum-Bronze   **Note:** Varieties exist.

Date	F	VF	XF	Unc	BU
1937-1946	0.50	1.00	2.00	4.00	—

Y# 112   KOPEK
Aluminum-Bronze **Obv:** Eight and seven ribbons on wreath **Note:** Varieties exist.

Date	F	VF	XF	Unc	BU
1948-1956	0.70	1.00	2.00	3.00	—

Y# 119   KOPEK
Aluminum-Bronze **Obv:** Seven and seven ribbons on wreath

Date	F	VF	XF	Unc	BU
1957	1.00	2.00	4.00	12.00	—

Y# 126   KOPEK
Copper-Nickel

Date	F	VF	XF	Unc	BU
1958	—	—	—	250	—

Y# 126a   KOPEK
Brass **Note:** Varieties exist.

Date	F	VF	XF	Unc	BU
1961-1991	0.10	0.15	0.20	0.30	—

Y# 77   2 KOPEKS
Bronze **Note:** Varieties exist.

Date	F	VF	XF	Unc	BU
1924	5.00	12.00	22.00	50.00	—

Y# 92   2 KOPEKS
Aluminum-Bronze **Note:** Varieties exist.

Date	F	VF	XF	Unc	BU
1926-1935	0.50	1.00	2.00	4.00	—

Y# 99   2 KOPEKS
Aluminum-Bronze **Note:** Varieties exist.

Date	F	VF	XF	Unc	BU
1935-1936	1.00	2.00	3.00	7.00	—

Y# 106   2 KOPEKS
Aluminum-Bronze

Date	F	VF	XF	Unc	BU
1937-1948	0.50	1.00	2.00	3.00	—

Y# 113   2 KOPEKS
Aluminum-Bronze **Obv:** Eight and seven ribbons on wreath **Note:** Varieties exist.

Date	F	VF	XF	Unc	BU
1948-1956	0.25	0.50	1.00	2.50	—

Y# 120   2 KOPEKS
Aluminum-Bronze **Obv:** Seven and seven ribbons on wreath

Date	F	VF	XF	Unc	BU
1957	1.00	2.00	4.00	9.00	—

Y# 127   2 KOPEKS
Copper-Nickel

Date	F	VF	XF	Unc	BU
1958	—	—	—	250	—

Y# 127a   2 KOPEKS
Brass **Note:** Varieties exist.

Date	F	VF	XF	Unc	BU
1961-1991	0.10	0.15	0.20	0.35	—

Y# 78 3 KOPEKS
Bronze **Note:** Varieties exist.

Date	F	VF	XF	Unc	BU
1924	6.00	12.50	25.00	65.00	—

Y# 93 3 KOPEKS
Aluminum-Bronze **Note:** Varieties exist.

Date	F	VF	XF	Unc	BU
1926-1935	0.75	1.50	3.00	5.00	—

Y# 100 3 KOPEKS
Aluminum-Bronze **Note:** Varieties exist.

Date	F	VF	XF	Unc	BU
1935-1936	1.00	2.00	5.00	10.00	—

Y# 107 3 KOPEKS
Aluminum-Bronze **Note:** Varieties exist.

Date	F	VF	XF	Unc	BU
1937-1948	0.50	1.00	2.00	3.00	—

Y# 114 3 KOPEKS
Aluminum-Bronze **Obv:** Eight and seven ribbons on wreath **Note:** Varieties exist.

Date	F	VF	XF	Unc	BU
1948-1957	0.50	1.00	2.00	3.50	—

Y# 121 3 KOPEKS
Aluminum-Bronze **Obv:** Seven and seven ribbons on wreath

Date	F	VF	XF	Unc	BU
1957	1.00	2.00	4.00	9.00	—

Y# 128 3 KOPEKS
Copper-Zinc

Date	F	VF	XF	Unc	BU
1958	—	—	—	250	—

Y# 128a 3 KOPEKS
Aluminum-Bronze **Note:** Varieties exist.

Date	F	VF	XF	Unc	BU
1961-1991	0.10	0.15	0.20	0.40	—

Y# 79 5 KOPEKS
Bronze **Obv:** Hammer and sickle national emblem **Rev:** Value, date within wheat stalks **Note:** Varieties exist.

Date	F	VF	XF	Unc	BU
1924	7.00	15.00	30.00	75.00	—

Y# 94 5 KOPEKS
Aluminum-Bronze **Obv:** Hammer and sickle national emblem **Rev:** Value, date **Note:** Varieties exist.

Date	F	VF	XF	Unc	B
1926-1935	1.00	2.00	3.00	6.00	—

Y# 101   5 KOPEKS
Aluminum-Bronze   **Note:** Varieties exist.

Date	F	VF	XF	Unc	BU
1935-1936	2.00	4.00	9.00	26.00	—

Y# 129a   5 KOPEKS
Aluminum-Bronze   **Note:** Varieties exist.

Date	F	VF	XF	Unc	BU
1961-1991	0.10	0.15	0.25	0.50	—

Y# 86   10 KOPEKS
1.8000 g., 0.5000 Silver .0289 oz. ASW   **Note:** Varieties exist.

Date	F	VF	XF	Unc	BU
1924-1930	1.00	2.00	5.00	8.00	—

Y# 108   5 KOPEKS
Aluminum-Bronze   **Note:** Varieties exist.

Date	F	VF	XF	Unc	BU
1937-1946	1.00	2.00	3.00	5.00	—

Y# 95   10 KOPEKS
Copper-Nickel   **Note:** Varieties exist.

Date	F	VF	XF	Unc	BU
1931-1934	1.00	2.00	3.00	4.00	—

Y# 115   5 KOPEKS
Aluminum-Bronze   **Obv:** Eight and seven ribbons on wreath **Note:** Varieties exist.

Date	F	VF	XF	Unc	BU
1948-1956	1.00	2.00	3.00	4.00	—

Y# 102   10 KOPEKS
Copper-Nickel

Date	F	VF	XF	Unc	BU
1935-1936	1.00	2.00	3.00	5.00	—

Y# 122   5 KOPEKS
Aluminum-Bronze   **Obv:** Seven and seven ribbons on wreath **Note:** Varieties exist.

Date	F	VF	XF	Unc	BU
1957	2.00	4.00	6.00	9.00	—

Y# 109   10 KOPEKS
Copper-Nickel   **Note:** Varieties exist.

Date	F	VF	XF	Unc	BU
1937-1946	0.50	1.00	2.00	3.00	—

Y# A110   10 KOPEKS
Copper-Nickel   **Obv:** Y102 **Rev:** Y109 **Note:** Mule.

Date	F	VF	XF	Unc	BU
1946 Rare	—	—	—	—	—

Y# 129   5 KOPEKS
Copper-Zinc

Date	F	VF	XF	Unc	BU
1958	—	—	—	375	—

Y# 116   10 KOPEKS
Copper-Nickel   **Obv:** Eight and seven ribbons on wreath **Note:** Varieties exist.

Date	F	VF	XF	Unc	BU
1948-1956	0.50	1.00	1.50	2.50	—

Russia

Y# 123　10 KOPEKS
Copper-Nickel　**Obv:** Seven and seven ribbons on wreath

Date	F	VF	XF	Unc	BU
1957	0.50	1.00	3.00	6.00	—

Y# A130　10 KOPEKS
Copper-Nickel

Date	F	VF	XF	Unc	BU
1958	—	—	—	350	—

Y# 130　10 KOPEKS
Copper-Nickel-Zinc

Date	F	VF	XF	Unc	BU
1961-1991	0.10	0.20	0.30	0.50	—

Y# 136　10 KOPEKS
Copper-Nickel-Zinc, 17 mm.　**Subject:** 50th Anniversary of Revolution

Date	F	VF	XF	Unc	BU
1967	—	0.20	0.30	—	—

Y# 87　15 KOPEKS
2.7000 g., 0.5000 Silver .0434 oz. ASW　**Note:** Varieties exist.

Date	F	VF	XF	Unc	BU
1924-1930	1.00	2.00	5.00	8.00	—

Y# 96　15 KOPEKS
Copper-Nickel　**Note:** Varieties exist.

Date	F	VF	XF	Unc	BU
1931-1934	1.00	2.00	3.00	5.00	—

Y# 103　15 KOPEKS
Copper-Nickel

Date	F	VF	XF	Unc	BU
1935-1936	1.00	2.00	3.00	5.00	—

Y# 110　15 KOPEKS
Copper-Nickel　**Note:** Varieties exist.

Date	F	VF	XF	Unc	BU
1937-1946	0.50	1.00	2.00	3.00	—

Y# 117　15 KOPEKS
Copper-Nickel　**Obv:** Eight and seven ribbons on wreath **Note:** Varieties exist.

Date	F	VF	XF	Unc	BU
1948-1956	0.50	1.00	2.00	3.00	—

Y# 124　15 KOPEKS
Copper-Nickel　**Obv:** Seven and seven ribbons on wreath

Date	F	VF	XF	Unc	BU
1957	1.00	2.00	3.00	5.00	—

Y# A131　15 KOPEKS
Copper-Nickel

Date	F	VF	XF	Unc	BU
1958	—	—	—	450	—

Y# 131　15 KOPEKS
Copper-Nickel-Zinc, 19.5 mm.

Date	F	VF	XF	Unc	BU
1961-1991	0.10	0.20	0.30	0.50	—

Y# 137   15 KOPEKS
Copper-Nickel-Zinc **Subject:** 50th Anniversary of Revolution
Rev: Statue of Laborers

Date	F	VF	XF	Unc	BU
1967	0.30	0.50	1.00	—	—

Y# 88   20 KOPEKS
3.6000 g., 0.5000 Silver .0578 oz. ASW

Date	F	VF	XF	Unc	BU
1924-1930	2.00	3.00	5.00	9.00	—

Y# 97   20 KOPEKS
Copper-Nickel **Note:** Varieties exist.

Date	F	VF	XF	Unc	BU
1931-1933	1.00	2.00	3.00	5.00	—

Y# 104   20 KOPEKS
Copper-Nickel **Note:** Varieties exist.

Date	F	VF	XF	Unc	BU
1935-1936	1.00	1.50	2.50	5.00	—

Y# 111   20 KOPEKS
Copper-Nickel **Note:** Varieties exist.

Date	F	VF	XF	Unc	BU
1937-1946	0.40	0.60	1.00	3.00	—

Y# 118   20 KOPEKS
Copper-Nickel **Obv:** Eight and seven ribbons on wreath **Note:**
Varieties exist.

Date	F	VF	XF	Unc	BU
1948-1956	0.50	0.75	1.25	2.00	—

Y# 125   20 KOPEKS
Copper-Nickel **Obv:** Seven and seven ribbons on wreath

Date	F	VF	XF	Unc	BU
1957	1.00	2.00	3.00	5.00	—

Y# A132   20 KOPEKS
Copper-Nickel

Date	F	VF	XF	Unc	BU
1958	—	—	—	450	—

Y# 132   20 KOPEKS
Copper-Nickel-Zinc **Note:** Varieties exist.

Date	F	VF	XF	Unc	BU
1961-1991	0.10	0.20	0.30	0.50	—

Y# 138   20 KOPEKS
Copper-Nickel-Zinc **Subject:** 50th Anniversary of Revolution
Rev: Cruiser "Aurora"

Date	F	VF	XF	Unc	BU
1967	0.40	0.60	1.00	—	—

Y# 89.1   50 KOPEKS
9.9980 g., 0.9000 Silver .2893 oz. ASW **Rev:** Hoe behind blacksmith at anvil **Edge Lettering:** Weight shown in old Russian units

Date	F	VF	XF	Unc	BU
1924	5.50	7.50	12.50	28.00	—

Y# 89.2   50 KOPEKS
9.9980 g., 0.9000 Silver .2893 oz. ASW **Edge Lettering:** Weight shown in Грамм (grams) only **Note:** Varieties exist.

Date	F	VF	XF	Unc	BU
1925-1927	5.50	7.50	12.50	28.00	—

Y# 90.1   ROUBLE
19.9960 g., 0.9000 Silver .5786 oz. ASW **Edge Desc:** 14 Zolotniks 21 Dolyas

Date	F	VF	XF	Unc	BU
1924 Rare	—	—	—	—	—

Y# 90.2   ROUBLE
19.9960 g., 0.9000 Silver .5786 oz. ASW **Edge Lettering:** 18 Грамм (grams) (43.21d) **Note:** Varieties exist.

Date	F	VF	XF	Unc	BU
1924	9.50	13.50	25.00	75.00	150

Y# 133a.1   50 KOPEKS
Copper-Nickel-Zinc **Edge:** Plain **Note:** Varieties exist.

Date	F	VF	XF	Unc	BU
1961	1.00	2.00	5.00	12.00	—

Y# 134   ROUBLE
Copper-Nickel

Date	F	VF	XF	Unc	BU
1958 Rare	—	—	—	—	—

Y# 134a.1   ROUBLE
Copper-Nickel-Zinc **Edge:** Plain

Date	F	VF	XF	Unc	BU
1961	2.00	3.50	6.00	15.00	—

Y# 133a.2   50 KOPEKS
Copper-Nickel-Zinc **Edge:** Lettered with date

Date	F	VF	XF	Unc	BU
1964-1991	0.15	0.25	0.50	1.00	—

Y# 134a.2   ROUBLE
Copper-Nickel-Zinc **Edge:** Lettered with date

Date	F	VF	XF	Unc	BU
1964-1991	0.25	0.50	1.00	2.50	—

Y# 139   50 KOPEKS
Copper-Nickel-Zinc **Subject:** 50th Anniversary of Revolution

Date	F	VF	XF	Unc	BU
ND(1967)	—	1.00	1.50	2.50	—

Y# 135.1   ROUBLE
Copper-Nickel-Zinc **Subject:** 20th Anniversary of World War II Victory

Date	F	VF	XF	Unc	BU
1965	—	0.50	1.00	2.50	—

Y# 135.2   ROUBLE
Copper-Nickel-Zinc **Edge Lettering:** 1988.N.

Date	F	VF	XF	Unc	BU
1965 Proof	Value: 3.50				

Y# 140.1 ROUBLE
Copper-Nickel-Zinc **Subject:** 50th Anniversary of Revolution
Edge: Lettered, with date

Date	F	VF	XF	Unc	BU
1967	—	0.50	1.00	2.50	—

Y# 140.2 ROUBLE
Copper-Nickel-Zinc **Edge Lettering:** 1988.N.

Date	F	VF	XF	Unc	BU
1967 Proof		Value: 4.00			

Y# 141 ROUBLE
Copper-Nickel-Zinc **Subject:** Centennial of Lenin's Birth

Date	F	VF	XF	Unc	BU
ND(1970)	—	0.50	1.00	2.50	—

Y# 142.1 ROUBLE
Copper-Nickel-Zinc **Subject:** 30th Anniversary of World War II
Victory **Rev:** Volgograd monument **Edge:** Date **Note:** Varieties
exist.

Date	F	VF	XF	Unc	BU
ND(1975)	—	0.50	1.00	2.50	—

Y# 142.2 ROUBLE
Copper-Nickel-Zinc **Edge Lettering:** 1988.N.

Date	F	VF	XF	Unc	BU
ND(1975) Proof		Value: 3.50			

Y# 143.1 ROUBLE
Copper-Nickel-Zinc **Subject:** 60th Anniversary of Bolshevik
Revolution **Rev:** Lenin, cruiser "Aurora"

Date	F	VF	XF	Unc	BU
ND(1977)	—	0.50	1.00	2.50	—

Y# 143.2 ROUBLE
Copper-Nickel-Zinc **Edge Lettering:** 1988.N.

Date	F	VF	XF	Unc	BU
ND(1977) Proof		Value: 3.50			

Y# A144 ROUBLE
Copper-Nickel-Zinc **Obv:** KM#143.1 **Rev:** KM#144

Date	F	VF	XF	Unc	BU
1977 Rare	—	—	—	—	—

Y# 144 ROUBLE
Copper-Nickel-Zinc **Series:** 1980 Olympics **Rev:** Emblem

Date	F	VF	XF	Unc	BU
1977	—	0.50	1.00	2.50	—

Y# 153.1 ROUBLE
Copper-Nickel-Zinc **Series:** 1980 Olympics **Rev:** Moscow Kremlin

Date	F	VF	XF	Unc	BU
1978	—	0.50	1.00	2.50	—

Y# 153.2 ROUBLE
Copper-Nickel-Zinc **Rev:** Clock on tower shows Roman numeral
6 (VI) instead of 4 (IV)

Date	F	VF	XF	Unc	BU
1978	—	8.00	16.00	25.00	—

Y# 164 ROUBLE
Copper-Nickel-Zinc **Series:** 1980 Olympics **Rev:** Moscow
University **Note:** Varieties in window arrangements exist.

Date	F	VF	XF	Unc	BU
1979	—	0.50	1.00	2.50	—

Russia

Y# 165 ROUBLE
Copper-Nickel-Zinc **Series:** 1980 Olympics **Rev:** Monument, Sputnik, and Sojuz

Date	F	VF	XF	Unc	BU
1979	—	0.50	1.00	2.50	—

Y# 177 ROUBLE
Copper-Nickel **Series:** 1980 Olympics **Rev:** Dolgorukij Monument

Date	F	VF	XF	Unc	BU
1980	—	0.50	1.00	2.50	—

Y# 189.1 ROUBLE
Copper-Nickel **Subject:** Russian-Bulgarian Friendship **Edge Lettering:** Cyrillic lettering

Date	F	VF	XF	Unc	BU
1981	—	0.50	1.00	4.00	—

Y# 189.2 ROUBLE
Copper-Nickel **Edge Lettering:** 1988.N.

Date	F	VF	XF	Unc	BU
1981 Proof		Value: 3.50			

Y# 178 ROUBLE
Copper-Nickel **Series:** 1980 Olympics **Rev:** Torch

Date	F	VF	XF	Unc	BU
1980	—	0.50	1.00	2.50	—

Y# 190.1 ROUBLE
Copper-Nickel **Subject:** 60th Anniversary of the Soviet Union **Edge Lettering:** Cyrillic lettering

Date	F	VF	XF	Unc	BU
ND(1982)	—	0.50	1.50	4.50	—

Y# 190.2 ROUBLE
Copper-Nickel **Edge Lettering:** 1988.N.

Date	F	VF	XF	Unc	BU
ND(1982) Proof		Value: 4.50			

Y# 188.1 ROUBLE
Copper-Nickel **Subject:** 20th Anniversary of Manned Space Flights **Rev:** Yuri Gagarin

Date	F	VF	XF	Unc	BU
ND(1981)	—	0.50	1.00	3.00	—

Y# 188.2 ROUBLE
Copper-Nickel **Edge Lettering:** 1988.N.

Date	F	VF	XF	Unc	BU
ND(1981) Proof		Value: 3.50			

Y# 191.1 ROUBLE
Copper-Nickel **Subject:** Death of Karl Marx Centennial **Edge:** Cyrillic lettering

Date	F	VF	XF	Unc	BU
1983	—	0.50	1.50	3.50	—

Y# 191.2 ROUBLE
Copper-Nickel **Edge Lettering:** 1988.N.

Date	F	VF	XF	Unc	BU
1983 Proof		Value: 4.50			

Y# 192.1 ROUBLE
Copper-Nickel **Subject:** 20th Anniversary of First Woman in Space **Rev:** Valentina Tereshkova

Date	F	VF	XF	Unc	BU
1983	—	0.50	1.00	4.00	—

Y# 192.2 ROUBLE
Copper-Nickel **Edge Lettering:** 1988.N.

Date	F	VF	XF	Unc	BU
1983 Proof		Value: 3.50			

Y# 195.1 ROUBLE
Copper-Nickel **Subject:** 125th Anniversary - Birth of Alexander Popov **Edge:** Cyrillic lettering

Date	F	VF	XF	Unc	BU
1984	—	0.50	1.00	3.00	—

Y# 195.2 ROUBLE
Copper-Nickel **Edge Lettering:** 1988.N.

Date	F	VF	XF	Unc	BU
1984 Proof		Value: 3.50			

Y# 193.1 ROUBLE
Copper-Nickel **Subject:** First Russian Printer **Rev:** Ivan Fedorov **Edge:** Cyrillic lettering

Date	F	VF	XF	Unc	BU
1983	—	0.50	1.00	3.00	—

Y# 193.2 ROUBLE
Copper-Nickel **Edge Lettering:** 1988.N.

Date	F	VF	XF	Unc	BU
1983 Proof		Value: 3.50			

Y# 196.1 ROUBLE
Copper-Nickel **Subject:** 185th Anniversary - Birth of Alexander Sergeevich Pushkin **Edge:** Cyrillic lettering

Date	F	VF	XF	Unc	BU
1984	—	0.50	1.00	3.00	—

Y# 196.2 ROUBLE
Copper-Nickel **Edge Lettering:** 1988.N.

Date	F	VF	XF	Unc	BU
1984-1985 Proof		Value: 3.50			

Y# 194.1 ROUBLE
Copper-Nickel **Subject:** 150th Anniversary - Birth of Dmitri Ivanovich Mendeleyev **Edge:** Cyrillic lettering

Date	F	VF	XF	Unc	BU
1984	—	0.50	1.00	3.00	—

Y# 194.2 ROUBLE
Copper-Nickel **Edge Lettering:** 1988.N.

Date	F	VF	XF	Unc	BU
1984 Proof		Value: 3.50			

Y# 197.1 ROUBLE
Copper-Nickel **Subject:** 115th Anniversary - Birth of Vladimir Lenin **Edge:** Cyrillic lettering

Date	F	VF	XF	Unc	BU
1985	—	0.50	1.50	5.00	—

Y# 197.2 ROUBLE
Copper-Nickel **Edge Lettering:** 1988.N.

Date	F	VF	XF	Unc	BU
1985 Proof		Value: 4.50			

Y# 198.1   ROUBLE
Copper-Nickel **Subject:** 40th Anniversary - World War II Victory
Edge: Cyrillic lettering

Date	F	VF	XF	Unc	BU
1985	—	0.50	1.00	3.00	—

Y# 198.2   ROUBLE
Copper-Nickel   **Edge Lettering:** 1988.N.

Date	F	VF	XF	Unc	BU
1985 Proof		Value: 3.50			

Y# 199.1   ROUBLE
Copper-Nickel **Subject:** 12th World Youth Festival in Moscow
Edge: Cyrillic lettering

Date	F	VF	XF	Unc	BU
1985	—	0.50	1.00	3.00	—

Y# 199.2   ROUBLE
Copper-Nickel   **Edge Lettering:** 1988.N.

Date	F	VF	XF	Unc	BU
1985 Proof		Value: 3.50			

Y# 200.1   ROUBLE
Copper-Nickel **Subject:** 165th Anniversary - Birth of Friedrich Engels

Date	F	VF	XF	Unc	BU
1985	—	0.50	1.50	4.50	—

Y# 200.2   ROUBLE
Copper-Nickel   **Edge Lettering:** 1988.N.

Date	F	VF	XF	Unc	BU
1983-1985 Proof		Value: 4.50			

Y# 201.1   ROUBLE
Copper-Nickel **Subject:** International Year of Peace **Edge:**
Cyrillic lettering **Note:** Rouble written with inverted "V" for Л.

Date	F	VF	XF	Unc	BU
1986	—	—	—	10.00	—

Y# 201.3   ROUBLE
Copper-Nickel **Note:** Rouble written РУБЛЬ.

Date	F	VF	XF	Unc	BU
1986	—	0.50	1.50	5.00	—

Y# 201.4   ROUBLE
Copper-Nickel **Edge Lettering:** 1988.N.

Date	F	VF	XF	Unc	BU
1986	—	0.50	1.50	5.00	—

Y# 202.1   ROUBLE
Copper-Nickel **Subject:** 275th Anniversary - Birth of Mikhail
Lomonosov **Edge:** Cyrillic lettering

Date	F	VF	XF	Unc	BU
1986	—	0.50	1.00	3.00	—

Y# 202.2   ROUBLE
Copper-Nickel **Edge Lettering:** 1988.N.

Date	F	VF	XF	Unc	BU
1986 Proof		Value: 3.50			

Y# 203   ROUBLE
Copper-Nickel **Subject:** 175th Anniversary - Battle of Borodino
- Soldiers **Edge:** Cyrillic lettering **Note:** Varieties with wheat in coat
of arms.

Date	F	VF	XF	Unc	BU
1987	—	0.50	1.00	3.00	—

Y# 204 ROUBLE
Copper-Nickel **Subject:** 175th Anniversary - Battle of Borodino
- Kutuzov Monument **Edge:** Cyrillic lettering **Note:** Varieties with
wheat in coat of arms.

Date	F	VF	XF	Unc	BU
1987	—	0.50	1.00	3.00	—

Y# 216 ROUBLE
Copper-Nickel **Subject:** 160th Anniversary - Birth of Leo Tolstoi
Edge: Cyrillic lettering

Date	F	VF	XF	Unc	BU
1988	—	0.50	1.00	3.00	—

Y# 205 ROUBLE
Copper-Nickel **Subject:** 130th Anniversary - Birth of Constantin
Tsiolkovsky **Edge:** Cyrillic lettering

Date	F	VF	XF	Unc	BU
1987	—	0.50	1.00	3.00	—

Y# 220 ROUBLE
Copper-Nickel **Subject:** 150th Anniversary - Birth of Musorgsky
Edge: Cyrillic lettering

Date	F	VF	XF	Unc	BU
1989	—	0.50	1.00	3.00	—

Y# 206 ROUBLE
Copper-Nickel **Subject:** 70th Anniversary of Bolshevik Revolution
Edge: Cyrillic lettering **Note:** Varieties with wheat in coat of arms.

Date	F	VF	XF	Unc	BU
1987	—	0.50	1.00	3.00	—

Y# 228 ROUBLE
Copper-Nickel **Subject:** 175th Anniversary - Birth of M.Y.
Lermontov **Edge:** Cyrillic lettering

Date	F	VF	XF	Unc	BU
1989	—	0.50	1.00	3.00	—

Y# 209 ROUBLE
Copper-Nickel **Subject:** 120th Anniversary - Birth of Maxin Gorky
Edge: Cyrillic lettering

Date	F	VF	XF	Unc	BU
1988	—	0.50	1.00	3.00	—

Y# 232 ROUBLE
Copper-Nickel **Subject:** 100th Anniversary - Birth of Hamza
Hakim-zade Niyazi **Edge:** Cyrillic lettering

Date	F	VF	XF	Unc	BU
1989	—	0.50	1.00	3.00	—

Y# 233 ROUBLE
Copper-Nickel **Subject:** 100th Anniversary - Death of Mihai
Eminescu **Edge:** Cyrillic lettering

Date	F	VF	XF	Unc	BU
1989	—	0.50	1.00	3.00	—

Y# 240 ROUBLE
Copper-Nickel **Subject:** 130th Anniversary - Birth of Anton
Chekhov **Edge:** Cyrillic lettering

Date	F	VF	XF	Unc	BU
1990	—	—	—	3.00	—

Y# 235 ROUBLE
Copper-Nickel **Subject:** 175th Anniversary - Birth of T.G.
Shevchenko **Edge:** Cyrillic lettering

Date	F	VF	XF	Unc	BU
1989	—	0.50	1.00	3.00	—

Y# 257 ROUBLE
Copper-Nickel **Subject:** 125th Anniversary - Birth of Janis Rainis
Edge: Cyrillic lettering

Date	F	VF	XF	Unc	BU
1990	—	—	—	3.00	—

Y# 236 ROUBLE
Copper-Nickel **Subject:** 100th Anniversary - Birth of
Tschaikovsky - Composer **Edge:** Cyrillic lettering

Date	F	VF	XF	Unc	BU
1990	—	—	—	3.00	—

Y# 258 ROUBLE
Copper-Nickel **Subject:** 500th Anniversary - Birth of Francisk
Scorina **Edge:** Cyrillic lettering

Date	F	VF	XF	Unc	BU
1990	—	—	—	3.00	—

Y# 237 ROUBLE
Copper-Nickel **Subject:** Anniversary - Marshal Zhukov **Edge:**
Cyrillic lettering

Date	F	VF	XF	Unc	BU
1990	—	—	—	5.00	—

Y# 260 ROUBLE
Copper-Nickel **Subject:** 550th Anniversary - Birth of Alisher Navoi
Edge: Cyrillic lettering

Date	F	VF	XF	Unc	BU
1990-1991	—	—	—	3.00	—

Y# 261 ROUBLE
Copper-Nickel **Subject:** 125th Anniversary - Birth of P. N. Lebedev **Edge:** Cyrillic lettering

Date	F	VF	XF	Unc	BU
1991	—	—	—	3.00	—

Y# 263.1 ROUBLE
Copper-Nickel **Subject:** 100th Birthday of Sergey Prokofiev **Edge:** Cyrillic lettering

Date	F	VF	XF	Unc	BU
1991	—	—	—	3.00	—

Y# 263.2 ROUBLE
Copper-Nickel **Subject:** 100th Birthday of Sergey Prokofiev **Note:** Error death date: 1952.

Date	F	VF	XF	Unc	BU
1991 Rare	—	—	—	—	—

Y# 282 ROUBLE
Copper-Nickel **Subject:** K. V. Ivanon **Rev:** K.T. Ivanov **Edge:** Cyrillic lettering

Date	F	VF	XF	Unc	BU
1991	—	—	—	3.00	—

Y# 283 ROUBLE
Copper-Nickel **Rev:** Turkman Poet Makhtumkuli **Edge:** Cyrillic lettering

Date	F	VF	XF	Unc	BU
1991	—	—	—	5.00	—

Y# 284 ROUBLE
Copper-Nickel **Subject:** 850th Anniversary - Birth of Nizami Gyanzhevi - Poet **Edge:** Cyrillic lettering

Date	F	VF	XF	Unc	BU
1991	—	—	—	5.00	—

Y# 289 ROUBLE
Copper-Nickel **Series:** Olympics **Rev:** Wrestlers

Date	F	VF	XF	Unc	BU
1991 Proof		Value: 5.50			

Y# 290 ROUBLE
Copper-Nickel **Series:** Olympics **Rev:** Javelin thrower

Date	F	VF	XF	Unc	BU
1991 Proof		Value: 5.50			

Y# 291 ROUBLE
Copper-Nickel **Series:** Olympics **Rev:** Cyclist and charioteer

Date	F	VF	XF	Unc	BU
1991 Proof		Value: 5.50			

Y# 299   ROUBLE
Copper-Nickel   **Series:** Olympics **Rev:** Weight lifters

Date	F	VF	XF	Unc	BU
1991 Proof		Value: 5.50			

Y# 300   ROUBLE
Copper-Nickel   **Series:** Olympics **Rev:** Broad jumpers

Date	F	VF	XF	Unc	BU
1991 Proof		Value: 5.50			

Y# 302   ROUBLE
Copper-Nickel   **Series:** Olympics **Rev:** Runners

Date	F	VF	XF	Unc	BU
1991 Proof		Value: 5.50			

Y# A134   2 ROUBLES
Copper-Nickel

Date	F	VF	XF	Unc	BU
1958	—	—	—	250	—

Y# B134   2 ROUBLES
Copper-Nickel

Date	F	VF	XF	Unc	BU
1958	—	—	—	—	—

Y# 207   3 ROUBLES
Copper-Nickel   **Subject:** 70th Anniversary - Bolshevik Revolution

Date	F	VF	XF	Unc	BU
1987	—	—	—	5.00	—

Y# 210   3 ROUBLES
34.5600 g., 0.9000 Silver 1.0000 oz. ASW   **Subject:** 1000th
Anniversary of Russian Architecture **Rev:** Cathedral of St. Sophie
in Kiev

Date	F	VF	XF	Unc	BU
1988 Proof		Value: 45.00			

Y# 211   3 ROUBLES
34.5600 g., 0.9000 Silver 1.0000 oz. ASW   **Subject:** 1000th
Anniversary of Minting in Russian **Rev:** Coin design of St. Vladimir,
977-1015

Date	F	VF	XF	Unc	BU
1988 Proof		Value: 42.50			

Y# 222   3 ROUBLES
34.5600 g., 0.9000 Silver 1.0000 oz. ASW   **Subject:** 500th
Anniversary United Russia **Obv:** State emblem and denomination
Rev: Kremlin

Date	F	VF	XF	Unc	BU
1989 Proof		Value: 32.50			

Y# 223   3 ROUBLES
34.5600 g., 0.9000 Silver 1.0000 oz. ASW   **Subject:** 500th
Anniversary of the First All-Russian Coinage

Date	F	VF	XF	Unc	BU
1989 Proof		Value: 37.50			

Y# 234   3 ROUBLES
Copper-Nickel   **Subject:** Armenian Earthquake Relief **Edge:**
Cyrillic lettering

Date	F	VF	XF	Unc	BU
1989	—	—	—	5.00	—

Y# 242   3 ROUBLES
34.5600 g., 0.9000 Silver 1.0000 oz. ASW   **Rev:** Capt. Cook on
Unalaska Island

Date	F	VF	XF	Unc	BU
1990 Proof		Value: 47.50			

Y# 247   3 ROUBLES
34.5600 g., 0.9000 Silver 1.0000 oz. ASW   **Subject:** World
Summit for Children

Date	F	VF	XF	Unc	BU
1990 Proof		Value: 37.50			

Y# 248   3 ROUBLES
34.5600 g., 0.9000 Silver 1.0000 oz. ASW   **Rev:** Peter the Great's
fleet

Date	F	VF	XF	Unc	BU
1990 Proof		Value: 30.00			

Y# 249   3 ROUBLES
34.5600 g., 0.9000 Silver 1.0000 oz. ASW   **Rev:** St. Peter and
Paul Fortress in Leningrad

Date	F	VF	XF	Unc	BU
1990 Proof		Value: 30.00			

Y# 262   3 ROUBLES
34.5600 g., 0.9000 Silver 1.0000 oz. ASW   **Rev:** Yuri Gagarin
Monument

Date	F	VF	XF	Unc	BU
1991 Proof	Value: 32.50				

Y# 264   3 ROUBLES
34.5600 g., 0.9000 Silver 1.0000 oz. ASW   **Rev:** Fort Ross in
California

Date	F	VF	XF	Unc	BU
1991 Proof	Value: 40.00				

Y# 274   3 ROUBLES
34.5600 g., 0.9000 Silver 1.0000 oz. ASW   **Rev:** Bolshoi Theater

Date	F	VF	XF	Unc	BU
1991 Proof	Value: 30.00				

Y# 275   3 ROUBLES
34.5600 g., 0.9000 Silver 1.0000 oz. ASW   **Rev:** Moscow's Arch
of Triumph

Date	F	VF	XF	Unc	BU
1991 Proof	Value: 30.00				

Y# 301   3 ROUBLES
Copper-Nickel   **Subject:** 50th Anniversary - Defense of Moscow
Edge: Cyrillic lettering

Date	F	VF	XF	Unc	BU
1991	—	—	—	5.00	—

Y# C134   5 ROUBLES
Copper-Nickel

Date	F	VF	XF	Unc	BU
1958	—	—	—	300	—

Y# 145   5 ROUBLES
16.6700 g., 0.9000 Silver .4824 oz. ASW   **Series:** 1980 Olympics
Rev: Scenes of Kiev

Date	F	VF	XF	Unc	BU
1977	—	—	—	5.50	—

Y# 146 5 ROUBLES
16.6700 g., 0.9000 Silver .4824 oz. ASW **Series:** 1980 Olympics
Rev: Scenes of Leningrad

Date	F	VF	XF	Unc	BU
1977	—	—	—	5.50	—

Y# 155 5 ROUBLES
16.6700 g., 0.9000 Silver .4824 oz. ASW **Series:** 1980 Olympics
Subject: Swimming

Date	F	VF	XF	Unc	BU
1978	—	—	—	5.50	—

Y# 147 5 ROUBLES
16.6700 g., 0.9000 Silver .4824 oz. ASW **Series:** 1980 Olympics
Rev: Scenes of Minsk

Date	F	VF	XF	Unc	BU
1977	—	—	—	5.50	—

Y# 156 5 ROUBLES
16.6700 g., 0.9000 Silver .4824 oz. ASW **Series:** 1980 Olympics
Subject: High Jumping

Date	F	VF	XF	Unc	BU
1978	—	—	—	5.50	—

Y# 148 5 ROUBLES
16.6700 g., 0.9000 Silver .4824 oz. ASW **Series:** 1980 Olympics
Rev: Scenes of Tallinn

Date	F	VF	XF	Unc	BU
1977	—	—	—	5.50	—

Y# 157 5 ROUBLES
16.6700 g., 0.9000 Silver .4824 oz. ASW **Series:** 1980 Olympics
Subject: Equestrian Show Jumping

Date	F	VF	XF	Unc	BU
1978	—	—	—	5.50	—

Y# 154 5 ROUBLES
16.6700 g., 0.9000 Silver .4824 oz. ASW **Series:** 1980 Olympics
Rev: Runner in front of stadium

Date	F	VF	XF	Unc	BU
1978	—	—	—	5.50	—

Y# 166 5 ROUBLES
16.6700 g., 0.9000 Silver 0.4824 oz. ASW **Series:** 1980 Olympics
Subject: Weight lifting

Date	F	VF	XF	Unc	BU
1979	—	—	—	5.50	—

Y# 167   5 ROUBLES
16.6700 g., 0.9000 Silver .4824 oz. ASW **Series:** 1980 Olympics
Subject: Hammer Throw

Date	F	VF	XF	Unc	BU
1979	—	—	—	5.50	—

Y# 179   5 ROUBLES
16.6700 g., 0.9000 Silver **Series:** 1980 Olympics **Subject:** Archery

Date	F	VF	XF	Unc	BU
1980	—	—	—	6.00	—

Y# 180   5 ROUBLES
16.6700 g., 0.9000 Silver **Series:** 1980 Olympics **Subject:**
Gymnastics

Date	F	VF	XF	Unc	BU
1980	—	—	—	6.00	—

Y# 181   5 ROUBLES
16.6700 g., 0.9000 Silver **Series:** 1980 Olympics **Subject:**
Equestrian - Isindi

Date	F	VF	XF	Unc	BU
1980	—	—	—	6.00	—

Y# 182   5 ROUBLES
16.6700 g., 0.9000 Silver **Series:** 1980 Olympics **Subject:**
Gorodki - Stick Throwing

Date	F	VF	XF	Unc	BU
1980	—	—	—	6.00	—

Y# 208   5 ROUBLES
Copper-Nickel **Subject:** 70th Anniversary - Bolshevik Revolution

Date	F	VF	XF	Unc	BU
1987	—	—	—	5.00	—

Y# 217   5 ROUBLES
Copper-Nickel **Rev:** Peter the Great mounted on horse in Leningrad

Date	F	VF	XF	Unc	BU
1988	—	—	—	5.00	—

Y# 218   5 ROUBLES
Copper-Nickel **Rev:** Novgorod Monument to the Russian millennium

Date	F	VF	XF	Unc	BU
1988	—	—	—	5.00	—

Y# 219 5 ROUBLES
Copper-Nickel **Rev:** St. Sophia Cathedral in Kiev

Date	F	VF	XF	Unc	BU
1988	—	—	—	5.00	—

Y# 221 5 ROUBLES
Copper-Nickel **Rev:** Pokrowsky Cathedral in Moscow

Date	F	VF	XF	Unc	BU
1989	—	—	—	5.00	—

Y# 229 5 ROUBLES
Copper-Nickel **Rev:** Samarkand

Date	F	VF	XF	Unc	BU
1989	—	—	—	5.00	—

Y# 230 5 ROUBLES
Copper-Nickel **Rev:** Cathedral of the Annunciation in Moscow

Date	F	VF	XF	Unc	BU
1989	—	—	—	5.00	—

Y# 241 5 ROUBLES
Copper-Nickel **Rev:** Petergoff Palace

Date	F	VF	XF	Unc	BU
1990	—	—	—	5.00	—

Y# 246 5 ROUBLES
Copper-Nickel **Rev:** Uspenski Cathedral **Edge:** Cyrillic lettering

Date	F	VF	XF	Unc	BU
1990	—	—	—	5.00	—

Y# 259 5 ROUBLES
Copper-Nickel **Rev:** Matenadarin Depository of Ancient Armenian Manuscripts

Date	F	VF	XF	Unc	BU
1990	—	—	—	5.00	—

Y# 268 5 ROUBLES
7.7758 g., 0.9990 Palladium .2500 oz. **Series:** Ballet

Date	F	VF	XF	Unc	BU
1991	—	—	—	150	—

Y# 271 5 ROUBLES

Copper-Nickel **Rev:** Cathedral of the Archangel Michael in Moscow **Edge:** Cyrillic lettering

Date	F	VF	XF	Unc	BU
1991	—	—	—	5.00	—

Y# 272 5 ROUBLES

Copper-Nickel **Rev:** State bank building in Moscow

Date	F	VF	XF	Unc	BU
1991	—	—	—	5.00	—

Y# 273 5 ROUBLES

Copper-Nickel **Rev:** David Sasunsky Monument **Edge:** Cyrillic lettering

Date	F	VF	XF	Unc	BU
1991	—	—	—	5.00	—

Y# 149 10 ROUBLES

33.3000 g., 0.9000 Silver .9636 oz. ASW **Series:** 1980 Olympics **Rev:** Scenes of Moscow

Date	F	VF	XF	Unc	BU
1977	—	—	—	11.50	—

Y# 150 10 ROUBLES

33.3000 g., 0.9000 Silver .9636 oz. ASW **Series:** 1980 Olympics **Obv:** Hammer and sickle national emblem divides CCCP, value below **Rev:** Map of U.S.S.R.

Date	F	VF	XF	Unc	BU
1977	—	—	—	11.50	—

Y# 158.1 10 ROUBLES

33.3000 g., 0.9000 Silver .9636 oz. ASW **Series:** 1980 Olympics **Subject:** Cycling **Obv:** Hammer and sickle national emblem divides CCCP, value below

Date	F	VF	XF	Unc	BU
1978	—	—	—	11.50	—

Y# 158.2 10 ROUBLES

33.3000 g., 0.9000 Silver .9636 oz. ASW **Series:** 1980 Olympics **Obv:** Hammer and sickle national emblem divides CCCP, value below **Rev:** Without mint mark

Date	F	VF	XF	Unc	BU
1978 Rare	—	—	—	—	—

Y# 159 10 ROUBLES

33.3000 g., 0.9000 Silver .9636 oz. ASW **Series:** 1980 Olympics **Subject:** Canoeing **Obv:** Hammer and sickle national emblem divides CCCP, value below

Date	F	VF	XF	Unc	BU
1978	—	—	—	11.50	—

Y# 160 10 ROUBLES
33.3000 g., 0.9000 Silver .9636 oz. ASW **Series:** 1980 Olympics
Subject: Equestrian Sport **Obv:** Hammer and sickle national emblem divides CCCP, value below

Date	F	VF	XF	Unc	BU
1978	—	—	—	11.50	—

Y# 169 10 ROUBLES
33.3000 g., 0.9000 Silver .9636 oz. ASW **Series:** 1980 Olympics
Subject: Volleyball **Obv:** Hammer and sickle national emblem divides CCCP, value below

Date	F	VF	XF	Unc	BU
1979	—	—	—	11.50	—

Y# 161 10 ROUBLES
33.3000 g., 0.9000 Silver .9636 oz. ASW **Series:** 1980 Olympics
Subject: Pole vaulting **Obv:** Hammer and sickle national emblem divides CCCP, value below

Date	F	VF	XF	Unc	BU
1978	—	—	—	11.50	—

Y# 170 10 ROUBLES
33.3000 g., 0.9000 Silver .9636 oz. ASW **Series:** 1980 Olympics
Subject: Boxing **Obv:** Hammer and sickle national emblem divides CCCP, value below

Date	F	VF	XF	Unc	BU
1979	—	—	—	12.50	—

Y# 168 10 ROUBLES
33.3000 g., 0.9000 Silver .9636 oz. ASW **Series:** 1980 Olympics
Subject: Basketball **Obv:** Similar to Y#149

Date	F	VF	XF	Unc	BU
1979	—	—	—	11.50	—

Y# 171 10 ROUBLES
33.3000 g., 0.9000 Silver .9636 oz. ASW **Series:** 1980 Olympics
Subject: Judo **Obv:** Hammer and sickle national emblem divides CCCP, value below

Date	F	VF	XF	Unc	BU
1979	—	—	—	12.50	—

Y# 172　10 ROUBLES

33.3000 g., 0.9000 Silver .9636 oz. ASW **Series:** 1980 Olympics
Subject: Lifting of the Weight **Obv:** Hammer and sickle national
emblem divides CCCP, value below

Date	F	VF	XF	Unc	BU
1979	—	—	—	12.50	—

Y# 185　10 ROUBLES

33.3000 g., 0.9000 Silver .9636 oz. ASW **Series:** 1980 Olympics
Subject: Reindeer Racing **Obv:** Hammer and sickle national
emblem divides CCCP, value below

Date	F	VF	XF	Unc	BU
1980	—	—	—	12.50	—

Y# 183　10 ROUBLES

33.3000 g., 0.9000 Silver .9636 oz. ASW **Series:** 1980 Olympics
Subject: Wrestling **Obv:** Hammer and sickle national emblem
divides CCCP, value below

Date	F	VF	XF	Unc	BU
1980	—	—	—	12.50	—

Y# 238　10 ROUBLES

15.5500 g., 0.9990 Palladium .5000 oz. **Subject:** Ballet **Obv:**
Hammer and sickle national emblem above CCCP, value below
Rev: Ballerina

Date	F	VF	XF	Unc	BU
1990	—	—	—	265	—

Y# 269　10 ROUBLES

15.5500 g., 0.9990 Palladium .5000 oz. **Subject:** Ballet **Rev:**
Ballerina

Date	F	VF	XF	Unc	BU
1991	—	—	—	265	—

Y# 285　10 ROUBLES

2.6600 g., 0.5850 Gold .0500 oz. AGW **Subject:** Bolshoi Ballet
Obv: Hammer and sickle national emblem above CCCP, value
below **Rev:** Ballerina

Date	F	VF	XF	Unc	BU
1991	—	—	—	55.00	—

Y# 184　10 ROUBLES

33.3000 g., 0.9000 Silver .9636 oz. ASW **Series:** 1980 Olympics
Subject: Tug of War **Obv:** Hammer and sickle national emblem
divides CCCP, value below

Date	F	VF	XF	Unc	BU
1980	—	—	—	12.50	—

Y# 212   25 ROUBLES
31.1000 g., 0.9990 Palladium 1.0000 oz.   **Rev:** Monument to
Vladimir, Grand Duke of Kiev and to the Millennium of Christianity
in Russia

Date	F	VF	XF	Unc	BU
1988	—	—	—	500	—

Y# 243   25 ROUBLES
31.1000 g., 0.9990 Palladium 1.0000 oz.   **Subject:** 250th
Anniversary - Discovery of Russian America **Rev:** Ship, St. Peter

Date	F	VF	XF	Unc	BU
1990 Proof		Value: 500			

Y# 224   25 ROUBLES
31.1000 g., 0.9990 Palladium 1.0000 oz.   **Subject:** 500th
Anniversary of Russian State **Rev:** Ivan III

Date	F	VF	XF	Unc	BU
1989 Proof		Value: 500			

Y# 244   25 ROUBLES
31.1000 g., 0.9990 Palladium 1.0000 oz.   **Subject:** 250th
Anniversary - Discovery of Russian America **Rev:** Ship, St. Peter

Date	F	VF	XF	Unc	BU
1990 Proof		Value: 500			

Y# 231   25 ROUBLES
31.1000 g., 0.9990 Palladium 1.0000 oz.   **Subject:** Ballet **Rev:**
Ballerina

Date	F	VF	XF	Unc	BU
1989	—	—	—	500	—

Y# 239   25 ROUBLES
31.1000 g., 0.9990 Palladium 1.0000 oz.   **Subject:** Ballet **Rev:**
Ballerina

Date	F	VF	XF	Unc	BU
1990	—	—	—	500	—

Y# 250   25 ROUBLES
31.1000 g., 0.9990 Palladium 1.0000 oz.   **Subject:** 500th
Anniversary of Russian State **Rev:** Peter the Great

Date	F	VF	XF	Unc	BU
1990 Proof		Value: 500			

Y# 265   25 ROUBLES
31.1000 g., 0.9990 Palladium 1.0000 oz.   **Note:** Three Saints
Harbor - Russian settlement in America.

Date	F	VF	XF	Unc	BU
1991 Proof		Value: 500			

Y# 266   25 ROUBLES
31.1000 g., 0.9990 Palladium 1.0000 oz.   **Note:** Novo
Archangelsk 1799 - three-masted ship

Date	F	VF	XF	Unc	BU
1991 Proof		Value: 500			

Y# 225   50 ROUBLES
8.6397 g., 0.9000 Gold .2500 oz. AGW   **Subject:** 500th Anniversary of Russian State **Obv:** State emblem and denomination **Rev:** Cathedral of the Ascension

Date	F	VF	XF	Unc	BU
1989 Proof			Value: 185		

Y# 270   25 ROUBLES
31.1000 g., 0.9990 Palladium 1.0000 oz.   **Subject:** Ballet **Rev:** Ballerina

Date	F	VF	XF	Unc	BU
1991	—	—	—	500	—

Y# 251   50 ROUBLES
8.6397 g., 0.9000 Gold .2500 oz. AGW   **Subject:** 500th Anniversary of Russian State **Rev:** Moscow Church of the Archangel

Date	F	VF	XF	Unc	BU
1990 Proof			Value: 185		

Y# 276   25 ROUBLES
31.1000 g., 0.9990 Palladium 1.0000 oz.   **Subject:** 500th Anniversary of Russian State - Abolition of Serfdom in Russia **Obv:** State emblem

Date	F	VF	XF	Unc	BU
1991 Proof			Value: 500		

Y# 277   50 ROUBLES
8.6440 g., 0.9000 Gold .2500 oz. AGW   **Subject:** 500th Anniversary of Russian State **Rev:** St. Isaac Cathedral in St. Petersburg

Date	F	VF	XF	Unc	BU
1991 Proof			Value: 185		

Y# 287   50 ROUBLES
13.3000 g., 0.5850 Gold .2500 oz. AGW   **Subject:** Bolshoi Ballet **Rev:** Ballerina

Date	F	VF	XF	Unc	BU
1991	—	—	—	250	—

Y# 287a   50 ROUBLES
7.7800 g., 0.9990 Gold .2500 oz. AGW   **Rev:** Ballerina **Edge Lettering:** Bolshoi Ballet

Date	F	VF	XF	Unc	BU
1991 Proof			Value: 450		

Y# 286   25 ROUBLES
5.3200 g., 0.5850 Gold .1 oz. AGW   **Subject:** Bolshoi Ballet

Date	F	VF	XF	Unc	BU
1991	—	—	—	110	—

Y# 286a   25 ROUBLES
3.1100 g., 0.9990 Gold .1 oz. AGW

Date	F	VF	XF	Unc	BU
1991 Proof			Value: 250		

Y# A163   100 ROUBLES
17.2800 g., 0.9000 Gold .5000 oz. AGW   **Series:** 1980 Olympics **Rev:** Symbols

Date	F	VF	XF	Unc	BU
1977	—	—	—	345	

Y# 213   50 ROUBLES
8.6397 g., 0.9000 Gold .2500 oz. AGW   **Subject:** 1000th Anniversary of Russian Architecture **Obv:** Similar to 100 Roubles, Y#A163 **Rev:** Cathedral of St. Sophia in Novgorod

Date	F	VF	XF	Unc	BU
1988	—	—	—	—	185

Russia

Y# 151   100 ROUBLES
17.2800 g., 0.9000 Gold .5000 oz. AGW **Series:** 1980 Olympics
Rev: Lenin Stadium

Date	F	VF	XF	Unc	BU
1978	—	—	—	345	—

Y# 186   100 ROUBLES
17.2800 g., 0.9000 Gold .5000 oz. AGW **Series:** 1980 Olympics
Rev: Torch

Date	F	VF	XF	Unc	BU
1980	—	—	—	345	—

Y# 162   100 ROUBLES
17.2800 g., 0.9000 Gold .5000 oz. AGW **Series:** 1980 Olympics
Rev: Waterside grandstand

Date	F	VF	XF	Unc	BU
1978	—	—	—	345	—

Y# 214   100 ROUBLES
17.2800 g., 0.9000 Gold .5000 oz. AGW **Series:** 1980 Olympics
Subject: 1000th Anniversary of Minting in Russia - Coin design
of St. Vladimir (977-1015) **Obv:** Similar to Y#186

Date	F	VF	XF	Unc	BU
1988	—	—	—	375	—

Y# 173   100 ROUBLES
17.2800 g., 0.9000 Gold .5000 oz. AGW **Series:** 1980 Olympics
Rev: Velodrome building

Date	F	VF	XF	Unc	BU
1979	—	—	—	345	—

Y# 226   100 ROUBLES
17.2800 g., 0.9000 Gold .5000 oz. AGW **Series:** 1980 Olympics
Subject: 500th Anniversary of Russian State **Obv:** State emblem
and denomination **Rev:** Seal of Ivan III

Date	F	VF	XF	Unc	BU
1989 Proof	Value: 450				

Y# 174   100 ROUBLES
17.2800 g., 0.9000 Gold .5000 oz. AGW **Series:** 1980 Olympics
Rev: Druzhba Sports Hall

Date	F	VF	XF	Unc	BU
1979	—	—	—	345	—

Y# 252   100 ROUBLES
17.2800 g., 0.9000 Gold .5000 oz. AGW **Series:** 1980 Olympics
Subject: 500th Anniversary of Russian State **Rev:** Peter the Great
monument

Date	F	VF	XF	Unc	BU
1990 Proof	Value: 450				

Y# 278 100 ROUBLES
17.2800 g., 0.9000 Gold .5000 oz. AGW **Series:** 1980 Olympics
Subject: 500th Anniversary of Russian State **Rev:** Tolstoi monument

Date	F	VF	XF	Unc	BU
1991 Proof		Value: 375			

Y# 288 100 ROUBLES
26.5900 g., 0.5850 Gold .5000 oz. AGW **Subject:** Bolshoi Ballet
Rev: Ballerina

Date	F	VF	XF	Unc	BU
1991	—	—	—	500	—

Y# 288a 100 ROUBLES
15.5500 g., 0.9990 Gold .5000 oz. AGW **Subject:** Bolshoi Ballet
Rev: Ballerina

Date	F	VF	XF	Unc	BU
1991 Proof		Value: 750			

Y# 152 150 ROUBLES
15.5400 g., 0.9990 Platinum .4991 oz. APW **Series:** 1980
Olympics **Rev:** Symbols over logo

Date	F	VF	XF	Unc	BU
1977	—	—	—	650	—

Y# 163 150 ROUBLES
15.5400 g., 0.9990 Platinum .4991 oz. APW **Series:** 1980
Olympics **Rev:** Throwing discus

Date	F	VF	XF	Unc	BU
1978	—	—	—	650	—

Y# 175 150 ROUBLES
15.5400 g., 0.9990 Platinum .4991 oz. APW **Series:** 1980
Olympics **Rev:** Greek wrestlers

Date	F	VF	XF	Unc	BU
1979	—	—	—	650	—

Y# 176 150 ROUBLES
15.5400 g., 0.9990 Platinum .4991 oz. APW **Series:** 1980
Olympics **Rev:** Roman chariot race

Date	F	VF	XF	Unc	BU
1979	—	—	—	650	—

Y# 187 150 ROUBLES
15.5400 g., 0.9990 Platinum .4991 oz. APW **Series:** 1980
Olympics **Rev:** Ancient Greek runners

Date	F	VF	XF	Unc	BU
1980	—	—	—	650	—

Y# 215 150 ROUBLES
15.5500 g., 0.9990 Platinum .5000 oz. APW **Subject:** 1000th
Anniversary of Russian Literature **Obv:** Similar to Y#187 **Rev:**
Chronicler writing epic about Grand Duke Igor

Date	F	VF	XF	Unc	BU
1988	—	—	—	650	—

Y# 227   150 ROUBLES
15.5500 g., 0.9990 Platinum .5000 oz. APW   **Subject:** 500th
Anniversary of Russian State **Obv:** State emblem and denomination
Rev: Ugra River encounter

Date	F	VF	XF	Unc	BU
1989 Proof		Value: 650			

Y# 245   150 ROUBLES
15.5500 g., 0.9990 Platinum .5000 oz. APW   **Subject:** 250th
Anniversary - Discovery of Russian America **Obv:** Similar to Y#187
Rev: Ship, St. Gavriil

Date	F	VF	XF	Unc	BU
1990 Proof		Value: 675			

Y# 253   150 ROUBLES
15.5500 g., 0.9990 Platinum .5000 oz. APW   **Subject:** 500th
Anniversary of Russian State **Rev:** Battle of Poltava River

Date	F	VF	XF	Unc	BU
1990 Proof		Value: 650			

Y# 267   150 ROUBLES
15.5500 g., 0.9990 Platinum .5000 oz. APW   **Subject:** 250th
Anniversary - Discovery of Russian America **Rev:** Bishop Veniaminov

Date	F	VF	XF	Unc	BU
1991 Proof		Value: 375			

Y# 279   150 ROUBLES
17.5000 g., 0.9990 Platinum .5000 oz. APW   **Subject:** 500th
Anniversary of Russian State - War of Liberation Against Napoleon

Date	F	VF	XF	Unc	BU
1991 Proof		Value: 650			

GOVERNMENT BANK ISSUES
1991-1992

Y# 296   10 KOPEKS
Copper Clad Steel   **Obv:** Kremlin tower and dome

Date	F	VF	XF	Unc	BU
1991	0.10	0.15	0.25	0.50	—

Y# 292   50 KOPEKS
Copper-Nickel

Date	F	VF	XF	Unc	BU
1991	0.15	0.25	0.35	1.00	—

Y# 293   ROUBLE
Copper-Nickel

Date	F	VF	XF	Unc	BU
1991	—	—	—	1.00	—

Y# 280   5 ROUBLES
Bi-Metallic Brass center in Copper-Nickel ring   **Series:** Wildlife
Rev: Blakiston's fish owl **Edge:** Alternating reeded and smooth

Date	F	VF	XF	Unc	BU
1991	—	—	—	3.00	6.00

Y# 281 5 ROUBLES
Bi-Metallic Brass center in Copper-Nickel ring **Series:** Wildlife **Rev:**
Mountain Goat, markhor **Edge:** Alternating reeded and smooth

Date	F	VF	XF	Unc	BU
1991	—	—	—	2.00	5.00

Y# 294 5 ROUBLES
Copper-Nickel **Edge:** Alternating reeded and smooth

Date	F	VF	XF	Unc	BU
1991	—	—	—	3.00	—

Y# 295 10 ROUBLES
5.9700 g., Bi-Metallic Copper-Nickel ring, Aluminum-Bronze
center **Edge:** Alternating reeded and smooth

Date	F	VF	XF	Unc	BU
1991-1992	0.50	1.00	2.00	3.00	—

RUSSIAN FEDERATION
Issued by БАНК РОССИИ
(Bank Russia)

STANDARD COINAGE

Y# 303 ROUBLE
Copper-Nickel **Subject:** Rebirth of Russian Sovereignty and
Democracy

Date	F	VF	XF	Unc	BU
1992	—	—	—	2.50	—

Y# 305 ROUBLE
Copper-Nickel **Subject:** 110th Anniversary - Birth of Jacob Kolas
Edge: Cyrillic lettering

Date	F	VF	XF	Unc	BU
1992	—	—	—	2.50	—

Y# 306 ROUBLE
Copper-Nickel **Subject:** 190th Anniversary - Birth of Admiral
Nakhimov **Edge:** Cyrillic lettering

Date	F	VF	XF	Unc	BU
1992	—	—	—	2.50	—

Y# 311 ROUBLE
Brass Clad Steel **Obv:** Double-headed eagle

Date	F	VF	XF	Unc	BU
1992	2.00	5.00	10.00	1.00	—

Y# 320 ROUBLE
Copper-Nickel **Rev:** Yanka Kupala **Edge:** Cyrillic lettering

Date	F	VF	XF	Unc	BU
1992 Proof	Value: 5.00				

Y# 321 ROUBLE
Copper-Nickel **Obv:** Double-headed eagle **Rev:** N. I. Lobachevsky

Date	F	VF	XF	Unc	BU
1992 Proof	Value: 5.00				

Y# 326 ROUBLE
Copper-Nickel **Obv:** Double-headed eagle **Rev:** K. A. Timiryazev

Date	F	VF	XF	Unc	BU
1993	—	—	—	2.50	—

Y# 319.1 ROUBLE
Copper-Nickel **Obv:** Double-headed eagle **Rev:** Vladimir Ivanovich Vernadsky

Date	F	VF	XF	Unc	BU
1993 Proof	Value: 5.50				

Y# 327 ROUBLE
Copper-Nickel **Rev:** V. Maikovski

Date	F	VF	XF	Unc	BU
1993	—	—	—	2.50	—

Y# 319.2 ROUBLE
Copper-Nickel **Obv:** Double-headed eagle, without mint mark below eagle's claw **Rev:** Vladimir Ivanovich Vernadsky

Date	F	VF	XF	Unc	BU
1993	—	—	—	2.50	—

Y# 335 ROUBLE
15.5500 g., 0.9000 Silver .4500 oz. ASW **Series:** Red Book Wildlife **Rev:** Tiger

Date	F	VF	XF	Unc	BU
1993 Proof	Value: 25.00				

Y# 325 ROUBLE
Copper-Nickel **Obv:** Double-headed eagle **Rev:** Gavrilla Romanovich Derzhavin

Date	F	VF	XF	Unc	BU
1993	—	—	—	2.50	—

Y# 336 ROUBLE
15.5500 g., 0.9000 Silver .4500 oz. ASW **Series:** Red Book Wildlife **Rev:** Blackiston's Fish Owl

Date	F	VF	XF	Unc	BU
1993 Proof	Value: 30.00				

Y# 337 ROUBLE
15.5500 g., 0.9000 Silver .4500 oz. ASW **Series:** Red Book
Wildlife **Rev:** Mountain goat (Markhor)

Date	F	VF	XF	Unc	BU
1993 Proof		Value: 25.00			

Y# 347 ROUBLE
Copper-Nickel **Obv:** Double-headed eagle **Rev:** A. P. Borodin

Date	F	VF	XF	Unc	BU
1993	—	—	—	2.50	—

Y# 348 ROUBLE
Copper-Nickel **Rev:** I. S. Turgenev

Date	F	VF	XF	Unc	BU
1993	—	—	—	2.50	—

Y# 372 ROUBLE
15.5500 g., 0.9000 Silver .4500 oz. ASW **Series:** Wildlife **Rev:**
Red-breasted Kazarka

Date	F	VF	XF	Unc	BU
1994 Proof		Value: 22.00			

Y# 373 ROUBLE
15.5500 g., 0.9000 Silver .4500 oz. ASW **Series:** Wildlife **Obv:**
Double-headed eagle **Rev:** Asiatic Cobra

Date	F	VF	XF	Unc	BU
1994 Proof		Value: 25.00			

Y# 374 ROUBLE
15.5500 g., 0.9000 Silver .4500 oz. ASW **Series:** Wildlife **Obv:**
Double-headed eagle **Rev:** Asiatic black bear

Date	F	VF	XF	Unc	BU
1994 Proof		Value: 25.00			

Y# 399 ROUBLE
Aluminum-Bronze **Subject:** WWII Victory **Rev:** Mother Russia
calling for volunteers

Date	F	VF	XF	Unc	BU
1995	—	—	—	1.50	—

Y# 446 ROUBLE
17.4600 g., 0.9000 Silver .5052 oz. ASW **Series:** Wildlife **Rev:**
Oriental White Stork

Date	F	VF	XF	Unc	BU
1995 Proof		Value: 25.00			

Y# 447 ROUBLE
17.4600 g., 0.9000 Silver .5052 oz. ASW **Series:** Wildlife **Obv:**
Double headed eagle **Rev:** Caucasian Black Grouse

Date	F	VF	XF	Unc	BU
1995 Proof		Value: 25.00			

Y# 494 ROUBLE
17.4600 g., 0.9000 Silver .5052 oz. ASW **Series:** Wildlife **Obv:**
Double-headed eagle **Rev:** Blind Mole Rat

Date	F	VF	XF	Unc	BU
1996 Proof		Value: 25.00			

Y# 448 ROUBLE
17.4600 g., 0.9000 Silver .5052 oz. ASW **Series:** Wildlife **Obv:**
Double-headed eagle **Rev:** Black Sea Dolphin

Date	F	VF	XF	Unc	BU
1995 Proof		Value: 25.00			

Y# 504 ROUBLE
Brass **Subject:** 300th Anniversary - Russian Fleet **Obv:** Double
headed eagle

Date	F	VF	XF	Unc	BU
1996	—	—	—	1.50	—

Y# 492 ROUBLE
17.4600 g., 0.9000 Silver .5052 oz. ASW **Series:** Wildlife **Obv:**
Double-headed eagle **Rev:** Peregrine Falcon

Date	F	VF	XF	Unc	BU
1996 Proof		Value: 25.00			

Y# 561 ROUBLE
8.4150 g., 0.9250 Silver .2502 oz. ASW **Subject:** 850th
Anniversary - Moscow **Obv:** Double-headed eagle

Date	F	VF	XF	Unc	BU
1997	—	—	—	—	10.00

Y# 562 ROUBLE
8.4150 g., 0.9250 Silver .2502 oz. ASW **Subject:** 850th
Anniversary - Moscow **Obv:** Double-headed eagle **Rev:** Cathedral
of the Kazan Icon of the Holy Virgin

Date	F	VF	XF	Unc	BU
1997	—	—	—	—	10.00

Y# 493 ROUBLE
17.4600 g., 0.9000 Silver .5052 oz. ASW **Series:** Wildlife **Obv:**
Double-headed eagle **Rev:** Turkmenian Gecko

Date	F	VF	XF	Unc	BU
1996 Proof		Value: 25.00			

Russia

Y# 563 ROUBLE
8.4150 g., 0.9250 Silver .2502 oz. ASW **Subject:** 850th Anniversary - Moscow **Obv:** Double-headed eagle **Rev:** State University

Date	F	VF	XF	Unc	BU
1997	—	—	—	—	10.00

Y# 576 ROUBLE
8.4150 g., 0.9250 Silver .2502 oz. ASW **Subject:** World Soccer Championship - Paris 1998 **Obv:** Double-headed eagle **Rev:** Soccer players, Eiffel Tower, globe in back

Date	F	VF	XF	Unc	BU
1997 Proof	Value: 17.50				

Y# 564 ROUBLE
8.4150 g., 0.9250 Silver .2502 oz. ASW **Subject:** 850th Anniversary - Moscow **Obv:** Double-headed eagle **Rev:** Bolshoi Theatre

Date	F	VF	XF	Unc	BU
1997 Proof	Value: 14.50				

Y# 577 ROUBLE
8.4150 g., 0.9250 Silver .2502 oz. ASW **Subject:** 1998 Winter Olympics - Ice Hockey

Date	F	VF	XF	Unc	BU
1997 Proof	Value: 17.50				

Y# 565 ROUBLE
8.4150 g., 0.9250 Silver .2502 oz. ASW **Subject:** 850th Anniversary - Moscow **Obv:** Double-headed eagle **Rev:** Resurrection Gate on Red Square

Date	F	VF	XF	Unc	BU
1997 Proof	Value: 14.50				

Y# 578 ROUBLE
8.4150 g., 0.9250 Silver .2502 oz. ASW **Subject:** 1998 Winter Olympics - Biathalon

Date	F	VF	XF	Unc	BU
1997 Proof	Value: 17.50				

Y# 566 ROUBLE
8.4150 g., 0.9250 Silver .2502 oz. ASW **Subject:** 850th Anniversary - Moscow **Obv:** Double-headed eagle **Rev:** Temple of Christ the Savior

Date	F	VF	XF	Unc	BU
1997 Proof	Value: 14.50				

Y# 579 ROUBLE
8.4150 g., 0.9250 Silver .2502 oz. ASW **Subject:** 1897 Soccer **Rev:** Three soccer players

Date	F	VF	XF	Unc	BU
1997 Proof	Value: 17.50				

Y# 580   ROUBLE
8.4150 g., 0.9250 Silver .2502 oz. ASW **Subject:** 1945 Soccer
Rev: Goalie

Date	F	VF	XF	Unc	BU
1997 Proof		Value: 17.50			

Y# 581   ROUBLE
8.4150 g., 0.9250 Silver .2502 oz. ASW **Subject:** 1956 Soccer
Rev: Players and kangaroo

Date	F	VF	XF	Unc	BU
1997 Proof		Value: 17.50			

Y# 582   ROUBLE
8.4150 g., 0.9250 Silver .2502 oz. ASW **Subject:** 1960 Soccer
Rev: Players, Eiffel Tower

Date	F	VF	XF	Unc	BU
1997 Proof		Value: 17.50			

Y# 583   ROUBLE
8.4150 g., 0.9250 Silver .2502 oz. ASW **Subject:** 1988 Soccer
Obv: Double headed eagle **Rev:** Three players

Date	F	VF	XF	Unc	BU
1997 Proof		Value: 17.50			

Y# 611   ROUBLE
17.5500 g., 0.9000 Silver .5078 oz. ASW **Series:** Wildlife **Obv:**
Double-headed eagle **Rev:** Two Greater flamingos

Date	F	VF	XF	Unc	BU
1997 Proof		Value: 25.00			

Y# 612   ROUBLE
17.5500 g., 0.9000 Silver .5078 oz. ASW **Series:** Wildlife **Obv:**
Double-headed eagle **Rev:** Goitered Gazelle

Date	F	VF	XF	Unc	BU
1997 Proof		Value: 24.00			

Y# 613   ROUBLE
17.5500 g., 0.9000 Silver .5078 oz. ASW **Series:** Wildlife **Obv:**
Double-headed eagle **Rev:** European Bison

Date	F	VF	XF	Unc	BU
1997 Proof		Value: 24.00			

Y# 342   2 ROUBLES
15.8700 g., 0.5000 Silver .2552 oz. ASW **Obv:** Double-headed
eagle **Rev:** Pavel Bazhov - Author of Ural Tales

Date	F	VF	XF	Unc	BU
1994 Proof		Value: 12.50			

Y# 343   2 ROUBLES
15.8700 g., 0.5000 Silver .2552 oz. ASW **Obv:** Double-headed
eagle **Rev:** Ivan Krylov - Author of Fables

Date	F	VF	XF	Unc	BU
1994 Proof		Value: 12.50			

Y# 344 2 ROUBLES
15.8700 g., 0.5000 Silver .2552 oz. ASW **Obv:** Double-headed eagle **Rev:** Nickolai Gogol - Writer

Date	F	VF	XF	Unc	BU
1994 Proof			Value: 12.50		

Y# 363 2 ROUBLES
15.8700 g., 0.5000 Silver .2552 oz. ASW **Obv:** Double-headed eagle **Rev:** Admiral Ushakov

Date	F	VF	XF	Unc	BU
1994 Proof			Value: 12.50		

Y# 364 2 ROUBLES
15.8700 g., 0.5000 Silver .2552 oz. ASW **Obv:** Double-headed eagle **Rev:** Ilya Repin - Painter

Date	F	VF	XF	Unc	BU
1994 Proof			Value: 12.50		

Y# 377 2 ROUBLES
15.8700 g., 0.5000 Silver .2552 oz. ASW **Obv:** Double-headed eagle **Rev:** A. S. Griboyedov

Date	F	VF	XF	Unc	BU
1995 Proof			Value: 14.50		

Y# 391 2 ROUBLES
15.8700 g., 0.5000 Silver .2552 oz. ASW **Subject:** WWII Victory Parade **Obv:** Kremlin

Date	F	VF	XF	Unc	BU
1995 Proof			Value: 16.50		

Y# 392 2 ROUBLES
15.8700 g., 0.5000 Silver .2552 oz. ASW **Series:** WWII **Obv:** Kremlin **Rev:** Marshal Zhukov on horseback

Date	F	VF	XF	Unc	BU
1995 Proof			Value: 16.50		

Y# 393 2 ROUBLES
15.8700 g., 0.5000 Silver .2552 oz. ASW **Series:** WWII **Obv:** Kremlin **Rev:** Nuremberg trial

Date	F	VF	XF	Unc	BU
1995 Proof			Value: 16.50		

Y# 414 2 ROUBLES
15.8700 g., 0.5000 Silver .2552 oz. ASW **Obv:** Double-headed eagle **Rev:** Sergei Esenin

Date	F	VF	XF	Unc	BU
1995 Proof			Value: 14.50		

Y# 415 2 ROUBLES
15.8700 g., 0.5000 Silver .2552 oz. ASW **Obv:** Double-headed eagle **Rev:** Field Marshal Kutozov

Date	F	VF	XF	Unc	BL
1995 Proof			Value: 13.50		

Y# 449 2 ROUBLES
15.8700 g., 0.5000 Silver .2552 oz. ASW **Obv:** Double-headed
eagle **Rev:** Ivan Bunin

Date	F	VF	XF	Unc	BU
1995 Proof		Value: 14.50			

Y# A391 2 ROUBLES
15.8700 g., 0.5000 Silver 0.2551 oz. ASW **Obv:** Double-headed
eagle **Rev:** Victory Parade **Note:** Mule of 1994 eagle obverse with
Y#391 Victory Parade reverse.

Date	F	VF	XF	Unc	BU
1995 Proof		Value: 250			

Y# 549 2 ROUBLES
15.8700 g., 0.5000 Silver .2552 oz. ASW **Obv:** Double-headed
eagle **Rev:** N. E. Zhukovsky

Date	F	VF	XF	Unc	BU
1997 Proof		Value: 25.00			

Y# 514 2 ROUBLES
15.8700 g., 0.5000 Silver .2552 oz. ASW **Obv:** Double-headed
eagle **Rev:** Nikolai Nekrasov

Date	F	VF	XF	Unc	BU
1996 Proof		Value: 25.00			

Y# 550 2 ROUBLES
15.8700 g., 0.5000 Silver .2552 oz. ASW **Obv:** Double-headed
eagle **Rev:** A. N. Skryabin - Musician

Date	F	VF	XF	Unc	BU
1997 Proof		Value: 25.00			

Y# 515 2 ROUBLES
15.8700 g., 0.5000 Silver .2552 oz. ASW **Obv:** Double-headed
eagle **Rev:** Fyodor Dostoevsky

Date	F	VF	XF	Unc	BU
1996 Proof		Value: 25.00			

Y# 551 2 ROUBLES
15.8700 g., 0.5000 Silver .2552 oz. ASW **Obv:** Double-headed
eagle **Rev:** A. L. Chizhevsky

Date	F	VF	XF	Unc	BU
1997 Proof		Value: 30.00			

Y# 558 2 ROUBLES
15.8700 g., 0.5000 Silver .2552 oz. ASW **Obv:** Double-headed
eagle **Rev:** Afanasi Nikitin - sailing ship

Date	F	VF	XF	Unc	BU
1997 Proof		Value: 28.00			

Russia

Y# 559 2 ROUBLES
15.8700 g., 0.5000 Silver .2552 oz. ASW **Obv:** Double-headed eagle **Rev:** Afanasi Nikitin - indian scene

Date	F	VF	XF	Unc	BU
1997 Proof		Value: 40.00			

Y# 584 2 ROUBLES
15.8700 g., 0.5000 Silver .2552 oz. ASW **Obv:** Double-headed eagle **Rev:** Cameo of A. K. Savrasov - church, trees

Date	F	VF	XF	Unc	BU
1997 Proof		Value: 40.00			

Y# 297 3 ROUBLES
Copper-Nickel **Subject:** International Space Year **Edge:** Cyrillic lettering

Date	F	VF	XF	Unc	BU
1992	—	—	—	3.50	5.00

Y# 298 3 ROUBLES
Copper-Nickel **Subject:** Battle of Chudskoye Lake **Edge:** Cyrillic lettering

Date	F	VF	XF	Unc	BU
1992	—	—	—	3.50	—

Y# 304 3 ROUBLES
Copper-Nickel **Series:** WWII **Rev:** Allied supply convoys to Murmansk

Date	F	VF	XF	Unc	BU
1992 Proof		Value: 5.50			

Y# 317 3 ROUBLES
Copper-Nickel **Subject:** 1st Anniversary - Defeat of Communist Attempted Coup

Date	F	VF	XF	Unc	BU
1992	—	—	—	3.50	5.00

Y# 349 3 ROUBLES
34.5600 g., 0.9000 Silver 1.0000 oz. ASW **Obv:** Double-headed eagle **Rev:** St. Petersburg Trinity Cathedral

Date	F	VF	XF	Unc	BU
1992 Proof		Value: 22.50			

Y# 350 3 ROUBLES
34.5600 g., 0.9000 Silver 1.0000 oz. ASW **Obv:** Double-headed eagle **Rev:** St. Petersburg Academy of Science

Date	F	VF	XF	Unc	BU
1992 Proof		Value: 25.00			

Y# 318   3 ROUBLES
Copper-Nickel   **Subject:** Battle of Stalingrad

Date	F	VF	XF	Unc	BU
1993	—	—	—	3.50	—

Y# 351   3 ROUBLES
34.5600 g., 0.9000 Silver 1.0000 oz. ASW   **Series:** Olympics
Subject: Soccer **Obv:** Double-headed eagle

Date	F	VF	XF	Unc	BU
1993 Proof		Value: 27.50			

Y# 323   3 ROUBLES
34.5600 g., 0.9000 Silver 1.0000 oz. ASW   **Subject:** Bolshoi Ballet
Rev: Ballet couple **Note:** Struck at Moscow without mint mark.

Date	F	VF	XF	Unc	BU
1993	—	—	—	14.50	—

Y# 328   3 ROUBLES
Copper-Nickel   **Subject:** 50th Anniversary - Battle of Kursk **Obv:**
Kremlin **Edge:** Cyrillic lettering

Date	F	VF	XF	Unc	BU
1993	—	—	—	3.50	—

Y# 409   3 ROUBLES
34.5600 g., 0.9000 Silver 1.0000 oz. ASW   **Series:** Wildlife **Obv:**
Double-headed eagle **Rev:** Brown Bear

Date	F	VF	XF	Unc	BU
1993 Proof		Value: 75.00			

Y# 340   3 ROUBLES
Copper-Nickel   **Subject:** 50th Anniversary - Kiev's Liberation from
German Fascists **Obv:** Kremlin

Date	F	VF	XF	Unc	BU
1993	—	—	—	3.50	—

Y# 450   3 ROUBLES
34.5600 g., 0.9000 Silver 1.0000 oz. ASW   **Subject:** Ballet **Rev:**
Ballerina - Anna Pavlova

Date	F	VF	XF	Unc	BU
1993 Proof		Value: 27.50			

Russia

Y# 451　3 ROUBLES
34.5600 g., 0.9000 Silver 1.0000 oz. ASW **Rev:** Fedor Schalyapin

Date	F	VF	XF	Unc	BU
1993 Proof		Value: 25.00			

Y# 464　3 ROUBLES
34.5600 g., 0.9000 Silver 1.0000 oz. ASW **Rev:** Sailing ships "Nadezhda" and "Neva" on world voyage

Date	F	VF	XF	Unc	BU
1993 Proof		Value: 32.50			

Y# 456　3 ROUBLES
34.5600 g., 0.9000 Silver 1.0000 oz. ASW **Obv:** Double-headed eagle **Rev:** Vasilyblazheny Cathedral, Moscow

Date	F	VF	XF	Unc	BU
1993 Proof		Value: 30.00			

Y# 465　3 ROUBLES
34.5600 g., 0.9000 Silver 1.0000 oz. ASW **Subject:** Russ-French Space Flight

Date	F	VF	XF	Unc	BU
1993 Proof		Value: 32.50			

Y# 341　3 ROUBLES
Copper-Nickel **Subject:** 50th Anniversary - Battle of Leningrad **Obv:** Kremlin

Date	F	VF	XF	Unc	BU
1994 Proof		Value: 5.50			

Y# 457　3 ROUBLES
34.5600 g., 0.9000 Silver 1.0000 oz. ASW **Obv:** Double-headed eagle **Rev:** Ivan the Great Cathedral, Moscow

Date	F	VF	XF	Unc	BU
1993 Proof		Value: 30.00			

Russia

Y# 345   3 ROUBLES
34.5600 g., 0.9000 Silver 1.0000 oz. ASW **Obv:** Double-headed eagle **Rev:** Cathedral of the Nativity of the Mother of God

Date	F	VF	XF	Unc	BU
1994 Proof			Value: 30.00		

Y# 346   3 ROUBLES
Copper-Nickel **Subject:** 50th Anniversary - Liberation of Sevastopol from German Fascists **Obv:** Kremlin

Date	F	VF	XF	Unc	BU
1994 Proof			Value: 5.50		

Y# 362   3 ROUBLES
Copper-Nickel **Subject:** Normandy Invasion **Obv:** Kremlin

Date	F	VF	XF	Unc	BU
1994 Proof			Value: 5.50		

365   3 ROUBLES
opper-Nickel **Series:** WWII **Subject:** Partisans Activities **Obv:** remlin **Edge:** Cyrillic lettering

ate	F	VF	XF	Unc	BU
994 Proof			Value: 5.50		

366   3 ROUBLES
opper-Nickel **Series:** WWII **Subject:** Liberation of Belgrade v: Kremlin

e	F	VF	XF	Unc	BU
4 Proof			Value: 5.50		

Y# 380   3 ROUBLES
Copper-Nickel **Series:** WWII **Subject:** Capture of Konigsberg **Obv:** Kremlin

Date	F	VF	XF	Unc	BU
1994-1995 Proof			Value: 6.00		

Y# 389   3 ROUBLES
34.8800 g., 0.9000 Silver 1.0093 oz. ASW **Subject:** Trans-Siberian railway **Obv:** Double-headed eagle

Date	F	VF	XF	Unc	BU
1994 Proof			Value: 35.00		

Y# 405   3 ROUBLES
34.5600 g., 0.9000 Silver 1.0000 oz. ASW **Subject:** Ballet **Obv:** Double-headed eagle **Rev:** Ballet couple

Date	F	VF	XF	Unc	BU
1994 Proof			Value: 25.00		

Y# 458   3 ROUBLES
34.5600 g., 0.9000 Silver 1.0000 oz. ASW   **Obv:** Double-headed eagle **Rev:** Pocrov Church on the Nerl

Date	F	VF	XF	Unc	BU
1994 Proof		Value: 35.00			

Y# 460   3 ROUBLES
34.5600 g., 0.9000 Silver 1.0000 oz. ASW   **Series:** Wildlife **Rev:** Sable

Date	F	VF	XF	Unc	BU
1994 Proof		Value: 50.00			

Y# 466   3 ROUBLES
34.5600 g., 0.9000 Silver 1.0000 oz. ASW   **Subject:** Discovery of Antarctica **Rev:** Sailing ships Vostok and Mirny

Date	F	VF	XF	Unc	BU
1994 Proof		Value: 37.50			

Y# 513   3 ROUBLES
34.6800 g., 0.9000 Silver 1.0034 oz. ASW   **Obv:** Double-headed eagle **Rev:** Smolny Institute & Monastery - St. Petersburg

Date	F	VF	XF	Unc	BU
1994 Proof		Value: 35.00			

Y# 520   3 ROUBLES
34.6800 g., 0.9000 Silver 1.0034 oz. ASW   **Obv:** Double-headed eagle **Rev:** Ryazan Kremlin - city view

Date	F	VF	XF	Unc	BU
1994 Proof		Value: 35.00			

Y# 528   3 ROUBLES
34.6800 g., 0.9000 Silver 1.0034 oz. ASW   **Obv:** Double-headed eagle **Rev:** Vassili Ivanovich Surikov; Siberian sled scene

Date	F	VF	XF	Unc	B
1994 Proof		Value: 30.00			

Y# 529   3 ROUBLES
34.6800 g., 0.9000 Silver 1.0034 oz. ASW   **Obv:** Double-headed eagle **Rev:** Alexander Andreyevich Ivannov

Date	F	VF	XF	Unc
1994 Proof		Value: 30.00		

Y# 378   3 ROUBLES
Copper-Nickel   **Subject:** Liberation of Warsaw **Obv:** Kremlin

Date	F	VF	XF	Unc	BU
1995 Proof		Value: 6.00			

Y# 383   3 ROUBLES
Copper-Nickel   **Series:** WWII **Subject:** Capture of Berlin **Obv:** Kremlin

Date	F	VF	XF	Unc	BU
1995 Proof		Value: 6.00			

Y# 379   3 ROUBLES
Copper-Nickel   **Subject:** Liberation of Budapest **Obv:** Kremlin

Date	F	VF	XF	Unc	BU
1995 Proof		Value: 6.00			

Y# 384   3 ROUBLES
Copper-Nickel   **Series:** WWII **Subject:** German Surrender **Obv:** Kremlin

Date	F	VF	XF	Unc	BU
1995 Proof		Value: 6.00			

Y# 381   3 ROUBLES
Copper-Nickel   **Series:** WWII **Subject:** Capture of Vienna **Obv:** Kremlin

Date	F	VF	XF	Unc	BU
1995 Proof		Value: 6.00			

Y# 385   3 ROUBLES
Copper-Nickel   **Series:** WWII **Subject:** Liberation of Prague **Obv:** Kremlin

Date	F	VF	XF	Unc	BU
1995 Proof		Value: 6.00			

Y# 382   3 ROUBLES
Copper-Nickel   **Series:** WWII **Rev:** American and Russian soldiers in front of their country's respective flag **Note:** 50-star U.S.A. flag.

Date	F	VF	XF	Unc	BU
1995 Proof		Value: 6.00			

Y# 386   3 ROUBLES
Copper-Nickel   **Series:** WWII **Subject:** Surrender of Japanese Army in Kwantung **Obv:** Kremlin

Date	F	VF	XF	Unc	BU
1995 Proof		Value: 6.00			

Y# 387   3 ROUBLES
Copper-Nickel, 33 mm. **Series:** WWII **Subject:** Japanese Formal
Surrender on Battleship U.S.S. Missouri **Obv:** Kremlin

Date	F	VF	XF	Unc	BU
1995 Proof		Value: 6.00			

Y# 388   3 ROUBLES
34.5600 g., 0.9000 Silver 1.0000 oz. ASW **Obv:** Double-headed
eagle **Rev:** Vladimir's Golden Gate

Date	F	VF	XF	Unc	BU
1995 Proof		Value: 37.50			

Y# 394   3 ROUBLES
34.5600 g., 0.9000 Silver 1.0000 oz. ASW **Subject:** Ballet -
Sleeping Beauty **Obv:** Double-headed eagle

Date	F	VF	XF	Unc	BU
1995 Proof		Value: 35.00			

Y# 407   3 ROUBLES
34.5600 g., 0.9000 Silver 1.0000 oz. ASW **Subject:** 50th
Anniversary - United Nations **Obv:** Double-headed eagle

Date	F	VF	XF	Unc	BU
1995 Proof		Value: 45.00			

Y# 445   3 ROUBLES
34.5600 g., 0.9000 Silver 1.0000 oz. ASW **Obv:** Double-headed
eagle **Rev:** Smolensk Kremlin

Date	F	VF	XF	Unc	B
1995 Proof		Value: 37.50			

Y# 459   3 ROUBLES
34.5600 g., 0.9000 Silver 1.0000 oz. ASW **Obv:** Double-headed
eagle **Rev:** Kizhi Church on Onega Lake

Date	F	VF	XF	Unc	
1995 Proof		Value: 37.50			

Russia

Y# 461 3 ROUBLES
34.5600 g., 0.9000 Silver 1.0000 oz. ASW **Obv:** Double-headed
eagle **Rev:** Arctic explorers, 1733-43

Date	F	VF	XF	Unc	BU
1995 Proof		Value: 37.50			

Y# 467 3 ROUBLES
34.5600 g., 0.9000 Silver 1.0000 oz. ASW **Subject:** Russian
Millennium of Belgorod **Obv:** Double-headed eagle

Date	F	VF	XF	Unc	BU
1995 Proof		Value: 35.00			

Y# 462 3 ROUBLES
34.5600 g., 0.9000 Silver 1.0000 oz. ASW **Obv:** Double-headed
eagle **Rev:** Roald Amundsen - Arctic Explorer

Date	F	VF	XF	Unc	BU
1995 Proof		Value: 40.00			

Y# 468 3 ROUBLES
34.5600 g., 0.9000 Silver 1.0000 oz. ASW **Subject:** Russian
Millennium **Obv:** Double-headed eagle **Rev:** Novgorod Kremlin

Date	F	VF	XF	Unc	BU
1995 Proof		Value: 35.00			

Y# 463 3 ROUBLES
34.5600 g., 0.9000 Silver 1.0000 oz. ASW **Subject:** 200th
Anniversary - Russian National Library **Obv:** Double-headed eagle

Date	F	VF	XF	Unc	BU
1995 Proof		Value: 50.00			

Y# 469 3 ROUBLES
34.5600 g., 0.9000 Silver 1.0000 oz. ASW **Subject:** Russian
Millennium **Obv:** Double-headed eagle **Rev:** Spaso -
Preobrazhensky Cathedral

Date	F	VF	XF	Unc	BU
1995 Proof		Value: 30.00			

Y# 473   3 ROUBLES
34.5600 g., 0.9000 Silver 1.0000 oz. ASW **Series:** Wildlife **Obv:**
Double-headed eagle **Rev:** Sable on branch

Date	F	VF	XF	Unc	BU
1995	—	—	—	27.50	—

Y# 477   3 ROUBLES
34.5600 g., 0.9000 Silver 1.0000 oz. ASW **Subject:** Combat
between Peresvet and Chelubey **Obv:** Double-headed eagle

Date	F	VF	XF	Unc	BU
1996 Proof		Value: 30.00			

Y# 478   3 ROUBLES
34.5600 g., 0.9000 Silver 1.0000 oz. ASW **Obv:** Double-headed
eagle **Rev:** Old Testament Trinity icon

Date	F	VF	XF	Unc	BU
1996 Proof		Value: 30.00			

Y# 474   3 ROUBLES
34.5600 g., 0.9000 Silver 1.0000 oz. ASW **Series:** Wildlife **Obv:**
Double-headed eagle **Rev:** Eurasian Lynx

Date	F	VF	XF	Unc	BU
1995	—	—	—	35.00	—

Y# 470   3 ROUBLES
34.5600 g., 0.9000 Silver 1.0000 oz. ASW **Rev:** Ilya the Prophet's
Church in Yaroslavl

Date	F	VF	XF	Unc	BU
1996 Proof		Value: 35.00			

Y# 482   3 ROUBLES
34.5600 g., 0.9000 Silver 1.0000 oz. ASW **Subject:** Nutcracke
Ballet **Obv:** Double-headed eagle

Date	F	VF	XF	Unc	B
1996 Proof		Value: 35.00			

Y# 483   3 ROUBLES
34.5600 g., 0.9000 Silver 1.0000 oz. ASW   **Subject:** Nutcracker
Ballet - Duel with Mouse King **Obv:** Double-headed eagle

Date	F	VF	XF	Unc	BU
1996 Proof		Value: 35.00			

Y# 510   3 ROUBLES
34.5600 g., 0.9000 Silver 1.0000 oz. ASW   **Obv:** Double-headed
eagle **Rev:** Alexander Column and Hermitage

Date	F	VF	XF	Unc	BU
1996 Proof		Value: 45.00			

Y# 490   3 ROUBLES
34.5600 g., 0.9000 Silver 1.0000 oz. ASW   **Obv:** Double-headed
eagle **Rev:** Kremlin of Kazan

Date	F	VF	XF	Unc	BU
1996 Proof		Value: 40.00			

Y# 511   3 ROUBLES
34.5600 g., 0.9000 Silver 1.0000 oz. ASW   **Subject:** 300th
Anniversary - Russian Navy **Obv:** Double-headed eagle **Rev:**
Icebreaker

Date	F	VF	XF	Unc	BU
1996 Proof		Value: 50.00			

Y# 491   3 ROUBLES
34.5600 g., 0.9000 Silver 1.0000 oz. ASW   **Rev:** Kremlin of
Tobolsk - city view

Date	F	VF	XF	Unc	BU
1996 Proof		Value: 30.00			

Y# 512   3 ROUBLES
34.5600 g., 0.9000 Silver 1.0000 oz. ASW   **Subject:** 300th
Anniversary - Russian Navy **Obv:** Double-headed eagle **Rev:**
Carrier ship

Date	F	VF	XF	Unc	BU
1996 Proof		Value: 50.00			

Y# 535   3 ROUBLES
34.5600 g., 0.9000 Silver 1.0000 oz. ASW **Series:** Wildlife **Obv:**
Double-headed eagle **Rev:** Amur tiger

Date	F	VF	XF	Unc	BU
1996 Proof	Value: 50.00				

Y# 560   3 ROUBLES
34.5600 g., 0.9000 Silver 1.0000 oz. ASW **Obv:** Double-headed
eagle **Rev:** Monastery in Yaroslavl

Date	F	VF	XF	Unc	BU
1997 Proof	Value: 45.00				

Y# 552   3 ROUBLES
34.5600 g., 0.9000 Silver 1.0000 oz. ASW **Subject:** 850th
Anniversary - Moscow **Obv:** Double-headed eagle **Rev:** Workers
rebuilding original Moscow, modern skyline behind

Date	F	VF	XF	Unc	BU
1997 Proof	Value: 30.00				

Y# 567   3 ROUBLES
34.5600 g., 0.9000 Silver 1.0000 oz. ASW **Subject:** Ballet - Swan
Lake **Obv:** Double-headed eagle **Rev:** Four ballerinas

Date	F	VF	XF	Unc	BU
1997 Proof	Value: 50.00				

Y# 553   3 ROUBLES
34.5600 g., 0.9000 Silver 1.0000 oz. ASW **Subject:** 850th
Anniversary - Moscow **Obv:** Double-headed eagle **Rev:** Riverside
city view

Date	F	VF	XF	Unc	BU
1997 Proof	Value: 30.00				

Y# 568   3 ROUBLES
34.5600 g., 0.9000 Silver 1.0000 oz. ASW **Subject:** Ballet - Swan
Lake **Obv:** Double-headed eagle **Rev:** Between Rothbart and
Prince Siegfried

Date	F	VF	XF	Unc	BU
1997 Proof	Value: 50.00				

Y# 575   3 ROUBLES

34.5600 g., 0.9000 Silver 1.0000 oz. ASW **Subject:** First
Anniversary - Russian-Belarus Treaty **Obv:** Double-headed eagle
Rev: Two city views

Date	F	VF	XF	Unc	BU
1997 Proof		Value: 50.00			

Y# 587   3 ROUBLES

34.5600 g., 0.9000 Silver 1.0000 oz. ASW **Subject:** Year of
Reconciliation **Obv:** Double-headed eagle

Date	F	VF	XF	Unc	BU
1997 Proof		Value: 60.00			

Y# 585   3 ROUBLES

4.5600 g., 0.9000 Silver 1.0000 oz. ASW **Subject:** Underroot
ativity of the Virgin Hermitage Monastery of Kursk **Obv:** Double-
eaded eagle **Rev:** Painting above monastery

ate	F	VF	XF	Unc	BU
997 Proof		Value: 45.00			

Y# 591   3 ROUBLES

34.5600 g., 0.9000 Silver 1.0000 oz. ASW **Obv:** Double-headed
eagle **Rev:** Solovetski Monastery

Date	F	VF	XF	Unc	BU
1997 Proof		Value: 45.00			

586   3 ROUBLES

.5600 g., 0.9000 Silver 1.0000 oz. ASW **Obv:** Double-headed
gle **Rev:** Sergy Julievich Witte

te	F	VF	XF	Unc	BU
7 Proof		Value: 50.00			

Y# 593   3 ROUBLES

34.5600 g., 0.9000 Silver 1.0000 oz. ASW **Series:** Wildlife **Obv:**
Double-headed eagle **Rev:** Polar bear watching walrus

Date	F	VF	XF	Unc	BU
1997 Proof		Value: 50.00			

Y# 312   5 ROUBLES
Brass Clad Steel   **Obv:** Double-headed eagle

Date	F	VF	XF	Unc	BU
1992	—	—	—	1.50	—

Y# 420   5 ROUBLES
7.7758 g., 0.9990 Palladium .2500 oz.   **Subject:** Ballet **Rev:** Ballerina

Date	F	VF	XF	Unc	BU
1993	—	—	—	150	—

Y# 322   5 ROUBLES
Copper-Nickel   **Subject:** Kazakhstan

Date	F	VF	XF	Unc	BU
1992	—	—	—	4.00	5.00

Y# 431   5 ROUBLES
7.7758 g., 0.9990 Palladium .2500 oz.   **Subject:** Ballet - Sleeping Beauty **Rev:** Ballerina

Date	F	VF	XF	Unc	BU
1994	—	—	—	150	—

Y# 324   5 ROUBLES
Copper-Nickel   **Subject:** Troitsk - Sergievsk Monastery

Date	F	VF	XF	Unc	BU
1993	—	—	—	6.00	7.00

Y# 400   5 ROUBLES
Aluminum-Bronze   **Series:** WWII **Rev:** Infantry officer leading attack

Date	F	VF	XF	Unc	BU
1995	—	—	—	1.50	—

Y# 435   5 ROUBLES
7.7758 g., 0.9990 Palladium .2500 oz.   **Rev:** Ballerina

Date	F	VF	XF	Unc	BU
1995 Proof	Value: 160				

Y# 339   5 ROUBLES
Copper-Nickel   **Subject:** 2500 Years of Merv Minaret, Turkmenistan

Date	F	VF	XF	Unc	BU
1993	—	—	—	4.00	5.00

Y# 505   5 ROUBLES
Brass   **Subject:** 300th Anniversary - Russian Fleet

Date	F	VF	XF	Unc	B
1996	—	—	—	2.50	—

Y# 307   10 ROUBLES
Bi-Metallic Aluminum-Bronze center in Copper-Nickel ring
Series: Wildlife **Rev:** Red-breasted goose **Edge:** Alternating
reeded and smooth

Date	F	VF	XF	Unc	BU
1992	—	—	—	2.50	5.00

Y# 308   10 ROUBLES
Bi-Metallic Aluminum-Bronze center in Copper-Nickel ring **Series:**
Wildlife **Rev:** Amur Tiger **Edge:** Alternating reeded and smooth

Date	F	VF	XF	Unc	BU
1992	—	—	—	3.00	5.00

Y# 309   10 ROUBLES
Bi-Metallic Aluminum-Bronze center in Copper-Nickel ring **Series:**
Wildlife **Rev:** Asian Cobra **Edge:** Alternating reeded and smooth

Date	F	VF	XF	Unc	BU
1992	—	—	—	3.00	5.00

Y# 313   10 ROUBLES
Copper-Nickel **Obv:** Double-headed eagle **Rev:** Denomination
Edge: Reeded **Note:** St. Petersburg minted coins have a round-
top 3 in date. Moscow minted coins have a flat-top 3 in date.

Date	F	VF	XF	Unc	BU
1992-1993	—	—	—	1.50	—

Y# 313a   10 ROUBLES
Copper-Nickel Clad Steel **Edge:** Plain **Note:** St. Petersburg
minted coins have a round-top 3 in date. Moscow minted coins
have a flat-top 3 in date.

Date	F	VF	XF	Unc	BU
1992-1993	—	—	—	1.50	—

Y# 352   10 ROUBLES
15.5517 g., 0.9990 Palladium .5000 oz. **Series:** Olympics **Rev:**
Cubertin and Butovsky

Date	F	VF	XF	Unc	BU
1993 Proof		Value: 250			

Y# 416   10 ROUBLES
1.5552 g., 0.9990 Gold .0500 oz. AGW **Subject:** Ballet **Rev:**
Ballerina

Date	F	VF	XF	Unc	BU
1993	—	—	—	50.00	—

Y# 421   10 ROUBLES
15.5500 g., 0.9990 Palladium .5000 oz. **Subject:** Russian Ballet

Date	F	VF	XF	Unc	BU
1993	—	—	—	250	—

Y# 424   10 ROUBLES
1.5552 g., 0.9990 Gold .0500 oz. AGW **Subject:** Russian Ballet

Date	F	VF	XF	Unc	BU
1994 Proof		Value: 60.00			

Y# 432   10 ROUBLES
15.5500 g., 0.9990 Palladium .5000 oz. **Subject:** Russian Ballet

Date	F	VF	XF	Unc	BU
1994	—	—	—	250	—

Y# 401   10 ROUBLES
Copper-Nickel **Series:** WWII **Rev:** Munitions workers

Date	F	VF	XF	Unc	BU
1995	—	—	—	2.00	—

Y# 436   10 ROUBLES
15.5500 g., 0.9990 Palladium .5000 oz. **Subject:** Ballet - Sleeping Beauty **Rev:** Ballerina

Date	F	VF	XF	Unc	BU
1995 Proof		Value: 275			

Y# 438   10 ROUBLES
1.5552 g., 0.9990 Gold .0500 oz. AGW **Subject:** Ballet - Sleeping Beauty

Date	F	VF	XF	Unc	BU
1995 Proof		Value: 60.00			

Y# 484   10 ROUBLES
1.5552 g., 0.9990 Gold .0500 oz. AGW **Subject:** Ballet - Nutcracker **Rev:** Nutcracker doll

Date	F	VF	XF	Unc	BU
1996 Proof		Value: 60.00			

Y# 506   10 ROUBLES
Copper-Nickel **Subject:** 300th Anniversary - Russian Fleet **Rev:** Cargo ship

Date	F	VF	XF	Unc	BU
1996	—	—	—	3.00	—

Y# 569   10 ROUBLES
1.5500 g., 0.9990 Gold .0498 oz. AGW **Subject:** Ballet - Swan Lake

Date	F	VF	XF	Unc	BU
1997 Proof		Value: 65.00			

Y# 314   20 ROUBLES
Copper-Nickel **Obv:** Double-headed eagle **Rev:** Denomination
Edge: Reeded and plain sections

Date	F	VF	XF	Unc	BU
1992	—	—	—	2.00	—

Y# 314a   20 ROUBLES
Copper-Nickel Clad Steel **Edge:** Plain

Date	F	VF	XF	Unc	BU
1993	—	—	—	2.50	—

Y# 402   20 ROUBLES
Copper-Nickel **Series:** WWII **Rev:** Soldiers and tanks

Date	F	VF	XF	Unc	BU
1995	—	—	—	3.00	—

Y# 507   20 ROUBLES
Copper-Nickel **Subject:** 300th Anniversary - Russian Fleet **Rev:** Scientific research ship

Date	F	VF	XF	Unc	BU
1996	—	—	—	4.50	—

Y# 353   25 ROUBLES
31.1035 g., 0.9990 Palladium 1.0000 oz. **Subject:** Age of enlightenment 17th century. **Rev:** Catherine II - Legislation

Date	F	VF	XF	Unc	B
1992 Proof		Value: 500			

Y# 395   25 ROUBLES
3.1104 g., 0.9990 Platinum .1000 oz. APW **Subject:** Russian Ballet **Rev:** Ballerina

Date	F	VF	XF	Unc	B
1993	—	—	—	185	—

Russia

Y# 422   25 ROUBLES
31.1035 g., 0.9990 Palladium 1.0000 oz. **Subject:** Russian Ballet
Rev: Ballerina

Date	F	VF	XF	Unc	BU
1993	—	—	—	500	—

Y# 406   25 ROUBLES
156.0400 g., 0.9990 Silver 5.0118 oz. ASW **Subject:** Russian
Ballet **Obv:** Bolshoi Theatre in Moscow **Rev:** Ballet couple **Note:**
Illustration reduced.

Date	F	VF	XF	Unc	BU
1993 Proof	Value: 95.00				

Y# 452   25 ROUBLES
31.1035 g., 0.9990 Palladium 1.0000 oz. **Subject:** Russian and
World Culture **Rev:** M.P. Musorgsky - composer

Date	F	VF	XF	Unc	BU
1993 Proof	Value: 500				

Y# 410   25 ROUBLES
3.1100 g., 0.9990 Gold .1000 oz. AGW **Series:** Wildlife **Rev:**
Brown bear

Date	F	VF	XF	Unc	BU
1993 Proof	Value: 125				

Y# 417   25 ROUBLES
3.1100 g., 0.9990 Gold .1000 oz. AGW **Subject:** Russian Ballet
Rev: Ballerina

Date	F	VF	XF	Unc	BU
1993	—	—	—	110	—

Y# 517   25 ROUBLES
31.1035 g., 0.9990 Palladium 1.0000 oz., 37 mm. **Subject:** First
Russian Global Circumnavigation **Rev:** Sloop "Nadyezhda" and
J.F. Krusenstern

Date	F	VF	XF	Unc	BU
1993 Proof	Value: 500				

Y# 518   25 ROUBLES
31.1035 g., 0.9990 Palladium 1.0000 oz., 37 mm. **Series:** First
Russian Global Circumnavigation **Rev:** Sloop "Neva" and Y.F.
Lisyansky

Date	F	VF	XF	Unc	BU
1993 Proof		Value: 500			

Y# 433   25 ROUBLES
31.1035 g., 0.9990 Palladium 1.0000 oz. **Subject:** Russian Ballet
Rev: Ballerina

Date	F	VF	XF	Unc	BU
1994	—	—	—	525	—

Y# 390   25 ROUBLES
172.8300 g., 0.9000 Silver 5.0009 oz. ASW **Subject:** 100th
Anniversary - Trans-Siberian Railroad **Rev:** Steam train, workers
laying ties and track

Date	F	VF	XF	Unc	BU
1994 Proof		Value: 185			

Y# 423   25 ROUBLES
172.8300 g., 0.9000 Silver 5.0009 oz. ASW **Subject:** Russian Ballet

Date	F	VF	XF	Unc	BU
1994 Proof		Value: 160			

Y# 425   25 ROUBLES
3.1100 g., 0.9990 Gold .1000 oz. AGW **Subject:** Russian Ballet
Rev: Ballerina

Date	F	VF	XF	Unc	BU
1994 Proof		Value: 115			

Y# 428   25 ROUBLES
3.1104 g., 0.9990 Platinum .1000 oz. APW **Subject:** Russian
Ballet **Rev:** Ballerina

Date	F	VF	XF	Unc	BU
1994 Proof		Value: 185			

Y# 521   25 ROUBLES
31.1035 g., 0.9990 Palladium 1.0000 oz. **Subject:** First Russian
Antartic Expedition, 1819-21 **Rev:** Sloop "Mirny" and M.P. Lazarev

Date	F	VF	XF	Unc	BU
1994 Proof		Value: 500			

Y# 522   25 ROUBLES
31.1035 g., 0.9990 Palladium 1.0000 oz. **Rev:** Sloop "Vostok"

Date	F	VF	XF	Unc	BU
1994 Proof		Value: 500			

Y# 524   25 ROUBLES
3.1103 g., 0.9990 Gold .1000 oz. AGW **Series:** Wildlife **Rev:**
Sable's head

Date	F	VF	XF	Unc	B
1994 Proof		Value: 110			

Y# 530   25 ROUBLES
31.1035 g., 0.9990 Palladium 1.0000 oz.   **Rev:** Andrei Rublev

Date	F	VF	XF	Unc	BU
1994 Proof		Value: 500			

Y# 534   25 ROUBLES
4.3198 g., 0.9000 Gold .1245 oz. AGW   **Rev:** Baikal railroad tunnel

Date	F	VF	XF	Unc	BU
1994 Proof		Value: 140			

Y# 437   25 ROUBLES
31.1035 g., 0.9990 Palladium 1.0000 oz.   **Obv:** Double-headed eagle **Rev:** Ballerina

Date	F	VF	XF	Unc	BU
1995 Proof		Value: 525			

Y# 439   25 ROUBLES
3.1100 g., 0.9990 Gold .1000 oz. AGW

Date	F	VF	XF	Unc	BU
1995 Proof		Value: 120			

Y# 442   25 ROUBLES
3.1104 g., 0.9990 Platinum .1000 oz. APW

Date	F	VF	XF	Unc	BU
1995 Proof		Value: 185			

Y# 471   25 ROUBLES
155.5000 g., 0.9000 Silver 4.4995 oz. ASW   **Series:** Wildlife **Obv:** Double-headed eagle **Rev:** Lynx on log **Note:** Illustration reduced.

Date	F	VF	XF	Unc	BU
1995 Proof		Value: 120			

Y# 472   25 ROUBLES
155.5000 g., 0.9000 Silver 4.4995 oz. ASW   **Subject:** First Station at North Pole **Obv:** Double-headed eagle **Rev:** Men, ship, and airplane

Date	F	VF	XF	Unc	BU
1995 Proof		Value: 175			

Y# 475   25 ROUBLES
31.1035 g., 0.9990 Palladium 1.0000 oz.   **Obv:** Double-headed eagle **Rev:** Alexander Nevski

Date	F	VF	XF	Unc	BU
1995 Proof		Value: 500			

Y# 536 25 ROUBLES
172.7972 g., 0.9000 Silver 5.0000 oz. ASW **Series:** Wildlife **Obv:**
Double-headed eagle **Rev:** Amur tiger **Note:** Illustration reduced.

Date	F	VF	XF	Unc	BU
1996 Proof		Value: 150			

Y# 479 25 ROUBLES
155.5000 g., 0.9000 Silver 4.4995 oz. ASW **Subject:** Battle of
Kulikova Plains **Obv:** Double-headed eagle **Note:** Illustration
reduced.

Date	F	VF	XF	Unc	BU
1996 Proof		Value: 175			

Y# 542 25 ROUBLES
172.7972 g., 0.9000 Silver 5.0000 oz. ASW **Subject:** Battle of
Gangut, 1714 **Obv:** Double-headed eagle **Note:** Illustration reduced.

Date	F	VF	XF	Unc	BU
1996 Proof		Value: 175			

Y# 485 25 ROUBLES
155.5175 g., 0.9990 Silver 5.0000 oz. ASW **Subject:** Ballet -
Nutcracker **Obv:** Double-headed eagle **Rev:** Children dancing
around tree **Note:** Illustration reduced.

Date	F	VF	XF	Unc	BU
1996 Proof		Value: 175			

Y# 486 25 ROUBLES
3.1103 g., 0.9990 Gold .1000 oz. AGW **Subject:** Ballet - Nutcracker
Obv: Double-headed eagle **Rev:** Marsha with nutcracker doll

Date	F	VF	XF	Unc	BU
1996 Proof		Value: 125			

Y# 543 25 ROUBLES
172.7972 g., 0.9000 Silver 5.0000 oz. ASW **Subject:** Battle of
Chesme, 1770 **Obv:** Double-headed eagle **Note:** Illustration reduced

Date	F	VF	XF	Unc	B
1996 Proof		Value: 175			

Y# 544   25 ROUBLES
172.7972 g., 0.9000 Silver 5.0000 oz. ASW **Subject:** Battle of Corfu, 1799 **Obv:** Double-headed eagle **Note:** Illustration reduced.

Date	F	VF	XF	Unc	BU
1996 Proof		Value: 175			

Y# 545   25 ROUBLES
172.7972 g., 0.9000 Silver 5.0000 oz. ASW **Subject:** Battle of Sinop, 1853 **Obv:** Double-headed eagle **Note:** Illustration reduced.

Date	F	VF	XF	Unc	BU
1996 Proof		Value: 175			

Y# 554   25 ROUBLES
172.7972 g., 0.9000 Silver 5.0000 oz. ASW **Subject:** 850th Anniversary - Moscow **Obv:** Double-headed eagle **Rev:** Monument

Date	F	VF	XF	Unc	BU
1997 Proof		Value: 155			

Y# 570   25 ROUBLES
172.7972 g., 0.9000 Silver 5.0000 oz. ASW **Subject:** Ballet - Swan Lake **Obv:** Double-headed eagle **Rev:** Prince Siegfried dancing with Odile **Note:** Illustration reduced.

Date	F	VF	XF	Unc	BU
1997 Proof		Value: 150			

Y# 571   25 ROUBLES
3.1103 g., 0.9990 Gold .1000 oz. AGW **Subject:** Ballet - Swan Lake **Rev:** Winged figure of Rothbart and swan

Date	F	VF	XF	Unc	BU
1997 Proof		Value: 175			

Y# 592   25 ROUBLES
172.7972 g., 0.9000 Silver 5.0000 oz. ASW **Series:** Wildlife **Obv:** Double-headed eagle **Rev:** Bear with cub **Note:** Illustration reduced.

Date	F	VF	XF	Unc	BU
1997 Proof		Value: 175			

Y# 354 50 ROUBLES
8.6397 g., 0.9000 Gold .2500 oz. AGW **Obv:** Double-headed
eagle **Rev:** Moscow's Pashkov Palace

Date	F	VF	XF	Unc	BU
1992 Proof			Value: 200		

Y# 594 25 ROUBLES
172.7972 g., 0.9000 Silver 5.0000 oz. ASW **Series:** Wildlife **Obv:**
Double-headed eagle **Rev:** Polar bear, caribou, seal

Date	F	VF	XF	Unc	BU
1997 Proof			Value: 175		

Y# 516 50 ROUBLES
8.6397 g., 0.9000 Gold .2500 oz. AGW **Obv:** Double-headed
eagle **Rev:** Chubuku (snow ram) on map **Note:** Yakutia.

Date	F	VF	XF	Unc	BU
1992 Proof			Value: 220		

Y# 329.1 50 ROUBLES
Aluminum-Bronze **Obv:** Double-headed eagle **Rev:**
Denomination **Edge:** Reeded and plain sections

Date	F	VF	XF	Unc	BU
1993	—	—	—	2.50	—

Y# 329.2 50 ROUBLES
Brass Clad Steel **Obv:** Double-headed eagle **Rev:** Denomination
Edge: Plain

Date	F	VF	XF	Unc	BU
1993	—	—	—	2.50	—

Y# 622 25 ROUBLES
173.2900 g., 0.9000 Silver 5.0143 oz. ASW **Series:** Wildlife **Obv:**
Double-headed eagle **Rev:** Sable

Date	F	VF	XF	Unc	BU
1997 Proof			Value: 185		

Y# 330 50 ROUBLES
Bi-Metallic Aluminum-Bronze center in Copper-Nickel ring **Series:**
Wildlife **Rev:** Asiatic black bear **Edge:** Alternating reeded and smooth

Date	F	VF	XF	Unc	BL
1993	—	—	—	2.50	4.00

Y# 315 50 ROUBLES
Bi-Metallic Aluminum-Bronze center in Copper-Nickel ring **Obv:**
Double-headed eagle **Rev:** Denomination **Note:** Off-metal strikes
exist from both mints. The strike is on the planchet reserved for
Y#316, 100 Roubles.

Date	F	VF	XF	Unc	BU
1992	0.50	0.75	1.00	2.50	—

Y# 331   50 ROUBLES
Bi-Metallic Aluminum-Bronze center in Copper-Nickel ring
Series: Wildlife **Rev:** Turkmenic Gecko **Edge:** Alternating reeded and smooth

Date	F	VF	XF	Unc	BU
1993	—	—	—	2.50	6.00

Y# 332   50 ROUBLES
Bi-Metallic Aluminum-Bronze center in Copper-Nickel ring
Series: Wildlife **Rev:** Caucasian black grouse **Edge:** Alternating reeded and smooth

Date	F	VF	XF	Unc	BU
1993	—	—	—	2.50	6.00

Y# 333   50 ROUBLES
Bi-Metallic Aluminum-Bronze center in Copper-Nickel ring   **Series:** Wildlife **Rev:** Oriental stork **Edge:** Alternating reeded and smooth

Date	F	VF	XF	Unc	BU
1993	—	—	—	2.50	6.00

Y# 334   50 ROUBLES
Bi-Metallic Aluminum-Bronze center in Copper-Nickel ring
Series: Wildlife **Rev:** Black sea porpoise **Edge:** Alternating reeded and smooth

Date	F	VF	XF	Unc	BU
1993	—	—	—	2.50	6.00

Y# 355   50 ROUBLES
8.6397 g., 0.9000 Gold .2500 oz. AGW   **Series:** Olympics **Rev:** Figure skater

Date	F	VF	XF	Unc	BU
1993 Proof	Value: 200				

Y# 356   50 ROUBLES
7.7758 g., 0.9990 Platinum .2498 oz. APW   **Series:** Olympics
Subject: Formal Riding

Date	F	VF	XF	Unc	BU
1993 Proof	Value: 285				

Y# 396   50 ROUBLES
7.7758 g., 0.9990 Platinum .2498 oz. APW   **Subject:** Bolshoi Ballet **Rev:** Ballerina

Date	F	VF	XF	Unc	BU
1993	—	—	—	350	—

Y# 411   50 ROUBLES
7.7800 g., 0.9990 Gold .2500 oz. AGW   **Series:** Wildlife **Rev:** Bear

Date	F	VF	XF	Unc	BU
1993 Proof	Value: 225				

Y# 418   50 ROUBLES
7.7800 g., 0.9990 Gold .2500 oz. AGW   **Subject:** Bolshoi Ballet **Rev:** Ballerina

Date	F	VF	XF	Unc	BU
1993	—	—	—	300	—

Y# 453   50 ROUBLES
7.7800 g., 0.9990 Gold .2500 oz. AGW   **Rev:** Sergei Rachmaninov

Date	F	VF	XF	Unc	BU
1993 Proof		Value: 200			

Y# 367   50 ROUBLES
Bi-Metallic Aluminum-Bronze center in Copper-Nickel ring   **Series:** Wildlife **Rev:** Blind mole rat **Edge:** Alternating reeded and smooth

Date	F	VF	XF	Unc	BU
1994	—	—	—	2.50	5.00

Y# 368   50 ROUBLES
Bi-Metallic Aluminum-Bronze center in Copper-Nickel ring   **Series:** Wildlife **Rev:** Bison **Edge:** Alternating reeded and smooth

Date	F	VF	XF	Unc	BU
1994	—	—	—	2.25	5.00

Y# 369   50 ROUBLES
Bi-Metallic Alunimum-Bronze center in Copper-Nickel ring   **Series:** Wildlife **Rev:** Goitered Gazelle **Edge:** Alternating reeded and smooth

Date	F	VF	XF	Unc	BU
1994	—	—	—	2.25	5.00

Y# 370   50 ROUBLES
Bi-Metallic Aluminum-Bronze center in Copper-Nickel ring   **Series:** Wildlife **Rev:** Peregrine falcon **Edge:** Alternating reeded and smooth

Date	F	VF	XF	Unc	BU
1994	—	—	—	2.50	5.00

Y# 371   50 ROUBLES
Bi-Metallic Aluminum-Bronze center in Copper-Nickel ring
Series: Wildlife **Rev:** Two Greater flamingos **Edge:** Alternating reeded and smooth

Date	F	VF	XF	Unc	BU
1994	—	—	—	3.00	5.00

Y# 426   50 ROUBLES
7.7759 g., 0.9990 Gold .2500 oz. AGW   **Subject:** Bolshoi Ballet **Rev:** Ballerina

Date	F	VF	XF	Unc	BU
1994 Proof		Value: 250			

Y# 429   50 ROUBLES
7.7759 g., 0.9990 Platinum .2500 oz. APW   **Subject:** Bolshoi Ballet **Rev:** Ballerina

Date	F	VF	XF	Unc	BU
1994 Proof		Value: 475			

Y# 525   50 ROUBLES
7.7759 g., 0.9990 Gold .2500 oz. AGW   **Series:** Wildlife **Rev:** Sable

Date	F	VF	XF	Unc	BU
1994 Proof		Value: 200			

Y# 531   50 ROUBLES
7.7759 g., 0.9990 Gold .2500 oz. AGW   **Rev:** Dimitri Grigorievich Levitsky

Date	F	VF	XF	Unc	BU
1994 Proof		Value: 225			

Y# 403　50 ROUBLES
Aluminum-Bronze　**Series:** WWII　**Rev:** Two sailors, ship, and plane

Date	F	VF	XF	Unc	BU
1995	—	—	—	4.00	—

Y# 480　50 ROUBLES
7.7800 g., 0.9990 Gold .2499 oz. AGW　**Rev:** Dmitri Donskoy Monument

Date	F	VF	XF	Unc	BU
1996 Proof		Value: 200			

Y# 408　50 ROUBLES
7.7800 g., 0.9990 Gold .2499 oz. AGW　**Subject:** 50th Anniversary - United Nations　**Note:** Similar to 3 Roubles, Y#407.

Date	F	VF	XF	Unc	BU
1995 Proof		Value: 215			

Y# 487　50 ROUBLES
7.7800 g., 0.9990 Gold .2499 oz. AGW　**Subject:** Ballet - Nutcracker　**Rev:** Marsha and Drosselmeyer with broken doll

Date	F	VF	XF	Unc	BU
1996 Proof		Value: 250			

Y# 440　50 ROUBLES
7.7800 g., 0.9990 Gold .2499 oz. AGW　**Subject:** Bolshoi Ballet - Sleeping Beauty　**Rev:** Ballerina

Date	F	VF	XF	Unc	BU
1995 Proof		Value: 350			

Y# 501　50 ROUBLES
8.6397 g., 0.9000 Gold .2500 oz. AGW　**Rev:** Church of the Savior on the Nereditza River

Date	F	VF	XF	Unc	BU
1996 Proof		Value: 185			

Y# 443　50 ROUBLES
7.7759 g., 0.9990 Platinum .2500 oz. APW　**Subject:** Bolshoi Ballet - Sleeping Beauty　**Rev:** Male dancer

Date	F	VF	XF	Unc	BU
1995 Proof		Value: 475			

Y# 508　50 ROUBLES
Aluminum-Bronze　**Subject:** 300th Anniversary - Russian Fleet　**Rev:** Submarine

Date	F	VF	XF	Unc	BU
1996	—	—	—	6.00	—

Y# 496　50 ROUBLES
8.6397 g., 0.9000 Gold .2500 oz. AGW　**Subject:** F. Nansen and the "Fram"

Date	F	VF	XF	Unc	BU
1995 Proof		Value: 200			

Y# A475　50 ROUBLES
7.7800 g., 0.9990 Gold .2499 oz. AGW　**Series:** Wildlife　**Rev:** Lynx

Date	F	VF	XF	Unc	BU
1995 Proof		Value: 200			

Y# 537　50 ROUBLES
7.7759 g., 0.9990 Gold .2500 oz. AGW　**Series:** Wildlife　**Rev:** Amur tiger

Date	F	VF	XF	Unc	BU
1996 Proof		Value: 200			

Y# 546   50 ROUBLES
8.6397 g., 0.9000 Gold .2500 oz. AGW **Rev:** Cruiser Varyag 1904

Date	F	VF	XF	Unc	BU
1996 Proof		Value: 250			

Y# 316   100 ROUBLES
Bi-Metallic Copper-Nickel center in Aluminum-Bronze ring **Obv:**
Double-headed eagle **Rev:** Denomination **Note:** Off-metal strikes
exist from the Moscow mint. The strike is on the planchet reserved
for Y#315, 50 Roubles.

Date	F	VF	XF	Unc	BU
1992	0.50	0.75	1.00	3.00	—

Y# 555   50 ROUBLES
8.6397 g., 0.9000 Gold .2500 oz. AGW **Subject:** 850th
Anniversary - Moscow

Date	F	VF	XF	Unc	BU
1997 Proof		Value: 200			

Y# 357   100 ROUBLES
17.5000 g., 0.9000 Gold .5000 oz. AGW **Obv:** Double-headed
eagle **Rev:** Michael Lomonosov

Date	F	VF	XF	Unc	BU
1992 Proof		Value: 350			

Y# 572   50 ROUBLES
7.7759 g., 0.9990 Gold .2500 oz. AGW **Subject:** Ballet - Swan
Lake **Rev:** Prince Siegfried with crossbow and swan

Date	F	VF	XF	Unc	BU
1997 Proof		Value: 225			

Y# 375   100 ROUBLES
17.5000 g., 0.9000 Gold .5000 oz. AGW **Obv:** Double-headed
eagle **Rev:** Wooly Mammoth **Note:** Yakutia

Date	F	VF	XF	Unc	BU
1992	—	—	—	375	—

Y# 595   50 ROUBLES
7.7759 g., 0.9990 Gold .2500 oz. AGW **Series:** Wildlife **Rev:**
Polar bear

Date	F	VF	XF	Unc	BU
1997 Proof		Value: 210			

Y# 338   100 ROUBLES
Copper-Nickel-Zinc

Date	F	VF	XF	Unc	BU
1993	0.25	0.50	1.00	3.00	—

Y# 712   50 ROUBLES
8.7500 g., 0.9000 Gold .2532 oz. AGW **Series:** Three
Millenniums **Subject:** Scientific and Technical Progress **Obv:**
Double-headed eagle **Rev:** Icarus and space travel

Date	F	VF	XF	Unc	BU
2000 Proof		Value: 250			

Y# 412 100 ROUBLES
15.5500 g., 0.9990 Gold .5000 oz. AGW **Series:** Wildlife **Rev:**
Asiatic black bear

Date	F	VF	XF	Unc	BU
1993 Proof		Value: 350			

Y# 526 100 ROUBLES
15.5500 g., 0.9990 Gold .5000 oz. AGW **Series:** Wildlife **Rev:**
Sable

Date	F	VF	XF	Unc	BU
1994 Proof		Value: 400			

Y# 419 100 ROUBLES
15.5500 g., 0.9990 Gold .5000 oz. AGW **Subject:** Bolshoi Ballet
Rev: Ballerina

Date	F	VF	XF	Unc	BU
1993	—	—	—	500	—

Y# 532 100 ROUBLES
15.5500 g., 0.9990 Gold .5000 oz. AGW **Rev:** Vassili Vassilievich
Kandinsky - The Blue Horse

Date	F	VF	XF	Unc	BU
1994 Proof		Value: 400			

Y# 454 100 ROUBLES
17.5000 g., 0.9000 Gold .5000 oz. AGW **Rev:** Peter Tchaikovsky

Date	F	VF	XF	Unc	BU
1993 Proof		Value: 500			

Y# 427 100 ROUBLES
15.5500 g., 0.9990 Gold .5000 oz. AGW **Subject:** Bolshoi Ballet
Rev: Ballerina

Date	F	VF	XF	Unc	BU
1994 Proof		Value: 550			

Y# 376 100 ROUBLES
1111.0861 g., 0.9000 Silver 32.1500 oz. ASW, 100 mm. **Series:**
Wildlife **Rev:** Mother brown bear with cubs **Note:** Illustration reduced.

Date	F	VF	XF	Unc	BU
1995 Proof		Value: 950			

Y# 404 100 ROUBLES
Copper-Nickel **Series:** WWII **Rev:** Berlin Soldier Monument

Date	F	VF	XF	Unc	BU
1995	—	—	—	5.00	—

Y# 497   100 ROUBLES
17.5000 g., 0.9000 Gold .5000 oz. AGW   **Rev:** Icebreaker "Krassin"

Date	F	VF	XF	Unc	BU
1995 Proof		Value: 500			

Y# 498   100 ROUBLES
912.3693 g., 0.9000 Silver 26.4000 oz. ASW   **Series:** Wildlife
Rev: Lynx with two kits

Date	F	VF	XF	Unc	BU
1995 Proof		Value: 950			

Y# 434   100 ROUBLES
912.3693 g., 0.9000 Silver 26.4000 oz. ASW, 100 mm.   **Subject:** Ballet - Sleeping Beauty **Note:** Illustration reduced.

Date	F	VF	XF	Unc	BU
1995 Proof		Value: 600			

Y# 499   100 ROUBLES
17.5000 g., 0.9000 Gold .5000 oz. AGW   **Series:** Wildlife **Rev:** Lynx

Date	F	VF	XF	Unc	BU
1995 Proof		Value: 500			

Y# 441   100 ROUBLES
15.5000 g., 0.9990 Gold .5000 oz. AGW   **Subject:** Ballet - Sleeping Beauty **Obv:** Ballerina

Date	F	VF	XF	Unc	BU
1995 Proof		Value: 695			

Y# 502   100 ROUBLES
17.5000 g., 0.9000 Gold .5000 oz. AGW   **Rev:** Badge and star of the Order of Alexander Nevsky

Date	F	VF	XF	Unc	BU
1995 Proof		Value: 500			

Y# A387　100 ROUBLES
1000.2108 g., 0.9000 Silver 28.9417 oz. ASW, 103 mm. **Series:**
WWII **Subject:** WWII Victory **Rev:** Allied commanders **Note:**
Illustration reduced.

Date	F	VF	XF	Unc	BU
1995 Proof		Value: 750			

Y# 481　100 ROUBLES
17.5000 g., 0.9000 Gold .5000 oz. AGW **Obv:** Double-headed
eagle **Rev:** All Saints Church in Kulishki

Date	F	VF	XF	Unc	BU
1996 Proof		Value: 350			

Y# 488　100 ROUBLES
1111.0861 g., 0.9990 Silver 32.1500 oz. ASW **Subject:** Ballet -
Nutcracker **Rev:** Marsha cradling nutcracker doll **Note:** Illustration
reduced.

Date	F	VF	XF	Unc	BU
1996 Proof		Value: 750			

Y# 489　100 ROUBLES
15.5517 g., 0.9990 Gold .5000 oz. AGW **Subject:** Ballet -
Nutcracker **Rev:** Dancing prince

Date	F	VF	XF	Unc	BU
1996 Proof		Value: 400			

Y# 495　100 ROUBLES
912.3693 g., 0.9000 Silver 26.4000 oz. ASW **Obv:** Double-
headed eagle **Rev:** Sables around walled city

Date	F	VF	XF	Unc	BU
1996 Proof		Value: 1,500			

Y# 509　100 ROUBLES
Copper-Nickel **Subject:** 300th Anniversary - Russian Fleet **Rev:**
Nuclear icebreaker "Arctica"

Date	F	VF	XF	Unc	BU
1996	—	—	—	7.00	—

Russia

Y# 538　100 ROUBLES
1111.0861 g., 0.9000 Silver 32.1500 oz. ASW **Series:** Wildlife
Rev: Amur tiger **Note:** Illustration reduced.

Date	F	VF	XF	Unc	BU
1996 Proof		Value: 750			

Y# 539　100 ROUBLES
15.5517 g., 0.9990 Gold .5000 oz. AGW **Series:** Wildlife **Rev:**
Amur tiger

Date	F	VF	XF	Unc	BU
1996 Proof		Value: 400			

Y# 556　100 ROUBLES
1111.0861 g., 0.9000 Silver 32.1500 oz. ASW **Subject:** 850th
Anniversary - Moscow **Obv:** Double-headed eagle **Rev:** Kuzma
Minin and Dmitri Pozharsky monument **Note:** Illustration reduced.

Date	F	VF	XF	Unc	BU
1997 Proof		Value: 750			

Y# 547　100 ROUBLES
912.3693 g., 0.9000 Silver 26.4000 oz. ASW **Obv:** Double-headed
eagle **Rev:** Warship - Poltava, 1712 **Note:** Illustration reduced.

Date	F	VF	XF	Unc	BU
1996 Proof		Value: 750			

Y# 557　100 ROUBLES
17.2890 g., 0.9000 Gold .5000 oz. AGW **Subject:** 850th
Anniversary - Moscow **Rev:** Yuri Dolgoruky monument

Date	F	VF	XF	Unc	BU
1997 Proof		Value: 500			

Y# 548　100 ROUBLES
17.5000 g., 0.9000 Gold .5000 oz. AGW **Subject:** Battleships of
WWII **Rev:** Destroyers "Gremyashij" and "Soobrazitelny"

Date	F	VF	XF	Unc	BU
1996 Proof		Value: 500			

Y# 573　100 ROUBLES
1111.0861 g., 0.9000 Silver 32.1500 oz. ASW **Subject:** Ballet -
Swan Lake **Obv:** Double-headed eagle **Rev:** Prince Siegfried
dancing with Odette **Note:** Illustration reduced.

Date	F	VF	XF	Unc	BU
1997 Proof		Value: 750			

Y# 574   100 ROUBLES
15.5517 g., 0.9990 Gold .5000 oz. AGW **Subject:** Ballet - Swan Lake **Rev:** Prince Siegfried and Odette's duet

Date	F	VF	XF	Unc	BU
1997 Proof		Value: 400			

Y# 597   100 ROUBLES
1111.0861 g., 0.9000 Silver 32.1500 oz. ASW **Series:** Wildlife **Obv:** Double-headed eagle **Rev:** Two polar bears

Date	F	VF	XF	Unc	BU
1997 Proof		Value: 750			

Y# 588   100 ROUBLES
1111.0861 g., 0.9000 Silver 32.1500 oz. ASW **Obv:** Double-headed eagle **Rev:** The Bark "Krusenstern" 4-masted ship **Note:** Illustration reduced.

Date	F	VF	XF	Unc	BU
1997 Proof	/	Value: 775			

Y# 623   100 ROUBLES
15.7200 g., 0.9990 Gold .5049 oz. AGW

Date	F	VF	XF	Unc	BU
1997 Proof		Value: 400			

Y# 596   100 ROUBLES
15.5517 g., 0.9990 Gold .5000 oz. AGW **Series:** Wildlife **Rev:** Polar bear on ice floe

Date	F	VF	XF	Unc	BU
1997 Proof		Value: 425			

Y# 699   100 ROUBLES
1111.1200 g., 0.9000 Silver 32.1510 oz. ASW, 100 mm. **Subject:** Russian Ballet **Obv:** Double-headed eagle **Rev:** Raymonda wedding scene **Edge:** Reeded **Note:** Illustration reduced.

Date	F	VF	XF	Unc	BU
1999 Proof		Value: 775			

Y# 358   150 ROUBLES
15.5517 g., 0.9990 Platinum .5000 oz. APW   **Subject:** Naval Battle of Chesme

Date	F	VF	XF	Unc	BU
1992 Proof		Value: 650			

Y# 430   150 ROUBLES
15.5517 g., 0.9990 Platinum .5000 oz. APW   **Subject:** Bolshoi Ballet **Rev:** Ballerina

Date	F	VF	XF	Unc	BU
1994 Proof		Value: 950			

Y# 397   150 ROUBLES
15.5517 g., 0.9990 Platinum .5000 oz. APW   **Subject:** Ballet **Obv:** Double-headed eagle **Rev:** Ballerina

Date	F	VF	XF	Unc	BU
1993	—	—	—	675	—

Y# 523   150 ROUBLES
15.5517 g., 0.9990 Platinum .5000 oz. APW   **Subject:** First Global Circumnavigation **Rev:** Sloops - "Mirny" and "Vostok"

Date	F	VF	XF	Unc	BU
1994 Proof		Value: 650			

Y# 455   150 ROUBLES
15.5517 g., 0.9990 Platinum .5000 oz. APW   **Rev:** Igor Stravinsky

Date	F	VF	XF	Unc	BU
1993 Proof		Value: 650			

Y# 533   150 ROUBLES
15.5517 g., 0.9990 Platinum .5000 oz. APW   **Subject:** Michail Alexandrowich Vrubel - The Demon

Date	F	VF	XF	Unc	BU
1994 Proof		Value: 650			

Y# 519   150 ROUBLES
15.5517 g., 0.9990 Platinum .5000 oz. APW   **Subject:** First Global Circumnavigation **Rev:** Sloops - "Nadyezdha" and "Neva"

Date	F	VF	XF	Unc	BU
1993 Proof		Value: 650			

Y# 444   150 ROUBLES
15.5517 g., 0.9990 Platinum .5000 oz. APW   **Subject:** Ballet - Sleeping Beauty **Rev:** Male dancer

Date	F	VF	XF	Unc	BU
1995 Proof		Value: 900			

Russia

Y# 503   150 ROUBLES
15.5517 g., 0.9990 Platinum .5000 oz. APW **Subject:** Battle of
the Neva River in 1240

Date	F	VF	XF	Unc	BU
1995 Proof	Value: 650				

Y# 540   200 ROUBLES
31.1035 g., 0.9990 Gold 1.0000 oz. AGW **Series:** Wildlife **Rev:**
Amur tiger

Date	F	VF	XF	Unc	BU
1996 Proof	Value: 1,200				

Y# 413   200 ROUBLES
31.1035 g., 0.9990 Gold 1.0000 oz. AGW **Series:** Wildlife **Rev:**
Bear with cub

Date	F	VF	XF	Unc	BU
1993 Proof	Value: 1,200				

Y# 598   200 ROUBLES
31.1035 g., 0.9990 Gold 1.0000 oz. AGW **Series:** Wildlife **Rev:**
Seated polar bear

Date	F	VF	XF	Unc	BU
1997 Proof	Value: 1,100				

Y# 527   200 ROUBLES
31.1035 g., 0.9990 Gold 1.0000 oz. AGW **Series:** Wildlife **Rev:**
Two sables

Date	F	VF	XF	Unc	BU
1994 Proof	Value: 1,200				

Y# 589   1000 ROUBLES
155.5000 g., 0.9990 Gold 4.9944 oz. AGW **Rev:** The Bark
"Krusenstern" - 4-masted ship

Date	F	VF	XF	Unc	BU
1997 Proof	Value: 5,000				

Y# 500   200 ROUBLES
31.1035 g., 0.9990 Gold 1.0000 oz. AGW **Series:** Wildlife **Rev:**
Seated lynx

Date	F	VF	XF	Unc	BU
1995 Proof	Value: 1,250				

Russia

Y# 541   10000 ROUBLES
1111.0861 g., 0.9990 Gold 35.6865 oz. AGW, 100 mm. **Series:** Wildlife **Obv:** Double-headed eagle **Rev:** Amur tiger with two cubs **Note:** Illustration reduced.

Date	F	VF	XF	Unc	BU
1996	—	—	—	—	24,000

Y# 599   10000 ROUBLES
1111.0861 g., 0.9990 Gold 35.6865 oz. AGW, 100 mm. **Series:** Wildlife **Obv:** Double-headed eagle **Rev:** Polar bear with two cubs **Note:** Illustration reduced.

Date	F	VF	XF	Unc	BU
1997 Proof		Value: 24,000			

REFORM COINAGE
January 1, 1998
1,000 Old Roubles = 1 New Rouble

Y# 600   KOPEK
Nickel **Obv:** St. George **Rev:** Denomination

Date	F	VF	XF	Unc	BU
1997-2004	—	—	—	0.25	0.35

Y# 601   5 KOPEKS
Nickel **Obv:** St. George **Rev:** Denomination **Edge:** Plain

Date	F	VF	XF	Unc	BU
1997-2005	—	—	—	0.35	0.50

Y# 602   10 KOPEKS
Brass **Obv:** St. George **Rev:** Denomination

Date	F	VF	XF	Unc	BU
1997-2005	—	—	—	0.50	0.75

Y# 603   50 KOPEKS
Brass **Obv:** St. George **Rev:** Denomination **Edge:** Reeded

Date	F	VF	XF	Unc	BU
1997-2004	—	—	—	0.75	1.00

Y# 604   ROUBLE
3.2500 g., Copper-Nickel-Zinc, 20.6 mm. **Rev:** Denomination **Edge:** Reeded

Date	F	VF	XF	Unc	BU
1997-1999	—	—	—	1.00	1.50

Y# 614   ROUBLE
8.5300 g., 0.9250 Silver .2357 oz. ASW **Series:** World Youth Games **Rev:** Female tennis player

Date	F	VF	XF	Unc	BU
1998 Proof		Value: 30.00			

Y# 615   ROUBLE
8.5300 g., 0.9250 Silver .2357 oz. ASW **Series:** World Youth Games **Rev:** Female gymnast

Date	F	VF	XF	Unc	BU
1998 Proof		Value: 30.00			

Y# 616 ROUBLE
8.5300 g., 0.9250 Silver .2357 oz. ASW **Series:** World Youth
Games **Rev:** Fencer

Date	F	VF	XF	Unc	BU
1998 Proof		Value: 30.00			

Y# 617 ROUBLE
8.5300 g., 0.9250 Silver .2357 oz. ASW **Series:** World Youth
Games **Rev:** Hammer thrower

Date	F	VF	XF	Unc	BU
1998 Proof		Value: 30.00			

Y# 618 ROUBLE
8.5300 g., 0.9250 Silver .2357 oz. ASW **Series:** World Youth
Games **Rev:** Female gymnast

Date	F	VF	XF	Unc	BU
1998 Proof		Value: 30.00			

Y# 619 ROUBLE
8.5300 g., 0.9250 Silver .2357 oz. ASW **Series:** World Youth
Games **Rev:** Volleyball player

Date	F	VF	XF	Unc	BU
1998 Proof		Value: 30.00			

Y# 628 ROUBLE
17.5500 g., 0.9000 Silver .5078 oz. ASW **Series:** Wildlife **Rev:**
Far Eastern Skink

Date	F	VF	XF	Unc	BU
1998 Proof		Value: 45.00			

Y# 629 ROUBLE
17.5500 g., 0.9000 Silver .5078 oz. ASW **Series:** Wildlife **Rev:**
Lavtev Walrus

Date	F	VF	XF	Unc	BU
1998 Proof		Value: 45.00			

Y# 630 ROUBLE
17.5500 g., 0.9000 Silver .5078 oz. ASW **Series:** Wildlife **Rev:**
Emperor Goose

Date	F	VF	XF	Unc	BU
1998 Proof		Value: 40.00			

Y# 640 ROUBLE
Copper-Nickel-Zinc **Obv:** Double-headed eagle **Rev:** Alexander
Pushkin portrait **Edge:** Reeded

Date	F	VF	XF	Unc	BU
1999	—	—	—	0.75	1.25

Y# 641 ROUBLE
17.4400 g., 0.9000 Silver .5046 oz. ASW **Series:** Wildlife **Obv:**
Double-headed eagle **Rev:** Daurian Hedgehog

Date	F	VF	XF	Unc	BU
1999 Proof		Value: 45.00			

Y# 720 ROUBLE
17.4400 g., 0.9000 Silver .5046 oz. ASW **Obv:** Double-headed
eagle **Rev:** Leopard Runner snake

Date	F	VF	XF	Unc	BU
2000 Proof		Value: 60.00			

Y# 642 ROUBLE
17.4400 g., 0.9000 Silver .5046 oz. ASW **Series:** Wildlife **Obv:**
Double-headed eagle **Rev:** Caucasian viper

Date	F	VF	XF	Unc	BU
1999 Proof		Value: 40.00			

Y# 721 ROUBLE
17.4400 g., 0.9000 Silver .5046 oz. ASW **Obv:** Double-headed
eagle **Rev:** Russian Desman

Date	F	VF	XF	Unc	BU
2000 Proof		Value: 60.00			

Y# 643 ROUBLE
17.4400 g., 0.9000 Silver .5046 oz. ASW **Series:** Wildlife **Obv:**
Double-headed eagle **Rev:** Ross's Gull standing on shore

Date	F	VF	XF	Unc	BU
1999 Proof		Value: 40.00			

Y# 731 ROUBLE
3.2100 g., Copper-Nickel, 20.7 mm. **Obv:** Double-headed eagle
Rev: Stylized design above hologram **Edge:** Reeded

Date	F	VF	XF	Unc	BU
2001	—	—	—	1.50	2.00

Y# 719 ROUBLE
17.4400 g., 0.9000 Silver .5046 oz. ASW, 33 mm. **Subject:**
Wildlife **Obv:** Double-headed eagle **Rev:** Two Black-hooded
cranes **Edge:** Reeded

Date	F	VF	XF	Unc	BU
2000 Proof		Value: 60.00			

Y# 732 ROUBLE
17.4300 g., 0.9000 Silver 0.5043 oz. ASW, 32.8 mm. **Subject:**
Sturgeon **Obv:** Double-headed eagle **Rev:** Sakhalin sturgeon and
other fish **Edge:** Reeded

Date	F	VF	XF	Unc	B
2001 Proof		Value: 40.00			

Y# 745 ROUBLE
17.4000 g., 0.9000 Silver 0.5035 oz. ASW, 32.8 mm. **Obv:**
Double-headed eagle **Rev:** Altai Argali sheep **Edge:** Reeded

Date	F	VF	XF	Unc	BU
2001 Proof		Value: 35.00			

Y# 746 ROUBLE
17.4000 g., 0.9000 Silver 0.5035 oz. ASW, 32.8 mm. **Obv:**
Double-headed eagle **Rev:** Two Eurasian Beavers **Edge:** Reeded

Date	F	VF	XF	Unc	BU
2001 Proof		Value: 40.00			

Y# 758 ROUBLE
17.4400 g., 0.9000 Silver 0.5046 oz. ASW, 33 mm. **Obv:** Double-
headed eagle **Rev:** Chinese Goral **Edge:** Reeded

Date	F	VF	XF	Unc	BU
2002 Proof		Value: 35.00			

Y# 759 ROUBLE
17.4400 g., 0.9000 Silver 0.5046 oz. ASW, 33 mm. **Obv:** Double-
headed eagle **Rev:** Sei Whale **Edge:** Reeded

Date	F	VF	XF	Unc	BU
2002 Proof		Value: 35.00			

Y# 760 ROUBLE
17.4400 g., 0.9000 Silver 0.5046 oz. ASW, 33 mm. **Subject:**
Golden Eagle **Obv:** Double-headed eagle **Rev:** Eagle with nestling
Edge: Reeded

Date	F	VF	XF	Unc	BU
2002 Proof		Value: 35.00			

Y# 770 ROUBLE
8.5300 g., 0.9250 Silver 0.2537 oz. ASW, 25 mm. **Subject:**
Ministry of Education **Obv:** Double-headed eagle **Rev:** Seedling
and open book **Edge:** Reeded

Date	F	VF	XF	Unc	BU
2002 Proof		Value: 50.00			

Y# 771 ROUBLE
8.5300 g., 0.9250 Silver 0.2537 oz. ASW, 25 mm. **Subject:**
Ministry of Finances **Obv:** Double-headed eagle **Rev:** Caduceus
in monogram **Edge:** Reeded

Date	F	VF	XF	Unc	BU
2002 Proof		Value: 50.00			

Y# 772 ROUBLE
8.5300 g., 0.9250 Silver 0.2537 oz. ASW, 25 mm. **Subject:**
Ministry of Economic Developement **Obv:** Double-headed eagle
Rev: Crowned double-headed eagle with cornucopia and
caduceus **Edge:** Reeded

Date	F	VF	XF	Unc	BU
2002 Proof		Value: 50.00			

Y# 773 ROUBLE
8.5300 g., 0.9250 Silver 0.2537 oz. ASW, 25 mm. **Subject:**
Ministry of Foreign Affairs **Obv:** Double-headed eagle **Rev:**
Crowned two-headed eagle above crossed **Edge:** Reeded

Date	F	VF	XF	Unc	BU
2002 Proof		Value: 50.00			

Y# 774 ROUBLE
8.5300 g., 0.9250 Silver 0.2537 oz. ASW, 25 mm. **Subject:**
Ministry of Internal Affairs **Obv:** Double-headed eagle **Rev:**
Crowned two-headed eagle with round breast **Edge:** Reeded

Date	F	VF	XF	Unc	BU
2002 Proof		Value: 50.00			

Y# 775 ROUBLE
8.5300 g., 0.9250 Silver 0.2537 oz. ASW, 25 mm. **Subject:**
Ministry of Justice **Obv:** Double-headed eagle **Rev:** Crowned
double-headed eagle with column on breast shield **Edge:** Reeded

Date	F	VF	XF	Unc	BU
2002 Proof		Value: 50.00			

Y# 776 ROUBLE
8.5300 g., 0.9250 Silver 0.2537 oz. ASW, 25 mm. **Subject:** Russian
Armed Forces **Obv:** Double-headed eagle **Rev:** Double-headed
eagle with crowned top pointed breast shield **Edge:** Reeded

Date	F	VF	XF	Unc	BU
2002 Proof		Value: 50.00			

Y# 797 ROUBLE
3.2500 g., Copper Nickel **Obv:** Curved bank name below eagle

Date	F	VF	XF	Unc	BU
2002	—	—	—	1.00	1.50

Y# 833 ROUBLE
3.2500 g., Copper-Nickel-Zinc, 20.6 mm. **Obv:** Two headed eagle
above curved inscription **Rev:** Value and flower **Edge:** Reeded

Date	F	VF	XF	Unc	BU
2002-2005	—	—	—	0.75	1.25

Y# 835 ROUBLE
7.7800 g., 0.9250 Silver 0.2314 oz. ASW, 25 mm. **Subject:** St.
Petersburg **Obv:** Double-headed eagle **Rev:** Sphinx

Date	F	VF	XF	Unc	BU
2002 Proof		Value: 15.00			

Y# 836 ROUBLE
7.7800 g., 0.9250 Silver 0.2314 oz. ASW, 25 mm. **Subject:** St.
Petersburg **Obv:** Double-headed eagle **Rev:** Small ship

Date	F	VF	XF	Unc	BU
2002 Proof		Value: 15.00			

Y# 837 ROUBLE
7.7800 g., 0.9250 Silver 0.2314 oz. ASW, 25 mm. **Subject:** St.
Petersburg **Obv:** Double-headed eagle **Rev:** Lion

Date	F	VF	XF	Unc	BU
2002 Proof		Value: 15.00			

Y# 838 ROUBLE
7.7800 g., 0.9250 Silver 0.2314 oz. ASW, 25 mm. **Subject:** St.
Petersburg **Obv:** Double-headed eagle **Rev:** Horse sculpture

Date	F	VF	XF	Unc	BU
2002 Proof		Value: 15.00			

Y# 839 ROUBLE
7.7800 g., 0.9250 Silver 0.2314 oz. ASW, 25 mm. **Subject:** St.
Petersburg **Obv:** Double-headed eagle **Rev:** Griffin

Date	F	VF	XF	Unc	BU
2002 Proof		Value: 15.00			

Y# A834 ROUBLE
7.7800 g., 0.9250 Silver 0.2314 oz. ASW, 0.25 mm. **Subject:** St.
Petersburg **Obv:** Double-headed eagle **Rev:** Angel on steeple of
Cathedral in fortress

Date	F	VF	XF	Unc	BU
2002 Proof		Value: 15.00			

Y# 814 ROUBLE
17.4000 g., 0.9000 Silver 0.5035 oz. ASW, 32.8 mm. **Obv:**
Double-headed eagle **Rev:** Two Arctic foxes **Edge:** Reeded

Date	F	VF	XF	Unc	BU
2003 Proof		Value: 30.00			

Y# 815 ROUBLE
17.4000 g., 0.9000 Silver 0.5035 oz. ASW, 32.8 mm. **Obv:**
Double-headed eagle **Rev:** Chinese Softshell turtle **Edge:** Reeded

Date	F	VF	XF	Unc	BU
2003 Proof		Value: 30.00			

Y# 816 ROUBLE
17.4000 g., 0.9000 Silver 0.5035 oz. ASW, 32.8 mm. **Obv:**
Double-headed eagle **Rev:** Pygmy Cormorant drying it's wings
Edge: Reeded

Date	F	VF	XF	Unc	BU
2003 Proof		Value: 30.00			

Y# 828 ROUBLE
17.2800 g., 0.9000 Silver 0.4499 oz. ASW, 33 mm. **Obv:** Two
headed eagle **Rev:** Amur Forest Cat on branch **Edge:** Reeded

Date	F	VF	XF	Unc	BU
2004 Proof		Value: 40.00			

Y# 883 ROUBLE
7.0100 g., 0.9250 Silver 0.2085 oz. ASW, 32.8 mm. **Obv:** Double-
headed eagle **Rev:** Asiatic Wild Dog **Edge:** Reeded

Date	F	VF	XF	Unc	BU
2005 Proof		Value: 25.00			

Y# 884 ROUBLE
7.0100 g., 0.9250 Silver 0.2085 oz. ASW, 32.8 mm. **Obv:** Double-
headed eagle **Rev:** Volkhov Whitefish **Edge:** Reeded

Date	F	VF	XF	Unc	BU
2005 Proof		Value: 25.00			

Y# 881 ROUBLE
7.4300 g., 0.9000 Silver 0.215 oz. ASW, 32.8 mm. **Obv:** Double-
headed eagle **Rev:** Natterjack Toad **Edge:** Reeded

Date	F	VF	XF	Unc	BU
2004 Proof		Value: 25.00			

Y# 605 2 ROUBLES
Copper-Nickel-Zinc **Rev:** Denomination **Edge:** Alternating
reeded and smooth

Date	F	VF	XF	Unc	BU
1997-2001	—	—	—	1.65	2.25

Y# 882 ROUBLE
7.0100 g., 0.9250 Silver 0.2085 oz. ASW, 32.8 mm. **Obv:** Double-
headed eagle **Rev:** Two Marbled Murrelet sea birds **Edge:** Reeded

Date	F	VF	XF	Unc	BU
2005 Proof		Value: 25.00			

Y# 607 2 ROUBLES
16.8108 g., 0.9250 Silver .4999 oz. ASW **Subject:** 100th
Anniversary - Sergei Eisenstein **Obv:** Double-headed eagle

Date	F	VF	XF	Unc	BU
1998	—	—	—	30.00	32.50

Y# 608 2 ROUBLES
16.8108 g., 0.9250 Silver .4999 oz. ASW **Subject:** 100th
Anniversary - Sergei Eisenstein **Obv:** Double-headed eagle

Date	F	VF	XF	Unc	BU
1998	—	—	—	30.00	32.50

Y# 609 2 ROUBLES
16.8108 g., 0.9250 Silver .4999 oz. ASW **Obv:** Double-headed
eagle **Rev:** K. S. Stanslavski

Date	F	VF	XF	Unc	BU
1998	—	—	—	30.00	32.50

Y# 610 2 ROUBLES
16.8108 g., 0.9250 Silver .4999 oz. ASW **Obv:** Double-headed
eagle **Rev:** Maxim Gorky play - Stanislavsky method

Date	F	VF	XF	Unc	BU
1998	—	—	—	30.00	32.50

Y# 620 2 ROUBLES
17.0000 g., 0.9250 Silver .5056 oz. ASW **Obv:** Double-headed
eagle **Rev:** Victor Mikhailovich Vasnetsov - three ancient warriors

Date	F	VF	XF	Unc	BU
1998	—	—	—	30.00	32.50

Y# 621 2 ROUBLES
17.0000 g., 0.9250 Silver .5056 oz. ASW **Obv:** Double-headed
eagle **Rev:** Victor Mikhailovich Vasnetsov - three seated figures

Date	F	VF	XF	Unc	BU
1998	—	—	—	30.00	32.50

Y# 649 2 ROUBLES
17.0000 g., 0.9250 Silver .5056 oz. ASW **Subject:** K. L.
Khetagurov 1859-1906 **Obv:** Double-headed eagle **Rev:** Portrait
with mountain tops and buildings

Date	F	VF	XF	Unc	BU
1999 Proof		Value: 50.00			

Y# 650 2 ROUBLES
17.0000 g., 0.9250 Silver .5056 oz. ASW **Subject:** N. K. Rerikh
1874-1947 **Obv:** Double-headed eagle **Rev:** Painter with
mountains in the background

Date	F	VF	XF	Unc	BU
1999 Proof		Value: 35.00			

Y# 651 2 ROUBLES
17.0000 g., 0.9250 Silver .5056 oz. ASW **Subject:** The Human
Acts by Rerikh. **Obv:** Double-headed eagle **Rev:** Detail from
painting, artist's portrait above

Date	F	VF	XF	Unc	B
1999 Proof		Value: 35.00			

Y# 652 2 ROUBLES
17.0000 g., 0.9250 Silver .5056 oz. ASW **Subject:** K. P. Bryulo
1799-1852 **Obv:** Double-headed eagle **Rev:** Portrait of painter

Date	F	VF	XF	Unc	B
1999 Proof		Value: 35.00			

Russia

Y# 653   2 ROUBLES
17.0000 g., 0.9250 Silver .5056 oz. ASW **Subject:** The Last Day
of Pompei **Obv:** Double-headed eagle **Rev:** Detail from painting,
portrait in exergue

Date	F	VF	XF	Unc	BU
1999 Proof		Value: 35.00			

Y# 654   2 ROUBLES
17.0000 g., 0.9250 Silver .5056 oz. ASW **Obv:** Double-headed
eagle **Rev:** Half bust of I.P. Pavlov, dog, books, cap, and gown

Date	F	VF	XF	Unc	BU
1999 Proof		Value: 35.00			

∤# 655   2 ROUBLES
∤7.0000 g., 0.9250 Silver .5056 oz. ASW **Obv:** Double-headed
∋agle **Rev:** Portrait and silence tower

∍ate	F	VF	XF	Unc	BU
∃999 Proof		Value: 35.00			

∤# 659   2 ROUBLES
∤7.0000 g., 0.9250 Silver .5056 oz. ASW **Subject:** Eugeny
∍bramovich Baratynsky **Obv:** Double-headed eagle **Rev:** Bust of
∍aratynsky at right, scenery at left **Edge:** Reeded

∍ate	F	VF	XF	Unc	BU
∐00 Proof		Value: 45.00			

Y# 660   2 ROUBLES
17.0000 g., 0.9250 Silver .5056 oz. ASW **Subject:** F. A.
Vassiliyev **Obv:** Double-headed eagle **Rev:** Cameo bust of
Vassiliyev left, dates below, scenery at left

Date	F	VF	XF	Unc	BU
2000 Proof		Value: 45.00			

Y# 662   2 ROUBLES
17.0000 g., 0.9250 Silver .5056 oz. ASW **Subject:** S. V.
Kovaleuskaya **Obv:** Double-headed eagle **Rev:** Cameo bust of
Kovaleuskaya right at left, academic items at right

Date	F	VF	XF	Unc	BU
2000 Proof		Value: 45.00			

Y# 663   2 ROUBLES
5.1000 g., Copper-Nickel-Zinc **Series:** World War II **Obv:**
Denomination **Rev:** Infantry assault at Stalingrad **Edge:** Reeded
and plain sections

Date	F	VF	XF	Unc	BU
2000	—	—	—	1.25	1.50

Y# 664   2 ROUBLES
Copper-Nickel-Zinc **Rev:** Cannon manufacturing scene in Tula
Edge: Alternating reeded and smooth

Date	F	VF	XF	Unc	BU
2000	—	—	—	1.25	1.50

Y# 665 2 ROUBLES
Copper-Nickel-Zinc **Rev:** Truck-mounted rocket launchers in Smolensk **Edge:** Alternating reeded and smooth

Date	F	VF	XF	Unc	BU
2000	—	—	—	1.25	1.50

Y# 704 2 ROUBLES
17.4400 g., 0.9250 Silver .5056 oz. ASW, 33 mm. **Subject:** M.I. Chigorin **Obv:** Double-headed eagle **Rev:** Cameo portrait and chess pieces **Edge:** Reeded

Date	F	VF	XF	Unc	BU
2000 Proof		Value: 45.00			

Y# 666 2 ROUBLES
Copper-Nickel-Zinc **Rev:** Murmansk ship convoy **Edge:** Alternating reeded and smooth

Date	F	VF	XF	Unc	BU
2000	—	—	—	1.25	1.50

Y# 675 2 ROUBLES
5.2000 g., Copper-Nickel, 23 mm. **Subject:** Yuri Gagarin **Obv:** Denomination and date **Rev:** Uniformed portrait **Edge:** Segmented reeding

Date	F	VF	XF	Unc	BU
2001	—	—	—	2.00	3.00

Y# 667 2 ROUBLES
Copper-Nickel-Zinc **Rev:** Defense of Moscow scene **Edge:** Alternating reeded and smooth

Date	F	VF	XF	Unc	BU
2000	—	—	—	1.25	1.50

Y# 730 2 ROUBLES
17.0000 g., 0.9250 Silver .5056 oz. ASW, 33 mm. **Subject:** V.I. Dal **Obv:** Double-headed eagle **Rev:** Portrait, book, signature, figures **Edge:** Reeded

Date	F	VF	XF	Unc	BU
2001 Proof		Value: 40.00			

Y# 668 2 ROUBLES
Copper-Nickel-Zinc **Rev:** Marine landing scene in Novorusiisk **Edge:** Alternating reeded and smooth

Date	F	VF	XF	Unc	BU
2000	—	—	—	1.25	1.50

Y# 742 2 ROUBLES
17.0000 g., 0.9250 Silver 0.5056 oz. ASW, 33 mm. **Subject:** Zodiac Signs: Leo **Obv:** Double-headed eagle **Rev:** Lion and symbol **Edge:** Reeded

Date	F	VF	XF	Unc	BU
2002 Proof		Value: 22.50			

Y# 669 2 ROUBLES
Copper-Nickel-Zinc **Rev:** Siege of Leningrad truck convoy scene **Edge:** Alternating reeded and smooth

Date	F	VF	XF	Unc	BU
2000	—	—	—	1.25	1.50

Y# 747　2 ROUBLES
17.0000 g., 0.9250 Silver 0.5056 oz. ASW, 33 mm. **Subject:** Zodiac
Signs **Obv:** Double-headed eagle **Rev:** Virgo **Edge:** Reeded

Date	F	VF	XF	Unc	BU
2002 Proof	Value: 25.00				

Y# 768　2 ROUBLES
17.0000 g., 0.9250 Silver 0.5056 oz. ASW, 33 mm. **Subject:**
Zodiac Signs **Obv:** Double-headed eagle **Rev:** Balance scale
Edge: Reeded

Date	F	VF	XF	Unc	BU
2002 Proof	Value: 22.50				

Y# 761　2 ROUBLES
17.0000 g., 0.9250 Silver 0.5056 oz. ASW, 33 mm. **Subject:** Zodiac
Signs **Obv:** Double-headed eagle **Rev:** Capricorn **Edge:** Reeded

Date	F	VF	XF	Unc	BU
2002 Proof	Value: 22.50				

Y# 793　2 ROUBLES
17.0000 g., 0.9250 Silver 0.5056 oz. ASW, 33 mm. **Subject:** L.P.
Orlova **Obv:** Double-headed eagle **Rev:** Actress' portrait **Edge:**
Reeded

Date	F	VF	XF	Unc	BU
2002 Proof	Value: 25.00				

Y# 798　2 ROUBLES
5.1000 g., Copper Nickel **Obv:** Curved bank name below eagle

Date	F	VF	XF	Unc	BU
2002	—	—	—	1.50	2.00

Y# 834　2 ROUBLES
5.1000 g., Copper-Nickel, 23 mm. **Obv:** Two headed eagle above
curved inscription **Rev:** Value and flower **Edge:** Segmented reeding

Date	F	VF	XF	Unc	BU
2002	—	—	—	4.00	5.00

Y# 762　2 ROUBLES
17.0000 g., 0.9250 Silver 0.5056 oz. ASW, 33 mm. **Subject:** Zodiac
Signs **Obv:** Double-headed eagle **Rev:** Sagittarius **Edge:** Reeded

Date	F	VF	XF	Unc	BU
2002 Proof	Value: 22.50				

Y# 766　2 ROUBLES
17.0000 g., 0.9250 Silver 0.5056 oz. ASW, 33 mm. **Subject:** Zodiac
Signs **Obv:** Double-headed eagle **Rev:** Scorpion **Edge:** Reeded

Date	F	VF	XF	Unc	BU
2002 Proof	Value: 22.50				

Y# 803　2 ROUBLES
17.1000 g., 0.9250 Silver 0.5085 oz. ASW, 32.8 mm. **Subject:**
Zodiac signs **Obv:** Double-headed eagle **Rev:** Pisces - 2 fish
Edge: Reeded

Date	F	VF	XF	Unc	BU
2003 Proof	Value: 35.00				

Y# 804   2 ROUBLES
17.1000 g., 0.9250 Silver 0.5085 oz. ASW, 32.8 mm. **Subject:**
Zodiac signs **Obv:** Double-headed eagle **Rev:** Aquarius kneeling
and pouring water from jar **Edge:** Reeded

Date	F	VF	XF	Unc	BU
2003 Proof		Value: 35.00			

Y# 820   2 ROUBLES
17.0000 g., 0.9250 Silver 0.5056 oz. ASW, 33 mm. **Obv:** Double-
headed eagle **Rev:** Crab and Cancer zodiac symbol **Edge:** Reeded

Date	F	VF	XF	Unc	BU
2003 Proof		Value: 25.00			

Y# 840   2 ROUBLES
16.8100 g., 0.9250 Silver 0.4999 oz. ASW, 33 mm. **Rev:** Guil
Yarovsky

Date	F	VF	XF	Unc	BU
2003 Proof		Value: 20.00			

Y# 841   2 ROUBLES
16.8100 g., 0.9250 Silver 0.4999 oz. ASW, 33 mm. **Rev:** Fedor
Tyutchev

Date	F	VF	XF	Unc	BU
2003 Proof		Value: 20.00			

Y# 844   2 ROUBLES
17.0000 g., 0.9250 Silver 0.5056 oz. ASW, 33 mm. **Subject:**
Zodiac Signs **Rev:** Aries

Date	F	VF	XF	Unc	BU
2003 Proof		Value: 22.50			

Y# 845   2 ROUBLES
17.0000 g., 0.9250 Silver 0.5056 oz. ASW **Subject:** Zodiac Signs
Rev: Taurus

Date	F	VF	XF	Unc	BU
2003 Proof		Value: 22.50			

Y# 846   2 ROUBLES
17.0000 g., 0.9250 Silver 0.5056 oz. ASW, 33 mm. **Subject:**
Zodiac Signs **Rev:** Gemini

Date	F	VF	XF	Unc	BU
2003 Proof		Value: 22.50			

Y# 842   2 ROUBLES
16.8100 g., 0.9250 Silver 0.4999 oz. ASW, 33 mm. **Rev:** V. P.
Tchkalov

Date	F	VF	XF	Unc	BU
2004 Proof		Value: 20.00			

Y# 843   2 ROUBLES
16.8100 g., 0.9250 Silver 0.4999 oz. ASW, 33 mm. **Rev:** Mikhail
Glinka

Date	F	VF	XF	Unc	BU
2004 Proof		Value: 20.00			

Y# 624   3 ROUBLES
34.5600 g., 0.9000 Silver 1.0000 oz. ASW **Obv:** Double-headed
eagle **Rev:** Officer Davydov

Date	F	VF	XF	Unc	BU
1998 Proof		Value: 35.00			

Y# 625   3 ROUBLES
34.5600 g., 0.9000 Silver 1.0000 oz. ASW **Obv:** Double-headed
eagle **Rev:** "Russian Sosaveta" sculpture

Date	F	VF	XF	Unc	BU
1998 Proof		Value: 35.00			

Y# 626   3 ROUBLES
34.5600 g., 0.9000 Silver 1.0000 oz. ASW **Obv:** Double-headed
eagle **Rev:** Archangel's head

Date	F	VF	XF	Unc	BU
1998 Proof		Value: 35.00			

Y# 627 3 ROUBLES
34.5600 g., 0.9000 Silver 1.0000 oz. ASW **Obv:** Double-headed
eagle **Rev:** "Merchant Woman Drinking Tea"

Date	F	VF	XF	Unc	BU
1998 Proof		Value: 35.00			

Y# 633 3 ROUBLES
34.8800 g., 0.9000 Silver 1.0093 oz. ASW **Subject:** Russian
Human Rights Year **Obv:** Double-headed eagle **Rev:** Document,
people, and map **Edge:** Reeded

Date	F	VF	XF	Unc	BU
1998 Proof		Value: 37.50			

Y# 631 3 ROUBLES
34.5600 g., 0.9000 Silver 1.0000 oz. ASW **Subject:** Nilo
Stolobenskaya Hermitage **Obv:** Double-headed eagle **Rev:** Saint

Date	F	VF	XF	Unc	BU
1998 Proof		Value: 37.50			

Y# 634 3 ROUBLES
34.7700 g., 0.9000 Silver 1.0061 oz. ASW **Subject:** 275th
Anniversary - St. Petersburg University **Obv:** Double-headed
eagle **Rev:** Four portraits and building

Date	F	VF	XF	Unc	BU
1999 Proof		Value: 40.00			

Y# 632 3 ROUBLES
34.5600 g., 0.9000 Silver 1.0000 oz. ASW **Obv:** Double-headed
eagle **Rev:** Church, view from bell tower

Date	F	VF	XF	Unc	BU
1998 Proof		Value: 45.00			

Y# 635 3 ROUBLES
34.7300 g., 0.9000 Silver 1.0049 oz. ASW **Obv:** Double-headed
eagle **Rev:** Mardjany Mosque in Kazan

Date	F	VF	XF	Unc	BU
1999 Proof		Value: 37.50			

Y# 636   3 ROUBLES
34.7300 g., 0.9000 Silver 1.0049 oz. ASW **Subject:** 200th
Birthday - A. S. Pushkin **Obv:** Double-headed eagle **Rev:** Pushkin
at his desk

Date	F	VF	XF	Unc	BU
1999 Proof		Value: 32.50			

Y# 637   3 ROUBLES
34.7300 g., 0.9000 Silver 1.0049 oz. ASW **Subject:** 200th Birthday
- A. S. Pushkin **Obv:** Double-headed eagle **Rev:** Pushkin standing

Date	F	VF	XF	Unc	BU
1999 Proof		Value: 32.50			

Y# 638   3 ROUBLES
34.7300 g., 0.9000 Silver 1.0049 oz. ASW **Subject:** First Tibet
Exhibition 1879-1880 **Obv:** Double-headed eagle **Rev:** Men on
horseback

Date	F	VF	XF	Unc	BU
1999 Proof		Value: 35.00			

Y# 639   3 ROUBLES
34.7300 g., 0.9000 Silver 1.0049 oz. ASW **Subject:** Second Tibet
Exhibition 1883-1885 **Obv:** Double-headed eagle **Rev:** Camp scene

Date	F	VF	XF	Unc	BU
1999 Proof		Value: 35.00			

Y# 644   3 ROUBLES
34.7100 g., 0.9000 Silver 1.0044 oz. ASW **Subject:** Science
Academy. **Obv:** Double-headed eagle **Rev:** Allegorical figure,
building, portraits, imperial double eagle

Date	F	VF	XF	Unc	BU
1999 Proof		Value: 50.00			

Y# 645   3 ROUBLES
34.7100 g., 0.9000 Silver 1.0044 oz. ASW **Subject:** Estada
Kuskovo Palace **Obv:** Double-headed eagle **Rev:** Palace from
three perspectives

Date	F	VF	XF	Unc	BU
1999 Proof		Value: 37.50			

Y# 646   3 ROUBLES
34.7100 g., 0.9000 Silver 1.0044 oz. ASW   **Subject:** Juryev Monastery, Movgorod **Obv:** Double-headed eagle **Rev:** Building view and detail from interior

Date	F	VF	XF	Unc	BU
1999 Proof		Value: 37.50			

647   3 ROUBLES
4.8800 g., 0.9000 Silver 1.0093 oz. ASW   **Subject:** 50th anniversary - Diplomacy wtih China **Obv:** Double-headed eagle **Rev:** Moscow Kremlin and Tiananmen gate

ate	F	VF	XF	Unc	BU
999 Proof		Value: 250			

657   3 ROUBLES
.7300 g., 0.9000 Silver 1.0049 oz. ASW   **Subject:** Ballet **Obv:** Double-headed eagle **Rev:** Sword fight

te	F	VF	XF	Unc	BU
99 Proof		Value: 45.00			

Y# 658   3 ROUBLES
34.7300 g., 0.9000 Silver 1.0049 oz. ASW   **Subject:** Ballet **Obv:** Double-headed eagle **Rev:** Couple dancing, Arabic soldiers in background

Date	F	VF	XF	Unc	BU
1999 Proof		Value: 45.00			

Y# 690   3 ROUBLES
34.7300 g., 0.9000 Silver 1.0049 oz. ASW, 38.8 mm.   **Subject:** Ufa Friendship Monument **Obv:** Russian eagle **Rev:** Five people and monument **Edge:** Reeded

Date	F	VF	XF	Unc	BU
1999 Proof		Value: 60.00			

Y# 661   3 ROUBLES
34.8800 g., 0.9000 Silver 1.0093 oz. ASW   **Subject:** World Ice Hockey Championship **Rev:** Two hockey players **Edge:** Reeded

Date	F	VF	XF	Unc	BU
2000 Proof		Value: 60.00			

Y# 671   3 ROUBLES
34.7600 g., 0.9000 Silver 1.0058 oz. ASW Series: Olympics Rev:
2000 Olympic design Edge: Reeded

Date	F	VF	XF	Unc	BU
2000 Proof		Value: 45.00			

Y# 673   3 ROUBLES
34.6700 g., 0.9990 Silver 1.1135 oz. ASW Subject: Soccer Obv:
Double-headed eagle Rev: Two soccer players, map, and net
Edge: Reeded

Date	F	VF	XF	Unc	BU
2000 Proof		Value: 60.00			

Y# 674   3 ROUBLES
34.9400 g., 0.9000 Silver 1.0110 oz. ASW Series: WWII Subject:
55th Anniversary - WWII Obv: Seated soldier Rev: Soviet Order
of Glory Edge: Lettered Edge Lettering: BANK of RUSSIA
THREE ROUBLES 2000

Date	F	VF	XF	Unc	BU
2000 Proof		Value: 42.50			

Y# 705   3 ROUBLES
34.8800 g., 0.9000 Silver 1.0093 oz. ASW, 39 mm. Subject: St.
Nicholas Monastery Obv: Double-headed eagle Rev: Saint and
buildings Edge: Reeded

Date	F	VF	XF	Unc	BU
2000 Proof		Value: 42.50			

Y# 706   3 ROUBLES
34.8800 g., 0.9000 Silver 1.0093 oz. ASW Subject: Novgorod
Kremlin Obv: Double-headed eagle Rev: Buildings

Date	F	VF	XF	Unc	BU
2000 Proof		Value: 42.50			

Y# 707   3 ROUBLES
34.8800 g., 0.9000 Silver 1.0093 oz. ASW Subject: City of
Pushkin Obv: Double-headed eagle Rev: Park and city view

Date	F	VF	XF	Unc	BU
2000 Proof		Value: 47.50			

Y# 708 3 ROUBLES
34.8800 g., 0.9000 Silver 1.0093 oz. ASW, 39 mm. **Series:** Third
Millennium **Subject:** Science **Obv:** Double-headed eagle **Rev:**
Astronaut, atomic elements chart, etc. **Edge:** Reeded

Date	F	VF	XF	Unc	BU
2000 Proof		Value: 42.50			

Y# 716 3 ROUBLES
34.8800 g., 1.0093 Silver **Subject:** Field Marshal Suvorov in
Switzerland **Obv:** Double-headed eagle **Rev:** Battle scene

Date	F	VF	XF	Unc	BU
2000 Proof		Value: 42.50			

Y# 709 3 ROUBLES
34.8800 g., 0.9000 Silver 1.0093 oz. ASW **Series:** Third
Millennium **Subject:** Human Role **Obv:** Double-headed eagle
Rev: People between cog wheel and computer

Date	F	VF	XF	Unc	BU
2000 Proof		Value: 42.50			

Y# 722 3 ROUBLES
34.8800 g., 0.9000 Silver 1.0093 oz. ASW **Subject:** Snow
Leopard **Obv:** Double-headed eagle **Rev:** Leopard on log

Date	F	VF	XF	Unc	BU
2000 Proof		Value: 45.00			

Y# 714 3 ROUBLES
34.8800 g., 0.9000 Silver 1.0093 oz. ASW **Subject:** 140th
Anniversary - State Bank of Russia **Obv:** Double-headed eagle
Rev: Seated allegorical woman

Date	F	VF	XF	Unc	BU
2000 Proof		Value: 60.00			

Y# 677 3 ROUBLES
34.8800 g., 0.9000 Silver 1.0093 oz. ASW, 39 mm. **Subject:** 225
Years - Bolshoi Theater **Obv:** Double-headed eagle **Rev:** Five
men, one with pole ax **Edge:** Reeded

Date	F	VF	XF	Unc	BU
2001 Proof		Value: 40.00			

Y# 680   3 ROUBLES

34.8800 g., 0.9000 Silver 1.0093 oz. ASW, 39 mm. **Subject:** 40th Anniversary of Manned Space Flight **Obv:** Double-headed eagle **Rev:** Uniformed portrait of Yuri Gagarin holding dove **Edge:** Reeded

Date	F	VF	XF	Unc	BU
2001 Proof		Value: 40.00			

Y# 682   3 ROUBLES

34.8800 g., 0.9000 Silver 1.0093 oz. ASW, 39 mm. **Subject:** Siberian Exploration **Obv:** Double-headed eagle **Rev:** Men riding horses, deer and sleds **Edge:** Reeded

Date	F	VF	XF	Unc	BU
2001 Proof		Value: 45.00			

Y# 733   3 ROUBLES

34.8800 g., 0.9000 Silver 1.0093 oz. ASW, 39 mm. **Subject:** 200th Anniversary of Navigation School **Obv:** Double-headed eagle **Rev:** Navigational tools and building **Edge:** Reeded

Date	F	VF	XF	Unc	BU
2001 Proof		Value: 40.00			

Y# 734   3 ROUBLES

34.8800 g., 0.9000 Silver 1.0093 oz. ASW, 39 mm. **Subject:** First Moscow Savings Bank **Obv:** Double-headed eagle **Rev:** Beehive above building **Edge:** Reeded

Date	F	VF	XF	Unc	BU
2001 Proof		Value: 40.00			

Y# 735   3 ROUBLES

34.8800 g., 0.9000 Silver 1.0093 oz. ASW, 39 mm. **Subject:** State Labor Savings Bank **Obv:** Double-headed eagle **Rev:** Dam, passbook and tractor **Edge:** Reeded

Date	F	VF	XF	Unc	BU
2001 Proof		Value: 40.00			

Y# 736   3 ROUBLES

34.8800 g., 0.9000 Silver 1.0093 oz. ASW, 39 mm. **Subject:** Savings Bank of the Russian Federation **Obv:** Double-headed eagle **Rev:** Chevrons above building **Edge:** Reeded

Date	F	VF	XF	Unc	B
2001 Proof		Value: 40.00			

Y# 737   3 ROUBLES
34.8800 g., 0.9000 Silver 1.0093 oz. ASW, 39 mm. **Subject:** 10th Anniversary - Commonwealth of Independent States **Obv:** Double-headed eagle **Rev:** Hologram below logo **Edge:** Reeded

Date	F	VF	XF	Unc	BU
2001 Proof		Value: 45.00			

Y# 755   3 ROUBLES
34.8800 g., 0.9000 Silver 1.0093 oz. ASW, 39 mm. **Subject:** Admiral Nakhimov **Obv:** Double-headed eagle **Rev:** Monument, Admiral with cannon and naval battle scene **Edge:** Reeded

Date	F	VF	XF	Unc	BU
2002 Proof		Value: 40.00			

Y# 738   3 ROUBLES
34.8800 g., 0.9000 Silver 1.0093 oz. ASW, 39 mm. **Subject:** Olympics **Obv:** Double-headed eagle **Rev:** Two cross-country skiers **Edge:** Reeded

Date	F	VF	XF	Unc	BU
2002 Proof		Value: 40.00			

Y# 756   3 ROUBLES
34.8800 g., 0.9000 Silver 1.0093 oz. ASW, 39 mm. **Subject:** Hermitage **Obv:** Double-headed eagle **Rev:** Statues and arch **Edge:** Reeded

Date	F	VF	XF	Unc	BU
2002 Proof		Value: 40.00			

Y# 744   3 ROUBLES
34.8800 g., 0.9000 Silver 1.0093 oz. ASW, 39 mm. **Subject:** St. John's Nunnery, St. Petersburg **Obv:** Double-headed eagle **Rev:** Nunnery and cameo portraits of John of Kronstadt **Edge:** Reeded

Date	F	VF	XF	Unc	BU
2002 Proof		Value: 45.00			

Y# 778   3 ROUBLES
34.8800 g., 0.9000 Silver 1.0093 oz. ASW, 39 mm. **Subject:** Kideksha **Obv:** Double-headed eagle **Rev:** Three churches on river bank **Edge:** Reeded

Date	F	VF	XF	Unc	BU
2002 Proof		Value: 40.00			

Y# 779   3 ROUBLES
34.8800 g., 0.9000 Silver 1.0093 oz. ASW, 39 mm.   **Subject:**
Iversky Monastery, Valdaiy **Obv:** Double-headed eagle **Rev:**
Building complex on an island in Lake Valdaiy **Edge:** Reeded

Date		F	VF	XF	Unc	BU
2002 Proof			Value: 40.00			

Y# 787   3 ROUBLES
34.8800 g., 0.9000 Silver 1.0093 oz. ASW, 39 mm.   **Subject:**
World Cup Soccer **Obv:** Double-headed eagle **Rev:** Soccer ball
center in circle of players **Edge:** Reeded

Date		F	VF	XF	Unc	BU
2002 Proof			Value: 25.00			

Y# 780   3 ROUBLES
34.8800 g., 0.9000 Silver 1.0093 oz. ASW, 39 mm.   **Subject:**
Miraculous Savior Church **Obv:** Double-headed eagle **Rev:**
Church with separate bell tower **Edge:** Reeded

Date		F	VF	XF	Unc	BU
2002 Proof			Value: 45.00			

Y# 801   3 ROUBLES
34.8000 g., 0.9000 Silver 1.007 oz. ASW, 38.7 mm.   **Subject:**
Veborg **Obv:** Double-headed eagle **Rev:** Sailing ships and
buildings **Edge:** Reeded

Date		F	VF	XF	Unc	BU
2003 Proof			Value: 50.00			

Y# 781   3 ROUBLES
34.8800 g., 0.9000 Silver 1.0093 oz. ASW, 39 mm.   **Subject:**
Works of Dionissy **Obv:** Double-headed eagle **Rev:** "The Crucifix"
Edge: Reeded

Date		F	VF	XF	Unc	BU
2002 Proof			Value: 40.00			

Y# 802   3 ROUBLES
34.7500 g., 0.9000 Silver 1.0055 oz. ASW, 38.7 mm.   **Subject**
Lunar Calendar **Obv:** National emblem **Rev:** Mountain goat in
crescent **Edge:** Reeded

Date		F	VF	XF	Unc	B
2003 Proof			Value: 50.00			

Y # 805   3 ROUBLES
34.8400 g., 0.9000 Silver 1.0081 oz. ASW, 38.8 mm. **Subject:**
Zodiac signs **Obv:** Double-headed eagle **Rev:** Leo - Lion **Edge:**
Reeded

Date	F	VF	XF	Unc	BU
2003 Proof		Value: 45.00			

Y # 808   3 ROUBLES
34.7400 g., 0.9000 Silver 1.0052 oz. ASW, 38.8 mm. **Obv:**
Double-headed eagle **Rev:** Ipatiyevsky Monastery in Kostroma
Edge: Reeded

Date	F	VF	XF	Unc	BU
2003 Proof		Value: 40.00			

 # 806   3 ROUBLES
34.7400 g., 0.9000 Silver 1.0052 oz. ASW, 38.8 mm. **Subject:**
Daniel's Monastery **Obv:** Double-headed eagle **Rev:** Statue
d monastery **Edge:** Reeded

te	F	VF	XF	Unc	BU
03 Proof		Value: 45.00			

Y # 809   3 ROUBLES
34.7400 g., 0.9000 Silver 1.0052 oz. ASW, 38.8 mm. **Subject:**
First Kamchatka Expedition **Obv:** Double-headed eagle **Rev:**
Natives drying fish, tall ship in background **Edge:** Reeded

Date	F	VF	XF	Unc	BU
2003 Proof		Value: 35.00			

807   3 ROUBLES
7400 g., 0.9000 Silver 1.0052 oz. ASW, 38.8 mm. **Subject:**
ld Biathlon Championships **Obv:** Double-headed eagle **Rev:**
eman and archer on skis **Edge:** Reeded

	F	VF	XF	Unc	BU
Proof		Value: 35.00			

Y # 810   3 ROUBLES
34.7400 g., 0.9000 Silver 1.0052 oz. ASW, 38.8 mm. **Subject:**
Zodiac signs **Obv:** Double-headed eagle **Rev:** Virgo - Stars and
seated allegorical woman **Edge:** Reeded

Date	F	VF	XF	Unc	BU
2003 Proof		Value: 30.00			

Y# 848　3 ROUBLES
34.5600 g., 0.9000 Silver 1 oz. ASW, 39 mm.　**Subject:** Zodiac
Signs **Rev:** Archer

Date	F	VF	XF	Unc	BU
2003 Proof		Value: 30.00			

Y# 849　3 ROUBLES
34.5600 g., 0.9000 Silver 1 oz. ASW, 39 mm.　**Subject:** Zodiac
Signs **Rev:** Capricorn

Date	F	VF	XF	Unc	BU
2003 Proof		Value: 30.00			

Y# 811　3 ROUBLES
34.7400 g., 0.9000 Silver 1.0052 oz. ASW, 38.8 mm.　**Subject:**
Zodiac signs **Obv:** Double-headed eagle **Rev:** Libra - scale and
stars **Edge:** Reeded

Date	F	VF	XF	Unc	BU
2003 Proof		Value: 30.00			

Y# 812　3 ROUBLES
34.7400 g., 0.9000 Silver 1.0052 oz. ASW, 38.8 mm.　**Subject:**
Diveyevsky Monastery **Obv:** Double-headed eagle **Rev:** Cameo
portrait above churches **Edge:** Reeded

Date	F	VF	XF	Unc	BU
2003 Proof		Value: 40.00			

Y# 885　3 ROUBLES
34.8000 g., 0.9000 Silver 1.007 oz. ASW, 38.7 mm.　**Subject:**
City of Pskov 1100th Anniversary **Obv:** Double-headed eagle **Rev:**
Pskov walled city view **Edge:** Reeded

Date	F	VF	XF	Unc	B
2003 Proof		Value: 55.00			

Y# 850　3 ROUBLES
34.5600 g., 0.9000 Silver 1 oz. ASW, 39 mm.　**Subject:** Lunar
Calendar **Rev:** Monkey

Date	F	VF	XF	Unc	
2004 Proof		Value: 35.00			

Y# 851　3 ROUBLES
34.5600 g., 0.9000 Silver 1 oz. ASW, 39 mm.　**Subject:** Zodiac
Signs **Rev:** Aquarius

Date	F	VF	XF	Unc	
2004 Proof		Value: 30.00			

Y# 852　3 ROUBLES
34.5600 g., 0.9000 Silver 1 oz. ASW, 39 mm.　**Rev:** Tomsk

Date	F	VF	XF	Unc	
2004 Proof		Value: 25.00			

Y# 853　3 ROUBLES
34.5600 g., 0.9000 Silver 1 oz. ASW, 39 mm.　**Subject:** Zodiac
Signs **Rev:** Pisces

Date	F	VF	XF	Unc	
2004 Proof		Value: 30.00			

Y# 854　3 ROUBLES
34.5600 g., 0.9000 Silver 1 oz. ASW, 39 mm.　**Rev:** Epiphany
Cathedral, Moscow

Date	F	VF	XF	Unc	
2004 Proof		Value: 25.00			

Y# 855　3 ROUBLES
34.5600 g., 0.9000 Silver 1 oz. ASW, 39 mm.　**Subject:** Zodiac
Signs **Rev:** Aries

Date	F	VF	XF	Unc	
2004 Proof		Value: 30.00			

Y# 813　3 ROUBLES
34.7400 g., 0.9000 Silver 1.0052 oz. ASW, 38.8 mm.　**Subject:**
Zodiac Signs **Obv:** Double-headed eagle **Rev:** Scorpio - scorpion
and stars **Edge:** Reeded

Date	F	VF	XF	Unc	BU
2003 Proof		Value: 30.00			

Y# 847　3 ROUBLES
34.5600 g., 0.9000 Silver 1 oz. ASW, 39 mm.　**Rev:** St. Trinity
Monastery

Date	F	VF	XF	Unc	BU
2003 Proof		Value: 25.00			

Y# 856　3 ROUBLES
34.5600 g., 0.9000 Silver 1 oz. ASW, 39 mm.　**Rev:** Soccer

Date	F	VF	XF	Unc	
2004 Proof		Value: 22.50			

Y# 857   3 ROUBLES
34.5600 g., 0.9000 Silver 1 oz. ASW, 39 mm.   **Subject:** Zodiac
Signs **Rev:** Taurus

Date	F	VF	XF	Unc	BU
2004 Proof		Value: 30.00			

Y# 858   3 ROUBLES
34.5600 g., 0.9000 Silver 1 oz. ASW, 39 mm.   **Rev:** Olympic torch

Date	F	VF	XF	Unc	BU
2004 Proof		Value: 25.00			

Y# 859   3 ROUBLES
34.5600 g., 0.9000 Silver 1 oz. ASW, 39 mm.   **Subject:** Zodiac
Signs **Rev:** Gemini

Date	F	VF	XF	Unc	BU
2004 Proof		Value: 30.00			

Y# 860   3 ROUBLES
34.5600 g., 0.9000 Silver 1 oz. ASW, 39 mm.   **Subject:** Zodiac
Signs **Rev:** Cancer

Date	F	VF	XF	Unc	BU
2004 Proof		Value: 30.00			

Y# 861   3 ROUBLES
34.5600 g., 0.9000 Silver 1 oz. ASW, 39 mm.   **Rev:** Church of the
Sign of the Holy Mother of God

Date	F	VF	XF	Unc	BU
2004 Proof		Value: 25.00			

Y# 862   3 ROUBLES
34.5600 g., 0.9000 Silver 1 oz. ASW, 39 mm.   **Rev:**
Transfiguration icon

Date	F	VF	XF	Unc	BU
2004 Proof		Value: 25.00			

Y# 863   3 ROUBLES
34.5600 g., 0.9000 Silver 1 oz. ASW, 39 mm.   **Rev:** Peter I's
monetary reform

Date	F	VF	XF	Unc	BU
2004 Proof		Value: 75.00			

 # 606   5 ROUBLES
opper-Nickel Clad Copper   **Rev:** Denomination **Edge:** Reeded
nd plain sections

ate	F	VF	XF	Unc	BU
997-1998	—	—	—	2.00	3.00

 # 799   5 ROUBLES
4500 g., Copper-Nickel Clad Copper, 25 mm.   **Obv:** Curved
ank name below eagle **Edge:** Segmented reeding

ate	F	VF	XF	Unc	BU
02	—	—	—	2.00	3.00

 # 829   5 ROUBLES
.2400 g., 0.9000 Bi-Metallic Gold And Silver .900 Silver 21.34g
nter in .900 Gold 25.9g ring 1.3669 oz., 39.5 mm.   **Obv:** Double-
eaded eagle **Rev:** Uglich city view **Edge:** Reeded

te	F	VF	XF	Unc	BU
04 Proof		Value: 850			

 # 695   10 ROUBLES
500 g., 0.9990 Gold .0499 oz. AGW, 12 mm.   **Subject:**
ssian Ballet **Obv:** Two headed eagle **Rev:** Standing knight Jean
Brienne **Edge:** Reeded

e	F	VF	XF	Unc	BU
9 Proof		Value: 65.00			

Y# 670   10 ROUBLES
8.2600 g., Bi-Metallic Copper-Nickel center in Brass ring   **Series:**
WWII **Subject:** 55th Anniversary - Victorious Conclusion of WWII
Obv: Denomination **Rev:** Infantry officer leading an assault **Edge:**
Reeded and lettered **Note:** Struck at St. Petersburg Mint.

Date	F	VF	XF	Unc	BU
2000	—	—	—	3.50	5.00

Y# 676   10 ROUBLES
8.2200 g., Bi-Metallic Copper-Nickel center in Brass ring, 27 mm.
Subject: Yuri Gagarin **Obv:** Denomination with latent image in
zero, and date **Rev:** Helmeted portrait **Edge:** Reeding over
denomination

Date	F	VF	XF	Unc	BU
2001	—	—	—	3.50	5.00

Y# 686   10 ROUBLES
1.6100 g., 0.9990 Gold .0517 oz. AGW, 12 mm.   **Subject:** Bolshoi
Theater 225 Years **Obv:** Double-headed eagle **Rev:** Building
above number 225 **Edge:** Reeded

Date	F	VF	XF	Unc	BU
2001 Proof		Value: 55.00			

Y# 739   10 ROUBLES
8.2200 g., Bi-Metallic Copper-Nickel center in Brass ring, 27 mm.
Subject: Ancient Towns - Derbent **Obv:** Denomination in wreath
Rev: City arms above walled city view **Edge:** Reeding over
denomination

Date	F	VF	XF	Unc	BU
2002	—	—	—	3.00	4.00

Y # 740   10 ROUBLES
8.2200 g., Bi-Metallic Copper-Nickel center in Brass ring, 27 mm.
Subject: Ancient Towns - Kostroma **Obv:** Denomination in wreath
Rev: Cupola, city arms and river view **Edge:** Reeding over
denomination

Date	F	VF	XF	Unc	BU
2002	—	—	—	3.00	4.00

Y # 741   10 ROUBLES
8.2200 g., Bi-Metallic Copper-Nickel center in Brass ring, 27 mm.
Subject: Ancient Towns - Staraya Russa **Obv:** Denomination in
wreath **Rev:** City arms and cathedral **Edge:** Reeding over
denomination

Date	F	VF	XF	Unc	BU
2002	—	—	—	3.00	4.00

Y # 748   10 ROUBLES
8.2200 g., Bi-Metallic Copper-Nickel center in Brass ring, 27 mm.
Subject: Ministry of Education **Obv:** Denomination **Rev:** Seedling
and open book **Edge:** Reeding over denomination

Date	F	VF	XF	Unc	BU
2002	—	—	—	2.00	2.50

Y # 749   10 ROUBLES
8.2200 g., Bi-Metallic Copper-Nickel center in Brass ring, 27 mm.
Subject: Ministry of Finance **Obv:** Denomination **Rev:** Caduceus
in monogram **Edge:** Reeding over denomination

Date	F	VF	XF	Unc	BU
2002	—	—	—	2.00	2.50

Y # 750   10 ROUBLES
8.2200 g., Bi-Metallic Copper-Nickel center in Brass ring, 27 mm.
Subject: Ministry of Economic Developement **Obv:** Denomination
Rev: Crowned double-headed eagle with cornucopia and
Caduceus **Edge:** Reeding over denomination

Date	F	VF	XF	Unc	BU
2002	—	—	—	2.00	2.50

Y # 751   10 ROUBLES
8.2200 g., Bi-Metallic Copper-Nickel center in Brass ring, 27 mm.
Subject: Ministry of Foreign Affairs **Obv:** Denomination **Rev:**
Crowned double-headed eagle above crossed palms **Edge:**
Reeding over denomination

Date	F	VF	XF	Unc	BU
2002	—	—	—	2.00	2.50

Y # 752   10 ROUBLES
8.2200 g., Bi-Metallic Copper-Nickel center in Brass ring, 27 mm.
Subject: Ministry of Internal Affairs **Obv:** Denomination **Rev:**
Crowned double-headed eagle with round breast shield **Edge:**
Reeding over denomination

Date	F	VF	XF	Unc	B
2002	—	—	—	2.00	2.5

Y # 753   10 ROUBLES
8.2200 g., Bi-Metallic Copper-Nickel center in Brass ring, 27 mm
Subject: Ministry of Justice **Obv:** Denomination **Rev:** Crowned
double-headed eagle with column on breast shield **Edge:** Reedin
over denomination

Date	F	VF	XF	Unc	
2002	—	—	—	2.00	2.

Y # 754   10 ROUBLES
8.2200 g., Bi-Metallic Copper-Nickel center in Brass ring, 27 mn
Subject: Russian Armed Forces **Obv:** Denomination **Rev:**
Crowned double-headed eagle with crowned pointed top shie
Edge: Reeding over denomination

Date	F	VF	XF	Unc	
2002	—	—	—	2.00	2

Russia

Y# 800   10 ROUBLES
8.4400 g., Bi-Metallic Copper-Nickel center in Brass ring, 27.1 mm. **Obv:** Value **Rev:** Coat of arms above walled city **Edge:** Reeding over lettering

Date	F	VF	XF	Unc	BU
2003	—	—	—	3.00	3.50

Y# 817   10 ROUBLES
8.3400 g., Bi-Metallic Copper-nickel center in Brass ring, 27 mm. **Obv:** Value **Rev:** Murom city view and arms **Edge:** Reeded and lettered

Date	F	VF	XF	Unc	BU
2003	—	—	—	3.00	3.50

Y# 818   10 ROUBLES
8.3400 g., Bi-Metallic Copper-Nickel center in Brass ring, 27 mm. **Obv:** Value **Rev:** Kasimov city view and arms **Edge:** Reeded and lettered

Date	F	VF	XF	Unc	BU
2003	—	—	—	3.00	3.50

Y# 819   10 ROUBLES
8.3400 g., Bi-Metallic Copper-Nickel center in Brass ring, 27 mm. **Obv:** Value **Rev:** Dorogobush monument, city view and arms **Edge:** Reeded and lettered

Date	F	VF	XF	Unc	BU
2003	—	—	—	3.00	3.50

Y# 824   10 ROUBLES
8.3300 g., Bi-Metallic Copper-Nickel center in Brass ring, 27 mm. **Subject:** Town of Ryazhsk **Obv:** Value **Rev:** City view **Edge:** Reeded and lettered

Date	F	VF	XF	Unc	BU
2004	—	—	—	3.00	3.50

Y# 825   10 ROUBLES
8.1300 g., Bi-Metallic Copper-Nickel center in Brass ring, 27 mm. **Subject:** Town of Dmitrov **Obv:** Value **Rev:** City view **Edge:** Reeded and lettered

Date	F	VF	XF	Unc	BU
2004	—	—	—	3.00	3.50

Y# 826   10 ROUBLES
8.1300 g., Bi-Metallic Copper-Nickel center in Brass ring, 27 mm. **Subject:** Town of Kem **Obv:** Value **Rev:** City view **Edge:** Reeded and lettered

Date	F	VF	XF	Unc	BU
2004	—	—	—	3.00	3.50

Y# 827   10 ROUBLES
8.4000 g., Bi-Metallic Copper-Nickel center in Brass ring, 27 mm. **Obv:** Value **Rev:** WWII eternal flame monument **Edge:** Reeded and Lettered

Date	F	VF	XF	Unc	BU
2005	—	—	—	3.00	5.00

Y# 886   10 ROUBLES
8.2300 g., Bi-Metallic Copper-Nickel center in Brass ring, 27 mm. **Obv:** Moscow coat of arms **Rev:** Value **Edge:** Reeded and lettered

Date	F	VF	XF	Unc	BU
2005	—	—	—	3.00	4.00

Y# 887   10 ROUBLES
8.2300 g., Bi-Metallic Copper-Nickel center in Brass ring, 27 mm.
Obv: Leningrad Oblast coat of arms **Rev:** Value **Edge:** Reeded and lettered

Date	F	VF	XF	Unc	BU
2005	—	—	—	3.00	4.00

Y# 891   10 ROUBLES
8.2300 g., Bi-Metallic Copper-Nickel center in Brass ring, 27 mm.
Obv: Tatarstan Republic coat of arms **Rev:** Value **Edge:** Reeded and lettered

Date	F	VF	XF	Unc	BU
2005	—	—	—	3.00	4.00

Y# 888   10 ROUBLES
8.2300 g., Bi-Metallic Copper-Nickel center in Brass ring, 27 mm.
Obv: Tverskaya Oblast coat of arms **Rev:** Value **Edge:** Reeded and lettered

Date	F	VF	XF	Unc	BU
2005	—	—	—	3.00	4.00

Y# 889   10 ROUBLES
8.2300 g., Bi-Metallic Copper-Nickel center in Brass ring, 27 mm.
Obv: Krasnodarskiy Kray coat of arms **Rev:** Value **Edge:** Reeded and lettered

Date	F	VF	XF	Unc	BU
2005	—	—	—	3.00	4.00

Y# 890   10 ROUBLES
8.2300 g., Bi-Metallic Copper-Nickel center in Brass ring, 27 mm.
Obv: Orlovskaya Oblast coat of arms **Rev:** Value **Edge:** Reeded and lettered

Date	F	VF	XF	Unc	BU
2005	—	—	—	3.00	4.00

Y# 691   25 ROUBLES
173.2900 g., 0.9000 Silver 5.0143 oz. ASW, 60 mm. **Subject:** Alexander Pushkin **Obv:** Double-headed eagle **Rev:** Walking figure with hat and cane **Edge:** Reeded **Note:** Illustration reduce

Date	F	VF	XF	Unc	E
1999 Proof		Value: 165			

Y# 696   25 ROUBLES
173.2900 g., 0.9000 Silver 5.0143 oz. ASW, 60 mm. **Subjec** Russian Ballet **Obv:** Double-headed eagle **Rev:** Raymonda a the knight dance scene **Edge:** Reeded **Note:** Illustration reduc

Date	F	VF	XF	Unc
1999 Proof		Value: 165		

Y# 697 25 ROUBLES
3.2000 g., 0.9990 Gold .1028 oz. AGW, 16 mm. **Subject:**
Russian Ballet **Obv:** Double-headed eagle **Rev:** Dancing Saracen
Edge: Reeded

Date	F	VF	XF	Unc	BU
1999 Proof		Value: 160			

Y# 715 25 ROUBLES
173.2900 g., 0.9000 Silver 5.0143 oz. ASW, 60 mm. **Subject:**
State Bank of Russia 140th Anniversary **Obv:** Double-headed
eagle **Rev:** Document, portrait and building **Edge:** Reeded **Note:**
Illustration reduced.

Date	F	VF	XF	Unc	BU
2000 Proof		Value: 500			

Y# 701 25 ROUBLES
173.2900 g., 0.9000 Silver 5.0143 oz. ASW, 60 mm. **Subject:**
Russian Exploers: N.M. Przhevalsky **Obv:** Double-headed eagle
Rev: Caravan in Central Asia **Edge:** Reeded **Note:** Illustration
reduced.

Date	F	VF	XF	Unc	BU
1999 Proof		Value: 165			

Y# 717 25 ROUBLES
173.2900 g., 0.9000 Silver 5.0143 oz. ASW, 60 mm. **Subject:** Field
Marshal Suvorov **Obv:** Double-headed eagle **Rev:** Suvorov with
maps and battle scene **Edge:** Reeded **Note:** Illustration reduced.

Date	F	VF	XF	Unc	BU
2000 Proof		Value: 185			

Y# 710 25 ROUBLES
173.2900 g., 0.9000 Silver 5.0143 oz. ASW, 60 mm. **Series:**
3rd Millennium **Subject:** Education **Obv:** Double-headed eagle
Rev: Ancient monk and modern student **Edge:** Reeded **Note:**
Illustration reduced.

Date	F	VF	XF	Unc	BU
2000 Proof		Value: 185			

Y# 723 25 ROUBLES
173.2900 g., 0.9000 Silver 5.0143 oz. ASW, 60 mm. **Subject:**
Snow Leopard **Obv:** Double-headed eagle **Rev:** Leopard on
branch **Edge:** Reeded **Note:** Illustration reduced.

Date	F	VF	XF	Unc	BU
2000 Proof		Value: 185			

Russia

Y# 678   25 ROUBLES
173.2900 g., 0.9000 Silver 5.0143 oz. ASW, 60 mm. **Subject:**
Bolshoi Theater 225 Years **Obv:** Double-headed eagle **Rev:**
Dancing couple scene **Edge:** Reeded **Note:** Illustration reduced.

Date	F	VF	XF	Unc	BU
2001 Proof		Value: 135			

Y# 683   25 ROUBLES
173.2900 g., 0.9000 Silver 5.0143 oz. ASW, 60 mm. **Subject:**
Siberian Exploration **Obv:** Double-headed eagle **Rev:** Standing
king and river boats **Edge:** Reeded **Note:** Illustration reduced.

Date	F	VF	XF	Unc	BU
2001 Proof		Value: 145			

Y# 687   25 ROUBLES
3.2000 g., 0.9990 Gold .1028 oz. AGW, 16 mm. **Subject:** Bolshoi
Theater 225 Years **Obv:** Double-headed eagle **Rev:** Ballerina
Edge: Reeded

Date	F	VF	XF	Unc	BU
2001 Proof		Value: 140			

Y# 794   25 ROUBLES
173.1300 g., 0.9000 Silver 5.0096 oz. ASW, 60.2 mm. **Subject:**
Foundation of Russian Savings Banks **Obv:** Double-headed eagle
Rev: Czar Nicholas I and document **Edge:** Reeded

Date	F	VF	XF	Unc	BU
2001 Proof		Value: 120			

Y# 743   25 ROUBLES
3.2000 g., 0.9990 Gold 0.1028 oz. AGW, 16 mm. **Subject:** Zodiac
Signs: Leo **Obv:** Double-headed eagle **Rev:** Lion and symbol
Edge: Reeded

Date	F	VF	XF	Unc	BU
2002 Proof		Value: 120			

Y# 763   25 ROUBLES
3.2000 g., 0.9990 Gold 0.1028 oz. AGW, 16 mm. **Subject:** Zodiac
- Capricorn **Obv:** Double-headed eagle **Edge:** Reeded

Date	F	VF	XF	Unc	BU
2002	—	—	—	—	120

Y# 764   25 ROUBLES
3.2000 g., 0.9990 Gold 0.1028 oz. AGW, 16 mm. **Subject:** Zodiac
Signs **Obv:** Double-headed eagle **Rev:** Virgo, seated woman
Edge: Reeded

Date	F	VF	XF	Unc	BU
2002	—	—	—	—	120

Y# 765   25 ROUBLES
3.2000 g., 0.9990 Gold 0.1028 oz. AGW, 16 mm. **Subject:** Zodiac
Signs **Obv:** Double-headed eagle **Rev:** Sagittarius the archer
Edge: Reeded

Date	F	VF	XF	Unc	B
2002	—	—	—	—	12

Y# 767   25 ROUBLES
3.2000 g., 0.9990 Gold 0.1028 oz. AGW, 16 mm. **Subject:** Zodiac
- Scorpio **Obv:** Double-headed eagle **Rev:** Scorpion **Edge:** Reede

Date	F	VF	XF	Unc	B
2002	—	—	—	—	12

Y# 769   25 ROUBLES
3.2000 g., 0.9990 Gold .1028 oz. AGW **Subject:** Zodiac Signs **Ob**
Double-headed eagle **Rev:** Libra, balance scale **Edge:** Reeded

Date	F	VF	XF	Unc	
2002	—	—	—	—	1

Y# 777   25 ROUBLES
173.2900 g., 0.9000 Silver 5.0143 oz. ASW, 60 mm. **Subject:** Czar Alexander I **Obv:** Double-headed eagle **Rev:** Portrait and Imperial eagle above document text establishing government ministries **Edge:** Reeded

Date	F	VF	XF	Unc	BU
2002 Proof		Value: 165			

785   25 ROUBLES
73.2900 g., 0.9000 Silver 5.0143 oz. ASW, 60 mm. **Subject:** dmiral Nakhimov **Obv:** Double-headed eagle **Rev:** Admiral atching naval battle **Edge:** Reeded **Note:** Illustration reduced.

ate	F	VF	XF	Unc	BU
002 Proof		Value: 150			

Y# 790   25 ROUBLES
173.2900 g., 0.9000 Silver 5.0143 oz. ASW, 60 mm. **Subject:** Hermitage **Obv:** Double-headed eagle **Rev:** Staircase viewed through door way **Edge:** Reeded **Note:** Illustration reduced.

Date	F	VF	XF	Unc	BU
2002 Proof		Value: 150			

Y# 821   25 ROUBLES
3.2000 g., 0.9990 Gold 0.1028 oz. AGW, 16 mm. **Obv:** Double-headed eagle **Rev:** Crab and Cancer zodiac symbol **Edge:** Reeded

Date	F	VF	XF	Unc	BU
2003	—	—	—	—	120

Y# 864   25 ROUBLES
172.8000 g., 0.9000 Silver 5.0001 oz. ASW, 60 mm. **Rev:** St. Sercius Monastery

Date	F	VF	XF	Unc	BU
2003 Proof		Value: 150			

Y# 865   25 ROUBLES
172.8000 g., 0.9000 Silver 5.0001 oz. ASW, 60 mm. **Rev:** Shlisselburg

Date	F	VF	XF	Unc	BU
2003 Proof		Value: 125			

Y# 866   25 ROUBLES
172.8000 g., 0.9000 Silver 5.0001 oz. ASW, 60 mm. **Rev:** Kamchatka

Date	F	VF	XF	Unc	BU
2003 Proof		Value: 150			

Y# 830   25 ROUBLES

177.9600 g., 0.9000 Bi-Metallic Gold And Silver .900 Silver 172.78g planchet with .900 Gold 5.18g insert 5.1494 oz., 60 mm. **Subject:** Monetary reform of Peter the Great **Obv:** Double-headed eagle **Rev:** Gold insert replicating the obverse and reverse designs of a 1704 one rouble coin **Edge:** Reeded **Note:** Illustration reduced.

Date	F	VF	XF	Unc	BU
2004 Proof		Value: 325			

Y# 867   25 ROUBLES

172.8000 g., 0.9000 Silver 5.0001 oz. ASW, 60 mm. **Rev:** Valaam Church

Date	F	VF	XF	Unc	BU
2004 Proof		Value: 150			

Y# 648   50 ROUBLES

8.7500 g., 0.9000 Gold .2532 oz. AGW **Subject:** 50th Anniversary - Diplomacy with China **Obv:** Double-headed eagle **Rev:** Moscow Kremlin and Tiananmen gate

Date	F	VF	XF	Unc	BU
1999 Proof		Value: 285			

Y# 692   50 ROUBLES

8.7500 g., 0.9000 Gold .2532 oz. AGW, 22.6 mm. **Subject:** Alexander Pushkin **Obv:** Double-headed eagle **Rev:** Portrait above quill and signature **Edge:** Reeded

Date	F	VF	XF	Unc	BU
1999 Proof		Value: 235			

Y# 698   50 ROUBLES

8.7500 g., 0.9990 Gold .2534 oz. AGW, 22.6 mm. **Subject:** Russian Ballet **Obv:** Double-headed eagle **Rev:** Raymonda and Saracen dancing **Edge:** Reeded

Date	F	VF	XF	Unc	BU
1999 Proof		Value: 235			

Y# 702   50 ROUBLES

8.7500 g., 0.9000 Gold .2532 oz. AGW, 22.6 mm. **Subject:** Russian Explorer N.M. Przhevalsky **Obv:** Double-headed eagle **Rev:** Portrait **Edge:** Reeded

Date	F	VF	XF	Unc	BU
1999 Proof		Value: 235			

Y# 672   50 ROUBLES

8.7100 g., 0.9000 Gold .2520 oz. AGW **Series:** Olympics **Obv:** Double-headed eagle **Rev:** Torch runner on map

Date	F	VF	XF	Unc	BU
2000 Proof		Value: 275			

Y# 718   50 ROUBLES

8.7500 g., 0.9000 Gold .2532 oz. AGW, 22.0 mm. **Subject:** Field Marshal Suvorov **Obv:** Double-headed eagle **Rev:** Portrait above cannons **Edge:** Reeded

Date	F	VF	XF	Unc	BU
2000 Proof		Value: 275			

Y# 725   50 ROUBLES

7.8900 g., 0.9990 Gold .2534 oz. AGW, 22.6 mm. **Subject:** Snow Leopard **Obv:** Double-headed eagle **Rev:** Leopard head **Edge:** Reeded

Date	F	VF	XF	Unc	BU
2000 Proof		Value: 250			

Y# 679   50 ROUBLES

8.7500 g., 0.9990 Gold .2532 oz. AGW, 22.6 mm. **Subject:** Bolshoi Theater 225 Years **Obv:** Double-headed eagle **Rev:** Dueling figures **Edge:** Reeded

Date	F	VF	XF	Unc	B
2001 Proof		Value: 200			

Y# 684   50 ROUBLES

8.7500 g., 0.9000 Gold .2532 oz. AGW, 22.6 mm. **Subject:** Siberian Exploration **Obv:** Double-headed eagle **Rev:** Portrait and boat **Edge:** Reeded

Date	F	VF	XF	Unc	
2001 Proof		Value: 200			

Y# 757   50 ROUBLES
8.6444 g., 0.9000 Gold 0.2501 oz. AGW, 22.6 mm. **Subject:**
Olympics **Obv:** Double-headed eagle **Rev:** Figure skater and flying
eagle **Edge:** Reeded

Date	F	VF	XF	Unc	BU
2002 Proof		Value: 250			

Y# 782   50 ROUBLES
7.8900 g., 0.9990 Gold 0.2534 oz. AGW, 22.6 mm. **Subject:**
Works of Dionissy **Obv:** Double-headed eagle **Rev:** Virgin of
Odygitriya **Edge:** Reeded

Date	F	VF	XF	Unc	BU
2002 Proof		Value: 235			

Y# 786   50 ROUBLES
8.7500 g., 0.9000 Gold 0.2532 oz. AGW, 22.6 mm. **Subject:**
Admiral Nakhimov **Obv:** Double-headed eagle **Rev:** Portrait above
flags and anchor **Edge:** Reeded

Date	F	VF	XF	Unc	BU
2002 Proof		Value: 235			

Y# 788   50 ROUBLES
8.7500 g., 0.9000 Gold 0.2532 oz. AGW, 22.6 mm. **Subject:**
World Cup Soccer **Obv:** Double-headed eagle **Rev:** Player kicking
soccer ball **Edge:** Reeded

Date	F	VF	XF	Unc	BU
2002 Proof		Value: 225			

Y# 822   50 ROUBLES
7.8900 g., 0.9990 Gold 0.2534 oz. AGW, 22.6 mm. **Obv:** Double-
headed eagle **Rev:** Seated "Virgo" and zodiac symbol **Edge:** Reeded

Date	F	VF	XF	Unc	BU
2003	—	—	—	—	200

Y# 823   50 ROUBLES
7.8900 g., 0.9990 Gold 0.2534 oz. AGW, 22.6 mm. **Obv:** Double-
headed eagle **Rev:** Balance scale Libra and zodiac symbol **Edge:**
Reeded

Date	F	VF	XF	Unc	BU
2003	—	—	—	—	200

Y# 868   50 ROUBLES
8.6400 g., 0.9000 Gold 0.25 oz. AGW, 23 mm. **Rev:** Peter I
monetary reform

Date	F	VF	XF	Unc	BU
2003 Proof		Value: 220			

Y# 869   50 ROUBLES
8.6400 g., 0.9000 Gold 0.25 oz. AGW, 23 mm. **Rev:** Ski race

Date	F	VF	XF	Unc	BU
2003 Proof		Value: 220			

Y# 870   50 ROUBLES
8.6400 g., 0.9000 Gold .2500 oz. AGW, 23 mm. **Rev:** Soccer player

Date	F	VF	XF	Unc	BU
2004 Proof		Value: 225			

Y# 871   50 ROUBLES
8.6400 g., 0.9000 Gold 0.25 oz. AGW, 23 mm. **Rev:** Olympic athletes

Date	F	VF	XF	Unc	BU
2004 Proof		Value: 220			

Y# 872   50 ROUBLES
8.6400 g., 0.9000 Gold 0.25 oz. AGW, 23 mm. **Rev:** Virgin of the
Son Icon

Date	F	VF	XF	Unc	BU
2004 Proof		Value: 220			

Y# 693   100 ROUBLES
1111.1200 g., 0.9000 Silver 32.1510 oz. ASW, 100 mm. **Subject:**
Alexander Pushkin **Obv:** Double-headed eagle **Rev:** Statue,
monuments and buildings **Edge:** Reeded **Note:** Illustration reduced.

Date	F	VF	XF	Unc	BU
1999 Proof		Value: 775			

Y# 694   100 ROUBLES
17.4500 g., 0.9000 Gold .5049 oz. AGW, 30 mm. **Subject:**

Alexander Pushkin **Obv:** Double-headed eagle **Rev:** Portrait and scenes **Edge:** Reeded

Date	F	VF	XF	Unc	BU
1999 Proof		Value: 420			

Y# 700   100 ROUBLES
15.7200 g., 0.9990 Gold .5049 oz. AGW, 30 mm. **Subject:** Russian Ballet **Obv:** Double-headed eagle **Rev:** Raymonda dancing alone **Edge:** Reeded

Date	F	VF	XF	Unc	BU
1999 Proof		Value: 420			

Y# 703   100 ROUBLES
17.4500 g., 0.9000 Gold .5049 oz. AGW, 30 mm. **Subject:** Russian Explorer N.M. Przhevalsky **Obv:** Double-headed eagle **Rev:** Two men viewing lake **Edge:** Reeded

Date	F	VF	XF	Unc	BU
1999 Proof		Value: 420			

Y# 711   100 ROUBLES
1111.1200 g., 0.9000 Silver 32.1510 oz. ASW, 100 mm. **Subject:** Russian State **Obv:** Double-headed eagle **Rev:** Mother Russia, mythological bird and map **Edge:** Reeded **Note:** Illustration reduced.

Date	F	VF	XF	Unc	BU
2000 Proof		Value: 775			

Y# 713   100 ROUBLES
17.4500 g., 0.9000 Gold .5049 oz. AGW, 30 mm. **Subject:** Department of Mining 300 Years **Obv:** Double-headed eagle **Rev:** Miner and equipment **Edge:** Reeded

Date	F	VF	XF	Unc	BU
2000 Proof		Value: 400			

Y# 724   100 ROUBLES
1111.1200 g., 0.9000 Silver 32.1510 oz. ASW, 100 mm. **Subject:** Snow Leopard **Obv:** Double-headed eagle **Rev:** Two leopards **Edge:** Reeded **Note:** Illustration reduced.

Date	F	VF	XF	Unc	BU
2000 Proof		Value: 775			

Y# 726   100 ROUBLES
15.7200 g., 0.9990 Gold .5049 oz. AGW, 30 mm. **Subject:** Snow Leopard **Obv:** Double-headed eagle **Rev:** Leopard on branch **Edge:** Reeded

Date	F	VF	XF	Unc	BL
2000 Proof		Value: 420			

Y# 729   100 ROUBLES
1111.1200 g., 0.9000 Silver 32.1510 oz. ASW, 100 mm. **Subjec** WWII Victory 55th Anniversary **Obv:** Russian soldier writing o Reichstag building pillar **Rev:** Conference scene **Edge:** Reede **Note:** Illustration reduced.

Date	F	VF	XF	Unc
2000 Proof		Value: 775		

Y# 681   100 ROUBLES
1111.1000 g., 0.9000 Silver 32.1504 oz. ASW, 100 mm. **Subject:** Yuri Gagarin **Obv:** Double-headed eagle **Rev:** Astronaut and rocket in space **Edge:** Reeded **Note:** Illustration reduced.

Date	F	VF	XF	Unc	BU
2001 Proof		Value: 800			

Y# 689   100 ROUBLES
1111.1000 g., 0.9000 Silver 32.1504 oz. ASW, 100 mm. **Subject:** Bolshoi Theater 225 Years **Obv:** Double-headed eagle **Rev:** Casino gambling scene **Edge:** Reeded **Note:** Illustration reduced.

Date	F	VF	XF	Unc	BU
2001 Proof		Value: 1,000			

Y# 685   100 ROUBLES
17.4500 g., 0.9000 Gold .5049 oz. AGW, 30 mm. **Subject:** Siberian Exploration **Obv:** Double-headed eagle **Rev:** Two portraits and sailboat **Edge:** Reeded

Date	F	VF	XF	Unc	BU
2001 Proof		Value: 375			

Y# 795   100 ROUBLES
1111.1200 g., 0.9000 Silver 32.151 oz. ASW, 100 mm. **Subject:** The Bark Sedov **Obv:** Double-headed eagle **Rev:** Cameo portrait and sailing ship **Edge:** Reeded **Note:** Illustration reduced.

Date	F	VF	XF	Unc	BU
2001 Proof		Value: 800			

Y# 688   100 ROUBLES
5.7200 g., 0.9990 Gold .5049 oz. AGW, 30 mm. **Subject:** Bolshoi Theater 225 Years **Obv:** Double-headed eagle **Rev:** Three dancers with swords **Edge:** Reeded

Date	F	VF	XF	Unc	BU
2001 Proof		Value: 375			

Y# 783   100 ROUBLES
1111.1200 g., 0.9000 Silver 32.151 oz. ASW, 100 mm. **Subject:** Works of Dionissy **Obv:** Double-headed eagle **Rev:** St. Ferapont Monastery in the center of a fresco covered cross **Edge:** Reeded **Note:** Illustration reduced.

Date	F	VF	XF	Unc	BU
2002	—	—	—	—	900

Y# 789   100 ROUBLES
1111.1200 g., 0.9000 Silver 32.151 oz. ASW, 100 mm. **Subject:**
World Cup Soccer **Obv:** Double-headed eagle **Rev:** Soccer ball
design with map and players **Edge:** Reeded **Note:** Illustration
reduced.

Date	F	VF	XF	Unc	BU
2002 Proof		Value: 900			

Y# 791   100 ROUBLES
1111.1200 g., 0.9000 Silver 32.151 oz. ASW, 100 mm. **Subject:**
Hermitage **Obv:** Double-headed eagle **Rev:** Statues and arches
Edge: Reeded **Note:** Illustration reduced.

Date	F	VF	XF	Unc	BU
2002 Proof		Value: 800			

Y# 792   100 ROUBLES
17.4500 g., 0.9000 Gold 0.5049 oz. AGW, 30 mm. **Subject:**
Hermitage **Obv:** Double-headed eagle **Rev:** Ancient battle scene
sculpted on comb **Edge:** Reeded

Date	F	VF	XF	Unc	BU
2002 Proof		Value: 375			

Y# 873   100 ROUBLES
1111.1200 g., 0.9000 Silver 32.151 oz. ASW, 100 mm. **Rev:** St.
Petersburg

Date	F	VF	XF	Unc	BU
2003 Proof		Value: 500			

Y# 874   100 ROUBLES
17.4500 g., 0.9000 Gold 0.5049 oz. AGW, 30 mm. **Rev:**
Petrozavodsk

Date	F	VF	XF	Unc	BU
2003 Proof		Value: 385			

Y# 875   100 ROUBLES
17.4500 g., 0.9000 Gold 0.5049 oz. AGW, 30 mm. **Rev:** Kamchatka

Date	F	VF	XF	Unc	BU
2003 Proof		Value: 385			

Y# 831   100 ROUBLES
1000.0000 g., 0.9000 Silver 28.9357 oz. ASW, 100 mm. **Obv:**
Double-headed eagle **Rev:** Panel of icons painted by Theophanes
the Greek **Edge:** Reeded **Note:** Illustration reduced.

Date	F	VF	XF	Unc	BU
2004 Proof		Value: 750			

Y# 832   100 ROUBLES
17.2800 g., 0.9000 Gold 0.5 oz. AGW, 30 mm. **Subject:** 2nd
Kamchatka Expedition **Obv:** Double-headed eagle **Rev:** Shaman
and two seated men **Edge:** Reeded

Date	F	VF	XF	Unc	BU
2004 Proof		Value: 375			

Y# 876   100 ROUBLES
1111.1200 g., 0.9000 Silver 32.151 oz. ASW, 100 mm. **Rev:**
Annunciation Cathedral Iconostasis

Date	F	VF	XF	Unc	BU
2004 Proof		Value: 700			

Y# 656   200 ROUBLES
3342.3899 g., 0.9000 Silver 96.7142 oz. ASW **Subject:** 275th
Anniversary - St. Petersburg Mint **Obv:** Double-headed eagle **Rev:**
Peter the Great, mint view, coin designs, and medal of the Imperial
Order **Note:** Illustration reduced.

Date	F	VF	XF	Unc	BU
1999 Proof		Value: 1,250			

Y# 727   200 ROUBLES
31.3700 g., 0.9990 Gold 1.0076 oz. AGW, 33 mm. **Subject:**
Snow Leopard **Obv:** Double-headed eagle **Rev:** Leopard on
branch **Edge:** Reeded

Date	F	VF	XF	Unc	BU
2000 Proof		Value: 775			

Y# 877   200 ROUBLES
3342.3899 g., 0.9000 Silver 96.7142 oz. ASW, 130 mm. **Rev:**
Peter I monetrary reform

Date	F	VF	XF	Unc	BU
2003 Proof		Value: 4,000			

Y# 878   1000 ROUBLES
156.4000 g., 0.9990 Gold 5.0233 oz. AGW, 50 mm. **Rev:** Cronstadt

Date	F	VF	XF	Unc	BU
2003 Proof		Value: 4,000			

Y# 728   10000 ROUBLES
822.8449 g., 0.9990 Gold 26.4551 oz. AGW, 100 mm. **Subject:**
Snow Leopard **Obv:** Double-headed eagle **Rev:** Leopard with two
cubs **Edge:** Reeded **Note:** Illustration reduced.

Date	F	VF	XF	Unc	BU
2000 Proof		Value: 18,000			

Y# 784   10000 ROUBLES
1001.1000 g., 0.9990 Gold 32.1539 oz. AGW, 100 mm. **Subject:**
Works of Dionissy **Obv:** Double-headed eagle **Rev:** Interior view
of the carved portal of the Virgin of the Nativity Church **Edge:**
Reeded **Note:** Illustration reduced.

Date	F	VF	XF	Unc	BU
2002	—	—	—	—	23,000

Y# 879   10000 ROUBLES
1001.1000 g., 0.9990 Gold 32.1539 oz. AGW, 100 mm. **Rev:** St.
Petersburg area map

Date	F	VF	XF	Unc	BU
2003 Proof		Value: 25,000			

Y# 880   10000 ROUBLES
1001.1000 g., 0.9990 Gold 32.1539 oz. AGW, 100 mm. **Rev:**
Church of the Transfiguration of the Savior, Novgorod

Date	F	VF	XF	Unc	BU
2004 Proof		Value: 25,000			

Slovakia

The Republic of Slovakia has an area of 18,923 sq. mi. (49,035
sq. km.) and a population of 4.9 million. Capital: Bratislava. Textiles, steel, and wood products are exported.

MINT MARK

Kremnica Mint

REPUBLIC
1939-45

STANDARD COINAGE
100 Halierov = 1 Koruna Slovenska (Ks)

KM# 8   5 HALIEROV
0.9400 g., Zinc, 14 mm. **Obv:** Slovak shield **Rev:** Large value
Edge: Plain

Date	F	VF	XF	Unc	BU
1942	3.00	5.00	15.00	30.00	—

KM# 1   10 HALIEROV
1.6600 g., Bronze, 16 mm. **Obv:** Slovak shield, wreath **Rev:**
Bratislava castle above Danube (Dunaj) and large value

Date	F	VF	XF	Unc	BU
1939-1942	1.50	2.00	4.00	8.00	—

KM# 4   20 HALIEROV
2.5000 g., Bronze, 18 mm. **Obv:** Slovak shield, wreath **Rev:** Nitra
Castle, large value **Edge:** Plain

Date	F	VF	XF	Unc	BU
1940-1942	1.25	2.00	3.00	6.00	—

KM# 4a   20 HALIEROV
0.6500 g., Aluminum, 18 mm. **Edge:** Plain **Note:** Varieties exist.

Date	F	VF	XF	Unc	BU
1942-1943	1.00	1.50	4.00	9.00	—

KM# 5   50 HALIEROV
3.3300 g., Copper-Nickel, 20 mm. **Obv:** Slovak shield, date below
Rev: Value above plow **Edge:** Plain

Date	F	VF	XF	Unc	BU
1940-1941	1.00	2.00	3.00	6.00	—

KM# 5a   50 HALIEROV
1.0000 g., Aluminum, 20 mm. **Edge:** Milled

Date	F	VF	XF	Unc	BU
1943-1944	1.00	1.50	2.50	5.00	—

KM# 6 KORUNA
5.0000 g., Copper-Nickel, 22 mm. **Obv:** Slovak shield within circle, date below **Rev:** Value above plow **Edge:** Milled

Date	F	VF	XF	Unc	BU
1940-1945	0.50	1.00	2.00	5.00	—

KM# 2 5 KORUN
Nickel, 27 mm. **Obv:** Slovak shield, wheat ears flanking, date below **Rev:** Bust of Andrej Hlinka **Edge:** Milled **Note:** Two varieties exist in the letter A in NAROD.

Date	F	VF	XF	Unc	BU
1939	1.50	2.00	3.50	10.00	—

KM# 9.1 10 KORUN
7.0000 g., 0.5000 Silver .1125 oz. ASW, 29 mm. **Obv:** Slovak shield within rays **Rev:** Prince Pribina standing, flanked by bishop with church building and knight **Edge:** Plain **Note:** Variety 1 - Cross atop church held by left figure.

Date	F	VF	XF	Unc	BU
1944	2.00	4.00	5.00	12.00	—

KM# 9.2 10 KORUN
7.0000 g., 0.5000 Silver .1125 oz. ASW **Note:** Variety 2 - Without cross atop church held by left figure.

Date	F	VF	XF	Unc	BU
1944	2.50	5.00	7.00	15.00	—

KM# 3 20 KORUN
15.0000 g., 0.5000 Silver .2411 oz. ASW, 31 mm. **Obv:** State emblem, date **Rev:** Dr. Jozef Tiso bust facing right **Edge:** Milled

Date	F	VF	XF	Unc	BU
1939	5.00	10.00	20.00	40.00	—

KM# 7.1 20 KORUN
15.0000 g., 0.5000 Silver .2411 oz. ASW, 31 mm. **Subject:** St. Kyrill and St. Methodius **Obv:** Slovak shield, date above, linden sprigs below **Rev:** Variety 1 - Single bar cross in church at lower right **Edge:** Milled

Date	F	VF	XF	Unc	BU
1941	3.00	4.00	6.00	15.00	—

KM# 7.2 20 KORUN
15.0000 g., 0.5000 Silver .2411 oz. ASW **Rev:** Variety 2 - Double bar cross

Date	F	VF	XF	Unc	BU
1941	4.00	6.50	20.00	50.00	—

KM# 10 50 KORUN
16.5000 g., 0.7000 Silver .3713 oz. ASW, 34 mm. **Subject:** 5th Anniversary of Independence **Obv:** Slovak shield within wreath **Rev:** Dr. Jozef Tiso bust right **Edge:** Milled

Date	F	VF	XF	Unc	BU
1944	5.00	6.00	8.50	17.50	—

REPUBLIC

STANDARD COINAGE
100 Halierov = 1 Slovak Koruna (Sk)

KM# 17 10 HALIEROV
Aluminum, 17 mm. **Obv:** Slovak shield **Rev:** 19th century wooden belfry from Zemplin **Edge:** Plain

Date	F	VF	XF	Unc	BU
1993-2003	—	—	—	0.35	—

KM# 18 20 HALIEROV
Aluminum, 19.5 mm. **Obv:** Slovak shield **Rev:** Tatra Mountain peak of Krivan **Edge:** Reeded

Date	F	VF	XF	Unc	BU
1993-2003	—	—	—	0.45	—

KM# 15 50 HALIEROV
Aluminum, 22 mm. **Obv:** Slovak shield **Rev:** Watch tower of Devin castle **Edge:** Plain

Date	F	VF	XF	Unc	BU
1993-1995	—	—	—	0.55	—

KM# 35 50 HALIEROV
2.8000 g., Copper Plated Steel, 18.7 mm. **Obv:** Slovak shield **Rev:** Watch tower of Devin Castle **Edge:** Milled and plain

Date	F	VF	XF	Unc	BU
1996-2005	—	—	—	0.60	—

KM# 12 KORUNA
Bronze Clad Steel, 21 mm. **Subject:** 15th Century of Madonna and Child **Obv:** Slovak shield **Edge:** Milled

Date	F	VF	XF	Unc	BU
1993-2005	—	—	—	0.75	—

KM# 13 2 KORUNA
4.4000 g., Nickel Clad Steel, 21.5 mm. **Obv:** Slovak shield **Rev:** 4th century B.C. Venus statue

Date	F	VF	XF	Unc	BU
1993-2005	—	—	—	0.85	—

KM# 14 5 KORUNA
5.4000 g., Nickel Clad Steel, 24.75 mm. **Obv:** Slovak shield **Rev:** 1st century Celtic coin of BIATEC **Edge:** Milled

Date	F	VF	XF	Unc	BU
1993-2005	—	—	—	1.25	—

KM# 11.1 10 KORUNA
6.6000 g., Brass, 26.5 mm. **Obv:** Slovak shield **Rev:** 11th century bronze cross

Date	F	VF	XF	Unc	BU
1993-2005	—	—	—	2.50	—

KM# 11.2 10 KORUNA
8.5000 g., 0.7500 Silver .2527 oz. ASW

Date	F	VF	XF	Unc	BU
1993 Proof		Value: 350			

KM# 67 20 KORUN
24.4800 g., 0.9250 Silver .7280 oz. ASW, 27.1 x 50.6 mm. **Series:** Banknotes **Obv:** Prince Pribina (800-861) **Rev:** Nitra Castle **Edge:** Plain

Date	F	VF	XF	Unc	BU
2003 Proof		Value: 20.00			

KM# 68 50 KORUN
26.6300 g., 0.9250 Silver 0.792 oz. ASW, 28.2 x 52.8 mm. **Series:** Banknotes **Obv:** Saints Cyril and Methodius (814-885) **Rev:** Two hands **Edge:** Plain

Date	F	VF	XF	Unc	BU
2003 Proof		Value: 25.00			

KM# 16   100 KORUN
13.0000 g., 0.7500 Silver .3135 oz. ASW, 29 mm. **Subject:** National Independence **Obv:** Slovak shield **Rev:** Map of Slovakia and three doves **Edge:** Milled **Note:** 7,450 uncirculated pieces melted in 2002.

Date	F	VF	XF	Unc	BU
1993	—	—	—	9.00	—

KM# 69   100 KORUN
28.8700 g., 0.9250 Silver 0.8586 oz. ASW, 29.3 x 55 mm. **Series:** Banknotes **Obv:** The Levoca Madonna **Rev:** St. James Church in Levoca **Edge:** Plain

Date	F	VF	XF	Unc	BU
2003 Proof	Value: 30.00				

KM# 19   200 KORUN
20.0000 g., 0.7500 Silver .4823 oz. ASW, 34 mm. **Subject:** 150th Anniversary of Slovak Language **Obv:** Slovak shield **Rev:** Creators of Slovak language: Hurban, Stur, and Hodza **Edge:** Plain with ornament **Note:** 5,682 uncirculated pieces melted in 2002.

Date	F	VF	XF	Unc	BU
1993	—	—	—	15.00	—

KM# 20   200 KORUN
20.0000 g., 0.7500 Silver .4823 oz. ASW, 34 mm. **Subject:** 200th Anniversary - Birth of Jan Kollar **Obv:** State emblem, value, date **Rev:** Windswept theatre mask **Edge Lettering:** SLAVME SLAVNE SLAVU SLAVOV SLAVNYCH **Note:** 10,065 uncirculated pieces melted in 2002.

Date	F	VF	XF	Unc	BU
1993	—	—	—	15.00	—

KM# 21   200 KORUN
20.0000 g., 0.7500 Silver .4823 oz. ASW, 34 mm. **Subject:** 100th Anniversary - Olympic Committee **Obv:** Olympic rings, state emblem **Rev:** Value, hockey player **Edge:** Snowflakes **Note:** 15,775 uncirculated pieces melted in 2002.

Date	F	VF	XF	Unc	BU
1994	—	—	—	15.00	—

KM# 22   200 KORUN
20.0000 g., 0.7500 Silver .4823 oz. ASW, 34 mm. **Subject:** 100th Anniversary - Birth of Poet and Painter Janko Alexy **Obv:** State emblem, value, head of young girl in winter **Rev:** Bust of Janko Alexy **Edge:** Plain with ornament **Note:** 12,400 uncirculated pieces melted in 2002.

Date	F	VF	XF	Unc	B
1994	—	—	—	15.00	—

KM# 23   200 KORUN
20.0000 g., 0.7500 Silver .4823 oz. ASW, 34 mm. **Subject:** 50th Anniversary - D-Day **Obv:** State emblem, value, date, stylized linden leaves **Rev:** Emblem of 312th Czechoslovak squadron **Edge Lettering:** SLOVACI PROTI FASISMU **Note:** 10,150 uncirculated pieces melted in 2002.

Date	F	VF	XF	Unc	BU
1994	—	—	—	20.00	—

KM# 26   200 KORUN
20.0000 g., 0.7500 Silver .4823 oz. ASW, 34 mm. **Subject:** European Environmental Protection **Obv:** State emblem, woodpecker feeding young **Rev:** Two storks and a swallow, value **Edge Lettering:** ENCY 1995 (3 fish) **Note:** 11,100 uncirculated pieces melted in 2002.

Date	F	VF	XF	Unc	BU
1995	—	—	—	20.00	—

KM# 24   200 KORUN
20.0000 g., 0.7500 Silver .4823 oz. ASW, 34 mm. **Subject:** 200th Anniversary - Birth of Pavol Jozef Safarik **Obv:** State emblem, date **Rev:** bust of Slovak scientist, Pavol Jozef Safarik **Edge Lettering:** ZAKLADATEL VEDECKEJ SLAVISTIKY **Note:** 8,700 uncirculated pieces melted in 2002.

Date	F	VF	XF	Unc	BU
1995	—	—	—	15.00	—

KM# 27   200 KORUN
20.0000 g., 0.7500 Silver .4823 oz. ASW, 34 mm. **Subject:** Centennial of Bratislava Electric Tram **Obv:** State emblem, value **Rev:** Two tram cars **Edge Lettering:** HLAVNE NADRAZIE TEREZIANSKA STVRT **Note:** 10,500 uncirculated pieces melted in 2002.

Date	F	VF	XF	Unc	BU
1995	—	—	—	15.00	—

KM# 25   200 KORUN
20.0000 g., 0.7500 Silver .4823 oz. ASW, 34 mm. **Subject:** 100th Anniversary - Birth of Mikulas Galanda **Obv:** State emblem, mother with child **Rev:** Head of Mikulas Galanda **Edge Lettering:** MIKULAS GALANDA - MALIAR A GRAFIK **Note:** 10,200 uncirculated pieces melted in 2002.

Date	F	VF	XF	Unc	BU
1995	—	—	—	15.00	—

KM# 30   200 KORUN
20.0000 g., 0.7500 Silver .4823 oz. ASW, 34 mm. **Subject:** 200th Anniversary - Birth of Samuel Jurkovic **Obv:** State emblem, date **Rev:** Head of Samuel Jurkovic **Edge Lettering:** V SLUZBACH NARODA **Note:** 10,700 uncirculated pieces melted in 2002.

Date	F	VF	XF	Unc	BU
1996	—	—	—	15.00	—

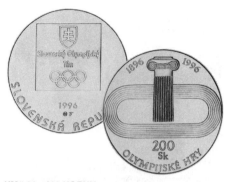

KM# 31   200 KORUN
20.0000 g., 0.7500 Silver .4823 oz. ASW, 34 mm. **Subject:** Olympic Games **Obv:** State emblem, olympic rings, date **Rev:** Oval track and greek column **Edge Lettering:** V DUCHU ODKAZU PIERRA DE COUBERTINA **Note:** 7,300 uncirculated pieces melted in 2002.

Date	F	VF	XF	Unc	BU
1996	—	—	—	16.50	—

KM# 34   200 KORUN
20.0000 g., 0.7500 Silver .4823 oz. ASW, 34 mm. **Subject:** 200th Anniversary - Birth of Moric Benovsky **Obv:** State emblem, clipper ship **Rev:** Portrait of Benovsky, value **Edge Lettering:** IN ADVERSIS ET PROSPERIS **Note:** 5,050 uncirculated pieces melted in 2002.

Date	F	VF	XF	Unc	BU
1996	—	—	—	15.00	—

KM# 32   200 KORUN
20.0000 g., 0.7500 Silver .4823 oz. ASW, 34 mm. **Subject:** 100th Anniversary - Birth of Jozef Ciger Hronsky **Obv:** State emblem, value **Rev:** Half face of Ciger and sun **Edge Lettering:** NIET KRAJSICH SLOV AKO SKUTKY **Note:** 10,700 uncirculated pieces melted in 2002.

Date	F	VF	XF	Unc	BU
1996	—	—	—	15.00	—

KM# 37   200 KORUN
20.0000 g., 0.7500 Silver .4823 oz. ASW, 34 mm. **Subject:** 150th Anniversary - Birth of Svetozar Hurban Vajansky 1847-1916 **Obv:** State emblem, value, date **Rev:** Head of Svetozar Hurban Vajansky **Edge Lettering:** POLITIK SPISOVATEL KRITIK NOVINAR **Note:** 4,000 uncirculated pieces melted in 2002.

Date	F	VF	XF	Unc	BU
1997	—	—	—	15.00	—

KM# 33   200 KORUN
20.0000 g., 0.7500 Silver .4823 oz. ASW, 34 mm. **Subject:** Centennial - Mountain Railway to Strba Lake **Obv:** State emblem, value, date **Rev:** Locomotive and passenger car at foot of Tatra mountain **Edge Lettering:** VYSOKE TATRY   VYSOKE TATRY **Note:** 5,850 uncirculated pieces melted in 2002.

Date	F	VF	XF	Unc	BU
1996	—	—	—	15.00	—

KM# 38   200 KORUN
20.0000 g., 0.7500 Silver .4823 oz. ASW, 34 mm. **Subject:** Banska Stiavnica - UNESCO **Obv:** State emblem, value, head gear tower **Rev:** Baroque building in Banska Stiavnica **Edge Lettering:** PATRIMOINE MODIAL

Date	F	VF	XF	Unc	BU
1997	—	—	—	15.00	—

KM# 40 200 KORUN
20.0000 g., 0.7500 Silver .4823 oz. ASW, 34 mm. **Subject:** 200th Anniversary - Birth of Stefan Moyzes, 1797-1997 **Obv:** Stylized national emblem in tree form **Rev:** Face of Moyzes, book, value **Edge Lettering:** PRVY PREDSEDA MATICE SLOVENSKEJ

Date	F	VF	XF	Unc	BU
1997	—	—	—	15.00	—

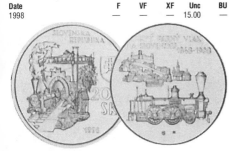

KM# 41 200 KORUN
20.0000 g., 0.7500 Silver .4823 oz. ASW, 34 mm. **Subject:** 50th Anniversary - Slovak National Gallery **Obv:** Madonna and child **Rev:** Daughters of King Lycomed **Edge Lettering:** GOTIKA A BAROK V ZBIERKACH SNG

Date	F	VF	XF	Unc	BU
1998	—	—	—	15.00	—

KM# 42 200 KORUN
20.0000 g., 0.7500 Silver .4823 oz. ASW **Subject:** 150th Anniversary - 1st Railroad in Slovakia **Obv:** State emblem, value, train emerging from tunnel **Rev:** Bratislava Castle and locomotive **Edge Lettering:** 150 ROKOV ZELEZNIC NA SLOVENSKU

Date	F	VF	XF	Unc	BU
1998	—	—	—	15.00	—

KM# 43 200 KORUN
20.0000 g., 0.7500 Silver .4823 oz. ASW **Subject:** 150th Anniversary - Slovak Revolt of 1848 **Obv:** State emblem, value,

date, seal of Slovenska Narodni Rada **Rev:** Slovak warrior **Edge Lettering:** ZA NARODNU SLOBODU

Date	F	VF	XF	Unc	BU
1998	—	—	—	15.00	—

KM# 44 200 KORUN
20.0000 g., 0.7500 Silver .4823 oz. ASW, 34 mm. **Subject:** UNESCO World Heritage site **Obv:** St. Martin's Cathedral towers **Rev:** Spis Castle and gothic window arch **Edge Lettering:** PATRIMONIE MONDIAL WORLD HERITAGE

Date	F	VF	XF	Unc	BU
1998	—	—	—	15.00	—

KM# 45 200 KORUN
20.0000 g., 0.7500 Silver .4823 oz. ASW, 34 mm. **Subject:** Centennial - Birth of Jan Smrek **Obv:** Seated female figure **Rev:** Bust of Jan Smrek **Edge Lettering:** BASNIK JAN SMREK 100 VYROCIE NARODENIA

Date	F	VF	XF	Unc	BU
1998	—	—	—	15.00	—

KM# 48 200 KORUN
20.0000 g., 0.7500 Silver .4823 oz. ASW, 34 mm. **Subject:** 150th Anniversary - Birth of Pavol Orszagh Hviezdoslav **Obv:** Portrait of face made with treetops **Rev:** Portrait of the artist **Edge Lettering:** HEROLD SVITAJUCICH CASOV

Date	F	VF	XF	Unc	BU
1999	—	—	—	15.00	—

KM# 49   200 KORUN
20.0000 g., 0.7500 Silver .4823 oz. ASW, 34 mm. **Subject:** 50th Anniversary - Slovac Philharmonic **Obv:** Pipe organ above national arms **Rev:** Reduta building bay window **Edge Lettering:** HUDBA-UNIVERZALNA REC LUDSTVA

Date	F	VF	XF	Unc	BU
1999	—	—	—	15.00	—

KM# 62   200 KORUN
20.3500 g., 0.7500 Silver 0.4907 oz. ASW, 34 mm. **Subject:** UNESCO World Heritage site - Vlkolínec **Obv:** Log building **Rev:** Wooden tower and denomination **Edge Lettering:** WORLD HERITAGE PATRIMONE MONDIAL

Date	F	VF	XF	Unc	BU
2002	—	—	—	15.00	—

KM# 65   200 KORUN
20.0000 g., 0.7500 Silver .4823 oz. ASW, 33.9 mm. **Subject:** Imrich Karvas **Obv:** Building, national arms and value **Rev:** Portrait **Edge:** Lettered **Edge Lettering:** NARODOHOSPODAR HUMANIST EUROPAN

Date	F	VF	XF	Unc	BU
2003	—	—	—	15.00	—

KM# 55   200 KORUN
20.0000 g., 0.7500 Silver .4823 oz. ASW, 33.9 mm. **Subject:** Juraj Fandly **Obv:** Radiant book above arms **Rev:** Portrait writing **Edge Lettering:** NIE SILOU ANI MOCOU, ALE MOJIM DUCHM

Date	F	VF	XF	Unc	BU
2000	—	—	—	15.00	—

KM# 66   200 KORUN
20.0000 g., 0.7500 Silver 0.4823 oz. ASW, 34 mm. **Obv:** Matica Slovenska building **Rev:** Jozef Skultety bust, value **Edge:** Lettered **Edge Lettering:** VYTRVALOST A VERNOST NARODNEMU IDEALU

Date	F	VF	XF	Unc	BU
2003	—	—	—	15.00	—

KM# 59   200 KORUN
20.0000 g., 0.7500 Silver .4823 oz. ASW, 34 mm. **Subject:** Alexander Dubcek **Obv:** National arms and tree **Rev:** Portrait **Edge Lettering:** "BUDSKOST SLOBODA DEMOKRACIA"

Date	F	VF	XF	Unc	BU
2001	—	—	—	15.00	—

KM# 60   200 KORUN
20.0000 g., 0.7500 Silver 0.4823 oz. ASW, 34 mm. **Subject:** L'udovit Fulla **Obv:** Two examples of modern art. **Rev:** Portrait and denomination. **Edge:** Lettered.

Date	F	VF	XF	Unc	BU
2002	—	—	—	20.00	—

KM# 70   200 KORUN
31.2100 g., 0.9250 Silver 0.9282 oz. ASW, 30.4 x 57.2 mm. **Series:** Banknotes **Obv:** Anton Bernolak (1762-1813) **Rev:** Trnava 18th Century city view **Edge:** Plain

Date	F	VF	XF	Unc	BU
2003 Proof		Value: 35.00			

KM# 75 200 KORUN
20.0000 g., 0.7500 Silver 0.4823 oz. ASW, 34 mm. **Obv:**
Kempelen's Chess Machine (1770) **Rev:** Inventor Wolfgang
Kemelen (1734-1804) above Bratislava city view **Edge:**
"VYNALEZCA - TECHNIK - KONSTRUKTER"

Date	F	VF	XF	Unc	BU
2004	—	—	—	15.00	—

KM# 78 200 KORUN
20.0000 g., 0.7500 Silver 0.4823 oz. ASW, 34 mm. **Subject:**
Slovakian entry into the European Union **Obv:** Circle of stars in
arch above national arms **Rev:** Map in arch above value **Edge:**
Lettered **Edge Lettering:** " ROZSIRENIE EUROPSKEJ UNIE O
DESAT KRAJIN "

Date	F	VF	XF	Unc	BU
2004	—	—	—	15.00	—

KM# 81 200 KORUN
18.0000 g., 0.9000 Silver 0.5208 oz. ASW, 34 mm. **Subject:**
Leopold I Coronation **Obv:** Value and partial castle view **Rev:** Coin
design of Leopold I in large size legend **Edge Lettering:**
"BRATISLAVSKE KORUNOVACIE"

Date	F	VF	XF	Unc	BU
2005	—	—	—	—	20.00

KM# 82 200 KORUN
18.0000 g., 0.9000 Silver 0.5208 oz. ASW, 34 mm. **Subject:**
Treaty of Pressburg **Obv:** Primate's Palace behind French military
standard **Rev:** Napoleon and Francis I of Austria **Edge Lettering:**
"26 DECEMBER. 5 MIVOSE AN 14"

Date	F	VF	XF	Unc	BU
2005	—	—	—	—	20.00

KM# 76 200 KORUN
20.0000 g., 0.7500 Silver 0.4823 oz. ASW, 34 mm. **Obv:** St.
Aegidius Church and Bardejov Town Hall **Rev:** Aerial view of
Bardejov circa 1768 **Edge:** Lettered **Edge Lettering:** "WORLD
HERITAGE - PATRIMOINE MONDIAL"

Date	F	VF	XF	Unc	BU
2004	—	—	—	15.00	—

KM# 77 200 KORUN
18.0000 g., 0.9000 Silver 0.5208 oz. ASW, 34 mm. **Obv:** "The
Segner Wheel" model **Rev:** Portrait of Segner wearing a fur hat
Edge: Lettered **Edge Lettering:** "VYNALEZCA - FYZIK -
MATEMATIK - PEDAGOG"

Date	F	VF	XF	Unc	BU
2004	—	—	—	15.00	—

KM# 28 500 KORUN
33.6300 g., 0.9250 Silver 1.0001 oz. ASW, 40 mm. **Subject:**
Slovensky Raj National Park **Obv:** State emblem, date, value,
flowers **Rev:** Machovy waterfall in gorge Vysny Kysel **Edge**
Lettering: OCHRANA PRIRODY A. KRAJINY **Note:** 11,200
Uncirculated pieces melted in 2002.

Date	F	VF	XF	Unc	BU
1994	—	—	—	35.00	—

KM# 39   500 KORUN
33.6300 g., 0.9250 Silver 1.0001 oz. ASW, 40 mm.   **Subject:**
Pieninsky National Park **Obv:** Swallowtail butterfly **Edge**
Lettering: OCHRANA PRIRODY A KRAJINY

Date	F	VF	XF	Unc	BU
1997	—	—	—	50.00	—

KM# 53   500 KORUN
33.6300 g., 0.9250 Silver 1.0001 oz. ASW, 40 mm.   **Subject:**
250th Anniversary - Death of Samuel Mikovini **Obv:** Allegorical
scene and map **Rev:** Portrait and cartographic instruments **Edge**
Lettering: KARTOGRAF - MATEMATIK - STAVITEL

Date	F	VF	XF	Unc	BU
2000	—	—	—	37.50	—

KM# 47   500 KORUN
33.6300 g., 0.9250 Silver 1.0001 oz. ASW, 40 mm.   **Subject:**
Tatransky National Park **Obv:** Two tatran chamois and
Leontopodium flowers **Rev:** Value, flower gentian **Edge Lettering:**
OCHRANA PRIRODY A KRAJINY

Date	F	VF	XF	Unc	BU
1999	—	—	—	40.00	—

KM# 50   500 KORUN
33.6300 g., 0.9250 Silver 1.0001 oz. ASW, 40 mm.   **Subject:**
500th Anniversary - First Thalers of Kremnica **Obv:** Mining scene
Rev: Old coin designs and city view **Edge Lettering:** GULDINER-
PREDCHODCA TOLIARA

Date	F	VF	XF	Unc	BU
1999	—	—	—	45.00	—

KM# 56   500 KORUN
33.6300 g., 0.9250 Silver 1.0001 oz. ASW, 40 mm.   **Subject:** Mala
Fatra National Park **Obv:** National arms center of beetle cross
Rev: Orchid with mountain background **Edge Lettering:**
OCHRANA PRIRODY A KRAJINY

Date	F	VF	XF	Unc	BU
2001	—	—	—	40.00	—

KM# 84   500 KORUN
33.6300 g., 0.9250 Silver 1.0001 oz. ASW, 40 mm. **Subject:**
Muranska Planina National Park **Obv:** Wildflowers and castle ruins
Rev: Two wild horses **Edge Lettering:** "OCHRANA PRIRODY A
KRAJINY"

Date	F	VF	XF	Unc	BU
2006	—	—	—	—	40.00

KM# 57   500 KORUN
31.1035 g., 0.9990 Silver 1.0000 oz. ASW, 45 mm. **Subject:**
Third Millennium **Obv:** "The Universe" **Rev:** Three hands **Edge:**
Plain **Shape:** 3-sided

Date	F	VF	XF	Unc	BU
2001	—	—	—	45.00	—

KM# 71   500 KORUN
33.6300 g., 0.9250 Silver 1.0001 oz. ASW, 31.5 x 59.4 mm.
Series: Banknotes **Obv:** Ludovit Stur (1815-1856) **Rev:** Bratislava
Castle view **Edge:** Plain

Date	F	VF	XF	Unc	BU
2003 Proof	Value: 40.00				

KM# 63   1000 KORUN
62.2070 g., 0.9990 Silver 1.998 oz. ASW, 43.6 x 43.6 mm.
Subject: 10th Anniversary of Republic **Obv:** National arms
between hands **Rev:** Denomination above map **Edge:** Segmented
reeding **Shape:** Square

Date	F	VF	XF	Unc	BU
2003 Proof	Value: 65.00				

KM# 72   1000 KORUN
43.9100 g., Bi-Metallic Gold And Silver .925 Silver 43.91g with .999 Gold .28g insert, 32.6 x 61.6 mm. **Series:** Banknotes **Obv:** Andrej Hlinka (1864-1938) **Rev:** The Madonna Protector and church of Liptovske Sliace **Edge:** Plain **Note:** Illustration reduced.

Date	F	VF	XF	Unc	BU
2003 Proof		Value: 60.00			

KM# 36   5000 KORUN
9.5000 g., 0.9000 Gold .2749 oz. AGW, 26 mm. **Subject:** Banska Stiavnica Historical Mines - UNESCO **Obv:** State emblem, value, date **Edge:** Milled

Date	F	VF	XF	Unc	BU
1997 Proof		Value: 325			

KM# 46   5000 KORUN
9.5000 g., 0.9000 Gold .2749 oz. AGW, 26 mm. **Subject:** Spissky Castle - UNESCO **Obv:** State emblem, lion, date **Edge:** Milled

Date	F	VF	XF	Unc	BU
1998 Proof		Value: 325			

KM# 54   5000 KORUN
9.5000 g., 0.9000 Gold .2749 oz. AGW, 26 mm. **Subject:** 500th Anniversary - Kremnica Mint **Obv:** Hungarian coin design **Rev:** Hungarian coin design **Edge:** Reeded

Date	F	VF	XF	Unc	BU
ND(1999) Proof		Value: 325			

KM# 51   2000 KORUN
124.4140 g., 0.9990 Silver 3.9960 oz. ASW, 65 mm. **Subject:** 2000 Bi-millennium **Obv:** National arms, denomination, historical scenes **Rev:** Jesus with churches **Edge:** Plain **Shape:** Octagon

Date	F	VF	XF	Unc	BU
MM(2000) Proof		Value: 450			

KM# 29   5000 KORUN
7.0000 g., 0.9000 Gold .2025 oz. AGW, 24 mm. **Subject:** 1100th Anniversary - Death of Great Moravian King Svatopluk **Obv:** State emblem, value, date **Rev:** Head of Svatopluk and ruin of castle Devin **Edge:** Milled

Date	F	VF	XF	Unc	BU
1994 Proof		Value: 500			

KM# 58   5000 KORUN
Tri-Metallic 31.1035, .999 Silver, 1.00 oz ASW with 6.22, .999 Gold, .20 oz AGW and .31, .999 Platinum, .10 oz. APW, 50 mm. **Series:**

Third Millennium **Obv:** "The Universe" **Rev:** Three hands **Edge:** Plain **Shape:** Triangular

Date	F	VF	XF	Unc	BU
2001 Proof		Value: 400			

KM# 61   5000 KORUN
9.5000 g., 0.9000 Gold 0.2749 oz. AGW, 26 mm. **Subject:** Vikolinec Village **Obv:** Enclosed communal well **Rev:** Window and fence **Edge:** Reeded

Date	F	VF	XF	Unc	BU
2002 Proof		Value: 325			

KM# 73   5000 KORUN
47.6340 g., Bi-Metallic Gold And Silver .925 Silver 46.65g with two .9999 Gold inserts .964g in total, 33.4 x 63.8 mm. **Series:** Banknotes **Obv:** Milan R. Stefanik **Rev:** Stefanik's grave monument **Edge:** Plain **Note:** Illustration reduced.

Date	F	VF	XF	Unc	BU
2003 Proof		Value: 85.00			

KM# 80   5000 KORUN
9.5000 g., 0.9000 Gold 0.2749 oz. AGW, 26 mm. **Subject:** Historic Town of Bardejov **Obv:** National arms and value left of Town Hall **Rev:** Zachariah in window frame left of St. Aegidius Church **Edge:** Reeded

Date	F	VF	XF	Unc	BU
2004 Proof		Value: 300			

KM# 83   5000 KORUN
9.5000 g., 0.9000 Gold 0.2749 oz. AGW, 26 mm. **Subject:** Leopold I Coronation **Obv:** Mounted Herald with Bratislava Castile in background **Rev:** Leopold I and Crown of St. Stephan **Edge:** Reeded

Date	F	VF	XF	Unc	BU
2005 Proof		Value: 350			

KM# 52   10000 KORUN
19.0000 g., 0.9000 Gold .5498 oz. AGW, 34 mm. **Subject:** 2000 Bi-millennium **Obv:** National arms, denomination, historical scenes **Rev:** Jesus with churches **Edge:** Milled **Note:** Similar to 2000 Korun, KM#51.

Date	F	VF	XF	Unc	BU
MM(2000) Proof		Value: 600			

KM# 64   10000 KORUN
17.1050 g., Bi-Metallic 1.555g, .999 Palladium round center in a 15.55g, .900 Gold square, 29.5 x 29.5 mm. **Subject:** 10th Anniversary of the Republic **Obv:** Girls portrait above national arms **Rev:** Bratislava castle above denomination **Edge:** Segmented reeding **Shape:** Square

Date	F	VF	XF	Unc	BU
2003 Proof		Value: 750			

KM# 79   10000 KORUN
24.8828 g., Bi-Metallic .999 Gold 12.4414g 23mm round center in .999 Palladium 12.4414g 40mm pentagon, 40 mm. **Subject:** Slovakian entry into the European Union **Obv:** National arms above entry date in center **Rev:** European map with entry date **Edge:** Plain

Date	F	VF	XF	Unc	BU
2004 Proof		Value: 800			

Spitzbergen

Spitzbergen (Svalbard), a Norwegian territory, is a group of mountainous islands in the Arctic Ocean 360 miles (579 km.) north of Norway. The islands have an area of 23,957 sq. mi. (62,050 sq. km.) and a population of about 4,000. West Spitzbergen, the largest island, is the seat of administration. Sealing and fishing are economically important. Despite rich carboniferous and tertiary coal deposits, coal mining, which was started on a commercial scale by the Arctic Coal Co. of Boston, Mass. in 1904, produces only small quantities.

Spitzbergen was probably discovered in 1194, but modern knowledge of it dates from its discovery by William Barents in 1596. Quarrels among the various nationalities involved in the whaling industry, which was set up in 1611, resulted in a de facto division of the coast, but despite diverse interests in, and claims to the islands by British, Dutch, Norwegians, Swedes, Danes, Russians and Americans, the question of sovereignty was not resolved until 1920, when a treaty agreed to by the claimants awarded the islands to Norway.

In 1932, the Russian mining company Arktikugol began operations in the islands. The tokens listed here were minted in Leningrad for use by the company in Spitzbergen.

RULERS
Norwegian, 1920-

LEGENDS
ШПИЦБЕРГЕН = Spitzbergen

АРКТИКУГОЛЬ = Artikugol = Arctic Coal Co.

РАЗМѢННЫЙ ЗНАК = Exchange Tokens

NORWEGIAN TERRITORY
TOKEN COINAGE
Catastrophe Memorial Issues

KM# Tn1   10 KOPEKS
Aluminum-Bronze

Date	F	VF	XF	Unc	BU
1946	15.00	25.00	45.00	115	—

KM# Tn2   15 KOPEKS
Aluminum-Bronze

Date	F	VF	XF	Unc	BU
1946	20.00	30.00	50.00	120	—

KM# Tn3   20 KOPEKS
Copper-Nickel

Date	F	VF	XF	Unc	BU
1946	22.00	38.00	60.00	135	—

KM# Tn4.1   50 KOPEKS
Copper-Nickel   **Obv:** Large star

Date	F	VF	XF	Unc	BU
1946	25.00	40.00	65.00	140	—

KM# Tn4.2   50 KOPEKS
Copper-Nickel   **Obv:** Small star

Date	F	VF	XF	Unc	BU
1946	25.00	40.00	65.00	140	—

KM# Tn5   10 ROUBLES
Copper-Nickel Clad Steel

Date	F	VF	XF	Unc	BU
1993	—	—	—	3.50	5.00

KM# Tn6   25 ROUBLES
Copper-Nickel Clad Steel

Date	F	VF	XF	Unc	BU
1993	—	—	—	4.50	6.00

KM# Tn7   50 ROUBLES
Copper-Nickel Clad Steel

Date	F	VF	XF	Unc	BU
1993	—	—	—	6.50	8.00

KM# Tn8   100 ROUBLES
Aluminum-Bronze

Date	F	VF	XF	Unc	BU
1993	—	—	—	9.00	11.00

Sweden

The Kingdom of Sweden, a limited constitutional monarchy located in northern Europe between Norway and Finland, has an area of 173,732 sq. mi. (449,960 sq. km.) and a population of *8.5 million. Capital: Stockholm. Mining, lumbering and a specialized machine industry dominate the economy. Machinery, paper, iron and steel, motor vehicles and wood pulp are exported.

MONETARY SYSTEM
100 Ore = 1 Krona

KINGDOM
REFORM COINAGE
1830-1855

KM# 656   1/6 SKILLING
Copper

Date	VG	F	VF	XF	Unc
1844-1855	0.90	1.75	4.50	13.00	—

KM# 657   1/3 SKILLING
Copper

Date	VG	F	VF	XF	Unc
1844-1855	1.00	2.00	6.00	18.00	—

KM# 658   2/3 SKILLING
Copper

Date	VG	F	VF	XF	Unc
1844-1845/4	2.50	5.00	15.00	45.00	—

KM# 663   2/3 SKILLING
Copper **Note:** Redesigned, smaller head.

Date	VG	F	VF	XF	Unc
1845-1855	1.50	3.00	10.00	35.00	—

KM# 659   SKILLING
Copper **Note:** Large head of Oscar I.

Date	VG	F	VF	XF	Unc
1844-1845/4	6.00	15.00	40.00	130	—

KM# 671   SKILLING
Copper **Note:** Redesigned, smaller head.

Date	VG	F	VF	XF	Unc
1847-1855	3.00	6.00	17.50	60.00	—

KM# 660   2 SKILLING
Copper

Date	VG	F	VF	XF	Unc
1844-1845	7.50	15.00	60.00	200	—

KM# 664   2 SKILLING
Copper **Obv:** Smaller head **Rev:** Similar to KM#442

Date	VG	F	VF	XF	Unc
1845-1855	7.50	10.00	32.50	100	—

KM# 672   4 SKILLING
Copper

Date	VG	F	VF	XF	Unc
1849-1855	4.00	10.00	30.00	125	—

KM# 681   1/32 RIKSDALER
1.0600 g., 0.7500 Silver .0255 oz. ASW

Date	VG	F	VF	XF	Unc
1852-1853	2.00	4.00	8.50	20.00	—

KM# 665   1/16 RIKSDALER
2.1300 g., 0.7500 Silver .0513 oz. ASW

Date	VG	F	VF	XF	Unc
1845-1855	2.00	5.00	12.50	37.50	—

KM# 682   1/8 RIKSDALER
4.2500 g., 0.7500 Silver .1024 oz. ASW

Date	VG	F	VF	XF	Unc
1852	40.00	80.00	175	425	—

KM# 669   1/4 RIKSDALER
0.5000 g., 0.7500 Silver .2049 oz. ASW

Date	VG	F	VF	XF	Unc
1846/4-1848/4	22.50	45.00	90.00	300	—

KM# 666   1/2 RIKSDALER
17.0000 g., 0.7500 Silver .4099 oz. ASW

Date	VG	F	VF	XF	Unc
1845-1852/45	50.00	100	200	400	—

KM# 661   RIKSDALER
34.0000 g., 0.7500 Silver .8198 oz. ASW

Date	F	VF	XF	Unc	BU
1844-1845	100	200	300	500	—

KM# 730   5 ORE
Bronze

Date	F	VF	XF	Unc	BU
1873/2	45.00	85.00	150	300	—

KM# 667   RIKSDALER
34.0000 g., 0.7500 Silver .8198 oz. ASW

Date	F	VF	XF	Unc	BU
1845-1855	60.00	125	250	475	—

REFORM COINAGE
1855-1873

100 Ore = 1 Riksdaler Riksmynt; 4 Riksdaler Riksmynt =
1 Riksmynt = 1 Riksdaler Specie

KM# 686   1/2 ORE
Bronze

Date	VG	F	VF	XF	Unc
1856-1858/7	0.90	1.50	3.50	8.00	—

KM# 715   1/2 ORE
Bronze

Date	VG	F	VF	XF	Unc
1867	7.50	15.00	32.00	60.00	—

KM# 687   ORE
Bronze

Date	F	VF	XF	Unc	BU
1856-1858/7	2.00	4.50	13.00	35.00	—

KM# 705   ORE
Bronze

Date	F	VF	XF	Unc	BU
1860-1872	1.50	2.50	15.00	30.00	—

KM# 728   ORE
Bronze

Date	F	VF	XF	Unc	BU
1873	5.00	9.00	45.00	110	—

KM# 688   2 ORE
Bronze

Date	F	VF	XF	Unc	BU
1856-1858/7	3.00	7.50	25.00	45.00	—

KM# 706   2 ORE
Bronze

Date	F	VF	XF	Unc	BU
1860-1872/1	2.00	5.00	10.00	27.50	—

KM# 729   2 ORE
Bronze

Date	F	VF	XF	Unc	BU
1873	6.00	17.50	40.00	100	—

KM# 690   5 ORE
Bronze

Date	F	VF	XF	Unc	BU
1857-1858/7	4.00	10.00	45.00	100	—

KM# 707   5 ORE
Bronze

Date	F	VF	XF	Unc	BU
1860-1872/66	3.00	10.00	25.00	55.00	—

KM# 683   10 ORE
0.8500 g., 0.7500 Silver .0204 oz. ASW

Date	F	VF	XF	Unc	BU
1855-1859/8	4.00	10.00	25.00	60.00	—

KM# 710   10 ORE
0.8500 g., 0.7500 Silver .0204 oz. ASW

Date	F	VF	XF	Unc	BU
1861-1871	3.00	6.00	20.00	45.00	—

KM# 727   10 ORE
0.8500 g., 0.7500 Silver .0204 oz. ASW

Date	F	VF	XF	Unc	BU
1872-1873	50.00	75.00	100	215	—

KM# 684   25 ORE
2.1300 g., 0.7500 Silver .0513 oz. ASW

Date	F	VF	XF	Unc	BU
1855-1859/8	5.00	12.00	40.00	80.00	—

KM# 712   25 ORE
2.1300 g., 0.7500 Silver .0513 oz. ASW

Date	F	VF	XF	Unc	BU
1862-1871/61	11.00	20.00	40.00	90.00	—

KM# 691   50 ORE
4.2500 g., 0.7500 Silver .1024 oz. ASW

Date	F	VF	XF	Unc	BU
1857	50.00	100	215	450	—

KM# 713   50 ORE
4.2500 g., 0.7500 Silver .1024 oz. ASW

Date	F	VF	XF	Unc	BU
1862	500	800	1,250	1,750	—

KM# 692   RIKSDALER RIKSMYNT
8.5000 g., 0.7500 Silver .2049 oz. ASW   **Obv:** Short goatee

Date	F	VF	XF	Unc	BU
1857	55.00	125	235	600	—

KM# 693   RIKSDALER RIKSMYNT
8.5000 g., 0.7500 Silver .2049 oz. ASW   **Obv:** Long goatee

Date	F	VF	XF	Unc	BU
1857	55.00	100	215	550	—

KM# 708 RIKSDALER RIKSMYNT
8.5000 g., 0.7500 Silver .2049 oz. ASW

Date	F	VF	XF	Unc	BU
1860-1871/61	40.00	80.00	160	275	—

KM# 731 RIKSDALER RIKSMYNT
8.5000 g., 0.7500 Silver .2049 oz. ASW **Obv:** Deepened hairlines

Date	F	VF	XF	Unc	BU
1873	350	600	1,000	1,300	—

KM# 694 2 RIKSDALER RIKSMYNT
17.0000 g., 0.7500 Silver .4099 oz. ASW

Date	F	VF	XF	Unc	BU
1857	85.00	175	375	800	—

KM# 714 2 RIKSDALER RIKSMYNT
17.0000 g., 0.7500 Silver .4099 oz. ASW

Date	F	VF	XF	Unc	BU
1862-1871	125	300	500	1,000	—

KM# 725 2 RIKSDALER RIKSMYNT
17.0000 g., 0.7500 Silver .4099 oz. ASW **Obv:** Small head **Rev:** Large date

Date	F	VF	XF	Unc	BU
1871	125	300	500	925	—

KM# 685 RIKSDALER SPECIE (4 Riksdaler Riksmynt)
34.0061 g., 0.7500 Silver .8201 oz. ASW **Obv:** Bust right with short goatee **Rev:** Crowned, supported arms, small mintmaster's initials

Date	F	VF	XF	Unc	BU
1856-1856/5	200	400	1,000	2,500	—

KM# 689 RIKSDALER SPECIE (4 Riksdaler Riksmynt)
34.0061 g., 0.7500 Silver .8201 oz. ASW **Obv:** Long goatee **Rev:** Large mintmaster's initials

Date	F	VF	XF	Unc	BU
1856-1859	85.00	175	240	500	—

KM# 711 RIKSDALER SPECIE (4 Riksdaler Riksmynt)
34.0061 g., 0.7500 Silver .8201 oz. ASW

Date	F	VF	XF	Unc	BU
1861-862/1	80.00	150	300	450	—

Sweden

KM# 726 RIKSDALER SPECIE (4 Riksdaler Riksmynt)
34.0061 g., 0.7500 Silver .8201 oz. ASW **Obv:** Larger head

Date	F	VF	XF	Unc	BU
1871	80.00	150	300	475	—

REFORM COINAGE
1873 - present

KM# 734 ORE
Bronze **Obv:** Small lettering

Date	F	VF	XF	Unc	BU
1874-1877	4.00	8.00	15.00	85.00	—

KM# 745 ORE
Bronze **Obv:** Large lettering

Date	F	VF	XF	Unc	BU
1877-1880	4.00	8.00	17.00	75.00	—

KM# 750 ORE
Bronze **Obv:** Legend lengthened

Date	F	VF	XF	Unc	BU
1879-1905	0.85	2.25	3.50	16.50	—

KM# 768 ORE
Bronze

Date	F	VF	XF	Unc	BU
1906-1907	0.20	0.50	2.00	12.50	—

KM# 777.1 ORE
Bronze **Obv:** Small cross

Date	F	VF	XF	Unc	BU
1909	6.00	9.00	18.00	100	—

KM# 777.2 ORE
Bronze **Obv:** Large cross **Edge:** Plain

Date	F	VF	XF	Unc	BU
1909-1950	0.10	0.25	0.50	1.50	—

KM# 789 ORE
Iron **Note:** World War I issues.

Date	F	VF	XF	Unc	BU
1917-1919	0.50	1.50	4.00	20.00	—

KM# 810 ORE
Iron **Note:** World War II issues. Similar to KM#777.

Date	F	VF	XF	Unc	BU
1942-1950	0.10	0.20	0.40	1.50	—

KM# 820 ORE
Bronze **Edge:** Plain **Note:** Varieties exist.

Date	F	VF	XF	Unc	BU
1952-1971	—	0.20	0.10	0.30	—

KM# 735 2 ORE
Bronze **Obv:** Small lettering

Date	F	VF	XF	Unc	BU
1874-1878	2.50	12.50	30.00	100	—

KM# 746 2 ORE
Bronze **Obv:** Large lettering

Date	F	VF	XF	Unc	BU
1877-1905	0.50	1.25	3.50	22.50	—

KM# 769 2 ORE
Bronze

Date	F	VF	XF	Unc	BU
1906-1907	0.30	0.60	2.50	15.00	—

KM# 778 2 ORE
Bronze

Date	F	VF	XF	Unc	BU
1909-1950	0.10	0.20	0.65	4.50	—

KM# 790 2 ORE
Iron **Note:** World War I issues. Similar to KM#553.

Date	F	VF	XF	Unc	BU
1917-1919	2.00	3.00	8.50	42.50	—

KM# 811 2 ORE
Iron **Note:** World War II issues.

Date	F	VF	XF	Unc	BU
1942-1950	0.15	0.30	0.75	7.00	—

KM# 821 2 ORE
Bronze **Edge:** Plain **Note:** Varieties exist.

Date	F	VF	XF	Unc	BU
1952-1971	0.10	0.10	0.10	0.45	—

KM# 736 5 ORE
Bronze **Obv:** Small lettering

Date	F	VF	XF	Unc	BU
1874-1889	4.00	20.00	60.00	160	—

KM# 757 5 ORE
Bronze **Obv:** Large lettering

Date	F	VF	XF	Unc	BU
1888-1905	1.00	4.00	12.50	50.00	—

KM# 770 5 ORE
Bronze

Date	F	VF	XF	Unc	BU
1906-1907	0.50	2.00	6.00	25.00	—

KM# 779.1 5 ORE
Bronze **Obv:** Small cross

Date	F	VF	XF	Unc	BU
1909	2.00	6.00	30.00	175	—

KM# 779.2 5 ORE
Bronze **Obv:** Large cross **Note:** Varieties exist.

Date	F	VF	XF	Unc	BU
1909-1950	0.20	0.25	0.75	6.00	—

KM# 791 5 ORE
Iron **Ruler:** Oscar II **Note:** World War I issues. Similar to KM#554.

Date	F	VF	XF	Unc	BU
1917-1919	4.00	8.00	18.00	70.00	—

KM# 812 5 ORE
Iron **Note:** World War II issues.

Date	F	VF	XF	Unc	BU
1942-1950	0.20	0.50	2.00	16.50	—

KM# 822 5 ORE
Bronze **Edge:** Plain

Date	F	VF	XF	Unc	BU
1952-1971	0.20	0.10	0.20	1.00	—

KM# 845 5 ORE
Bronze

Date	F	VF	XF	Unc	BU
1972-1973	—	—	0.10	0.25	0.60

KM# 849 5 ORE
Copper-Tin-Zinc **Edge:** Plain

Date	F	VF	XF	Unc	BU
1976-1981	—	—	0.10	0.25	0.60

KM# 849a 5 ORE
Copper-Zinc

Date	F	VF	XF	Unc	BU
1981-1984	—	—	0.10	0.20	0.60

KM# 737 10 ORE
1.4500 g., 0.4000 Silver .0186 oz. ASW **Obv:** Small lettering

Date	F	VF	XF	Unc	BU
1874-1876/5	6.00	20.00	55.00	140	—

KM# 755 10 ORE
1.4500 g., 0.4000 Silver .0186 oz. ASW **Obv:** Large lettering
Note: Varieties exist.

Date	F	VF	XF	Unc	BU
1880-1904	0.75	1.50	8.50	25.00	—

KM# 774 10 ORE
1.4500 g., 0.4000 Silver .0186 oz. ASW

Date	F	VF	XF	Unc	BU
1907	0.45	1.25	5.00	20.00	—

KM# 780 10 ORE
1.4500 g., 0.4000 Silver .0186 oz. ASW

Date	F	VF	XF	Unc	BU
1909-1942	0.25	0.40	1.00	6.00	—

KM# 795 10 ORE
Nickel-Bronze

Date	F	VF	XF	Unc	BU
1920-1947	0.10	0.30	0.75	6.00	—

KM# 813 10 ORE
1.4400 g., 0.4000 Silver .0185 oz. ASW **Note:** Varieties exist.

Date	F	VF	XF	Unc	BU
1942-1950	BV	0.30	0.75	4.00	—

KM# 823 10 ORE
1.4400 g., 0.4000 Silver .0185 oz. ASW

Date	F	VF	XF	Unc	BU
1952-1962	—	BV	0.60	3.50	—

KM# 835 10 ORE
Copper-Nickel

Date	F	VF	XF	Unc	BU
1962-1973	0.10	0.25	0.15	0.25	1.00

KM# 850 10 ORE
Copper-Nickel **Edge:** Plain

Date	F	VF	XF	Unc	BU
1976-1991	—	—	0.10	0.15	0.30

KM# 738 25 ORE
2.4200 g., 0.6000 Silver .0467 oz. ASW **Obv:** Small lettering

Date	F	VF	XF	Unc	BU
1874-1878/7	6.00	30.00	65.00	240	—

KM# 739 25 ORE
2.4200 g., 0.6000 Silver 0.0467 oz. ASW **Obv:** Large lettering

Date	F	VF	XF	Unc	BL
1874-1905	1.75	5.50	18.50	70.00	—

KM# 775 25 ORE
2.4200 g., 0.6000 Silver 0.0467 oz. ASW

Date	F	VF	XF	Unc	BF
1907	0.75	2.00	6.00	42.50	—

KM# 785 25 ORE
2.4200 g., 0.6000 Silver 0.0467 oz. ASW

Date	F	VF	XF	Unc	B
1910-1941	BV	1.00	2.50	7.00	—

KM# 798 25 ORE
Nickel-Bronze

Date	F	VF	XF	Unc	
1921-1947	0.15	0.30	1.25	9.00	

KM# 816   25 ORE
2.3200 g., 0.4000 Silver .0298 oz. ASW

Date	F	VF	XF	Unc	BU
1943-1950	—	BV	1.25	3.50	—

KM# 824   25 ORE
2.3200 g., 0.4000 Silver .0298 oz. ASW   **Obv:** Plain

Date	F	VF	XF	Unc	BU
1952-1961	—	BV	1.00	2.50	—

KM# 836   25 ORE
Copper-Nickel

Date	F	VF	XF	Unc	BU
1962-1973	—	0.20	0.15	0.45	—

KM# 851   25 ORE
Copper-Nickel

Date	F	VF	XF	Unc	BU
1976-1984	—	—	0.10	0.30	—

KM# 740   50 ORE
5.0000 g., 0.6000 Silver .0965 oz. ASW

Date	F	VF	XF	Unc	BU
1875-1899	6.00	30.00	95.00	300	—

KM# 771   50 ORE
5.0000 g., 0.6000 Silver .0965 oz. ASW

Date	F	VF	XF	Unc	BU
1906-1907	2.00	5.00	32.50	125	—

KM# 788   50 ORE
5.0000 g., 0.6000 Silver .0965 oz. ASW

Date	F	VF	XF	Unc	BU
1911-1939	—	BV	2.50	18.00	—

KM# 796   50 ORE
Nickel-Bronze   **Note:** Varieties exist.

Date	F	VF	XF	Unc	BU
1920-1947	0.25	1.00	4.00	20.00	—

KM# 817   50 ORE
4.8000 g., 0.4000 Silver .0617 oz. ASW

Date	F	VF	XF	Unc	BU
1943-1950	BV	1.00	1.50	10.00	—

KM# 825   50 ORE
4.8000 g., 0.4000 Silver .0617 oz. ASW

Date	F	VF	XF	Unc	BU
1952-1961	—	BV	1.50	8.50	—

KM# 837   50 ORE
Copper-Nickel

Date	F	VF	XF	Unc	BU
1962-1973	0.15	0.15	0.20	0.60	—

KM# 855   50 ORE
Copper-Nickel   **Edge:** Plain

Date	F	VF	XF	Unc	BU
1976-1991	—	0.15	0.10	0.20	—

KM# 878   50 ORE
Bronze

Date	F	VF	XF	Unc	BU
1992-2005	—	—	0.10	0.15	0.25

KM# 741 KRONA
7.5000 g., 0.8000 Silver .1929 oz. ASW

Date	F	VF	XF	Unc	BU
1875-1876/5	7.00	60.00	175	525	—

KM# 747 KRONA
7.5000 g., 0.8000 Silver .1929 oz. ASW **Obv:** OCH replaces "O" in royal title

Date	F	VF	XF	Unc	BU
1877-1889	17.00	70.00	200	650	—

KM# 760 KRONA
7.5000 g., 0.8000 Silver .1929 oz. ASW **Ruler:** Oscar II **Obv:** Without initials below bust

Date	F	VF	XF	Unc	BU
1890-1904	3.50	15.00	80.00	285	—

KM# 772 KRONA
7.5000 g., 0.8000 Silver .1929 oz. ASW **Ruler:** Oscar II

Date	F	VF	XF	Unc	BU
1906-1907	3.50	14.00	60.00	245	—

KM# 786.1 KRONA
7.5000 g., 0.8000 Silver .1929 oz. ASW **Ruler:** Gustaf V **Obv:** With dots in date

Date	F	VF	XF	Unc	BU
1.9.1.0-1.9.2.4	2.25	6.50	17.50	100	—

KM# 786.2 KRONA
7.5000 g., 0.8000 Silver .1929 oz. ASW **Ruler:** Gustaf V **Obv:** Without dots in date

Date	F	VF	XF	Unc	BU
1924-1942	—	BV	3.00	6.00	—

KM# 814 KRONA
7.0000 g., 0.4000 Silver .0900 oz. ASW **Ruler:** Gustaf V

Date	F	VF	XF	Unc	BU
1942-1950	—	BV	1.50	6.00	—

KM# 826 KRONA
7.0000 g., 0.4000 Silver .0900 oz. ASW **Ruler:** Gustaf VI

Date	F	VF	XF	Unc	BU
1952-1968	—	BV	1.25	2.25	—

KM# 826a KRONA
Copper-Nickel Clad Copper **Ruler:** Gustaf VI

Date	F	VF	XF	Unc	BU
1968-1973	—	0.30	0.40	1.50	—

KM# 852 KRONA
Copper-Nickel Clad Copper **Ruler:** Carl XVI Gustaf

Date	F	VF	XF	Unc	BU
1976-1981	—	0.30	0.40	0.75	—

KM# 852a KRONA
Copper-Nickel **Ruler:** Carl XVI Gustaf

Date	F	VF	XF	Unc	BU
1982-2000	—	0.30	0.30	0.25	—

KM# 897 KRONA
6.9800 g., Copper-Nickel, 24.9 mm. **Ruler:** Carl XVI Gustaf
Subject: Millennium **Obv:** Head of King Carl Gustav XVI left **Rev:**
Crowned monogram **Edge:** Reeded

Date	F	VF	XF	Unc	BU
2000	—	—	—	2.00	3.00

KM# 894 KRONA
6.9800 g., Copper-Nickel, 24.9 mm. **Ruler:** Carl XVI Gustaf **Obv:**
King's new portrait **Rev:** Crown and denomination **Edge:** Reeded

Date	F	VF	XF	Unc	BU
2001-2005	—	—	—	0.65	1.00

KM# 742 2 KRONOR
15.0000 g., 0.8000 Silver .3858 oz. ASW

Date	F	VF	XF	Unc	BU
1876-1880	20.00	100	450	1,000	—

KM# 749 2 KRONOR
15.0000 g., 0.8000 Silver .3858 oz. ASW **Obv:** OCH replaces
"O" in royal title

Date	F	VF	XF	Unc	BU
1878-1880	40.00	190	725	1,800	—

KM# 761 2 KRONOR
15.0000 g., 0.8000 Silver .3858 oz. ASW **Obv:** Without initials
below bust

Date	F	VF	XF	Unc	BU
1890-1904	12.00	40.00	145	465	—

KM# 762 2 KRONOR
Silver **Ruler:** Oscar II **Subject:** Silver Jubilee

Date		VG	F	VF	XF	Unc
ND(1897)		9,876	6.50	9.00	15.00	40.00

KM# 773 2 KRONOR
15.0000 g., 0.8000 Silver .3858 oz. ASW **Ruler:** Oscar II

Date	F	VF	XF	Unc	BU
1906-1907	6.50	18.50	75.00	320	—

KM# 776 2 KRONOR
15.0000 g., 0.8000 Silver .3858 oz. ASW **Ruler:** Oscar II
Subject: Golden Wedding Anniversary **Edge:** Reeded

Date	F	VF	XF	Unc	BU
1907	BV	6.50	11.50	22.50	—

KM# 787 2 KRONOR
15.0000 g., 0.8000 Silver .3858 oz. ASW **Ruler:** Gustaf V

Date	F	VF	XF	Unc	BU
1910-1940	—	BV	5.50	14.00	—

KM# 799 2 KRONOR
15.0000 g., 0.8000 Silver .3858 oz. ASW **Ruler:** Gustaf V
Subject: 400th Anniversary of Political Liberty

Date	F	VF	XF	Unc	BU
1921	BV	4.25	8.50	20.00	—

KM# 805   2 KRONOR
15.0000 g., 0.8000 Silver .3858 oz. ASW   **Ruler:** Gustaf V
Subject: 300th Anniversary - Death of Gustaf II Adolf

Date	F	VF	XF	Unc	BU
1932	BV	4.50	10.00	27.50	—

KM# 807   2 KRONOR
15.0000 g., 0.8000 Silver .3858 oz. ASW   **Ruler:** Gustaf V
Subject: 300th Anniversary - Settlement of Delaware **Rev:** The ship "Calmare Nyckel"

Date	F	VF	XF	Unc	BU
ND(1938)	BV	4.25	9.00	20.00	—

KM# 815   2 KRONOR
14.0000 g., 0.4000 Silver .1800 oz. ASW   **Ruler:** Gustaf V

Date	F	VF	XF	Unc	BU
1942-1950/1	—	BV	2.75	8.50	—

KM# 827   2 KRONOR
14.0000 g., 0.4000 Silver .1800 oz. ASW   **Ruler:** Gustaf VI

Date	F	VF	XF	Unc	BU
1952-1966	—	—	BV	4.50	—

KM# 827a   2 KRONOR
Copper-Nickel   **Ruler:** Gustaf VI

Date	F	VF	XF	Unc	BU
1968-1971	0.45	0.55	0.70	2.25	—

KM# 756   5 KRONOR
2.2402 g., 0.9000 Gold .0648 oz. AGW

Date	F	VF	XF	Unc	BU
1881-1899	BV	50.00	80.00	175	—

KM# 766   5 KRONOR
2.2402 g., 0.9000 Gold .0648 oz. AGW   **Ruler:** Oscar II

Date	F	VF	XF	Unc	BU
1901	BV	45.00	65.00	100	—

KM# 797   5 KRONOR
2.2402 g., 0.9000 Gold .0648 oz. AGW   **Ruler:** Gustaf V

Date	F	VF	XF	Unc	BU
1920	BV	45.00	65.00	100	—

KM# 806   5 KRONOR
25.0000 g., 0.9000 Silver .7234 oz. ASW   **Ruler:** Gustaf V
Subject: 500th Anniversary of Riksdag

Date	F	VF	XF	Unc	BU
ND(1935)	BV	7.50	12.50	22.50	—

KM# 828   5 KRONOR
22.7000 g., 0.4000 Silver .2920 oz. ASW   **Ruler:** Gustaf VI
Subject: 70th Birthday of Gustaf VI Adolf **Edge:** Plain

Date	F	VF	XF	Unc	B
ND(1952)	3.50	7.50	13.50	30.00	

Sweden

KM# 829   5 KRONOR
18.0000 g., 0.4000 Silver .2315 oz. ASW   **Ruler:** Gustaf VI **Edge**
Lettering: PLIKTEN FRAMFOR ALLT **Note:** Regular issue.

Date	F	VF	XF	Unc	BU
1954-1971	—	BV	2.75	6.00	—

KM# 830   5 KRONOR
18.0000 g., 0.4000 Silver .2315 oz. ASW   **Ruler:** Gustaf VI
Subject: Constitution Sesquicentennial

Date	F	VF	XF	Unc	BU
1959	—	BV	4.50	8.50	—

KM# 838   5 KRONOR
18.0000 g., 0.4000 Silver .2315 oz. ASW   **Ruler:** Gustaf VI
Subject: 80th Birthday of Gustaf VI Adolf **Rev:** Pallas Athena
holding shield and owl

Date	F	VF	XF	Unc	BU
ND(1962)	3.75	7.50	13.50	35.00	—

KM# 839   5 KRONOR
18.0000 g., 0.4000 Silver .2315 oz. ASW   **Ruler:** Gustaf VI
Subject: 100th Anniversary of Constitution Reform **Edge:**
horizontal wavy lines

Date	F	VF	XF	Unc	BU
1966	—	BV	2.75	5.00	—

KM# 846   5 KRONOR
Copper-Nickel Clad Nickel   **Ruler:** Gustaf VI

Date	F	VF	XF	Unc	BU
1972-1973	—	1.25	1.25	2.00	—

KM# 853   5 KRONOR
Copper-Nickel   **Ruler:** Carl XVI Gustaf

Date	F	VF	XF	Unc	BU
1976-1992		16.50	27.50	0.75	1.25	—

KM# 853a   5 KRONOR
Copper-Nickel Clad Nickel, 28.5 mm.

Date	F	VF	XF	Unc	BU
1993-2003	—	—	—	1.00	1.25

KM# 885   5 KRONOR
Copper-Nickel Clad Nickel   **Ruler:** Carl XVI Gustaf **Subject:** 50th
Anniversary - United Nations

Date	F	VF	XF	Unc	BU
ND(1995)	—	—	1.00	3.50	4.50

KM# 732   10 KRONOR
4.4803 g., 0.9000 Gold .1296 oz. AGW

Date	F	VF	XF	Unc	BU
1873-1876	—	BV	100	200	—

KM# 743   10 KRONOR
4.4803 g., 0.9000 Gold .1296 oz. AGW   **Obv:** OCH substituted for "O" in royal title

Date	F	VF	XF	Unc	BU
1876-1895	—	BV	90.00	150	—

KM# 767   10 KRONOR
4.4803 g., 0.9000 Gold .1296 oz. AGW   **Ruler:** Oscar II **Obv:** Large head

Date	F	VF	XF	Unc	BU
1901	—	BV	85.00	125	—

KM# 847   10 KRONOR
18.0000 g., 0.8300 Silver .4803 oz. ASW   **Ruler:** Gustaf VI
Subject: 90th Birthday of Gustaf VI Adolf

Date	F	VF	XF	Unc	BU
1972	—	BV	5.00	8.50	—

KM# 877   10 KRONOR
Copper-Aluminum-Zinc   **Ruler:** Carl XVI Gustaf

Date	F	VF	XF	Unc	BU
1991-2000	20.00	30.00	2.00	1.75	—

KM# 895   10 KRONOR
6.5700 g., Copper-Aluminum-Zinc, 20.4 mm.   **Ruler:**
Carl XVI Gustaf **Obv:** King's new portrait **Rev:** Three crowns and denomination **Edge:** Reeded and plain sections

Date	F	VF	XF	Unc	BU
2001-2005	—	—	—	1.75	2.00

KM# 733   20 KRONOR
8.9606 g., 0.9000 Gold .2593 oz. AGW

Date	F	VF	XF	Unc	BU
1873-1876/5	—	BV	225	450	—

KM# 744   20 KRONOR
8.9606 g., 0.0000 Gold .2593 oz. AGW   **Rev:** Arms wider

Date	F	VF	XF	Unc	BU
1876-1877	—	BV	220	400	—

KM# 748   20 KRONOR
8.9606 g., 0.9000 Gold .2593 oz. AGW   **Obv:** OCH substituted for O in royal title

Date	F	VF	XF	Unc	BU
1877-1899	—	BV	200	325	—

KM# 765   20 KRONOR
8.9606 g., 0.9000 Gold .2593 oz. AGW   **Ruler:** Oscar II **Obv:** Large head

Date	F	VF	XF	Unc	BU
1900-1902	—	BV	160	245	—

KM# 800   20 KRONOR
8.9606 g., 0.9000 Gold .2593 oz. AGW   **Ruler:** Gustaf V

Date	F	VF	XF	Unc	BU
1925	165	320	465	765	—

Sweden

KM# 848   50 KRONOR
27.0000 g., 0.9250 Silver .8029 oz. ASW **Subject:** Constitutional Reform

Date	F	VF	XF	Unc	BU
1975	—	BV	8.50	12.00	—

KM# 854   50 KRONOR
27.0000 g., 0.9250 Silver .8029 oz. ASW **Subject:** Wedding of King Carl XVI Gustaf and Queen Silvia

Date	F	VF	XF	Unc	BU
ND(1976)	—	BV	8.00	11.50	—

KM# 910   50 KRONOR
22.0000 g., Brass, 36 mm. **Ruler:** Carl XVI Gustaf **Obv:** Playful young girl **Rev:** Astrid Lindgren **Edge:** Plain

Date	F	VF	XF	Unc	BU
ND (2002)	—	—	—	—	8.50

KM# 915   50 KRONOR
22.0000 g., Brass, 36 mm. **Ruler:** Carl XVI Gustaf **Obv:** Winged letter flying over landscape **Rev:** Sweden's first postage stamp design **Edge:** Plain

Date	F	VF	XF	Unc	BU
ND (2005)	—	—	—	—	8.50

KM# 861   100 KRONOR
16.0000 g., 0.9250 Silver .4759 oz. ASW **Subject:** Parliament

Date	F	VF	XF	Unc	BU
1983	—	—	—	18.50	20.00

KM# 863   100 KRONOR
16.0000 g., 0.9250 Silver .4759 oz. ASW **Subject:** Stockholm Conference

Date	F	VF	XF	Unc	BU
1984	—	—	—	18.50	20.00

KM# 864   100 KRONOR
16.0000 g., 0.9250 Silver .4759 oz. ASW **Subject:** International Youth Year

Date	F	VF	XF	Unc	BU
1985	—	—	—	20.00	22.50

KM# 865   100 KRONOR
16.0000 g., 0.9250 Silver .4759 oz. ASW **Subject:** European Music Year

Date	F	VF	XF	Unc	BU
1985	—	—	—	20.00	22.50

KM# 866   100 KRONOR
16.0000 g., 0.9250 Silver .4759 oz. ASW **Subject:** International Year of the Forest

Date	F	VF	XF	Unc	BU
1985	—	—	—	22.50	25.00

KM# 867.1 100 KRONOR
16.0000 g., 0.9250 Silver .4759 oz. ASW **Ruler:** Carl XVI Gustaf
Subject: 350th Anniversary of Swedish Colony in Delaware **Obv:**
Large head

Date	F	VF	XF	Unc	BU
ND(1988)	—	—	—	27.50	30.00

KM# 867.2 100 KRONOR
16.0000 g., 0.9250 Silver .4759 oz. ASW **Ruler:** Carl XVI Gustaf
Obv: Small head

Date	F	VF	XF	Unc	BU
ND(1988)	—	—	—	22.50	25.00

KM# 860 200 KRONOR
27.0000 g., 0.9250 Silver .8029 oz. ASW **Ruler:** Carl XVI Gustaf
Subject: Swedish Royal Succession Law

Date	F	VF	XF	Unc	BU
1980	—	—	—	30.00	40.00

KM# 862 200 KRONOR
27.0000 g., 0.9250 Silver .8029 oz. ASW **Ruler:** Carl XVI Gustaf
Subject: 10th Anniversary of Reign

Date	F	VF	XF	Unc	BU
1983	—	—	—	35.00	42.50

KM# 869 200 KRONOR
27.0000 g., 0.9250 Silver .8029 oz. ASW **Subject:** Ice Hockey

Date	F	VF	XF	Unc	BU
1989	—	—	—	32.50	40.00

KM# 875 200 KRONOR
27.0000 g., 0.9250 Silver .8029 oz. ASW **Ruler:** Carl XVI Gusta
Subject: Warship - Vasa

Date	F	VF	XF	Unc	B
1990	—	—	—	35.00	40.0

KM# 879   200 KRONOR
27.0000 g., 0.9250 Silver .8029 oz. ASW **Subject:** 200th
Anniversary - Death of Gustaf III

Date	F	VF	XF	Unc	BU
ND(1992)	—	—	—	35.00	40.00

KM# 886   200 KRONOR
27.0000 g., 0.9250 Silver .8029 oz. ASW **Ruler:** Carl XVI Gustaf
Subject: 1000th Anniversary - Swedish Coinage

Date	F	VF	XF	Unc	BU
ND(1995)	—	—	—	—	40.00

KM# 881   200 KRONOR
27.0000 g., 0.9250 Silver .8029 oz. ASW **Ruler:** Carl XVI Gustaf
Subject: 20th Anniversary of Reign

Date	F	VF	XF	Unc	BU
1993	—	—	—	35.00	40.00

KM# 888   200 KRONOR
27.0000 g., 0.9250 Silver .8029 oz. ASW **Ruler:** Carl XVI Gustaf
Subject: 50th Birthday - King Carl XVI Gustaf

Date	F	VF	XF	Unc	BU
ND(1996)	—	—	—	—	40.00

KM# 882   200 KRONOR
27.0000 g., 0.9250 Silver .8029 oz. ASW **Subject:** 50th Birthday
- Queen Silvia

Date	F	VF	XF	Unc	BU
ND(1993)	—	—	—	—	40.00

KM# 890   200 KRONOR
27.0000 g., 0.9250 Silver .8029 oz. ASW **Ruler:** Carl XVI Gustaf
Subject: Kalmar Union **Obv:** King's portrait **Rev:** Queen
Margareta's portrait and castle

Date	F	VF	XF	Unc	BU
1997	—	—	—	35.00	45.00

KM# 892   200 KRONOR
27.0000 g., 0.9250 Silver .8029 oz. ASW **Ruler:** Carl XVI Gustaf
Subject: 25th Anniversary - Reign of Carl XVI Gustaf **Obv:** King Carl XVI Gustaf

Date	F	VF	XF	Unc	BU
1998	—	—	—	35.00	40.00

KM# 898   200 KRONOR
27.0300 g., 0.9250 Silver 0.8039 oz. ASW, 36 mm. **Ruler:** Carl XVI Gustaf **Subject:** Millennium **Obv:** Conjoined busts of King Gustaf and Crown Princess Victoria **Rev:** Arms **Edge:** Plain

Date	F	VF	XF	Unc	BU
1999	—	—	—	30.00	—

KM# 896   200 KRONOR
27.2500 g., 0.9250 Silver .8104 oz. ASW, 36 mm. **Ruler:** Carl XVI Gustaf **Subject:** 25th Wedding Anniversary **Obv:**

Conjoined busts of King Carl Gustaf and Queen Silvia **Rev:** National arms **Edge:** Plain

Date	F	VF	XF	Unc	B
ND(2001)	—	—	—	35.00	45.0

KM# 908   200 KRONOR
27.0000 g., 0.9250 Silver 0.803 oz. ASW, 36 mm. **Ruler:** Carl XVI Gustaf **Subject:** 750th Anniversary of Stockholm **Obv:** City seal with three towers and gate **Rev:** Three towers of city ha **Edge:** Plain

Date	F	VF	XF	Unc	B
ND (2002) Proof	Value: 35.00				

KM# 902   200 KRONOR
Silver **Ruler:** Carl XVI Gustaf **Subject:** 30th Anniversary of Reig

Date	F	VF	XF	Unc	B
2003	—	—	—	35.00	45.0

KM# 904   200 KRONOR
27.0300 g., 0.9250 Silver, 36 mm. **Ruler:** Carl XVI Gustaf **Subject:** 700th Anniversary, St. Birgitta **Obv:** Cross in circle abov value **Rev:** St. Birgitta **Edge:** Plain

Date	F	VF	XF	Unc	B
ND (2003)	—	—	—	35.00	45.0

KM# 911   200 KRONOR
27.0000 g., 0.9250 Silver 0.803 oz. ASW, 36 mm. **Ruler:** Carl XVI Gustaf **Subject:** Royal Palace in Stockholm 250th Anniversary **Obv:** Two antique keys over map **Rev:** Royal Palac in Stockholm **Edge:** Plain

Date	F	VF	XF	Unc	B
ND (2004) Proof	Value: 35.00				

KM# 906   200 KRONOR
27.0300 g., 0.9250 Silver, 36 mm. **Ruler:** Carl XVI Gustaf **Subject:** Centennial of the end of the Union between Norway an Sweden **Obv:** Split disc **Rev:** Flag on pole and two clouds

Date	F	VF	XF	Unc	B
2005	—	—	—	35.00	45.0

KM# 913   200 KRONOR
27.0000 g., 0.9250 Silver 0.803 oz. ASW, 36 mm. **Ruler:** Carl XVI Gustaf **Obv:** Stylized flames **Rev:** Dag Hammarskjold **Edge:** Plain

Date	F	VF	XF	Unc	B
ND (2005) Proof	Value: 35.00				

KM# 868   1000 KRONOR
5.8000 g., 0.9000 Gold .1678 oz. AGW **Ruler:** Carl XVI Gusta **Subject:** 350th Anniversary of Swedish Colony in Delaware

Date	F	VF	XF	Unc	I
ND(1988)	—	—	—	235	2

KM# 870   1000 KRONOR
5.8000 g., 0.9000 Gold .1678 oz. AGW **Subject:** Ice Hockey

Date	F	VF	XF	Unc	I
1989	—	—	—	175	2

KM# 876   1000 KRONOR
5.8000 g., 0.9000 Gold .1678 oz. AGW   **Ruler:** Carl XVI Gustaf
Subject: The Vasa - Arms

Date	F	VF	XF	Unc	BU
1990	—	—	—	185	250

KM# 880   1000 KRONOR
5.8000 g., 0.9000 Gold .1678 oz. AGW   **Subject:** 200th
Anniversary - Death of Gustaf III

Date	F	VF	XF	Unc	BU
ND(1992)	—	—	—	185	250

KM# 883   1000 KRONOR
5.8000 g., 0.9000 Gold .1678 oz. AGW   **Ruler:** Carl XVI Gustaf
Subject: 20th Anniversary of Reign   **Obv:** King's bust

Date	F	VF	XF	Unc	BU
1993	—	—	—	175	225

KM# 884   1000 KRONOR
5.8000 g., 0.9000 Gold .1678 oz. AGW   **Subject:** 50th Birthday
of Queen Silvia

Date	F	VF	XF	Unc	BU
ND(1993)	—	—	—	—	225

KM# 887   1000 KRONOR
5.8000 g., 0.9000 Gold .1678 oz. AGW   **Ruler:** Carl XVI Gustaf
Subject: 100th Anniversary - Swedish Coinage

Date	F	VF	XF	Unc	BU
ND(1995)	—	—	—	—	225

KM# 889   1000 KRONOR
5.8000 g., 0.9000 Gold .1678 oz. AGW   **Ruler:** Carl XVI Gustaf
Subject: 50th Birthday - King Carl XVI Gustaf

Date	F	VF	XF	Unc	BU
ND(1996)	—	—	—	—	225

KM# 891   1000 KRONOR
5.8000 g., 0.9000 Gold .1678 oz. AGW   **Ruler:** Carl XVI Gustaf
Subject: Kalmar Union - Queen Margareta   **Obv:** King's bust

Date	F	VF	XF	Unc	BU
1997	—	—	—	150	190

KM# 893   1000 KRONOR
5.8000 g., 0.9000 Gold .1678 oz. AGW   **Subject:** 25th
Anniversary - Reign of King Carl XVI   **Obv:** King Carl XVI Gustaf

Date	F	VF	XF	Unc	BU
1998	—	—	—	150	190

KM# 899   2000 KRONOR
13.0000 g., 0.9000 Gold 0.3762 oz. AGW, 26 mm.   **Ruler:**
Carl XVI Gustaf   **Subject:** Millennium   **Obv:** Conjoined busts of King
Gustaf and Crown Princess Victoria left   **Rev:** Arms   **Edge:** Plain

Date	F	VF	XF	Unc	BU
1999	—	—	—	260	—

KM# 909   2000 KRONOR
12.0000 g., 0.9000 Gold 0.3472 oz. AGW, 26 mm.   **Ruler:** Carl
XVI Gustaf   **Subject:** 750th Anniversary of Stockholm   **Obv:** City seal
with three towers and gate   **Rev:** Three towers of city hall   **Edge:** Plain

Date	F	VF	XF	Unc	BU
ND (2002) Proof		Value: 350			

KM# 903   2000 KRONOR
Gold   **Ruler:** Carl XVI Gustaf   **Subject:** 30th Anniversary of Reign

Date	F	VF	XF	Unc	BU
2003	—	—	—	260	—

KM# 905   2000 KRONOR
12.0000 g., 0.9000 Gold, 26 mm.   **Ruler:** Carl XVI Gustaf
Subject: St. Birgitta's 700th Anniversary of birth   **Obv:** Gothic letter
B above value   **Rev:** St. Birgitta   **Edge:** Plain

Date	F	VF	XF	Unc	BU
ND (2003)	—	—	—	260	—

Sweden

KM# 912   2000 KRONOR
12.0000 g., 0.9000 Gold Royal Palace in Stockholm 250th
Anniversary 0.3472 oz. AGW, 26 mm.   **Ruler:** Carl XVI Gustaf
Subject: Two antique keys over map **Rev:** Royal Palace in
Stockholm **Edge:** Plain

Date	F	VF	XF	Unc	BU
ND (2004) Proof		Value: 350			

KM# 907   2000 KRONOR
12.0000 g., 0.9000 Gold, 26 mm.   **Ruler:** Carl XVI Gustaf
Subject: Centennial of the end of the Union between Norway and
Sweden **Obv:** Split disc **Rev:** Flag pole dividing two clouds

Date	F	VF	XF	Unc	BU
2005	—	—	—	260	—

KM# 914   2000 KRONOR
12.0000 g., 0.9000 Gold 0.3472 oz. AGW, 26 mm. **Ruler:**
Carl XVI Gustaf **Obv:** Stylized flames **Rev:** Dag Hammarskjold
Edge: Plain

Date	F	VF	XF	Unc	BU
ND (2005) Proof		Value: 350			

TRADE COINAGE

KM# 716   CAROLIN (10 Francs)
3.2258 g., 0.9000 Gold .0933 oz. AGW

Date	F	VF	XF	Unc	BU
1868-1872	70.00	125	225	400	—

KM# 662   DUCAT
3.4856 g., 0.9760 Gold .1094 oz. AGW **Obv:** Large head of Oscar
I right

Date	VG	F	VF	XF	Unc
1845/4	125	300	600	650	—

KM# 668   DUCAT
3.4856 g., 0.9760 Gold .1094 oz. AGW **Obv:** Smaller head

Date	VG	F	VF	XF	Unc
1845-1859	75.00	150	250	420	—

KM# 709   DUCAT
3.4856 g., 0.9760 Gold .1094 oz. AGW

Date	VG	F	VF	XF	Unc
1860-1868	75.00	125	250	425	—

KM# 680   2 DUCAT
7.0000 g., 0.9860 Gold .2219 oz. AGW

Date	VG	F	VF	XF	Unc
1850-1857	375	700	1,375	1,725	—

KM# 670   4 DUCAT
13.9424 g., 0.9760 Gold .4376 oz. AGW

Date	VG	F	VF	XF	Unc
1846-1850	500	1,000	2,000	3,200	—